The Autumn of Italian Opera

The Autumn of Italian Opera

FROM VERISMO TO MODERNISM, 1890–1915

Alan Mallach

Northeastern University Press
BOSTON

Published by University Press of New England
Hanover and London

Northeastern University Press
Published by University Press of New England,
One Court Street, Lebanon, NH 03766
www.upne.com

Library of Congress Cataloging-in-Publication Data

Mallach, Alan.
The autumn of Italian opera from verismo to modernism, 1890–1915 / Alan
Mallach.
    p. cm.
Includes bibliographical references (p.) and index.
ISBN–13: 978–1–55553–683–1 (cloth : alk. paper)
ISBN–10: 1–55553–683–2 (cloth : alk. paper)
1. Opera—Italy—19th century.   2. Opera—Italy—20th century.   I. Title.
ML1733.4M35 2007
782.10945′09034—dc22   2007027452

Contents

Part II: The Operatic Landscape

Part III: After 1900

Illustrations and Tables

Tables

Figures

Préface and Acknowledgments

In writing my earlier book on Pietro Mascagni, I learned that the world of Italian opera in which he thrived, during the years from the end of the nineteenth century up to the outbreak of the First World War, was at least as rich and intriguing as my subject's own multifaceted musical career and complicated personal life. It was a world in which art and commerce, money, publicity and celebrity were all interwoven in ways that were both very familiar and yet alien to a twenty-first–century scholar, all of it unfolding against the backdrop of an Italian nation that had only come into being a few years earlier, and that was laboriously and painfully trying to turn itself from a collection of squabbling fiefdoms and provincial loyalties into a modern country. It was, in short, a wonderful subject for a book.

The time was, moreover, a distinctive autumnal moment in the history of Italian opera. These were the last truly creative years of Italian opera, the years during which the so-called Young School or *giovane scuola*, with Puccini at its head, but including also Mascagni, Leoncavallo, Giordano, Franchetti and Cilèa, brought forth a rich, varied body of operas that are still an important part of the international operatic repertoire more than a hundred years later. After decades during which the Italian public had had little to look forward to beyond the rare works that emerged at ever longer intervals from the aging Verdi, its world once again seemed to overflow with young composers full of talent and energy, with exciting new works following one upon the other from their pens in rapid succession.

Despite the importance of these composers' works in the contemporary repertoire, this period and its leading figures have yet to be examined with the seriousness they deserve. Although audiences still flock to *Pagliacci*, *Andrea Chénier*, or *Adriana Lecouvreur*, they know little about the operas' composers or the cultural and social setting in which they were formed, and that accounts for so much of the distinctive quality of their operas. While Puccini, once taboo among serious scholars, has become a popular subject not only for biography but for serious musicological research, rarely if ever does he appear in his true musical and cultural context: one member of a larger body of composers, working in a common milieu, and maintaining a common perspective on the composition of opera and on the musical world of which they were a part. While far more needs to be done, including biographical and musical studies of the key figures of the period, I hope that this book will begin to fill the vacuum that currently exists, for both the composers and the larger Italian operatic world to which they were critical.

While it rarely is possible to put precise starting and ending dates on a complex cultural phenomenon, in this case the period — although spilling over its bounds, both before and after — is clearly bounded. It began with the premiere of Mascagni's *Cavalleria rusticana* in May 1890, an operatic bombshell establishing that a new generation, if perhaps not Mascagni himself, was ready to inherit the mantle of Verdi. It ended in May 1915, when Italy entered the First World War, a self-destructive decision on the part of its leaders that put an end to the nation's uneasy prewar social peace, setting Italy irrevocably on the path to fascism. Even before the war, however, the cinema had already begun to supplant the opera as the nation's quintessential art form, ushering in the end of a tradition that had lasted more than three hundred years.

Opera had always had a cultural resonance in Italy that made it a more important part of the national psyche than in any other country. Although that was soon to change, the last years of the nineteenth century were the high point in the diffusion of opera throughout Italian society. Through the proliferation of popular opera houses, where operas were offered at prices affordable to bank clerks, tailors, or factory workers, and the spread of civic bands and choral societies, Italians of modest means, in small towns as well as large cities, were able to participate in operatic life, to hear the evergreen classics of Verdi and Donizetti, sing the immortal words of "Va, pensiero," or listen to the town band play a medley from *Cavalleria rusticana*. In a new nation still unsure of its bearings, and divided by a daunting number of social, economic, and geographic fault lines, this was no small thing.

This last flowering of Italian opera, as both a creative and cultural phenomenon, could not last. For all the excitement that their works generated, the composers of the *giovane scuola*, with their synthesis of Verdi, Wagner, Massenet, and Bizet, were not so much providing a foundation for future generations as exhausting the resources of their tradition. Although one of their number, Puccini, was a genius whose operas will live as long as there are singers, opera houses, and audiences, his genius was individualistic and idiosyncratic. Although there were younger composers who sought to continue in the footsteps of the *giovane scuola*, such as Zandonai or Montemezzi, they are little more than epigones, adding a layer of Debussy and Richard Strauss onto the tradition that they inherited. By the second decade of the twentieth century, the world of music was changing in ways that none of them anticipated, or could surmount.

Not long into the new century, with the tradition of opera as both an art and a popular entertainment under attack from a rising generation of younger intellectuals, and challenged by emerging composers with modernist values and aspirations, the flow of successful new operas began to slow. At the same time, the freshness, immediacy, and spectacle of the cinema drew the mass audience away from the opera. By 1915, when Italy made its ill-fated entrance in the First World War, the moment that had begun in 1890 with the premiere of *Cavalleria* was all but over. With Puccini's death, and the posthumous premiere of his unfinished *Turandot*, it truly came to an end. New operas were no longer part of a vital artistic tradition or an activity that still carried meaning for the larger society. By the late twentieth century Italy's operatic culture was much like that of any other country. There was little left to show, except for the monumental opera houses and the memorials to the great composers of yesteryear, that for hundreds of years Italy had been the land of opera, the font from which nearly the entire world drew not only operas, singers, and conductors, but even the very idea of what constituted an opera, and the operatic experience.

This book attempts to capture the essence of this brief era, not only the operas and their composers, but the nature of the opera industry and the social framework in which it first thrived and then withered. I have always been fascinated by the extent to which opera historically has been not only an art, but an industry, not to mention a not always passive reflection of its social and economic milieu. Between 1890 and 1915, opera was intensely part of the social and economic fabric of Italy, a period during which the laborious, uneven project of nation-building that had begun in 1860 with unification came close to unraveling in the 1890s, and was carefully but only temporarily patched up in the first decade of the twentieth century. As cultural power moved from the aristocracy to the rising bourgeoisie, opera followed suit, commercialized and marketed by the two dominant figures of the opera industry of the age, the publishers Giulio Ricordi and Edoardo Sonzogno. A book about opera of this period would be incom-

plete if it failed to make the connections between opera and the larger society, and between opera as art and opera as an intense, cutthroat but
wildly lucrative business. I have tried to make these connections while
being careful not to take the spotlight away from the essence of the subject,
the operas themselves.

I am grateful for the assistance of Dr. Lorenza Guiot, of the Fondo Leoncavallo of the Sistema Bibliotecario Ticinese, to Piero Ostali, Jr., of the Casa
Musicale Sonzogno, to Konrad Claude Dryden, Roger Flury, and particularly to the always-helpful staff of the superb Music Division of the Library
of Congress, where I was able to read through such long-forgotten works
as Leoncavallo's *Mameli* or Franchetti's *Glauco*. I am also grateful to the
Princeton University Library for the access to their collections that they
provided me as an unaffiliated scholar. My deepest gratitude, as always,
goes to Robin, whose support and encouragement has been my mainstay
for many years, and who read and commented on many of the initial drafts
of the chapters of this book, pointing out ambiguities, repetitions, and the
excessive use of commas and semicolons, all of which I have tried to correct. It is to her that this book is dedicated.

Roosevelt, New Jersey
December 2006

Part I

Before 1900

Chapter 1

Prologue: The Unification of Italy and the World of Opera to 1890

Opera and Society on the Eve of Unification

Italy became a nation at 8:30 in the morning of October 26, 1860, on a dusty road in front of a modest tavern outside the town of Teano, twenty-five miles north of Naples.[1] On that road Giuseppe Garibaldi met Vittorio Emanuele II, king of Sardinia and soon to become king of a unified Italy. After the two men had embraced, leaning across to each other from the saddles of their horses, the grizzled warrior presented the king with Naples and the lands to the south, which Garibaldi had taken in a lightning campaign after landing in Sicily only five months before. Although it would be ten more years before Rome would be taken from the pope and joined to the new nation, at Teano the battle for a unified Italy came to an end. The Risorgimento, Italy's resurgence as a single unified nation, the dream of poets, intellectuals, and revolutionaries for generations, had become a reality.

It is not clear whether the Risorgimento leader Massimo D'Azeglio ever actually quipped, "we have made Italy, now we must make Italians," but the phrase reflected a painful truth. The Italian nation was more an idea than a reality, an idea shared by few beyond the small elite from which the new nation's leadership was drawn. For most Italians, rich or poor, their country was their region, their city, or even their native village. The great majority of Italians were illiterate, while outside of Tuscany, whose Florentine vernacular had been adopted by the nation's literati as the official Italian language, nearly everyone spoke regional dialects, many unintelligible to one another. Italy now had a flag and a king, and would soon have a parliament, an army, and a common currency, but the process of making Italians had barely begun.

Yet beneath this fragmented picture, there was clearly something that could be considered an Italian national culture, a shared identity, however

The encounter at Teano: Giuseppe Garibaldi and Vittorio Emanuele establish the Italian nation. *(Alinari Archive)*

inchoate and indistinct, that extended beyond the native city or region. What the Italian identity was, precisely, and how widely it was shared, was then and is still hard to define. What is apparent, however, is that close to the heart of that cultural identity, one of the few ways in which it found concrete representation, was the institution of Italian opera. Opera was an art form shared by the entire peninsula. Although it emerged from a variety of regional styles, such as the Venetian operas of Monteverdi and Cavalli or the *commedia per musica* of Naples, during the course of the eighteenth century it became well established as the national art par excellence, as a common body of operas made their way along with their singers throughout the Italian lands. Italian opera developed an international following and became an important export industry during the same period, as Italian composers, singers, and instrumentalists, from the grandest sopranos to the humblest journeyman violinists, became a fixture, and something of a stereotype, in every European capital from London to Saint Petersburg. Opera was an Italian invention, and it would hardly have occurred to Handel or Gluck, until the French operas with which he ended his career, to have set libretti in any other language.

Italian opera arguably found its golden age during the first half of the nineteenth century. From 1810, when Rossini's first opera, *La cambiale di matrimonio*, appeared, Rossini, Bellini, Donizetti, and Verdi presented the Italian stage with a seemingly inexhaustible series of operatic masterworks. Italian opera was now a thoroughly national, even international industry. Bellini was Sicilian while Donizetti was born in the shadow of the Alps, yet they shared a common language and were part of the same world. Their operas would be premiered in Milan, Naples, or Venice, or, in order to earn fees that were well beyond what Italy's theaters offered, in Paris or Vienna. After the first performance, they spread rapidly to the many other opera houses that dotted the peninsula, to other European capitals, and to American cities such as New York, New Orleans, or Buenos Aires. New Orleans saw Rossini's *Le Comte Ory* less than two years after its first performance in Paris,[2] while within less than ten years, *Lucia* had appeared not only on virtually every Italian stage, but in theaters in Austria, Spain, Portugal, Germany, the Netherlands, Scandinavia, Russia, Poland, and the Americas.[3]

The explosion of new operas and the increasing popularity of their composers coincided with the restoration of the aristocracy after the upheavals of the Napoleonic wars, leading to a proliferation of new theaters in the Italian states Between 1821 and 1847 some one hundred new theaters were built, nearly doubling the number of operatic venues available to the Italian public. By midcentury, nearly 120 theaters around the peninsula had regular opera seasons, with at least that many again housing intermittent or sporadic seasons. During 1846, Verdi's *Ernani*, which had first appeared in Venice in March 1844, was performed in sixty-two different Italian theaters, from those in major cities such as Milan or Naples to theaters in towns barely larger than villages, such as Pallanza, Recanati, or Stradella.[4]

Over the twelve months beginning in December 1846, Livorno, a prosperous Tuscan mercantile city of 82,000, saw seventeen different operas, presented in three different theaters.[5] Eleven of the operas were by the "big four" composers, with Donizetti heading the list with five of his works. Fifteen of the operas staged in Livorno that year were written by Italian composers; of the two operas that were not, one was de facto Italian, having been written to an Italian libretto by a young Polish composer living in nearby Florence, and the other was Meyerbeer's operatic spectacle *Robert le diable*, chosen to grace the dedication of Livorno's newest opera house, the Teatro Leopoldo. Needless to say, it was sung in Italian, as *Roberto il diavolo*. While only limited information is available on the number of performances each production received, what figures do exist suggest that the

Livornese were offered the impressive total of 120 and 150 operatic performances during the course of the year.[6]

Livorno was perhaps more prosperous and more sophisticated than the
average Italian city of moderate size, but not atypical. Nearly every city, or
large town, had its own opera house, while larger cities had two, three, or
more competing theaters. Milan in the 1860s and 1870s contained six
or more theaters offering reasonably regular operatic seasons, ranging
from La Scala, hub of the city's aristocratic life, to the modest Teatro
Re, built and operated by Carlo Re, a successful shoemaker with artistic
pretensions.[7]

Opera houses before unification were the playground of the aristocracy,
but they made room for an operagoing audience that went well beyond
the local nobility, the more prominent local officials, and the well-heeled
merchants. The people who filled the stalls, or, where it was provided,
the gallery, were not the wealthy or powerful. They are well described by
Roselli: "The stalls were for [the] middle class (wives and daughters included in some towns), for students, travelers, officers; these last were
sometimes allowed to monopolize the front rows, where they would ogle
the ballerinas and occasionally stand so as to block everyone else's
view. . . . The gallery, where there was one, was for shopkeepers, artisans,
soldiers, servants."[8]

Neither the agricultural smallholders, landless farmworkers or sharecroppers, however, nor the lowest strata of the urban population, made up
of porters, day laborers, and market vendors, were likely ever to set foot in
an opera house.[9] That does not mean they were unaware of opera, either
as an institution or as music. While the extent to which opera was disseminated to this large substratum of the Italian population before unification
is uncertain, opera cut across many of the fault lines created in Italian society by illiteracy and by the pervasive presence of local dialects. Even illiterate peasants in midcentury knew of Verdi, while their counterparts fifty
years later knew of Mascagni as a figure to revere, along with the king and
Garibaldi. People who might be unable to carry on a conversation in standard Italian could nonetheless understand it well enough to follow the language of their operatic heroes and heroines, nor was illiteracy a barrier to
enjoying the music or the spectacle offered by the peninsula's opera
houses. With the spread of operatic music through military bands, barrel
organs, and broadsheets, as well as the thousands of impromptu renditions
of arias by those who had been to the opera house the evening before,
opera was, at least in urban Italy, something close to a universally shared
experience.[10]

Unification and Its Discontents

The new nation that was created with a roadside embrace at Teano and called Italy was cobbled together from two kingdoms, three duchies, chunks of the Austrian empire, and the Papal States, the secular property of the pope reaching from south of Rome as far north as Bologna. While the northwestern region of Piedmont, officially known for complex dynastic reasons as the Kingdom of Sardinia, had had a measure of representative democracy since 1848, the rest of the peninsula was ruled despotically by aristocrats or foreign dynasties, occasionally benign but more often oppressive. The new country was largely agricultural, and desperately poor, a land where nearly 10 percent of the population suffered annually from malaria, and malnutrition and epidemics were all but universal. Three-quarters of the adult population of the new nation could neither read nor write, while south of Naples 90 percent of the population was illiterate.[11]

Those Italians who had expected unification to bring with it a dramatic change in their lives, or even any change for the better, were soon disappointed. While the country was now a constitutional monarchy with an elected parliament,[12] only 500,000 propertied men out of 27 million Italians had the right to vote, and barely half of them bothered to exercise it. With little debate, the new nation's leaders scrapped proposals for a federal system in favor of tightly centralized rule, under which Italy's provinces were ruled by prefects appointed by the central government, accountable not to the people but to the new class of bureaucrats. In the old Kingdom of Naples, overwhelmed but not truly won over by Garibaldi, unification led to a protracted guerrilla war, pitting a motley collection of brigands, Bourbon sympathizers, demobilized soldiers, and discontented peasants against the greater part of the new state's armed forces. The war raged for a decade until 1871, ravaging the countryside, poisoning the political landscape, and widening the north-south divide that has plagued Italy ever since.

The new nation was all but bankrupt. Its war debts, coupled with the exorbitant demands of a new army and bureaucracy, added up to far more than a poor agricultural country could comfortably handle. The nation's first leaders, men for the most part of high moral principles preoccupied with building a firm foundation for the new state and largely indifferent to public opinion, imposed painful new taxes on the country's people and their economic life. Most bitterly resented by the nation's peasants, most of whom were already desperately poor, was the notorious flour tax, which led to meters being installed and taxes imposed on every grain mill in the country. In the Po Valley, Italy's breadbasket, the flour tax set off peasant demonstrations that turned into a violent uprising. It was brutally repressed by the government at a cost of more than 250 lives.[13]

Driven by poverty and hunger, by the end of the 1860s more than 100,000 Italians were leaving their country each year in hopes of finding a better life elsewhere. By the end of the century, emigration had became a flood, with more than 300,000 Italians leaving each year in the 1890s. Although emigration was a painful wound to the new nation's pride, the remittances sent home helped bolster the nation's shaky finances. It also built the overseas audience for Italian opera. When Pietro Mascagni landed in Buenos Aires in 1911 for the premiere of his new opera *Isabeau*, he found himself in a city where one out of four of its residents had been born in Italy, and where Italian opera was the heart of the city's cultural and social life.

While it is unclear how much the potential emigrant, who was most often a peasant from the hills of southern Italy, knew of national politics, urban Italians were all too familiar with what, in Martin Clark's words, had become "a gray, ignoble business of granting favors and buying support, of job-seeking and compromise."[14] By the mid-1870s, the nation's founders had left the scene, and Italy had settled into a routine of corrupt and unstable governments, mostly led by the shifty, manipulative Agostino DePretis, constantly changing yet remaining the same through a process of building and subverting coalitions known as *trasformismo*, a process that uncannily prefigured the more familiar Italian governmental scene after World War II.

And yet, it is hard to decide which was the more significant development between unification and the end of the century, the extent of corruption and sheer mismanagement of the nation's affairs, or the degree to which, despite everything, a modern Italian state somehow began to emerge from the patchwork of its origins. Between 1860 and 1890, the face of the country changed significantly. Railroads, a major priority of the new government, were built across Italy, with the national network growing from 2,000 kilometers in 1860 to nearly 8,000 by 1876.[15] While the new trains were neither particularly fast nor reliable, they transformed the society and the economy in a land where inland travel, by cart, by carriage, or on horseback, had been excruciatingly slow, uncomfortable, and often dangerous. The industrial economy grew, and the number of industrial workers reached three million by the end of the century. The nation's major cities such as Milan, Rome, and Turin all grew rapidly, with new public buildings and new residential quarters in grand Victorian style, as pompous blocks of apartment buildings, wide boulevards, and tramways replaced suburban villas, vineyards, and dirt paths.

Alongside Italy's physical transformation, an inexorable process of social change was taking place. Traditional social hierarchies were breaking down, and new classes were coming to power, armed with a compelling body of convictions about society, politics, and art. Between 1860 and 1890, the values and tastes of the new class redefined the practice of the arts in Italy: its writing, its painting, and not least, the new world of opera that emerged near the end of the century. Without a discussion of these values it is difficult if not impossible to understand why the composers of the 1890s wrote the operas they did, and why they found such a passionate response in the Italian audience of the day.

Positivism and Naturalism: The New Class and Its Doctrines

The Italian states before 1860 were agrarian societies ruled by aristocrats, who ranged from the feudal counts and marquises of the Kingdom of the Two Sicilies to the more cultivated nobility of the Grand Duchy of Tuscany, who read the French *philosophes* and engaged in agricultural experiments on their estates. The nobility dominated political and social life, setting standards for art and culture, and enforcing a traditional code of behavior based on the teachings of the all-but-pervasive Catholic Church. The church, ruled absolutely by the pope, was as much a part of the system as any nobleman, buttressing aristocratic rule with its teachings, and being supported by the aristocracy in their turn. Nowhere, indeed, was the ancien régime more persistent, and conditions more oppressive, than in the priest-run Papal States, where cardinals of noble descent played the role of the provincial aristocracy, Jews were confined to ghettos until 1848, and public executions went on long after they had been abolished elsewhere in western Europe.

These Italian states had their bourgeois class, a small stratum of professionals and merchants, but it counted for little politically or socially. Under the aristocratic system, lawyers, notaries, and doctors were little more than well-educated servants, useful people to keep the system moving, but far from social equals. The same was largely true of merchants outside a handful of entrepôts, of which Livorno, an anomaly in an agrarian land, was the most notable. Livorno was a city of merchants and traders, with few aristocrats, described by one observer as a place "one could breathe freely, where . . . one need no longer feel mortified before the monuments of the great nor belittled by family names crowned by five centuries of admiration."[16]

All of this changed with unification. Although the new nation was a monarchy, the new order over which the king nominally presided was a resolutely bourgeois one, dominated by professionals, most notably lawyers, and bureaucrats. While the aristocracy retained their lands and much of their standing in provincial society, the agricultural depressions of the 1870s and 1880s caused their economic position and the value of their lands to diminish, along with much of the appeal of their way of life. Verdi, whose consciousness was formed by the old agrarian society, used the profits from his operas to buy land and become a country squire, but none of the younger generation of wealthy composers showed any interest in following in his path.

The new class took control of the government, the bureaucracy, and a growing share of the economy. More than one-third of the deputies in the first Italian parliament held law degrees, a figure that rose to more than half by 1890.[17] With the new class came a new set of convictions and attitudes, resolutely challenging the values and beliefs on which the older, aristocratic Italian society had been built. As these convictions were translated into an artistic credo, that credo became the matrix within which the operas of the next generation were written.

The dominant ideology of the new class was a curious philosophy known as *positivism*, particularly popular among nation-building elites in hitherto backward nations, particularly in southern Europe and Latin America.[18] As with so many Italian cultural developments of the time, it originated in France. As its Italian adherents absorbed it from the French philosopher Auguste Comte (1798–1857), positivism was a doctrine made to order for a body of people who, having overthrown the old order, were determined to build a new society on its ruins.

Comte laid down, as a matter of natural law, that humanity is destined to progress through three states, from the theological to the metaphysical and finally to the positivistic state, where the certainties of science have triumphed over the fantasies of theology and the speculations of metaphysics.[19] This doctrine resonated with the new nation's leaders, who saw most of their country as being mired in the theological state, under the thumb of the Catholic Church and the pope, who, unwilling to accept the changed order of things, continued to snipe at the new nation from behind the Vatican walls.

Progress, a moral as well as material goal, was most powerfully evident to its devotees in the new technologies that were the fruits of the scientific revolution of their time, particularly the engineering works that were transforming the country's transportation network. To Italy's new elite, every railroad line, every bridge and tunnel, was another battle won against the forces of reaction. No more perfect expression of these convictions can be found than the ballet *Excelsior*, which made its Milan debut at La Scala in 1881, and was perhaps the single most popular Italian theatrical event of the decade of the 1880s. Its creator, Luigi Manzotti, described his work vividly in the preface he wrote to the ballet's program book:

> Look at the monument raised in Turin in honor of the magnificent Mont Cenis tunnel and imagine the choreographic work you are about to see. It is the titanic battle waged by *Progress* against *Reaction* that I am presenting to this intelligent public; it is the grandeur of *Civilization* that defeats, beats down and destroys, for the good of the people, the historic power of *Obscurantism* that has kept them in the darkness of servitude and ignominy. Beginning with the age of the Spanish Inquisition, I arrive at the Mont Cenis tunnel, demonstrating the wondrous discoveries and awe-inspiring achievements of our century [all emphases in original].[20]

In addition to the tunnel under the Alps, the ballet depicts the invention of the steam engine, Volta's discovery of the electric battery, and the digging of the Suez Canal, all culminating in a grand tableau in which the Genius of Humanity is flanked by Science, Progress, Brotherhood, and Love. *Excelsior* was given at La Scala more than one hundred times in 1881 alone, after which it was taken up all over Italy and the rest of the world, running in London for seven straight months.[21]

Excelsior was not the only Italian artistic work written to pay homage to modern transportation. While it is hard to imagine an opera being commissioned today to mark a new link in the interstate highway system, the great Verdi was commissioned to write *Aida* to celebrate the opening of the Suez Canal; on a more modest scale, Ponchielli wrote a "Triumphal Hymn" to commemorate the inauguration of the railroad line through the Gotthard tunnel in 1882, of which the teen-aged Mascagni wrote dismissively to his teacher back in Livorno, "Ponchielli's piece is no big deal. It starts well. A big theme grows, and grows, but ends poorly. Then he works the Italian and Swiss anthems together. . . . A lot of noise."[22]

The positivist corollary to the idea of progress and the glorification of science was the replacement of imagination and speculation with a theory of knowledge as being firmly grounded in facts, or the real; as one commentator writes, "observation of what exists is to replace the imagination,

Illumination in the form of electricity triumphs over obscurantism: a scene from the ballet *Excelsior* as depicted in a contemporary illustration. *(Library of Congress)*

which hitherto had arbitrarily claimed freedom in the shaping of social and political affairs."[23] Ultimately, the positivists expected, scientific rules would be established to govern human society much as, thanks to the century's discoveries in physics and chemistry, they had come to be seen as governing the physical universe. Those rules would emerge from the new discipline Comte had invented, called *sociology*.

While sociology was to prove unsuccessful at finding universal laws of social behavior, the positivist doctrine of the real was to have a dramatic effect on the arts, by spawning the movement known in France as naturalisme, which was in turn to inspire the Italian movement known as *verismo*. Naturalism, as described by its primary inventor, Emile Zola, went beyond realism, the attempt to depict reality without frills, "as it was." Naturalism added a scientific dimension, as Zola wrote about his novel *Thérèse Raquin*, "my goal was a scientific one above all. . . . I simply subjected two living bodies to the same analysis that surgeons perform on cadavers."[24]

Through the works of its leading writers such as Giovanni Verga and Luigi Capuana, verismo gave voice to the lives of humble peasants and workers, the victims of society's pressures and the weight of a hostile environment. More important, however, than the choice of subject was the writers' attitude toward their subjects, whether poor peasants or Milan industrialists. Their focus was on the real, the tangible, unmediated by the author. As Verga wrote in a famous passage: "the triumph of fiction [will take place] when the honesty of its reality will be so clear, and its manner and raison d'être so necessary, that the hand of the author will remain utterly invisible, and the . . . work of art will seem to have been *created by itself* (emphasis in original)."[25]

Life is what is, not what should be according to an arbitrary value system or moral order. Life is a struggle, in which there are winners and losers for reasons that have nothing to do with whether they are good or bad people, or whether they behave according to the accepted moral code. In another famous passage, in which he introduced *I Malavoglia*, the first part of what he intended to be his summa, a five-novel depiction of the struggle for survival in post-unification Italy, Verga wrote: "He who observes this spectacle has no right to sit in judgment; at most, to remove himself briefly from the field of battle in order to study it without passion, and render the scene clearly. . . . so that the work represents reality as it truly was, or as it has to have been."[26] Of the many currents making up Italian literary culture as the century neared its end, verismo was the perspective at the heart of the operas of the new generation.

The idea that a moral order existed underlying all things was deeply embedded in the operas of earlier generations, from the recurrent conflict of love and honor with which baroque opera busied itself up to and most emphatically including Verdi himself. Verdi's operas, indeed, would be largely incomprehensible without the presence of an underlying moral order, which leads Riccardo to renounce Amelia in *Un ballo in maschera*, drives Violetta to do the right thing in *La traviata*, or traces the ultimate consequences of a crime, albeit an unintentional one, across the decades in *La forza del destino*.

Under the influence of naturalism and verismo, as well as the works deeply steeped in naturalism of the French composers Bizet and Massenet that entered the Italian repertory in the 1880s, the subject matter as well as the musical vocabulary of Italian opera changed dramatically. The moral order with its strong Catholic connections, so central to the works of Verdi and his predecessors, all but disappears from the operas of Puccini, Mascagni, and their contemporaries. Instead, life is what it is. In *La bohème*, Rodolfo and Mimì meet, fall in love, quarrel, and separate. Some months later, Mimì returns, and dies. It is beautiful and sad, but it reflects a world from which deeper moral or ethical principles are absent. Life is sad, life is uncertain, nothing more.

We shall return to this theme in the following chapters, as we explore the operas of this period and their reception by the operatic audience of the time, now dominated by the new class. At this point, it is appropriate to turn to what was going on in the world of Italian opera, while Italian society and its values were shifting around it.

Italian Opera in Crisis: 1860–1890

The Italian operagoer of 1860 might have sensed little difference between the opera world of his day, and that of fifteen or twenty years earlier. Donizetti and Bellini were both gone, while Rossini was living in peaceful retirement in his Parisian villa, but Verdi was not only alive, but producing masterworks of such a quality and at such a pace that the continuation of the golden age of opera seemed assured. Between 1849 to 1859, in addition to a number of works less well known today,[27] the Italian audience was presented with *Luisa Miller, Les vêpres siciliennes, Un ballo in maschera* and, above all, the immortal trilogy of *Rigoletto, Il trovatore,* and *La traviata.*

Verdi's remarkable achievement obscured the reality that Italian opera had never fully recovered from the unrest that gripped much of the country from 1848 to the early 1850s, or that the opera industry was heading into even more stormy waters.[28] The opera industry had been a major beneficiary of the aristocratic system that dominated Italian life before unification. Not only did aristocratic families support opera through their purchase of boxes and payment of substantial annual fees, the aristocratic states, led as often as not by the boxholders themselves, supported opera generously from the public purse with subsidies and guarantees to impresarios. While the history of impresarios' constant struggles to keep their heads above water suggests that the level of support was often inadequate, that support nonetheless represented a major financial commitment for agrarian societies of modest means.

With unification, all of that came to an end. The national government, which had inherited the obligations of the former despotic states, including their subsidies to their opera houses, soon washed its hands of the matter, unilaterally handing responsibility for the opera houses to the nation's municipal governments (*comuni*). With the finances of the *comuni* typically even more strained than those of the national government, it was not long before opera houses across the peninsula began to find themselves in increasingly difficult financial straits. The 1870s and 1880s saw a growing number of houses close their doors, either temporarily or permanently; where they stayed open, the number of performances declined, and the standard of performance became increasingly erratic and unpredictable.

As the economic foundations of the traditional Italian opera world began to crumble, the creative underpinnings of that world began to look more and more uncertain, an uncertainty that was to grow into a full-fledged crisis over the next two decades. While Verdi had produced operas steadily up to the early 1860s, by the end of the decade he was more and more the squire of Sant'Agata and less and less the hardworking operatic composer of earlier years. After *La forza del destino* in 1862, the Italian audience had to wait until nearly the end of the decade for *Don Carlo*, written for the Paris Opéra rather than an Italian house. The 1870s brought *Aida* alone.

Meanwhile, the remarkable insularity of the Italian opera world was coming to an end; the Italian operagoing public was finally exposed to the operas being written elsewhere not as a rare curiosity, but as a steady part of the operatic diet. As Julian Budden writes: "Gounod, together with Meyerbeer and followed at some distance by Thomas, remained the strongest of strictly operatic influences during the 1870s. *Faust*, composed in 1859 . . . had already bid fair to replace *Il trovatore* as the most popular opera in the European repertory. . . . By the end of the decade every one of Meyerbeer's French operas was in the repertory of the larger Italian theaters."[29]

The penetration of foreign opera during these years can be vividly seen in the repertory of the conservative Livorno theaters. During the entire decade of the 1850s only one opera by a non-Italian composer, Meyerbeer's *Le prophète*, appeared in Livorno. Productions of operas by foreign composers increased to five in the 1860s, nine in the 1870s and fifteen in the 1880s. The choice of operas was characteristic of Italian houses. Putting aside a single production of Nicolai's *Il templario* (which is actually an Italian opera),[30] Livorno saw twenty-nine productions of twelve foreign operas, nearly all French, and nearly half by Meyerbeer.[31]

While Livorno saw *Carmen*, a major influence on the younger generation of Italian composers, in 1884 and again in 1888, it is perhaps a reflection of its conservative tastes that it failed to make the acquaintance of Massenet until the mid-1890s. Although Massenet never became quite so popular in Italy as Gounod or Meyerbeer, his *Roi de Lahore* was first performed in Milan in 1879, while his *Hérodiade*, a sultry but not scandalous precursor of Strauss's *Salome*, also became popular in Italy during the

1880s, exerting a not insignificant influence on the works of the young Catalani and Puccini.

Even before the premiere of *Carmen* and the rise of Massenet as the principal French opera composer of the age, Italians were increasingly looking to French opera for new dramatic and musical directions, seeing the grandiloquence of Meyerbeer and the sentimental romanticism of Gounod and Thomas as correctives to the backward state of Italian opera. While the works of these composers filled the void that had emerged in the Italian opera world, it is hard not to believe that at least some of the admiration for their works may have been driven more by the taste for things French that permeated Italian cultural and intellectual life than by the merits of these operas. Italians devoured the products of French artistic and intellectual life, not only the positivist philosophy of Auguste Comte, but also the novels of Emile Zola and the works of the symbolist poets. Italy's own artistic movements, from the bohemian *Scapigliatura* of Milan to the literary verismo of Verga and Capuana, were modeled after their French counterparts. For all the new nation's political independence, artistic Italy remained in many ways a French colony.

The other, far more significant and complex influence on Italian opera that began to emerge during this period was that of the German titan, Richard Wagner. The first performance of a Wagner opera in Italy took place when *Lohengrin* appeared in Bologna in 1871, twenty-one years after its Weimar debut. Bologna, the home base of the publisher Giovannina Lucca, a passionate Wagnerite and the owner of the Italian rights to his works, was, moreover, after years of confinement in the cultural backwater of the Papal States, eager to asset a strong cultural role in the new Italian nation, and perhaps even upstage Milan as Italy's principal cultural center.[32] With assiduous promotion by Lucca, Bologna became the center of Wagnerism in Italy, with *Lohengrin* followed over the next few years by productions of *Tannhäuser, Rienzi,* and *Der fliegende Holländer.*

Although *Lohengrin* was greeted enthusiastically in Bologna, its reception when it reached Milan two years later was very different. Even before the opera's appearance at La Scala, it had already become the focus of a heated controversy, albeit one less musical than political or cultural. While the first performance, although regularly interrupted by a mixture of catcalls, whistles, and applause, was greeted at the end with respect if not enthusiasm by the audience, matters deteriorated with every subsequent performance. The fifth saw a fistfight in the stalls, while during the seventh, "at the point in the second act when Telramund challenges Lohengrin . . . the tumult reached such threatening proportions that the curtain was brought down."[33] Milan did not see another Wagner opera until 1888, fifteen years later.

During the nearly two decades bracketed by the 1871 Bologna premiere and the 1888 La Scala revival of *Lohengrin,* as the German master's operas slowly moved into the Italian repertoire, Wagner and Wagnerism became a major intellectual and cultural bone of contention in Italy — although one, as Miller points out, that "had precious little to do with music per se."[34] For many intellectuals, their support for or opposition to Wagner reflected either their identification with Italy's traditional musical institutions and figures, or their adversarial stance toward those same figures and institutions. The young Milanese bohemians known as the Scapigliati, (disheveled ones) saw Wagner as a cudgel with which to attack the ossified conventions of the opera of their time, while others, including Giulio Ricordi, saw Wagner as a threat to the integrity of Italy's cultural traditions. During the 1870s Ricordi's house organ, the *Gazzetta musicale di Milano,* published a "torrent of articles denouncing Wagner and all his works."[35]

Independently of the polemics that surrounded his name, Wagner's music was having a powerful effect on the Italian composers coming of age in the 1870s and 1880s, although few actually heard the German composer's mature operas until the late 1880s and 1890s, when *Tristan* and *Die Meistersinger* finally reached Italian opera houses.[36] As Budden writes, "for Puccini's entire generation from Catalani to Mascagni his operas possessed a deep and abiding fascination."[37] Catalani's works, up to his last opera *La Wally,* show their Wagnerian allegiance openly, but he was not alone. The young Mascagni, who as a student in Milan pooled his and Puccini's meager funds to purchase a copy of the vocal score for *Parsifal,* was so deeply moved by Wagner's death that he rushed to his room and in a few intensely emotional days composed an elegy for orchestra in the composer's memory.[38] Puccini's *Preludio Sinfonico,* written in 1882 while a student at the Milan Conservatory, shows its debt to *Lohengrin* openly. By the 1890s Wagner was unequivocally part of the shared heritage of Italy's younger composers, and was becoming an increasingly common visitor to the nation's opera houses.

For all the new operas arriving from France or Germany, and the Wagnerian controversy playing out in the pages of Italy's newspapers and musical magazines, the Italian operatic world was still fundamentally Italian. Through the 1880s, works by Italian composers continued to make up the overwhelming majority of the repertory. In 1875, only twelve of the seventy-seven different operas performed in Italian opera houses that year were by foreign composers — and almost half were, as in Livorno, Meyerbeer's.[39] Along with the evergreen works of Verdi, Donizetti, and Rossini, new operas by younger Italian composers continued to form the bulk of the repertory. Indeed, two-thirds of the Italian works performed in 1875 were by living composers, including such once respected and now forgotten figures as Cagnoni, Petrella, Pacini, and the two Ricci brothers, Luigi and Federico.

The problem was not one of quantity, but of quality. By the 1870s and 1880s it had become clear that these composers and their colleagues, although talented men who worked hard, and made at least some modest effort to stay au courant, had nothing of significance to add to the course of Italian music. A partial exception must be made for Boito's *Mefistofele*, whose 1868 premiere at La Scala raised high expectations and drew intense interest, not least because of the controversy stirred up by its supposedly Wagnerian character, and by the composer's anti-Verdi pronouncements.[40] As Francesco D'Arcais, a prominent critic, wrote, "all during the performance, the piazza was thronged with people anxiously awaiting news of the performance; along with messengers who, at the end of each act, carried news of the battle to the farthest quarters of the city."[41] The opera, however, was a failure, damned by most critics and spurned by the audience. The chastened Boito extensively rewrote his opera for its reappearance in 1875 and again in 1876, removing its most demanding sections and adding crowd-pleasing arias and set pieces such as "Lontano, lontano." While it was far more successful in its new garb, it had become a largely conventional opera, saying little that Verdi had not already said far better in his 1871 *Aida*.

The two new composers that attracted the most attention during the 1870s were Antonio Carlos Gomes and Amilcare Ponchielli. Although both raised initially high expectations, neither, in the final analysis, had more than a transitory effect on the course of Italian music. Indeed, as I have written elsewhere, they were "little more than Verdian epigones, seeking new and superficially different ways of manipulating a vocabulary that by 1870 even the great Verdi had transcended."[42]

Gomes was a Brazilian whose initial successes in his homeland had prompted the emperor of Brazil to finance his further studies in Italy. In 1870, his opera *Il Guarany* made a spectacular debut at La Scala; during the following years he produced a number of other operas, of which *Salvator Rosa* (1874) was most successful. While the music of *Il Guarany* shows great charm and melodic flair, which, along with the exoticism of its setting in the jungles of South America, may account for its enthusiastic initial reception, it is also derivative, almost to the point of parody. One cannot listen to *Il Guarany* without being constantly reminded of early- or middle-period Verdi, or even at times Donizetti. While Gomes's later operas display a more sophisticated vocabulary, in the process they lost the freshness that made *Il Guarany* so appealing. By the end of the decade, he was already a spent force in Italian opera, and soon forgotten.

Ponchielli is a more substantial musical figure. Although his first success, a setting of Manzoni's iconic novel *I promessi sposi*, is no less derivative than *Il Guarany*, his slow, methodical pursuit of the operatic craft bore fruit in *La Gioconda*, his one opera that remains on the fringe of today's operatic repertory. Ponchielli's mastery of the techniques and resources of the grand opera tradition are apparent on virtually every page of that massive score. Yet *La Gioconda* would not have survived, however tenuously, did it not offer much more than solid craftsmanship. Boito's libretto is far better than is often recognized. Keeping its Grand Guignol tendencies carefully under control, it offers strong and well-differentiated characters, well-organized scenes, and powerful dramatic confrontations. Ponchielli rose to the occasion, pouring his not inconsiderable musical gifts into the opera, attaining a level he had never reached before, and was never to reach again. If *La Gioconda's* strength lies in its intensity, one of its greatest defects is its tendency to hyperbole, which prefigures some of the excesses of the next generation of Italian composers. Ponchielli's music is constantly in motion, his scenes constantly building to ever greater dramatic intensity, his wide-ranging melodic lines possessed of an unswerving determination to reach a vocal climax above the staff.

Ponchielli is a far more significant transitional figure than Gomes. Gioconda's aria "Suicidio," which dominates the final act of *La Gioconda*, bridges the defile between the generation of Verdi and that of Puccini and Mascagni, both in its wild melodic leaps and in the manner in which it creates its undeniable dramatic effect. Its echoes can be found in many of the pages of the younger generation, not least in Mascagni's *Cavalleria rusticana*.

Another generation of composers began to emerge in the 1880s, notably Catalani, Franchetti, and Puccini (all of whom will be discussed in chapter 3). As the decade came to an end, however, none of them looked likely to offer a solution to the conundrum that was increasingly preoccupying the Italian musical world: the key to the future of Italian opera. The void that had begun to appear thirty years earlier was turning into a chasm. By 1890, Verdi was seventy-seven years old, and still the most dynamic, creative, and original figure in Italian opera. For thirty years, the Italian public and musical world had been looking without success for that key; wondering, in the words of the critic Primo Levi, where is "the man destined to remain? To extend, or better, to begin anew, the tradition of our great ones, to open it to the future? To demonstrate if there will be an opera of tomorrow, and what it will be?"[43]

The first answer to Levi's question was given on May 17, 1890, at Rome's Costanzi opera house.

Chapter 2

"Abbiamo Un Maestro": *Cavalleria Rusticana* and Its Progeny

The Premiere of Cavalleria rusticana

May 17, 1890, was a beautiful warm spring day in Rome. As the conductor Leopoldo Mugnone stepped onto the podium in the Costanzi opera house that evening to conduct the first performance of Pietro Mascagni's *Cavalleria rusticana*, the house was not even half-full, few people having found themselves drawn on such a delightful evening to hear a new unheralded opera by an unknown composer. Those in attendance "had gone out of a vague sense of a painful duty to be done, or out of polite obedience to the demands of the privileged few who had attended the rehearsals."[1] As the first bars of the Prelude were heard, the listeners fell silent; a few minutes later, as one observer wrote: "When after a few harp arpeggios, the melody of the 'Siciliana' sung by Roberto Stagno unfolded from behind the curtain . . . more than applause, more than a shout, but a thundering outcry exploded in the theater, as everyone, jumping to their feet, burst out in an ovation the likes of which had not been heard in an opera house for years."[2] At the end of the opera, the composer and the performers were called back for sixty curtain calls; Gemma Bellincioni, the first Santuzza, wrote, "the spectators seemed literally to go crazy. They screamed, they waved their handkerchiefs, in the corridors strangers embraced, crying 'Abbiamo un maestro!' [We have a maestro!] Hurrah for the new Italian maestro!"[3] It was a triumph of unheard-of proportions, which was not only to transform an unknown small-town musician into an international celebrity, but would remake the Italian operatic world.

That *Cavalleria* was being performed at all was the result of an unusual venture by an unusual figure in the Italian operatic world, the publisher

Edoardo Sonzogno (1836–1920). A passionate opera lover and bon vivant, he had arrived on the opera scene by buying the Italian rights to much of the French operatic repertory, including works by Offenbach and Thomas, and in 1879, Bizet's *Carmen*. In 1883 Sonzogno announced a competition for the best one-act opera by a young unpublished Italian composer, offering the winner a prize of 2,000 lire[4] and a performance in a Milan theater. Although one-act operas were not common in Italian opera, they were a good test of a young composer's skills and could, in any event, be combined with a ballet for an evening's theater.[5] Although the 1883 contest is still best known for having inexplicably overlooked Puccini's *Le Villi*, awarding the prize to two lesser and quickly forgotten works, Sonzogno persevered.

In 1888, he announced a second competition, with the first prize increased to the substantial sum of 3,000 lire. Under the rules of the competition, three finalists would be selected by the jury to have their operas performed at Rome's Costanzi opera house, after which the jury would reconvene to pick the grand-prize winner. Reflecting the publisher's desire that the competition be seen as credible by the rest of the musical world, the jury included some of Italy's most distinguished musical figures, including Giovanni Sgambati, professor at Rome's Santa Cecilia conservatory; Pietro Platania, director of the Naples Conservatory; and the eminent critic Francesco D'Arcais, Marquis of Valverde.

Seventy-three composers submitted operas by the deadline at the end of May 1889. After winnowing the scores down to eighteen, the jury invited those composers to Rome to present their works, announcing the three finalists in mid-March 1890. They were Mascagni's *Cavalleria rusticana*, Nicola Spinelli's *Labilia*, and *Rudello* by Vincenzo Ferroni, a professor at the Milan conservatory. Not among the prizewinners, but singled out for special mention by the jury, was an opera by a young student at the Naples Conservatory, Umberto Giordano.

Sonzogno, who had taken over management of the Costanzi opera house the year before, had engaged the well-known husband-and-wife team of Roberto Stagno and Gemma Bellincioni to sing the leading roles in the three operas. Stagno, a scion of the Sicilian aristocracy, was fifty-four and perhaps past his prime; as one writer has noted, "He belonged, notoriously, to that category of singer associated with the school . . . of ardent temperament, rather than having the pure resources of a truly privileged voice."[6] The much younger Bellincioni, considered but rejected by Boito for the role of Desdemona in the premiere of Verdi's *Otello*, was to go on to a major career in verismo roles, her somewhat thin voice more than compensated for by her powerful stage presence. Although neither may have been among the era's great voices, both were popular figures and compelling operatic actors.

Sonzogno had done his work, and the jury theirs, in creating the conditions for the triumph of May 17, 1890. To understand that moment, however, we must turn to the individual directly responsible, the composer of *Cavalleria rusticana*. Who was Pietro Mascagni, and what was different, even unique, about his new opera?

Pietro Mascagni

Pietro Mascagni (1863–1945), composer of *Cavalleria rusticana*, was the most vivid, theatrical figure among the composers of the generation that emerged toward the end of the century, and who came to be known as the *giovane scuola* (Young School). As a conductor, educator, orator, and polemicist, as well as a composer, he was an omnipresent figure in Italian musical life from 1890 until well into the dark days of World War II, a combative figure around whom controversy swirled, evoking passionate admiration and adoration from many, and equally intense scorn and contempt from others. Although the musical world soon came to recognize that Puccini was the greater composer, Mascagni was the more beloved public figure, whose every action or quip was newsworthy, and whose features graced the domestic altars of the homes of Italy's peasants and workers, alongside the picture postcards of Garibaldi and the king.

He was born on December 7, 1863, in a Livorno tenement overlooking the Piazza delle Erbe, the city's busy market square, the second son of a baker, Domenico Mascagni, and his wife Emilia Rebua, who died of tuberculosis when Pietro was only nine years old, leaving her husband with five small children. Domenico Mascagni, although an artisan of modest means, was better educated than most men of his class, and harbored ambitions for his family beyond the baker's trade. Having decided that his intelligent, energetic, and mischievous son Pietro would become a lawyer, he scraped together the funds to pay the substantial fees to enroll him in the *ginnasio* (classical middle school), the starting point on the path to a university degree and entry into the prosperous bourgeoisie.

Domenico Mascagni's plans, however, were in vain. Although he had initially encouraged his son's musical studies, he did not expect them to lead to a musical career. With no musical tradition or history of musical talent in the Mascagni family, he is unlikely to have expected that his son would find music more than an ornament to the solid bourgeois life planned for him.

Pietro Mascagni at the time of *Cavalleria rusticana*. *(Museo Mascagnano, Bagnara di Romagna)*

By the age of thirteen, however, little else mattered to young Pietro other than studying, playing, and above all composing music. It was at that point that he found a kindred spirit in a young graduate of the Milan conservatory named Alfredo Soffredini, who had recently arrived in Livorno to open the city's first true music school, the Istituto Luigi Cherubini.

Soffredini recognized the young composer's talent, and quickly became the leading figure in his early musical life. Soon, Pietro was neglecting his nonmusical studies in order to devote his time to his compositions and his studies with Soffredini. That choice led to a violent rupture with his father, and ultimately to his leaving his father's house and moving into the home of his bachelor uncle, his father's older brother Stefano. From that point on, particularly after his graduation from the *ginnasio* in 1879, he lived and breathed music, as he described many years later: "My uncle said to me, . . . "I'll give you a key to the house and subscriptions to all the theaters . . . you go to the theaters, and I'll see you back home whenever you feel like." For me, this was a dream come true. Still just a kid, I was free to live the life I wanted. I played [the piano] from morning to evening, I went to my piano teacher, and I went to . . . Soffredini."[7]

Mascagni had a precocious gift. A four-movement symphony composed at sixteen — although the product of an environment in which Haydn and Mozart, with a touch of Schubert and Mendelssohn, were his models — is a substantial and convincing work. A dramatic cantata, *In filanda* [In the spinning mill], which was presented at the Casino di San Marco shortly after his seventeenth birthday, made him a local celebrity. It was followed a year later by an even more ambitious work, a setting of Schiller's *Ode to Joy* that was performed in Livorno's Avvalorati theater in March 1882.

That performance marked the end of the young composer's life in Livorno. He had learned what he could from Soffredini, while his growing ambitions demanded a wider stage for their realization. Invited to Milan by Ponchielli, now the distinguished professor of composition at the Milan conservatory, he lost no time arranging his affairs and making his farewells. With three hundred lire from performances of the *Ode to Joy* and another three hundred from a local magnate, Count Florestano de Larderel, in his pocket, he left for Milan early in May.

Mascagni's early years illustrate not only his prodigious musical gifts, but also his grandiosity, his impatience, and his lack of self-discipline, traits understandable in a precocious teenager, but that would remain part of his personality all his life. While *In filanda* is a charming work, effective within its modest compass, the *Ode to Joy* is an exercise in overreaching, as the composer's search for a musical language worthy of the text leads him regularly into domains beyond his reach, his best ideas dissolving into noise and bombast. In the same vein, when he arrived in Milan at eighteen he fully expected to be recognized by the musical world as the composer he already felt himself to be. Instead, he discovered that even the warmly disposed Ponchielli saw him not as a finished composer, but as a gifted adolescent ready to begin his serious musical education. He was back in Livorno by late July, having run through his six hundred lire in less than three months, chastened but not really humbled.

Reassured by a 150-lire monthly stipend from de Larderel, he returned to Milan in October to enroll in the conservatory. Although he remained there for more than two years, studying intermittently, he could never bring himself to accept the discipline the institution sought to impose on him, or resolve the conflict between his self-image and the student's role he was expected to play. His ultimate departure from the Milan conservatory, in the spring of 1885, came less from conflict with his teachers than an impulsive reaction to a sudden opportunity that he believed would permit him to make his way in the musical world without the need for degrees or certificates.

For all his frustration at the conservatory, life in Milan agreed with Mascagni. Milan was the center of the Italian musical world, the one city where not only operas, but orchestral and chamber music, could regularly be heard. During 1883, his first full year in Milan, the city's six active opera houses put on thirty-two different operas, including three world premieres, most notably Catalani's *Dejanice* (which both Mascagni and Puccini admired), eight French operas, and Beethoven's *Fidelio*.[8] During the same year, a concertgoer could have heard five of Beethoven's symphonies, five Wagner overtures, including *Tristan* and *Parsifal*, excerpts from *Die Walküre* and *Götterdämmerung*, and major chamber works by Haydn, Mozart, Mendelssohn, Schubert, and Schumann.[9] It was in his first year in Milan that Mascagni came under the spell of Wagner, whom he described in a latter to his friend Gianfranceschi as "the Pope [*il papa*] of all musicians present and future."[10] It was the beginning of a lifelong love-hate relationship.

Milan was also home to the Scapigliatura, the nearest thing Italy offered to a bohemian subculture; its members welcomed the handsome, dashing young student into their circles as they had the young Catalani ten years earlier. As we saw in chapter 1, the Scapigliati rejected the bourgeois, positivist ethos of post-unification Italy. They saw it as a betrayal of the people's dreams, as reflected in a famous poem by Emilio Praga, perhaps their quintessential figure:

> We are the sons of diseased parents,
> Eagles whose feathers are falling off;
> We fly about aimlessly, silent, stupefied,
> Famished, above our god's death struggle.[11]

Although much of their energy was dissipated in self-destructive behavior in imitation of the French *poètes maudits*, some Scapigliati espoused a body of more or less coherent artistic ideas. Led by Boito and Faccio, they sought to bring new ideas, largely derived from Wagner, into Italian opera, including the use of leitmotifs, a continuous orchestral texture and an end to closed forms, a greater emphasis on the meaning and poetry of the libretto, and a search for new, exotic themes and settings. Although their heyday had passed by the 1880s, Mascagni came under the spell of their ideas, closely reflected in his early opera *Guglielmo Ratcliff.*

Mascagni discovered Andrea Maffei's Italian translation of Heinrich Heine's "dramatic ballad" "Guglielmo Ratcliff" during his second year in Milan. Although Maffei's translation was in *endecasillabi,* an Italian verse form using eleven-syllable lines roughly comparable to English iambic pentameter blank verse (and equally difficult to set to music), Mascagni was transfixed by the work, identifying closely with its obsessed central figure, a rebel who goes to his doom eloquently condemning the society that has rejected him. As he wrote a few years later, "Maffei's verses seemed so beautiful. . . . I declaimed them all night, walking back and forth in my room, and they set me so much on fire . . . that I dreamed of nothing but . . . the fantastic passion of Guglielmo."[12] When Mascagni left the conservatory the following year, and began his travels as a wandering musician, the valise with the ever-growing score of *Guglielmo Ratcliff* was his constant companion. Although he set it aside for *Cavalleria,* he picked it up again in 1893, and conducted its first performance at La Scala in February 1895.

Mascagni also met Puccini in Milan, forming a friendship that, although often strained in later years, was never completely broken. They shared rooms during Puccini's last year at the conservatory; a year later, Mascagni stood next to his friend in the wings of the Dal Verme theater as Puccini's *Le Villi* was first performed. Although Puccini's first opera would have some influence on Mascagni's musical vocabulary in *Cavalleria,* its immediate effect was to make his frustration even more painful, as a letter he wrote not long afterward makes clear: "Here I was watching my dearest friend reach the goal that I myself have dreamed of for so long, and I was burning with the desire to imitate him, and yet I could not see any possibility of doing so. . . . Oh, art! My beautiful art! Would I never, then, be able to reach the glory that I longed for, which I dreamed about even wide awake?"[13] His moment of glory would come, but not for six long years.

In the spring of 1885, Mascagni finally broke with the conservatory. Invited by a friend to conduct an operetta company for a night in nearby Cremona, he soon found himself caught up in the raffish world of traveling operetta companies, in which diplomas mattered little. Offered an assistant conductor's job, he accepted with a mixture of bravado and embarrassment, and was soon on the road with his new companions. He soon discovered, however, that for all its freemasonry, the world he was now part of was a world of "brutal poverty, homelessness and humiliation."[14] Operetta was a marginal pursuit in Italy, offering its practitioners little status or dignity. Companies came and went, many promoters were corrupt or incompetent, bookings were uncertain, and payment erratic or nonexistent. Over the next two years, Mascagni lived a desperate, hand-to-mouth existence as the conductor of one company after another, often stranded penniless and far from home, rejected by family and friends.

His wanderings came to an end in February 1887. Tired of life on the road, and now traveling with a young woman who had joined him the summer before and who was carrying his child, he was offered an irresistible opportunity: to settle in the small Apulian market town of Cerignola, reopen the town's music school, and organize a student orchestra. Hired by the town at the modest stipend of 100 lire per month, which he supplemented by giving piano lessons to young women from the area's more prosperous families, he soon became a part of Cerignola's small cultural and intellectual circle.

Although life in Cerignola started well, it soon wore thin. He found it more and more difficult to support his new family on his modest earnings, while he soon became bored with the provincial society of a small southern town far from Milan. As he later wrote, "I was totally aware that for my artistic aspirations . . . a little provincial spot like Cerignola was the kiss of death."[15] In his desperate state of mind, the announcement of the second Sonzogno competition in July 1888 was more than an opportunity; it was a life preserver thrown to a drowning man.

By the time Mascagni had convinced his childhood friend Giovanni Targioni-Tozzetti to write his libretto and the two had settled on Verga's *Cavalleria rusticana* as their subject, it was already January 1889. Less than five months were left until the deadline. Targioni-Tozzetti enlisted a young Livorno poet named Guido Menasci to help him, and over the next two months, the two writers sent the composer the libretto in bits and pieces, often no more than a few lines at a time on the back of a postcard. Writing at feverish speed, setting a libretto that was still being written as he was composing the music, Mascagni wrote and scored *Cavalleria* in four months. On the evening of May 27, 1889, a fair copy of the full score, a piano-vocal score, and a clean copy of the libretto as required by the competition, were in the mail on their way to Milan. Although he would wait for word with increasing impatience until February 1890, his path to fame and fortune had begun.

Cavalleria Rusticana, *a Transformative Opera*

Giovanni Verga's story *Cavalleria rusticana* is more than a powerful story; it is the iconic work of Italian literary naturalism, or verismo.[16] It is a work of stark realism, told in clipped but vivid dialogue as if from inside the minds of his characters, offering neither moral judgments nor commentary. It offers no conventional description, its brief descriptive phrases capturing only those things that matter to the characters or illuminate their world. It has little sense of time or place. The events of the story that lead to the final confrontation could be taking place over weeks, months, or even years.

The story, which Verga based on an incident in his hometown of Viz-zini, is a simple one. Turiddu Macca, a handsome but idle young man, has returned home from the army to find his former sweetheart Lola married to Alfio, a wealthy carter. He begins to court Santuzza, but Lola is still drawn to him. With Alfio away from town, they become lovers, and Turiddu abandons Santuzza. When Alfio returns, Santuzza tells him about Lola and Turiddu. Alfio challenges Turiddu, who accepts the challenge. They walk to an orchard outside the village, take out their knives, and fight. A few moments later, Turiddu is lying dead on the ground.

In 1883, when Verga decided to embark on a career as a playwright in the hope of earning more from the theater than he could as a writer of fic-tion, he chose to make a dramatization of *Cavalleria* his first theatrical project. The play, which made its debut in Turin in January 1884 with Eleanora Duse as Santuzza and the Sicilian Flavio Andò as Turiddu, was a spectacular success, and soon became a staple of the Italian theater. Duse performed it throughout the world, and innumerable companies toured with it up and down the peninsula.

Verga, with sure theatrical instinct,[17] rather than attempting literally to dramatize his story, wrote a new play based on the story, concentrating on the Easter morning confrontations that lead to the final, fatal encounter between Turiddu and Alfio. In making *Cavalleria* into a play, Verga also created four omnipresent secondary characters, a small-town Greek cho-rus who, although having no direct role in the events of the play, are nonetheless intimately involved as observers and minor participants in the drama emerging before their eyes; they are, as Vallora writes, "active wit-nesses, informers, primitive country Iagos,"[18] reminding one that in the Si-cilian village everything is already known, except perhaps to the protago-nists. This change, indeed, is largely responsible for the play's escaping the status of crude melodrama.

Copertina della seconda edizione dello spartito di Cavalleria rusticana. *Nella fotografia i primi interpreti: Gemma Bellincioni e Roberto Stagno*

Stagno and Bellincioni depicted in a scene from *Cavalleria rusticana,* from the cover of the second edition of the piano-vocal score. *(Casa Musicale Sonzogno)*

Although some references refer to the libretto of *Cavalleria rusticana* as having been based on Verga's original story, Targioni-Tozzetti and Menasci based their libretto directly on the play, making little change to its structure, but giving greater weight to some episodes, and reducing others nearly to the vanishing point. In converting the play to a libretto, their most serious problem was the secondary characters. While it would be difficult to retain the flavor of Verga's village Iagos in an opera, if no one was to remain but the protagonists, *Cavalleria* would not only lose any sense of dramatic balance in its headlong rush to the end, but also lose the sense of the omnipresence of the community, so central to its meaning.

The librettists' solution was to create an all but omnipresent chorus of villagers, who appear in a series of set numbers framing the confrontations between the opera's protagonists. While formally these numbers are highly conventional, and have been criticized for sanitizing the harsh reality of Sicilian peasant life,[19] they allowed the librettists to convey much of the sense of the constant presence of the community, both because of the way the choral episodes break up the events of the drama, and the sheer mass of choral writing. Few operas devote so much time to choral music, and so little to the protagonists, as *Cavalleria*.

It was inevitable, of course, that Mascagni's librettists, two proper young Tuscan gentlemen, would soften Verga's material to some extent. The greatest softening, however, had already taken place in Verga's own transformation of his story into a play, in the course of which the dialogue lost much of its pungency,[20] the powerful undercurrents of wealth and poverty in the story were muted if not eliminated, and the final knife fight moved offstage. The librettists' writing for the protagonists, however, while following Verga closely in substance, is far more pedestrian in its language, while the choruses, which are the librettists' original work, are conventional, even clichéd. In the final analysis, however, for the purpose of supplying words that Mascagni could set to music, the libretto is an effective, well-crafted effort.

From this libretto, Mascagni crafted an opera that remains as powerful today as it was when first performed in 1890 — although the reasons for its power, and the influence it had on the operatic world of the time, continue to elude the musicological world, which has for the most part treated *Cavalleria* with condescension, if not outright contempt. I have has written about the features that give this opera its distinctive quality and power elsewhere,[21] but a few words are important here.

More than that of any other opera written before, the experience of *Cavalleria* is that of a single uninterrupted dramatic arc. Such an experience was new for an 1890 audience, and largely responsible for their passionate response to the work, described by one participant as "an almost orgiastic festival, an almost religious rite."[22] While it is not possible to construct a work of more than a few minutes that actually follows a continuous dramatic trajectory, in *Cavalleria* Mascagni brilliantly builds and then releases tension in precisely measured quantities, creating the overwhelming effect of an inexorable, cumulative buildup of dramatic intensity over the course of an hour and a quarter.

If the sheer unrelieved dramatic power of *Cavalleria* is one part of its appeal, another comes from the freshness and novelty of its musical language. While all of its musical materials were recognizable, *Cavalleria* sounded like no opera that had ever been written before. As the prominent critic Guido Pannain wrote, looking back fifty years later: "It was like a door that suddenly blew open onto a sealed room. A fresh, cool wind from the country blew away the faint smell of mildew that was beginning to spread. . . . It was a furious exaltation of song. The public, which was the people, heard their voice in it and were overwhelmed."[23] Although the sounds of popular music, or even operetta, had occasionally found their way into opera, they had always been used as self-conscious interpolations, such as the *banda* music in early Verdi. Here instead was an opera that spoke the plebian language of the composer's working-class childhood on the streets of Livorno and his immersion in the operetta world, combining the sounds of popular song and operetta almost seamlessly with a more conventional, operatic language pared down to the bone, and all but devoid of ornamentation or display.

This is not local color. There are no Sicilian songs or dances in *Cavalleria*, the way Neapolitan songs and tarantellas decorate Giordano's *Mala vita* and so many of the verismo operas to come in *Cavalleria*'s wake. Even if Mascagni, who had never been to Sicily when he wrote the work, could have introduced Sicilian motifs or rhythms, there is no reason to believe he would have done so. Indeed, it was his design to avoid anything that would distance the audience from the immediacy of the events taking place. Lola's ditty and Turiddu's serenade are the two most vivid examples of popular song in the opera, but the one is a Tuscan *stornello* and the other, notwithstanding its Sicilian words,[24] more or less Neapolitan. Both genres were not exotic but familiar, plebian sounds of Italian life

This familiar language does not reflect any lack of mastery of the techniques of conventional opera, but a deliberate simplification of means, designed to create a language for *Cavalleria* that would give the impression, however illusory, that the composer's hand was indeed invisible. That language, however simplified, is nonetheless grounded in a network of leitmotifs and thematic connections reflecting the composer's familiarity with the works of Wagner. These connections carry through the entire work, from its opening phrase to its final chords, adding immeasurably to the sense of overall unity and cohesion that the listener experiences.[25]

In the final analysis, however, *Cavalleria* does not represent, nor does it claim to represent, the harsh, oppressive reality of Sicilian life in 1890. Although Mascagni, living as he was in an economically depressed southern town, undoubtedly had some inkling of that reality, such concerns were alien to his intentions in writing *Cavalleria*. If he was familiar with Verga's original story at all, it made little difference. His intentions were (1) to create an opera that would gain its power from the emotional confrontations between its protagonists; (2) to appeal to an audience that, he rightly surmised, was eager for redder operatic meat than it was being offered; and (3) to win the Sonzogno competition.

The charge that *Cavalleria* fails to represent the social reality behind its story has less to do with the opera than with the iconic position of that story in the Italian literary consciousness, and the perception that the opera is somehow a "betrayal" of its initial literary source. No other opera of the period addresses the social reality of its setting any better (with the possible exception of Giordano's 1892 *Mala vita*, for which Sansone makes a credible case).[26] No other opera, however, was based on such a sacred text. Moreover, while it may be stretching a point to argue that writing an opera that truly conveys the underlying social reality of its setting is not possible, the fact remains that the musical vocabulary available to Mascagni and his contemporaries, with its overwhelming emphasis on cantabile melody, was exceptionally ill-suited to the task.

Italian opera, of course, was a business as much as an artistic pursuit. While the intellectual and literary elite filled the pages of the better newspapers and literary magazines, the growing middle class filled the seats of the theaters. Although Mascagni and his short, potent opera were denounced by Italy's littérateurs — most notably by the rising young poet Gabriele D'Annunzio in a famous diatribe "Il capobanda" (The bandmaster) — it drew a mass audience to the opera houses, not only in Italy but throughout the world. By contrast, *Mala vita*, although a rough-edged apprentice work unlikely to have found a place in the repertoire in any event, was denounced at its Naples premiere for having brought "the pestilential slums of Naples onto the splendid stage of the San Carlo," and soon disappeared from the scene.[27] Warts and all social realism was not to the bourgeois audience's taste; what they did want, and why, will be taken up in a later chapter.

Diffusion and Imitation

Cavalleria rusticana spread like wildfire. From the fall of 1890, when Italy's opera houses reopened after their summer break, the pace of new productions steadily grew. In the year beginning in September 1890, *Cavalleria* was staged in forty-one cities in Italy alone, not only all of its major centers, but also dozens of smaller cities where opera was rarely heard. By the end of 1893, it had already been staged four times in Rome and Milan, and three times each in Buenos Aires, Saint Petersburg, and Oporto, Portugal. While *Cavalleria* is Italian to the core, its popularity in Germany and Austria equaled its success at home. As Conati writes, "in the German lands, the initial interest prompted by the sudden appearance of 'verismo' opera . . . reached levels of unprecedented fervor, reflected by the overwhelming success within a few months throughout Central Europe first of *Cavalleria*, followed by *Pagliacci*."[28] First produced in Berlin in October 1891, by the following November *Cavalleria* had been performed in the German capital one hundred times; as the papers noted, one could see *Cavalleria* in the German capital one night out of every three.[29]

Within the next few years, the spectacular and unexpected success of *Cavalleria* had spawned a flood of imitations, as a host of composers sought to capture the same magic for themselves by writing what had come to be called verismo opera: compact, violent dramas of plebian life. Mascagni did not invent plebian opera. Verismo was in the air. Little more than a month before the premiere of *Cavalleria*, another treatment of Verga's play, the opera *Mala pasqua* by the composer Stanislao Gastaldon, had made its debut at the same theater; it was received, however, with little enthusiasm. The second-prize winner in the Sonzogno competition, *Labilia*, was a setting of a similar, although less compelling, story of peasant love and violence set in Corsica, a story uncannily similar to that of Mascagni's 1895 opera *Silvano*. Other titles from the list of competition entries, including *Rita*, *Marina*, and *Carmela*, suggest that it was not unique. The emergence of the "aesthetic of the knife" (*l'estetica del coltello*), in Tedeschi's dismissive phrase, was driven by more than *Cavalleria*'s success.

Scardovi's study of the genre identified forty-nine Italian "plebian" operas that were written and performed in the nation's opera houses between 1892 and 1899, of which ten, prompted by the immediate stimulus provided by *Cavalleria*, made their debut in 1892 alone.[30] These operas are set for the most part in Italy's impoverished countryside or in Naples, the urban surrogate for the violent rural society depicted in *Cavalleria*. The protagonists are members of the lower social classes, poor peasants and farm laborers, fishermen, or urban street vendors or day laborers, along with a scattering of mafiosi, smugglers, and other criminals. The plots are stripped down to the essence of sexually based conflict leading to a violent end. Indeed, many of them could better be characterized as "situations" rather than plots, particularly those used for one-act operas: they offer no character development, no intrigue or complexity, and as often as not, no particular dramatic logic, as in *Tristi nozze* (Sad nuptials) by Dallanoce, set ostensibly in Sardinia:

> Rilla and Severo love one another, but are blocked by her brother Flavio, who hates Severo and wants Rilla to marry Toto. Toto arrives, and the fishermen and sailors celebrate the forthcoming wedding. Severo comes looking for Rilla but finds Flavio, who explains the reason for his hatred — the woman he loved admitted to him on her deathbed that she had always loved Severo. The two fight, and Severo is killed, despite Rilla's vain efforts to save him.[31]

Someone is always killed off in the operas of this genre. In contrast to the inevitability of the outcome in *Cavalleria*, however, there is rarely any compelling logic to who is killed, and who does the killing. Finally, local color through the use of folkloric elements, loosely defined, is a pervasive theme of the genre, ranging from the interpolation of popular songs or dances (most often tarantellas, which were seen as a shorthand musical characterization of the south), and the depiction of distinctive regional customs, such as the gathering of the Camorristi in Spinelli's *A basso porto*.

While the great majority of these operas were ephemeral, trivial, efforts, some were substantial works, such as Giordano's *Mala vita* or Smareglia's *Nozze istriane*, which attracted serious attention and a respectable number of performances, at least for a while. In the end, though, only one of the plebian operas that followed *Cavalleria rusticana* has lasted: Ruggero Leoncavallo's *Pagliacci*.

Ruggero Leoncavallo and Pagliacci

In contrast to Mascagni, whose vivid individuality still comes across powerfully after more than a century, Ruggero Leoncavallo's personality remains obscure and hard to characterize. His photographs depict a pleasant, avuncular man with a Falstaffian belly and impressive handlebar mustaches, looking more like a provincial stationmaster or a retired sergeant major than an artist. Although described as pleasant, courteous, and charming in his manner, there is an air of passivity about him, an uncertainty about who he was both as person and artist that, were it not for his one bold stroke with *Pagliacci*, might have left him unknown to posterity, a modest figure occupying the penumbra of the Italian operatic world. This uncertainty carries over to much of the most basic information about the first thirty-five years of his life up to the premiere of his one truly successful opera — in large part because of the web of misinformation spun by the composer himself.[32]

Leoncavallo was a compulsive fabricator of his life, inventing degrees and encounters, even cutting a year off his life in his autobiographical accounts, claiming to have been born in 1858 rather than 1857.[33] Where attempts have been made to verify his accounts, such as his claim to a degree from the University of Bologna, or the date of his marriage — or even the given name of his wife — they have been called into question. As a result, it is difficult to describe his life before *Pagliacci*, except in broad outline. Even that outline, however, makes clear that these years were difficult ones, despite seemingly auspicious beginnings.

Ruggero Leoncavallo was a product of the Neapolitan elite, born in the last days of the Bourbon monarchy before its overthrow by Garibaldi. His father, a scion of the Apulian aristocracy, was a judge, while his mother came from a prominent artistic family in Naples. Her painter father was a professor at the Royal Academy of Fine Arts, while her sister Carolina had a brief career at the San Carlo opera house, singing in the premiere of Donizetti's *Il fortunato inganno* before leaving the stage for marriage and respectability. After spending much of his childhood in Italy's remote Basilicata region, where his father, who retained his judgeship after unification, was serving, Ruggero returned at eleven to Naples, where he began his musical studies. Although it is unclear whether he ever received a conservatory diploma, there is no question that his musical training was a thorough one, and that he became a more than competent pianist as well as a polished musical craftsman.

In contrast to his peers, whose musical training at the conservatory typically made up most of their formal learning, the young Leoncavallo had a classical as well as musical education, studying piano and composition at the conservatory while going through the prescribed courses at the *liceo*, the classical high school. After presumably graduating from the *liceo*, and spending some time living in the remote town of Potenza with his recently widowed father, in 1877 he left the south at the age of twenty to study in Bologna. It is not clear precisely what Leoncavallo did in Bologna, and it is doubtful that he was ever formally enrolled at the university, but it was in Bologna where he first began to think of himself as a serious composer, and where his earliest musical ideals were molded, under the influence of the dominant figure in that city's cultural life, Giosuè Carducci.

In the 1870s and 1880s Carducci was Italy's most famous poet, a writer who has been compared in his poetic scope and in the passionate intensity of his language to Walt Whitman.[34] For Carducci, poetry was a public, political undertaking; from his chair in literature at the University of Bologna he preached a doctrine of an engaged art for more than three decades, calling on young poets, painters, and musicians to depict Italy's mythic origins and glorious history as a way of remaking Italy's national consciousness — never more necessary than in the gray years that followed unification.

Under Carducci's influence, Leoncavallo embarked on a project that was to engage him off and on for the next fifteen years: an epic historical trilogy on the Italian Renaissance, modeled both dramatically and musically after Wagner's *Ring*; as its author wrote some years later, "faithful to the principles of the genius of Bayreuth."[35] In explicit homage to the master's *Götterdämmerung*, the work was to be entitled *Crepusculum*, and was intended to contain three operas, *I Medici*, *Savonarola*, and *Cesare Borgia*.[36] As did his contemporaries, Leoncavallo held Wagner in awe, in later years recounting an almost certainly apocryphal story of how in the course of an encounter in Bologna, the Master had personally blessed his trilogy.[37]

Only *I Medici* would ever be written, however, and that only many years later. After having conceived the trilogy, Leoncavallo set it aside in order to write a less ambitious opera, a romantic opera based on the story (taken from a play by Alfred de Vigny) of the doomed eighteenth-century English poet Thomas Chatterton, who died by his own hand at the age of eighteen. As with all his major operas, Leoncavallo wrote his own libretto. Although a production of *Chatterton* was announced for Bologna's Teatro del Corso, in what was to be the first of a series of disappointments, it failed to materialize.[38]

From Bologna he retreated to his father's home in Potenza, and from there to Egypt, where an uncle had a position as a musician in the khedive's court. Leoncavallo spent the next three years as a musician in Cairo, leaving in 1882 under somewhat unclear circumstances and washing up in Marseille, once again all but destitute. Making his way to Paris, he lived the *vie de bohème* for the next few years, combining the excitement of being a young artist in the City of Light with the uncertainty and misery of grinding poverty. Starting out as a piano player in cheap cafés, he accompanied singers and wrote songs. He gradually moved up to become a singing teacher, accompanist, and coach to many of the more prominent singers at the Opéra, becoming part of the Parisian musical scene and meeting the woman he would marry, either then or later.[39] Paris molded Leoncavallo's musical language more deeply than he ever cared to acknowledge: the pervasive waltz rhythms of so much of his music (particularly in his *La bohème*,) and the feeling given off by so many of his cantabile moments that one is never far away from the sawdust and marble-topped tables of the Parisian cabaret, are the legacy of his Paris years.

Even in his darkest days, Leoncavallo had never wavered in his conviction that his mission was to create the epic Italian historical trilogy that he had sketched years earlier in Bologna. In Paris, he completed the libretto for *I Medici*, which he showed to Victor Maurel, the baritone who had only a few months before created the role of Iago in Verdi's *Otello*. Impressed, Maurel arranged an introduction for the composer to Giulio Ricordi. Returning to Italy with his household, which included his wife and her mother, as well as a young woman adopted by his mother-in-law, Leoncavallo signed a contract for *I Medici* with Ricordi in April 1889, including a stipend of 200 lire per month for a year. He was now thirty-two, and this was the first point in his musical career at which he could allow himself to hope that his life would be more than the humdrum existence of a voice teacher, accompanist, and occasional songwriter.

He finished the score in the middle of 1890, submitted it to Ricordi, and waited, making ends meet once again by accompanying singers and giving voice lessons. After a number of false starts, he was finally convinced in October 1891 that Ricordi was going to have *I Medici* performed the following spring — only at the last minute to learn that Ricordi had decided to mount a revised version of Puccini's *Edgar* in its place. It was the ultimate disappointment in a life of growing desperation. As he wrote, a few years later, "it was the collapse of a thousand dreams, it was the sudden realization that I had thrown away years of work and pointless waiting."[40]

Pagliacci was fueled by Leoncavallo's desperation, not unlike that of Mascagni in his Cerignola exile, but made that much more intense by Leoncavallo's being ten years older, with the galling example of Mascagni's runaway success in front of his eyes. Putting his epic trilogy aside, Leoncavallo set down to create a plebian opera that would, if anything out-*Cavalleria Cavalleria*. Having nimbly extricated himself from his contract with Ricordi, he wrote both libretto and music for *Pagliacci* in five months and submitted it to Sonzogno, who accepted the opera immediately. Wasting no time, Sonzogno presented it at Milan's Teatro Dal Verme on May 21, 1892 (almost precisely two years after the debut of *Cavalleria rusticana*) under Toscanini's baton with Maurel as Tonio. The opera was a great success, and soon spread across Italy and central Europe, where its reception paralleled that of *Cavalleria* two years earlier.

The success of *Pagliacci* prompted enough interest in *I Medici* to lead to its debut at the Dal Verme in November 1893, but both then and in an 1895 revival at La Scala it was received coldly by both audience and critics. Whether Leoncavallo finally realized that his talents lay elsewhere, or concluded that audiences were looking for something other than historical epics, is unclear; what *is* clear is that he abandoned the remaining parts of the projected trilogy, and devoted the rest of his career to bourgeois opera and operetta.

After a prologue, in which Tonio explains that the opera we are about to see is a "slice of life," *Pagliacci* proper opens in a small town in Calabria, where Canio's troupe of traveling players has come to perform. Nedda, tired of her husband Canio's jealousy and brutality, loves a villager, Silvio. Tonio, a hunchbacked clown in the company, also loves Nedda, who despises him and rejects his advances. Seeing her with Silvio, Tonio tells Canio, who rushes in only to hear Nedda's final words to him, "tonight, and I shall be yours forever" as Silvio disappears in the night.

After Canio's famous aria "Vesti la giubba" and the obligatory intermezzo, the company's performance begins, with Canio playing Pagliaccio, the cuckolded husband, and Nedda Columbina, the cheating wife. When Canio hears Columbina repeat the same phrase in the play he heard her say earlier, he loses control of himself, and demands the name of her lover. Nedda tries to remain in character, but Canio is overcome by jealousy. As she tries to run away, he drives his knife into her back. As Silvio rushes up, his knife drawn, Canio stabs him in the heart. As the audience screams, Canio says the final words of the opera, the famous line "la commedia è finita."[41]

The source of Leoncavallo's libretto soon spawned a controversy that has never completely disappeared. When the French edition of *Pagliacci* appeared in 1894, the French playwright Catulle Mendès accused the composer of plagiarism, claiming that Leoncavallo had taken the plot of *Pagliacci* from Mendès's play *La femme de Tabarin*, which had appeared in Paris in the fall of 1887. Leoncavallo responded indignantly, asserting that the story was based on an episode that he had heard as a child sitting in his father's courtroom in Montalto; adding, furthermore, that in any event, Mendès's play was based on still another play, the popular *Un drama nuevo* (A new play) by the Spanish playwright Manuel Tamayo y Baus.[42] Although Mendès did not pursue the matter further, questions remained, largely because of the inconsistencies in Leoncavallo's own claims.

By 1900, still stung by the accusations that would not go away, Leoncavallo gave a far more detailed account of the "episode," now claiming that he had actually witnessed the murder, which he described in detail, and that the character of Silvio in the opera was none other than a young man named Gaetano Schiavelli, a servant who worked in the Leoncavallo household.[43] For good measure, the composer added that prior to the composition of *Pagliacci* he had never seen either *La femme de Tabarin* or *Un drama nuevo*.

It is hard to see Leoncavallo's assertions as anything but more of his compulsive fabrications. The murder of Gaetano Scavello (not Schiavelli) was nothing but a grim, pathetically ordinary *crime passionnel*, bearing no resemblance whatsoever to either the facts or the setting of *Pagliacci*.[44] The composer's accounts, both the more laconic 1894 one and the graphically depicted 1900 version, are made up of whole cloth. Similarly, his assertion that he had never seen *La femme de Tabarin*, a highly publicized play by a prominent author produced in Paris when he was not only an active member of that city's musical world but an assiduous theatergoer, is implausible at best.[45]

In all likelihood, Leoncavallo concocted his libretto from a number of sources. He relied on *La femme de Tabarin* as well as a slightly earlier version of the same story, an opera entitled *Tabarin* that appeared in Paris in 1885, and that Leoncavallo presumably also saw.[46] Both tell the story of the jealous clown Tabarin, a historical figure in seventeenth-century Paris, and his unfaithful wife Francisquine, although in the former work Tabarin kills his wife, and in the latter they are reconciled at the end. As Sansone demonstrates, despite the different ending, the libretto of the opera *Tabarin* is far closer to that of *Pagliacci*, including the content of the "play-within-the-play" and many specific points of wording, including Tabarin's closing lines, "la pièce est jouée, mes bons messieurs" (the play is over, my good sirs). Leoncavallo may also have used Tamayo's work (which also features the device of a play-within-the play), in which the action of the play parallels the entanglements of the characters offstage, and in which the entanglements closely resemble those of the characters of *Pagliacci*.[47]

In the end, however, the ultimate point of the controversy is that there is none. Leoncavallo took themes, including the image of the clown, the contrast between real life and the stage, and the play-within-a-play (all of which were common enough currency in the theater of the time), and wove them into a tight and effective story, set in a Calabria he knew just well enough to make both vivid and convincing. Without the composer's determination to muddy the waters with his implausible fabrications, it is unlikely that there ever would have been a controversy.

Leoncavallo was something of a creative magpie with respect to his music as well as his literary efforts.[48] Extensive passages in his libretto for *I Medici* are pastiches or outright borrowings of the poetry of Lorenzo de' Medici and of his court poet Poliziano. Similarly, the score of that opera is not only replete with borrowings from Wagner's operas, but contains a number of passages derived from, of all things, Schumann's *Novelette*, Op. 21, no. 3.[49] Even a cursory survey identifies many similar borrowings that can be found in *Pagliacci*: the famous "ridi, pagliaccio," phrase, which comes from act 3 of Verdi's *Otello*; the "Din Don" chorus, which appears to be taken from Chabrier's *España*; one extended passage from the Nedda-Silvio duet that unmistakably comes from Mendelssohn's Piano Trio in D Minor;[50] and a shorter one derived from Beethoven's Piano Sonata in A Major, op. 101.[51]

None of this has any bearing on why *Pagliacci* has not only survived but thrived, while its equally veristic contemporaries withered. Its success is not fortuitous. *Pagliacci* is an impressively crafted work, weaving together arias, choruses, and ensembles into large continuous scenes that are consistently effective; the extent to which it is far more technically sophisticated than *Cavalleria* is a staple of the critical literature, offering guilty pleasures to those who feel the need to denounce the crudities of the latter work. Although Leoncavallo's melodic vein is less original than Mascagni's, it is genuine; his motifs are distinctive, and the melodic high points such as Nedda's *Ballatella* and her duet with Silvio are powerful, even when they may be faintly reminiscent of something or someone else.

Pagliacci is a work of tremendous energy and impetus, far more vigorous than any other work of the composer—which may be attributable, as with Mascagni's similar work, to the hurried and desperate circumstances of its composition. The crowd scenes that open both acts are full of vitality and plebian flavor, while the final confrontation, as reality seeps into the play-within-the-play, remains one of the most gripping scenes in Italian opera. Finally, in Nedda, with her independent spirit and her yearning for a better life, Leoncavallo has created one of opera's most beautifully realized female characters, the near-equal of Violetta or Butterfly. In the end, after Canio has once again reminded her that he rescued her from the gutter, and demanded her lover's name, she replies:

> I may be contemptible, whatever you say,
> But I am not dishonorable, by God!
> My love is stronger than your contempt for me,
> Even if you kill me, I will not speak!

Her spirit has transcended the sordid frame from which she has emerged, and is consumed in an ecstasy that is all the more powerful for being a matter of a few seconds, rather than hours.[52]

Verismo Opera: Fact or Fancy?

In 1910, while composing his "leggenda drammatica" *Isabeau*, Mascagni was asked by Arnaldo Fraccaroli of the *Corriere della sera* if his new work was a return to romanticism. He responded "Absolutely; and imagine, I began with verismo! But verismo kills music. It is in poetry, in romanticism, that inspiration finds its wings."[53] Mascagni always resisted being characterized as a verismo composer, and if verismo is defined as the plebian genre of *Cavalleria* and *Pagliacci*, his point is well-taken. Although Puccini was still to extract one last drop of life from the genre with *Il tabarro*, the self-limiting musical and dramatic vocabulary that characterized the operatic exploration of society's lower depths quickly condemned it to the margins of Italian operatic life.

The term *verismo* is widely used, however, in a far broader sense than as a reference point for a small collection of violent operas that, whatever their historical significance, was but a minor genre of the period, let alone in the history of Italian opera. When used narrowly as a defining term for what we have earlier called plebian opera, it has at least the virtue of clarity, in that those operas are clearly the descendants, however attenuated in spirit, of the literary verismo of Verga and his contemporaries. When the term is applied more broadly, particularly when used to characterize the entire output of the composers of the *fin de siècle*, it becomes more problematic, raising two questions: Is there in fact enough common ground between these composers to justify their being categorized by a single term? And, if so, is "verismo" an appropriate term by which to categorize them?

The plots and settings of the operas of the time are hardly uniform, ranging from the exotic Japan of Puccini's *Madama Butterfly* and Mascagni's *Iris* to the Parisian music hall ambience of Leoncavallo's *Zazà*, from the contemporary setting, all but ripped from the headlines, of Giordano's *Fedora*, to the gloomy medieval castles of Zandonai's *Francesca da Rimini*. While exotic settings were hardly unknown in earlier operatic eras, the sheer variety of settings, as composers engaged in a hectic search for the new and different, is a distinguishing characteristic of the period. No composer searched harder than Puccini, placing his amorous heroes and suffering heroines in the Rome of 1800, contemporary Japan, a timeless mythic China, nineteenth-century Paris, and the American Wild West.

The search for newer and more unusual settings, which took opera to the Siberian taiga and the garrets of starving artists, was one manifestation of a central distinguishing feature of the operas of the Indian summer: the never-ending effort by their composers to provide their demanding new audiences with ever stronger and more powerful sensations. The most notable musical features of the operas of this period and the most notable departures from the musical language inherited from Verdi and his predecessors included octave doublings, pedals, and ostinato rhythms, as well as the increasing use of short, intense vocal phrases, often sung "quasi parlato" (almost spoken) or shouted, as in Santuzza's "A te la mala Pascua!" All served to further the central goal of magnifying the immediate dramatic effect of the music, intensifying the already superheated emotional climate of a dramatic vocabulary that was simultaneously becoming more violent and more sentimental.

Many of these same musical features, while accentuating the melodrama that lies at the heart of so many of the operas of the time, also function in ways that make the events depicted on stage more immediate, or more "real," and less part of a formalized musical frame. Beginning with the premise that the orchestra functions as narrator, Corazzol points out that "the orchestra's harmonic and rhythmic gestures in verismo opera are . . . regressive and simplifying . . . giving it an oral character, almost one of direct speech — gestural rather than abstract or logical."[54] The use of the orchestra as narrator or as the composer's voice, coupled with the fragmentation and intensification of the vocal language — all worked to break down the formal frame that separated the audience from unmediated experience of the events depicted on stage, creating a parallel of sorts with the verismo fiction of Verga or Capuana.

Even so, it would be misleading to draw that parallel too tightly. In contrast to the depiction of social reality that Verga and his peers strove for, the verismo composers strove for what might be called a melodramatic reality, attempting to create the illusion of unmediated reality in service of melodramatic artifice, rarely more effective, but also rarely more patently artificial, than the way emotional intensity is blended with the intrigue of a *roman policier* in the famous confrontation between Loris and the eponymous heroine of Giordano's *Fedora* to the accompaniment of a Chopinesque piano solo performed onstage.

As a popular genre, the operatic aesthetic of the time, with its poles of exoticism and bourgeois sentimentality, is far closer to the popular fiction of its time—epitomized by Emilio Salgari, Antonio Fogazzaro, or Gero-lamo Rovetta[55]—than to Verga's stark and unsentimental depiction of Si-cilian reality. Salgari, arguably the most popular writer in Italy during the 1890s (and sometimes called the Italian Jules Verne), wrote adventure and science fiction novels set in exotic locations in India, Malaysia, or the Caribbean. Fogazzaro's and Rovetta's novels were more intimate, depict-ing the conflicts within bourgeois families; or, in Fogazzaro's famous tril-ogy beginning with *Piccolo mondo moderno*, the conflicts between reli-gious yearnings and the desires of the flesh. While writers like Fogazzaro and Rovetta were not insensitive to the social realities and class conflicts of their time, those realities exist in their works largely as a frame within which the emotional conflicts of their characters are set, much as the French Revolution exists to frame the *Liebestod* of Andrea Chénier and Maddalena, and Russian nihilism is used even more tenuously to move the somewhat creaky gears of Giordano's *Fedora*.

In that respect, it is essential to remember that Italian opera, particularly in the last years of the nineteenth century, was as much a commercial ven-ture as it was an art form. The test of an opera was the enthusiasm with which it was greeted by the public; if it failed to engage its audience, it would not survive, whatever the verdict of the critics and intellectuals. The audience was increasingly a bourgeois audience, looking for stronger sen-sations and an intensified emotional experience from their nights at the opera. That audience was in some respects more sophisticated, but in other respects less so, than the earlier aristocratic audience. They were more likely to be readers, but their reading was more likely to be Salgari's stories of Sandokan, the "Tiger of Malaysia," than Verga or Tolstoy. They were more aware of the larger world, but their knowledge of that world was likely to be superficial and drawn heavily from the illustrated supplements that began to appear in the Italian press in the 1890s. Above all, they were less rooted in the traditional values of the church, the land, and the hierarchal ordering of society than their predecessors; their values, as we have noted before, belonged to a world of neutral facts and behaviors rather than moral principles, change and progress rather than stability and permanence— values derived, however tenuously, from the pervasive influence of posi-tivism in the bourgeois culture of the time.

In verismo opera, the traditional moral order has been replaced with a positivist view of human behavior, as significant a common ground among the composers of this period as the similarities in vocal technique or plot construction, and radically different from that of the operatic world of the past. It is impossible to make any sense of Mozart's operas, whether the affirmation of *Die Zauberflöte* or the subversion of *Così fan tutte*, outside the framework of a firmly grounded and universally understood moral order. The same is true, as noted earlier, of Verdi's works. The extent to which this changed by the end of the century can be seen in a comparison between the final scenes of Verdi's *La traviata* and Puccini's *La bohème*, thoroughly different despite their superficial likeness.

Both scenes, of course, depict the death of a beautiful young woman from tuberculosis, a common disease and frequently used dramatic trope of the time.[56] Both are sad, and likely to prompt much dabbing of moist eyes with handkerchiefs even among a hardened audience. Violetta's death, however, occurs within a larger moral universe. The audience, along with Alfredo and Germont, know of her renunciation, understand its significance, and read her death not only as a redemption, but as a transfiguration made possible by her sacrifice. The entire scene is inconceivable without reference to a potent, shared religious value system.

By contrast, in Puccini's *La bohème*, poor Mimì simply dies, accompanied by a texture of musical details and thematic reminiscences, in which, as Girardi points out, "all the emotions that the death of a loved one can provoke are arranged in such a way as to arouse the deepest response from the broadest possible audience,"[57] culminating in the classic verismo gesture, Rodolfo's desperate fortissimo cry of "Mimì!"[58] Puccini's sincerity is not at issue. One cannot doubt that Puccini, the quintessential bourgeois *homme moyen sensuel*, was deeply moved by Mimì's death; as the master craftsman he was, he made certain that his audience would feel the same. At the same time, neither he nor his librettists suggest that any larger meaning can be found in Mimì's death, or seek anything more from their audience than a purely emotional response to a heartbreaking moment.

Similar, although less deeply moving, episodes can be found throughout the operatic repertory of the period. A far more explicit statement of the positivist worldview appears in Mascagni's 1898 *Iris*, an emblematic work that while rarely seen today was regularly performed in Italy in the first decades of the twentieth century. *Iris* is the grim, sordid tale of an innocent Japanese maiden, kidnapped and taken to an Edo brothel, who dies in a trash heap on the edge of the city in the last act. As she dies, she hears from afar the voice of the wealthy libertine who arranged her kidnapping, summing up their story in librettist Illica's overripe fin de siècle language:

> Everyone follows their path, driven by their fatal nature.
> Your sweet manner, indifferent to divine desire, is an inhuman torture.

You die like a flower picked for its sweet smell.
In my darkness, I will now carry my smile and ghostly song elsewhere.
That is life. . . . Farewell . . .

Così la vita. That is life.

In short, for all the many variations in style and quality between the operas of the Indian summer, there is more than enough common ground to consider them a single movement, or school. There are exceptions, most notably in the work of Franchetti, but they are rare. Indeed, from the beginning of their rise to fame, Puccini, Mascagni, and their contemporaries were widely and appropriately seen as a school, known as the *giovane scuola* (Young School) of Italian composers, presumably to distinguish them from their older colleagues. Such a term could have been limited in its utility as the "Young School" grew older, and a new generation began to bark at their heels. Yet that was not the case. Indeed, as the term *giovane scuola* was still in use by the time the next generation (those born in the 1880s) began to emerge, those of the new generation who appeared to share common values were dubbed *la generazione dell'ottanta* (the generation of the eighties).

While it may appear difficult if not impossible to coin a neologism that would successfully replace the all but universal use of "verismo opera" to characterize the works discussed in these pages, either as a simple descriptor or a term of opprobrium, I remain deeply uncomfortable with the term. To characterize the works of these composers as "verismo operas" is inherently unsatisfactory: first, because "verismo" has already been applied to a literary movement with which they and their creators have little in common; and, second, because the re-creation of some sort of literal truth, as distinct from the construction of an emotionally compelling facsimile of that truth, is remote from their composers' intentions.

The term *verismo opera* will undoubtedly survive, not only because it has already lasted more than a hundred years, but because it is a straightforward, concise way of referring to a group of composers and operas that share substantial ground. There is enough validity to the term, moreover, to keep it from being entirely misleading. Without trying to repudiate it, however, I shall largely avoid using it in these pages, preferring the neutral *giovane scuola* in its place.

Chapter 3

Catalani, Franchetti, and the Rise of Puccini

Catalani, Puccini, and Franchetti in 1890

B y the 1880s, the last heroes of the Risorgimento were gone. Vittorio Emanuele had died in 1878, and Garibaldi, to the end denouncing how his revolution had been corrupted, died on his island of Caprera in 1882. A new generation was emerging that had known no country other than a united Italy, for whom the corrupt, oppressive governments of the time mattered more than the bygone heroics of the Risorgimento. In the cities and the countryside, peasants and workers were beginning to find their voice and build their own organizations, often triggering a violent reaction from the authorities. A younger, more cosmopolitan, generation of artists and intellectuals was coming of age. In the opera houses, the works of Massenet, Bizet, and Wagner were steadily moving into the Italian repertoire.

It was all but inevitable that a new body of composers, far more attuned to the international opera world than their predecessors, and eager to fill the void in Italian opera with their particular vision of the future, would emerge. During the 1880s three such composers appeared on the Italian scene, each with his partisans and detractors. By 1890, although all three had received considerable attention and were seen as composers of promise, none had yet demonstrated the ability to set a creative course for the future of Italian opera. Nor were any seen as likely to become, in the phrase that was beginning to circulate, "Verdi's heir." Still, until *Cavalleria rusticana* permanently changed the landscape of Italian opera, these three figures were seen, at least briefly, as representing its future.

The three composers were Alfredo Catalani (1854–1893), Alberto Franchetti (1860–1941), and Giacomo Puccini (1858–1924). While today it has long since been established that Puccini was the leading figure of his generation, that conclusion would not have been obvious to an observer of the

Italian operatic scene in 1890. Indeed, of the three, Catalani, although hardly a household name, was by far the most prominent. Since the premiere of his first opera, *Elda*, in 1880, three more substantial works of his had appeared on Italian stages, culminating in the successful debut of *Loreley* at Turin's Teatro Regio in February 1890. By comparison, Franchetti and Puccini were still both emerging composers. Although Puccini's first work, the one-act opera *Le Villi*, had been warmly received in its 1884 Milan debut, it had failed to engender sustained interest. It received a tepid response from the Turin audience the following year, while its Naples appearance in 1888, where it was greeted with hisses and catcalls, was a true fiasco. His first full-length opera, *Edgar*, was no more successful. Although Franchetti was represented only by a single opera, the 1888 *Asrael*, its ambitious quasi-Wagnerian musical and dramatic scope had attracted much critical attention, if not yet widespread public recognition.

By 1893, the situation had changed dramatically. By the end of that year, Puccini had clearly established himself with *Manon Lescaut* as the dominant figure among the younger generation of Italian composers. Catalani was dead at thirty-nine, the victim of the tuberculosis that had afflicted him since his teens,[1] while Franchetti's 1892 opera *Cristoforo Colombo*, although winning him a measure of popular attention, served even more to demonstrate his creative limitations. Although he would continue to compose operas for the next three decades, he would soon come to be seen as a secondary, although never uninteresting, figure on the Italian musical landscape.

Alfredo Catalani, Poet of Melancholy

Alfredo Catalani was born on June 19, 1854, in Lucca, the small Tuscan city that had given birth to Boccherini and would greet Puccini's arrival four years later. Although the Catalani family, like that of Puccini, were musicians, their role in Lucca's musical life was less elevated; Catalani's father was a music teacher and occasional composer, while his grandfather had been a piano teacher and piano tuner.[2] Intelligent, studious, and musically gifted, the young Catalani both studied music and pursued a classical education, enrolling both in the Liceo Machiavelli, the city's classical high school, and Lucca's conservatory, the Istituto musicale Pacini,[3] where his teacher was Fortunato Magi, Puccini's uncle. Catalani received his diploma with honors from the *liceo* in 1871, followed in 1872 by his diploma, along with the top prize in his class, from the conservatory. At his graduation concert, he presented a Symphony for Large Orchestra in F Major,[4] and a "Romanza" for baritone and orchestra. A warmly received Mass for soloists, chorus, and orchestra followed a few months later.

Catalani was clearly gifted with talents well beyond those of a small-town musician. Reflecting the changing cultural climate, he was encouraged by Magi to study at the Paris Conservatory rather than continue his studies elsewhere in Italy. Although Catalani remained in Paris less than a year, and does not appear ever to have enrolled in the conservatory,[5] the intense cultural stimuli offered by the French capital had a powerful effect on the sensitive youth from a provincial Italian town. Indeed, one biographer suggests that he cut short his stay in Paris in large part because he was overwhelmed by the sheer variety of the city's artistic and cultural life.[6] When he returned to Italy in 1873 to study at the Milan Conservatory, however, he was far more prepared for the city's turbulent artistic life than he would have been the year before. Handsome and articulate, he was soon a presence in the circles of the Scapigliati, and a welcome visitor to Countess Maffei's elegant salon. It was in these circles that he also met and became the lover of Teresa Garbagnati, who married his close friend Benedetto Junck, initiating a discreet triangular relationship that lasted off and on to the end of the composer's life.

As a sign of the esteem in which the young composer was held by the Scapligiati, their most prominent member, the poet and composer Arrigo Boito, wrote the libretto for Catalani's graduation work, an "Oriental eclogue" or one-act opera entitled *La falce* (The scythe). *La falce*, which was performed to much acclaim at the conservatory in July 1875, is a short two-character work set in the Arabian desert. The sole survivor of a battle between Muslims and idolaters encounters a mysterious solitary figure holding a scythe in the midst of the desert. Although she believes him to be Death, he encourages her to embrace life and love once again; at the end the two head off together into the desert. The work is introduced by a massive Prologue, a symphonic poem depicting the battle, based on a scenario prepared by Boito.

Aware of the young composer's promise, Milan's musical establishment turned out en masse for the event. The reviews were glowing. Filippo Filippi, dean of Milan's music critics, wrote "At twenty, and not yet graduated from the Conservatory, he is the absolute master of his art, fully in control of every resource, subordinating his means to the most elevated concepts."[7] Catalani was the musical hero of the hour. The conductor Franco Faccio led a performance of the Prologue with the prestigious Società del Quartetto, which subsequently appointed Catalani their artistic director. Giovannina Lucca, whose publishing firm was second in Italy only to the Casa

Ricordi, purchased the score of *La falce*, and commissioned a full-length opera from the young composer, whose diploma from the conservatory was still barely dry.

In some respects the summer of 1875, Catalani's twenty-first birthday, may have been the high point of his short life. He was not yet immersed in the drudgery of earning a living with his music, nor were the effects of his declining health and his increasingly difficult personality yet visible. Over the coming years, he would find himself more and more isolated, as his physical debility, his emotional dependency, and his resentment of his contemporaries and contempt for their works, would drive away all but a small body of loyal friends and admirers. In *L'edera* (The ivy), a famous 1878 painting by the Scapigliato painter Tranquillo Cremona, Catalani is portrayed as a pathetic figure, clinging desperately to a young woman, who has turned her face away from him with a look of indifference.[8] The image of the composer as a clinging vine grasping for strength from others rang profoundly true to his contemporaries.

Although Catalani had signed a contract with Lucca for an opera in 1875, it was two years before he was able to begin, a period largely devoted to an effort to convince Boito to write another libretto for him. Unsuccessful, Catalani settled for a libretto by Carlo D'Ormeville, a well-respected Milan impresario and theatrical manager, who was also a competent producer of libretti for a variety of Italian composers from the 1860s through the 1880s. The work, entitled *Elda*, was a treatment of the story of the Lorelei based loosely on the famous Heine poem, relocated to a vaguely defined setting along the Baltic Sea. Both the choice of subject and its setting reflected not only Catalani's own preferences, but a broader predilection among the Scapigliati for northern themes and settings. To the Scapigliati, the north was not only the land of Wagner, but the land of mystery, romanticism, and melancholy — all features they found in short supply in Italy, a land too brightly lit for their crepuscular tastes. *Elda* was the first of a series of such Nordic operas to appear over the next ten-plus years, while Mascagni's *Guglielmo Ratcliff,* begun in 1884 but not completed and performed until 1895, was the last to attract any notice.

Completed late in 1878, *Elda* was given its first performance, after substantial cuts and changes had been made to the score, at Turin's Teatro Regio in January 1880. The opera was well received by the critics, and at least moderately so by the Turin public. For all its weaknesses of form and organization, it revealed a fresh new voice in Italian opera, a composer who was more than another imitator of Verdi, alive to the influence of Wagner and the French composers yet still at his core Italian. Extensively

Catalani as a clinging vine in the painting *L'edera* (The ivy) by Tranquillo Cremona.
(Galleria Civica d'Arte Moderna e Contemporanea, Turin)

rewritten, *Elda* reappeared ten years later as *Loreley*, one of the two Catalani operas (the other being *La Wally*,) that deserve to be heard more often
by modern audiences.

Elda's success led to a contract with Lucca for a second Catalani opera.
Boito, once again rebuffing Catalani's pleas for a libretto, prepared a scenario for him entitled *Dejanice*, which was turned into a libretto by Angelo
Zanardini, who had recently written the libretto for Ponchielli's *Il figliuol
prodigo*.[9] Boito's scenario is a perfunctory rehash of *La Gioconda*, which
he had written nearly ten years before for Ponchielli, relocated in time and
space to the Greek colony of Syracuse in Sicily of 400 B.C.E.[10] Although he
was later to speak scornfully of the libretto, Catalani went to work without
hesitation, finishing his new opera in March 1882. Assiduously promoted
by Faccio and D'Ormeville, *Dejanice* made its debut a year later at La
Scala. Although it found some admirers, including two young conservatory
students named Puccini and Mascagni, the critical and public reaction
was lukewarm, and the opera soon disappeared from the boards.

Neither the unconvincing classical setting nor the hackneyed plot drew
the composer's best efforts. Although it has some inspired passages, much
of *Dejanice* sounds like an exercise in "composing-by-the-numbers," in
which the composer produced formulaic music to accompany each scene
or passage, appropriately violent, exotic or romantic, with little concern for
the overall dramatic arc or progression of the music. Although *Dejanice*
shows some growth in the composer's musical craft, it was a backward step
for Catalani after the freshness and appeal of *Elda*.

Giovannina Lucca remained faithful to her composer, and commissioned another opera from his pen. By now Boito was working with Verdi
on *Otello*, and suggested that Catalani seek a libretto from Antonio Ghislanzoni, librettist of *Aida*. Ghislanzoni offered him a libretto that he had
written some years before for another composer but that had never been
used; that libretto, entitled *Edmea* and based on the play *Les Danicheffs*
by Alexandre Dumas *fils*, became Catalani's new opera.[11] Although Ghislanzoni was a competent versifier, he was a child of an earlier era. His
libretto was an old-fashioned effort, with a clichéd plot, set arias and ensembles, and a mad scene, reminiscent of libretti written by Romani and
others for Bellini, Donizetti, and their contemporaries early in the century.[12] While Catalani was drawn to this story by the melancholy pathos of
the heroine and the Germanic setting, he was also comfortable with its
conventional cut; he felt, as he wrote to his faithful friend Giuseppe Depanis, the impresario of Turin's Teatro Regio, "the need for a quick and immediate success to make my name with the wider public."[13] Although his po-

sition as the most promising composer of the younger generation was not yet threatened by others, he was acutely aware that, nearly nine years after his auspicious debut, he had yet to create a work that was more than at most a succès d'estime.

Edmea is a much more convincing work than *Dejanice*. It is laced throughout with appealing music, including an exquisite love duet between Edmea and Oberto and a solo scene for Oberto, reminiscent of Alvaro's famous "La vita è inferno all'infelice" from *La forza del destino*, but a fine fusion of recitative, arioso, and orchestral comment in its own right. The mad scene, understated rather than histrionic, is quietly moving, while the opera as a whole moves smoothly and effectively to its equivocally happy ending. For all its beauties, however, the opera is curiously pallid and highly forgettable. There is little that is musically distinctive about it; while the occasional modulation reminds us that we are in the 1880s, the work breathes the air of an earlier era. As in the operas of the early nineteenth century, dramatic confrontations predictably evolve into formal ensembles, while orchestra and soloist alike regularly pause and take a deep breath between the end of each recitative and the beginning of the next aria.

Another problem, notable not only in *Edmea*, but in all of Catalani's works until *La Wally* as well as in the works of his contemporaries, is the unevenness between the music written to express emotional states, and that written to accompany action. By *Edmea*, the musical vocabulary that Catalani deploys for his lyrical effusions has become highly sophisticated. Adding his own particular sensibility to a vocabulary borrowed in part from Verdi and in part from French models, Catalani's rhythmically flexible melodic line is supported by a varied harmonic texture and a rich orchestral fabric that has become an increasingly important part of the drama itself. In *Edmea*, he is able to create not only moving and expressive moments, but entire scenes with a continuous texture and dramatic arc. In this respect, he is an important predecessor to and influence on his younger contemporaries, including Puccini and Mascagni.

Catalani, however, has found no comparable musical language to give his scenes of action and dramatic conflict vitality and individuality. In comparison to his lyric moments, these scenes depend on a series of instrumental clichés, string tremolos, sforzando diminished chords, and trumpet calls occasionally given weight by doubled trombones intoning short portentous motives, while the vocal line pursues a restricted, unimaginative, line on top of the orchestral racket. Although he came close in *La Wally*, Catalani never truly overcame this problem, which was solved only by Puccini in his mature operas beginning with *Manon Lescaut*.

Edmea was substantially more successful than its predecessors, with a respectable number of performances not only in major Italian cities, but also in cities as far-flung as Saint Petersburg, Moscow, and Mexico City. The Turin performance was Arturo Toscanini's Italian conducting debut, and led to a warm friendship between Toscanini and the composer. Toscanini remained devoted to Catalani's memory long after the composer's death, naming his children Walter and Wally, after the protagonists of Catalani's two most successful operas.

Although *Edmea* soon faded, it had the desired effect of sustaining Giovannina Lucca's faith in his future.[14] Instead of a new opera, however, he embarked on the reworking of *Elda*, which, by the end of 1887, had been recast as *Loreley*. With the help of Zanardini and further assistance by Giuseppe Giacosa and Luigi Illica, it was extensively rewritten and restored to its traditional setting along the Rhine.[15] The new opera's debut, however, was delayed by the acquisition of the Lucca publishing firm by the House of Ricordi in the spring of 1888. In contrast to the almost maternal support that Giovannina Lucca had given the composer, Guilio Ricordi was remote and uncommunicative; that fall Catalani wrote Depanis, "my new master is like a sphinx: he never lets you get a glimpse of him, and you can never speak with him. I don't even know if he knows that I've had *Loreley* ready to go for a year now."[16] Catalani by this time was increasingly embittered by his lack of popular success and by his failing health, which began to deteriorate badly in 1889. He was convinced, not without reason, that Ricordi had other favorites, writing Depanis in August, "there is only one publisher, and this publisher won't hear mention of anybody else but Puccini."[17]

Loreley finally caught Ricordi's eye, making its successful debut in February 1890 at Turin's Teatro Regio, more than two years after it had been finished. Although it shares some of the defects of its predecessors, it was Catalani's strongest opera to date, melodically richer and far more inventive harmonically than anything he had written before. It continues to be preferred by many listeners, including the author, to the more finely crafted but less spontaneous *La Wally*. The pervasive influence of Wagner is particularly notable in *Loreley*, far more so than in any of Catalani's earlier operas. While the Wagnerian echoes are predominately those of *Tannhäuser* and *Lohengrin*, Catalani's familiarity with Wagner's later works, *Tristan und Isolde* and the *Ring* (both all but unknown to Italian audiences) is also apparent. While it would not be unreasonable to characterize *Loreley* as thus more derivative than Catalani's previous works, Wagner's influence has a paradoxically liberating effect on the composer. The conventional harmonies of the earlier operas are replaced by a new chromatic complexity and freedom of modulation, while his melodies have a new breadth and expansiveness, even when they do not stray far from Wagnerian models.

Loreley does not maintain its high level throughout: the third act, although containing a moving funeral scene that left a strong imprint on Puccini's funeral music in *Edgar*,[18] is thinner musically than the first two — a not unusual phenomenon in operas of the period. It is redeemed, however, by its magical ending. As the Rhine flows over Walter's body, the orchestral tumult dies down and we hear the voice of Loreley singing pianissimo; as her voice dies away in turn, the upper strings and harp intone an exquisitely ethereal postlude, the music disappearing into all but nothingness with the final curtain.[19]

Catalani began to cast about for a new subject as soon as *Loreley* was finished, without waiting for its future to be resolved. Although Boito once again turned down the composer's request for a libretto, he urged Catalani to work with a young librettist named Luigi Illica, suggesting as a subject *Die Geyer-Wally*, a romantic novel by the Bavarian writer Baroness von Hillern that had recently been translated into Italian and serialized in the Milan newspaper *La Perseveranza*.[20] Illica, a vivid, combative figure who would soon become the premier librettist to the rising generation of Italian opera composers, already had a modest reputation in Milan as a playwright. He brought a fresh, creative voice to the craft of libretto-writing, something Catalani desperately needed after years of dealing with the Zanardinis and Ghislanzonis of the world. Illica completed the libretto early in 1889, and Catalani went immediately to work.

La Wally, as the opera was titled, is set in the Tyrol, where Wally wanders her native mountains with her androgynous companion Walter. Rejecting a match with the forester Gellner, she leaves the parental home. Wally is secretly in love with Hagenbach and follows him to a village fair, where Gellner warns her that Hagenbach is betrothed to Afra. Hagenbach steals a kiss from the virginal Wally, who vows vengeance, telling Gellner that she will marry him if he kills Hagenbach. As Hagenbach follows Wally home to seek her forgiveness, Gellner ambushes him and throws him into a ravine. Wally discovers that Hasenbach is still alive, and pulls him out of the ravine. She then leaves her home for the mountains, where Hagebach follows her. As a storm breaks out they declare their love. When an avalanche buries Hagenbach, Wally throws herself to her death.

La Wally was a desperate gamble driven by Catalani's need to compose, whatever the outcome of his efforts might be. With his health steadily deteriorating, Catalani may have had at least some premonition that this would be his last opera. Although his immediate economic needs were met by the stipend from the Milan Conservatory where he had begun to teach in 1888, he had no contract for the new opera, and no assurances that Ricordi would purchase it or arrange for it to be performed. As he worked on *La Wally* from 1889 to 1891, he was increasingly convinced that everything and everyone was conspiring against him; it seemed that every few months another composer arrived on the scene, more favored by publishers, critics, and even by the great Verdi,[21] than himself. Puccini's *Edgar*, Franchetti's *Asrael*, and above all, Mascagni's *Cavalleria rusticana*, sent Catalani into spasms of fury and disgust, expressed in the letters he sent nearly daily to Giuseppe Depanis.[22]

In this difficult atmosphere, Catalani set himself the task of writing an opera that would be his masterpiece, by which he would be remembered and which would remind the Italian musical world of how much they would lose by his passing. Every page of *La Wally* shows careful attention to the smallest detail. In his final opera, Catalani has finally broken free of the weight of his influences, from Verdi to Wagner, creating a seamless musical language in which each act follows a single dramatic and musical arc, blending orchestra, chorus, and protagonists in a flexible, constantly changing musical texture. All this, however, is not enough; as Budden has written, "though he finally solved all the problems of scale and dramatic continuity and won through to a new freedom of expression, his own artistic personality emerges curiously pallid and insubstantial . . . [his] own voice remains elusive and his ideas mostly unmemorable."[23]

As Zurletti has aptly observed, "*La Wally* is Catalani's masterpiece, but it is not a masterpiece."[24] The music of *La Wally* is consistently good, but rarely more than good. Indeed, the contrast between the body of the opera and its one truly inspired moment, the famous aria "ebben? . . . N'andro lontana" (well then? . . . I will go far away.) is painful. This aria is sung by Wally near the end of the first act, when she tells her father that she will leave her home rather than marry the odious Gellner. As its first lustrous notes are heard, the listener is suddenly aware that she is in the presence of truly beautiful music, compared to which everything that has gone before is merely ordinary. This aria, however, was not written for *La Wally*, but was a reworking of a song originally entitled "Chanson Groënlandaise" that Catalani had written during his student years, fifteen or more years before.[25] As many of the best ideas in *Loreley* had already appeared in *Elda* ten years earlier, it is hard not to conclude that, although Catalani had perfected his craft in *La Wally*, his creative vein had grown weaker over the years.

Catalani finished *La Wally* in May 1891, and played it for Ricordi, who agreed to publish and present the opera. Hedging his bets, however, Ricordi forced Catalani to accept an unusual contract under which, rather than receive the customary flat payment on delivery of the opera, his fee would be deferred and paid out in three installments, after the twentieth, fortieth, and sixtieth performances respectively of the opera.[26] *La Wally* made its debut in January 1892 at La Scala, where it was warmly received, and given eighteen performances. It made the rounds of the Italian opera houses, and in 1893, received a warm welcome in Hamburg, the first German production of a work by Italy's most Germanophile composer. By this point, however, Catalani's health was failing. A last trip to the mountains in the hope of regaining his health was unsuccessful, and he was brought back to Milan, where he died on August 7, 1893, only thirty-nine years old.

Although an important transitional figure, whose music prefigures much of that of Puccini and his generation, Catalani remains a secondary figure in Italian operatic history. Although he commands respect for his ability to create atmosphere and convey the themes of romantic yearning and melancholy, his range is narrow, and his ability to create fully realized characters to which the audience could respond all but nonexistent, something where not only Puccini, but even lesser verismo composers such as Cilea and Leoncavallo surpass him. His characters are largely shadowy, insubstantial, figures; Walter and Loreley, Oberto and Edmea are little more than personifications of their thwarted romantic yearnings. When Catalani finally took on a more muscular subject in *La Wally*, little changed. For all its difference in tone, its underlying theme is the same as in the earlier operas; in this case, Wally's obsessive yearning for the unattainable Hagenbach. Wally and Hagenbach are creatures of bizarre caprice and extreme emotional states, rather than credible personalities. For all the tight musical organization of that opera, its dramatic logic is unconvincing. Still, the beauty of his best music in *Loreley* and *La Wally* is such that he will never be entirely forgotten by the world of opera.

Alberto Franchetti and the Last Grand Opera

Most Italian opera composers of the period were products of the nation's small middle class, often from families with long musical histories. Of the composers who came to public notice in the 1880s and 1890s, Puccini and Catalani were from musical families. Cilèa, Leoncavallo, and Giordano had solid middle-class roots, while Mascagni was the sole member of the group whose origins were in Italy's large working class. Baron Alberto Franchetti was from the opposite end of the social spectrum. A member of the Jewish titled aristocracy, one of nineteenth-century Europe's smallest and most exotic clubs, he was raised in a world of wealth and privilege beyond the imagination of most Italians. While the claim that Baron Raimondo Franchetti, the composer's father, could travel from Tuscany to Venice without leaving his landholdings was an exaggeration,[27] the phrase "ricco come Franchetti" (as rich as Franchetti) reputedly could once be heard in some parts of central Italy.[28]

The Franchetti family, whose origins can be traced back to medieval southern France, were merchants and bankers in Livorno, pillars of that city's Jewish community by the eighteenth century. In 1858, the composer's grandfather, Abramo Franchetti, a financier and a pioneer in developing Italy's railway network, was made a baron by Vittorio Emanuele, king of Sardinia and future king of Italy. Three weeks after the family was ennobled, Abramo's son Raimondo, the composer's father, married the daughter of Baron Anselm von Rothschild of the Vienna Rothschilds, joining two of Europe's most potent financial clans. Their oldest son, Alberto, was born in Turin in 1860, but was raised in Venice, where the family had extensive holdings, including a Murano glassworks.[29] It was in Venice that he began his musical studies, and published his first small works at family expense, under various pseudonyms.[30]

It does not appear that Franchetti was ever under any pressure to pursue a more respectable profession; on the contrary, both his father, who was a passionate opera lover and part-time impresario, and his mother, a talented amateur pianist,[31] appear to have encouraged him throughout his musical career, and were content to provide him with financial support well into his middle years. After completing his military service, Franchetti went to Germany to continue his musical studies, beginning in Munich with Josef Rheinberger and continuing in Dresden under Felix Draeske, contemporaries of Brahms and both highly regarded symphonists of the time.

Wagner notwithstanding, Italians saw Germany as the land of the symphony, and the choice of Germany for musical study suggests that the young Franchetti may have felt at least some ambivalence at the time about an operatic career. Indeed, his graduation work at Munich, a Symphony in E Minor, shows him to be a promising symphonist. It is an appealing, well-crafted four-movement work in the German mainstream, comparable to the works of Reinecke, Raff, or the young Richard Strauss.[32]

Franchetti, however, had no desire to become or be seen as a dilettante composer, dabbling in symphonies and string quartets while living off his father's money. While still in Germany, he realized that if he were to be recognized in his homeland as a serious composer, he would have to conquer the world of opera. Early in 1884, Franchetti asked his father to obtain a libretto for him. Raimondo Franchetti initially sought a libretto from Boito, who was unavailable or uninterested, and who recommended the Scapigliato poet and playwright Ferdinando Fontana, who had prepared the libretto for Puccini's *Le Villi* the year before.[33]

Fontana (1850–1919) was a prominent figure in the Milan musical and literary scene until 1898, when, fearing prosecution for his political activities in the repressive climate of that time, he fled Italy, spending the rest of his life in exile in Switzerland. He was perhaps the last of the true Scapigliati, pursuing not only radical politics and fantastic literary dreams, but also the hand-to-mouth existence of an improvident bohemian, long after those pursuits had ceased to be in fashion in Milan. Generous, warmhearted, and idealistic, he not only reduced his fee for the impecunious Puccini — although not for Franchetti — but was largely responsible for raising the funds and organizing the Milan premiere of *Le Villi* that saved that opera from obscurity and set Puccini on the path to fame. Sadly, Fontana was not a good librettist, combining a taste for overelaborate and grandiloquent verse with a nearly total lack of dramatic acumen, weaknesses apparent in his libretto for *Asrael* and in his subsequent effort for Puccini, *Edgar*.

Although one contemporary source describes Fontana's libretto as based on "a Flemish legend of 1300 and the episode of Farat and Nama in Thomas Moore's *Loves of the Angels*,"[34] a reading of that poem shows no connection with the opera other than, at most, a certain atmosphere.[35] The two scenes of the first act are set in hell, from which the demon Asrael returns to Earth to seek his heavenly spouse Nefta; and in heaven, from which Nefta returns to Earth in hopes of saving him. The rest of the opera takes place in medieval Brabant, part of modern Belgium, and better known operatically as the setting of *Lohengrin*.

Asrael bests the wicked Princess Lidoria,[36] who has chosen the magic arts over marriage, but rejects her hand. The ensuing melee, in which Loretta, queen of the Gypsies and her band take his side, is halted by Sister Clotilde, Nefta in earthly form. In the third act, Loretta has fallen in love with Asrael, but Lidoria warns her that he is a demon who will steal her soul, giving Loretta a flask of holy water to pour over him. After an ecstatic love duet, Asrael falls asleep. Loretta empties the flask over him, and he cries out in agony. Angels and demons battle over him, as Sister Clotilde rescues him. In the final act, despite Asrael's conviction that he is damned,

Clotilde finally convinces him to pray for salvation. As he prays, heavenly trumpets are heard. Clotilde is transformed back into Nefta, and welcomes Asrael into heaven, as the opera ends in a blaze of choral and orchestral sound.

This libretto, however preposterous, offered the young Franchetti the opportunity to tackle almost every form and genre known to Italian opera of the time; infernal music for the hosts of hell, antiphonal choruses for the saints and virgins in heaven, ceremonial marches, battle scenes, numerous solos including a Gypsy air for Loretta, and an extended love duet for Loretta and Asrael. Taking full advantage of those opportunities, Franchetti composed a massive, audacious, work, demonstrating an astounding mastery of choral textures and orchestral technique, as well as the ability to construct effective, if not often memorable, vocal lines.

Back in Italy, Franchetti completed *Asrael* in the fall of 1887. The new opera made its debut in February 1888 in the central Italian city of Reggio Emilia, where the composer's father dabbled as the theater's impresario between 1887 and 1893. It was given an impressive production, with an orchestra of 90, chorus of 100, and an additional complement of 22 trumpeters and bandsmen.[37] Greeted enthusiastically, the score was purchased and published by Ricordi, and staged again in Bologna in March. *Asrael* reached La Scala in December, where it opened the 1889 season with an impressive seventeen performances. In January 1889 *Asrael* was produced at the Teatro Carlo Felice in Genoa, in October of that year in Treviso,[38] and in the fall of 1890 it opened the Metropolitan Opera season in New York. *Asrael* immediately placed Franchetti in the front rank of Italy's younger composers, sparking a predictably wounded outburst from the embittered Catalani.[39]

With the exception of Boito's *Mefistofele*, to which it bears some resemblance, no Italian opera composer had ever begun his career so ambitiously, nor had any composer demonstrated such mastery of means in his debut work. It is easy to understand the enthusiasm with which *Asrael* was greeted, particularly given the moment in which it appeared, when the yearning of the Italian musical world for new composers to carry on the work of Verdi was turning into desperation. Looked at from today's vantage point, however, while one must admire the sheer energy of the work, it is impossible to share that enthusiasm, not only because of the weakness of the libretto, but because of the limitations of the music. Deeply influenced by *Mefistofele*, *Faust*, and above all by the Wagner of *Lohengrin* and *Tannhäuser*, the opera goes on far too long, with Franchetti simply unable to produce music compelling enough to sustain interest in his overwrought drama. *Asrael* more than amply illustrates his most glaring limitations as a composer, the lack of distinction in his melodic line, and the squareness of his rhythmic impulse. He enlivens his melodies with unusual harmonies and modulations, some of which are highly effective while others are forced and artificial; the melodies themselves, however, have little dynamism or forward motion, often losing impetus after a series of symmetrical four-bar phrases.

One should not, however, dismiss Franchetti. Even in his first opera, he was a master of operatic architecture, and it is likely that many of his grand ensembles and choral scenes are far more effective in performance than they may appear on the printed page.[40] The extended love scene between Asrael and Loretta in the third act, where Franchetti reached lyrical heights that he would rarely achieve in his subsequent works, is also fine music of a Wagnerian, *Tristan*esque hue. *Asrael* also signaled that Franchetti's artistic sensibility was quite different from that of the other composers of his generation. Although he would grapple with a veristic subject years later in *La figlia di Jorio*, the effort was unsuccessful and uncongenial to his temperament. His operatic predilections were those of a vanishing tradition, comfortable with the formal ensembles and concertati that his contemporaries rejected, and with the traditional themes, such as the conflict of love and honor or the nobility of sacrifice, that animated opera from the days of the opera seria through Verdi.[41]

The course from *Asrael* to Franchetti's next work was fast and direct. In 1889, the city of Genoa was looking for a composer from whom to commission an opera on the life of Christopher Columbus, in honor of the forthcoming 400th anniversary of the discovery of America. When consulted by the city fathers, Verdi, who had attended the Genoa performance of *Asrael* and admired the work, recommended Franchetti.[42] Franchetti accepted the commission, for which he was paid the substantial sum of 35,000 lire, put aside his plans for an opera on the life of Zoroaster, and began immediately to set the libretto by Luigi Illica, who had won a libretto competition held by the city.[43]

Cristoforo Colombo was conceived as a semihistorical pageant-opera in the grand manner. In the course of four acts and an epilogue, it takes Columbus from his first meeting with Queen Isabella to the Americas and back to his death in Spain, abandoned by all but his faithful lieutenant Guevara. The first act depicts Columbus's rebuff by the Council of Salamanca and his rescue by Queen Isabella, while the second act, which takes place at sea, ends with the first sighting of America, just in time to quell a mutiny led by Roldano, who appears throughout the opera as

Columbus's nemesis. While these two acts are loosely based on the historical account, the third and fourth acts, set in America ten years later, are
based more on Illica's rummaging through his predecessors' efforts than
on the historical record, depicting a complex tangle of plots and counter-
plots between the Spaniards and the Indians.[44] An Indian uprising is
thwarted by the love between Guevara and the Indian princess Iguamota,
but Columbus is disgraced and sent home in chains. In the epilogue, Guevara leads the ailing explorer to seek Isabella's help once again; as they
learn that the queen has just died, Columbus falls dead on her tomb.

Mounted in Genoa in October 1892 as the centerpiece of yearlong festivities, *Cristoforo Colombo* was given a star-studded performance, with
Giuseppe Kaschmann as Columbus, Edoardo Garbin as Guevara, and
Francesco Navarrini as Roldano, under the direction of the distinguished
conductor Luigi Mancinelli. The audience was enthusiastic, particularly
after the first two acts. Although some fatigue was evident as the evening
wore on, the end of the opera was greeted with prolonged applause, as the
audience remained in the hall, calling the composer and the performers
back time and again, until well after two in the morning. The production
then moved to Milan, where it opened the La Scala season, again to acclaim tempered with fatigue.

The opera was clearly too long, and despite its warm reception in
Genoa and Milan, Italy's other houses showed little interest in putting it
on. Franchetti and Illica made extensive cuts to the third and fourth acts,
reworking them into a single act, and reducing the opera's length by nearly
an hour. Even then, it was still too long for some audiences, and many
houses, with the composer's permission, performed a truncated version
consisting of the first two acts and the epilogue, a version that captures the
opera's best music, but lacks dramatic shape or coherence. In one version
or the other, *Colombo* began to make its way slowly across the peninsula in
1894 and 1895. Although it never truly caught on with the Italian public,
Colombo received a handful of productions in Italy and Argentina during
the years preceding the First World War.[45]

Colombo is an impressive achievement, and contains much of the best
music Franchetti was to write. At the same time, it is less a single coherent
work than two radically different operas combined into one. The first two
acts, which contain little action but much fine music, are more oratorio
than opera, dominated by the omnipresent chorus, the backdrop against
which Columbus appears as a solitary hero moving toward his destiny.
Franchetti's ability to control large forms is never better displayed, as these
two acts form a single, sweeping, musical-dramatic whole, leading inex-

orably to the climax of the second act, the discovery of America. The third and fourth acts, by contrast, are full of often muddled action, written in a vocabulary that is less Wagnerian than that of Ponchielli and middle-period Verdi, during which Columbus is subordinated — until nearly the end of the two acts — to a host of newly introduced characters whose roles and relationships to one another are not always clear.

Franchetti identified fully with Columbus. His lines have a nobility that is rare in the music of the period, and in the epilogue they take on a deeply moving pathos. Franchetti's muse is less effective, however, in capturing either Roldano's wickedness or Guevara's youthful passion. Columbus is the opera's center, and when he yields the stage in the third and fourth acts, the opera loses its bearings. The epilogue attempts to provide the resolution that will unify the two halves. While it contains some of Franchetti's best music, the task, in the final analysis, is impossible. Despite his repeated efforts to rework his opera, which led ultimately to his composing a completely new third act to supersede entirely the two American acts,[46] Franchetti was never able to find a solution.

While Franchetti's strengths and weaknesses, including his fatal limitations as a melodist, are much the same as in *Asrael, Colombo* is ultimately brought down by its archaic form and content. While a grand opera-pageant may have been what the Genoese city fathers wanted to glorify their city's history — and to further the project, dear to the politicians of the time, of building a new Italian identity — it was not something that held any real interest for the bourgeois audience of the 1890s. The age of grand opera, or *opera-ballo* as it was known in Italy, was over. Its dramatic themes, particularly the patriotic themes that serve as the subtext of *Colombo*,[47] did not appeal to the new audience, while the musical vocabulary that emerged in the 1890s was ill-suited to the genre. Neither Franchetti nor any other Italian composer of note was ever to attempt another work of this sort. *Cristoforo Colombo* was the last Italian grand opera.

Despite *Cristoforo Colombo*'s equivocal reception, it established Franchetti as a major figure on the Italian opera scene. During the coming decade he would be regularly identified in the same breath as Mascagni and Puccini as a leading member of the *giovane scula*,[48] and in 1902 his *Germania* would give him another significant although short-lived success. In the meantime, his personality and appearance became well known in Italy. His long black beard gave him the look of an Old Testament prophet, while his eccentricities and his association with that newfangled invention, the motor car, made him grist for the popular media. A founder of the Italian Touring Club, he was one of Italy's pioneering motorists and racers,

The *giovane scuola* at the piano: Mascagni, Franchetti, and Puccini in 1896. *(Museo Mascagnano, Livorno)*

winning the Brescia Grand Prix in 1900 at the wheel of a twelve-horse-power Panhard Levassor, averaging better than thirty-three miles per hour over the 138-mile course.[49]

Giacomo Puccini Makes His Operatic Debut

The third composer to come to public attention during the 1880s, and the one who would finally be recognized as not only the dominant Italian composer of his generation, but one of Italy's greatest musical figures, was Giacomo Puccini.[50] Puccini was born on December 22, 1858, in Lucca, the same small Tuscan city that had given birth to Catalani four years earlier. For four generations, members of the Puccini family had been church composers and organists in Lucca, beginning when the composer's name-sake, Giacomo Puccini, came to Lucca from the hill town of Celle in 1739 to take the position of organist at the Church of San Martino. Puccini's father Michele was the organist of Lucca Cathedral and a distinguished local music teacher.

Michele died when the future composer was only five, leaving Puccini's mother, Albina Magi, a widow with five daughters and two sons. Puccini, the older son, was the fifth child. The Lucca authorities assumed that young Puccini would inherit his father's position, appointing a replacement subject to the proviso that he "must hand over the post of Organist and *Maestro di Cappella* to Signor Giacomo, son of the aforementioned defunct master, as soon as the said Signor Giacomo be able to discharge such duties."[51] The young Signor Giacomo began music study at age six with his father's replacement, his uncle Fortunato Magi, former teacher of Catalani and future teacher of Franchetti. While neither particularly diligent nor seeming visibly precocious, he made steady progress. By his teens he was studying music full-time, playing organ in the churches of Lucca and the surrounding towns, and helping his mother make ends meet by playing the piano in hotels, cafés, and houses of ill-repute in Lucca and Bagni di Lucca, the nearby bathing resort.

At twenty-one, completing his studies at the Istituto Pacini, he presented a *Messa a quattro voci* on the Feast of San Paolino, Lucca's patron saint, achieving the same local fame that Catalani had gained eight years before. Although it shows few signs of the signature that instantly identifies Puccini's later works as his own, the Mass is a strong work, full of fresh musical ideas supported by solid craftsmanship. A frugal husband of his musical resources from the beginning, Puccini would mine its material extensively later for his first two operas, *Le Villi* and *Edgar*.

Although financial reasons alone would have made further study in France or Germany impossible, by 1880 the Milan Conservatory was no longer a compromise. With the composers Antonio Bazzini[52] and Ponchielli as its leading lights, it had become the outstanding music school in Italy, just as Milan had become the Italian city with the broadest, richest, musical life. That winter, La Scala presented the premiere of Ponchielli's new Orientalist epic, *Il figliuol prodigo* and the revised version of Verdi's *Simon Boccanegra*. In Milan, Puccini found himself at home among his fellow Tuscans, receiving initial encouragement from the older Catalani, and forming a close friendship with the younger Mascagni. Puccini and Mascagni shared a room for a year, and their escapades à la *bohème* form the subject of numerous anecdotes.[53]

For all his occasional bohemian tendencies, Puccini was an assiduous student, particularly of those aspects of music that interested him most, and his graduation piece, a *Capriccio sinfonico*, is an impressive effort, although not without crudities and traces of immature bombast. He was acclaimed by Filippi in *La Perseveranza* as "a decisive and rare musical temperament and one which is especially symphonic,"[54] and the piece was taken up by Franco Faccio, and performed again in the summer and fall of 1883. Puccini, however, subsequently found it more valuable as raw material for his subsequent works than as a composition in its own right. A number of its ideas found their way into *Edgar*, while the principal theme of the Allegro has become better known as the opening motif of *La bohème*.

Opera had always been Puccini's goal, however, and while Giovannina Lucca bought the rights to the *Capriccio sinfonico*, neither Lucca nor Ricordi showed any interest in commissioning an opera from the aspiring young graduate. His opportunity would come instead from the upstart publisher Sonzogno's first competition for a new one-act opera. The competition was announced in April 1883, shortly before Puccini's graduation. Ponchielli introduced Puccini, who was eager to compete, to the obliging Ferdinando Fontana, who agreed to write him a libretto. Fontana and the composer took to each other, and the poet generously accepted a reduced fee; confident of Puccini's talent, he agreed to defer the balance to be paid from the composer's winnings.

Fontana's libretto was a representative product of the Scapigliatura; a Nordic romantic subject treated in a way that would expand the role both of dance and of the orchestra. For his subject, he drew on the legend of the Willis, the girls who avenge themselves after death on their unfaithful lovers, from a version by the French author Alphonse Karr.[55] *Le Villi* is much the same story as Heine's *Lorelei* or Adam's popular 1841 ballet, *Giselle, ou Les Willis*. As the story opens, Roberto is bidding farewell to his beloved Anna on his departure from his native village for Mainz, where he has inherited money from an aunt. In Mainz, he is seduced by a siren and loses his money, while the abandoned Anna dies in despair, episodes that are depicted in the first of two intermezzi. When Roberto returns to the village, Anna and the Willis draw him into their dance of vengeance, and he dies. A thin story, but more than adequate for a one-act opera, with many opportunities for atmospheric and descriptive music. Puccini was delighted, writing his mother in July that "it is a fine little subject . . . it truly pleases me a lot, and will give me a lot to do in the descriptive symphonic style, which suits me well."[56] The opera was written in great haste, and barely reached the jury by the deadline, the end of 1883.

Puccini was optimistic about the outcome. Aside from the merits of his opera, four of the five judges were associated with the Milan Conservatory, two of whom, Faccio and Ponchielli, were particularly friendly to him. As a result, he and Fontana were both amazed and dejected when the winners of the competition were announced and *Le Villi* was not among them. This outcome, all the more surprising because the two winners were thoroughly mediocre and forgettable works,[57] has widely been attributed to

Puccini's haste; specifically, that he was unable to make a fair copy of his score, and that the score he submitted was so illegible that the judges were unable to decipher it.[58]

Girardi has cast doubt on this story, establishing through an examination of the score that it was in fact not illegible, and pointing out that in February 1884, while the jury was still deliberating, Ponchielli (quite irregularly) arranged for Puccini to meet Sonzogno's archrival Giulio Ricordi and, one assumes, play him some of the music from *Le Villi*. Although Girardi presents his ideas circumspectly, he allows the reader to draw the inference that Ponchielli may have rigged the competition in order to ensure that Ricordi would obtain the rights to *Le Villi*, which, if Puccini had won the competition, would have belonged to Sonzogno.[59]

Be that as it may, the disappointed Fontana took matters into his own hands, organizing a soiree at the home of Marco Sala, a popular journalist and amateur musician, to permit Puccini to present his opera to members of Milan's cultural elite, including Boito, Catalani, and Giovannina Lucca. The evening was a success; within days, Fontana was able to raise the 450 lire needed to put on the opera, Ricordi agreed to publish the libretto without charge,[60] and Boito convinced the manager of the Dal Verme theater to add the work to a program already scheduled for the end of May. On May 31, 1884, only two months after the winners of the Sonzogno competition had been announced, *Le Villi* made its debut.

The new opera was greeted enthusiastically. The second intermezzo, the "Tregenda" or "Witches' Sabbath" was repeated three times, and at the end, Puccini took eighteen curtain calls. The next day, Gramola in the *Corriere della sera* wrote a laudatory review, concluding, "it is a work so elegant, so refined, that from time to time it seems that one is hearing not a young student, but a Bizet, a Massenet."[61] The next day Ricordi invited Puccini to his villa on Lake Como. A week later the *Gazzetta musicale di Milano* announced that Ricordi had bought the rights to *Le Villi* and commissioned Puccini both to expand his work to a full evening's entertainment, and to write a second, full-length, opera to a libretto by Fontana. In order to enable Puccini to work, Ricordi gave him a monthly stipend of 200 lire, not overgenerous, but enough for a frugal young man to make do.

The revised version of *Le Villi* made its debut in Turin in December, where it was greeted without enthusiasm, but a January 1885 production at La Scala, after further revisions, was more successful. Despite the 1888 Naples fiasco, it made its way slowly around Italy, and after Puccini's name had become internationally famous, around the world, although never becoming truly part of the operatic repertory, either in Italy or elsewhere.

The revised version, dubbed an "opera-ballo," expanded the work into two acts, adding two of its most beautiful numbers, the soprano aria "Se come voi piccina" in the first act, and the tenor *romanza* "Torna ai felici di," in the second.

Although the term "opera-ballo" was widely used in Italy to refer to French grand opera, here it meant something very different; *Le Villi* is an opera in which dance is not only very much present, but is central to the unfolding of the drama itself, from the opening village dance through the "Tregenda" intermezzo and the final scene, where the Willis dance Roberto to his death.[62] The dance element is one of many features that give *Le Villi* an unusual sense of almost symphonic unity and integration. Although at one level *Le Villi* is a number-opera, with discrete arias and duets ending in distinct musical periods, as Girardi notes, "cross-references create semantic links that undermine the work's frame as a 'number opera,' and succeed in forging a dramatic cohesion made by interweaving melodic threads."[63] Even beyond the obvious cross-references, the thematic unity of the work is enhanced by the ubiquity of short symmetrical archphrases, as in Anna's "Non ti scordar di me" (do not forget me), which is echoed by Roberto's "Ah dubita di Dio, ma no dell'amor mio" (Doubt God, but not my love), which returns, sung half-bitterly and half-wistfully by Anna at the end, before she and her Willis deliver the coup de grâce to poor Roberto.

As the first opera of a young man barely out of the conservatory, *Le Villi* is an exceptional achievement. In addition to its tight structure, it is rich in expressive melody, not only in the two solos mentioned earlier, but in the choral prayer "Angiol di Dio," and in the first of the two intermezzi, "L'abbandono," which depicts Anna's abandonment and death. It is effectively scored, with many touches that justify Gramola's praise for its elegance and refinement. At the same time, as can be expected, it is far more derivative than the mature Puccini operas. As he remained throughout his life, Puccini was already au courant with the newest Italian, French, and German operas. Echoes of French composers, from Gounod to Bizet, abound, along with an undeniable reference to the *Abendmahl-motiv* from Parsifal.[64] Guglielmo's act 2 solo is almost stereotypically Verdian in style, while Roberto's *romanza* takes its inspiration from Admeto's aria "Mio bianco amore" from Catalani's *Dejanice*. Puccini's aria, however, is far superior to its model.

In the final analysis, however, despite its many merits, *Le Villi* is largely lacking in dramatic effect. For all of its often frenetic dancing and movement, it is fundamentally static, more a secular cantata in two tableaux — Rodolfo's farewell, and Rodolfo's death — than an opera. It is not inconceivable that *Le Villi* was actually more effective in its original one-act version: in its extended form it is far too exiguous dramatically to hold the stage for an entire evening. While some of the opera's weakness can be blamed on the libretto, the music plays its part as well. Although much of it is beautifully written, it rarely goes beneath the surface to engage the emotions of an audience. With the exception of Anna's and Roberto's solos, which deal with the sort of elemental sentiment that always brought out the best in Puccini, much of the rest of the music is decorative, neither deeply felt or expressed. Nordic supernaturalism à la Catalani, in the final analysis, was not Puccini's forte.

In addition to introducing Puccini to the Italian opera world, *Le Villi* had an important effect on his friend and ultimate rival Mascagni. The younger man found in *Le Villi* both a goad to his own ambitions, and a source of musical ideas that would play a role in both his *Gugliemo Ratcliff* and, more important, *Cavalleria rusticana*. The unusual chord with which Puccini opens "L'abbandono"[65] made a particularly strong impression on Mascagni, who used the same chord both in the intermezzo from *Gugliemo Ratcliff* known as "Ratcliff's Dream," written the following year, and in the opening bars of *Cavalleria rusticana*.[66] Although this is only one of a number of echoes of *Le Villi* in Mascagni's work, Puccini's later comment, "*Le Villi* initiated the style that today they call "Mascagnian" and no one has ever done that fact justice,"[67] is baseless; the spirit of the two works is so utterly different that any thematic or harmonic borrowings pale into insignificance by comparison.

Edgar *and* Manon Lescaut: *Puccini's path to creative maturity*

Fontana quickly found a subject for his new libretto in an unusual philosophical verse drama entitled *La coupe e les lèvres* by the French poet Alfred de Musset, a figure popular with the Scapligliati for both his hyperromantic verse and his outré lifestyle. In the meantime, however, Puccini's life had become far more complicated. Shaken badly by his mother's death in July 1884, an affair with a married woman that he embarked on that autumn in Lucca would thoroughly unsettle his life for the next few years.[68] He had initially met Elvira Gemignani some time earlier, when he had given her piano and voice lessons; two years younger than Puccini, with two small children, she was an imposing woman, described by Budden as "tall, dark-eyed, full-figured with regular features and a Roman nose."[69] The affair turned into a deeper relationship, and by mid-1886, with Elvira pregnant with Puccini's child, the couple fled Lucca, taking her daughter Fosca but leaving her son behind with her estranged husband. Their son Antonio, known as Tonio, was born in Monza, a suburb of Milan where Fontana had found lodgings for the fugitive couple, in December 1886.

Ricordi's stipend, however, was hardly adequate to enable Puccini to cover the cost of supporting a woman with two small children, as well as his younger brother Michele, who was now a student himself at the Milan Conservatory. Courting their neighbors' disapproval, Puccini and Elvira soon moved back to Lucca, moving in with his sister Ramelde and her husband. That soon proved uncomfortable, and the couple decided to separate temporarily, with Elvira moving in with relatives in Florence, and the composer returning to Milan. In the meantime, work moved forward unevenly on the new opera, which Fontana had entitled *Edgar*.

Musset's drama, never intended for performance, is a bizarre farrago of incidents, encounters, and philosophical reflections,[70] rendered even more chaotic by Fontana's inept efforts to compress it into an operatic libretto. As it is perhaps the worst libretto of any set by a major composer of the era, it may be worth describing in somewhat more detail.

As the first act opens, a tender scene between Edgar and Fidelia is interrupted by Tigrana, who reminds him of his onetime infatuation with her. Edgar denounces her and leaves. Her current lover Frank enters, and curses her for the misery she causes him. Tigrana disrupts a church service, and the villagers attack her. She flees to Edgar, who emerges from his house, threatens the villagers with his sword, sets fire to his house, and announces that he and Tigrana are leaving together. Frank tries to block his way; they fight and Edgar wounds him. As the couple leave, Frank curses Tigrana. In the second act, Edgar has tired of the sensual life with Tigrana. As a band of armed men pass their palace, he invites in their captain, who turns out to be Frank. Frank greets him as a comrade in arms, telling Edgar that by wounding him, Edgar had cured his obsession with Tigrana. Edgar leaves for the war with Frank, ignoring Tigrana's pleas.

The third act begins with a funeral procession for Edgar. As Frank praises Edgar's bravery, a hooded friar denounces Edgar's sins, but Fidelia defends him. Tigrana arrives, mourning Edgar. The friar and Frank try to convince her to denounce Edgar. She refuses at first, but worn down by their pleas and attracted by their bribes, she finally does so. As she does, the friar reveals that he is Edgar, and that the funeral was a ruse. Denouncing Tigrana, he draws Fidelia to his side and announces that they will begin a new life together. As they leave, Tigrana pulls out a dagger and kills Fidelia.

Fontana was occupied with revisions to the libretto of *Le Villi* through the spring of 1885, and Puccini only received the final libretto of *Edgar* in November 1885, more than a year after he had begun work. From that point on, between moves and domestic complications, Puccini worked steadily on the opera, finishing the short score by the fall of 1887. The orchestration took shape only gradually, however, and was not complete until November 1888, while proposals for the opera's first performance came and went. Finally, the opera made its debut at La Scala on Easter Sunday of 1889, nearly five years after the debut of its predecessor. Despite a publicity barrage by Ricordi, and a first-rate performance under Franco Faccio's baton, *Edgar*'s debut, if not quite a fiasco, was far from successful. After three performances, the opera was withdrawn.

Ricordi, despite opposition from his board of directors, maintained his faith in Puccini, whom he had now been supporting for five years with little financial return.[71] He immediately encouraged both the composer and the reluctant Fontana to revise and tighten the opera, while setting in motion a commission for a third opera. Subsequently, *Edgar* was drastically revised and reduced to three acts, in the process eliminating much of Tigrana's part, an extended banquet scene, as well as the lengthy preludes to the second, third, and fourth acts. Although Puccini continued to tinker with it through 1905, the revised version performed in 1892 fundamentally represents the opera as it is known today.

Edgar represents in almost all respects a step backward from *Le Villi*. Faced with a libretto crammed with violent but inconsistent and unmotivated action, little of which appears to have engaged his deepest feelings, Puccini took refuge in composing generic — although often effective — music, interspersed with many of the action clichés, the trumpet calls, drumrolls, and tremolos of his predecessors. The texture of cross-references that was one of the great strengths of *Le Villi* is far thinner in *Edgar*, replaced in large part by repetition of themes or short motifs, often brought back in seemingly arbitrary fashion.

Puccini's melodic ideas have grown richer in *Edgar*, and at their best have a passionate quality that is largely lacking in *Le Villi*. Their musical quality, however, is rarely put to strong dramatic effect; Fidelia's two third-act scenes, "Addio, addio, mi dolce amor" and "Nel villaggio d'Edgar" contain some of Puccini's most beautiful music, but are the only truly outstanding solos in a long opera. Tigrana and Edgar's second-act duet, "Dal labbro mio," is musically superb and clearly intensely felt by the composer, but dramatically absurd. Sounding like a conventional love duet, only a close reader of the libretto could even imagine that while Tigrana is singing "in my lips, find oblivion" he is singing in unison, to this exquisite sensual melody, "will I never be able to flee this abyss of shame and hor-ror?" It comes as little surprise that this scene was originally written as a closing love duet for Edgar and Fidelia, and recycled into the second act after Puccini's suppression of the fourth act. While much of the third act is musically strong and, with the byplay between Frank and the monk, the choral interjections, and the interweaving of roles for Fidelia and Tigrana, grounded in a formal structure that is both innovative and complex, its dra-matic effect is negated by the sheer pointlessness of the events being de-picted and the insufferable self-absorption of its eponymous hero.

Ultimately, it is the drama that must bear the brunt of the blame for *Edgar*'s failure. The audience can forgive the coincidence of Frank turn-ing up as the captain in the second act, but not the absurdity of his thank-ing Edgar for all but killing him in the first. The transformation of Edgar from a dreamy romantic to a berserk killer in the first act, or his running off with Tigrana after having cursed her only a few minutes earlier, make no more sense than the elaborate charade of the empty coffin and the fake funeral, which seem to serve no purpose other than to further shame the by now thoroughly disgraced Tigrana. Indeed, the treatment of Tigrana throughout the opera is perverse and misogynistic. Although it is generally accepted that Fontana modeled her character on Carmen, there is noth-ing of the free spirit or life force about her; there is little in her lines or in the music Puccini wrote for her to suggest that she is anything more than a highly sexual woman, utterly dependent on the men in her life.[72] Despite this, she is treated time and again with vicious contempt by everyone in the opera, and finally humiliated by Edgar in front of the entire company. It is not surprising that she lashes out at the end of the opera; one is only disap-pointed, however, that she attacks poor, innocent Fidelia instead of putting a well-deserved end to her tormenter Edgar.

While Puccini continued for some time to tinker with *Edgar*, he soon came to recognize its weakness, writing famously in the margins of the vocal score he gave Sybil Seligman many years later, "E Dio ti GuARdi da quest'opera" ("May God preserve you from this opera").[73] While Gi-rardi aptly points out that "the experience with Fontana . . . was beneficial to Puccini at least inasmuch as it obliged him to test his strength within a form of vast proportions,"[74] the experience was most valuable in that it taught Puccini not only to look far more closely and critically at any fu-ture libretto, scrutinizing the story as a whole as well as the individual words themselves, but also to understand the true nature of his abilities and to concentrate on the subjects that would bring out his strengths and minimize his limitations. He also learned that Fontana, for all his comradely warmth and ingratiating manner, was not a suitable collaborator. Although Fontana repeatedly sought to work with Puccini in years to come, suggesting a variety of subjects for the composer's approval, Puccini rebuffed his efforts. At least two of the subjects suggested by Fontana, however, *Manon Lescaut* and *Tosca*, became Puccini operas with libretti by other hands.[75]

From the premiere of *Edgar* to that of *Manon Lescaut* was less than four years, but they were four critical years. Between 1889 and 1893, the world of Italian opera was transformed with the arrival of *Cavalleria rusticana*, as well as *Pagliacci* and a host of lesser works. As these works appeared and were acclaimed by the Italian public, the pressure on Puccini to realize his potential was intense: for all Ricordi's faith in him, that faith was not unlimited. While Puccini's domestic circumstances, other than the continual effort to stretch Ricordi's stipend to cover the expenses of his young family, had become somewhat less chaotic, the process of selecting a new opera and finding a librettist were more difficult. Although Puccini had expressed an interest in the abbé Prévost's novel, the *Histoire du Chevalier Des Grieux et de Manon Lescaut*, even before *Edgar*'s debut, Ricordi was doubtful, reluctant to complete with Massenet's *Manon*, which had been steadily moving into the repertory since its 1884 debut. Ricordi suggested other subjects, but the composer insisted on *Manon*, reputedly telling his mentor, "a woman like Manon can have more than one lover."[76]

Ricordi acceded to Puccini's desires, and by mid-1889, Marco Praga, a young poet and the son of the Scapigliato poet Emilio Praga, had begun work on the libretto. Over the next three years, the libretto would take many forms, and go through the hands of at least four writers, including a playwright recruited by Praga named Domenico Oliva,[77] the composer Ruggero Leoncavallo, the extent of whose contribution is still impossible to determine,[78] and Luigi Illica. In the end, a few lines were contributed by Puccini himself, and even by Ricordi, who added the lines that the Captain says to Des Grieux, welcoming him aboard the ship to America at the end of the third act, "So, young man, you want to populate the Americas? Well, so be it." While it appears that Oliva and Illica were responsible for the greater part of the work, the libretto was ultimately published without attribution. Puccini began work in 1890, and had all but completed the first act by January 1891, even though the libretto did not take its final form until 1892.

The story of Manon and her lover Des Grieux was perfectly suited to Puccini's sentimental streak. Manon is the first of his great doomed heroines, from Mimì to Liù, while Des Grieux is the first and perhaps most be-

Giacomo Puccini at the time of *Manon Lescaut,* with an affectionate dedication to Giulio Ricordi. *(Ricordi Archive)*

sotted of his ardent tenor lovers. The opera opens at a coach stop in Amiens where Manon, bound for the convent, meets the young Des Grieux. Despite the intrigues of her brother Lescaut, and the elderly but rich tax collector Geronte, she and Des Grieux run off to Paris, as Lescaut consoles Geronte that ultimately Manon's taste for luxury will win her over. In the second act, she has left Des Grieux and is now Geronte's mistress, but despite her jewels and finery, she is unhappy and pines for her lover. Lescaut arranges for a visit by Des Grieux; as the lovers embrace, Geronte arrives, followed by the police. Manon delays their departure as she gathers her jewels, and is arrested as a prostitute and a thief. The third act takes place at the port of Le Havre. Manon has been sentenced to be transported to the colonies. After an attempt to rescue her fails, she is taken onboard a ship for America, followed by Des Grieux. In the last act, set in the "wastelands of Louisiana,"[79] Manon dies, and Des Grieux falls senseless on her lifeless body.[80] Except for the first act, Puccini's librettists were able to avoid duplicating any of the scenes in Massenet's work — at the cost, however, of creating an opera that is more a series of disconnected scenes than an organic whole.

Because the La Scala management was concentrating on preparations for the premiere of Verdi's *Falstaff*, Ricordi decided to present *Manon Lescaut* to the public in Turin rather than Milan. The opera made its debut at the Teatro Regio on February 1, 1893, with a well-prepared and capable although far from stellar cast. It was a unqualified success. Puccini was called back for thirty curtain calls, while the critics were unanimous in their praise; as Budden notes, "for the only time in Puccini's career, press and public were of one mind."[81] The authoritative Colombani of the *Corriere della sera* wrote that the music "has all the developmental style of the great symphonies, without on that account rejecting the need for dramatic expression — or indeed what is generally termed 'italianità.'"[82] From Turin, *Manon Lescaut* soon spread across Italy and Europe, including London's Covent Garden, after which George Bernard Shaw wrote his famous line, "on this and other accounts, Puccini looks to me more like the heir of Verdi than any of his rivals."[83] In one night, Puccini had gone from being seen as a talented composer seeking to find his way to recognition as a mature, fully formed master.

Manon Lescaut represents a remarkable creative leap from its predecessor, as Giovanni Pozza, also writing in the *Corriere della sera*, noted, "Between *Edgar* and *Manon*, Puccini jumped across an abyss. One can consider *Edgar* a necessary preparatory step, full of redundancies, flashes and hints. *Manon* is the work of a self-confident genius, master of his art, creator and perfectionist."[84] From the exuberant, brilliant opening bars of the short orchestral prelude (based on a theme taken by Puccini from a minuet written some years earlier and subtly transformed), the listener is aware that she is in the hands of a master. The orchestra weaves a seamless web in which first Edmondo, then the students, and then Des Grieux appear, moving effortlessly between vivid scherzando and lyrical cantabile, creating a rich, complex texture of motives that simultaneously establish the eighteenth-century atmosphere of the work, the carefree revels of the students, and Des Grieux's romantic yearnings, while foreshadowing the deeper drama to come. All of this leads up to Manon's arrival, which sets the plot in motion and introduces her distinctive motif, which becomes not just a recurrent motto theme, but a true Wagnerian leitmotif, deeply interwoven into the very texture of the opera, subtly transformed to reflect the unfolding of her story and her pathetic end.[85]

From there to the end of the act, the dramatic momentum and musical variety never flag, as Des Grieux and Manon's unfolding love blends with the overlapping intrigues of Geronte, Lescaut, and Edmond — all to the backdrop of the students' gaiety, and the sounds and smells of the spring evening. The rest of the opera is nearly at the same level as the first act. Although the second act, with its hairdressers, singers, and dancing masters may lack the same degree of cohesion, the third act at Le Havre, with its superb roll-call scene, is easily the equal of the first.

For all the talent on display in *Le Villi* or in *Edgar*, nothing in either opera suggests that their composer could be capable of the fusion of drama and music, singers and orchestra, action and repose, and intrigue and sentiment that takes place in the first act of *Manon Lescaut*. Puccini had learned a great deal from the ubiquitous Wagner. He had not only achieved a mastery of Wagnerian procedures, but integrated them into an innately Italian — and distinctly personal — melodic vocabulary, as well as adapting them to the dramatic themes with which he was most at home. While Puccini had been familiar with Wagner's music since his student days, he benefited greatly from an unusual and unique interaction with the German composer as he set out to write *Manon Lescaut* in 1889.

In the aftermath of the *Edgar* fiasco, Ricordi sent Puccini to Bayreuth to hear Wagner's *Die Meistersinger von Nürnberg*, subsequently commissioning the young composer to prepare a reduced edition of the opera for presentation at the opening of the 1889–90 La Scala season.[86] As a result, Puccini was deeply engaged throughout 1889 in an intimate study of the Wagner opera most closely aligned in spirit to the work on which he would soon embark. The lessons of *Die Meistersinger*, assimilated thoroughly and made Puccini's own, pervade *Manon Lescaut*, from the manner in which Wagner weaves scherzando and cantabile motifs into his orchestral texture to the way in which the German composer creates the effect of a concertato in "real time" (as distinct from the Italian practice of frozen time) as a model for the deservedly famous roll-call scene. Even Puccini's central "Manon" leitmotif may have been prompted by recollections of *Die Meistersinger*, where that same distinctive two-note motif appears often, most prominently as it announces Walther in the act 1 trial scene, reappearing moments later in a distorted version that accompanies Beckmesser as he steps into the Marker's box.

Manon Lescaut is the first opera in which Puccini found his most congenial dramatic theme, that of young love undone. In contrast to operas such as *Tosca* and *Butterfly*, where love is undone by villainy or treachery, the lovers in *Manon Lescaut* are undone by Manon's own nature. She is little more than a creature of her appetites, her almost unconscious passion and cupidity. As a result, unlike both Tosca and Cio-Cio-San, who establish their own powerful individual identities in the face of the forces undoing them, Manon remains a poorly defined, passive figure. *Manon Lescaut* is Des Grieux's opera. Almost throughout the opera, we see Manon through his eyes, as the object of his obsessive and somewhat inexplicable adoration.

Manon Lescaut's structure suffers by comparison to Puccini's later operas, made up as it is of four discrete scenes lacking clear dramatic connection or continuity from one to the next, culminating in an act of which Budden aptly notes, "18 minutes is distinctly long for an act in which nothing happens apart from the heroine's death."[87] For all its beautiful music, the fourth act is ultimately let down by its lack of dramatic movement or tension. Manon's indistinct nature, however, is another reason why *Manon Lescaut*, for all its mastery, has never entered the public's heart to quite the same extent as Puccini's subsequent operas. By the time she comes alive as a character in the fourth act, as she sings "Sola, perduta, abbandonata" in the Louisiana wastelands, she is less than ten minutes from her death, and it is too late for the audience to begin making the emotional connections that would make them truly committed to the work.

Manon Lescaut, nonetheless, is a masterpiece, and was recognized as such by Italy's public and critics alike. It established Puccini as the leading composer of his generation, and put an end to the financial worries that had dogged his steps since childhood. With the proceeds, he was now able to repay nearly a decade of Ricordi's stipends, and buy back the family home in Lucca, which had been sold after his mother's death. In the meantime, he had come to spend more and more of his time on the shores of Lake Massaciuccoli, not far from Lucca, where he was able to indulge his pastimes of hunting and card-playing. Perhaps as a way of getting exercise, he also invested the substantial sum of 220 lire — more than a month's income for him only a short while before — to buy a Humber bicycle.[88]

Chapter 4

The *Giovane Scuola* Comes of Age: Giordano, Cilèa and the House Of Sonzogno

The giovane scuola *Emerges*

Pietro Mascagni's status as a singular, trailblazing figure in the Italian operatic world in the wake of *Cavalleria* did not last long. Within only two years, the new wave in Italian opera that had begun with *Cavalleria rusticana* had grown into a large enough movement that the Italian media could not unreasonably dub its adherents the *giovane scuola*, the "Young School" of Italian composers. In addition to Mascagni, whose 1891 *L'amico Fritz* added to his reputation, the *giovane scuola* included Puccini, Franchetti, Leoncavallo, and two figures whose first operas appeared in 1892: Umberto Giordano and Francesco Cilèa. Both would play important roles in the coming decade; Cilèa's star, however, would fade not long after the turn of the century, while Giordano would remain prominent in Italian musical life through the 1920s.

The manner in which this school emerged represented a characteristically fin de siècle blend of art and commerce. While it was propelled by the creative energy of a new generation of composers, it was in equal part the commercial creation of Edoardo Sonzogno, and his application of a new entrepreneurial model to the discovery, promotion, and nurturing of operatic talent. Sonzogno, mentioned briefly in chapter 2, was one of the remarkable personalities of the age. The third generation of a respectable but stodgy Milan publishing dynasty, he founded *Il Secolo*, Italy's first mass-circulation newspaper in 1866. Appealing to the growing Italian middle class with a blend of culture, entertainment, serialized fiction, and radical republican politics, by the 1880s it had the largest circulation of any Italian newspaper. He was also the first Italian publisher to offer prizes to subscribers, ranging from modest awards such as inexpensive books and re-

Edoardo Sonzogno *(Museo Mascagnano, Livorno)*

productions of classic paintings to a villa in San Remo or an alpine chalet overlooking Lake Como.[1]

In a nation where reading had traditionally been seen as an elite pursuit, he was the first publisher who fully grasped the economic implications of the rapid growth in literacy that began in Italy in the 1860s and 1870s and steadily gained momentum during the last decades of the century. Redirecting the energies of the family publishing firm to the growing middle-class market, he released inexpensive editions of both classic and modern authors under the rubric of La biblioteca del popolo (The people's library) along with a voluminous catalogue of manuals and popular guides to music, history, philosophy, science, and agriculture.

Sonzogno himself, although in his youth an unsuccessful dabbler in the theater, had no musical background or training. His engagement with the Italian opera industry was encouraged and assisted by the composer Amintore Galli (1845–1919), a former *garibaldino* who became the music critic for *Il Secolo* in 1874, at the age of twenty-eight. Galli became Sonzogno's principal musical adviser and the musical director of the publisher's new venture, the Casa Musicale Sonzogno, holding that position for three decades until his retirement in 1904.[2] Under Galli's astute guidance, Sonzogno initiated his musical activities by acquiring the rights to a large number of French operas and operettas—including Bizet's *Carmen*, an opera that soon became widely popular in Italy. In 1881, with Galli as editor, he launched a musical magazine, *Il Teatro illustrato*, designed to compete directly with Ricordi's well-established *Gazetta musicale di Milano*.

While up to 1883 Sonzogno largely imitated the established publishers Ricordi and Lucca, his decision to hold a national competition for new one-act operas was a venture of a fundamentally different nature. At the time, the publishers' custom was to wait until a new composer's works had been performed in one of the peninsula's opera houses, an event that typically took place when the composer was able to convince an impresario to perform the work, either on its merits or with the help of a subsidy (often substantial) from the composer. If the work was successful, the publisher would then approach the composer with an offer; if not, it was quickly forgotten. Sonzogno not only recognized that the system clearly favored the more established publishers over any newcomer, but may have recognized as well that with the emergence of a repertory of works by Verdi, Rossini, and Donizetti and the growing popularity of foreign operas, the space within which new operas and composers might "naturally" emerge was becoming more limited.

A competition would bypass this process, not only expanding the oppor-

tunity for young composers to find their market, but providing Sonzogno
with privileged access to the winners' works for his publishing house, as
well as a variety of opportunities for ancillary publicity, for the competition
as well as for Sonzogno's other ventures. The benefits to the publisher,
however, were even greater: the competition also enabled Galli to scrutinize
the efforts of numerous young composers on his employer's behalf, giving
him the opportunity to identify promising talents among them, including
works that might not be selected, for one reason or another, as competition
winners. Although the process was not perfect, and, as has been discussed,
the first competition may well have been hijacked by Ponchielli on behalf
of Sonzogno's competitor Ricordi, it was an important departure in the
Italian opera industry. Moreover, despite the first competition's forgettable
outcome, Sonzogno persevered, mounting a second, even more ambitious,
competition five years later.

The second competition not only yielded a spectacularly successful
winner in Mascagni's *Cavalleria rusticana*, it enabled Galli to spot a second promising talent in the person of a young Neapolitan conservatory student, Umberto Giordano. Although the student's entry failed to win even
an honorable mention — a failure attributed to a libretto that Galli later described as "a subject utterly lacking in interest, without dramatic life, without characters or atmosphere"[3] — the critic recognized Giordano's ability
and alerted Sonzogno to the young composer's potential value. Sonzogno
subsequently invited Giordano to Rome in May 1890 and, upon the composer's graduation from Naples' San Pietro a Maiella Conservatory that fall,
commissioned him to compose a full-length opera for the firm. Although
the work, *Mala vita*, a crude but intense verismo opera set in Naples' lower
depths, established Giordano as a composer more of promise than solid
achievement, he would become a major moneymaker for Sonzogno over
the next decade with *Andrea Chénier*, *Fedora*, and *Siberia*.

Francesco Cilèa (1866–1950), the next member of the Sonzogno "stable"
came to the publisher's attention in similar fashion. Although Cilèa, Giordano's fellow student at San Pietro a Maiella, did not enter the competition, he had composed an opera entitled *Gina*, which had been presented
at the conservatory early in 1889. Aware of Sonzogno's search for promising musical talent, Paolo Serrao, Cilèa's professor at the conservatory and
a well-known figure in Italian musical life, took it upon himself to travel to
Rome in October 1890 in order to alert Sonzogno to his student's potential. After meeting with Sonzogno, Serrao immediately wrote Cilèa back
in Naples: "get on the train and come here as soon as possible, at most
within six days. I won't tell you that this trip will make you money, or guar-

antee your future, but it will give you a chance to make yourself known and appreciated by the one individual in a position to help out a young person with real talent. So wake up and don't quibble!"[4] Cilèa rushed to Rome, where Sonzogno also offered him a commission for a full-length opera.[5] While *Tilda*, also in the verismo vein, was not successful, it paved the way for Cilèa's more successful works, *L'Arlesiana* and *Adriana Lecouvreur*.

By the end of 1890, Sonzongo had on commission at least four works in progress. In addition to the operas by Cilèa and Giordano, they included two works by Mascagni, *L'amico Fritz* and *I Rantzau*. With his activities widely known in the small world of Italian opera, it was all but inevitable that Leoncavallo, his ambitions frustrated by Ricordi, would turn to Sonzogno with his proposal for *Pagliacci*. It was equally inevitable that Sonzogno would accept the proposal with alacrity. By mid-1892 five new operas by four young composers had appeared under Sonzogno's banner, and references to them as the *giovane scuola*, led by the now world-famous Mascagni, had begun to appear.[6]

Cementing his position as the individual responsible for bringing a new generation of Italian composers into being, Sonzogno took a bold step to introduce his composers as a "school" on the world stage by presenting them at the International Theater and Music Exposition in Vienna in September 1892, renting the small theater on the Prater's exposition grounds for a sixteen-day season of their works.[7] It was a venture designed to yield publicity for Sonzogno and his composers rather than any financial return to the firm. Indeed, financial losses were all but certain, as the theater's seating was limited and Sonzogno was determined to spare no expense, recruiting a body of singers that included not only the famous husband-and-wife team of Stagno and Bellincioni, but outstanding singers such as the tenor Fernando De Lucia, the baritone Antonio Cotogni, and the soprano Fanny Torresella. As had become his practice, Sonzogno subsidized this project as well as many others with the considerable profits being generated by his nonmusical ventures.

Cavalleria and *L'amico Fritz* were both already well known to the Viennese audience. *Cavalleria* had appeared there first in March 1891, and by the fall of 1892 had already been performed nearly one hundred times in the Austrian capital, while *Fritz* had made its successful debut there in the spring of 1892.[8] The other works, however, were new for Vienna, and the local audience responded enthusiastically to them. The season was a triumph for Sonzogno, and for the visceral, direct style of the new Italian operas, which came as a welcome change of pace for a Viennese audience accustomed to a diet of turgid post-Wagnerian drama leavened with frivolous Strauss operettas. It was also a personal triumph for Mascagni and, to a lesser extent, Giordano. As Mascagni described his experience, "I had barely arrived in Vienna when a huge crowd formed in front of the hotel to see me. I couldn't take a step without people jumping in front of me to get my autograph. At my hotel three or four hundred letters, mostly from women, arrived every day."[9] As a recent writer has noted, "Vienna was embarking on what was to be a long love affair with Mascagni."[10]

The season opened with *L'amico Fritz*, followed by *Pagliacci*, *Tilda*, *Cavalleria*, and *Mala vita*, all playing to packed houses in the small theater. *Tilda* was only moderately well received, but *Mala vita* was greeted enthusiastically. Giordano wrote his father the next day, "The opera pleased [the audience] from the first to the last note, while in two or three spots their enthusiasm reached the level of delirium. I'm not exaggerating, because you know me too well. It was like a thunderclap in a clear sky. I arrived here almost unknown . . . now I have become a somebody in Vienna."[11] Unlike *Cavalleria* and *Pagliacci*, whose popularity in Austria and Germany soon equaled that of *Cavalleria*, *Mala vita* soon disappeared from the stage. While the authoritative critic Hanslick found it effective, and had nothing but praise for Bellincioni's performance in the difficult role of Christina, his ultimate verdict was dismissive: "[Giordano's] dramatic spirit is stronger than his musical creativity, his temperament more powerful than his art . . . the music appears no more than the obedient, diligent handmaiden of the dialogue."[12]

It made little difference. Sonzogno's season was a brilliant publicity stroke, establishing in the world of opera not only that *Cavalleria* was no fluke and that Italy had become once again a vibrant creative force in the world of opera, but that he, Edoardo Sonzogno, was to be recognized as the impresario of this new generation, the individual whose vision and money had made it all possible. From this point on, the battle, not so much for the operatic world's soul, perhaps, as for its pocketbook, would be a battle of equals between Sonzogno and Ricordi.

Umberto Giordano

Umberto Menotti Maria Giordano was born in the Apulian city of Foggia on August 28, 1867, into a solid Southern bourgeois family. His father was a pharmacist, owner of his own store. Neither of his parents were native to Foggia; his mother's family was from Naples, while his paternal grandfather had come to Foggia from Lecce, further south in the heel of Italy's boot. Foggia itself, the principal city of the fertile Apulian plain known as the Tavoliere, was a clean, prosperous but unprepossessing small city of some 35,000 population,[13] less than twenty-five miles across the plain from the town of Cerignola, where Mascagni wrote *Cavalleria rusticana.*

Born at a time when Italy's unification was still fresh in people's minds, and the Southern "brigands" were still waging their guerilla war against the central government, Giordano's name suggests unusual sympathies on his parents' part, as well as a strong desire to identify with the new nation, rather than the former Bourbon kingdom. He was named Umberto for the Italian crown prince, Menotti for Garibaldi (Menotti being Garibaldi's middle name), and Maria for Foggia's patron saint, Saint Mary of the Seven Veils. With no musical tradition in the family, and with his family eager to improve their social and economic standing, his father dreamed of his becoming a lawyer or a doctor, or, according to one doubtful source, a fencing master.[14]

There seems to be no clear explanation why an intense, all-consuming drive to write music will well up in one particular child who seems no different from, and has had no more or less exposure to music than, thousands of other children in the same time and place, but that is what happened to Giordano as it had with Mascagni in Livorno a few years earlier. As with Mascagni, Giordano also faced predictable parental opposition to his desire to devote himself to music. A sympathetic neighbor's intervention, however, ultimately persuaded his father. As the composer later put the matter, typical of his lifelong, cool self-confidence, "the means at his disposal to make me change direction were utterly inadequate to make my passion submit to his will."[15] After two years of elementary music study in Foggia, he won a place as a boarding student at the San Pietro a Maiella Conservatory in Naples, which he entered in 1882 at the age of fourteen.

In 1882, Naples was still Italy's largest city.[16] Although the demise of the royal court and its subsidies had sent the famous San Carlo theatre into a precipitous decline, the city was still a major center with a flourishing musical culture. Not only could opera still be heard at the Teatro Nuovo and Teatro Fondo, in addition to intermittently at the San Carlo, but Naples had begun to experience a strong revival of instrumental music in the last third of the century, led by the pianist and scholar Alessandro Longo and the remarkable Giuseppe Martucci, Italy's leading instrumental composer of the nineteenth century and a spectacular pianist and adventuresome conductor.[17] Longo, who later prepared the first complete edition of Scarlatti's sonatas, was a classmate of Giordano's at San Pietro a Maiella, while the precocious Martucci had begun to teach there in 1880 at twenty-four, after returning from nearly a decade of concertizing throughout Europe.

In addition to his substantial musical gifts, Giordano was a diligent, hardworking student who received consistently outstanding grades and was the delight of his teachers, a demanding body of serious musicians. No accounts of student escapades similar to those of Mascagni or Puccini are recorded about the youthful Giordano. From his early years, he appears to have become the solid, ambitious, self-controlled figure that he remained all his life; as one biographer describes him, his "physical appearance . . . reflected the presence of perfect internal equilibrium and absolute self-discipline."[18] A handsome young man with a prominent handlebar mustache, which he would later relinquish for a more "international" clean-shaven appearance, he had also begun to develop something of a reputation as a ladies' man.[19] Giordano was not yet twenty, and still two years from graduation, when he decided to compete in the second Sonzogno competition, submitting an opera entitled *Marina* with a libretto by the Neapolitan librettist Enrico Golisciani, who had composed the libretto for Ponchielli's last opera, *Marion Delorme*, only a few years earlier.[20] Although *Marina* was withdrawn by its composer and has long since disappeared, it led directly to the composition of his first performed opera, *Mala vita*.

Sonzogno hired Nicola Daspuro, a Neapolitan journalist who acted as Sonzogno's representative in Naples, to adapt *Mala vita*, a successful 1889 play by the Neapolitan poet and writer Salvatore Di Giacomo, which the author had adapted in turn from his short story "Il voto" (The Vow). The story was one of a series that Di Giacomo called "scene popolari," depicting life among the poor in Naples' lower depths. The libretto, largely faithful to its literary source, is a sordid tale, set in a square in one of the city's more wretched quarters.[21]

Vito, a dyer suffering from consumption, makes a vow to the Virgin that if she cures him, he will make an honest woman out of a prostitute by marrying her. When he encounters Cristina, a young prostitute who works in the brothel facing the square, he offers to save her. They promise to be true to one another, despite the sneers of the coachman Annetiello. In the second act, in her miserable apartment, Amalia, Annetiello's wife and Vito's mistress, begs Cristina to give up Vito. When she refuses, Amalia seduces Vito, as Cristina looks on from outside. The third act opens back in the square with Neapolitan songs and a tarantella, heralding the annual Piedigrotta song festival. Vito rejects Cristina's pleas, and goes off with Amalia to Piedigrotta. In despair, Cristina curses her fate, and as the curtain falls, is seen knocking on the brothel door, seeking her job back.

In its way, *Mala vita* is a slice of life in society's lower depths that is far more uncompromising than *Cavalleria*, or any other opera that had been seen on the Italian stage to that point. While *Cavalleria*'s denouement embodies a crude but clear notion of morality and justice, and *Pagliacci* distances the audience from its sordid outcome with its proto-Pirandellian devices, *Mala vita* offers no similar consolations. It presents an amoral world without catharsis or redemption. As Sansone writes: "the characters are . . . trapped in the inescapable prison of their wretched condition. Debauchery, callousness, cowardice are permanent blemishes for which they pay a daily toll of bitterness and misery."[22] For all of Vito's brave words, he is a pathetic coward, while Amalia is a possessive, jealous virago and her husband Annetiello a complaisantly cuckolded boor. Only Cristina, in her dream of a better life with Vito, is sympathetic, but if there is any point to the story at all, it is that people like Cristina are destined to be ground under by life, and their dreams destroyed.

Mala vita made its debut in Rome's Teatro Argentina on February 21, 1892, with Stagno and Bellincioni creating the roles of Vito and Cristina. The Roman audience was enthusiastic, and the composer and singers were called back for twenty-four curtain calls. From Rome, the opera traveled to Naples, where it appeared at the San Carlo on April 27. If the composer had anticipated a triumphal return to the city where he had lived for a decade and in which the opera was set, he was sharply disappointed. The evening was a debacle; as described vividly by Eugenio Sacerdoti: "From the beginning the San Carlo was like a kennel of barking dogs. Most of the Neapolitan public felt that their moral values had been offended, forgetting that the same play, in prose, had been applauded throughout Italy and abroad as a lively, strong, depiction of local customs. . . . My efforts to listen to the music were in vain; vulgar howling resounded ominously in the air all evening, like an insistent undertone of whistles and ocarinas."[23] Giordano took the situation in stride, calmly writing his sometime mentor Rocco Pagliara, the librarian at San Pietro a Maiella, who had written a thoughtful, although far from uncritical, review of the new opera, "I can sincerely assure you that the cries and whistles of those savages have not discouraged me in the least. *Mala vita* is not yet destroyed, nor is its composer."[24]

The composer's faith in his work was restored by its warm reception in Vienna in September, which was followed by generally successful appearances in Berlin in December, and in Milan the following January.

Mala vita largely disappeared from the stage, however, at that point. Although it reappeared, extensively reworked and rendered less offensive, as *Il voto* in 1897, the new version sacrificed many of the original's strengths without remedying its weaknesses, and has vanished as well from the operatic scene.

Mala vita, although full of promise, is a crude student work, rather than the work of a mature composer in full command of his craft. Hanslick's comments noted earlier, and a reviewer's comment at its premiere, that "it moves forward largely by reinforcing the dialogue, accentuated by cadences and accompanied by orchestral racket,"[25] are not far from the mark. It has more than its share of derivative passages, including some of the most prominent sections of the opera. The extended choral set piece that Giordano constructs around Vito's vow is highly reminiscent of the Easter Sunday music in *Cavalleria*, while the principal theme of Vito and Christina's duet, which is repeated almost ad nauseum, is more than reminiscent of Delilah's famous aria from Saint-Saëns' *Samson et Dalila*, "Mon coeur s'ouvre à ta voix."[26]

Mala vita has many virtues. The obligatory folkloric elements, in this case the Neapolitan songs and tarantella that take up much of the final act, are effective and full of vivacity, while the insidious theme of Vito's *canzone* might well have helped inspire Di Capua's famous Neapolitan song, "O sole mio," written six years later. Most important, it has an energy and impetus about it that move it powerfully forward. *Mala vita* makes it clear that Giordano was a born operatic composer. His ability to pace and shape each dramatic scene and encounter is uncanny, even when the limitations of the music lead to results that fall short of his intentions. *Mala vita* clearly identified Giordano as a composer whose next work would be closely watched.

In view of the nature of the work, and its gritty depiction of Naples' lower depths, its reception sheds light on a number of features of the culture and musical life of the time. In retrospect, its rejection by Naples is easier to understand than its initially enthusiastic welcome in Rome, Vienna, and elsewhere. Clearly, part of that enthusiasm, which most contemporary critics failed to share, can simply be attributed to the visceral effect of Giordano's theatricality, and to music that, for all its limitations, moved the drama forward expeditiously and efficaciously. It is a short opera that does not overstay its welcome, and for the most part makes its points succinctly and effectively: although it is divided into three acts, the actual duration of the music — leaving intermissions aside — is less than that of many performances of *Cavalleria*.[27] In the climate of 1892, where any new opera in the veristic genre of *Cavalleria* (particularly one by a young man barely into his twenties) could be assured of a potentially receptive audience, *Mala vita*'s modest virtues were more than enough to ensure an enthusiastic response.

Even so, there are arguably more factors at work in the opera's initial reception. While the Neapolitan audience reacted angrily to seeing the misery and depravity of their city's poor depicted on the operatic stage, that picture might well not only *not* offend, but might even add to the opera's appeal elsewhere. As Sacerdoti had noted, the play from which it was derived "had been applauded throughout Italy and abroad as a lively, strong, depiction of local customs." The northern Italian audience — and even more the Viennese audience — not only did not identify with the poor of Naples but, as reflected in the famous mot "l'Europe finit à Naples, et même elle y finit assez mal" (Europe ends at Naples, and ends there very badly), saw them as almost a species apart.[28]

This perception was reinforced by positivist doctrine, which encouraged "modern" people, such as Italy's bourgeois audience, to distinguish themselves from primitive cultures, such as that of Naples' wretched quarters. As did Di Giacomo's play, the opera confirmed its audience's stereotypes of Naples' poor. The amorality of their behavior and their religiosity, depicted in *Mala vita* as little more than a tissue of superstitions, further confirmed the audience's belief that the subjects of the opera were different from them in kind, not merely in degree.

Ultimately, however, naturalism was not enough. Not only was Giordano's opera, in the final analysis, not strong enough to sustain a place in the Italian audience's heart, the subject itself was thoroughly without catharsis or redemption. After the initial frisson of excitement and titillation, the mixture that Hanslick dubbed "at the same time fascinating and disgusting" was an experience the audience was reluctant to repeat. While Di Giacomo's play held its audience with a variety of minor characters, folkloristic effects, and melodramatic contrivances, these were largely absent in the opera, leaving — except for ten minutes of Neapolitan folkloristic music — little but human misery in their place.

Sonzogno, however, was more than satisfied with Giordano's debut, and was eager to have another opera from his latest protégé. Turning to Mascagni's librettists Targioni-Tozzetti and Menasci for a new libretto for Giordano, Sonzogno was unusually candid, writing Menasci in June 1892, "the problem is that Giordano does not really know what he wants, and it will not be easy to satisfy him. His lack of culture prevents him from framing a clear idea of what he feels, what he wants and what is more or less readily adaptable to a libretto. Patience is needed, since he has other gifts and qualities as a musician.[29]

Giordano finally decided, peculiarly, on Donizetti's *Maria de Rohan* as his subject. The work, a conventional early-romantic mixture of love, honor, and intrigue, was reworked for him by Targioni-Tozzetti and Menasci, renamed *Regina Diaz*, and moved from Paris to Naples. The opera was stillborn. Saddled by a weak, uncongenial libretto, Giordano was unable to recapture the passion and intensity of *Mala vita*, composing a stiff, awkward work, of which the well-disposed but objective Rocco Pagliara wrote, "he has composed a Romantic melodrama, . . . but by plunging himself into utter conventionality . . . has been unable to achieve anything that would even polish or illuminate the stale and the conventional."[30] The opera was a failure in its Neapolitan debut, and Sonzogno pulled it off the boards after the second performance.

Giordano, at twenty-seven, was young and provincial, with little formal education outside of his musical training, and little knowledge of the world north of Naples. That would soon change. Within little more than two years, the success of his next opera, *Andrea Chénier*, followed by his marriage to a Milan heiress, would open a dramatic new chapter in his life. The crude verismo of *Mala vita*, and indeed Naples and the south, would soon become very much part of his past.

Francesco Cilèa

Francesco Cilèa was born in Palmi, a small Calabrian coastal town at the southwestern tip of the Italian peninsula, on July 23, 1866. Palmi, a pleasant, prosperous town surrounded by olive groves, lies in the shadow of Calabria's rugged Aspromonte mountains, which were still haunted in 1866 by brigands and guerillas making their final effort to fend off the arrival of the Italian state. It is doubtful that Cilèa, the oldest of a prosperous attorney's five children, was much aware of this as a child. With his mother ailing, he and his younger brother were sent off to a boarding school in Naples at an early age, where at the age of nine he began to write short pieces for the piano, and decided that he wanted to devote his life to music.

In what has become a familiar story, Cilèa's father, who expected his son to follow in his footsteps and become an attorney, objected strongly. Music, for all the respect that Italians felt for the great Verdi and his famous operatic antecedents, was far from a distinguished profession. Few musicians earned a stable, respectable income, either as composers or as professors at

Francesco Cilèa flanked by librettists Arturo Colautti (*left*) and Ettore Moschino (*right*). (*Casa Musicale Sonzogno*)

one of Italy's conservatories. Far more were journeymen eking out a meager living, either more or less predictably as a music teacher or church organist, or irregularly as a member of one of the innumerable orchestras, bands, or operetta companies dotting Italy's cultural landscape. To Giuseppe Cilèa, a member of a respected profession, for his son to become a musician was not an appealing prospect. As happened with Mascagni and Giordano, an outside party intervened, in this case a Neapolitan doctor named Giacomo Correale, a distant relative of the Cilèa family. Correale, who was the personal physician of Francesco Florimo, the elderly musicologist who was perhaps Naples' most highly esteemed musical figure, was taken with the young man's talent and seriousness of purpose, and arranged for him to be examined by the eighty-year-old musician.

Florimo, a fellow Calabrian who had studied at the Naples Conservatory with the composer Bellini and who revered the Sicilian composer's memory, was impressed both by Cilèa's precocious talent and by his fervent admiration for the composer of *Norma*;[31] he urged Cilèa's father to allow him to begin serious musical studies. Reluctant to openly refuse Florimo's request, Cilèa's father equivocated for the next two years, finally allowing his son to enter the San Pietro a Maiella Conservatory in 1879 at thirteen, with Dr. Correale as guarantor of his son's tuition and good behavior. According to one biographer, Cilèa was a driven student, all but obsessed with the need to excel, not only to satisfy himself and his teachers, but to prove to his father that his choice of a musical career had been a sound one.[32] His father, however, would not live to see the outcome of his son's choice, dying in 1884 when Cilèa was only eighteen. His mother, and two of his sisters, had died some years earlier.

Cilèa's first operatic venture took place in 1889, while he was still at the conservatory. The custom at San Pietro a Maiella was to name the outstanding student in the school "primo alunno maestrino," or "first student and junior maestro."[33] The honor fell in 1887 to the young Cilèa, whose Suite for Orchestra had just won a national competition sponsored by the Ministry of Public Education. It was more than an honor, as it carried with it both rewards and responsibilities. While the "first student" was expected to supervise the work of his juniors, and to see that administrative orders were carried out, the title also entitled the bearer to leave the school at will and, above all, to free admission to the operas at the San Carlo theater.[34] It also led the school authorities to have him compose a full-length opera, rather than the usual operatic *scena*, as his graduation exercise.

The opera was *Gina*, with a libretto commissioned by the conservatory from Enrico Golisciani, who would next provide Cilèa's fellow student Giordano with the libretto for his one-act opera *Marina*. The libretto was an adaptation of *Cathérine, ou le croix d'or* by the mid-nineteenth-century French playwright Mélésville, a play in the genre, old-fashioned even then, known as *vaudeville*, a mixture of light, fast-moving ensembles and lyrical solos and duets, usually on a sentimental theme.[35]

Gina made its debut on February 9, 1889 at the conservatory, receiving not only local attention, but an extended, favorable review in Ricordi's *Gazzetta musicale di Milano*. Working with an old-fashioned, conventional libretto, Cilèa composed a highly conservative score in the tradition of Neapolitan light opera, but one full of sparkling buffa touches and appealing melody, as well as occasional inventive harmonic touches and an unexpected affinity for remote keys, such as D-flat and G-flat. A number of scenes, such as Lilla's third-act romanza and the second-act finale, stand out for the warm sentiment of their melodic lines, while Cilèa later used an important phrase from the opera to good effect in his *Adriana Lecouvreur.*

For all the acclaim *Gina* received, the self-critical Cilèa's own assessment was restrained. As he wrote later: "*Gina* was sure to please because of its melodic abundance and spontaneity, and the self-confidence with which I had set the three acts; but this little opera, despite the generosity of the critics, must be considered a simple youthful experiment — an experiment that enabled me to learn through practice many things that I could not have learned in school."[36] Indeed, *Gina's* composer may not have had any serious operatic aspirations at this point. As a composer, Cilèa seemed more drawn to instrumental music, which by this time included in addition to the Suite, a competent Piano Trio, and a stronger and considerably more sophisticated Sonata for Violoncello and Piano. It is likely, moreover, that he saw his future career more as pedagogue than composer. Even before graduating, he had put himself forward for a teaching position at the Santa Cecilia Conservatory in Rome; remarkably, he was found to be qualified, and although he did not get the position, ranked fourth among the twelve candidates.[37] After graduation, rather than taking any steps toward an operatic career, he took a position as a part-time faculty member at the Naples Conservatory while spending his leisure time writing short piano pieces, a number of which were published by Ricordi.

Cilèa was willing, however, to take the opportunity given him by Sonzogno to compose an opera, even though he was unhappy with the libretto for *Tilda,* which he not unreasonably characterized as "rather vulgar verismo." The libretto, indeed, is a crude attempt by the elderly Zanardini to adapt his old-fashioned language to the new demands of the popular verismo style by reworking his libretto for Catalani's *Dejanice,* which was, in turn, a reworking of Boito's libretto for *La Gioconda.* Cilèa seriously considered rejecting Sonzogno's offer, but encouraged by the publisher, who urged him to "follow the trend," ultimately accepted the commission, recognizing the rare opportunity it offered him to establish himself in the opera world.[38]

The opera is set in and around Rome at the end of the eighteenth century. Tilda, a street singer, is in love with the French officer Gastone, who is engaged to Agnese and treats Tilda with contempt. Tilda, seeking revenge, frees Gasparre, a captured brigand, and takes him into her service. In the second act, outside Rome, a band of brigands led by Gasparre waylay Gastone and Agnese's carriage, and take them to Tilda. Although she tries to attract his interest, Gastone insults her. She frees him, but keeps Agnese, telling Gastone to bring the ransom the next day. Tilda is on the verge of killing Agnese, but seeing Agnese pray, she is moved and joins her prayer. In the third act, Tilda declares her love, but Gastone again insults her. She then tells him that she has killed Agnese, at which point he stabs her. Agnese arrives and Gastone realizes his error. Tilda dies in their arms, wishing the future bride and groom well.

Cilèa faced a difficult task with the libretto, which was not only uncongenial to his tastes but which superimposed a thin verismo veneer on melodramatic clichés. His solution, if it could be called that, was to accentuate the old-fashioned character of the opera, while layering it with the full panoply of decorative genre pieces characteristic of the verismo vein. As a result, *Tilda* contains long stretches of conventional, even archaic, recitative and traditional *pezzi chiusi* (self-contained arias and ensemble numbers), interspersed with an equally long series of genre numbers, including a prayer scene and a *brindisi*, both in the vein of *Cavalleria*. There are two saltarelli (a dance once popular in Rome whose fast music in 6/8 time in Cilèa's treatment is indistinguishable from that of the tarantella) and even a Neapolitan *canzone*, despite the Roman setting of the opera, a charming number, "Ciociara bella," sung by Tilda's goddaughter Cecilia.

Cilèa finished *Tilda* within a year, and the opera made its debut at the Teatro Pagliano in Florence on April 7, 1892, with Fanny Torresella as Tilda, under the baton of Rodolfo Ferrari. It was received cordially, but without the excitement with which audiences responded to *Pagliacci* or Giordano's *Mala vita*, both of which appeared at roughly the same time. At *Tilda's* Vienna debut that fall it was dismissed by Hanslick, who wrote, after savaging the libretto, "this bloody, stupid action moves forward with the greatest ponderousness; every scene is drawn out with flabby, dragging music dripping with sentimentality." Yet," he conceded, "in a few places, the composer shows a delicate lyrical vein and an expert musical hand.[39] He made a point of singling out the "Ave Maria" sung by Agnese, Tilda, and Cecilia in the second act for praise.

Although *Tilda* soon began to appear in opera houses here and there in Italy, Cilèa was not happy with his work and, as soon as it was opportune, suppressed the opera. As far as it is known, the work has not been performed since 1893; according to at least one source, the orchestral score has since been lost or destroyed.[40] Cilèa was to be more satisfied with his next opera, *L'Arlesiana,* based on the stories of Alphonse Daudet. This work will be discussed in chapter 6.

Costume Drama and Cinematic Opera: Giordano's Andrea Chénier

The operatic world, with its love of the melodramatic, has long cherished not only operas themselves, but also the stories of how operas, particularly those that subsequently became famous, came into being. This tendency became particularly pronounced toward the end of the nineteenth century, as the emerging machinery of popular publicity, exemplified most prominently in the growing number of newspapers and illustrated supplements, turned operatic composers into popular celebrities. The archetype of this phenomenon in the 1890s was Pietro Mascagni. By mid-decade, the handsome, voluble Mascagni had become a figure of extraordinary visibility and popularity (as well as intermittent controversy) and the rags-to-riches story of the composition of *Cavalleria rusticana* had become a staple of the popular press. The *Cavalleria* trope, with its distinctive themes — the discovery of the perfect libretto, the privations suffered by the composer, and the fortuitous intervention that made the ultimate success possible — was repeated by the story of *Pagliacci,* and further elaborated in the story of the composition of *Andrea Chénier.* The story also illustrates the solidarity that existed, at least at this early point in their careers, among the composers of the *giovane scuola.*

Sonzogno's hostility in the wake of *Regina Diaz*'s failure had put Giordano's professional future in doubt, with one account even suggesting that the composer had begun to make plans to abandon his operatic career and compete for a bandmaster's position.[41] Whether or not this was true, he was desperately in need of an opportunity to redeem himself with his publisher. While he had been in touch with Luigi Illica since late 1893, he had neither a libretto nor any firm prospects of one. At this point, only a month after the *Regina Diaz* fiasco, fortune intervened.

In April 1894, Alberto Franchetti and Luigi Illica were both in Naples: Franchetti for the Naples debut of his new opera *Fior d'Alpe,* and Illica to assist with the staging of a new opera by the Greek-Italian composer Spyros Samara, *La martire,* for which he had written the libretto.[42] Giordano described the event some years later: "One beautiful day, under the bright sun, the three of us were together in one of those enchanting *trattorie,* on the terraces from which Vesuvius rises . . . Franchetti showed an interest in my situation, and, in a moment of altruism, offered to give me the rights to the libretto for *Chénier,* for which he had a contract with Illica."[43] Most probably then and there at the trattoria, Franchetti picked up his pen and wrote: "Dear Giordano, knowing that you are in need of a libretto, I am quite happy to cede you my rights for *Andrea Chénier,* based on a scenario by Luigi Illica, as long as you reimburse me the 200 lire that I paid Illica for the exclusive rights to the above libretto."[44] It took two months of effort by Illica to gain Sonzogno's attention, but finally by July 26, he was able to report to Giordano that the publisher had read the scenario, and had agreed to contract with Illica and Giordano for the new opera.

Andrea Chénier is the story of two lovers caught up in the turmoil of the French Revolution. While the opera itself, as will be discussed below, is full of incidents, some contributing to the drama but most atmospheric, the heart of the opera is found in the vicissitudes of the opera's three central figures. The first act, a prologue to the action in which the three principal characters are introduced, is set in the Château de Coigny on the eve of the Revolution. The poet Chénier sings passionately of love and human dignity (the famous *Improvviso*), deeply stirring the feelings of the beautiful young Maddalena de Coigny. As the guests dance, the servant Gérard escorts a crowd of beggars into the ballroom, denounces the aristocracy, and leaves, throwing off his livery.

The rest of the opera takes place after the Revolution, under the Terror. In the second act, Chénier, who is under suspicion for opposing Robespierre, has received letters from an unknown woman, who turns out to be Maddalena. Gérard, who has become a powerful figure in the Revolution and who is in love with Maddalena, has been hunting for her in Paris. Maddalena and Chénier meet, and pledge their love unto death. Gérard arrives, and tries to seize Maddalena. He and Chénier fight a duel. Gérard is lightly wounded, but allows Chénier to flee with Maddalena.

In the third act, Chénier has been arrested. Gérard, in order to lure Maddalena to him, denounces Chénier. Maddalena arrives, and offers herself to Gérard in return for Chénier's freedom. Gérard, moved by her story and her love for Chénier, vows to try to free Chénier. Despite Gérard's efforts, Chénier is pronounced guilty and sentenced to death. In the last act, Maddalena joins Chénier in prison, having bribed the jailer to let her substitute for a woman scheduled to die the next morning. As dawn comes, their names are called, and as the curtain falls they leave to face the guillotine together.

Illica was a busy man who by this point in his career, to his composers' dismay, was accustomed to working on more than one libretto at a time.

He had only just finished the libretto for Antonio Smareglia's *Nozze istri-ane*,[45] and was still far from having completed the numerous changes Puccini needed in the libretto for *La bohème*. By fall, Giordano realized that he would have to be in Milan, by Illica's side, in order to ensure that the writer would devote time to *Chénier* rather than his other projects. As he wrote later,

> at that time, Illica lived in an apartment in a building a few steps from the Monumental Cemetery. I went to find a room of some sort in that building, in order to be close to Illica, but none were available. I insisted. The owner left and came back with an enormous key. "Come with me," he said. We walked across the courtyard, and I found myself in front of a heavy, rough wooden door. He opened it. We walked in. It was a vast, poorly lit store-room, used to store gigantic mortuary statues in various heart-breaking poses. "There," he said, "that's all I have." I didn't know what to say, but I thought of *Chénier* and decided. That night, when I came back to my lugubrious lodgings, I felt as if I'd walked into a cemetery.[46]

Cellamare, a hagiographic but usually not inaccurate biographer, adds details, describing it as a "room with a dirt floor, one rickety window opening on the courtyard, and spider webs in the corners and on the ceilings." Giordano set up his cot, a table and a few chairs, a gas lamp, a zinc bathtub, and an upright piano in the room and set to work.[47] He was desperately poor. Although Sonzogno had resumed paying his 300-lire monthly stipend, the composer was sending 200 lire per month to help his family in Foggia get through severe financial difficulties, leaving hardly enough for the bare necessities.

Although his relationship with Illica was a stormy one, demanding that he spend much of his time and energy pressing Illica to produce the libretto,[48] *Chénier* moved steadily forward, and was completed by the end of January 1896, less than a week before the premiere of Puccini's *La bohème*. In the meantime, Sonzogno, who had taken charge of La Scala a year earlier, announced that the opera's premiere would take place at that theater in March. Another fortuitous intervention would still be needed, however, for the opera to reach the stage.

Although the opera's premiere had already been announced, when the score was actually in the publisher's hands, Amintore Galli rejected it, telling Sonzogno, according to one source, "this *Chénier* is worthless. It's unperformable."[49] Sonzogno, who relied completely on Galli's musical judgment, immediately withdrew the opera. The desperate Giordano convinced Sonzogno to listen to a second opinion, and sought out Mascagni, then in Florence.[50] Rushing back to Milan with Giordano, Mascagni argued passionately on behalf of the opera, finally convincing Sonzogno that the work should be performed. The opera was restored to the La Scala season, and, although not without further complications,[51] made its debut on March 28, 1896, with two outstanding young singers, Giuseppe Borgatti as Chénier and Mario Sammarco as Gérard, in the cast. It was a great success, with twenty curtain calls for the young composer at the end of the opera. The following day, Colombani wrote in the *Corriere della sera*: "[Giordano] has been revealed as a strong, skilled musician; his opera has real value and undeniable importance, and in these times, after *so many* disappointed hopes, it gladdens the heart to hear it. . . . Its greatest virtue is that of theatricality, understood and demonstrated with enormous confidence by Giordano. He has reached that point through a simple means: that of composing straightforwardly and sincerely."[52] The opera was performed eleven times, redeeming what had otherwise been a largely dismal season at La Scala. Within the next year, *Andrea Chénier* would not only return to La Scala for another eleven performances, but would appear in Genoa, Parma, Brescia, Mantua, Turin, Cremona, Rome, Naples, New York, Budapest, Saint Petersburg, and Moscow. It has been a part of the international operatic repertoire ever since.

The initial reviews consistently stressed the sheer dramatic intensity and pace of *Andrea Chénier*; in addition to Colombani, *Il Secolo* noted that "the dramatic interest does not fall off for an instant," and Nappi, in *La Perseveranza*, summed up a long review by commenting "among its virtues . . . are its concision, the precise balance of each scene, the leanness of its contours."[53] These comments all reflected the fact that in *Andrea Chénier*, the audience was hearing something new in Italian opera: something that would herald a shift in the choice of operatic subject and its treatment that would presage the cinema and set the stage for the transition by which the cinema ultimately supplanted opera in Italy as the iconic dramatic form. *Chénier* can not unreasonably be called the first cinematic opera.[54]

The story itself falls in a genre — lovers caught up in a violent, dangerous social or political environment — that has become a familiar cinematic subject today, whether set in the revolutionary Russia of *Doctor Zhivago* or the 1960s Indonesian civil war depicted in *The Year of Living Dangerously*. The genre itself belongs far more to the world of popular romantic fiction than to either verismo or serious literature; other than the familiar trope of revolutionary ideals betrayed, Illica and Giordano's French Revolution has no particular political content. What interests them is the *atmosphere* of the Terror, and its effect on the two star-crossed lovers who find themselves caught in its turmoil.

Illica was the most cinematic of Italian librettists, both in terms of his seeing scenes or entire acts not only as coherent dramatic wholes, but even more as visual sequences. To assist the reader or performer, he was in the habit of adding detailed stage directions and commentary (*didascalie,* in Italian) to his libretti, a forerunner of the instructions that characteristically appear on screenplays. He was also fond of giving the historic times or exotic places in which his libretti were set the appearance of verisimilitude by adding atmospheric details to his text based on his sporadic research. The dialogue between the Abbé and his rapt audience in Act I is typical:

"Necker?"
"Don't speak of him!"
"That Necker!"
"We have a Third Estate!"
"Ah . . ."
"And I have seen defaced. . . ."
"What?"
" . . . the statue of Henry the Fourth!"

In his libretto for *Andrea Chénier,* written for a composer who was far less demanding than Puccini and who rarely challenged his decisions, Illica gave full rein to his cinematic instincts. The opera is crammed both with incidents and telling visual details, including the atmospheric use of patrols and lamplighting in the second act, and the emotionally stirring scene of the mother offering her small son to the Revolution in the third. The arresting scene of the elderly servant struggling with a heavy piece of furniture that comes soon after the opening of the first act is particularly worth noting. This moment, a powerful example of the way Illica uses a fleeting but telling visual image for dramatic effect, is far more characteristic of film than it is — or had been up to that point — of opera. Similarly, it is hard to think of an Italian opera before *Chénier* in which the changes in light from day to night, and from night to dawn, are used as dramatic elements,[55] or where the story cuts so quickly from one contrasting scene or moment to the next, or from the background to the lovers in the foreground. All of these scenes give a sense of depth and complexity to the background against which the tragic love story is played out, which has the effect of magnifying its impact, at least at the level of melodrama, as well as making it easier for the audience to overlook its somewhat uncertain plausibility.

Within this quasi-cinematic framework, Illica reworks the conventional tenor-soprano-baritone triangle familiar to opera lovers to create three characters able to engage the audience's sympathies. Chénier is not only a poet, but a self-consciously romantic figure who attempts to mold his life to match his poetic sensibility; while Gérard, torn by the conflict between his revolutionary and his sexual passions, who repents of his villainy and vainly tries to free Chénier, is far more appealing that the usual evil baritone. Only Maddalena is a conventional operatic heroine in the mold of Leonora in *Trovatore*, but no less sympathetic for that.

This libretto perfectly fit a composer whose dramatic acumen, as Hanslick had recognized in *Mala vita*, exceeded his musical creativity. Giordano had substantially broadened his musical horizons, however, since the beginning of the decade. Not only was Giordano more familiar with Wagner's music than he had been five years earlier, he had the far more salient example of Puccini's *Manon Lescaut*, and its use of Wagnerian techniques to express an Italian sensibility, close at hand. From its opening notes, *Andrea Chénier* is deeply indebted to Puccini's path-breaking opera, with its rich orchestral texture, and its seamless shifts from *parlante* declamation to *cantabile* arioso.

Each act, with its many quick cuts back and forth from foreground to background, forms a single continuous dramatic unit, largely driven by the orchestra, that, like the soundtrack of many a film, is all but continuous, stopping only for brief moments where silence enhances the dramatic effect of a few well-chosen words. While much of the orchestral music is not melodic as such and, indeed, is recognizable as the customary fill material — tremolos, sforzando chords, and such — of Italian opera, in many of *Chénier*'s most important scenes the melodic content of the music is in the orchestra, rather than the vocal line.

Andrea Chénier, like any successful Italian opera of the period, is ultimately driven by melody. Giordano often seems more interested in melody per se than in melody as a vehicle for characterization, or for capturing and enhancing the precise meaning of the words (unlike, notably, Verdi or Mascagni). Recognizing that it is the melody that is moving the drama forward and that captures the audience's attention, he is more concerned with its contour than with reflecting verbal details or even with vocal prosody, readily breaking vocal phrases in midsentence or otherwise distorting the verbal sense of the phrase in the interest of the musical.[56] Even a careful listener, however, may not notice these deficiencies, as Illica's words tend to fall into insignificance in the face of Giordano's sweeping melodic lines.

Although Giordano could at times spin a strong extended melody, many of his longer melodies tend to dissipate their energies after a strong opening. His true forte was for the short melodic cell, rarely more than two bars in length, that could be used to set off a longer *parlante* passage as in Chénier's first-act *Improvviso*, or used to build an extended arioso as in Maddalena's "La mamma morta." In *Andrea Chénier*, he used that strength to great advantage, building on his unerring instincts for dramatic effect by constructing his solos not as discrete, formally shaped numbers, but as more informally organized narratives or monologues modeled after Wagner's narratives in *Lohengrin* or *Tannhäuser*. Consider the famous *Improvviso*: this narrative builds to its first climax at bar 24, with a viscerally powerful two-bar phrase;[57] it then begins again and after an intervening section where a new melodic idea — which returns momentously later in the opera — is heard in the orchestra, builds to a second, even more powerful, climax on the same two-bar phrase, as it returns in bar 73 with the words "amor, divino dono" (love, divine gift).[58] Although the *Improvviso* is largely *parlante*, it is transformed by these brief melodic moments that cast a melodic aura, as it were, over the entire narrative.

A similar melodic cell, this time in four bars, serves as the climax to Chénier's second-act monologue, in which he talks about his yearning for love, and his hopes for the mysterious stranger whose letters he has been receiving. The distinctive drop of a fourth in this phrase, to the words "Credi all'amor, Chénier! Tu sei amato!" (Believe in love, Chénier! You are loved!), becomes the motivic source for the final *Liebestod* duet, and the subject of the inevitable closing orchestral peroration. These narratives are not only musically effective, but serve a critical dramatic purpose. They establish Chénier's character as that of someone who is so enamored, not only of love itself, but with the idea of living a life devoted to love and if need be giving up his life for love, that he could subsequently and plausibly sing "we will be together until death" to a woman he has barely known for five minutes.

Plausibly, but only barely so. Indeed, the entire connection between Chénier and Maddalena must be taken on faith, because — after their initial encounter in the Prologue — they have only two encounters in the entire opera, one in which they pledge their undying love, and the other in which they go to the guillotine, singing, in unison at the top of their lungs, "Viva la morte insiem!" (long live death, together! — an admittedly literal translation) Just as it is hard to believe in the substance of this relationship, it is hard to take the story any more seriously than any of the penny-dreadful novels that Giordano was trawling for an operatic subject before *Chénier* appeared.[59] That is, indeed, the ultimate weakness of

Umberto Giordano in the garden of his Villa Fedora on Lago Maggiore. *(Casa Musicale Sonzogno)*

the opera: for all Giordano's considerable ability, and the movement, the color, and the visceral excitement that he generates with his music, the music never goes below the surface, adding little depth of characterization beyond that already provided by Illica's libretto.

A comparison of *Andrea Chénier* with *Tosca,* an opera with which it has much in common dramatically, consistently works to the disadvantage of the former work. Both follow the same "lovers in peril" model; yet, while the atmosphere of Puccini's opera is no more compelling than that of Giordano's and the action no more viscerally compelling, Cavaradossi, Tosca, and Scarpia become infinitely more real and more intensely present as human beings than Chénier, Maddalena, and Gérard. This is the achievement of Puccini's music: to interweave a rich texture of leitmotifs with expansive as well as distinctive melodies that capture the individuality of each of the opera's figures.

Ultimately, Giordano's melodies are generic ones, forming an interchangeable sort of music. At their best, they represent generalized sentiments rather than being individualized to the characters or their particular emotions; at worst, they are effective but superficial note-spinning. Giordano's gifts are many, but so are his limitations. While his strengths include a genuine ability to create distinctive melodic ideas harnessed to a sophisticated musical technique, his weakness are more those of an intellectual or cultural, even spiritual, nature. Giordano was, more than any of his colleagues, both product and creator of the popular culture of his time. Lacking in aesthetic or cultural vision, he was the consummate manufacturer of operas, creating finely burnished mechanisms that work perfectly, yet in the end, leave behind little emotional residue.

Giordano captured the spirit of the moment with *Andrea Chénier*.[60] The brief moment of plebian opera had passed. Although *Cavalleria rusticana* and *Pagliacci* were solidly established in the repertory, and minor composers would continue to turn out operas about sordid affairs and peasant vendettas for some time, the vogue was over. As the end of the century approached and Italy lurched toward economic and social crisis, the operatic audience was looking less for grim naturalism than for stories into which they could escape, containing characters with whom they could identify. The successful operas of the next decade, into the early years of the twentieth century, tended to be either domestic dramas of bourgeois life or costume operas set in exotic places or historic times. Their common denominator was their direct, unswerving focus on the personal and the passionate, and on love and death unmediated by larger social, political, or spiritual concerns.

Chapter 5

The Greatest Living Italian:
The Last Decade of Giuseppe Verdi

The Last Hero

As the grim years of the 1890s began, Italy's people had few heroes. The nation's leaders of the day inspired little respect, and no visible affection. King Umberto was a stolid figure, "without intellectual or artistic interests of any kind,"[1] militaristic in his pursuits, and with no personal traits that might endear him to his nation. The devious, manipulative Agostino Depretis, who had dominated Italy's political life since the 1870s, died in 1887 only to be replaced by the Sicilian Francesco Crispi, a one-time *garibaldino* who brought an authoritarian streak and a touch of megalomania to the intrigues of the Italian parliamentary system. As the decade continued, a deadly mixture of civil strife, scandal, foreign adventurism, and governmental incompetence combined to bring Italy to its most perilous position since the formation of the Italian state.

The one individual whom the entire nation saw as a hero, one who, in Parker's words, "had become a national monument,"[2] was Giuseppe Verdi. The awe Italians felt for Verdi went far beyond his being Italy's greatest composer — a position more than amply reinforced by the 1887 premiere of his *Otello*, an opera that towered over anything being written by his contemporaries. While his works dominated the repertory of Italy's opera houses, it was his persona, carefully crafted over the decades, first as the "bard of the Risorgimento" and then as the personification of the traditional, unpretentious, but solid country values of the "real Italy," that established his hold on the hearts of the Italian people. Every literate Italian knew that the initials V.E.R.D.I, stood for "Vittorio Emanuele, re d'Italia," while by the end of the century the account of how Verdi's "Va, pensiero" chorus from *Nabucco* had served as a rallying cry for unification was thoroughly ingrained in the Italian national consciousness.[3]

The image of the elderly Verdi recognized by everyone, an elderly figure thin as a rail, ramrod straight, in his black "peasant go-to-market" suit,[4] his snow-white beard, and his broad-brimmed black hat, symbolized his status as the embodiment of Italy's traditional values, prized all the more as they appeared to recede into Italy's preindustrial history. He was the man of the people, yet, as befits an iconic figure, he projected a remote austerity. He might stop in the railroad station buffet in Genoa for a modest lunch like any traveler or workingman, but people soon learned that if he were approached directly, or even recognized, he would coldly turn away, and quickly flee.[5]

By 1890, Verdi was seventy-seven years old. While seventy-seven is not seen as a particularly old age today, matters were different in nineteenth-century Italy. Barely one out of every hundred Italians living in 1890 reached the age of seventy-five.[6] Only a handful of Italians could aspire to a life span such as Verdi seemed to have achieved almost without effort. Nearly a third of all Italian infants died by the age of five, and the survivors could expect a total life span of no more than fifty more years. Italians were carried away by the thousands in their youth and in middle age by infectious diseases. Intestinal infections such as cholera were the single greatest killer, with pneumonia, tuberculosis, diphtheria, and malaria all not far behind.[7]

Early deaths were the rule, rather than the exception, at all social and economic levels; almost every one of the composers of the *giovane scuola*, before he was out of his teens, experienced the death of one parent. Puccini's father died at fifty-one, when his son was only five; Mascagni's mother died in her thirties of tuberculosis when her son was nine, while three of his four siblings died in their teens. Cilèa's father, a prosperous attorney, died when his son was eighteen; Leoncavallo's mother died at forty, when her son was sixteen.[8] It was not only Verdi's great age, though, but his extraordinary vigor, coupled with his remoteness and austerity, that served to add to his legend, giving him the almost superhuman aura of someone who had in some mysterious fashion held back the inexorable forces of time and nature.

Verdi's great age meant that he saw Italian society from a perspective very different from that of the great majority of educated, urban Italians. Born in 1813 and raised in the picturesque but backward Duchy of Parma, he was the product of a preindustrial, almost feudal era, a world far removed from the industrializing and rapidly urbanizing Italy of the 1890s. Although, like many restless young men of his time, he developed strong radical republican and anticlerical beliefs, his values remained rooted in the agrarian society of his youth. In 1848, at the height of the revolutionary agitation

The elderly Verdi, in Giulio
Ricordi's garden in Milan.
(Ricordi Archive)

that was sweeping Italy, he bought his first properties outside the village of
Sant'Agata, south of Cremona, the beginning of a series of land purchases
that made him one of the largest landowners in the region by the 1880s.[9]
In Sant'Agata he re-created a paternalistic way of life based less on the reality than on his idealized image of the feudal nobility of his childhood. As
he wrote in a letter to Arrivabene in 1881: "Last year I built a dairy, this year
two that are even larger. There are about two hundred laborers . . . to
whom I have to give instructions for future works, as soon as the frost permits. . . . These buildings won't give me another cent of income from the
land, but in the meantime the people are earning money and aren't emi-
grating from my village.[10] Sant'Agata was a busy working farm, but it was
also an estate, with an unpretentious but comfortable manor house and a
two-acre park in the informal English garden style, including a grotto and
a pond set off by willows and poplar trees, as on the estates of the resented
yet admired role models of his younger days.

   Although during the heady days of the Risorgimento Verdi had briefly
allowed himself, at Cavour's urging, to become involved in politics, by the
1880s he had become thoroughly disenchanted with Italian political life,
withdrawing from public affairs and sending out periodic jeremiads from

Sant'Agata or his winter residence in Genoa. His principal sounding board was Giuseppe Piroli, a longtime member of the Italian Parliament, who had become a close friend during Verdi's brief foray into politics.[11] In one 1888 letter to Piroli he denounced the Italian government's colonial adventures: "The war in Africa? . . . It was an idiotic venture at the beginning, and continuing it could become an even more idiotic venture! So many people and so much money thrown away, while we just might have the need for those people and money here at home. And why? Ah, Glory! Ah, much could be said about that ugly word!"[12]

Verdi's distinctive perspective on Italian society, combining humanitarian concerns with an unconscious nostalgia for an agrarian world that had all but disappeared, appears in a well-known letter of 1889, written from Genoa at the height of Italy's rural agitation and unrest, and worth quoting at some length:

> A sad business, that unfortunately will lead to worse! They repress, they make arrests, they exile people, but it does no good. Certainly, among the masses there are agitators, bad actors, thieves, but almost always there is also *hunger*.
>
> I have no love for politics, but I admit its necessity . . . forms of government, Patriotism, Dignity, etc., etc. but above all, people *must be able to live*. From my window every day I see a ship, and sometimes two, each one filled with a thousand emigrants! *Misery and hunger!* In the countryside I see the landowners of a few years ago reduced today to peasants, day-laborers and emigrants (*misery and hunger*). The wealthy, whose fortunes diminish each year, can't spend the way they used to; therefore, *misery and hunger!*
>
> And how can we go forward? It will certainly not be our industries that will save us from ruin! You say that I'm a pessimist! . . . No, no. . . . I believe it is the utter truth, saying that I am profoundly convinced, that this path will lead us to total ruin. Perhaps, you, a politician, will say that *"there's no other way."* Well, if that's true, we had better prepare for total disorder and chaos, first in one city and then in another, then in the villages and then in the countryside, and then *the deluge!* (all emphases in original)[13]

Italy's national hero, with his Utopian vision of an agrarian society of benevolent landowners and a contented peasantry, was deeply estranged from the nation that unification had brought into being. At the same time, he was no pensioner counting the days to his death. Well into his eighties, he remained actively engaged with the management of Sant'Agata and continued to compose, following *Falstaff* with the superb *Quattro pezzi sacri*. Driven both by his humanitarian values and his disenchantment with the Italian state, he channeled his energies into a growing number of charitable and philanthropic pursuits. In addition to innumerable small acts of benevolence and generosity, these pursuits included his building a hospital in a village near Sant'Agata and the Casa di Riposo, the Milan retirement home for impoverished elderly musicians that continues to serve that purpose over a hundred years later.

While Verdi was living the life of a country squire, his operas had come to represent a significant part of the Italian operatic repertory. During the 1880s, a Milan operagoer could attend five or six Verdi operas in the course of a typical year, ranging from the perennially popular "trilogy" of *Rigoletto*, *La traviata*, and *Il trovatore* to less-often-heard fare such as *Luisa Miller* or *Attila*. All in all, fifteen different Verdi operas appeared in Milan in the 1880s, representing slightly less than one out of every five operas performed in Milan during the decade. Verdi's domination of the repertory was even more pronounced in cities like Genoa and Livorno, which had an active operatic life, but which were more conservative in their tastes. During the 1880s, a quarter of all of the operas presented in Genoa, and nearly one of three operas seen in Livorno were Verdi operas.[14]

Not all Verdi operas were created equal. The backbone of the repertory remained *Rigoletto*, *La traviata*, and *Il trovatore*, accounting for more than half of all Verdi productions in most Italian cities between 1880 and 1909. Among the operas of Verdi's early "galley years" before *Rigoletto* set him free, *Ernani*, with its pageantry and gripping romantic theme, was by far the most popular, far outstripping *I Lombardi* or *Nabucco*, both of which had begun to fade from the repertory by the end of the century.[15] Among his later operas, *Aida*, *La forza del destino* and *Un ballo in maschera* were the most popular. Operas such as *Simon Boccanegra* and *Don Carlo* were still rarely heard, while *I vespri siciliani* was all but unknown. *Don Carlo* was not heard at Rome's Costanzi opera house until 1910, when it appeared there under Mascagni's baton.

In major operagoing cities such as Milan or Genoa, one could expect to see at least two of the three "trilogy" operas every year. These productions, as well as those of his earlier operas, rarely took place in La Scala or the Carlo Felice that today's audiences associate with these cities, but in one of the many less prestigious and less expensive theaters of the city, particularly those known as *Politeamas*, large, unpretentious structures used not only for opera, but for operetta, prose theater, and even music hall and circus performances. Indeed, Toscanini's decision to present *Trovatore*, which Sachs describes as having become "the most down-trodden and battle-weary work in the repertoire," at La Scala in 1902 was as controversial in its way as a presentation of some radical new opera from across the Alps.[16]

Verdi and the giovane scuola

Although Verdi's giant shadow loomed over the younger generation of opera composers, his own engagement with their music was limited to little more than a sort of distant paternal interest, occasionally encouraging but often casually dismissive. Although during an 1894 Paris visit, he asserted to a French interviewer: "I do not know the music of either Mascagni or Leoncavallo . . . and I have never heard their operas,"[17] he was clearly being disingenuous. There is little doubt that he made some effort to keep abreast with their works. Although he attended the opera rarely in his later years, he saw Franchetti's *Asrael* and *Cristoforo Colombo*, and Puccini's *Manon Lescaut*, and was familiar with many of the scores of the *giovane scuola*, including Mascagni's *Cavalleria rusticana* and *L'amico Fritz*. It is doubtful, however, that he ever saw either of those two operas, or any of Mascagni's later works.

It is harder, however, to assess what Verdi thought of their music. His famous letter to Arrivabene about Puccini's *Le Villi* is often cited:

> I have heard much good about the composer Puccini . . . He follows modern tendencies, which is natural, but he remains attached to melody, which is neither modern nor old. It seems, though, that the symphonic element is predominant in [his music]! Nothing wrong with that. Only, one must be careful with that. Opera is opera: symphony is symphony, and I don't believe that in an opera it's a good idea to make a symphonic racket, just for the fun of seeing the orchestra dance.[18]

This letter, however, reads very much as if he had not heard a note of the work, but was relying on the words of others. Similarly, when he wrote dismissively of Catalani's *La Wally* to a Genoese critic in 1892, he had most probably neither seen nor read it:

> [I have no interest] in hearing the new German opera by that half-pint composer [*maestrino*] from Lucca. . . . The public wants Italian music, and not counterfeit German operas in disguise. Something other than "the music of the future" is called for! . . . I don't think it will last, because without heart and inspiration, living music cannot be made. These young people who want

to innovate and rush down new paths, who seem to me rather poorly advised and overly trusting in the future, will end up losing even the present.[19]

Both letters reflect a deeply rooted, almost instinctive reluctance on the elderly Verdi's part to grapple seriously with the music of the younger generation, music that reflected not only stylistic choices, but underlying musical values very different from those that Verdi had absorbed in his youth, and to a large extent still held.

While Bellini and Donizetti were distant historical figures to the *giovane scuola*, they were near-contemporaries to Verdi. He was eighteen when *Norma* made its debut, and nearly twenty-two when *Lucia di Lammermoor* first appeared; his *I Lombardi* and Donizetti's *Don Pasquale* are almost exact contemporaries. While Verdi's musical vocabulary and concept of operatic form steadily evolved over the next half-century, to the extent he absorbed ideas from his contemporary Richard Wagner, or from French composers such as Thomas or Gounod, they were integrated slowly and systematically into a musical foundation that never lost touch with its origins in the Italian traditions of early *ottocento* opera. His musical worldview was rooted in that period, in sharp contrast to the cosmopolitan world of the young composers of the 1890s, for whom Wagner and Bizet were as much a part of their musical heritage as Donizetti and Bellini — or, for that matter, Verdi himself.

For the most part, Verdi avoided commenting on the music of the *giovane scuola*; indeed, his comment to the French interviewer was most probably designed to deflect the inevitable questions that the interviewer would otherwise pose. The only composer who offers something of an exception is Mascagni, whose *Cavalleria rusticana* and *L'amico Fritz* were the subject of such attention on their appearance that Verdi's interest, or at least his curiosity, was piqued. The story that Verdi had said "now I can die content" — which made the rounds soon after the debut of *Cavalleria*, — was patently apocryphal and an annoyance to the older composer.[20] Verdi did, however, gave the Mascagni score close study, as he described to Giovanni Tebaldini some years later:

> Hearing about the immense uproar and the great success of *Cavalleria*, I wanted to find out about the new opera immediately, so I began to read it through together with Boito. The Prelude, lovely, fresh, supple; the idea of Turiddu's Serenade was a great idea [*ben trovato*]. The first chorus, also very fine, with its thoroughgoing folk feeling. Then came the "carter's song." What's this about? . . . When we got to the Easter chorus, that would have

liked to be a concertato, it was starting to get on my nerves, and I said to Boito, "Enough. Put it down." But during the night I couldn't sleep. There was something there that wouldn't let me go. And in the morning, I got up early, picked up *Cavalleria* and went back to the garden to read it. When I got to the "Addio alla madre," I burst out, by God, this is theater!"[21]

While Verdi clearly had mixed feelings about the music of *Cavalleria*, as a practical man of the theater, he recognized and admired its dramatic power. The same was not true, however, of Mascagni's next opera. Reading the score of *L'amico Fritz* at the time of the work's premiere in the fall of 1891, he wrote Ricordi:

> I have in my life read very, very, very many bad libretti, but never have I read such a silly libretto such as this. As for the music, I have made some headway, but I soon tired of so many dissonances, those false modulations, suspended cadences and tricks, and then, so many changes of tempi in almost every bar — all most appetizing, but they offend one's sense of rhythm and hearing. . . . The music may be very beautiful, but I have my own view of things.[22]

Verdi's is an astonishing reaction to the music — if not necessarily the libretto — of this gentle opera. *L'amico Fritz*, although dramatically exiguous, is nonetheless all but universally recognized today as a work of great lyrical grace and tenderness, suffering if anything from a surfeit rather than a dearth of bel canto lyricism and harmonic consonance.

Mascagni's harmonic vocabulary, however conservative it may appear to modern ears, was as alien to Verdi as that of Stravinsky would be to Mascagni. While *L'amico Fritz* is clearly tonal (as are all of the works of the *giovane scuola,*), it adheres to a very different idea of tonality than that of the *ottocento*. From the opening bars of the Preludietto, the music of *Fritz* inhabits a world of harmonic ambiguity and modal flavor, where major and minor are constantly interwoven, and where chromatic and enharmonic shifts are regularly employed, and where cadences rarely flow directly from dominant to tonic, but where the tonic is reached, if at all, through other, more remote progressions.

Although Verdi and Mascagni gradually developed a warm personal relationship, the older composer appears to have largely lost interest in Mascagni's music after *Fritz*. In 1895 or 1896, he told the writer Gino Monaldi, "What a pity! He is a young man, whose feeling for music exceeds his knowledge of it. . . . He could achieve much . . . but . . . I think he has now lost his way."[23]

Verdi's interest in the personal welfare of the younger composers, however, was a different matter. Although he found much about their music
alien and disconcerting, he saw the composers themselves as kindred
spirits, young men dedicated to the future of Italian opera, seeking to find
their path and build their careers much as he had done half a century before. Although he may have written dismissively about Catalani's operas,
that composer's premature death prompted a deeply felt note to the conductor Mascheroni: "Poor Catalani! Such a decent fellow and *excellent
musician!* . . . Do thank Giulio [Ricordi] for the few, fine words he said
about that *poor soul!* What a shame!"[24]

Verdi encouraged the efforts of the younger composers, recommending
Franchetti for the commission to write an opera for the 400th anniversary
of the discovery of America, offering to withdraw a production of *Falstaff*
to avoid upstaging Puccini's *Manon Lescaut*,[25] and offering Mascagni
the materials he had collected for an opera on Shakespeare's *King Lear*.[26]
He urged Giordano to consider Sardou's *Madame Sans-Gêne*, set in the
Napoleonic era, as a subject. Giordano described the conversation, which
took place only a few weeks before Verdi's death:

> "Why don't you tackle *Madame Sans-Gêne?*"
> "And what about Napoleon, maestro?" And Verdi, with the intuition of a
> genius, replied, "I could not imagine Napoleon coming to the footlights to
> sing a romance with his hand across his heart. Certainly not. But a Napoleon
> who uttered dramatic recitative would be perfectly fitting, even in an opera."[27]

Giordano did ultimately set *Madame Sans-Gêne*, although not until 1915.

Among the young composers of the time, Verdi formed personal relationships with Franchetti, Giordano, and Mascagni.[28] While Franchetti's
ties to the older composer dated back to the late 1880s, Verdi's bonds with
both Giordano and Mascagni were formed in the mid-1890s. Giordano's
connection with Verdi began during the days of *Andrea Chénier*, when he
was courting Olga Spatz, the daughter of the Swiss proprietor of the Hôtel
de Milan, which Verdi made his home in Milan. According to one account, Spatz, reluctant to have his daughter marry a musician, asked Verdi
to look at the score of *Chénier*, in order to advise him whether Giordano
would be a suitable son-in-law.[29] Whether or not that episode actually took
place, Giordano and his bride were warmly welcomed by Verdi and his
wife when they visited the couple in Genoa on their honeymoon near the
end of 1896.[30] That initial visit led to regular calls by Giordano on the older
composer through January 1901, a few weeks before his death.

While Verdi may have been impressed by *Cavalleria*, he was initially put off by Mascagni's brash and aggressive manner. When a Genoa newspaper reported that the young composer, when asked at a banquet in 1892 what opera he would write next, quipped, "a *Nerone*, for which the honorable maestro Boito has allowed me plenty of time," Verdi was offended, and lost no time urging Boito to finish his *Nerone*, as a "reply to [Mascagni's] impertinences."[31] The following year, Verdi reputedly snubbed Mascagni at a Milan banquet, a gesture noticed by much of Milan's artistic elite. Mascagni's first encounter with Verdi most probably took place in 1895, not long after the premiere of *Ratcliff*. While Verdi may or may not have uttered the praise attributed to him about this strong but problematic opera,[32] he may well have felt a particular kinship with this most Verdian of Mascagni's works, both for its Romantic sensibility, and for its connection with Verdi's longtime friend Andrea Maffei.[33]

After the ice was broken, Mascagni visited Verdi often when the two men were both in Milan. Mascagni would take a room in the Hôtel de Milan,[34] and the two would meet for conversation late in the afternoon, before dinner, in Verdi's rooms. For the emotionally needy and insecure Mascagni, Verdi's friendship was a gift of incalculable value: as he wrote, years later, Verdi became "the man I came to know personally, the man who gave me the honor and the good fortune to take me into his confidence, whose voice taught me so many things that have become my guides in both my life and my art."[35] Their conversations, as reported by Mascagni, ranged from the importance of studying Bach to the merits of various violinmakers. If Verdi expressed any judgments on the music of any of Mascagni's contemporaries, it is tactfully not mentioned.

As a tribute to his friend and mentor, Mascagni, who was by now director of the Rossini Conservatory in Pesaro, made a performance of Verdi's last work, the *Quattro pezzi sacri*, the centerpiece of the 1899 spring concerts at the conservatory. Although Verdi had initially hoped to attend, he was unable to, sending Mascagni instead a rueful letter: "Despite my sincere wishes, my years condemn me to quiet, to rest, and to inertia. I praise and rejoice in these wonderful musical exercises you are leading, that are so full of Italian blood, and so valuable to our art." He closed with best wishes to Mascagni's wife, and "a kiss to your sweet children."[36] The performance was exceptionally well received, with the *Stabat Mater* and *Te Deum* both repeated.

Verdi's affection for Mascagni's three small children, whom their father had brought to meet the elderly composer the year before at his Milan hotel, adds a touching albeit sentimental twist to the story of Verdi and

Mascagni. Three years after that encounter, on Verdi's death in January 1901, Mascagni entered Verdi's rooms, which had been transformed into a funeral chamber, for the last time. Looking at Verdi's writing desk, he was astonished and moved to see laid out there three handwritten notes from Verdi to his three children, thanking them for their New Year's presents, along with three small envelopes, waiting to be mailed.[37]

Va, vecchio Giuseppe . . . Falstaff and the Apotheosis of Giuseppe Verdi

As Verdi approached his eightieth birthday, he was far from through with music. In contrast to the long years of near-silence after *Aida*, not long after the successful debut of *Otello* Boito's gentle but insistent pressure had begun to lead Verdi to entertain the thought of writing another opera. While the first direct reference to *Falstaff* appears in a letter from Verdi to Boito on July 6, 1889, the tone of the letter suggests that the project had already been the subject of some discussion between the two collaborators; only a few days later, after a further exchange, Verdi wrote Boito again, "Let us do *Falstaff* then! We will not think for the moment about the obstacles, age, illnesses!!"[38]

Boito began work on the libretto in August, delivering the first two acts to Verdi in November 1889. Verdi completed the first act in March 1890. While a variety of interruptions resulted in his achieving little more during that year, he worked intensely, in a remarkable sustained creative effort, through most of 1891 and 1892 completing the entire opera by the end of summer 1892. With Giulio Ricordi taking charge of every detail, Verdi's first comic opera since his unsuccessful youthful effort *Un giorno di regno* made its debut at La Scala on February 9, 1893, nine days after the Turin premiere of Puccini's *Manon Lescaut*.[39]

The first public notice that a new Verdi opera was in the making appeared in November 1890 in the pages of the *Corriere della sera*, which reported that the composer was working on an opera buffa "in the broadest sense of the word." This was followed in a few days by a report in Ricordi's house magazine, the *Gazzetta musicale di Milano*, that the opera was indeed *Falstaff* but "no one knows when Verdi will decide to have it performed, because the composer has repeatedly stated that he has begun it purely for his pleasure, with no idea when or whether he will finish it."[40] During the months after the *Gazzetta* article, Verdi, while readily acknowledging the project, was uncharacteristically coy about its status and his intentions. He wrote the Roman impresario Gino Monaldi, who was angling for the premiere, "I am having fun writing the music . . . and I don't even know if I will finish it. . . . I repeat: I am having fun."[41]

Part of Verdi's diffidence can be attributed to his recurrent fear that illness or infirmity might keep him from finishing *Falstaff*; it may also, however, reflect his awareness of the low esteem in which opera buffa was held by the Italian opera world of the time. Outside of Naples, where the buffa tradition clung, although with waning energy, to life, it was a moribund genre. Italian opera buffa was a genre frozen in time, with its clichéd plots, formulaic sentimental romances, and staccato patter numbers, unimaginative harmonic vocabulary, and repetitive rhythms. By the end of the century it was closer in both style and reception to the French operettas being put on in provincial houses by ramshackle touring companies than to the "serious" operas being produced by the *giovane scuola*.

From the standpoint of the public, however, what mattered was that it was a new opera by the great Verdi, whatever the genre. As the date of the premiere drew closer, the anticipation, both from the Italian public and from the European cultural and musical world, was considerable. Although Verdi had initially wanted the premiere of *Falstaff* to take place at a smaller, more intimate, theater, Ricordi had prevailed upon him to allow the opera to make its debut at La Scala. Taking full advantage of the opportunity, the management increased the price of orchestra seats from the regular 5 lire to an unprecedented 200 lire, while selling box seats for 250 lire and the poorest places in the gallery for 30 lire.[42] Despite the prices, on opening night every seat in the theater was taken, with Italy's nobility brushing elegant shoulders with critics from every part of Europe. Mascagni, Puccini, and the French verismo composer Alfred Bruneau were in attendance, as were literary figures such as Giosuè Carducci and Giuseppe Giacosa.

Falstaff made its triumphal debut on February 9, 1893. Applause and the cries of "Verdi! Verdi!" reverberated through the theater at the end of each act, as Verdi came forward from the wings time after time, together with the singers, with the conductor Mascheroni, with Boito, and finally by himself. At the telegraph station that had been set up for the press in a side room, more than three hundred telegrams were sent off to every corner of the world, the longest — 830 lines — being sent by the English composer Charles Villiers Stanford to London's *Daily Graphic*. At the end of the performance, while Verdi, Giuseppina, and Boito attempted to slip out of the theater unnoticed, their carriage was soon surrounded by a throng of admirers, who accompanied them in a triumphal procession to the hotel, where thousands of people were already gathered waiting for the composer. At the hotel, Verdi had to appear three times on the balcony to respond to the crowd of cheering well-wishers, who then slowly dispersed into the night.[43]

In order to capitalize on the immense public interest in Verdi's new opera, Ricordi and Piontelli, the La Scala impresario, arranged for the entire production to go on tour, a practice that would become more common in the next century, but was rare at that time. After twenty-two performances in Milan, the La Scala forces, singers, chorus, orchestra, sets, and costumes, traveled to Genoa, where they performed *Falstaff* four times at the Teatro Carlo Felice. The tour then moved on to Rome, where the tour's triumphal aspect took on a more overtly nationalist character.[44] The *Falstaff* tour was more than an economic venture on Ricordi's part; it was an extended national act of homage to the great composer, the greatest living Italian, in which his appearance in Italy's capital was to play a central part. Knowing that Verdi, by now comfortably back home in Genoa, was reluctant to travel to Rome, Ricordi wrote him a long, obsequious letter in his distinctively convoluted style, playing on his patriotism:

> Can you explain why we [referring to himself and Boito] earnestly feel the need for your presence in Rome? . . . I base myself on all of Italy's quite fervent, almost inexplicably intense desire to see the most glorious of her sons in Rome, in the capital. . . . Why not acknowledge this universal sentiment as a new token of affection toward you on the part of the Italians? . . . In Rome! . . . a magic word that is now repeated for Verdi, quite naturally in view of all of the extraordinary circumstances soon to be realized — two truly eminent persons, the King and the Queen, the Senate, the Ministry, look forward to seeing Italy's most honored man in Rome! . . . and you, Maestro, wish to remain insensitive to these voices, which emanate from Vittorio Emanuele's famous cries of pain?[45]

Although Verdi hesitated for a week, he finally acceded to Ricordi's wishes, and arrived in Rome on April 13, two days before the first performance.

From his arrival, where a crowd of thousands had formed on the station platform, to his departure a week later, Verdi was the center of a series of demonstrations all but unprecedented in Italian history. At the performance of *Falstaff* on April 15, King Umberto called Verdi to the royal box, where he came forward, holding the composer's hand, and presented him to the audience, which responded with a long ovation.[46] As Phillips-Matz writes, "With the sovereign, dozens of royal and noble families, and all of Rome's national government . . . in the audience, this grand gala at the Teatro Costanzi represented a national recognition and apotheosis of Verdi that had never been tendered him before."[47] The next evening, as thousands of onlookers gathered around the Hotel Quirinale, the orchestra of the Teatro Costanzi assembled on the hotel terrace under Verdi's window, and played selections from his operas in his honor. For the duration of the composer's stay, an honor guard of Roman police in full dress uniform stood in front of the hotel.

The Roman celebrations completed the process of transforming Verdi into a national symbol. While Verdi's persona had first become part of the Italian collective consciousness as something separate from his musical achievements years before, his "apotheosis" meant that although still alive and vigorous as he approached his eightieth birthday, to the Italian people he was now more a historical figure than a living, breathing human being. From this point on, no more ceremonies or celebrations would be needed, and had they been proposed, it is likely that Verdi would have been most reluctant to participate. Fixed in the pantheon of great Italians of the ages, the one remaining ceremony in which he would be called upon to take part, and in which he would have no choice about his participation, would be his funeral, eight years later.

In the accounts of the Roman celebrations, *Falstaff* often seems to be put to one side, almost as if it were the pretext for this remarkable act of national homage rather than of any particular importance in itself. Although that may seem an exaggeration, it reflects the fact that, for all the sincerity and passion in the nation's tribute to Verdi, the opera itself was seen with considerable uncertainty and ambivalence. As Piamonte writes, many of the reviews "often allowed a glimpse of an undercurrent of perplexity, hidden beneath the layer of devoted admiration and homage to the eighty year old Giuseppe Verdi."[48]

Even at the premiere of *Falstaff* at La Scala, an astute observer noted that the opera's reception was less unequivocal than the official story: "When the opera reached its end, there followed a moment of general, awkward silence. But fortunately, the audience was not lacking knowledgeable musicians and learned critics who appreciated the opera's beauties. And then, realizing that Verdi was there, just in the wings. . . . Then the applause burst forth."[49] Mascagni, one of the knowledgeable musicians in the audience, made the same point in a letter to his wife after the performance: "the opera is one of miraculous beauty, but the Milan public neither understood or appreciated its value." He added insightfully, "it will be some years, but *Falstaff* will be recognized as Verdi's masterpiece. But it will never be destined for the popularity of *Trovatore, Rigoletto,* or *Aida.*"[50]

Even after prices at La Scala had been reduced, although not to their

normal level, the theater was half-empty for many of the subsequent performances of the opera. After the excitement of the opera's initial appearance had worn off, the same experience was repeated in cities throughout
Italy. In January 1895, after *Falstaff*'s first return to Genoa after the initial
La Scala tour, Verdi wrote Ricordi, his pen dripping with angry sarcasm:

> Last evening at the Carlo Felice, *Falstaff* was reduced, not his belly, but his
> price!! I dare not say it! 1.50 Lire. Result? The same. If I were Piontelli [the
> impresario], I would try something else. I would remove all the seats from
> the theater. I would put in a large bar near the orchestra, with six or more
> barmaids, and four newsboys outside the theater shouting "Gentlemen,
> come in, come into the theater gratis!! All you pay for is the beer, five cen-
> times a mug!!! Step right up, step right up, gentlemen!! A real bargain!! With
> this trick, Piontelli might see a few pennies in his box.[51]

Genoa was unusual, in that *Falstaff* reappeared there not long after its initial production. While many Italian opera houses presented *Falstaff* during the year or so after its Milan debut, few brought it back for a second
look until decades later, if ever. Even in Verdi's homeland of Parma, after
its 1895 debut, *Falstaff* did not appear again until 1913, and then only as part
of a gala historic retrospective commemorating the centenary of Verdi's
birth.[52] Among important secondary opera centers, Bari did not see *Falstaff* until 1925, while the work has yet to be performed in Livorno. As his
letter suggests, the outcome of his last opera was deeply disappointing to
Verdi. Whatever personal significance *Falstaff* held for him, its composer
never lost track of the importance of the box office.

While generally recognized today as a masterpiece, Verdi's *Falstaff* is in
many respects a difficult work. While the audiences of the 1890s clearly
failed to respond to its reinterpretation of the opera buffa genre as a modern genre with a continuous, complex orchestral texture and an absence of
closed forms and stock numbers, the difficulties of *Falstaff* extend to the intensely personal, and in an important sense political, nature of the work.
Indeed, *Falstaff* should be read at three levels beyond the obvious delights
of its music and drama: (1) as a polemic, albeit a good-humored one,
against the musical trends of the time; (2) as a statement about politics and
society; and (3) as a personal testament, Verdi's self-conscious closing of the
book on an operatic career lasting more than half a century. It is in this
light, as Parker has pointed out, that it is necessary to read the composer's
repeated statements, during the composition of the opera, that he was writing *Falstaff* for himself, as a personal pastime for his pleasure.[53]

Parker has also noted the extent to which *Falstaff* is "an elaborate essay written against the grain of contemporary opera; more than any other Verdi work, a kind of manifesto, an ideological statement, an attempt to influence the story of Italian opera."[54] For some time, Verdi had denounced the spread of foreign influences on Italian composers, and on what he saw as the distinctly Italian art of opera. The examples of Catalani, Franchetti, and the Puccini of *Le Villi* and *Edgar*, with their highly visible and poorly assimilated debt to the French composers and to Wagner, were much on his mind as he set to work on *Falstaff*.[55] The problem, for Verdi, was not only their modernism, but what he saw as their almost willful rejection of the central Italian opera tradition, of that essential *italianità* that was their artistic and cultural heritage, in their pursuit of trendy and inappropriate foreign models.

The choice of opera buffa, a genre that reached back nearly to the roots of Italian opera and that was central to its identity up to the middle of the nineteenth century, was very much a part of Verdi's polemical scheme. Ironically, this rationale was articulated only eight years later by Pietro Mascagni, who saw his comedy *Le Maschere* (The masks) in ideological terms that paralleled those of *Falstaff*. As he told an interviewer, "today the public goes to the theater to feel anguish, to ruin their digestions with violent feelings. We composers no longer know how to laugh: people say that the wonderful vein of Italian humor dried up with Rossini."[56] While Mascagni's opera was based on Illica's attempt to re-create the traditional Italian genre of the commedia dell'arte, Boito had based his libretto on Shakespeare; just the same, however, Verdi saw the story as being an Italian one, asserting with some vehemence to a French interviewer: "Do you know what *Falstaff* is? It is nothing other than an ancient Italian comedy, written in a very ancient language long before Shakespeare! Shakespeare took the material and added the character of Falstaff. . . . The rest of the play is practically identical."[57]

To both Verdi and Mascagni opera buffa meant a return to a purer Italian opera, free from the contamination of both French *grand opéra* and Wagnerian opera that had so transformed serious Italian opera by the late nineteenth century. That demanded in turn an appropriate musical language. *Falstaff* is an uncommonly diatonic work by the standards of the time, in which chromaticism is all but purely decorative, and which, to quote Parker once again, "is obsessed by cadence, forever punctuated by unequivocal gestures of closure."[58] At the same time, *Falstaff* is not an attempt to re-create in literal fashion either the language or forms of eighteenth- or early-nineteenth-century opera buffa, as is Mascagni's *Le*

Maschere. Verdi's genius lies in his fusion of old and new, in the way each of the characteristics of the opera buffa — the patter number for the buffo bass, the sentimental romance for the ingénue, the grand finale — has been reimagined and reinvented, within the framework of continuous texture characteristic of the times. Twenty years earlier, Verdi had written famously, "torniamo all'antico, sarà un progresso" (return to the past, [and] that will be progress).[59] *Falstaff* is Verdi's way of demonstrating how one could actually accomplish that seeming contradiction, and produce a unique synthesis of old and new.

If the musical polemic in *Falstaff*, symbolized by the constant play of dominant-tonic cadences, is fairly clear, the social and political commentary is more veiled, but nonetheless significant. For all that the opera's story can be taken as a delightful romp, many ambiguities exist beneath its surface, not least the ambiguity in Sir John Falstaff's status and his relationship to the people of Windsor among whom he mysteriously finds himself. Sir John Falstaff, for all that he is old, fat, and broke, is an aristocrat, cast among the bourgeoisie: when he sings to Alice, "quando ero paggio al Duca di Norfolk, ero sottile" (when I was a page to the Duke of Norfolk, I was thin) he is not only remembering his slender youth, he is reminding her — and the audience — that he is part of another world, the world of the nobility, of pages and palaces. In contrast to that other famous comedy of aristocrats and commoners, *Le nozze di Figaro*, where the commoner is clever and the nobleman obtuse, in *Falstaff* it is the bourgeois men — Ford and Dr. Caius — who are fools, and Falstaff clever. Falstaff and Figaro are clever, however, they are no more than that; it is the women of both operas who are wise, rather than merely clever.

While the juxtaposition of Figaro and Almaviva in *Figaro* serves as a reminder that their underlying class conflict can be patched over, but cannot be resolved except by revolution, the roles of the parties in *Falstaff* tell us precisely the opposite. Sir John's presence graces and enhances the lives of the men and women of Windsor, as he reminds them near the end of the opera:

> All sorts of common folk mock me, and glory in it,
> But without me, those braggarts' lives would lack even a pinch of salt.
> It is I, I alone, who make you lively,
> It is my sharp wit that makes you witty.

His presence is the fulcrum of their lives, not only giving them the dash of salt they cannot provide by themselves, but providing the way by which the women of Windsor can restore the balance in their world, and allow the young love of Fenton and Nanetta to triumph.

Falstaff provides us with a window into Verdi's vision of an ideal world, the same vision of a benevolent feudal society that Verdi sought to bring into being at Sant'Agata. In *Falstaff*, social order is threatened, but easily restored. Class conflict is an illusion, laughter is wisdom, and in the end, aristocrats and bourgeoisie alike all go off arm in arm to dinner. It is a lovely vision, but one badly at odds with the grim realities of the age into which *Falstaff* was born.

Finally, though, there is another important sense in which Verdi can be said to have written *Falstaff* for himself: as his personal testament, the work with which he consciously ended the operatic career he had begun with *Oberto, Conte di San Bonifacio* in 1839, fifty-four years earlier. While it would be too much to suggest that Verdi saw himself literally as Sir John, there is far more of Verdi in "pancione" (big-belly), as he affectionately called him, than in any other of the long list of memorable characters that he had created in his long life. Falstaff is a rogue, to be sure, but he is an inexhaustible life force. He may be old, fat, and broke, but he is unbowed, confident — if deluded — that his powers are still intact, and that he still has much to offer the world. He is Verdi crying, "I'm still here" as he approached eighty.

Final testimony of Verdi's deep identification with his character comes from the note, paraphrasing the famous lines from the opera beginning "Va, vecchio, John," (go, old John) which he jotted down at the end of the last sections of the manuscript that he sent Ricordi in the fall of 1892:

It's all over.
Go, go, old John,
Keep moving on your way as long as you can.
Entertaining rogue
Forever true under all of your masks
In every time, every place.
Go, go, keep moving.
Farewell.[60]

The last lines should be given to Giuseppina, who wrote to Giuseppe De Santis, Verdi's godson, a year after the premiere of *Falstaff*: "Have no illusions about future operas. Verdi has worked enough and has every right to rest. Let others follow in his example, not only in regard to his activity, but to his *honest* character in every sense of the word."[61]

Chapter 6

The Rise of Bourgeois Opera
in a Changing Nation

The Crisis of the Fin de siècle

Italy in the mid-1890s was a nation in the throes of massive social, economic, and political change. The pain that inevitably accompanies rapid social and economic change was exacerbated by the behavior of the nation's narrow-minded and often corrupt and incompetent ruling class. From the late 1880s a pointless, vindictive tariff war with France had undermined Italy's agriculture, further impoverishing an already straitened peasant population. Thousands left the countryside for the nation's cities, while thousands more emigrated, abandoning their homeland in the hopes of a better life in the Americas. Meanwhile, an equally pointless series of colonial adventures in East Africa drained the nation's treasury, culminating in the March 1896 Adowa disaster, where the Italian army was routed by the Abyssinians under King Menelik, leaving five thousand dead on the field.

While the population growth and industrialization of cities such as Milan, Genoa, and Turin was building a large, self-aware bourgeois class, it was also creating a growing disenfranchised urban working class living on the edge of destitution and hunger. Workers and peasants began to organize, and in 1892, delegates representing more than three hundred local associations met in Genoa to form the Italian Socialist Party.[1] Widespread uprisings took place in Sicily in 1893, as the discontented peasants and workers of the island began to form themselves into *fasci* (literally, "bundles," meaning alliances), often under socialist or anarchist leadership. Their strikes and demonstrations spread across the island, often turning into violent riots.

Early in 1894, the government moved to suppress the *fasci*, putting Sicily under martial law and sending 40,000 troops to the island, exiling thousands of suspected rioters to isolated outposts without trial, and sentencing their leaders to long prison terms. Although there was no evidence of any direct connection, the Italian authorities used the Sicilian riots as an excuse to dissolve the Socialist Party, arrest its leaders, and purge the electoral rolls of known Socialist Party supporters. While quiet appeared to prevail for the time being, the insecure and unrepresentative Italian government, led by the unstable Francesco Crispi, was incapable of resolving the situation. By 1896, paralyzed by the Adowa disaster and Crispi's subsequent resignation, the Italian government could do nothing to address the challenges it faced, responding only with violence and repression.

The next wave of popular unrest was not far away. In the fall of 1897, a poor grain harvest, coupled with the government's failure to take timely measures to import wheat, led to widespread hunger throughout the Italian countryside. Although the first uprisings were quickly put down, they resumed with greater intensity in April 1898, spreading from the Po Valley and Puglia throughout southern and central Italy. Although lacking any central organization or leadership, what began as a pure "protest of the stomach" developed broader political overtones.[2]

When the unrest spread to Milan early in May, the Socialist leaders tried desperately to calm the populace, but without success. As thousands of men, women, and children filled the streets, shouting slogans and blocking traffic, the government placed the city under martial law and turned matters over to the army. Over the course of a few gruesome days, still known in Italy as the *fatti di Maggio* (Events of May), General Bava-Baccaris led the army in a wave of bloody attacks, shooting volley after volley into unarmed crowds. The official count was 80 dead and 450 wounded in Milan, with another 51 dead elsewhere in Italy, figures most authorities consider substantially understated. As with the suppression of the Sicilian *fasci*, thousands of demonstrators, so-called ringleaders, and innocent bystanders — including the entire Socialist Party leadership — were sentenced to prison or exile by military tribunals with little pretense of a fair trial.[3] Nearly three thousand workers' councils, peasant leagues, and other "subversive" organizations were forcibly dissolved.[4]

There was no insurrection, nor was there any conspiracy beyond that in the minds of a handful of semirational anarchists — one of whom subsequently assassinated King Umberto in 1900. Indeed, Italy's Socialist leadership, despite a political system rigged against them, was overwhelmingly committed to nonviolent organizing and political action. As Giovanni Giolitti, a rising establishment figure, admitted years later, "Among the ruling class, a state of mind that was intensely fearful of any expressions of popular agitation was pervasive; the government, responding to those sentiments, acted excessively."[5] Under Giolitti's leadership, early in the twentieth century, Italy would finally begin to open up the franchise beyond the narrow electorate of propertied men; radicals, Socialists, and even Catholics, despite the pope's anathema, would gradually begin to be absorbed into the system. Along with a dramatic increase in economic growth, these measures brought a degree of social peace to the nation. It was a fragile peace, however, and was brutally ruptured by World War I and its aftermath. In the 1890s, however, that was still far in the future.

Opera for the Changing Tastes of the Bourgeoisie

It would be a mistake, however, to look at the decade entirely through the prism of social conflict, which was for the most part beneath the surface, and which impinged only intermittently on the consciousness of the urban bourgeoisie. Within the major cities of northern and central Italy, this period also saw the growth of a stronger, more self-aware bourgeois class, along with a burgeoning lower-middle class of shopkeepers, clerks, and lesser functionaries who modeled their behavior and tastes after those of the professionals, civil servants, and industrialists in their midst.

Existing on top of the large struggling substratum of laborers, servants, and the unemployed, these classes had more money to spend, and more leisure to spend it on. People took up pastimes such as Alpine hiking and bicycling (immortalized in Giordano's *Fedora*), went to spas or bathing beaches, or simply promenaded in the new parks *à l'anglaise* that were being laid out in the nation's cities. Huge, ornate new theaters, such as Rome's Costanzi, Catania's Bellini, and Palermo's Massimo, were being built, along with the music halls and *cafés chantants* depicted in *La bohème* and in Leoncavallo's *Zazà*.

There was no single bourgeois culture. The Italian bourgeoisie was a social class in transition, full of inconsistencies and seeming contradictions. The connections between the urban bourgeoisie and their roots in the traditional Italian society of small-town life and extended family relationships were weakening; in their place, they sought not only the often sexually charged popular entertainment offered by the *cafés chantants*, but followed their counterparts in France and England in building a culture of domesticity around the home and the nuclear family. Children became a center of attention, and the focus of sentimental feeling. The end of the nineteenth century saw a huge industry develop for the care and feeding of the offspring of the bourgeoisie, including clothing, toys, and books, among which were the two most prominent children's books of the era, Collodi's subtly subversive *Pinocchio* and De Amicis' thoroughly establishment *Cuore*

(Heart), with its relentlessly patriotic nation-building message. Although largely forgotten today, the latter was far more popular well into the twentieth century. The year 1891 also saw the appearance of Italy's first domestic cookbook, Artusi's *La scienza in cucina e l'arte di mangiar bene* (Science in the kitchen and the art of eating well), which had gone through five editions by the decade's end.

The bourgeois audience was drawn to the sentimental and the melodramatic. No longer rooted in the traditional values of the church or of a hierarchal, traditional society, they sought entertainments that would provoke emotional release rather than moral resolution, craving the tender feelings engendered by a sentimental scene or the frisson of excitement prompted by a whiff of illicit sexuality or the appearance of a particularly loathsome villain. To a remarkable degree, this was precisely what the operas written between 1896 and 1900 offered. Of the many new operas that appeared during these five years, eight stand out in that they became — some only for a while and others permanently — a part of the Italian repertory. All of them reflected directly the tastes and preferences of the bourgeois audience, in many cases offering them a mirror in which they could see themselves, and in the process introducing new themes and subject matter into the world of Italian opera.

None of these operas follow the short, violent model made briefly popular by Mascagni's *Cavalleria rusticana* and Leoncavallo's *Pagliacci*. While those two operas had firmly entrenched themselves in the repertory, none of the many similar works that followed them attracted more than brief attention. Although examples of the genre would continue to appear over the following decades, culminating with Puccini's superb *Il tabarro*, the

Table 1

Major New Operas and Their First Performances 1896–1900

Opera	Composer	Librettist	Date	Location
La bohème	Puccini	Illica & Giacosa	Feb. 1, 1896	Regio, Turin
Andrea Chénier	Giordano	Illica	Mar. 28, 1896	La Scala, Milan
La bohème	Leoncavallo	Leoncavallo	May 6, 1897	Fenice, Venice
L'Arlesiana	Cilèa	Marenco	Nov. 27, 1897	Lirico, Milan
Fedora	Giordano	Colautti	Nov. 17, 1898	Lirico, Milan
Iris	Mascagni	Illica	Nov. 22, 1898	Costanzi, Rome
Tosca	Puccini	Illica & Giacosa	Jan. 14, 1900	Costanzi, Rome
Zazà	Leoncavallo	Leoncavallo	Nov. 10, 1900	Lirico, Milan

fad for operas of brutish lower-class violence that began with *Cavalleria* was a thing of the past. While two notable later operas, Cilèa's *L'Arlesiana* and Mascagni's *Amica*, have rural settings, they have nothing else in common with the verismo genre to which they are sometimes inappropriately assigned. They are operas of family relationships and doomed romantic aspirations, not violence and *crimes passionels*.

While it is possible that the growing reality of peasant unrest in 1890s Italy may have made a genre whose stock-in-trade was rural violence less tenable as a popular, escapist entertainment, more significant were the inherent limitations of the genre itself. Plebean opera, with its crude settings emphasizing the poverty and backwardness of the protagonists and their world, lent itself neither to the sentimental representations of the sorrows and struggles of everyday life nor to the creation of the complex melodramatic intrigues that the audiences wanted. Equally important, it failed to offer creative scope to the talents of the composers of the *giovane scuola*, most of whom, including Mascagni, found the genre and its subject matter thoroughly uncongenial. *Cavalleria*, although a decisive turning point in Italian opera, was less the first exemplar of an important new operatic genre — much as it might have briefly appeared so — than a harbinger of a new way of thinking about opera that bore fruit in bourgeois opera. In many respects, operas like *La bohème* and *Zazà*, with their attention to the modest details of urban life, were truer to the credo of verismo than the violent but superficial rural tales they displaced.

Within the realm of bourgeois opera, it is appropriate to distinguish between two genres, one of which can be characterized as sentimental or domestic opera, and the other as melodramatic opera. Among the eight listed above, both Puccini's and Leoncavallo's *La bohèmes*, *L'Arlesiana*, and *Zazà* can be characterized as sentimental opera, while *Andrea Chénier*, *Tosca*, and *Fedora* are melodramatic, although not lacking in sentimental elements, particularly in *Fedora*. *Iris*, although sharing both sentimental and melodramatic elements, is sui generis, fitting neatly into neither genre. It creates its own imaginative world, drawn from the emerging imagery of art nouveau, reflecting both the librettist Illica's bent for dramatic experimentation and Mascagni's restless, adventuresome spirit.

Tender Feelings and Everyday Objects

Although less famous today than other operas of the period, the archetypal opera of bourgeois domesticity is Cilèa's *L'Arlesiana*, which made its debut in November 1897 at the Teatro Lirico Internazionale in Milan, the former

Teatro alla Canobbiana, dating from 1778. Used for little more than carnival balls and light entertainment by the early 1890s,[6] it was acquired and rebuilt by Edoardo Sonzogno, who reopened it in 1894 as a showcase for the works of his firm's stable of composers, both the Italian *giovane scuola* and French composers such as Bizet, Massenet, and Godard. The Lirico's 1897 season, in addition to Cilèa's new opera, included the premiere of Giordano's *Il voto* (his reworking of *Mala vita*), the Milan debut of Leoncavallo's *La bohème*, and three Massenet operas.

Although Sonzogno had proposed to Cilèa that he set a play entitled *Celeste* by Leopoldo Marenco,[7] the composer chose instead Alphonse Daudet's play, *L'Arlésienne*, made famous by Bizet's incidental music, which Marenco then adapted for him.[8] Still smarting from his unfortunate experience with the uncongenial libretto for *Tilda*, Cilèa was drawn by the two female characters in Daudet's play, writing that he "was struck by the pure love of Vivetta and the powerfully passionate maternal love of Rosa Mamai. These two noble expressions of eternal sentiment, *so different from the violent and bloody scenes of the libretti of the day*, pushed me to choose [Daudet's play]" (my emphasis)."[9]

L'Arlesiana is set in Provence, on the farm of the wealthy Rosa Mamai, whose son Federico has fallen in love with a woman from Arles (the "Arlesiana" of the title). Although Rosa has never met the woman, she reluctantly gives her consent to their marriage. As they celebrate, Metifio, a horse-wrangler from the Camargue, arrives and shows Rosa letters from the woman from Arles proving that she has shared her favors with Metifio. Federico reads the letters, and curses her. In the second act, Federico laments his fate. A wise old shepherd the Baldassare, Rosa, and Vivetta, who has loved Federico since childhood, all try to console him. After initially resisting their efforts, he finally realizes that he has been bewitched, and accepts Vivetta's love in order to end the spell the woman from Arles has over him.

In the third act, as all are celebrating the betrothal of Federico and Vivetta, Metifio arrives to get his letters back, and announces that he is on his way to Arles to carry her off. Federico, in a fit of jealousy, attacks Metifio. He is dragged away, and led to his room for the night. In the morning, he climbs to the top of the farm tower, and ignoring Rosa's and Vivetta's pleas, he throws himself to his death.

L'Arlesiana is about social class, the bourgeois family, and appropriate behavior. All of the important family connections are accounted for, including the widow Rosa Mamai;[10] her older son Federico; Baldassare, the elderly family retainer; and Vivetta, Rosa's goddaughter, who is, significantly, from a lower social class than Rosa and her family. There is an important but largely symbolic secondary role for Rosa's simpleminded younger son, "L'innocente" (the Innocent), and a small role for her brother Marco, who offhandedly gives his blessing to Federico's marriage before Metifio's arrival. Within this family setting—which has nothing especially rural about it and could easily be transplanted intact to a Milan apartment— only one thing is at issue: the classic bourgeois question of the suitable marriage.

The conflict, however, is not the seemingly obvious one between Federico's desire to marry the woman from Arles and his mother's reluctance to accept her. After reading the letters, Federico fully recognizes that she is unacceptable, not to his mother, but to himself; when Rosa, pained by his misery, suggests he marry her just the same, he replies:

> Oh no! That is not possible, mother!
> You know well what kind of woman she is!

The conflict is between Federico's obligation to his family, which he not only accepts but fully internalizes, and the misery it causes him. There is never any question of not doing one's duty; the true theme of the opera is not the conflict between desire and duty, but the psychic cost exacted by doing what one must.

As a study of the psychic cost of appropriate behavior, it is notable that the two high points of the opera, musically and dramatically, are the two soliloquies in which first Federico, and then Rosa, give voice to the unhappiness of their lives. In the second act, Federico's famous *Lamento* poignantly conveys his misery and his yearning for relief in sleep or death from the state that has engulfed him since he learned of the Arles woman's treachery. In the third act, in "Esser madre è un inferno" (being a mother is hell), Rosa vents her desperation; speaking to God, she says:

> You know that I have given up piece after piece of my soul,
> To make him a man who would be strong and honest, my love and my pride;
> . . . .
> You know that, if he dies, I will not survive him by an hour, and will die damned!

These two soliloquies, while musically not unconventional for the time, are an expression of something new and different in Italian opera. They are self-referential expressions of psychological states, unconnected to any particular dramatic moment or event. They express the state of mind of every unhappy lover or desperate mother, inviting members of the audience, whether sensitive young men or worried mothers, to identify directly with the characters.

In some respects, Rosa's soliloquy, although perhaps less musically distinguished than Federico's Lament, is more important. For all the central roles played by the mother in Italian society, mothers were rare in Italian opera. With the exception of Azucena, a questionable role model, live mothers — as distinct from memories of beloved but departed ones — play no important part in any Verdi opera;[11] while Mamma Lucia is an important presence in *Cavalleria rusticana,* Mascagni never allows her anything more than a few scattered interjections. Rosa Mamai finally brings the long-suffering Italian mother who lives for her sons into full operatic prominence. A mother is a central figure in many subsequent operas, including Giordano's *Mese Mariano,* Leoncavallo's *Zazà,* Puccini's *Suor Angelica,* and Mascagni's *Il piccolo Marat.*

The role of the Innocent, the simpleminded child, is equally important. While the loss of a child, as in Donizetti's *Lucrezia Borgia* or Verdi's *Simon Boccanegra,* could become a fulcrum of the drama, children themselves, as objects of sentimental attention or dramatic interest, are largely absent from earlier Italian opera. The mother-child scene in the last act of *L'Arlesiana,* where the Innocent regains his reason, and comes into his mother's room in an attempt to console her, is tender, verging on the sentimental; as his mother kisses him, he exclaims:

> Oh, such sweet kisses you give me,
> I have never had such loving kisses before.

The scene plays not only on childhood innocence to tug at the audience's heartstrings, but also on their knowledge of how badly he has been neglected by his mother in favor of her older son.

L'Arlesiana is far from a fully realized opera. Despite the presence of Caruso in the title role, its debut was only moderately successful; even after extensive revisions the following year (including the fortuitous addition of "Esser madre è un inferno"), it failed to gain more than a toehold in the Italian repertory.[12] It lacks consistent dramatic impetus, and many of the action scenes fall back on the tired clichés of the genre. Just the same, it is an opera of considerable merit. Cilèa's great lyrical gifts as a composer are apparent throughout the opera. In addition to Federico's Lament, *L'Arlesiana* has many beautiful lyrical passages: Rosa's "Era un giorno di festa" (It was a holiday), in which she tells Vivetta how Federico met the woman from Arles; Baldassare's "Vieni con me sui monti" (Come with me to the mountains), in which he evokes the peace of the mountains as surcease to Federico's troubled soul; and the duet between Federico and Vivetta that opens the third act. Cilèa's melodies are unlike those of any of his contemporaries; often, as in the Lament, he will begin with a simple, usually stepwise, melodic line, which will then move in some unexpected, yet thoroughly apposite and effective, direction. Although the Lament has become a staple of the tenor literature, the opera as a whole deserves better than the oblivion into which it has largely fallen.

As one turns from *L'Arlesiana* to Puccini's *Bohème*, one enters another world. Not only does Cilèa's music seem naïve and almost amateurish by comparison with Puccini's brilliant interweaving, in Girardi's words, of "broad lyric melodies, mutable motivic cells, tonality with a semantic function, and bright and varied orchestral colors,"[13] but Puccini's characters inhabit a radically different environment from that of Cilèa. For all that it is set in the verdant Provençal countryside, *L'Arlesiana* is an almost claustrophic opera, subordinating action to its preoccupation with the internal emotional states of its leading characters. *Bohème* is an urban opera, the first opera to put the world inhabited by the urban bourgeoisie on the operatic stage, and present the rich panorama of that world in its full variety and flavor. Although nominally set in 1830s Paris, there is nothing about the setting of *Bohème* that could not be 1890s Milan — which, as Puccini certainly remembered from his own student days, had its own Bohemia in the back alleys of the Brera quarter or along the canals beyond the Porta Ticinese.[14]

The Bohemians themselves are, as Budden points out, nothing more than "young men of the middle class sowing their wild oats";[15] as D'Amico writes, *Bohème* depicts "youth as the happy season of irresponsible freedom, without burdens or commitments, whose very adversities will reappear, in later memory, transfigured by an indulgent smile."[16] It is not hard to envisage the Bohemians twenty years after the events depicted in *Bohème*, with Rodolfo a successful hack journalist, and Marcello a successful academic painter, both with respectable wives and children and comfortable apartments, thinking back on their youthful escapades, and remembering Mimì and Musetta through a pleasant nostalgic haze. The respectable bourgeois paterfamilias taking his family to see *Bohème* at the opera could easily discern echoes of his own youth in the Bohemians' antics; at the same time his son, sitting beside him in the theater, could imagine himself one of them, sharing an existence that might be slightly outré but not beyond the pale of bourgeois respectability.

Scene from act 3 of *La bohème,* from a contemporary postcard. *(Author's Collection)*

In many respects, Puccini's *Bohème* comes closest of all the bourgeois operas to being, more than any of the plebian operas to which that epithet has most often been given, a true verismo opera, both in its representation of the larger world its characters inhabit, and its depiction of the nuances of their emotional lives. In light of the many excellent commentaries that have been written on *Bohème,* a detailed discussion here would be excessive. Still, a few words on its status as the finest of the bourgeois operas are appropriate.[17]

The second act is a riotous re-creation of a festive urban scene, in all its multifarious details and confusion, with street vendors, urchins, mothers, soldiers, and their music overlapping and crossing in wild — but perfectly controlled — exuberance. It is the world of the urban bourgeoisie at play, re-created in clearly recognizable fashion on the operatic stage. Although the germ of this act can be traced back to the encampment scenes from Verdi's *La forza del destino,* with Preziosilla as a sort of proto-Musetta, Verdi's peddlers and camp followers are far removed from Puccini's world. Moreover, the power of the act lies not in the brilliant depiction of the Parisian street scene (which would not in itself sustain an entire act), but in the way it is interwoven with the stories of the two couples: the tender blossoming of the love between Rodolfo and Mimì — and the purchase of the pink bonnet — and the joyous but rather less tender game of love played by Musetta and Marcello.

While the second act brings the representation of the world onstage, the scene between Rodolfo and Mimì in the first act captures the nuances of those characters' relationship in a unique fashion. The sheer familiarity of such passages as "Che gelida manina" and "Mi chiamano Mimì" should not be allowed to obscure the remarkable qualities of this scene, both musical and dramatic. In the course of slightly less than twenty minutes, in a seamless web of parlando, recitative, and arioso woven over some 350 bars, Puccini depicts the process by which two total strangers make a connection, first tentative, then coy, and finally passionate, from the first hesitant gestures and introductions to the ultimate avowal of love.

While the scene is musically superb, its dramatic innovations are more significant. Nearly all operatic love scenes before Puccini were largely static representations of a love that was already manifest, if not perhaps yet given voice. Even where a love scene projected a dynamic tension, as in the first act of *La traviata* or, rather differently, the first act of *Die Walküre*, it tended to represent an idealized — or mythologized — love. In contrast, *Bohème*, depicts the way in which ecstasy can emerge for two ordinary people from the everyday moments of life, growing from such small things as a candle and a misplaced key. As Rodolfo and Mimì connect with one another, every member of the audience who has ever had a romantic experience feels a frisson of recognition and familiarity, while the younger listeners can experience a feeling of anticipation of joys to come. In either case, the artifice of Puccini and his librettists have made it *real*, within the emotional ambit of the bourgeois audience. Rodolfo and Mimì are themselves the members of that audience, as they were or would hope to be.

The ecstasies of young love, and the delights of the Parisian street, are fleeting. The third act is a dark mirror to the second. The hollow fifths we hear from the orchestra as it opens mimic the brassy triads that opened the previous act. Street cries and snatches of song follow, again reminiscent of the earlier street scene, but now scattered and fragmentary in the cold winter air. Similarly, the fourth act is the tragic mirror of the first, back in the Bohemians' garret, to which Mimì returns to die in Rodolfo's arms. At this point, and arguably for the first and only time in the opera, the careful auditor cannot avoid a glimpse of the sentimental machinery at work: as Rodolfo and Mimì revisit their initial meeting, the orchestra plays reminiscences of "Che gelida manina" and "Mi chiamano Mimì," and Rodolfo puts the pink bonnet, the talisman of their love, on her head. Puccini, however, transforms the scene. As Mimì dies, the orchestra dies away; there is silence, interrupted only by Rodolfo's anxious muttering. Suddenly, the orchestra reappears fortissimo, and a moment later we hear Rodolfo's scream of "Mimì!' cutting through the orchestral texture, which gradually dies away as the curtain falls. It is a blatant, even crass, verismo gesture, and yet it burns away the sentimental haze that has built up far more powerfully than if the opera had been allowed to end quietly — as a more self-consciously tasteful composer might have done.

Puccini's opera was not the only opera based on Henri Murger's *Scènes de la vie de Bohème* to appear in 1890s Italy. More or less simultaneously, Ruggero Leoncavallo also decided to set Murger's stories. Although it is unclear who had the idea first, after Leoncavallo — or his publisher Sonzogno — had widely publicized his plans in March 1893, Puccini wrote a resentful letter to the *Corriere della sera*:

> [I]f Maestro Leoncavallo . . . had confided in me before suddenly letting me know the other evening, I would never have given Murger's *Bohème* a thought. Now — for reasons easy to understand — I am no longer inclined to be as courteous to him, as a friend and a composer, as I would have liked. . . . He'll compose, I'll compose. The public will judge. In art, precedence does not imply that one must interpret the same subject with the same artistic intentions.[18]

While neither composer had yet written a note, the race was on. Although *Il Secolo* had announced that Leoncavallo's opera would be performed in 1894, it did not appear at Venice's Teatro La Fenice until May 1897, more than a year after Puccini's opera. By that time, Puccini's *Bohème* was steadily moving into the repertory; leaving nothing to chance, Ricordi arranged for a lavishly staged production of Puccini's opera to appear in the nearby Teatro Rossini a week before the debut of the rival work.[19] Delighted with the outcome, Puccini sent a few lines of doggerel to his sister Ramelde, playing on his rival's name, "lion-horse":

> The lion flunked out,
> The horse was beaten up,
> There's only one *Bohème* . . .
> All the rest is a lagoon.[20]

Although Leoncavallo's opera has many charms, including a moving death scene for Mimì, its emotional and musical range is far more limited than that of Puccini's work; too often it lapses into a kind of glib *café chantant* melody that was gradually becoming Leoncavallo's "default mode" of lyrical writing. Although Sonzogno later renamed the work *Mimì Pinson* in the hope of better distinguishing it from Puccini's opera, it never escaped the shadow of its more famous sister.

Leoncavallo returned to a world much like his Bohemia in his next opera, *Zazà*, based on a French play by Pierre Berton and Charles Simon that had first appeared in Paris only two years before. The play had been a smash hit, appearing the next year on Broadway in an adaptation by David Belasco and on the Italian stage, performed by the famous Virginia Reiter. Within a few years it had made the rounds of the world's theaters, translated into, among other languages, Yiddish, Russian, and Hungarian.[21] Aside from the obvious commercial advantages offered by setting such a popular play, for Leoncavallo, *Zazà*'s music hall milieu may well have stirred nostalgic memories of the Parisian world of his youth.

Zazà is the story of a music hall artiste in a provincial theater who yearns for the life of a respectable wife and mother; she has fallen in love with Milio Dufresne, a bourgeois businessman who frequents the theater. The first act, which is set backstage amid music hall turns and the usual theatrical chaos, ends as he declares his love for her. In the second act, which takes place three months later, he tells Zazà that he must leave on a long business trip for America. Cascart, Zazà's onstage partner and former lover, tells her that he has seen Dufresne in Paris with another woman. Seeing her dream of love and marriage threatened, Zazà rushes off to Paris to confront the woman she believes to be Dufresne's mistress.

The third act is set in the sitting room of Dufresne's elegant Parisian apartment. Dufresne and his wife leave, and Zazà arrives. She is welcomed by a charming small child, Totò, whom Zazà soon realizes is Dufresne's daughter. After a tender scene, Zazà realizes that she cannot bring herself to destroy Totò's happiness by breaking up her family, and leaves. In the final act, she sends Dufresne away, bursting into bitter tears as she watches him disappear down the street.

Zazà is a synthesis of all of the themes of bourgeois opera, the first opera of the time set in a milieu that has been stripped of even the most minimal distance from its audience. After the first act with the color provided by the music hall milieu has run its course, the opera devolves into a domestic drama. An archetypal contemporary bourgeois family — husband, wife, and child — appears onstage; the equivocal position of the husband is resolved firmly in favor of hearth and family; and the sentimental tropes of sanctified motherhood and childhood innocence are carried far beyond their use in any previous opera.

Leoncavallo, in preparing his own libretto, made important changes from the Berton and Simon play. While some, such as the removal of the fifth act, an epilogue in which Dufresne, now a widower, seeks Zazà out years later only to be rejected tearfully by the now-famous chanteuse, make the drama tighter and more effective, most are clearly made to enhance its sentimental nature. Zazà's character is softened, and her immoral past, a central theme of the play, is no longer mentioned. The role of the Duke de Brissac, a noble admirer who also seeks Zazà's favors, has been entirely excised from the opera. In a significant but telling detail, rather than having Zazà be seen as a kept woman by moving into an apartment rented for her by Dufresne, in the opera Dufresne moves into — or at least spends nights in — Zazà's modest but respectably furnished apartment.

The most significant change Leoncavallo made, however, was to another character. In the play, Zazà's Aunt Rosa, a tippling, spendthrift busybody hanging onto a marginal position in the music hall milieu, is a purely comic character, intriguing to win Zazà's favors for the Duke. Leoncavallo has changed her to Anaide, Zazà's mother. While she has a comic dimension, she has become a sentimental figure as well; when Zazà's longtime friend and confidant Cascart criticizes her drinking, Zazà bursts out: [D]on't torture me! . . . she's my mother . . . and has smiled so little in her younger years! . . . Do you know what it means when a man runs away leaving you with a little child, all by yourself? . . . What is she to do, where is she to go, tell me, a mother with a frightened child in her arms!" It is indeed the "back story" of Zazà's unhappy childhood, carted around by her mother to sing in taverns, seeing their earnings evaporate into her mother's drunken binges, that drives Zazà's dreams of seeing herself some day as Dufresne's "adored white-haired wife and mother," and that ultimately leads to her renunciation of her lover.

In all of this, *Zazà's* defining moment, and indeed the iconic scene of fin de siècle operatic sentimentality, is the scene in the opera's third act, little more than ten minutes long, that follows the departure of Dufresne and his wife for the railroad station. Zazà and her maid Natalie arrive in the living room of Dufresne's apartment on the Quai Mazarin,[22] with its "very elegant [*elegantissimi*] furnishings." A little girl enters, and walks toward the piano. By this point, Zazà, having read a letter left open on the table, knows that Dufresne is married, and that the woman she thought was his lover is actually his wife. The child, Totò, sees the women, and a conversation between her and Zazà follows. Throughout, Totò is a speaking role, while Zazà begins *parlante*:

ZAZÀ: Totò! Tell me . . .

TOTÒ: You called me "tu"! . . . Why?

ZAZÀ: Because . . . because . . . you resemble . . . one I love so much!

TOTÒ: One you love? I look like my papà! Do you know him?

ZAZÀ: No! . . .

TOTÒ: He loves me so much! . . . He is so good! I didn't see him for six
months, you know . . .

ZAZÀ: (*under her breath*) Six months!

TOTÒ: Now I am seeing him again, and I am happy.

This is only the beginning. Under Totò's gentle questioning, Zazà's vocal
line gradually shifts to an increasingly intense arioso as she tells Totò the
story of her youth, a story that the audience already knows:

ZAZÀ: I never had [a mother]! . . . You know, little one, that there are
people one must love deeply! They may be bad . . . and the world may
look down on them . . . but they have suffered so much in their youth!

TOTÒ: Children without bread or a roof?

ZAZÀ: (*in anguish*) There are children who lack even more than that!

TOTÒ: Are they the children who lack a father's love?

ZAZÀ: Fatherless children! You understand! (*almost crying*) You understand! That is the worst thing for a child! But you can live in peace, dear
creature, no one . . . no one . . . will take your father from you!

The music, which has gradually built up both in dramatic intensity and volume, reaches its climax, as the sobbing Zazà holds the child tightly to her.

The scene is dramatically effective, perhaps even moving, although the
manner in which Leoncavallo uses the contrast between the child's spoken
dialogue and Zazà's impassioned arioso to manipulate the audience's emotions is far from subtle. Precisely at this point, however, Leoncavallo twists
the emotional knife another turn. Zazà asks the child to play something
on the piano. As Totò begins to play a simple "Ave Maria" by Cherubini,
Zazà, once again *parlante*, sings "It is over . . . Married! And an angel for
a daughter! . . . I had a dream." The piano continues, as richly scored
strings enter in a sonic precursor of the once-famous Warsaw Concerto;
Zazà's line once again shifts to arioso, and the music swells to a second,
greater climax on her closing line, delivered half-singing, half-crying, "What
will become of me?" After this, in many respects the last act, although it
contains Cascart's famous aria "Zazà, piccola zingara" (Zazà, little Gypsy),
comes as a distinct anticlimax.

Zazà was Leoncavallo's last successful opera, catching the public's favor
with its adroit juxtaposition of pathos and the affirmation of conventional
bourgeois values. Reworked by the composer to trim the first act, which
was an hour long at the work's premiere,[23] *Zazà* soon caught on, and for
the next decade was regularly produced, not only in Italy but throughout
the operatic world, retaining some popularity with operatic audiences well

into the 1920s. The role of Zazà, which was created by Rosina Storchio, is a demanding but effective vehicle for a soprano with the appropriate vocal equipment and temperament. It attracted many noted singers, above all Emma Carelli, who was closely identified with the part, and upon whose retirement *Zazà* began to fade from the scene.[24]

Leoncavallo's score offers the listener numerous pleasures, with its many set numbers and almost operetta-like infectious waltz rhythms. Both "Zazà, piccola zingara" and Dufresne's aria that opens act 3, as he contemplates never seeing his lover again, "Mai più, Zazà" (Never again, Zazà), became popular recital and recording numbers. As with Leoncavallo's other scores, *Zazà* contains borrowings from numerous other composers, in this case including Rossini, Waldteufel, and Mozart, and a most probably deliberate allusion to Verdi's *Falstaff*.[25] It also represents, to some extent, a willed simplification of Leoncavallo's musical language after the relatively ambitious as well as complex *La bohème*. *Zazà* forms a bridge between the ambitious efforts of the composer's first decade on the operatic scene and the depressing downward trajectory of the years until his death in 1919, during which his energies were increasingly devoted to a long series of gradually less successful and more trivial operettas.

Sexuality, Violence and Melodrama

For all the preoccupation with home, family, and outward decorum, bourgeois Italy was highly sexualized, although in an ambivalent, compartmentalized fashion. Female nudity was common not only in monumental sculpture but also in advertising posters and illustrations, particularly as the art nouveau style or *stile liberty*, with its heady blend of sexuality and floral imagery, became popular toward the end of the century.[26] As suggested by the Café Momus scene in *Bohème* and the first act of *Zazà*, the worlds of the café and the music hall were highly charged with sexuality, while prostitution was widespread, open, and legal in late-nineteenth-century Italy. The sexual exploits of the poet Gabrielle D'Annunzio and the affairs of the actress Eleanora Duse, with each other and with others, were followed by the public — male and female — as assiduously as modern Americans follow the amatory adventures of Hollywood stars. As D'Annunzio's longtime associate and confidante Tom Antongini later wrote, "in all justice to the Poet we should not forget that, in those days, to be loved by a beautiful woman, to 'conquer' her, was the chief ambition and the all-absorbing preoccupation of every man between the ages of sixteen and thirty."[27] Couples living together without benefit of marriage were not unusual, particularly in the "artistic" milieu of writers, musicians, and painters, where virtue was believed to be defined more flexibly than in the homes of the bourgeoisie. Verdi, Puccini, and Mascagni all lived for years with women they would ultimately marry before officially tying the knot.

The line of demarcation between "good" and "bad" women was still very real, as the popular writer Luigi Barzini, himself the product of a classic Milan bourgeois upbringing, wrote: "European children took for granted, years ago, that there were two kinds of women: women like one's mother, aunts, grandmothers, sisters, cousins, family friends; and the others. The others were habitually called "them," *une d'elles, una di quelle,* were the common euphemisms."[28] The line, however, was blurring. Beneath the code of respectability, proper married women had affairs and, if given the opportunity, threw themselves at D'Annunzio. Answering the question of when a lady ceased to become a lady, Barzini adds, "the common rule was that a lady could have any number of lovers, one after the other or all at the same time, and keep her rank; but she would lose it automatically the moment she accepted the first precious gift."[29]

Love, romance, or passion — pure or profane — were all abundantly in earlier Italian opera, yet sexuality was all but absent. The sole significant exception to which one can point was Verdi's *La traviata.* That opera, however, rather than treating Violetta's sexuality and her liaison with Alfredo as a normal matter without passing judgment, used it as the starting point for a series of moral lessons requiring her sacrifice of both love and life, and even implying a connection between her licentious life and her sickness and premature death. By contrast, Musetta in *Bohème* wears her sexuality openly, even proudly, as she sings in the famous "Waltz Song":

> When I walk alone down the street, men stop and stare,
> And check me out from head to foot.
> And I relish their secret desire, which I read in their eyes
> And their gestures, to know my hidden charms.
> The outpouring of their desire surrounds me, and fills me
> With delight. [30]

Musetta is definitely one of "them." It is Mimì, the good girl, at least in relative terms, however, who dies of tuberculosis. In *Bohème,* though, tuberculosis is a disease, not a moral judgment on the patient.

Sexuality in *Bohème* is easygoing, accepted as part of the lives of the Bohemians. The same is true of the music hall world in Leoncavallo's *Zazà*, or Tosca's relationship with Cavaradossi, who sings famously of his love:

> She entered, fragrant, and fell into my arms . . .
> O sweet kisses, slow caresses, while I, trembling,
> Loosened the veils from her beautiful body.

All of these characters are artists, for whom the world of the time permitted a certain license; through them, the audience could vicariously experience a freer and more casual sexuality than the mores of the society permitted the straitlaced bourgeoisie.

Giordano's *Fedora*, based on a popular Sarah Bernhardt vehicle by the wildly successful French playwright Victorien Sardou, offers a variation on this theme, blending sentimental and melodramatic elements. With its "ripped from the headlines" Russian setting, it brought onto the operatic stage as well a touch of the emerging literary genre known as the *roman policier*, or detective story.

The libretto by Arturo Colautti,[31] which follows Sardou's play closely, opens in Saint Petersburg. When Princess Fedora Romazov's fiancé, Count Vladimir Andreyevich, is murdered, suspicion falls on Count Loris Ipanov, who is believed to be a Nihilist. Fedora vows to track him down and bring him to justice. By the second act, in Paris, to which she has followed him, Loris has fallen in love with her. She extracts a confession from him, and sets a trap for him, meanwhile sending a letter back to Russia denouncing Loris for the murder. When Loris returns, he shows her letters proving that he killed Andreyevich not for political reasons, but because he was having an affair with Loris's wife. With her feelings for Andreyevich turned to hatred, Fedora realizes that she truly loves Loris. Knowing that the house is surrounded by Russian agents, she convinces him to spend the night, falling into his arms at the curtain.

The third act takes place in Fedora's villa in Switzerland, where Loris and Fedora are living in idyllic contentment. Loris learns that his brother has been arrested and died in prison, and that his mother has died of grief, all as a result of an anonymous letter sent from Paris. He curses and threatens the unknown woman. Fedora, abandoning hope, takes poison. Too late, Loris realizes he loves her just the same, and she dies in his arms.

At the end of the second act, Fedora has lured Loris back to her Parisian house late at night, having instructed the Russian detective Grech to surround the house with his men. At this point, however, she realizes that she loves Loris, leading to the following exchange:

FEDORA: Stay! I am afraid. . . . You are running into a trap, perhaps even
   to your death . . .

LORIS: Do you want to make me look dishonorable?

FEDORA: You are, if you leave me . . .

LORIS: They'll say, Fedora, that I'm your lover!

FEDORA: What does it matter, if you live?

As the third act opens, they are living happily without official sanction in
her Alpine villa. Their life, as depicted in this scene, is a romantic fantasy
of kisses and embraces; as their friend Olga comes out the door, she finds
them in a slow, passionate kiss in the yard, prompting the following:

OLGA: Still at it?

FEDORA (laughing): Always!

LORIS (kissing her again): Always!

The setting of this last act is thoroughly up-to-date, not only in its nonjudg-
mental attitude to its characters' sexuality, but in its portrayal of the trappings of 1890s haute bourgeois life: the vacation villa in the popular
Bernese Oberland, and the bicycles that the secondary characters wheel
on- and offstage during the course of the act. These homely details, along
with a Swiss mountain song sung offstage, are all designed to set the sudden irruption of tragedy into this placid scene into sharp relief. The setting,
however, in some respects only accentuates the conventional nature of a
denouement that would not be out of place in a minor Donizetti opera,
leaving behind an air of contrivance rather than tragedy. After the powerful dramatic tension that was built up in the first two acts, the third act
comes as something of an anticlimax.

   The conventionality of *Fedora* extends to the Russian setting. Although
the first act, with its whispers of Nihilist assassinations, is richly atmospheric, it soon becomes apparent as the opera progresses that the Nihilist
theme is nothing but a red herring. As soon as Fedora learns that Loris had
killed her fiancé because he was the lover of Loris's wife's, she exclaims, in
language that could, once again, have come out of a Donizetti opera:

> I believed you a vile slave of a different hatred,
> But you were [instead] a strong, a noble, a holy
> Instrument of punishment . . . [*sacro punitor*]

As is true of *Tosca* and *Andrea Chénier*, the political dimension in *Fedora*
is little more than superficial *couleur locale*. Even more than in those two
operas, however, here it is only the thinnest of veneers over a series of
melodramatic clichés.

Fedora has its high points, particularly in the second act, which in addition to the popular tenor aria "Amor ti vieta" and the passionate closing duet, also includes a highly cinematic scene in which Fedora extracts Loris's confession while an onstage pianist plays a Chopinesque nocturne. Overall, however, Colautti's libretto offered Giordano far less scope for his musical imagination than did Illica's libretto for *Andrea Chénier.* Although Giordano's unfailing dramatic instincts ensure that *Fedora* engages its audience, it is musically far thinner than the composer's previous opera. It survives on its dramatic qualities and its undeniable effectiveness as a star vehicle for a soprano of ardent temperament — as it was in its original version for Sarah Bernhardt.

Sexuality in *Fedora* is tender and sentimental. It takes on a different, far less sentimental coloration in Puccini's *Tosca* and Mascagni's *Iris,* where it reflects the dark side of fin de siècle sexuality, reminding us that this was also the era of Jack the Ripper and Krafft-Ebing's *Psychopathia Sexualis.* The predatory male who craves the tenor's woman and seeks to win her through intrigue or violence, most famously in the person of the Conte di Luna in *Trovatore,* had long since been a staple of Italian opera. He was now invested with a new quality: the figures of Osaka in *Iris* and Scarpia in *Tosca* are the first in which the predatory male is presented in explicitly sexual, or even pathological terms.

Scarpia is first described early in act 1, when Cavaradossi reacts to Angelotti's mention of his name:

> Scarpia? That bigoted[32] satyr who uses religious practices to refine
> His libertine lusts, and uses the confessor and the executioner
> As tools of his lascivious urges!

Scarpia himself, in lines that have become famous, delights in his predatory nature, singing:

> The violent conquest has a stronger savor
> Than sweet consent . . .
> I pursue what I desire, I sate myself, and throw it away . . .

Just as Scarpia's religiosity is no more than a camouflage for his sexual urges, politics and religion in *Tosca* are merely the decorative frame within which the real story, the typical Sardou mixture of predatory sex, gruesome violence, and intrigue takes place. The specific political context with its references to Napoleon and the battle of Marengo has no greater signifi-

Act 2 of *Tosca*, from the souvenir postcard series designed by Leopoldo Metlicovitz.
(Author's Collection)

cance than does Russian Nihilism in *Fedora*. The religious dimension is more important: the implicit connection drawn between Scarpia's religiosity and his brutal sexuality lends the opera a distinct anticlerical aura. That aura, however, was neither unusual nor reprehensible in respectable bourgeois circles in 1890s Italy; as a prominent historian has written, "it is noteworthy how 'official,' how 'bourgeois,' anticlericalism was in the late nineteenth century."[33]

The juxtaposition of Scarpia's "erotic perversion tinged with sadism"[34] and his seemingly absolute, arbitrary power, make *Tosca* a prototypical picture of life under the nightmare of totalitarian rule, a precursor to *Wozzeck*, Dallapiccola's *Il prigioniero*, or Orwell's *1984*.[35] Before the first act is over, it is apparent that Cavaradossi and Tosca, two innocents in a malevolent world, will be caught up in Scarpia's web and destroyed. The gulf between the victims and the oppressive state, and the extent to which they cannot even comprehend the evil at its core, have rarely been better conveyed than in Tosca's famous "Vissi d'arte:"

> I lived for art, I lived for love,
> I've never done wrong to a living soul! . . .
> . . . Why, Lord, why, do You repay me in this way?

"Vissi d'arte" is far more than a diva's showpiece, it is the *cri de coeur* of every decent person who has found herself caught inadvertently in the tentacles of evil.

Tosca stands in sharp contrast to *Andrea Chénier*, which on the surface covers much the same ground, but which, for all its cinematically vivid images of the Revolution has far less emotional impact. Leaving aside the effect of Puccini's music, Gérard is far too decent to symbolize the totalitarian state, and Chénier and Maddalena far too caught up in their romantic obsession with love and death, for there to be any resonance to the relationship between the doomed lovers and the larger social or political setting. In *Tosca*, the lovers want to live, and they fight for life. Their death is not a sentimental *Liebestod*, but the result of the workings of arbitrary power.

Puccini adapted his musical technique brilliantly to a story of violent passions and almost incessant action, in almost every way the opposite of the sentimental, leisurely *Bohème*. Unlike the earlier opera, where motifs were subordinated to the flow of cantabile melody, *Tosca*'s musical essence is found in the many short motifs, beginning with the three chords — B, A, and E — that stand for Scarpia, and are powerfully intoned *fff* by a bass-heavy full orchestra to open the opera. The interweaving of motifs create an almost Wagnerian texture; as Jürgen Maehder has noted, "in *Tosca*, even the more cantabile themes seem to be constructed from short motivic cells; through transforming, recombining, and transposing these cells, Puccini creates a musical organism of great dramatic power."[36]

In contrast to *Bohème*, where set pieces grow seamlessly from the dramatic arc of the opera, most of *Tosca*'s most famous cantabile moments exist outside the drama, even interrupting it. While "Vissi d'arte" is dramatically apposite and powerful, both "Recondita armonia" and "E lucevan le stelle" are fundamentally disconnected from the texture of the work, grafted onto it either to slow down the otherwise breakneck pace of the opera, or provide applause opportunities for the principal tenor. While wonderful music, they stand in marked contrast to the seamless integration of such moments in the texture of *Bohème*.

Tosca is a brilliant opera. Time after time, Puccini finds exactly the right musical gesture to correspond to and amplify the dramatic events taking place onstage. At the same time, the fact that so much of the music exists to amplify the drama, rather than being a generative force in itself as in *Bohème*, argues for placing *Tosca* below the earlier opera in a larger assessment of Puccini's *oeuvre*. As Budden writes, "no-one would claim *Tosca* as its composer's masterpiece."[37] Just the same, it is a work of remarkable musical and dramatic impact, as well as a window onto the dark side of power and sexuality at the end of the nineteenth century.

Sex, Violence and Symbolism in Mascagni's Iris

Much the same can be said about Mascagni's *Iris*, which made its debut in Rome in November 1898, slightly more than a year before *Tosca*. Although *Iris* is far less known than Puccini's opera today, it is a work of considerably more than historical interest.[38] With it, Mascagni began a fifteen-year collaboration with Luigi Illica, a period of intense shared creative activity, as well as regular periods of strain and open conflict that one might expect from two such volatile individuals. *Iris* is the first of the three operas, along with *Le Maschere* and *Isabeau*, that Mascagni wrote with Illica; all must be ranked among the composer's more distinctive and original works.

By mid-decade, although recognized as the premier librettist on the Italian scene, Illica was a deeply frustrated man. Blessed with a vivid albeit undisciplined imagination, he found his ideas kept firmly in check by Puccini and Giacosa, while he was sought out by others largely for melodramas or adaptations of popular plays and novels. He longed for the opportunity to take opera in new, untried directions, as he wrote in a note to himself: "Idea of a new [type of] opera. New form. Opening new horizons, a new form of expression. . . . An idea in which there is no longer any need for the usual plots, set in motion one way or another, with such and such cardboard characters as a pretext for a certain [type of] music. Plots . . . under which the calculations being made, the sensations one wants to excite in the audience, are visible."[39] In Mascagni, Illica found a composer who shared his frustration with the conventions of 1890s opera, and who was willing to embrace his vision of introducing into Italian opera the expressionistic, decadent themes of such writers as Huysmans or Maeterlinck, whom Illica saw as models for emulation.

Mascagni, with his restlessness, his romanticism, and his craving for innovation, was an unlikely figure to have come to symbolize realistic, verismo opera. *Cavalleria* had been for him a *pièce d'occasion*, rather than a reflection of deeply rooted convictions. Since *Cavalleria* he had floundered, reluctant to repeat himself, recognizing the need for a new direction, but with no idea how or where to find it. In the absence of a clear path forward, he had turned backward, devoting most of his energy between 1893 and 1895 to recasting his youthful romantic drama *Guglielmo Ratcliff*, most of which had been written in the years before *Cavalleria*. Simultaneously, he had also composed, reluctantly and under intense pressure from Sonzogno, a second verismo opera, a pallid drama of Apulian fishermen entitled *Silvano*.[40] Although *Ratcliff* was a succès d'estime at its Milan debut early in 1895, *Silvano*, which followed a month later, found little favor with either critics or public. Years later, the critic Giannotto Bastianelli acutely noted that, "If *Silvano* has any value at all, it is that of having demonstrated fully to Mascagni his duty to renew himself."[41]

In the spring of 1895, Mascagni and Illica were brought together by Giulio Ricordi, to whom Mascagni owed an opera as a result of a complicated series of circumstances.[42] Although the two quickly found themselves to be kindred spirits, Mascagni's new duties as director of the Rossini Conservatory in Pesaro, a position he assumed in October 1895, delayed any progress toward a new opera. Mascagni finally accepted Illica's proposal for an opera with a Japanese setting in March 1896. Written largely during the many extended breaks in the conservatory's schedule, *Iris* was not completed until October 1898, by far the longest period of gestation for any of Mascagni's operas.

Although Illica, in an 1894 note, refers to *Iris* as being based on a Japanese legend,[43] the story is far more likely to have been Illica's invention, perhaps inspired by an episode in Joris-Karl Huysmans's *À rebours* (Against the

Osaka and Kyoto spying on Iris, from act 1 of *Iris*, from the souvenir postcard series designed by Adolfo von Hohenstein. *(Mascagni.org)*

grain), a wildly popular 1884 novel about the Baron Des Esseintes, a bored, enervated aesthete who is clearly the model for the figure of the wealthy libertine Osaka in the opera. Although Illica sprinkles the story with enough Japanese words (mostly used with fair accuracy)[44] to give the setting a minimally credible Japanese atmosphere, his pre-Western, timeless Japan is an otherworldly, metaphorical land, rather than an attempt to re-create a real time and place.

The first act is preceded by a long prelude that builds to a grandiose climax, as it depicts night giving way to dawn, and the sun restoring life to the earth. In the morning light, we see the beautiful young Iris in the garden of the cottage in the shadow of Mount Fuji, where she lives with her blind father. Osaka, who desires her, arranges for the Edo brothel-keeper Kyoto to abduct her and take her to the Yoshiwara, Edo's pleasure quarter. Believing that his daughter has left him of her free will, Iris's father sets out for Edo after her, not to rescue her, but to curse her for abandoning him.

In the second act, Osaka attempts to seduce Iris, praising her beauty and plying her with expensive gifts. When he realizes he cannot penetrate her innocence, he rejects her disdainfully. Kyoto, to recoup his investment, places her on display in the balcony of the brothel. As crowds gather to admire her beauty, Osaka's lust is rekindled, and he demands her back. As her father arrives, Iris cries out with joy, but he curses her for leaving him, pelting her with clods of mud. Iris screams, throwing herself from the balcony into the sewer, which carries her away.

The third act is set in the Edo sewers. As she lies in the darkness, ragpickers surround her. Thinking her dead, they strip the jewels and finery from her body. As she stirs, they flee in horror. She slowly rises. Crying "perchè? (why?), she hears the cold, brutal voices of her father, Osaka, and Kyoto, reminding her of the cruelty of life. As the sun begins to rise, she extends her arms, and dies as the scene is flooded with golden light, and flowers emerge from the ground, wrapping around her dead body and carrying her soul to the sun.

The number of different themes or ideas interwoven in Illica's libretto is such that they are difficult to separate into distinct strands. While the substructure is a grim tale of an innocent girl destroyed by sexual predators — to the extent that one American writer could sum it up as "a tale of veristic horror Mongolized"[45] — that story is in many respects only a frame for an elaborate symbolic edifice with its roots partly in French decadent poetry and partly in the visual imagery of the art nouveau movement, which was in turn deeply influenced by the art flowing from Japan into Europe during the last third of the nineteenth century. As I have previously written, "Illica's libretto, with its luxuriant floral imagery, its vampires, and its juxtapositions of light and darkness, blood and tears, lies squarely at the intersection of art nouveau with the symbolist, decadent poetry of Baudelaire, Mallarmé and Rimbaud. *Iris* is the supreme reflection of art nouveau on the operatic stage."[46] The iris, in particular, with its sinuosity and distinctive patterning, often depicted in the Japanese *ukiyo-e* prints reaching the West at the time, was the emblematic flower of the art nouveau movement.

At the same time, the story of sexual victimization that lies at the heart of *Iris* needs to be taken seriously; beneath its symbolic trappings, it tells a story that was far from alien to the Italian bourgeois world. as Orselli aptly notes, "In *Iris*, we find plainly expressed the creed of a *Belle époque* seducer . . . the Green Houses [of the Yoshiwara] are an elegant *fin de siècle* Roman bordello, barely disguised."[47] Voyeurism forms a major subtext of this story, from the first act when Osaka and Kyoto spy on Iris in her cottage, to the beginning of the second act where they observe the sleeping Iris. A few moments later, Osaka faces her, and sings:

> Oh, how your slender body is enfolded,
> And how it shapes that clinging nightgown!
> My eyes are fixed on you, from head to foot.[48]

Later in that same act, Kyoto puts Iris on display on the balcony of the bordello

> In clothes even more transparent,
> As if she were wearing nothing.

The story of *Iris* parallels the story of *Tosca*, but with Iris triply exploited: by Osaka, the voracious sexual predator; Kyoto, the cynical sexual profiteer; and finally her father, who is not only blind in the physical sense but blind to other human beings, a figure of almost perfect selfishness. All three are monsters, without a glimmer of human feeling.

Both Tosca and Iris ultimately arrive at the same point of utter incomprehension in their inexorable downward path, and both ask "why?" of an indifferent world. While Scarpia brushes off the question, in the more self-consciously philosophical *Iris* the dying girl hears the voices of her three torturers, each one explaining to her that life is brutal and callous, and that, in Osaka's words, she is fated to "die like a flower that's picked for its sweet smell."

Illica's libretto inspired Mascagni to his most sustained and successful creative effort since *Cavalleria*; indeed, in many respects, far outstripping that early opera in terms of both the sophistication of his musical language and his ability to weave together musical ideas to build long, extended scenes to powerful dramatic effect. The scene in which Osaka attempts to seduce Iris in the second act, which extends for more than four hundred bars, and ends in Osaka's disgusted

> She's bored me for a whole hour!
> She's a puppet from a play! A wooden puppet!

is a sustained series of beautifully interwoven threads. While utterly different in its dramatic effect, the scene can legitimately be compared in the quality of its musical organization to Rodolfo and Mimì's scene in the first act of Puccini's *Bohème*.

From the first notes of the tonally ambiguous, growling double bass line that opens *Iris*, it is clear that this is an opera unlike any other of its time. In order to create a musical counterpart for this complex mélange of realism, exoticism, and symbolism Mascagni crafted music with a distinctive *tinta* of sinuous, chromatic, melodic lines, often resting on top of unstable, constantly shifting, and uncertain harmonic structures. Although *Iris* contains fewer of the long-limbed melodies that characterized Mascagni's earlier operas, in their place he has "strewn his score so liberally with short motives, themes, melodies and ideas of such variety that much of the opera has an almost shimmering quality."[49] In Iris's famous "Aria della piovra" (Octopus aria), the axis around which the seduction scene revolves, Mascagni created a dramatic arc of overwhelming power without melody as such, driven by a play of constantly shifting harmony and steady rhythmic impulse.

Mascagni's search for innovation reaches its apex in the orchestral prelude to the third act. This prelude, portraying the sinister night in the sewers of Edo, blends highly ambiguous chromaticism with unusual orchestral timbres to create a unique atmosphere of otherworldly mystery. Although Mascagni had experimented with the whole-tone scale before (including a charming choral sequence in his 1892 *I Rantzau*), here the whole-tone scale is no longer decorative but the essence of the work itself, as reflected in the central theme, a haunting, evocative motif based on the tritone, with its underlying harmony slowly shifting back and forth between G flat and C.

The drama of the first two acts of *Iris*, for all its symbolism, still provides the audience with clear points of reference to the familiar, while its vocabulary, for all its chromatic and exotic elements, remains grounded in the musical language of the time. The third-act prelude, however, was by far the most radical music ever to be presented to a mass audience in Italy, and the scene that follows as the curtain rises, in which the ragpickers root for treasure in the sewers of Edo and strip Iris's comatose body, may well be perhaps the most scabrous moment that had yet appeared on the Italian operatic stage. At the opera's debut at Rome's Costanzi opera house, after greeting the opening "Inno del sole" (Hymn of the sun) and the first two acts enthusiastically, the audience's mood underwent a marked shift as the first notes of the third act were heard. As the critic Alberto Gasco wrote, "in the course of a few moments, the thermometer went from the boiling point to freezing."[50] Within minutes, coughing, muttering, and shouting matches between those eager to hear the music and those who disapproved of it, turned the theater into near-pandemonium. Only as Iris's final aria began, and the strains of the reprise of the "Inno del sole" were heard, did the house calm down, with strong but hardly universal applause at the end.

Although the critical reaction to Mascagni's music was mixed, ranging from passionate admiration to outright, almost contemptuous dismissal, hardly anyone had anything good to say about Illica's libretto. Puccini, in a letter to Alberto Crecchi, who was friendly with both Puccini and Mascagni, wrote: "For me, this opera that contains so many beautiful things, and such brilliant dazzling orchestral colors, starts with a fundamental defect: a story without interest spread out thinly over three acts. . . . Even if the Good Lord Himself had set this libretto, He would not have been able to do any more with it than Pietro has."[51]

Despite the cool critical reaction, Italian audiences, after some initial hesitation, warmed to Illica and Mascagni's strange work. Newspaper accounts note with some bemusement that at each subsequent performance, both in Rome and two months later in Milan, the audiences were more and more enthusiastic. *Iris* soon moved into the repertory both in Italy and in South America, where it had an enthusiastic following. Although never quite so popular as the best-known operas of Verdi or Puccini, it became nearly a standard work through the 1920s. Its demanding title role was popular with sopranos from the Romanian Hericlea Darclée, who created the role, to such singers as Emma Eames, Lucrezia Bori, and Elisabeth Rethberg, all of whom sung Iris at the Metropolitan Opera, to Magda Olivero. Nearly every ambitious tenor of the early twentieth century, even those who never sang the role of Osaka on stage, included his serenade "Apri la tua finestra" on their programs — although few of them did its subtleties justice.[52]

While Mascagni's often superb music clearly deserves the greater part of the credit for *Iris*'s becoming part of the Italian repertory, it would appear that Illica's libretto did not represent an insuperable obstacle. In an age of rapid social dislocation, in which the exploitation of women was a sad but commonplace reality, the symbolic trappings of Iris's story did not prevent it from resonating with the audiences of its time. Indeed, by surrounding the story with a symbolic aura, on the one hand, and the prurient frisson of voyeurism on the other, Illica was able to obscure the reality that the story itself is little more than a cliché, and Iris herself a character without individuality, in Osaka's words, a wooden puppet. Ultimately, that reality would become apparent. When the painful process of winnowing down the Italian operatic repertory began — a process that lasted from the 1920s through the 1960s — *Iris*, except for the occasional revival, did not survive. Although it is not likely to return to the standard repertory in the future, I still hold firmly to my earlier opinion, that "of all the less-known operas of Mascagni, there is none more worthy of regular revival than *Iris*, for the sheer quality of its music, and, despite its weaknesses, for its strange, compelling power as a work of musical theater."[53]

Part II

The Operatic Landscape

Chapter 7

The Land of Opera

O pera was a pervasive presence in late-nineteenth-century Italy. Although every nation that followed the European model of civilization had its opera houses, in no other nation did opera play so prominent a role in the society, or in the lives of its citizens beyond the cultural or aristocratic elite. From the wealthy industrialists attending performances in their La Scala boxes to the farmer listening to the village band play in the piazza on market day, opera was intimately woven into the fabric of Italian society through a rich and complex hierarchy of operatic places and activities, highly diverse, stratified by social class, and to an even larger extent, by geography.

In the 1890s an official register listed a total of 1,055 theaters, including but not limited to opera houses, in 775 Italian towns and cities,[1] linked in a hierarchy both formal and informal. At the top were the eleven theaters of the top rank in the nation's major cities, often referred to as *teatri massimi*, (grand theaters). Below those magnificent houses spread a vast array of theaters, ranging from the second-rank theaters in the great cities (such as Milan's Dal Verme), many of which presented seasons similar in scale and quality to those of the *massimi*, to small houses in small towns and villages, where years might go by between rudimentary operatic performances.

Italian opera houses were ornate, lavishly decorated jewel boxes, designed with high ceilings to accommodate tiers of boxes, and in most theaters, an open gallery or *loggione* above the boxes. Although 3,000 spectators could fit into the San Carlo in Naples, most major theaters seated about 2,000, with theaters in smaller cities making room for 1,000 to 1,500 seats. The stalls were far shallower, from the orchestra pit to the rear wall, than in modern theaters; the Teatro Argentina, Rome's principal theater during most of the nineteenth century, offered only thirteen rows of orchestra seating. More than half of most theaters' seats were in boxes, which rose in four, five, or even six tiers, forming a grand and largely private horseshoe-shaped ring around the orchestra.

The physical form of the opera house, as it emerged during the eighteenth and early nineteenth century, was a visual representation of its social structure. The local aristocracy, along with prosperous merchants in cities like Livorno, was the most prominent audience for opera and its principal means of support. Opera houses were designed for their comfort and convenience. The leading families of each town generally owned their boxes, decorated them to their taste, and carried on much of their social life within them,[2] chattering away during the performance, only falling silent when the orchestra took up the introduction to a particularly prized aria or ensemble. For their further convenience, the theaters provided foyers and pantries, where their servants could prepare their meals and drinks or simply wait for instructions, and salons where the local nobility and their guests could repair during intermission for eating, drinking, or gambling.

Although they made room, as we have seen, for the middle class and for a handful of artisans and servants, the theaters of the early nineteenth century belonged to the aristocracy. This was, if anything, even more true in the smaller cities such as Ferrara or Parma, where the local aristocracy was even more dominant in their narrow sphere, and the local bourgeoisie, always with the exception of Livorno, was even more subservient to the nobility.[3] After the Risorgimento, as the middle class gradually came to dominate Italian society, the opera audience broadened, and became more middle class and less aristocratic, as the more prosperous bourgeois families began to replace the nobility in the boxes of La Scala or Genoa's Carlo Felice. The majority of Italians who were engaged in agriculture (smallholders, landless farm workers or sharecroppers) or the lowest strata of the urban population (porters, day laborers and market vendors) were unlikely ever to set foot in an opera house; through a variety of means, however, ranging from the ubiquitous village bands to choral societies and street musicians, all but the most culturally or geographically isolated Italian could share in the operatic experience.

Temples of opera

In 1893 the *teatri massimi* included La Scala, the Comunale in Bologna, the Bellini in Catania, La Pergola in Florence, the Carlo Felice in Genoa, the San Carlo in Naples, the Bellini in Palermo, the Argentina and the

Costanzi in Rome, the Regio in Turin, and La Fenice in Venice.[4] In 1897, Palermo's Bellini was replaced by the far larger, and far more pretentious, Teatro Massimo. While many of these theaters had distinguished historical traditions, their status was determined as much by their location in Italy's major centers as their physical proportions — in which respect they were not markedly different from the principal theaters in many smaller cities, such as Livorno's Goldoni or Parma's Regio, which often had their own distinguished history and tradition. While their seasons were often shorter, the quality of their productions was often comparable to those taking place at the *massimi*, particularly when run by a competent and energetic impresario. The oldest of the *massimi* was the elegant but tiny Teatro alla Pergola in Florence, which had been constructed in 1656, and served for generations as the court theater of the dukes of Tuscany. The youngest, the Teatro Massimo of Palermo, was also the largest.

Palermo's decision to build a new opera house reflects both the social importance of opera in post-unification Italy, and the use of opera as a means of defining civic consciousness in the new nation. Although Palermo had a small eighteenth-century opera house, the municipal government had already begun to make plans to build a major opera house by 1862, less than two years after Garibaldi first landed on the shores of Sicily. As the theater's official history puts it, "Palermo, in the second half of the 19th century, was engaged in getting itself a new identity in light of the new national unity."[5] More than any other single gesture, a new opera house symbolized that identity. In order to serve as an adequate representation of the city's new modern identity, the theater and its precincts had to be both large and impressive, in this case requiring the removal of nearly the entire old San Giuliano quarter and demolition of one of the remaining ancient city gates, the Porto Maqueda.

The new opera house came into being slowly, however, dogged by a seemingly never-ending series of controversies and conflicts. Although a design competition was held in 1864, the winner was not announced until 1868, and construction did not begin until 1875. Construction stopped in 1882 with the building less than half finished, and did not resume again until 1890, and then only as a result of pressure from a prominent local magnate. The theater finally opened, with a production of Verdi's *Falstaff*, in May 1897, thirty-five years after initially proposed. Grandiose in appearance, laid out in traditional style with five tiers of boxes and a gallery, and seating more than three thousand, the house was heralded as the largest in Italy, second in Europe only to the Opéra in Paris.[6]

While the Massimo was driven by the desire of Palermo's civic fathers to show the rest of the nation that theirs was a modern and in particular an *Italian* city, Rome's Teatro Costanzi, which largely replaced the Argentina as the city's principal operatic venue by the end of the century, was the work of a property developer and contractor, a product of the speculative building fever that transformed Rome after its designation as Italy's capital in 1870. One of many builders pushing urban Rome eastward along the Via Nazionale and the Via Cavour, Domenico Costanzi constructed his opera house as the centerpiece of a new residential quarter of the city, near the new Piazza della Republica and central train station, on the site of the former villa of the mad Roman emperor Heliogabalus far from the city's historic center.[7]

The Costanzi, which was constructed in a mere eighteen months, was also large by Italian standards, seating 2,200 people. Unlike Palermo's Massimo or the older opera houses, however, it was designed to accommodate a more diverse audience, ranging from the nouveaux riches to struggling bank clerks and minor civil servants, by providing a far larger number of inexpensive seats, with an amphitheater and two galleries, and only three tiers of boxes. The opera house was clearly intended to add distinction to the new area, and by extension, enhance the value of its properties. At the same time, it was widely seen as a quixotic venture; Constanzi was unable to find a single partner to share the cost of the project with him, while the municipality, despite his pleas, was willing to do no more than make a contribution toward the cost of street improvements to the area.[8]

With the royal family in attendance, the new opera house opened in 1880 with a performance of Rossini's *Semiramide*. To Costanzi's disappointment, however, the city was willing neither to purchase the theater from him, take responsibility for it, nor reimburse him for his costs. As a result, he retained ownership of the theater, seeking to make ends meet as best he could, making the Costanzi available to accommodate the less-prestigious genres of operetta and prose theater during the summer and fall of each year.

With the sole exception of the Bologna Comunale, which held its season in the autumn, the opera season at all the *massimi* was the same; known as the *carnevale–quaresima* (Carnival–Lent season), it ran from Christmas to Easter, with most seasons opening on Saint Stephen's Day, December 26.[9] While in earlier times a distinction had been made between the types of opera performed during Carnival and during Lent—with the Lenten season devoted to serious opera and oratorio—that distinction had disappeared by the late-nineteenth century, and the two periods were treated as a single season. The schedule (*cartellone*) was a limited one; as Fontana wrote disapprovingly in 1881: "While [outside Italy] twenty or more operas might rotate in the repertory over less than two months, at La Scala it is always the usual drastically limited [*ristretissimo*] number of operas and ballets, just as in all the major theaters of other Italian cities, just like minor provincial theaters in other countries."[10] A typical season at La Scala during the 1880s and 1890s — except for the three years when the house was controlled by Sonzogno, who presented more operas but fewer performances of each — consisted of five or six different operas and two full-length ballets. The impresario's contract at Genoa's Carlo Felice stipulated that each year five serious operas were to be presented, one of which would be a local premiere; one *opera-ballo* (a grand opera with ballet in the Parisian style), and two ballets. The new works were to be "preferably by Genoese composers."[11] Seasons at Venice's La Fenice during the 1880s and 1890s were even shorter, often including only three or four operas, along with a ballet.

It was at the *massimi* where the production values, the sets and costumes, were most elaborate, where one heard the most famous singers, and where the most important conductors directed the performances. It was also there that the Italian audience was introduced not only to the most important new works by the younger Italian composers such as Puccini, Mascagni, and Giordano, but to the important works coming into Italy from across the Alps, works by Wagner and Massenet, and later by Strauss and Debussy. Although the new operas of the *giovane scuola* and a few foreign works, such as Massenet's *Werther* or *Thaïs*, would gradually work their way down to the secondary theaters, more challenging operas such as *Tristan* or *Elektra* would remain the preserve of the *massimi* and their more sophisticated audiences.

Despite the theaters' ambitions, there was still much that was haphazard about their efforts. Neither the number of performances of each opera nor the opening nights of new productions — after the season's opening night — were set firmly in advance.[12] The run of a popular opera might be extended to fifteen, twenty, or more performances — while an unsuccessful one might be pulled from the boards after three, or even two performances, as Sonzogno did with Giordano's failed *Regina Diaz* in Naples in 1894 and Ricordi with *Madama Butterfly* at La Scala in 1904. A long run of a particularly successful work might push back, or displace entirely, a previously scheduled production of another opera, while a failure would force the impresario to fill the gap, usually by adding a production of a standard opera such as *Trovatore* or *Lucia* that almost every Italian singer could be counted on to know from memory. For subscribers, in particular, the unpredictable nature of their theater's schedule was a constant source of frustration, as they would have little idea at the onset of a new season, what works — or perhaps more important, which singers — they would end up getting to hear.

Audiences at the *massimi* in the 1890s had a wide variety of seating and pricing alternatives from which to choose. Following the traditional model, all of the major opera houses had an orchestra section, boxes — often as many as two hundred — and a gallery for standees high above the last tier of boxes. In the latter years of the century, in a move prompted largely by economic reasons, but to some extent as well by the cautiously egalitarian impulses of the new municipal administrations, theaters such as La Scala, La Fenice, and the Regio all removed the highest tier of boxes in order to create a second gallery, an open balcony that offered seating at prices higher than those of the *loggione*, but lower than those of the orchestra or boxes.

A spectator generally paid one charge to enter the theater, and a second charge that varied depending on the nature of the preferred accommodation, a practice dating back to the days when many people would go to the opera to gamble or socialize in the foyers and salons, rather than listen to the opera. In 1900 at La Fenice the charge to enter the theater for most productions was 3 lire, except for entry to the *loggione*, which was only 1 lira. Additional charges depended on location, the nature of the seating, and whether one wanted a reserved seat or the right to sit in unreserved areas, either in the orchestra, the balcony, or the *loggione*, and ranged from 1.5 lire for a reserved spot in the *loggione* to 10 lire for a relatively comfortable reserved seat in the orchestra, which was often divided into sections of varying degrees of price and comfort. By this time, however, the *massimi* had also begun to offer *rappresentazioni popolari*, or popular — reduced price — performances, usually toward the end of an opera's run. For such a performance, at the end of a run of Mascagni's *Iris* at La Fenice in February 1900, the general entry charge was reduced to 2 lire, orchestra seats were reduced from 10 to 5 lire and seats in the balcony from 2 lire to 1 lira.

These prices were popular only in relative terms, and were still far beyond the reach of the typical working-class family. At the turn of the century, such a family in Milan, with both husband and wife working full-time, might typically earn 2.5 lire per day, or 750 lire per year, of which nearly four-fifths was consumed by food, rent, heat, and lighting. With perhaps 150 lire per year (or 3 lire per week) available for everything else, including clothing, travel, and health care for the couple and their children, such a family could not expect ever to set foot in La Scala, or its equivalent in other Italian cities.[13] There were, however, other, less expensive places in Milan where less prosperous opera aficionados could hear operatic performances. Indeed, as many of the *massimi* found themselves in increasing financial difficulties (a topic that will be discussed later in this chapter), the secondary theaters often found themselves called upon to fill an embarrassing void in a city's operatic life.

The Second Tier

Historically, the *massimi*, along with the more distinguished provincial theaters, have always received the lion's share of attention, both from contemporary commentators and subsequent generations of writers and historians. They were not, however, the only theaters in major cities such as Milan or Genoa; houses such as La Scala or the Carlo Felice did not even account for a majority of the operatic productions offered the citizens of those cities. While the activities of many theaters in smaller towns and cities have been well documented over the years, secondary theaters in the major cities represented an important and largely undocumented means by which Italian audiences, particularly those who could not afford the prices at the *massimi*, experienced opera.[14]

Between 1886 and through 1895, ten different theaters in Milan presented at least one opera, while in the average year five or six different venues offered operatic productions, ranging from a single work to more than twenty different operas over the course of a number of months. While a few of these theaters presented opera only rarely, others offered a steady diet of Verdi, Rossini, and Donizetti "standards," while the Dal Verme and the Lirico offered frequent and often quite elaborate productions that included both world premieres and operas new to Milan. Taken as a whole, these theaters offered the Milanese audience a greater variety and number of operas than were given at La Scala, while reaching a wider spectrum of Milan's social and economic classes.

The most prominent of Milan's secondary opera houses, the Teatro Dal Verme, was built in the early 1870s on the site of the Circo Ciniselli, a ramshackle barnlike structure built in the early 1860s for equestrian performances by Gaetano Ciniselli, a riding master and member of a prominent circus family. Finally demolished after years of public complaints, it was replaced by a handsome opera house built by Count Dal Verme, which opened in 1872. Dal Verme's opera house, which Fontana described in 1881 as "the most beautiful opera house he had ever seen,"[15] was large and elaborately decorated, with a total capacity of nearly three thousand. It contained only two rows of boxes, above which extended an enormous open balcony capable of accommodating 1,400 spectators. It quickly supplanted the Teatro Carcano, which had been Milan's semiofficial "second house" earlier in the century, but which had become increasingly decrepit over the course of the years. By the 1880s the Dal Verme had established a reputation as an adventuresome house with a open-minded audience, as Fontana wrote: "Its greater popular element makes the Dal Verme's audience less pedantic, less supercilious, and more open to excitement and feeling, and thus more agreeable [*simpatico*]. In its few years of existence, [the Dal Verme] has established a number of solid reputations, now recognized and approved by all, including those of the composers Ponchielli and Auteri, and, although of less artistic importance . . . that of the choreographer Manzotti."[16] Another contemporary described it as the most heavily patronized theater in Milan, even more than La Scala.[17]

In addition to the staples of the repertoire, the Dal Verme presented numerous first performances of new operas by young Italian composers, making the theater and its resources available to composers willing to pay for the privilege. Between 1880 and 1889, the Dal Verme presented nineteen premieres, all ephemeral works except for Puccini's *Le Villi*, which made its debut there in May 1884, as a last-minute addition to the program. The commercial venality of this practice, and the failure of the theater to demand any minimum artistic standard of the works chosen to be performed, was deplored by more serious-minded observers.[18]

In the mid-1890s, the role of the Dal Verme was diminished by the opening of Edoardo Sonzogno's showcase, the Teatro Lirico Internazionale, created out of the old Cannobbiana. From 1894 through 1907, the Lirico presented a repertory made up largely of works by the *giovane scuola*, along with French composers of the present and the recent past, particularly Massenet, whose *Manon* appeared there in 1894, 1895, 1896, and 1897. Seating two thousand, the Lirico, like the Dal Verme, had only two tiers of boxes, with two balconies and a *loggione*. Heavily subsidized by Sonzogno, the Lirico saw the premieres of many notable operas, including *Adriana Lecouvreur*, *Fedora*, and *Zazà*, as well as the debut of the iconic tenor of the age, Enrico Caruso. In the early years of the twentieth century, Eleanora Duse's theater company also appeared often at the Lirico, which saw the debut of D'Annunzio's *La città morta*, and the Italian premieres of Maeterlinck's *Monna Vanna* and Ibsen's *Rosmersholm*.[19] During the second decade of the twentieth century, as the cinema began to supersede opera in the hearts of the Italian public, it became a sought-after venue for the premieres of important motion pictures.

A step down from the Dal Verme and Lirico were smaller theaters such as the Fossati in the Brera quarter, which alternated seasons of opera with operetta and Milanese dialect theater, or the centrally located Manzoni, which alternated opera with mainstream prose theater. Their seasons drew largely from the classic repertoire of Bellini, Rossini, Donizetti, and Verdi, with the addition of opere buffe by the likes of Sarria or the Ricci brothers, interspersed with the occasional novelty from little-known composers like Leoni or Cippollini.[20] By the latter part of the century, such theaters, in Milan and elsewhere, had come to be seen as the natural habitat of the most popular Verdi operas, in particular *Rigoletto*, *Ernani*, and *Il trovatore*, which were now rarely given at the *massimi*. The 1894 season at the Fossati was summed condescendingly up by the *Gazetta musicale di Milano* as "bringing forth the old Verdian repertoire; its public, sick of theoretical-modernist elucubrations, felt their heart beat faster hearing the inspired melodies of *Lombardi*, *Trovatore*, etc., etc., serviceably performed. They run in, besiege the theater, enjoy themselves, applaud, and everyone is happy."[21] To the La Scala audience, Toscanini's decision to add *Trovatore* to the season in 1902 was arguably in its way a more radical gesture than the inclusion of an avant-garde opera from Germany or eastern Europe.

The last third of the century saw the construction of multipurpose theaters known as *politeamas*: large, often unpretentious structures designed to be used not only for opera, but for operetta, prose theater, and even circuses, equestrian shows, or music hall entertainment. Such theaters were often larger than the *massimi*; the Politeama Vittorio Emanuele II in Florence seated six thousand, while the Politeama Genovese, only one of a number of such theaters in that city, seated three thousand. Both of these theaters were initially constructed as open-air arenas.

The Politeama Genovese was constructed in 1870 on the site of an old outdoor arena; although an elegant neoclassical structure with a painted curtain depicting the Triumph of Peace, it was also open to the elements. While the open roof made possible one of the theater's most attractive features, a large open-air café in place of the customary *loggione*, it also created serious difficulties, as described in one report of a performance of Petrella's *I promessi sposi*, just three weeks after the theater's grand opening:

> Last night [the weather] made the worst mess ever at the Politeama. After having permitted the . . . opera to begin, thunder and lightning burst out along with a downpour that made the orchestra go silent. The performance had to be halted, but all that was needed was to wait a short while for the rain

to let up, and the performance to resume. A small part of the audience did
not understand this, and they began to demand that the lights be turned
back on, and that they get their money back. They began to make an unholy
racket, and, what's worse, vandalize the place. . . . Two squads of soldiers
had to enter the theater to reestablish order and quiet. [22]

A mobile, retractable roof was erected over the Politeama Genovese in
1874. It seems to have worked adequately, because it remained in place for
more than twenty years until it was replaced with a permanent roof in 1895.
The *politeama* in Florence, which is today the city's Teatro Comunale, received its roof in 1882.

Despite its somewhat uncertain beginnings, and its plebian character,
at least by comparison with the elegant Carlo Felice, the Politeama Genovese played a major role in Genoa's operatic life from the 1880s well into
the twentieth century. Not only did it stage ten to twenty productions a
year, in contrast to four to six at the Carlo Felice, but many important operas made their first Genoa appearance there, including Massenet's *Manon*,
Puccini's *La Bohème* and *Tosca*, and Giordano's *Andrea Chénier*. Toscanini
conducted its orchestra, and a number of distinguished singers appeared
there, including Stagno and Bellincioni, Emma Nevada, Giuseppe Borgatti, Fanny Torresella, and Emma Carelli. Unusual among Italian opera
houses of the time, it operated year-round. In 1903, for example, the Politeama opened on December 24 with *Fedora*, offering six operas during
the *carnevale–quaresima* season, through February. It reopened in April,
with four more operas through the end of May; it then reopened in July,
and offered nine operas through the end of November. The season included five operas new to Genoa, including Cilèa's *Adriana Lecouvreur*
with Adelina Stehle.[23] As was true of *politeamas* generally, it was a private
venture, operated — presumably at a profit — by the redoubtable local entrepreneur Giovanni Chiarella.

Genoa, which was both a mercantile and an industrial center, had
many more theaters than just the Carlo Felice and the Politeama Genovese. During the 1850s — a period that saw the city's first major industrial
plants and its first major railroad connections — no fewer than four separate theaters were constructed, ranging from the 800 seat Modena to the
2000-seat Andrea Doria. By the end of the century, all four were still going
strong and presenting operas to the Genoese public, although the Andrea
Doria had been acquired in 1885 by Chiarella's cousin Danielle, rebuilt,
and renamed the Politeama Margherita, in honor of Italy's queen. Operas
were even occasionally presented at the Alcazar, an entertainment com-

plex built by the Chiarellas featuring not only a theater and *café chantant*, but a swimming pool, billiard parlor, and skating rink.

Even suburban, largely working-class districts of Genoa such as Sampierdarena and Sestri had their own *politeamas* where operas could be seen. While the prosperous, well-educated merchant watching *Die Walküre* from his box at the Carlo Felice may well have disdained the machinist or longshoreman watching *Il trovatore* from the gallery of the Politeama Sampierdarenese, they were both a part of the greater opera public, stratified by social class, means, and tastes, but sharing a passion for the quintessential Italian musical experience.

The number of *politeamas*, arenas, neighborhood theaters, and other venues presenting operas in small and large cities, and the number of performances that took place, makes it clear that opera was a mass entertainment, at least for the population of Italy's larger cities. To cite one admittedly exceptional case, in August and September 1898 the Politeama Livornese, a theater seating two thousand that sold an average of one thousand tickets a performance,[24] put on thirty-one performances of *La bohème*. During the same year, the Politeama presented twenty-six performances of other operas, including ten of the perennial *Cav* and *Pag*, while during the summer, the open-air Arena Alfieri presented a total of twenty-three performances of the staple operas *Rigoletto*, *Trovatore*, and *Lucia*. All in all, during the course of the year, the city's two "plebian" theaters presented eighty operatic performances, offering roughly 160,000 tickets to a city of 100,000 population.

Even if we assume that many in the audience were repeat visitors — not unlikely for a relatively new and much-heralded work like *Bohème*[25] — it is nonetheless apparent that a very large part of the city's population, including much of its working class, must have attended one or more opera performances during the course of the year. The tenor Galliano Masini, then an illiterate dockworker, was first exposed to opera at one of those thirty-one performances, a performance of *Bohème*, having been taken to the show by a fellow longshoreman who was an opera fan and member of the local choral society.[26] While we do not have detailed information on the pricing of these performances, they were clearly within the means of the greater part of the city's population.

Yet another body of operatic venues, closer to the *massimi* in their style and audience than to the *politeamas*, were the principal theaters in Italy's small cities, where they were often the only venues presenting opera on a regular basis. Nearly every city of any size in Italy had an opera house, which served as the center of entertainment and culture for the provincial aristocracy. Many of these theaters, often beautifully restored, remain in use today, hosting a variety of activities that may or may not include the occasional operatic festival or performance.

Many of the theaters were constructed in the eighteenth or early-nineteenth century as smaller versions of the theaters being built in the peninsula's capital cities. The Teatro Comunale in Treviso, a northeastern city of thirty-four thousand in 1901, was first built in 1692 and then rebuilt in 1836 after being nearly destroyed by fire. The Teatro Comunale in Ferrara opened its doors in 1797, designed in part by Piermarini, the architect of La Scala. The provincial theaters were generally far smaller than those of the metropolitan areas. Treviso's theater seated only six hundred, while Ferrara's held no more than nine hundred spectators.

At the beginning of the twentieth century, many of these theaters were still presenting regular opera seasons, rarely including more than four or five operas. The works of the *giovane scuola* were popular in the provincial theaters, which typically scheduled the latest works of Puccini, Mascagni, and their contemporaries within a year or less after they first appeared at La Scala or the Costanzi. The rest of their repertoire tended by depend on the traditional Italian staples, enlivened by the occasional opera buffa.

While we have less information about the audience in these theaters, their small size, the limited number of performances, and the traditional and elitist social aura that still surrounded many of them, suggests that far fewer of the less prosperous citizens of Treviso or Ferrara attended opera than their counterparts elsewhere. While a shopkeeper, artisan, or even a longshoreman might attend opera performances in Genoa or Livorno, his or her counterpart in a smaller city would be far less likely to do so. The gap would be even greater in the south, where operatic seasons of any kind outside the major cities of the region were rare.

Finally, even smaller towns and villages saw occasional opera performances. A production of *Fra diavolo* was mounted for the Carnival season in Poggibonsi, a Tuscan town of eight thousand in 1901, while a production of *La bohème* in the historic but even smaller Tuscan village of Sansepolcro in 1899 was the venue for the soprano Maria Farneti's stage debut. These small towns had theaters, but no regular opera seasons. Many of these productions were staged to commemorate a special event such as the dedication of a public building, as was the case with the 1873 performance of *Luisa Miller* in the small shoemaking town of San Elpidio al Mare that launched the conductor Mancinelli's career. In this last case, it is perhaps less notable that the town would commission an operatic performance than that the city fathers could find in nearby Ancona, a modest port city of thirty-three thousand, a local impresario with the ability to assemble an entire cast of singers, chorus, and orchestra on short notice.

The Crisis of the teatri massimi *and the Decline
and Fall of the Teatro alla Scala*

Italy's grand opera houses were the products of an aristocratic society, designed to serve the pleasures of that society with their secluded boxes, their salons, foyers, and gambling halls. These opera houses, whether in major capitals like Naples or provincial cities such as Parma or Lucca, typically came about through a partnership between a royal or ducal court and the local aristocracy. While the details varied, the pattern was generally the same: the cost would be divided in some fashion between the court and the individual aristocratic or mercantile families in their capacity as the theater's future boxholders. The ownership of the theater, while in some cases retained either by the government or the boxholders, would often be divided, with the boxholders owning the boxes and the government the rest of the theater. At La Scala,[27] which opened in 1778, replacing the old court theater (which had suspiciously burned to the ground in February 1776), ownership was shared between the court, represented by the Austrian emperor's viceroy, and the boxholders, all but eight of whom were members of the nobility.[28]

The boxholders and the government would share the cost and responsibility of maintaining the theater. Each year the government would provide a *dote*, an "endowment" or subsidy, while the boxholders would raise a further sum through a levy on the individual boxes. These funds would then be provided to the impresario retained to present the season. At those times and places where it was permitted, the impresario would also generally be given the concession to run the lucrative gambling salon, a fixture of eighteenth-century opera houses. Under the most auspicious circumstances, the profits from the gambling concession made a *dote* unnecessary. In Milan, when the Emperor Joseph II in the 1790s forbade gambling in the theaters, a subsidy from the viceroy's court made up the difference; after Napoleon's army had occupied Milan, and gambling was restored, the new impresario was not only willing to do without a subsidy, but agreed to pay the government 75,000 lire for the privilege.[29]

It was not an easy life for the impresario, but for the most part, allowing for a modicum of haggling among boxholders, court officials, and impresarios over the size of the subsidy, the cost of the season, or the quality of the singers, the system worked well. The court or the government — which were one and the same — shared the boxholders' interests; both demanded lavish operatic entertainments, particularly during the *carnevale–quaresima* season, and both were willing to devote substantial resources to ensuring that those entertainments would be available. Moreover, prior to 1848, no Italian state was subject to anything other than absolutist rule.[30] If the king or duke was accountable to anyone, such as a privy council, its members would invariably be the same individuals who spent their evenings in the court opera house's boxes.

This cozy state of affairs came to an end in 1861. With unification, the national government inherited the obligations of the former despotic states, including the subsidies they provided to their opera houses. The 1862 national budget included 1.1 million lire in theatrical subsidies, from which Milan's La Scala and Naples' San Carlo received more than 400,000 lire each.[31] With the new state facing intense financial pressures and deeply in debt, those subsidies quickly became a major bone of contention. By 1867, maintaining the peninsula's opera houses had come to be seen by the government as an untenable burden. That year, by a vote of 172 to 90, the Italian parliament washed its hands of the matter, unilaterally turning over the nation's stake in its opera houses to its municipal governments, the *comuni*.[32] Adding insult to injury, a year later the national government, in its constant search for additional revenues, imposed a 10 percent tax on the gross receipts of theaters and opera houses.

Municipal finances were even more strained than those of the Italian state. With few sources to draw upon, and with their citizens demanding clean water, better roads, and schools, cities were reluctant to devote large sums to activities that were widely seen as frills benefiting only an increasingly irrelevant aristocracy.[33] They began to whittle away at their operatic subsidies, while the nation's recurrent financial and agricultural crises meant that a growing number of opera's traditional aristocratic patrons were no longer able to pay the considerable sums needed to maintain their own positions as boxholders. While in the booming commercial cities of Milan or Genoa their places might be taken by members of the new commercial and manufacturing elite, there was no substitute for their presence in the smaller cities. Meanwhile, operatic expenditures continued to rise, as the audience developed a taste for grand opera on the Parisian model, which demanded a larger orchestra and chorus, more elaborate sets and costumes, and a full-fledged corps de ballet.[34]

La Scala and the other *massimi* supported themselves from a combination of box office receipts, boxholder contributions, and municipal subsidy —

an unstable combination that ultimately disintegrated toward the end of the century. Other theaters, however, lacked well-heeled boxholders, and for the most part received no municipal support. Except when a Maecenas like Sonzogno was available to underwrite their costs, houses such as the huge *politeamas* in cities such as Florence or Genoa had to support themselves entirely from box office receipts, offering more modest productions of crowd-pleasing operas, with heavy doses of standard Verdi works and opera buffa, performed by singers of at most local reputation. Less scrupulous managers would even make ends meet by accepting payment from would-be opera stars of little talent to permit them to appear in a *Rigoletto* or a *Barbiere*, and in at least one case, in an opera newly composed as a vehicle for the aspiring singer.[35]

The roster of opera houses that found themselves in difficulty in the 1870s and 1880s reads like an honor roll of Italian opera. Florence's Pergola closed its doors intermittently after 1877, while the Carlo Felice in Genoa was dark from 1879 to 1883, shut down as a by-product of litigation of *Bleak House* proportions between the theater's boxholders and the municipality.[36] Rome's Apollo, for decades the capital's principal opera house, closed in 1884, while La Fenice in Venice was unable to present a carnival season on thirteen occasions between 1872 and 1897.[37] Performances at Naples' San Carlo became so erratic that one wag wrote in *La gazzetta musicale di Milano* in 1878: "The management of the San Carlo should hang a permanent sign by the entrance to the theater: 'No performance today; come back tomorrow.' It would be more economical and more honest."[38] Even where the theaters stayed open, the number of performances dropped sharply from earlier years; while La Fenice typically presented twelve to sixteen operas and ballets annually during the 1840s, of which nine or ten were offered during the *carnevale–quaresima* season, by the 1880s that season was reduced to three to five operas and one or two ballets, and the traditional April–May spring season had all but disappeared.

Milan's La Scala was one of the few major houses to keep its doors consistently open through the 1870s and 1880s. It would ultimately melt down, however, in highly melodramatic fashion, shortly before the end of the century. The story of the crisis of La Scala, or the *"questione della Scala,"*[39] as it was characterized in the news articles and commentaries of the time is not only far better documented than that of other theaters, but, as Tabanelli writes, in his typical lawyer's style: "[Because] La Scala is the greatest of Italian theaters, not so much because of its magnitude, but owing to its artistic importance . . . the *questione della Scala* has particular importance . . . both from a legal and an artistic standpoint, to such an extent that one can well argue that it takes on such gravity as to surpass the city's boundaries, and become a question of national concern."[40] The decline of La Scala during the 1890s, leading to its collapse and closing in 1897, and its resurgence little more than a year later, encapsulates the forces affecting opera in Italy at the end of the nineteenth century.

When the Italian government ended its subsidies in 1867, Milan's municipal government somewhat grudgingly assumed the responsibility for providing an annual subsidy to the opera house, entering into periodic agreements with the boxholders through 1887, when a municipal subsidy of 240,000 lire a year through 1897 was approved over the vocal opposition of a small minority of the municipal council.[41] Opera seasons continued, but became shorter. The traditional fall season became shorter and shorter, disappearing entirely by the late 1870s. By the end of that decade, the pattern of a single *carnevale–quaresima* season, with five or six operas and two ballets, and a total of fifty-five to sixty opera performances, had become the norm.[42] Although the theater opened its doors for some orchestral concerts and the occasional gala or benefit event after the season was over, it was largely dark from April to December.

By the 1880s, it was painfully apparent that the La Scala problem was not only one of quantity, but of quality. As Fillipo Fillipi, a prominent critic of the time, wrote in 1881: "It is not possible to have any faith in the complete success of any season, and it happens far too often that spectacular triumphs, with the hall bursting with spectators, are followed by flaccid performances, highly-promoted fiascos, pitiful renditions, with the stalls empty, and the boxes deserted."[43] Antolini adds that "performances continually rescheduled because of singers' illnesses, frequent and unexpected changes in performers, new operas promised and cancelled at the last minute, were typical of La Scala seasons during the 80's."[44]

Seasons were entrusted to less than capable impresarios, including Luigi Piontelli, of whom Verdi wrote Ricordi, when plans were being made for the premiere of *Falstaff:* "I read that Piontelli will be the manager of La Scala! I regret this for the theater, because he is not a good manager, but personally I am almost pleased, because it relieves me of a great embarrassment, or to put it better, of some indecision."[45] Edoardo Sonzogno's efforts to run the house during 1895 and 1896 were no more successful, and after two years, he withdrew from the fray by somehow convincing Enrico Corti[46] and Temistocle Pozzali to step into his shoes for the last year of his contract. The authoritative critic Colombani denounced the new management: "even more than their predecessors, they have subordinated the city's opera house exclusively to their own interests . . . in open violation of

their obligations, not only contractually, but morally."[47] It was in this climate that Milan's city council took up the question of whether to renew
the municipal subsidy to La Scala.

By 1897, social and political conditions in Milan were very different
from 1887, when the municipal subsidy had last been debated. Although
the streets of Milan would not explode until the following spring, the nation's growing social and economic crisis was much on the minds of the
city's political leaders. More important, the makeup of those leaders, and
the framework of public opinion that guided their behavior, had changed
dramatically over the previous decade. Although the city's administration
was still in the hands of conservative parties, their power was on the decline, and that of not only the "historic" Left of Radicals and Republicans,
but the new Socialist and Catholic Worker forces, growing.

An ever-increasing number of daily newspapers and weekly magazines
had begun to appear, propagating the ideas of the new populist and Socialist movements, denouncing the ancien régime and calling upon the city to
take responsibility for more than the maintenance of law and order. To
many of the writers in these newspapers, the idea of a subsidy to La Scala,
while urgent social needs remained unmet, was a scandal. As the Republican *L'Italia del Popolo* thundered:

> While the city is taking on new debts, and preparing to impose new
> taxes . . . while there are not enough schools, and many of them are un-
> healthy, while far too many children do not get enough to eat to benefit from
> school, the subsidy to La Scala is going to be continued so that the box-
> holders will have one more place to spend their winter evenings, their ladies
> an excuse to show off their décolletage, so Sonzogno can carry out his dubi-
> ous experiments there, or Ricordi can play tyrant when he's in charge, or
> boycott it when he can't get his hand into its pocket! A good use, for God's
> sake, of the city's money![48]

From April through June, as the date of the city council vote approached,
the polemic over the future of the subsidy filled the city's newspapers. Virtually all of the forces on the Left opposed continuing the subsidy in its
present form, with only a few suggesting that it could perhaps be maintained if there were to be a thoroughgoing reform of the institution itself,
widely seen as decadent, disorganized, and rudderless.

Although the mayor argued in favor of maintaining the subsidy, his proposal found little support. After voting down two Radical proposals, one to
sell the theater outright and another to expropriate the boxes, at their July

1 session, the council voted by 31 to 22, with 8 abstentions, to reject the mayor's proposal and abolish the subsidy in its entirety. In all likelihood, had the membership of the council more accurately represented the city's entire population, the vote would have been far less close. On December 26, the traditional opening day of the season, a black-bordered card, similar to those used for death notices, appeared on the main door of the theater. It read:

> LA SCALA THEATER
> CLOSED BECAUSE OF THE DEATH OF FEELING
> FOR ART,
> OF CIVIC DIGNITY, AND COMMON SENSE

For the first time in the memory of anyone living, in 1898 there would be no *carnevale–quaresima* season at La Scala.

Bringing La Scala Back to Life

The failure of La Scala to open its doors on December 26 galvanized the Milan establishment into action. Less than two weeks later, on January 8, 1898, a distinguished body of Milan's good and great met and formed the Comitato Pro-Scala (Committee for La Scala), dedicated to bringing about the reopening of the theater on the basis of a continuing but reduced municipal subsidy, and a reorganization of the theater on the basis of "criteria of maximum modernity and efficiency"[49] A private corporation was established to operate La Scala under the leadership of the wealthy and widely respected Duke Guido Visconti di Modrone.[50]

Visconti di Modrone moved quickly. By the end of May, 316,500 lire in capital had been raised for the new corporation; by the end of June, he had obtained the approval of the city council—with only three dissenting votes—both for the reduced subsidy and for a contract with the corporation to run La Scala for three years. By mid-July, he had obtained the box-holders' unanimous approval, and recruited Giulio Gatti-Casaza, a twenty-nine-year-old former naval officer, who had made a great impression during his short tenure managing Ferrara's Teatro Communale, to manage the opera house. Within hours after his arrival in Milan in early July, Gatti-Cassaza was on his way to Turin to hire Arturo Toscanini as La Scala's new artistic director.

In less than a year, the Milan municipal council had dramatically reversed itself, with all factions of the Left other than the Socialists concurring in the decision to restore the subsidy to La Scala, while those who had offered tepid support to the subsidy before were now openly enthusiastic about Visconti di Modrone's proposal. Many of those most familiar with conditions at La Scala believed, not without reason, that the team that Visconti di Modrone had assembled would mount seasons far more worthy of La Scala's name and tradition than had the collection of improvident and irresponsible impresarios that had run the theater in recent years. To those observers, the increased contribution from the boxholders and the reduced municipal subsidy also carried weight. Intangible considerations, however, were equally important. La Scala mattered; as Fontana observed sarcastically, "La Scala takes up two-thirds (putting it mildly!) of the lives of the Milanese, something, given how many other subjects worthy of human thought exist in the world, seems to me to be a bit much."[51] Even for people who might frequent La Scala rarely, it was a defining point of Milan's identity, a central element in the Milanese sense of itself as Italy's "moral capital" — as distinct from Rome, its political capital. That La Scala *might* close, as was the case the year before, was far less traumatic to the Milanese psyche than that La Scala *had* closed, as was now the case. Although in theory the decisive January 8 meeting could have taken place at any time after the council vote in July 1897, it was only after the absence of a La Scala season that Milan's establishment was galvanized into action.

The moral significance of La Scala was enhanced rather than diminished by the *fatti di Maggio*, still brutally reverberating through the city's consciousness. De Herra, a Radical city-council member and a leader of the opposition in 1897, explained the change in his position by saying that "in a land where the tax collector's bills and the soldiers' swords have become the only unshakable institutions, we have an obligation to support the arts."[52] To Visconti Venosta, a leader of the committee, the reopening of La Scala was needed to lift the city's spirits, to heal what he characterized as a state of "profound depression."[53] Another member of the committee suggested in a more positive vein that "this vote . . . is the surest way to let the entire world know that elevated pursuits, concord of spirits, and a solid commitment to order and to work still reign here." He added, somewhat dubiously, that "in six months, the city will have forgotten these sad days, and regained its busy life, its throngs of foreign visitors, and all the signs of its economic vitality."[54]

There is a strongly delusional element to this rhetoric, in its manifest lack of understanding of the underlying issues that led to the *fatti di Mag-*

gio and the vast social and economic fault lines in the society. At the same time, it shows a civic commitment that, however misguided in some respects, is in other respects admirable, grounded as it is in the shared premise that the well-being of the city as a whole depended on the vitality of its opera house.

On December 26, 1898, La Scala opened its doors for the 1898–1899 *carnevale–quaresima* season with a production of *Die Meistersinger* conducted by Toscanini. It was clear that things had changed dramatically at the theater. Attendance at performances, which had dropped off — except for first nights — during the previous years, increased dramatically. Audiences found the productions to be better prepared and more finished, the staging more elaborate. Moreover, as one critic noted with amazement, "the notorious placard announcing the cancellation of a performance because of the 'sudden indisposition' of a singer, had not appeared *even once* during the long season" (emphasis in original).[55] Much of this is to the credit of Gatti-Cassazza, who found a theater, in his words: "almost abandoned . . . ; no scenery, chorus, ballet, ballet school, orchestra, stage crew; everything gone and everything to be reorganized; publishers in bad humor; press anything but friendly; no ledgers showing expenses or receipts.[56] He took responsibility for reorganizing all of the theater's departments, turning La Scala for the first time in years — if not decades — into a truly functioning artistic organism.

Perhaps the most important feature of the first three years during which Visconti di Modrone, Toscanini, and Gatti-Cassazza ran La Scala was the demonstration that a major opera house could be run professionally, bringing a level of both quality and integrity to the business of opera that was a distinct rarity in Italian opera history. To Toscanini and his colleagues, the purpose of an opera house was to present operas in the best way and under the best circumstances possible. That purpose was reflected in the care taken with the preparation of each opera — including devoting an entire month, all but unprecedented, to rehearsals for *Die Meistersinger* — as well as in Toscanini's order that the house be darkened, so that the audience would concentrate more on the opera than on one another, and that ladies sitting in the orchestra seats would take their hats off during the performances. It was also reflected in Toscanini's practice of performing even the longest operas with at most minimal cuts, out of respect for the composer's intentions.

Although the new regime was both an artistic and public success, it was far less successful financially. Although prices were raised steadily during the three years, with a season subscription for the best orchestra seats going

La Scala at the beginning of the twentieth century. *(Alinari Archive)*

from 225 to 375 lire, expenses constantly outpaced revenues. At the end of the first year, despite the funds from the municipality and the boxholders, and an infusion of over 100,000 lire of the corporation's capital to cover operating costs, the season was more than 100,000 lire in the red. The books were only balanced by a major fund-raising effort, to which Visconti di Modrone contributed 75,000 lire of his own money. The financial outcome of La Scala's second and third years was not substantially different. By the end of the third year, the corporation's capital was exhausted, while political support for continued municipal subsidies was, if anything, even less than it had been three years earlier.[57] Visconti di Modrone, who was already suffering from his final illness, reorganized the corporation, raising 500,000 lire in new capital through a second stock offering, and enlisting a small group of his fellow industrialists to guarantee with him the all but inevitable future operating deficits.

The following seasons saw the dissolution of the triumvirate. Visconti di Modrone died, mourned by all Milan, in November 1902. His eldest son Uberto, who took his place at the head of the corporation, brought neither his father's personal qualities nor his passionate commitment to La Scala

to the position, although he took a particular interest in the theater's ballerinas.[58] For Toscanini, who had held Uberto's father in deep respect, it
was a major blow. During 1903, his personal life—divided between his
wife and his relationship with Rosina Storchio, who was about to bear his
child—was in chaos; in addition, he bitterly resented the fact that he had
not been offered an increase in pay since taking the position in 1898. On
April 14, 1903, at the season-ending performance of Verdi's *Un ballo in
maschera*, after a battle with the audience over an encore, he stormed off
the stage at the end of the second act, refusing to return to finish the opera.
The next day, he left for a tour of South America, and did not return to La
Scala until the 1906–1907 season. He remained there for two years before
leaving for New York with Gatti-Cassazza, who had been appointed director of the Metropolitan Opera. Toscanini's departure deprived La Scala not
only of a conductor who brought a distinctive sensibility and excitement to
the repertory, but also of his unique organizing abilities.

Although Uberto Visconti di Modrone may not have had his father's
qualities, he ultimately developed a strong commitment to La Scala,
which he led and supported financially until 1917. Steady increases in
ticket prices and boxholders' contributions, combined with an increase in
the municipal subsidy in 1911 and the continued support of the Visconti di
Modrone family and their industrialist friends and colleagues, enabled the
theater to remain afloat until the darkest days of World War I, when Uberto
reluctantly withdrew. The opera house was closed and remained dark, except for an abbreviated fall 1918 season, until 1921.

The experience of La Scala after 1898 demonstrated that it was possible in Italy to organize an opera house on sounder artistic and manage-
rial principles, and present opera seasons of higher quality and greater
consistency than those to which most Italian audiences of the 1890s were
accustomed. It failed, however, to resolve the larger question of whether
it was possible to sustain those principles in the face of the fundamentally
irrational underpinnings of the Italian opera world. The power of the
publishers, the unnatural marriage in which municipalities and boxholders were yoked together, and, above all, the uncertain role not only of
La Scala, but all the *teatri massimi* in each city's civic life and in Italian
culture generally, were not addressed by Visconti di Modrone and his
colleagues, nor could they be. Although the unnatural marriage of boxholders and local governments was put to an end in the 1920s, by which
time the duopoly of the publishers was gradually disappearing as a by-
product of social and economic change, the question has yet to be answered even today.

Bands, Choral Societies, and Opera outside the Opera Houses

The many Italians who lacked the geographic opportunity or the financial means to set foot inside an opera house were nonetheless exposed to a steady diet of opera. As the century ended, the music they heard or played, and even the stories they told, were increasingly likely to be drawn from an operatic repertoire that was steadily infiltrating Italian popular culture.[59] The music Italians were most likely to hear was that performed by one of the thousands of bands that grew up throughout the peninsula during the century. An 1872 survey found more than 1,600 civic brass and wind bands in Italy, with nearly 43,000 musicians, along with another more than 100 military bands employing nearly 3,000 musicians.[60] By 1889, the number of civic bands had grown to more than 2,200,[61] suggesting that 35 new bands were being formed each year during the 1870s and 1880s, a process characterized by one author as the "great Italian band phenomenon of the 19th century."[62]

The tradition of band music in Italy dates back to the late eighteenth century, with many town and village bands tracing their origins to the military bands of the Napoleonic era — and in Saluzzo, to a "Turkish band" modeled after those popular in eighteenth-century Vienna. The band of Acquaviva delle Fonti, a small Apulian hill town, was established in 1797, a way of expressing local republican sentiments and a gesture of support for the short-lived Napoleonic Parthenopean Republic. Despite its origins, it was allowed to remain intact by the restored Bourbon monarchy; its members, as recorded after the restoration in 1805, included five cobblers, four tailors, three blacksmiths, two cabinetmakers, and two schoolboys, aged nine and ten respectively. The oldest member was twenty-seven, and the average age was eighteen.[63] Band music continued to be associated with revolutionary, republican sentiments; an observer of a public event during the 1849 republican uprising in Livorno described how "the festive numbers of the band echoed the joy of the public, so deeply felt, so energetically expressed."[64]

Although many bands originated as part of military or police detachments, during the nineteenth century the character of the Italian band became decidedly civilian, with little but the military character of the uniforms and an extensive repertory of marches to reflect their martial roots. From the beginning, they were seen, in Carlini's words, as "interclass organisms, where the factory worker sat beside the artisan, and the peasant alongside the bourgeois."[65] Riccardo Zandonai's father, a poor cobbler, expressed his

The municipal band of Cavour, near Turin, late in the nineteenth century. *(Banda musicale "San Lorenzo," Cavour)*

"passion for music by playing the bombardon [a bass tuba] in the local band" in the village of Sacco, in the foothills of the Tyrol.[66] In order to render band membership accessible even to musicians of the most modest attainments, many band arrangements provided for the simplest possible accompaniments, requiring no more than the "reproduction of the basic rhythm while using an extremely limited number of notes."[67] Given the desire of even villages of a few hundred people to have their own band, this was not only a democratic gesture but an accommodation to reality.

From the earliest days, operatic music was one of the three mainstays of the band repertoire along with dance music and marches. An 1817 account from Genoa mentions a band performance of "diverse orchestral selections, drawn specifically from Rossini's *Cenerentola*,"[68] while over the course of the century, village and town bands were increasingly drawn into the opera house to perform as the *banda*, or stage band, whose use in opera grew in parallel with the growth in the number of bands outside the opera house. With their wildly unpredictable membership and instrumental combinations, the use of town bands for the *banda* led to the practice, customary until near the end of the nineteenth century, of composers scoring *banda* music in two staves similar to a piano score, leaving it to the local bandmaster to arrange it for the particular combination of instruments available locally.

By the latter part of the century, the typical band drew upon an extensive operatic repertory, making up anything from a quarter to a half of their total inventory of musical numbers. Operatic arrangements came in three general categories, the most widely heard being transcriptions of specific numbers, including overtures, arias, and ensembles. In addition, large numbers of operatic fantasies, "potpourris," or reminiscences were offered, as well as transcriptions of complete acts or entire operas. During most of the century arrangements were typically made by local bandmasters, working from a copy of the piano-vocal score, perhaps supplemented from notes jotted down during a performance. Publishers appeared to have allowed the practice, difficult in any event to combat in the unsettled state of copyright law that obtained in Italy until 1882. Unauthorized band transcriptions of numbers from Verdi's *Don Carlos* were being performed in Novara and Treviso only a few months after the work's 1867 Paris debut.[69] During the last decades of the century, both Ricordi and Sonzogno began to publish their own band arrangements, and at least intermittently prosecute copyright violators.

In September 1890, less than five months after the triumphal debut of *Cavalleria rusticana*, the Roman band performed a "Reminiscences of *Cavalleria*," arranged by its leader, Alessandro Vessella, to a wildly enthusiastic crowd that filled the Piazza Colonna, the seats of every café, and every balcony and window in the buildings surrounding the piazza.[70] Although Vessella was perhaps the most respected bandmaster of the age, and although the work was described by the critic "Tom" as "done with true artistic intent, with scrupulous respect, and with singular mastery,"[71] Edoardo Sonzogno objected strongly, bringing a legal action to block further performances of the work. The wave of public protest that ensued ultimately forced the publisher to back down. After Mascagni had intervened, listening to the work at a private audition and offering his compliments to Vessella, the strains of *Cavalleria* were once again heard in Roman piazzas.[72] Sonzogno subsequently published his firm's own band arrangements of the opera, which are still in print.[73]

Notably, although perhaps with less than prophetic judgment, "Tom" added that "the descent of *Cavalleria* from the luminous space of the theater to the piazza should be the most effective means of ensuring its long-lasting popularity." Although *Cavalleria* has lasted anyway, bands had become the principal means by which operatic music was diffused beyond the opera houses. In 1880s Modena, the municipal band entertained visi-

tors to the city's Public Garden with complete renditions of Verdi's *Aida*
and *La forza del destino*, transcribed by their energetic leader, Ubaldo Reg-
giani.[74] While such marathons were unusual, a typical band concert, even
in the smallest villages, would include a variety of operatic numbers; by
1890, not only piazzas, but also the newly opened parks and public gardens
across Italy were ringing with the sound of operatic band music, providing
listeners with extensive selections from both the classic repertoire and the
latest works of the *giovane scuola*.

Participation as a band member was a way of being part of a national
musical community while continuing to express classic Italian sentiments
of engagement with one's native community; perhaps, it was also, as Carlini suggests, a means by which a new nation propagated both social discipline and bourgeois values among the peasantry and working-classes.[75]
Whatever their social motivation, for the many thousands of Italian band
members — largely members of the working class and the most modest
ranks of the bourgeoisie — performance of operatic music linked them
meaningfully to the art they perceived as their nation's highest artistic
achievement. At the same time, to their audiences, in Leydi's words, the
bands moved "the opera repertory . . . from the opera house to the streets,"[76]
giving nearly every Italian the opportunity to hear the music of the popular operas, not as an isolated event, but on a regular basis.

While the band was the most important vehicle for social diffusion of
opera, it was not the only one. A second important means of operatic diffusion emerged in the 1870s and 1880s in the form of the choral society.
While Italy had an ancient, albeit uneven, tradition of sacred choral singing,
secular choral societies were something new in Italian musical life. Much as
bands emerged initially from the heady blend of military music and revolutionary ferment of the Napoleonic era, choral societies were a product of
the growth of civic and working-class association in the years following unification and the beginnings of Italy's industrial revolution, often with a
strong Socialist identity.[77] Indeed, the choral society in the Tuscan town of
Bagno a Ripoli was established in 1902 as a choral and mutual aid society,
with the ambitious vision of "promoting recreation, instructing and training
the members in the demands of modern life, reclaiming civic and social
participation, to the end of gradually achieving all possible human demands."[78] As one writer comments, "male-voice music touched off con-
viviality on the one hand and revolutionary determination on the other."[79]

The earliest choral societies date to the 1870s. The "Constanza e con-
cordia" chorus of Livorno, later renamed the "Pietro Mascagni" chorus,
was established in 1877, while the "Guido Monaco" chorus in the small

Tuscan industrial city of Prato, was founded in 1878. The latter was founded by a group of young men who had come to know one another in an orphanage where they had learned music, and who first came together when recruited to sing in the debut of an opera by a local musician at the city's Teatro Metastasio. Their leader was a cobbler, whose workshop became the choral society's first meeting place. Each member paid ten centesimi a week to provide a modest stipend for the professional musician they hired to train and conduct them.[80] Apparently, the appetite for choral music in Prato was not yet satisfied, since in 1902, a second choral society, also made up of factory workers and artisans, was established. The "Giuseppe Verdi" choral society made its home in a tailor's workshop, setting as its mission the straightforward task of "singing the choruses from the most famous operas."[81]

While choral societies were consistently "popular" in their membership, not all were operatic in their interests. Some, known as polyphonic choirs, concentrated on church music, while a few, particularly in the northern mountain valleys of Lombardy, devoted their efforts to choral renditions of local folkloric and traditional music.[82] Many, however, focused on the operatic repertory, often participating in performances at the local opera house, as well as giving concerts in which operatic choruses and scenes, such as finales, in which the chorus had a prominent role, were featured. While choral societies did not play so great a role as bands in the dissemination of opera to the masses, they contributed not insignificantly to that effort; moreover, they were an important vehicle by which working-class men — and later, gradually, women as well — not only gained exposure to operatic music, but were given the opportunity to participate in operatic performances, often in theaters to which they would otherwise have had difficulty gaining admission.

Bands and choral societies formed vast networks of sustained dissemination of opera, spreading across Italy during the late-nineteenth century. During the same period, a vast array of more modest vehicles added to the process of dissemination, from printed materials such as postcards, cigarette cards, and inexpensive "novelizations" of opera stories, to the adaptation of operatic stories, with little or no musical accompaniment, by puppet theaters, a popular working-class entertainment in many late-nineteenth-century Italian cities.[83] Operatic music worked its way into the church, where operatic arias were interpolated into the service, or portions of the service were set to opera melodies. In a mass at the Orvieto Cathedral in 1891, the Intermezzo from *Cavalleria rusticana* was performed during the elevation of the Host.[84]

Street musicians, including Neapolitan urchins and the famous traveling harpists from the small Basilicata town of Viggiano, mixed operatic numbers with their more traditional repertory of folk and popular songs. At the same time, not only was popular music infiltrating opera, as in *Cavalleria* and Giordano's *Mala vita*, but popular music, particularly in Naples, was becoming more "operatic," as exemplified by the Neapolitan songs written toward the end of the century — the first "crossover" music to become part of the repertoire of opera as well as popular singers.

In some fashion, however attenuated and simplified it may have become as it worked its way down the social and geographic ladder, opera reached the great majority of Italians. At the end of the nineteenth century, even rural and working-class Italians were familiar with the principal tunes of the popular operas, and made a connection, however tenuous, with the stories and principal characters of the operas. As Leydi demonstrates, operatic characters like Rigoletto, Radamès and Aida, or Turiddu and Santuzza, became part of the popular patrimony, appearing in their stories, plays, and poetry.[85] When the time came, however, the connection was easily broken. It was not long before the mass of Italians changed their allegiance from opera to the new medium of the cinema, a process that took place with astonishing rapidity during the early decades of the twentieth century.

Chapter 8

Performing Opera

The Operatic Octopus

Opera was more than a business in late-nineteenth-century Italy; it was a force that affected the lives of hundreds of thousands of Italians, an economic octopus whose tentacles reached into sectors far removed from the opera houses themselves. The lavishly rewarded diva with her palatial hillside villa overlooking Lake Como and the seamstress coughing in her freezing garret, sewing embroidery on the diva's costume, were equally dependent on the opera industry for their livelihood.

The tentacles of the operatic octopus reached farthest in Milan, which by the 1890s was the unchallenged operatic capital of Italy, the center of an operatic universe that covered the greater part of the known world.[1] Singers, conductors, and entire opera companies were hired in the offices of Milan's booking agents to perform in Spain, Portugal, Egypt, Greece, Latin America, the United States, and wherever else Italian opera was in demand. Every spring, as the principal season wound down in the Italian opera houses, more than a thousand Italian singers and other musicians boarded ocean liners at Genoa for South America, where they would perform until it was time to return in the fall for the next year's Italian season openings at the end of December. It was on such a tour in 1886 that Arturo Toscanini, then a nineteen-year-old cellist, made his impromptu conducting debut in Rio de Janeiro.

Italy was still a poor country, with little to offer the rest of the world other than its agricultural products and its people. Opera was a major export industry, with millions of lire making their way each year into the Italian economy from the earnings of Italian musicians abroad. In the 1890s Milan contained eleven major booking agencies, and innumerable lesser ones, from prosperous firms with lavishly decorated offices down to the lowliest members of the profession, men in threadbare suits who prowled the Galleria, hoping to convince an impresario to give a break to some promising young singer they were trying to promote.

Inside Milan, the number of separate businesses that were supported by the opera industry was almost beyond counting. In addition to the principal ones, which included the theatrical costumers and set builders, the publishers, and the workshops for the manufacture and repair of musical instruments, a 1901 account lists "outfitters, makers of fringes and ribbons, hosiers, dyers and printers, hairdressers, shoemakers, jewelers, embroiderers, florists, haberdashers, hat makers, modistes, and furriers."[2] In addition to La Scala's own work force of nearly 1,100 people, more than 1,000 people were employed in Milan and environs to supply the opera house's needs. The La Scala production of the 1897 ballet spectacular *Sport* provided employment for 1,500 people over the course of its preparation, rehearsal, and performance. The costumes alone required the work of 200 people for three months, as well as 50,000 feet of silk, 16,000 feet of velvet, and 10,000 ribbons.[3] While much of this work was seasonal — most of the jobs at La Scala lasted for at most six months of the year — they were both stable and relatively well paid by the standards of the time, in which job security and steady wages were still an aspiration rather than a reality for most of the urban working class.

The opera industry extended even further into the Milanese economy. Not only was it a mainstay of the city's tourist trade, on which numerous hotelkeepers, carriage-owners, storekeepers, restaurateurs, and others depended; it made Milan a destination of choice for hundreds of aspiring young singers from Europe and the Americas. As one commentator noted: "These folk come to Milan, and live here for year after year . . . not because their own countries, or places closer to home, lack musical institutions quite as good as those found here; but because it has become an unchallenged proposition, recognized internationally, that the one place in the world where one must study music and where one can most readily find the path to a spectacular artistic career is the city of La Scala."[4]

Although the role of opera in Milan's economy was magnified by the city's unique national and international role, including not only the booking agents and managers, but the two major publishers Ricordi and Sonzogno, each of whom employed hundreds of people, the same picture was reproduced on a more modest scale in each of Italy's other major cities. As was La Scala in Milan, each one of Italy's major opera houses, whether the Regio in Turin, the Carlo Felice in Genoa, or the San Carlo in Naples, was a major employer in its own right, as well as an important source of business for a network of local firms that provided the goods and services that each opera house needed. Opera was big business in Italy. Ultimately it rested, however, on the shoulders of the people who actually made opera: the singers, conductors, musicians, and others for whom making opera was their daily work.

Singers

Singers have always been the heart of the operatic experience and the operatic industry.[5] No other operatic profession has ever received either the adulation or the scorn lavished on singers: even today, when opera is far from central to most people's lives, terms like "diva" or "prima donna" are common currency, while three tenors, or even a single one, can become mass marketing phenomena. That was far more the case, of course, at the end of the nineteenth century, when the most famous sopranos and tenors were figures of not only national but international renown. At the same time, for every world-famous diva there were dozens if not hundreds of aspiring singers barely making ends meet, or singing in a chorus at night while working in a menial job by day, hoping against the odds to be discovered by an impresario or wealthy connoisseur.

Singers in Italy were far more likely than other operatic figures to come from the world of artisans and laborers that made up the great majority of Italians, a circumstance that undoubtedly added to the affection they inspired among the Italian people. Italy's greatest Wagnerian tenor, Giuseppe Borgatti (1871–1950), according to the traditional account, "was chipping stones in a mason's yard when a local Marchese, an aficionado of the opera, chanced by and heard the young man singing away at the top of his voice."[6] The marquis arranged for him to take lessons with Alessandro Busi in Bologna, and a few years later, young Borgatti made his operatic debut in 1892 at twenty-one in the title role of *Faust* at the theater in the small town of Castelfranco Veneto near Treviso. Caruso came from a working-class, although not impoverished, family in Naples, while Francesco Tamagno's father was an innkeeper in Varese, near Turin. Francesco Marconi was a carpenter, while Titta Ruffo, perhaps the greatest baritone of his generation, was a blacksmith.

The Livorno tenor Galliano Masini (1896–1986) offers an even more dramatic and better documented rags-to-riches story. The son of a desperately poor factory worker, he was taken out of school after the second grade and put to work, first as a delivery boy, and then in a variety of odd jobs, ending up as a longshoreman on the city's docks. Gifted with a huge voice,

Lina Cavalieri and Enrico Caruso in *Fedora*, 1905 or 1906. *(Casa Musicale Sonzogno)*

Titta Ruffo in the role of Cascart from *Zazà*. *(Baskerville Publishers)*

he often sang popular songs in a downtown bar, where he attracted the attention of a number of well-to-do young men, who took him under their wing and induced him to join a local choral society, from which he was recruited to sing a short but pivotal passage in a local production of Mascagni's *Lodoletta*.

Masini was already twenty-five, and had never studied. Indeed, he was barely literate in Italian, and it is doubtful that he even knew how to read music.[7] Friends of Mascagni, however, were in the theater for the performance, and arranged for the young singer to meet the composer, who listened to him, and pronounced, "it would be a crime not to make him study." After a period of local study, the longshoremen's union and the choral society were able to raise just enough funds to enable him to study in Milan. Three difficult and privation-filled years later, he made his debut, singing Cavaradossi in a special performance at Livorno's Teatro Goldoni underwritten by his local friends and admirers. It was not until five more years singing in provincial opera houses that he was recognized as a singer of the first rank.[8] By that point, he was already thirty-three.

Not all tenors came from struggling, impoverished backgrounds. Fernando De Lucia's family, from Naples' solid middle class, was able to send him to a private school in his early teens, and to the San Pietro a Maiella Conservatory.[9] Roberto Stagno (1840–1897), who created the role of Turiddu in *Cavalleria*, was the oldest son of a noble family that had come to Sicily from Spain early in the sixteenth century. His family would not accept his dream of a musical career, considering it to be inappropriate, even indecent, for a man of his standing. Cut off without a penny and disinherited by his father, he too had to struggle both economically and artistically before achieving success.[10]

Tenors appear to have been more likely to come from humble backgrounds than sopranos. Although Rosina Storchio, who originated the title roles in *Butterfly* and *Zazà*, was the daughter of an officer in the *carabinieri*, Italy's national police force, she faced no serious impediments, economic or otherwise, to her pursuing a singing career.[11] Gemma Bellincioni was the daughter of a successful singer, from a Florentine family that, although in straitened circumstances, was solidly middle-class, while Emma Carelli was the daughter of a prominent singing teacher, a professor at San Pietro a Maiella and a pillar of respectable Neapolitan society. Rosa Raisa (1893–1963) was a special case. Born Rosa Burchstein in Bialystok, Russia, she and her family fled the poverty and pogroms of their native land, winding up in Naples in 1907 when she was fourteen. Sponsored by a wealthy Neapolitan who paid for her training at San Pietro a

Maiella, she was subsequently discovered by the conductor Cleofonte Campanini, who hired her for the Chicago Opera in 1914. Renamed Rosa Raisa, she went on to a major career, largely in the New World rather than in Italy.

The training of singers in late-nineteenth-century Italy was still an informal, highly personalized, process, often rendering access to a singing career easier for young people without money or connections. Although a growing number of singers were attending conservatories, particularly San Pietro a Maiella and the Liceo Rossini in Pesaro, many still studied independently, with one or more of the host of singing teachers that could be found in every major Italian city and many smaller towns. Caruso, who had already obtained some local renown in Naples as a singer of cabaret songs in the city's *cafés-chantants*, was accepted by a well-regarded teacher, Guglielmo Vergine, at the age of seventeen. Because Caruso had no money to pay for his lessons, he signed an agreement with Vergine that in return for four years of lessons, the teacher would receive 25 percent of his earnings for five years of singing. Unconscionably, the contract was not for 25 percent of his earnings over his first five years as a singer, but for *five years of singing*; that is, more than 1,800 performances.[12] Masini's teacher in Milan, Giovanni Laura, gave him free lessons after learning how desperately poor the young man was.[13] By contrast, Beniamino Carelli charged the substantial sum of 10 lire per lesson, "as much," in his son's account, "as a visit to the most illustrious doctor of the period."[14]

The teaching of singing was shifting, however, to the conservatories. The Liceo Rossini in Pesaro, a newcomer in the ranks of Italy's conservatories, became increasingly known as a school that produced singers, particularly during the years toward the end of the century when Mascagni was at its helm. During that period, the Liceo's graduates included sopranos Celestina Boninsegna, Maria Farneti, and Tina Poli-Randaccio, and tenor Piero Schiavazzi. Other conservatories also had their distinguished graduates. Titta Ruffo studied at Rome's Santa Cecilia, while Eugenia Burzio was a product of the Milan Conservatory. For most vocal students, however, the conservatory was little more than their teacher's home base; as Roselli writes, "the memoirs of singers who trained in the decades up to the 1930's . . . treat their conservatory experience as one incident among others in their training, notable chiefly for encounters with an individual singing teacher, good or bad."[15]

The demand for gifted singers was strong, and once such a singer had finished his or her training, the path to the top was often swift. Preceded by recommendations from their teachers, they usually began in provincial theaters, not with minor parts, but with leading roles. Maria Farneti (1877–1955) made her debut as Mimì in *La bohème* in the Tuscan town of Sansepolcro in the fall of 1899. At that point, she had already been signed to create the title role in the first Turin performance of Mascagni's *Iris* in December, on her twenty-second birthday. Within a year, she was singing leading roles not only at the Teatro Regio but at the Carlo Felice and at La Fenice. In her case, there is little doubt that her speedy rise was assisted by Mascagni, who had already singled her out for attention while she was a student at the Liceo Rossini, and recommended her for the Turin role.[16] Perhaps because of the speed of her rise to fame, Farneti had a brilliant but short career. By 1914 she was clearly in decline; as one writer puts it, "not absolutely because of vocal decline, but rather from a certain general tiredness."[17] She performed rarely from then on and retired from the stage in 1917. Married to a prosperous attorney, she spent the rest of her life in comfortable retirement in a palatial villa on the banks of Lake Como. She did return briefly to the recording studio in 1930, demonstrating that she was still capable of turning in a riveting performance when she cared to do so.

Celestina Boninsegna (1877–1947) made her debut at nineteen, singing Gilda in the theater in Fano, a small city in the Marche. After a season singing in provincial theaters, she decided, unusually for a budding diva, that she needed more training, and went back to Milan for further study. In later years, she referred to her performance three years later in Piacenza as the Queen of Sheba in Goldmark's *La regina di Saba* as her "real" debut.[18] By the following year she was singing at Milan's Dal Verme, and a year later, at the Teatro Costanzi.

Tenors' careers tended to move only slightly more slowly. De Lucia, after singing for more than a year in concerts and churches, and becoming known throughout Naples for his suave renditions of Tosti's songs, made his debut at twenty-four at the Teatro San Carlo as Faust in Gounod's opera. Within the year, he was singing leading roles in Bologna and Florence, and in the spring of 1886, a year after his debut, he was on his way to South America with a troupe of Italian singers, singing leading tenor roles in *Faust*, *L'ebrea* (La juive), *Lucrezia Borgia*, *La favorita*, and *La Gioconda*. Amadeo Bassi (1872–1949) made his debut at twenty-five in Marchetti's *Ruy Blas*, still a popular opera at the time, in Castelfiorentino. He spent 1898 and 1899 in the "provinces" before being hired by the conductor Luigi Mancinelli to sing at Naples' San Carlo in 1900.

Perhaps the most spectacular career path of the period was that of Emma Carelli (1877–1928), who received both a thorough vocal training from her father and a solid general education at one of Naples' most prestigious private schools. She made her debut in Mercadante's *La Vestale* at Altamura, near Bari, shortly after her eighteenth birthday. At twenty, she was singing at Sonzogno's Teatro Lirico in Milan; at twenty-one she was acclaimed for her renditions of Iris and of Margherita in Boito's *Mefistofele* at Rome's Teatro Costanzi. An intelligent, strong-willed woman, she already had clear ideas about the roles she was interpreting, writing about the jail scene in *Mefistofele:* "Specifically, I wanted this: that when the curtain came up, even before I sung or spoke, the public had the feeling that they were facing the ruin of an anguished life, and saw on the ground a poor undone creature with the straw of the pallet in her hair, with her eyes fixed in the stare of a madwoman."[19] Recognizing that her interpretation might be controversial at a time when Margherita was generally depicted as a passive, innocent victim, she took the precaution of writing Boito, receiving back a generous letter from the composer: "Your artistic concept, which you have courteously chosen to confide to me . . . could not be more aptly thought out or more clearly and expressed. If you have indeed carried it out (which I do not doubt), you fully deserve the clamorous triumph that you have received. I rejoice with you and for you."[20] At twenty-two she opened the La Scala season as Desdemona in Verdi's *Otello* under Toscanini's baton. Hired initially at 10,000 lire for the season, before the season was over, Gatti-Cassazza, the general manager of La Scala, had offered her 40,000 lire to come back for the 1900–1901 season.[21]

In the meantime, at the end of the La Scala season, Carelli was off to South America. By the end of the century, foreign travel, particularly to South America, was part of the routine for every Italian opera singer of any stature. Once the *carnevale–quaresima* season at the major Italian opera houses was over, there was no good reason for any major singer to remain in Italy. No secondary theater and no summer or fall season in Italy offered either the fees or the publicity that could be garnered from a season in Buenos Aires, Madrid, or New York. Indeed, to the embarrassment of Italian patriots, a not insignificant number of important Italian singers chose to make their careers largely or entirely overseas. These including the soprano Luisa Tetrazzini and, most famously, the great tenor Enrico Caruso, about whom many Italians felt, in Greenfield's words: "he had betrayed his country by surrendering to the temptations of the American dollar."[22] Another notable Italian singer, Regina Pacini (1871–1965), built a distinguished career in South America, retiring from the stage in 1907 to marry Marcelo Alvear, a prominent Buenos Aires politician who later became president of Argentina.[23]

Latin American tours took many forms. Some singers might be recruited by a Buenos Aires impresario for an entire season at one theater, with perhaps a side trip to Montevideo, while others might spend a season in Santiago, Havana, or Mexico City. Others covered a significant part of the continent. The tours organized by Walter Mocchi in the second decade of the twentieth century were particularly ambitious. Over a six-month period, the 1911 company led by Pietro Mascagni went, after a seven-week season in Buenos Aires, to Rosario (Argentina's second city), to Rio di Janeiro and São Paolo in Brazil, from there to Montevideo, across the mountains to Santiago and Valparaiso, until returning to Buenos Aires and embarking for Genoa. Over six months, Mascagni conducted 163 operatic performances and eleven concerts; as he wrote Anna Lolli, "I am working constantly: I rehearse from noon to six, then I go have a bite and take a nap in an armchair; at 8:30 I'm back in the theater for the performance and leave at one in the morning. That's my life, without a single day off."[24]

The singers were well paid for their hard work. De Lucia was paid 150,000 lire for a four-month season in Buenos Aires and Montevideo in 1889, from which he returned to Italy to sing in the *carnevale–quaresima* season at Naples' San Carlo for 75,000 lire, a figure close to the pinnacle of the Italian fee structure.[25] Titta Ruffo, who as a baritone could not expect to be paid as much as a tenor, nonetheless received an amount he characterizes as "greater than" 50,000 lire for a 1908 season at Buenos Aires' Teatro Colón, performing roughly fifty times over three and a half months. In his last full season in Italy, at La Scala in 1904, he had been paid 10,000 lire.[26]

Ruffo entitled his autobiography *La mia parabola* (My parabola), which is an apt way to describe his earning power as he rose to fame. His first extended engagement, in a minor theater in Livorno in 1898, paid the modest sum of 10 lire per performance, to which the impresario, after the young baritone's pleas, added "a *caffelatte* in the morning and meat for my midday meal."[27] His first South American contract, in 1900, paid 2,700 lire per month. Five years later, he was earning more than 100,000 lire for a season in Saint Petersburg, singing sixty-six times, in an environment he described as "heavy, dismal and sad."[28]

Russia before the revolution was another highly lucrative destination for Italian singers. As one writer has described it: "The pride of the Theater Directorate was St. Petersburg's Italian Opera, which performed only foreign works, and which enjoyed the enthusiastic support of the royal court. . . . Vast sums were spent to provide the Italian Opera with an excellent orchestra, elaborate sets and costumes, and the best foreign artists, often engaged at exorbitant fees."[29] What is exorbitant, however, is in the eyes of the beholder. While these sums were large, they reflected a market in which the demand for outstanding singing abilities outstripped by a substantial margin the supply of singers with those abilities. Although Italy might be the source of operatic talent, it could not compete in the international market. Wealthy elites, whether the tsar's court in Russia, Wall Street plutocrats in New York, or multimillionaire *latifundistas* (estate-owners) in Buenos Aires, had both far greater resources and fewer constraints on their spending than did Italy's beleaguered opera houses, dependent on dwindling aristocratic patronage and grudging governmental support.

Only a handful of singers could command such fees. Fees dropped off rapidly from the top. For the 1899–1900 *carnevale–quaresima* season, La Scala spent 293,000 lire on the "compagnia di canto," or roughly one-third of the opera house's total budget for the year. For this sum, they hired eighteen singers for roles substantial enough to receive billing, along with some six to ten *comprimarii*. Francesco Tamagno, who sang seven performances of *Otello* for 10,000 lire each, received nearly a quarter of the total, while Carelli and Borgatti divided a roughly similar amount between them. With two or three other singers, including Darclée and Pini-Corsi, able to demand at least 20,000 lire each, the remaining billed singers earned 5,000 to 8,000 lire for their seasons. While this was a comfortable if not lavish salary, the *comprimarii* earned far less. They, along with billed singers at the smaller provincial opera houses, rarely made more than 300 to 500 lire for the season, barely enough to escape penury.

At the Metropolitan Opera the range was even greater. In the 1890s Melba was making $1600 (L. 8,000–9,000) per performance, while a decade later, Caruso received $2500 (L. 13,000–14,000) per performance, a figure that could have been far greater had he been more demanding of his principal employer.[30] Meanwhile, Eugenia Mantelli, a highly regarded contralto, was singing important roles for $48 per performance. Some *comprimarii* at the Met made as little as eight dollars a week for five performances.[31]

Fully 1,106 singers were on the books of Milan theatrical agencies in 1896–1897. Their rosters included gifted singers in their prime, older singers desperately holding to the shreds of a voice, and a steady stream of young aspirants, many from outside Italy, drawn to the heart of the Italian opera world. A handful of these singers had brilliant international careers and bought grandiose villas, of which the grandest may have been Caruso's Villa Bellosguardo in Tuscany: "[It] stood in the midst of a huge park; there were formal gardens, many acres of vineyards, and . . . several lawn tennis courts. . . . On the ground floor were two salons, a chapel, a forty foot drawing room, kitchens, a baggage room and a completely separate servants' quarters. On the second floor there were twenty more rooms, among them a gallery of arms, a gallery of paintings, an Arabian conservatory, a special room for his growing coin collection . . . and an immense studio."[32] A somewhat larger number earned enough to maintain a solid middle-class lifestyle and a comfortable retirement; for many sopranos, the glamour of their operatic careers, however modest, paved the way to an economically successful marriage. A far larger number, though, lived a hand-to-mouth existence for some number of years, ultimately drifting back to their native city or village with nothing but the memory of having once sung Manrico or Violetta on the boards of one or another of the many small, poorly paying, provincial opera houses that could be found across the peninsula.

Conductors

While the history of singing as a profession goes back to the earliest days of opera, the profession of conductor was still a young one in Italy in the late nineteenth century. Until midcentury, indeed, the conductor in the modern sense hardly existed in Italian opera houses. The orchestra was generally led by the *capo d'orchestra e primo violino* (orchestra leader and first violin), who gave the tempi by gesticulating with his bow, nodding his head, or tapping his feet. The *capo d'orchestra*, however, played little part in the preparation and rehearsal of the opera, which was the duty of the *maestro concertatore* or répetiteur,[33] who would conduct the rehearsals from behind his piano or harpsichord. When a new opera was being prepared for its debut, the composer would often play the role of *concertatore*, and take responsibility for leading the first three performances.

The man generally recognized as the first Italian conductor, in the sense of a musician whose activities and responsibilities largely resembled those of a modern conductor, was Angelo Mariani (1821–1873). Although he combined the roles of conductor and *concertatore* as early as 1844 in Messina, he was still conducting from the first violin desk at that time; one scholar admits that "it is not known exactly when he truly assumed the prerogatives of a modern conductor."[34] He had clearly begun to do so, however, when he took over the position at the Carlo Felice in Genoa in 1852, followed by the Comunale in Bologna in 1860. As Phillips-Matz writes, with slight and pardonable exaggeration, "he lived for his work, rehearsed his ensemble until it was perfect and used his extraordinary personal charm to persuade everyone in the production that opera was more than a collision of random elements."[35] The modern conductor only arrived at La Scala, however, in 1868, when the position was established by Alberto Mazzucato (1813–1877), who was already a distinguished teacher at the conservatory and a prominent Milan musical figure. Mazzucato most probably did not see conducting as a career, and soon returned to the Milan Conservatory, where he served as its director until his death. Franco Faccio (1840–1891), who began conducting at La Scala in 1871 and remained there through 1890, was the one who firmly established that the conductor at La Scala was to be the animating and presiding musical spirit of the opera house.

Faccio was struck down at an early age by tertiary syphilis, but by the 1890s a growing number of younger Italian musicians had begun to build careers as conductors, both in Italy and abroad. These musicians included such figures as Luigi Mancinelli, Leopoldo Mugnone, Edoardo Mascheroni, Pietro Mascagni (who had a major career as a conductor separate from his composing career) and, most famously, Arturo Toscanini.

There was no recognized path by which one became a conductor, nor did any conservatory offer courses in conducting to its students. Mugnone and Mascagni both learned their trade by conducting pit bands in traveling operetta companies, an arena in which a young conductor could develop his skills in an environment that was relatively undemanding, at least from an artistic standpoint. The path by which Luigi Mancinelli (1848–1921), who was the dean of Italian conductors after the death of Faccio, became a conductor, although different, was not atypical.[36]

Mancinelli, the son of a prosperous music-loving Orvieto businessman, was drawn to music at an early age. After early studies in Orvieto, he moved to Florence, where he studied cello and composition privately, the latter with Teodulo Mabellini, a distinguished professor at the conservatory and a friend of the family. At nineteen, he became a member of the cello section of the Pergola opera house in Florence, earning 90 lire per month. In 1871, he moved to Rome, becoming second chair in the cello section at the Teatro Apollo at the more substantial salary of 190 lire per month. In both cases, Mancinelli received a salary only for those months when the opera season was taking place; the rest of the year he sought work elsewhere, playing in spring and summer seasons in smaller cities around the peninsula.

It was on such an occasion, when he was playing in a theater in Ancona in the summer of 1873, that he had his first opportunity to conduct an operatic performance. A nearby small town, San Elpidio al Mare, had hired an Ancona impresario to stage a performance of Verdi's *Luisa Miller* in honor of the dedication of the town's new theater. The impresario offered the young cellist the conducting position, which he accepted, and apparently carried off capably.[37] Although that minor provincial performance did not lead directly to further conducting engagements, by the time Mancinelli returned to Rome in the fall, his horizons had begun to extend beyond his chair in the cello section of the orchestra.

The following summer, while playing in a production of *Aida* in Perugia organized by the Roman impresario Gino Monaldi, Mancinelli had a second, and more lasting opportunity. Mancinelli's biographer tells the story: "Coming back from a party organized for the artists by Count Oddi at his villa on Lake Trasimeno, Usiglio[38] [the conductor], having enjoyed Bacchus too much, was unable to conduct the opera. Someone mentioned to Monaldi that he had seen the young cellist playing Verdi's opera from memory on the piano, and the impresario suggested that he conduct the opera. Mancinelli accepted; the performance went magnificently, and that date . . . represented the beginning of a series of triumphs."[39] On his return to Rome he became assistant conductor to Usiglio at the Teatro Apollo. The young musician was not only talented, however, but a gifted intriguer. By the following year, he had not only caught Giulio Ricordi's eye, but maneuvered both Usiglio and the former music director, Eugenio Terziani, out of the way in order to become conductor and music director of the Apollo, one of Rome's two principal opera houses, at a salary of 4000 lire for the season. He was twenty-seven years old.

Mancinelli and his younger contemporaries all achieved substantial recognition as conductors at an early age. Toscanini made his conducting debut at nineteen, and reached the pinnacle of the profession as music director of La Scala at thirty-one. Edoardo Mascheroni, who conducted Verdi's *Macbeth* and *Un ballo in maschera* in Brescia at the age of twenty, became principal conductor at Rome's Teatro Costanzi in 1885 at twenty-six. When he moved on, three years later, he was replaced by the thirty-year-old Leopoldo Mugnone.[40] While there is no question that these young men were talented, their rapid rise was attributable more to the fact that theirs was a new profession, for which the increasing complexity of the operatic scores being performed had created a new demand. The field was clear. With few exceptions, such as the faltering Terziani at the Apollo, there were no established older conductors in Italy that might resist and only grudgingly give way to the younger generation.

It was not only the composers who realized, as Mariani writes, that "the outcome of their works had come to depend not only on the singers, but also on the preparation and the conducting,"[41] but the all-powerful publishers. Both Ricordi and Sonzogno realized the importance of having capable conductors on hand to perform not only the newest works of their

house composers, but also the complex works of composers such as Meyerbeer, Massenet, and above all, Wagner that made up a growing part of the
Italian repertory. Ricordi cultivated both Mancinelli and Mascheroni, to
whom he entrusted the prima of Verdi's *Falstaff,* while Sonzogno did the
same with Mugnone, retaining him in 1888 as the firm's house conductor.

The tradition that composers led the first performances of their works,
however, was still alive, and all of the leading composers of the time except
for Puccini did so at one time or another. With the boundaries between the
roles of the conductor and the composer still imprecisely defined, this tradition could lead to conflict, particularly when both the composer and the
conductor were famously volatile personalities. In 1892, when Toscanini
was conducting at Rome's Costanzi, Mascagni sought to exercise his composer's prerogative to conduct the first three Rome performances of his
new opera *I Rantzau.* Toscanini, who had a modern rather than a traditional sense of his prerogatives as a conductor, objected strenuously. He
withdrew entirely from the production, venting his displeasure in an open
letter to *La Tribuna,* writing that "Mascagni wanted to keep for himself the
honor of the first three performances. . . . I, on my part, beg him to take on
the remaining ones as well."[42] At the time, Mascagni was twenty-eight and
Toscanini twenty-five years old.

An even more acrimonious conflict erupted between Mascagni and
Mascheroni six years later, over the premiere of *Iris.* Mascagni had objected strongly to Ricordi's decision to hire Mascheroni, writing the publisher resentfully in the summer of 1898:

> I won't hide from you that I learned of his hiring with some sadness, consid-
> ering that in Milan . . . I let you know that Mascheroni is no Saint in my cal-
> endar; Mascheroni screwed me [*me ne fece una grossa*] when he conducted
> the Barcelona premiere of *Cavalleria* . . . making a fool of my music and
> myself . . . *Iris* is exceptionally difficult to pull together, and above all, to in-
> terpret: I do not believe that Maestro Mascheroni is capable of understand-
> ing it. . . . Finally, from the standpoint of the publisher, I do not understand
> the point of hiring a conductor who up to now has been going around
> spreading slurs about my opera, which he is scheduled to conduct only a few
> months from now.[43]

When rehearsals began, Mascagni was constantly on the scene, making
changes and criticizing Mascheroni's work. After two weeks of rehearsal,
Illica, cast in the ill-fitting role of peacemaker, write Giulio Ricordi in
desperation: "The moment one incident is over, another begins, and these

incidents are far from the usual cases of nerves, bad tempers, and gossiping. Everything is completely insane here. . . . Tito [Ricordi] has lost six kilos, and I am nearly worn out from running from one person to another, placating this one, calming down that one. . . . If I had to give you my judgment, I would say that *Iris* is fit only for the madhouse.[44] Ricordi rushed to Rome, but it was too late to repair matters between Mascagni and Mascheroni. On November 12, after one last fight, Mascheroni put down his baton — according to another version, he snapped it into pieces and threw them at the composer — and stormed out of the theater. Returning to his lodgings, he packed quickly, and left Rome. The following day, an open letter from Mascheroni appeared in *La Tribuna*, followed by an equally tart response from the composer.[45] When *Iris* appeared on November 22, Mascagni was on the podium. For the Milan premiere of *Iris* the following January, which was to be conducted by Toscanini, Ricordi took the drastic step of barring Mascagni from La Scala for both the rehearsals and the first performance. Although Mascagni bombarded Ricordi with petulant letters from Livorno, the publisher ignored them, and the performance went off without overt conflict or difficulty.

Puccini shared Mascagni's reservations about Mascheroni. Many years later, he wrote Tito Ricordi in a tone reminiscent of Mascagni's letter to Tito's father: "Is it true that *Fanciulla* is being done in Barcelona soon? And that Mascheroni is conducting? Be careful, because he has never done the opera, and I remember a *Bohème* in Rome, what tempi. . . . You must arrange to send someone to help him. With Mascheroni alone, it is a disaster."[46]

Many of this group of conductors were also composers. Mancinelli received favorable notice for his works, notably his 1906 opera *Ero e Leandro*, which was performed not only in a number of Italian opera houses, but also in London's Covent Garden and at the Metropolitan Opera. Mancinelli's composing, however, was a sideline to his conducting. Mascagni, who was a major presence throughout Europe as both a symphonic and operatic composer from the mid-1890s through the 1930s, was the only Italian musician to combine two such full-time careers successfully. Conducting, indeed, became an economic necessity for Mascagni given his expensive lifestyle, particularly during the many periods when he was either in conflict with his publishers, or when they (as with the Casa Sonzogno in the second decade of the twentieth century) were in financial difficulty and paying royalties irregularly or not at all. Leoncavallo, who suffered from chronic financial difficulties during the last decade of his life, wrote a friend late in 1914 that "Mascagni is lucky he's a conductor — otherwise he would be in the same financial situation that I'm in."[47]

Important as conductors were becoming, in the 1890s they were not yet stellar figures comparable to the important singers and a few notable composers. Mancinelli's salary of 4000 lire as principal conductor at the Apollo was at most three times the salary of a member of his orchestra, while orchestra members had far greater opportunities to supplement their salary with teaching and freelance work.[48] Toscanini's salary when first hired as music director of La Scala in 1898 was 12,000 lire for the season — a substantial salary for six months' work by conventional middle-class standards, but far less than the star singers in his company were paid. By the 1902–1903 season, his resentment of La Scala's refusal to raise his salary to a level he considered appropriate contributed to his sudden and unexpected departure from the theater at the end of that season.[49] As time went on, the chance of greater remuneration drove nearly all of Italy's most distinguished conductors to spend more and more of their time conducting abroad. Between 1886 and 1905 Luigi Mancinelli was a virtual exile from his homeland, conducting largely in Spain, Great Britain, and the United States, returning to Italy for only four short seasons over twenty years.[50]

It was Toscanini who, by sheer force of personality as much as talent, changed the status of the conductor in Italy. While his achievement was considerable, to write, as one scholar does, that "it was Toscanini who brought into the mainstream of Italian opera the principles . . . that opera was a musical form . . . and that what the composer has written is what should be performed," is an egregious overstatement.[51] Toscanini did not spring from nowhere, but built on the achievements of a generation of conductors, from Mariani and Faccio to Mancinelli. All of these conductors certainly sought to be faithful to the composers' intentions, and did so with considerable competence and dedication. At the same time, there is no question that Toscanini raised the standard of performance to a higher level, significantly insisting that the same high standard should be maintained not only for the premieres and the "important" operas, but for an entire season, and that a chestnut like *Trovatore* was worthy of the same respect and careful preparation as a *Falstaff* or *Meistersinger*.

Toscanini was driven by unshakable self-confidence and absolute conviction. In an unprecedented gesture, he cancelled an entire La Scala production of *Norma* during the dress rehearsal, because he decided that the singer of the title role, the well-known soprano Ines de Frate, was not capable of performing the part to his satisfaction. When the La Scala board, appalled by the lost income, as well as the potential litigation and bad publicity, suggested that the performance go forward under another man's baton, he replied icily that "he had personal responsibility for the entire organization, and could not therefore permit, even in an emergency, a performance that he considered unworthy of the dignity of La Scala."[52]

Toscanini's determination that the singers would sing their roles as he, not they, saw fit, was a dramatic departure. Even highly respected conductors tended to allow star singers to have their way; Carelli may have consulted Boito about her interpretation of Margherita at the Costanzi, but does not appear to have consulted Mugnone. Similarly, Titta Ruffo describes his battle with Mancinelli over his interpretation of the title role in Thomas's *Hamlet*. Finally, "at the end of my tirade Mancinelli exclaimed, in an unexpectedly soft Roman accent, 'Know what I've got to say to you, my son? Do as you please. You'll answer to your public. I wash my hands of it.'"[53] It is impossible to imagine Toscanini ever saying anything similar to a singer, however prominent; it is equally impossible to imagine any singer haranguing Toscanini as Ruffo did Mancinelli.

Toscanini drove his musicians ruthlessly, as described by the conductor Tullio Serafin, who played viola under him at La Scala: "Against . . . laxity, laziness, inattentiveness, and false tradition, Toscanini fought like a lion. He was after one thing only: respect for art. But in his anxiety to get it, or rather to force it to happen, he exercised no self-control: he shouted, imprecated, even insulted. . . . his impatience made him go too far." Yet the force of his charisma was such that, as Serafin adds, "A special pride, a point of honor, a sort of 'esprit de corps' existed among La Scala's personnel from that time on."[54]

His conducting, although widely acclaimed, was not always received without reservations. Giulio Ricordi, in a famously scathing review of Toscanini's revival of *Falstaff*, wrote: "It is undeniable that rigidity was characteristic of last Saturday's interpretation . . . the orchestra, precise to a fault, lacked those delicate shades, that sweetness of sound, that elasticity of movement, that are all essential qualities of the Italian orchestra. . . . [W]e might say that the overall effect of sounds and coloring, rather than the effect produced by a masterly hand on the piano, was rather that of a gigantic mechanical piano!"[55] Similarly, a number of the reviewers of *Tosca*'s Milan debut under Toscanini compared it unfavorably to Mugnone's conducting at the opera's premiere in Rome a few months earlier, with one concluding that "for me, Mugnone is the greatest [Italian] conductor; he has fire and spirit, and no one can bring his élan [*slancio*] to the passionate works of our composers."[56] Two years earlier, Mascagni had written Ricordi that "Toscanini is a fine conductor, accurate, precise to a fault, but a bit hard, angular, and [the sound] of his orchestra never has that elasticity which for me is essential to music."[57] Notably, the most frequent criticism of Mascagni's conducting was the opposite, his tendency to linger over particular passages, shaping them in ways that, however beautiful in themselves, detracted from the larger continuity of the work.

Needless to say, it will never be possible to reach a firm conclusion with respect to the merits of these comments. It is hard enough to reconstruct isolated snippets of singers' repertory from early-twentieth-century recordings; to reconstruct the sound and texture of a Toscanini performance of the time, and compare it to one by Mascagni, or by any of their contemporaries such as Mancinelli or Mugnone, is clearly impossible.

Toscanini's growing reputation, however, had as much to do with his persona as with his performances. His instructions that the house lights be doused and that women remove their hats during performances were part and parcel with the shouting matches, tantrums, and thrown batons, all of which unquestionably reflected the seriousness with which he took operatic performance. Even more, they built his image as a selfless, if highhanded, avatar of art: one can only speculate on the extent to which Toscanini was consciously seeking to construct a particular image for himself, not only for personal aggrandizement, it must be added, but in the interest of his art.

Whatever legitimate criticisms can be made of his conducting, there is no doubt that Toscanini was a great conductor. His importance, however, in the Italian opera world at the beginning of the twentieth century, lies even more in what he symbolized, and what that in turn meant for the still-emerging role of the conductor. He offered a generation of Italians a vision of way of performing opera entirely devoted to the search for beauty, shorn of the web of small compromises and adjustments that were typical of the operatic life of their time; in that vision, the role of the conductor was that of a sort of secular priest, responsible for marshalling the talents and energies of all those involved to that end. To the extent that he was able to play that role, he was unique in his world.

Staging and the disposizione scenica

Almost all writing on the history of opera concerns itself with the music, either as written by the composer or as performed by the various singers that have brought the composer's creative efforts to life. Opera is also, however, and has been from its earliest days, *theater*, a dimension of its history that has been given far less attention, at least until recent years.[58] It is difficult to reconstruct the appearance and movement of an operatic production from a bygone era — far more difficult than to reconstruct the notes of the music that were performed. A further difficulty is posed by our inability to assign clear responsibility for the staging of opera, as we can for the music or its performance.

The role of the stage director as a distinct position or profession in the Italian opera house — let alone as a creative artist in his or her own right — did not come into being until after World War I, or by a stricter definition, even until the 1950s. Up to that point, the responsibility for staging operas had always devolved on an individual whose principal duties associated with the performance were either literary or musical. Indeed, the contemporary idea of *Regieoper* or *Regietheater*, opera in which the stage director drives all aspects of the production according to his or her conception of the work, would have been unthinkable to anyone involved with opera in the eighteenth or nineteenth century.

During the eighteenth-century heyday of the librettist, staging was often the responsibility of the *poeta del teatro* (theater poet), a versifier or librettist who was employed by the theater to "rewrite and add recitatives and arias at the request of the singers, but also to coordinate the scenic realization of the performances."[59] As Vienna's theater poet, Metastasio staged the operas written to his libretti, while Carlo Goldoni practiced the same profession in the 1730s and 1740s at various theaters in Venice. The theater poet's work, however, most probably had less to do with direction in the modern sense as it did with stage management, as suggested by the lines spoken by a theater poet in Goldoni's comedy *L'impresario delle Smirne*:

> . . . I teach the musicians their movements,
> And direct the stage, and run behind the wings,
> To warn the leading lady that it's almost time she sings.
> I deal with extras and whistle as a cue
> To advise all concerned that a change of scene is due.[60]

The position of theater poet, with responsibility for staging, continued to exist at many opera houses well into the nineteenth century. Francesco Maria Piave, Verdi's librettist, who was theater poet at La Scala in the 1860s, described his duties in anticipation of taking up the position: "Hold the rehearsals necessary to stage the entire opera . . . assisted, as needed by the *maestro al cembalo* [coach]. Partial rehearsals will be held with the individual artists, explaining to them the import of the action and the way of representing it to the spectators, then rehearsing with the *masse* [chorus and extras]; finally, with everyone together."[61] As the status of the librettist declined, the role of the theater poet gradually diminished. By midcentury, only the most important theaters employed poets. Elsewhere, staging was more likely to be a part of the duties of the *concertatore*, something to be done as an adjunct to the musical preparation of the production.

With the rise of the conductor, the job of staging operas became the conductor's responsibility. The major conductors of the 1880s and 1890s, from Faccio through Toscanini, all took responsibility for the scenic and dramatic as well as the musical dimensions of the operas they conducted. The conductor was expected to be a jack-of-all-trades, as Ricordi's magazine *Ars et Labor* described Mascagni on his arrival as music director of the Costanzi theater in 1909: "Here is Mascagni in his brand-new role as administrator, conductor, stage director, etc., etc. . . . ; here is Mascagni on stage, supervising the work of renovating the theater; therefore, also as architect, electrician, engineer."[62] Toscanini was notable for the control he exercised over every aspect of La Scala's productions, and the detail with which he made his wishes known. Toti dal Monte, a prominent singer of the second and third decades of the twentieth century, described how Toscanini taught Galeffi, the Rigoletto in a 1922 production, "his entire third act scene, transforming himself into Rigoletto, demonstrating every gesture, every expression, every spoken word, every anguished outburst of wrath."[63]

A singular exception to the picture described above applied when a new opera was making its debut, when it was customary that the composer would step in, take responsibility for preparing the opera both musically and dramatically, and often conduct the first performance himself. As a rule, the composer was assisted in his task by the librettist, who was often in charge of the staging. Although Verdi rarely chose to conduct the premieres of his operas, he was intimately involved in their preparation. He began preparations for staging *Falstaff* four months before the first performance, working with models of the sets and props that were delivered to his home in Sant'Agata, subsequently beginning piano rehearsals with the principals in Genoa.[64] For a month before the work's debut on February 7, he spent nearly every waking moment at La Scala, supervising all aspects of the production, with Ricordi, Boito, Mascheroni, and the set and costume designer Hohenstein, at his side. To Verdi, no arbitrary division existed between the musical and dramatic sides of his opera; both were totally interwoven in his vision of his opera. Although Hepokoski accurately writes, "Verdi wished the gestures to arise spontaneously from an understanding of the words and music," the composer was careful to provide detailed guidance toward that end.[65]

In the right hands, with enough expenditure of time and money, the Italian system could result in performances that were dramatically as well as vocally compelling. Nonetheless, it was fundamentally flawed. As Hepokoski writes, apropos of *Otello*, "by 1887 the staging of an opera — in particular the premiere of a towering masterpiece — had become a vexedly complex operation, far beyond the control of any single individual."[66] Few conductors possessed Toscanini's power and authority; even Toscanini lacked the time and energy to ensure that every production at La Scala was up to his high standards. Elsewhere, the situation was often worse, particularly with respect to the standard operas that made up the backbone of the repertory. Performances were staged with few rehearsals, allowing singers to rely on a handful of stock gestures, in the hopes — presumably realized some of the time — that the music would carry the drama. One account describes how, at La Scala before the days of Toscanini, one might see "a love duet sung from opposite ends of the stage, because the tenor was used to singing that scene downstage right and the soprano, unfortunately, downstage left."[67] To at least some powerful Italian musicians, it was an unacceptable state of affairs.

An attempt at a solution was broached by Verdi, who proposed in 1855 to Ricordi that the publisher adopt the French practice of publishing what were known in France as *Livrets de mise-en-scène* (staging books), which would provide impresarios and others involved in the opera industry with detailed, specific instructions on the dramatic presentation of his operas. These *Livrets* had come into use in Paris at the beginning of the eighteenth century, and by the 1830s were available for some two hundred or more grand operas and opéras comiques.[68] Such a staging book had been prepared by Louis Paliati, the regisseur of the Paris Opéra, for the premiere of Verdi's *Les Vêpres siciliennes*, prompting Verdi to remark to Piave that armed with Paliati's staging book, a child could mount *Les Vêpres*.[69]

Ricordi followed Verdi's advice. Over the next roughly thirty years, such books entitled *Disposizioni sceniche* — which can be roughly translated as "staging arrangements" — were published for all of Verdi's operas from *I vespri siciliani* to *Otello*, as well as for other important operas, such as those of Puccini, controlled by the Casa Ricordi. Sonzogno followed Ricordi's lead, and began issuing staging books for his operas in the 1890s, translating the French term for his products into Italian: *Messa in iscena* (or *scena*).[70]

Depending on the length and complexity of the opera, production books could be from forty to fifty pages to well over one hundred pages long. Typically, they contained detailed specifications for the sets, props, and costumes that were to be used; the staging book for *Fedora* also contained detailed descriptions of the wigs, shoes, jewelry, and flowers to be worn or held by the chorus and extras. The *Aida* staging book added a series of small drawings showing how the extras must hold their axes and standards in the second-act procession.[71] The *Fedora* staging book also specified that the onstage piano for the second act must be a *"real* grand piano" and that the pianist, who performs a Chopinesque nocturne as the backdrop to the intrigue between Fedora and Loris, must be "a *real* pianist, just as the piano must be real" (emphases in original).[72] For the actor playing the pianist to fake the performance, while the nocturne was played by a pit pianist, was not acceptable. In the case of a similar piano played by the little girl Totò in the third act of Leoncavallo's *Zazà*, however, the staging book was more flexible, allowing the piano to be either "real or fake," so that the little girl playing the part need not also be able to play the piano.[73] Printed in the staging book, or provided separately but in conjunction with the staging book by the publisher, were the drawings of the sets (*bozzetti*) and the drawings of the costumes for the principal characters (*figurini*).

The publishers expected the instructions to be followed to the letter, as the text of the *Aida* staging book indicates: "The stage director will not permit, under any circumstances or for any reason, any artist, member of the chorus or the ballet, etc., etc. to alter in the slightest degree the costumes, the wigs, the jewelry, all of which have been scrupulously executed according to the costume designs, which were prepared with great care, and carried out by famous artists with scrupulous historic precision."[74]

The greater part of the staging book was devoted to the actual staging of the opera, and provided instructions for the movements and gestures of the singers, chorus and extras. Some books provided a guide that followed the libretto (in italics below) line by line, as seen in this extract from Ricordi's staging book for Massenet's *Le roi de Lahore:*

On the words: *Chi mai sei tu?* (Who, then, are you?)
  Indra makes a gesture to Alim to get up, and he, with a supplicating gesture, says:
A me sorrideva la vita (Life smiled on me)
On the words: *O re dei re* (O king of kings)
  Alim prostrates himself once again in front of Indra, who responds calmly and seriously:
Suo di non giunse ancor (His day has not yet arrived)
  Alim gets up again, and takes one step forward to say:
Ma la grazia che imploro (But the mercy I beg)

Then, with great resolution, advances further exclaiming:
Dammi eterno dolor . . . (Give me eternal sorrow . . .)
General stupor at these words. The chorus and the corps de ballet should take an active part in this scene. (etc., etc.)[75]

In other cases, diagrams were provided for the use of the stage manager. The *Aida* staging book provides no fewer than 94 separate diagrams, ranging from small sketches that show how two characters are to move during a duet, to large-scale drawings showing the position of as many as 150 soloists, choristers, and extras during the second-act processional scene. The direction in which all characters, represented by small circles, squares, or diamonds, are to face is shown with tiny arrows. The scene between Aida and Amonasro in the third act contains seven separate diagrams, each one set off by words taken from the libretto. Sonzogno's staging book for *Isabeau* is similar, providing five diagrams for the third-act love duet between Isabeau and Folco, and specifying positions for more than two hundred soloists, choristers, and extras in the first-act tournament scene, laid out on a detailed bird's-eye view of the stage set.

The *Isabeau* staging book is unusual, not only in that it was prepared by Illica and Antonio Rovescalli, the stage designer, under the eyes of Mascagni himself, rather than by one or more largely anonymous functionaries in the publisher's office, but that it was prepared well before the first performance, rather than, as was the usual case, afterward. As Alberti writes, "the staging of *Isabeau* was born on a tabletop, not on stage. It was based on a clear vision of the stage, and a considered directorial plan, but it lacked the reality test of an actual staging. It was *a priori*."[76] As such, it may be seen to represent an idealized vision, perhaps, of the opera rather than a realistic guide in all respects to its performance.

This, of course, raises the tantalizing questions we cannot answer. First, to what extent were the staging books literally followed by the theaters that performed these operas? Second, what did these operas actually look like on stage? There is evidence, at least with respect to set design, that the staging books were often treated as little more than general guides — or set aside entirely at some major theaters, often with the approval of the composer or publisher.[77] Conversely, it is hard to imagine that some of the more modest theaters that staged Verdi's *Aida* or Mascagni's *Isabeau* had the financial and technical resources to follow the staging books to the letter. While Ricordi exercised his prerogatives to block productions of operas under his control because of the inadequacy of a singer, or the general incapacity of a theater's forces, I am unaware of any case in which he

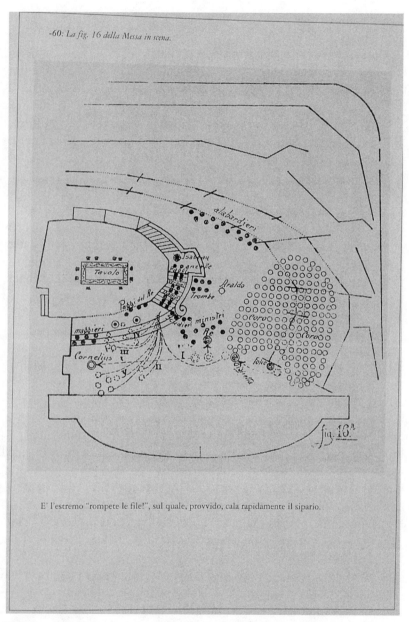

-60: La fig. 16 della Messa in scena.

E' l'estremo "rompete le file!", sul quale, provvido, cala rapidamente il sipario.

Closing scene of act 1, from the staging book for Mascagni's *Isabeau*. *(Casa Musicale Sonzogno)*

used his power to prevent a production because of inadequacies of the mise-en-scène.

Moreover, given the egos typically found in the operatic world, it is hard to imagine almost anyone responsible for a production — from the conductor or stage manager — literally staging the opera with book in hand, just as no one can imagine the typical diva passively accepting the instructions. The reaction of the soprano Rosa Raisa, who sang Francesca at the La Scala premiere of *Francesca da Rimini* in 1916, to Tito Ricordi's directorial instructions, was probably not atypical: "Tito Ricordi called me, saying that when I say '*ah tu mi svegli*' to Samaritana, he wanted me to be on the first step. Somehow this seemed a very unreasonable demand, which irritated me greatly at that moment. I answered that I was a spontaneous artist, that I sang with sincerity, not according to rules or directions, and I never knew on what step I will finish what phrase . . . With that I walked off."[78] If a soprano could react that way to the imposing head of the Casa Ricordi, she was not likely to be any more subservient to instructions read out of a book.

While drawings, paintings, and photographs of sets and costumes exist in great number, testifying to the highly realistic, three-dimensional, scenic imagery popular at least in Italy's major opera houses, far greater uncertainty surrounds the actual staging of the operas in these houses. Staging is rarely, if ever, described in detail in the operatic reviews of the time. A literal application of the instructions in the staging books, with their schematic "take one step forward, one to the side" manner, would almost certainly appear highly mechanical, not only to a modern audience, but in all probability to the audiences of the time. In the best-prepared performances, however, it is likely that the director synthesized the prescribed movements — assuming that he followed the staging book at all — into a flowing, continuous motion, much as is true of the best operatic performances today. Those, however, in all likelihood, were rare. The typical performance would probably strike modern audiences as intolerably static, only partially compensated by the grandeur of the sets and beauty of the costumes.

This does not mean that the operatic experience was not intensely dramatic. The drama, to a large extent, lay less in the ensemble than in the individual performances, particularly by those singers — of whom there were far more at the time — who invested their singing and physical being with dramatic intensity. What contemporary chronicles attest to repeatedly is the intensely *dramatic* effect of the great singers in their great roles, such as Caruso's Canio, or Bellincioni's Santuzza. A description of De Lucia as Don José in *Carmen* captures this power: "Many of his finest and most impressive moments were when he was practically doing nothing and his enormous dramatic force came from mere facial expression and an essentially dramatic presence. . . . But the picture he gave of the gradual moral deterioration and crumbling away of Don José's character under the influence of balked passion and jealousy, his ever-growing abject misery of soul, and frantic desperation, was admirably fine, powerful and artistic."[79] Another example is Emma Carelli's Margherita, in Boito's *Mefistofele*, of which Rome's *Il Messaggero* wrote: "Carelli's interpretation captured faithfully [Margherita's] personality, reaching its highest point in the jail scene. The character came across to the spectator's eyes with clear contours, precise, with everything that would could imagine to be most true and most human."[80]

We cannot tell how we would react to Carelli's Margherita or De Lucia's Don José today, but we can be sure that for the audiences of the time they were the quintessence of a dramatic as well as musical experience in the theater.

Chapter 9

Ricordi, Sonzogno, and the Power of the Publishers

The Publishing Duopoly

I f opera houses formed the physical center of the Italian operatic world, the publishers formed the economic center. In truth, their power went far beyond that: publishers dictated which operas were to be performed and which singers and conductors would perform them in the theaters of the peninsula. For all the vast reach and diversity of Italy's operatic life at the end of the nineteenth century, it was controlled by two publishing firms to a degree that today seems hard to imagine — indeed, not so much controlled by the firms as by the two energetic and bitterly competitive individuals heading those firms: Giulio Ricordi and Edoardo Sonzogno.

Ricordi and Sonzogno were vastly different personalities, each giving his firm its distinctive character. Ricordi, although younger and of a family background much the same as that of Sonzogno,[1] was a pillar of the Milanese establishment, a member of the municipal council and founder and president of the Società orchestrale del Teatro alla Scala. A professionally trained and not untalented composer in his own right, as the third generation of a family to publish music in Milan he saw himself as the upholder of a cultural tradition stretching back over nearly a century. Austere and reserved in his manner except to a handful of intimates, Ricordi's personality was reflected in the character of his firm, which was described by the distinguished critic Leone Fortis in 1894:

> The Casa Ricordi is justly proud of its long-standing artistic nobility, and of those severe and austere publishing traditions that have already lasted through three generations, preserving that . . . character intact — traditions that are today almost the motto of the family and the firm — as a result of which the publisher's freedom of movement is limited, making it seem slow-moving and late-coming . . . in the frantic race of modern competition.[2]

Giulio Ricordi *(Ricordi Archive)*

By contrast, Edoardo Sonzogno was something of an upstart, both in the world of music and in Milan society. A bon vivant and cosmopolitan, he was a music lover rather than a musician, happier in Paris than in Milan. Despite his wealth, he was a man of the political Left, in contrast to the conservative, even reactionary Ricordi. His newspaper, *Il Secolo,* was for decades the principal voice of republican sentiment in Italy, a sounding board for the Radical Party of Felice Cavallotti, the firebrand politician, poet, and playwright known as the "bard of democracy."[3] To Fortis, Sonzogno's firm was the antithesis of Ricordi's:

> The Casa Sonzogno, as a music publisher, has no genealogy, no history —...
> —it lacks the *impediments* [emphasis in original] imposed by tradition —
> and in its place it has the self-assurance of its youth — that sometimes looks

A luncheon at Edoardo Sonzogno's Milan townhouse in 1906. Among those present, Boito, Mascagni, Giordano, Cilèa, and Sonzogno's two nephews Lorenzo and Riccardo. *(Casa Musicale Sonzogno)*

like boasting or imprudence — with which it confronts the hardest risks, often going from audacity to recklessness. . . . It is not for me to judge the direction that the Casa Sonzogno takes with its brave initiatives, its bold investments, its high-risk attempts. . . . But even this old curmudgeon [*brontolone*] can do no less than recognize that the Casa Sonzogno has shocked the young art of music out of the torpor of depression into which it had been abandoned.[4]

Before Sonzogno's arrival on the scene, Ricordi's principal rival had been the firm founded in 1825 by Francesco Lucca, a former Ricordi employee. After Lucca's death in 1872, the firm become a serious competitor to Ricordi under the management of his capable widow Giovannina,[5] who actively promoted the works of Wagner, for which she owned the Italian rights, and nurtured young talents like Catalani. In 1888, however, in her midseventies and lacking an heir, Giovannina Lucca retired, selling the business to Ricordi for the considerable sum of 1,500,000 lire.[6]

The power of the publishers rested in their control of the operatic repertory, which they obtained through their contracts with composers. This control reflected, in turn, a gradual transformation of the opera industry during the nineteenth century from one focused entirely on novelty to one in which an operatic repertory — and thus a growing market for scores and parts for operas that had already been performed elsewhere — was coming into being. An important part of this transformation was the adoption of copyright law, a fitful process in Italy that was not fully resolved until 1882.

In the first half of the nineteenth century it was customary for an impresario to commission an opera from a composer for a particular season at a particular opera house, and only afterward, if ever, for the rights to be assigned to a publisher and the score published. By the 1890s the practice had been reversed, with dramatic implications for both publishers and impresarios. The publisher, as we have already seen, now contracted directly with the composer, before the time and place of the first performance had been determined, or even given much consideration — indeed, in the case of well-established composers, before the opera had even been written. Once that contract had been entered into, the opera could not be performed — nor for that matter, could any selection from the opera be performed — without the permission of the publisher who held the rights to the opera.

Publishers were zealous guardians of their authority, as a 1901 court case illustrates. In a not unusual practice, the management of a Bologna theater announced that at the end of a performance the tenor Alessandro Bonci would sing a few songs, accompanied by the conductor at the piano. Among the "songs" Bonci sang, however, were arias from *La bohème* and *Rigoletto*, both operas being the property of the Casa Ricordi. When Ricordi found out, he immediately brought suit against not only the impresario, but the tenor and the pianist, all three of whom were hauled into police court, and fined 150 lire each. The not insubstantial fines were subsequently upheld on appeal by the Bologna district court. While some took issue with the court's decision to fine the singer and the pianist, rather than only the impresario, the impropriety of the singer's choice of repertoire, and Ricordi's right — even duty — to enforce his rights, were not challenged.[7]

Their control of a hundred years' worth of operatic repertory meant that it was effectively impossible to break the Ricordi/Sonzogno duopoly. In 1890, an Argentine millionaire named Arturo Demarchi attempted to do just that, buying Milan's Alhambra Theater, publishing a musical magazine in competition with Ricordi's *Gazzetta musicale di Milano* and Sonzogno's *Teatro illustrato*, and buying the rights to whatever few operas had somehow been overlooked by Ricordi and Sonzogno. He was unable to make headway against the duopoly, and committed suicide in 1899, after his firm had gone into bankruptcy.[8] An exploratory proposal in 1901 and 1902 by Mascagni to organize a sort of composers' publishing cooperative, with the financial backing of the wealthy Sicilian industrialist Florio, was never seriously pursued.[9]

Ricordi owned the rights to nearly all of the traditional Italian repertory, including the works of Rossini, Bellini, Donizetti, and Verdi; and through Lucca, the Italian rights to Wagner's operas. Sonzogno, beginning in 1874, had acquired the Italian rights to the works of virtually the entire body of contemporary French composers, including Bizet, Massenet, and Thomas.[10] Among the emerging composers of the 1880s and 1890s, Puccini was the prize of Ricordi's "stable," which also included Franchetti as well as Catalani, whom he had inherited from Lucca. Sonzogno, who was far more aggressive in seeking out younger composers, had nearly the entire *giovane scuola* under contract, including Mascagni, Leoncavallo, Giordano, Cilèa and a number of lesser-known figures such as Orefice and Samara.

Through their control of the repertory, the publishers were in a position to control almost everything that took place in the opera houses. As Roselli writes, "publishers decided where operas were to be done, controlled casting, supplied set and costume designs, and often directed the production, if not in person then through the issue of detailed production books."[11] Contracts between publishers and impresarios provided, in return for renting the impresario the score and parts for the opera, for approval of casts by the publisher, as well as clauses binding the impresario not to make cuts or add interpolations to the opera, and to strictly follow the instructions of the detailed *disposizioni sceniche* provided by the publisher. Thus, Ricordi could indignantly telegraph the impresario of Rome's Teatro Argentina in 1896: "*Manon* outcome thoroughly displeasing. You must not go forward with Beduschi ill as you are obligated to provide a proper company, not singers who are hoarse or blockheads [*salami*]. If management cannot provide what is needed to produce *Manon* or prepare *Bohème* I will take back the score." When the soprano Eugenia Burzio was unavailable for the role of Minnie, Ricordi forced a delay in the La Scala premiere of Puccini's *La fanciulla del West* in 1912.[12]

The publishers' control went beyond individual operas to cover the entire seasons at many, even most, Italian opera houses. It is not clear when the practice formally began, but by the 1890s it was common for Ricordi, as a condition imposed on impresarios seeking to perform operas under his control, to prohibit them from putting on any operas rented from Sonzogno. Because Ricordi controlled the Verdi operas that formed the heart of the Italian repertory, as well as the inexpensive Rossini and Donizetti operas that filled up much of the rest of the season, he was in a far stronger position to impose this condition, at least during the early years of the Ricordi/Sonzogno rivalry, than his competitor. Later, once the body of *giovane scuola* operas controlled by Sonzogno had reached a certain critical mass, that publisher appears to have followed suit; a review of the 1907–1908 season across the peninsula shows that many houses, including those in cities such as Bari, Cagliari, Cremona, Genoa, Messina, and Pavia, were all presenting seasons made up entirely of Sonzogno's operas.[13] While demands for exclusivity were imposed more strictly on theaters in smaller cities rather than on the *teatri massimi*, the major theaters were not immune; despite their popularity elsewhere in Italy, not a single opera from Sonzogno's "stable" appeared at La Scala between 1892 and 1894 or at the Costanzi between 1895 and 1899.

Rental fees for scores and parts varied widely, and often idiosyncratically. As a general rule, new operas were more expensive than older ones, major houses were charged higher rentals than smaller or more modest theaters, and rentals were higher for the *carnevale–quaresima* season than for the "lesser" seasons. While standard operas by Verdi or Donizetti might be rented to small provincial theaters for as little as 200 or 300 lire, a new opera by a major composer might command a rental fee that could range from 6000 to well over 10,000 lire. Naples' San Carlo paid 11,000 lire to present Giordano's 1903 much-awaited *Siberia*, his first opera since *Fedora*, three months after its La Scala debut.[14] These fees, however, were highly negotiable; Ricordi regularly reduced his fees, either to reward a favored impresario, to induce the impresario to enter into an exclusivity agreement, or simply to ensure that the opera was performed. At times, however, he could take the opposite approach, and raise the rental fee in order that an opera *not* be performed. In 1901, Ricordi set a fee of 30,000 lire to Turin's Regio for the rental of Wagner's *Ring*, nearly double the price quoted a year earlier, explaining that he considered it "inappropriate, in the year of Verdi's death, to put on a Wagner cycle, rather than properly honoring the Italian composer."[15]

The publishers' power did not do away with the impresario's role. Impresarios were still needed to deal with singers, municipalities, and the thousand details of putting on opera seasons, as well as to assume such financial risk as was not taken up by the municipality and the boxholders. They were no longer free agents, however, but were thoroughly subordinated to the publishers. Ricordi created a "stable" of impresarios (such as Piontelli), whom he controlled and used as his de facto agents. Sonzogno, while dealing with impresarios wherever he could, realized that as the upstart challenging Ricordi's de facto monopoly, he would have to engage directly in operatic production in order to ensure that his operas saw the light of day.[16] He became his own impresario, taking on the responsibility himself, or placing responsibility in the hands of trusted subordinates like Nicola Daspuro. Beginning modestly in 1875 with a season of light opera and operetta at Milan's small Santa Radegonda theater, between 1883 and 1897 Sonzogno presented one or more seasons in nearly every major Italian city, often simultaneously presenting operas in two or three different theaters across the peninsula. In 1893 he presented a *carnevale–quaresima* season at the Dal Verme, a *quaresima* season at La Fenice in Venice, a spring season at the Politeama Rossetti in Trieste, and a fall season at Milan's Carcano theater. After opening his Teatro Lirico in 1894, his activity as an impresario elsewhere declined sharply, but not before presenting two seasons, in 1895 and 1896, at La Scala, still the ultimate prize for an impresario.[17]

La Scala had been a bone of contention between Ricordi and Sonzogno since 1890. For the most part, during the 1880s, La Scala operated as an adjunct of the Casa Ricordi. Although Ricordi would permit the theater's impresarios to mount the occasional opera from Sonzogno's list, such as Bizet's *Carmen*, which opened the 1886 season, or the works of Lucca's protégé Catalani, these were relatively rare. The La Scala repertory was heavy with works by Verdi and Donizetti, while the world outside Italy was largely represented by the operas of Meyerbeer and Halévy's *La juive*. Except for the disastrous 1873 production of *Lohengrin*, not one Wagner opera appeared at La Scala until 1888, after Giovannina Lucca had sold her firm, and the Italian rights to Wagner's operas, to Ricordi.

In 1891, in order to ensure a place for *Cavalleria rusticana* in the La Scala repertory, Sonzogno took the drastic step of buying the right to select the season's operas from the house's impresarios, the Corti brothers. Although *Cavalleria*, which was given twenty-three performances, was successful, the rest of the season, made up entirely of operas owned by Sonzogno, was not. A production of Gluck's *Orfeo e Euridice* and the premiere of Samara's *Lionella* were both fiascos. Both were withdrawn after a single performance, and the former replaced by a hastily mounted production of *Lohengrin*.[18]

Having launched *Cavalleria* in Milan, Sonzogno withdrew at the end of the 1891 season. Ricordi, back in control through his henchman Piontelli, had his revenge. During the next three seasons, not one opera controlled by Sonzogno appeared on the La Scala boards. When Piontelli's contract ended, at the end of the 1894 season, Sonzogno presented himself as his replacement, offering to produce the season for substantially less than the customary municipal subsidy, and, moreover, present more operas than the usual five or six.[19] Although his other conditions, which included giving him the right to operate without interference or supervision, were the source of some objections, the municipality named Sonzogno impresario for the following three years.[20]

During the next two years, Sonzogno presented what can only be characterized as a thoroughly bizarre repertory. The La Scala audience was accustomed to a solid diet of Italian classics leavened with the works of a few younger Italian composers, along with regular productions of Meyerbeer, and more recently Wagner. With Ricordi refusing to make any of his operas available to La Scala under Sonzogno's management,[21] operagoers were given a massive dose of contemporary French opera, including works by Massenet, Bizet, Saint-Saëns, and a few lesser lights; Italy was represented only by Mascagni's three most recent operas and single works by Leoncavallo and Giordano. As the Casa Sonzogno house history comments, with considerable understatement, "the level of appreciation on the public's part did not correspond to [Sonzogno]'s great productive effort."[22] Saint-Saëns' *Samson et Dalila* was popular, but was no novelty, while Mascagni's *Guglielmo Ratcliff* was no more than a succès d'estime. Most of the other productions, including Leoncavallo's Renaissance epic *I Medici* and productions of Massenet's *Manon* and *La Navarraise*, were outright failures. The only truly notable success of Sonzogno's two years at the helm of La Scala was his final production, the premiere of Giordano's *Andrea Chénier*.

Sonzogno's seasons, which often featured prominent singers in elaborate productions, were a showcase for the operas of his "stable" more than a business venture. Sonzogno subsidized them heavily from his nonmusical ventures, spending 300,000 lire out of his pocket for the 1890 season at Rome's Costanzi and Argentina theaters, and another 500,000 for his theatrical ventures in Florence, Rome, Venice, and Paris the year before. As one account of his ventures concluded, "Sonzogno, bless him, is not afraid of spending money, because he's a millionaire."[23]

The publishing firms were simultaneously personal fiefdoms and modern industrial enterprises. Ricordi's factory, built in 1884, covered an acre of ground near the heart of Milan; centrally heated and lit by electricity generated by its own plant, it employed more than two hundred workers, and was fitted out with the most modern printing technology available anywhere in Europe. While Giulio Ricordi was a benevolent employer, offering his workers retirement and other benefits rare at the time, he was in other respects typical of his class. When the typesetters in his plant went on strike in 1895, he fired the workers and permanently shut down the typography department rather than negotiate with them.[24] Sonzogno went Ricordi one better, and bought a paper mill on the shores of Lake Orta, creating a fully integrated industrial system under his control from the raw material to the finished product.[25]

Publishers and their Composers

Composers played little part in this process, other than being called upon at the publisher's discretion to conduct their operas, or assist in their staging or preparation. While publishers could, when they chose, ensure adequate performances of the operas they controlled, the composer had no recourse if the publisher chose not to do so; Cilèa's experience with the premiere of L'Arlesiana was not unusual: "From a series of small episodes and ambiguous comments I quickly realized the miserable effort that was being made with my work, to which few resources were being devoted, and which was going to be put on quickly and on the cheap. The female roles were all given, indeed, to three beginners: the protagonist a certain Trassy, a young American, with a miserable voice and grotesque pronunciation."[26] Cilèa's only recourse was to write a half-indignant, half-pleading letter to Sonzogno: "Does it seem to you, in good conscience, that L'Arlesiana and I could be content with the way we have been treated? I will not rebel against you, because that is something I do not know how to do, but I am dejected by the spectacle of seeing three years of my hard, conscientious, work destroyed."[27] Sonzogno's response was to demand that the opera be cut from four to three acts, which the unhappy but obedient Cilèa subsequently did without further complaint.

Ricordi could be even more arbitrary. While going to extraordinary lengths to accommodate Puccini, and ensure that his operas were performed as often as possible under the most auspicious circumstances, he could allow the completed manuscripts of Catalani's Loreley and Leoncav-

Tito Ricordi and Puccini in a motorboat. *(Ricordi Archive)*

allo's *I Medici* to languish for years after inheriting the one, and commissioning the other. As a well-informed French observer commented in 1904, "it would appear that, Verdi having died, the House of Ricordi, having chosen Puccini, set aside more or less systematically everything that was not signed by that composer."[28]

Under the standard contract, the composer relinquished *all* of his rights under law to the publisher: "The Composer . . . as of this moment cedes, sells and transfers to the Publisher the full, absolute, universal and exclusive property of his opera; and thus for all countries, including in this cession all of the rights of performance, execution, printing, translation, publication and reduction in all forms, as specific and protected by all laws in effect and all international conventions."[29] In return for ceding all rights to his opera, a composer with recognized box office power typically received a cash payment of 20,000 to 50,000 lire, and royalties in the form of a percentage of the rentals of the opera, generally 30 percent. Except where a contract made specific provision to the contrary, the composer did not share in any of the proceeds from the works sold by the publisher, such as the arrangements of the score and its more popular selections for various instrumental combinations. The term of royalties also varied; while in later years, Puccini's royalties lasted for the duration of the copyright period, his contract for *Edgar* provided that he would receive 30 percent of the rental income only for the first eight years after the work's premiere.[30] Mascagni's initial contracts with Sonzogno specified the composer would be entitled to 30 percent of the opera's rental income for twenty years.[31]

The most highly paid librettists received both an initial fee and royalties on the rentals of the opera, both of which were customarily 10 percent or less of the composer's fee and royalties; Luigi Illica received a cash payment of 3000 lire and 3 percent of the rental fees for his libretto for Mascagni's *Le Maschere*.[32] Because both Illica and Giacosa demanded a full librettist's share of 3 percent for their work on *Tosca*, Puccini received a cash advance of 40,000 lire but only 28 percent of the rental income to reflect the fact that Ricordi was paying a double librettist's fee.[33] This agreement was unusual, reflecting the exceptional value placed on both Illica's and Giacosa's contributions. More ordinary librettists received only a one-time fee, usually on completion, with no continuing share in the income from the finished product, with Ricordi typically paying 500 lire an act, or 1500 lire for a three-act opera.[34] At the other extreme, the famous writer Gabriele D'Annunzio, whose financial needs were as great as his fame, demanded and usually received 25,000 lire in advance for a libretto, although Tito Ricordi convinced him to accept 20,000 to make *Francesca da Rimini* available to Zandonai.

Their contracts could make even a moderately successful composer a wealthy man by contemporary standards. The earnings over five years from the royalties from a single opera receiving ten performances a year, along with a representative cash payment of 30,000 lire, would enable a composer to earn 24,000 lire per year, or roughly ten times a typical middle-class salary.[35] Puccini, Mascagni, and Giordano all earned far more than that amount. Whether the composer would actually receive all of the funds to which he was entitled, however, was another matter. Mascagni found that Sonzogno, in addition to routinely subtracting a 5 percent "commission" not provided for in the contract, frequently delayed quarterly payments, failed to include all of the performances for which royalties were due, and on at least one occasion withheld payment entirely in an effort to coerce the composer into postponing delivery on an opera Mascagni owed his rival Ricordi.[36]

Mascagni's travails with his publishers began within days after *Cavalleria* had made its spectacular debut. Although Sonzogno had not yet offered him a contract for *Cavalleria*, when Mascagni was approached by Ricordi's agent, he rejected his offer out of a sense of obligation to Sonzogno. In lieu of *Cavalleria*, Mascagni signed a contract with Ricordi for his still-unfinished *Guglielmo Ratcliff*. In 1892 or 1893, under somewhat obscure circumstances, Sonzogno demanded that Mascagni retrieve the rights to *Ratcliff* from Ricordi. Ricordi agreed to relinquish the opera in return for a commitment that Mascagni would compose a new opera for the Casa Ricordi, an opera that became the 1898 *Iris*. Although a provision of Mascagni's 1894 contract with Sonzogno, covering *Ratcliff, Silvano,* and subsequent operas, clearly gave Ricordi's opera priority over operas to be written for Sonzogno after *Silvano,* Sonzogno accepted that provision with ill-concealed distaste. Over the next few years he made repeated efforts to delay or, if possible, prevent the completion of *Iris.* Meanwhile, even before *Iris* was completed, Mascagni had begun work on a new opera for Sonzogno, first known as the "commedia" and ultimately as *Le Maschere* (The masks).

Throughout the decade, Mascagni's personal relationship with Sonzogno — whom he had seen almost as a surrogate father during the years immediately after *Cavalleria,* and who was godfather to Mascagni's second son, had been deteriorating. By the time of the 1901 premiere of *Le Maschere,* which, as will be described later, was one of the most spectacular fiascos in Italian operatic history, the two men were barely on speaking terms. In the aftermath of that fiasco, Sonzogno broke off his ties with Mascagni, making it clear that he would publish no more of the composer's operas.

By 1901, *Iris* had begun to move into the repertory, and Ricordi was more than willing to add another Mascagni opera to his catalogue. He initially enlisted Giacosa to combine with Illica on Mascagni's behalf, as he had with Puccini, but Giacosa soon withdrew, under pressure to complete his work on Puccini's *Butterfly.* Illica, meanwhile, had begun work on a new libretto, a elephantine historical drama on the life of Marie Antoinette that he and Ricordi both pressed on Mascagni. Although Mascagni soon realized that the subject and its treatment were both utterly alien to his talents and needs, he was unable to convince either Illica or Ricordi to reconsider. As a result, by 1903, on his return from an ill-fated tour of the United States, he found himself with no prospect of writing an opera for either Ricordi or Sonzogno; that is, effectively unemployed and unemployable. As he summed up his situation in a 1904 article, "in Italy, the composer without a publisher does not exist, and cannot exist."[37]

This statement was literally true. Publishers had an absolute veto over every performance in every opera house in Italy. No impresario, even at the most modest theater, would dare put on an opera without the permission of the publisher who was providing him with his repertory, which permission was unlikely to be granted in the case of an experienced and recognized composer like Mascagni. The only exceptions to this rule were newcomers, young composers seeking to have their first works performed, and who were willing and able to pay a fee to the impresario and bear the entire cost of the production. Ermanno Wolf-Ferrari, who subsequently became prominent among his generation of opera composers, paid the impresario Cesari 10,000 lire to have his first opera, *Cenerentola*, performed at La Fenice in 1900.[38] Even then, as he later wrote Mascagni, "I had good relations with Ricordi at the time, so I knew that on top of what I had to pay, *propriety demanded* [emphasis in original] that Cesari ask Ricordi whether he had any reason to object (!) if [Cesari] were to present my opera in Venice."[39] Wolf-Ferrari was fortunate to have had wealthy parents and friends. Faced with a similar situation a few years later, the young Italo Montemezzi, with fewer means, raised the money to have his first opera performed through a public appeal to his Verona compatriots. Even a modest percentage of the sum required would have been out of the reach of most young Italian musicians.

Mascagni's situation changed a few years later.[40] In 1906, a chance meeting between him and Tito Ricordi, Giulio Ricordi's son, reopened communications between the composer and the Casa Ricordi; at the same time, Edoardo Sonzogno's astute nephew Lorenzo, who was playing a growing role in the firm's business, was eager to recapture the still-productive composer. Offering the composer the substantial incentive of extending his royalties for the entire length of the copyright period, with respect to both operas previously written and future operas, he soon brought Mascagni back into the fold. The composer's new contract, in addition to extending the royalties on all of the operas from *Cavalleria* to *Le Maschere*, provided a cash payment of 40,000 lire, royalties of 30 percent on rental fees, and, as a sort of bonus, royalties of 30 percent on overseas sales of printed materials.[41] Mascagni's hopes of a comfortable financial future, however, were not to be realized. Although it might have seemed as solid as ever to the outside observer, the Casa Sonzogno was already badly overextended financially. Within less than a decade, it would begin to disintegrate.

A New Generation Takes Over

In the early years of the twentieth century, both Ricordi and Sonzogno, conscious of their advancing age, began to relinquish control of the firms that they had built and run for years with an iron hand. For many years before his death in 1912, Giulio Ricordi had been gradually turning more of the firm's management over to his eldest son Tito — or Tito II as he is grandiloquently known in histories of the Casa Ricordi, to distinguish him from his grandfather Tito I. Tito was a complex figure who, as the house history of the firm tactfully notes, "lacked the gifts of refined equilibrium that in his mature and older years had made [his father] so celebrated."[42] Mosco Carner describes him less tactfully but more forthrightly: "Unlike Giulio, Tito was impulsive, short-tempered, intransigent and dictatorial. The wealth and fame of his family had engendered in him an arrogance which made him both feared and hated." Carner goes on, however, to point out that he "was a man of drive and initiative."[43] Tito saw himself as a man of the new century, a modern businessman in contrast to his father, whom he considered old-fashioned, even provincial; as the Ricordi house history comments, "he was the first to want to run the firm along lines that one could call American."[44]

Closely attuned to the new musical currents emerging throughout Europe, he was far more interested than his father in recruiting new talent, bringing younger composers such as Alfano, Montemezzi, and Zandonai, whom he saw as the future of Italian opera, into the firm. He lavished particular attention on Riccardo Zandonai, visualizing himself as playing the same role of artistic mentor and fatherly guide with Zandonai that his father had played with Puccini. Tito had little respect, however, for Puccini, seeing the composer as belonging to an outmoded and irrelevant generation.

Tito was also a man of some literary skill, capable of adapting D'Annunzio's *Francesca da Rimini* into a libretto for Zandonai to the satisfaction of both the author and the composer. He was also, as Carner writes, "one of the first persons in Italy to realize the importance of good acting and careful production for the success of a realistic opera."[45] While perhaps not quite "the founder of modern Italian stage direction," as the Ricordi house history calls him, he was one of the first to see stage direction as a distinctive body of skills and talents of its own, to be exercised in the theater independently of — but closely tied to — the musical and scenic dimensions of the production.[46] From the time of the 1900 Rome premiere of *Tosca* to the debut of Italo Montemezzi's gargantuan spectacle *La nave* (The ship) at La Scala in 1918, Tito Ricordi would regularly leave the firm in the hands of his assistants in order to devote weeks or even months to staging the latest opera from a member of the Ricordi stable.

For all Tito's energy and ability, however, his push for unbridled expansion and modernization, his explosive, abrasive personality, and his increasing inattention to the details of the firm's business rendered the firm dangerously overextended — precisely as the First World War was undermining the international connections he had worked so hard to establish. Under increasing pressure from the firm's shareholders, he stepped down early in 1919, and the Casa Ricordi, after four generations, passed out of the control of the Ricordi family.[47] Under the competent leadership of Carlo Clausetti and Renzo Valcarenghi, the two executives of the firm who stepped into the family's shoes, the Casa Ricordi regained its balance. It remained a solid firm, although never recapturing — for reasons both internal and external — the power it wielded at the turn of the century.[48] Tito Ricordi himself lived on until 1933, a sad, lost figure hovering on the fringes of the Milan musical world.

Despite the effects of the war and Tito's excesses, the Casa Ricordi weathered the storm, and emerged into the 1920s and beyond largely intact. Conditions were very different across town at the Casa Sonzogno, where the advent of a new generation led to a protracted crisis that all but destroyed the grand but rickety edifice that Edoardo Sonzogno had built. Lacking children of his own, and with two energetic, ambitious, nephews in the wings, in 1909 Sonzogno turned responsibility for the family firm over to them — while retaining, however, ultimate control. Riccardo Sonzogno, son of his brother Alberto, was given responsibility for the printing and nonmusical book publishing, while Lorenzo, son of his brother Giulio Cesare, was given responsibility for the firm's musical activities.

The firm, however, had already begun to lose ground. The last opera competition took place in 1903, while Sonzogno's activities as an impresario ended in 1907 with his last season at the Teatro Lirico. The flagship of his publishing empire, the newspaper *Il Secolo*, had been losing circulation since the mid-1890s to Luigi Albertini's more modern and less overtly polemical *Corriere della sera*; in 1909, Sonzogno sold *Il Secolo* — linotypes, archive, masthead, and all — to raise capital. By then, the paper mill on Lake Orta had already been sold, and a mortgage taken out for 650,000 lire on the firm's offices in the Via Pasquirolo.

At the point that the two nephews took over the firm at the end of 1909, it was clear that nothing short of a determined and unified effort on their part would have been capable of rectifying the situation and restore the firm to health. Unfortunately, the two nephews loathed one another and were incapable of working together. In July 1910, Mascagni, who was completing his new opera *Isabeau* for the firm, wrote Lorenzo Sonzogno:

> I am in a state of continual anxiety about the situation at the firm, and have no idea how this terrible conflict can be resolved. All I know is that matters are going downhill in a hurry [*a rotta di collo*] and I see my own future,

[which is] totally in the hands of the Casa Sonzogno, jeopardized in an alarming manner. . . . Because, dear Renzo, the battle between you and Riccardo is becoming a matter of such pigheadedness, backbiting, and personal nastiness that the interests of the poor composers are completely ignored.[49]

Lorenzo himself wrote a desperate appeal to his uncle around the same time:

The Casa Sonzogno crisis is entirely out in the open. Everybody is talking about it, everywhere. I am scared for the future of the firm, and I assure you that this is not to influence you, or force your hand. The business is a shambles. . . . Riccardo is so busy collecting non-existent evidence to justify his lies about me, [he] has no time to take care of business.[50]

Edoardo Sonzogno, however, took Riccardo's side and accepted the evidence Riccardo offered him of Lorenzo's financial irregularities. At the end of 1910, barely a year after having entrusted the firm to the two nephews, he returned from Paris, summarily fired Lorenzo, and placed his cousin in complete charge of the Casa Sonzogno.

Whether or not the accusations had merit, it was a bad business decision. In mid-1912, Count Suzani, a Piacenza industrialist closely associated with the firm, wrote his friend Luigi Illica, who had taken Riccardo's side in the dispute: "It is a shipwreck. And at the helm of the ship that is taking in water from every direction is Riccardo, a man without energy, without initiative, I would even say without a brain had he not translated Baudelaire into Italian prose. . . . There was one man — and everybody knows it — who could restore the fortunes of the firm, Lorenzo Sonzogno, intelligent, unscrupulous, a practical businessman."[51]

Lorenzo immediately went into competition with his cousin, establishing the Casa Musicale Lorenzo Sonzogno, and soon enticing both Mascagni and Leoncavallo away from his uncle's firm.[52] Over the course of the next few years, he presented an impressive body of works new to the Italian public, including operas by Richard Strauss, Paul Dukas, and Nikolay Rimsky-Korsakov, Italian composers such as Respighi and Wolf-Ferrari, and the premiere of Mascagni's most ambitious opera, *Parisina*. Lorenzo also invested in two operetta companies, putting on a season of operettas in Paris in 1913, and in the new emerging cinema industry. In the meantime, conditions at the firm he had left continued to deteriorate; on Riccardo's unexpected death in 1915 at the age of forty-four, the firm was scheduled for liquidation.

Edoardo and Lorenzo, who had achieved a sort of rapprochement, intervened. The last nonmusical assets of the firm were sold off,[53] and the firm reorganized once again, now under the complete control of Lorenzo; the nearly eighty-year-old Edoardo returned to the life he was now living as an aging Parisian boulevardier, remaining in Paris until his death in 1920.[54] The firm was a shadow of its former self, however; when Lorenzo himself unexpectedly died at his American mistress's apartment little more than a week after his uncle's death, the Casa Musicale Sonzogno was insolvent, burdened with more than four million lire in debt.[55] In 1923, Milan industrialist Piero Ostali bought the firm to keep it from being sold to German investors and restored it, much diminished, to fiscal solvency, selling the Teatro Lirico, its last concrete asset, to the city of Milan in 1926. The Casa Musicale Sonzogno di Piero Ostali survives to this day, a small firm largely devoted to living off its illustrious past.[56]

Of the two publishers who dominated Italian opera at the end of the nineteenth century, Edoardo Sonzogno was the one entrepreneur. Seen purely from a business standpoint, Giulio Ricordi was an inheritor, capitalizing on the legacy of his forebears, except for the one stroke of luck or brilliance that led to Puccini's operas becoming the legacy that he left to the next generation. Verdi and Puccini works were indispensable to the opera repertory of the 1890s and 1900s; without them, it is more than likely that his firm would have collapsed under the pressure of Sonzogno's energy and determination. Even in an age rich with entrepreneurs, Sonzogno stood out as a remarkable, creative figure.

Ricordi's true legacy, however, was not financial but artistic. His literary skills and musical judgment made him not merely a publisher, but a true collaborator with his composers — particularly Puccini — and their librettists. His role as midwife to the Verdi-Boito collaboration that yielded *Otello* and *Falstaff*; his nurturing Puccini's genius; his collaboration with Illica and Giacosa that led to *Bohème*, *Tosca*, and *Madama Butterfly* — these were his true, unique, and invaluable contributions to Italian opera and the world of music. Edoardo Sonzogno, for all his brilliance and entrepreneurial spirit, left no comparable legacy behind.

Chapter 10

Librettists and Libretti

The Librettists

Since the beginning of opera, composers and librettists have been yoked together in a symbiotic but stressful relationship. Much as the relationship between words and music in opera has shifted back and forth over the centuries, the relationship between the composer and the librettist has shifted as well, along with the status of the librettist and his position in the culture and society of his time.[1] In the mid-eighteenth century librettists were more famous than composers, and Pietro Metastasio, today little more than a faint memory, was, in the words of Vernon Lee, "famous throughout Europe, adored in Italy."[2] Metastasio, as court poet for the Hapsburg emperor, did little but write libretti; yet, as a librettist, he "was petted by kings and empresses and popes, and looked up to like a sort of prophet by his countrymen; while Voltaire . . . said that he was greater than the Greeks; and Rousseau . . . declared that he was the only living poet who was a poet of the heart."[3] His elegantly crafted opere serie were the collective cultural property of eighteenth-century opera. They were repeatedly set to music by one composer after another. More than half had thirty or more settings, while the most popular, *Artaserse*, was the subject of nearly ninety different musical versions between 1730 and 1806.[4]

By the mid-nineteenth century, the status of the librettist had badly deteriorated. Professional librettists such as Cammarano and Piave, famous today for their association with Donizetti and Verdi, were poorly paid and overworked, employed by opera houses to produce libretti on demand, described by one early writer as "veritable slaves, at the beck of composer or manager."[5] Whether respected as solid craftsmen or derided as hacks, there was no question that their work was subordinated to that of the composer, particularly when the composer was a Verdi or a Donizetti. Two of the last members of this generation of professional librettists, Antonio

Ghislanzoni, who wrote the libretto for *Aida*, and Angelo Zanardini, who devoted most of his energy to translating French and German operas for the Italian market, both retired around 1890. One of Zanardini's last efforts as a librettist was the initial adaptation he prepared for Edoardo Sonzogno in 1890 of the French play that would ultimately become Mascagni's *L'amico Fritz*. Mascagni's reaction to Zanardini's libretto reflects the changed taste of a new generation of composers. As he wrote a friend: "I loved the subject, but the lines. . . . My God, what stuff! Poor old Zanardini! — you bring Piave back to life — Imagine: 'a re-greening of baby leaves and a heart that throbs ardently with shame!!'"[6] Sonzogno soon arranged for Nicola Daspuro, a Neapolitan journalist who doubled as his theatrical representative in Naples, to step in and rework Zanardini's libretto into a form more acceptable to the young composer.

With the rise of the publishers toward the end of the century, theaters no longer had any reason to employ librettists. Although Sonzogno at first commissioned libretti from various authors, particularly Zanardini, he soon abandoned the practice. The last professional librettist of the old school was the Neapolitan Enrico Golisciani (1848–1919), who turned out more than eighty works during his long career. A literary chameleon, he could produce whatever the market demanded, from grisly one-act verismo dramas to bubbly operettas. By the late nineteenth century, however, a career such as his could not have happened anywhere in Italy other than Naples, with its steady demand for opera buffa as well as more serious works. Golisciani is remembered today, if at all, for the libretti he wrote for Wolf-Ferrari late in his career, most notably the one-act comedy *Il segreto di Susanna* and his collaboration with the much younger Carlo Zangarini on Wolf-Ferrari's steamy Neapolitan verismo opera, *I gioielli della Madonna*.

While there were librettists for hire in the 1890s — such as Ferdinando Fontana, an endearing person but poor dramatist who concocted the sorry libretti for Puccini's *Le Villi* and *Edgar* — they were few and far between, and for the most part were not sought out by the more substantial composers of the day. Although Fontana's other clients included Franchetti and Samaras, his roster was largely made up of the operatic unknowns and wannabes of the 1880s and 1890s, forgotten names such as Ferrari, Buzzi-Peccia, or Pacchierotti. The only professional librettist of significance during the years between 1890 and 1915 was Luigi Illica, to whom we will turn later.

With no organized market for libretti, many composers, including the most established ones, found their librettists informally, through friendships or chance encounters. The writers they found did not see themselves as librettists first, or even at all; instead, they were people from all literary walks of life who dabbled in writing libretti, as a favor for a friend, to become part of the exciting theatrical milieu, or for the money.

When Mascagni needed a libretto for an opera to submit to the Sonzogno competition, he turned to his childhood friend, Giovanni Targioni-Tozzetti (1863–1934). Targioni-Tozzetti, child of an old and distinguished Tuscan family, subsequently enlisted a young poet of his acquaintance named Guido Menasci to assist him in preparing the libretto for *Cavalleria rusticana*. While the composer's initial choice of librettists was driven as much by his poverty as by friendship, after the success of *Cavalleria* Mascagni continued to work with Targioni-Tozzetti, and occasionally with Menasci, for his entire career. Over the next forty years, they produced four more libretti for their favored composer, while supplementing, rewriting, or adapting five other libretti written principally by others.[7]

Targioni-Tozzetti had a full and distinguished career outside of opera. He was a professor at the Naval Academy in Livorno, and a prominent local public figure, serving twice as the city's mayor.[8] Writing libretti as such was of little interest to him; with the exception of Giordano's *Regina Diaz*, written at Sonzogno's behest, he wrote no libretti for other composers. His work as a librettist was motivated by one concern alone: in the words of a mutual friend, "satisfying his Pietro."[9] It was quite literally a lifelong pursuit; three weeks before his death, he was still able to find the energy to make the last revisions Mascagni needed on the libretto for *Nerone*, his last opera.

Mascagni realized relatively early in his career that for all his devotion, Targioni-Tozzetti was no more than a mediocre writer, whose verses had a distinctly conventional stamp and who lacked dramatic imagination and flair. The last libretto he accepted from Targioni-Tozzetti and Menasci was the 1896 *Zanetto*, a straightforward adaptation of a modest two-character play by the French François Coppée. From that point onward, Mascagni sought out more gifted dramatists for his libretti, including Illica and D'Annunzio, and in later years proficient younger writers such as Giovacchino Forzano and Arturo Rossato. Still, Targioni-Tozzetti was always "on call," as it were, to write or rewrite a line, a page, or an entire scene to Mascagni's satisfaction — although to the outrage of Forzano or Rossato. When Mascagni, unhappy with Rossato's work on *Nerone*, replaced him with Targioni-Tozzetti in 1933, the incensed Rossato wrote the composer's cousin Mario: "If *Nerone* ever comes out, he will have a brand on his forehead and a court order of attachment on his toga. . . . I have written sixty libretti and never has anyone told me he wouldn't use one."[10] Rossato did not pursue the matter, however, and in the end, his considerable contribution received no recognition. When the opera was published, Targioni-Tozzetti was given full credit as the librettist.

Other composers also sought out their friends to write their libretti. The libretti for Wolf-Ferrari's first two comedies, including his most successful opera, *I quattro rusteghi* (The four bumpkins), were both adapted from Goldoni's original plays by his friend Luigi Sugana, a well-known Venetian dialect playwright and poet, as well as a successful painter. Similarly, the symbolist poet Silvio Benco, a friend of James Joyce who was to become a prominent literary and cultural figure in Trieste, wrote the libretti for the Istrian composer Antonio Smareglia's last three operas between 1897 and 1914. Benco was twenty years younger than Smareglia and thoroughly in awe of the composer, whose local — if not national — fame was considerable.

The connection between a third composer of the period, Giacomo Orefice, and his librettist Angiolo Orvieto (1869–1967), although not precisely known, was almost certainly personal rather than professional. Orvieto was a distinguished Florentine poet and cultural figure, founder of the journal *Vita Nuova* and editor of *Il Marzocco*, who has been characterized as having had a "vast influence on Italian literary culture during the early twentieth century."[11] Not noted for any particular interest in opera, Orvieto wrote three libretti for Orefice between 1901 and 1907, including the composer's two most successful works, *Chopin* and *Mosè*. Both Orvieto and Orefice were members of Italy's tiny Jewish minority community, a connection that may have led to their artistic collaboration. As with Targioni-Tozzetti, Sugana, and Benco, Orvieto wrote no libretti for any other composer.

Many occasional librettists were journalists, a career that tended to encourage literary pretensions. Most prominent among these was Arturo Colautti, for many years editor of the Neapolitan newspaper *Corriere del mattino*, who wrote more than a dozen libretti in all, adapting Sardou's play *Fedora* for Giordano and *Adriana Lecouvreur* by Scribe and Legouvé for Cilèa. Similarly, the Milanese freelancer Cesare Hanau adapted Tolstoy's novel *Resurrection* for Franco Alfano, and Daspuro reworked Di Giacomo's *Mala vita* for Giordano. Journalist-librettists tended to produce straightforward melodramatic works, usually staying close to their sources, as suggested by the title page for *Adriana Lecouvreur*: "Dramatic play by E. Scribe and E. Legouvé reduced in four acts for the operatic stage by Arturo Colautti."

At the opposite end of the poetic spectrum were distinguished literary figures, drawn to opera either for economic reasons or out of a fascination with the operatic world. By the 1880s and 1890s, libretto-writing was no longer seen as a shameful activity for a serious poet or novelist. Novelists such as Verga and Di Giacomo had already begun to adapt their works for the prose theater, in large part for financial reasons. From there the writing of libretti was a short step. Although Verga never wrote an operatic libretto himself, he dabbled repeatedly with the idea, going as far as to sign a contract with Ricordi to adapt his story "La lupa" (The wolf) for Puccini. In 1884, he wrote his fellow verismo writer Luigi Capuana, urging him to consider writing a libretto for Filippo Marchetti and admonishing him "not to turn up his nose at an operatic proposal." Almost in the same breath, however, he adds, "if you prefer, it will be possible to refrain from mentioning that the verses are yours."[12] Salvatore Di Giacomo, a prominent Neapolitan playwright, adapted his own work *O Mese Mariano* into a libretto for Giordano. Even Giovanni Pascoli — who stood with D'Annunzio and Carducci at the apex of Italian poetry at the end of the nineteenth century — tried his hand not once but twice at libretto-writing.

The most prominent literary figure to write libretti, however, was Gabriele D'Annunzio. While D'Annunzio's work, and his influence on the Italian opera world of the early-twentieth century, will be discussed in detail in a later chapter, it should be noted that he was responsible for four of the more substantial operas to appear on the Italian stage between 1906 and 1915: Franchetti's *La figlia di Jorio*, Mascagni's *Parisina*, Pizzetti's *Fedra*, and Zandonai's *Francesca da Rimini*, the only one of the four to retain even a bare toehold in today's repertory. D'Annunzio was a passionate music lover and operagoer, and something of a composer manqué; in his megalomaniac fashion, much as he saw himself as the preeminent Italian poet, novelist, and playwright of the time, he was eager to demonstrate that he was also its outstanding librettist. Always in need of money to support his extravagant lifestyle, he weighed financial considerations heavily in his decision to engage in libretto-writing, an arena where he was acutely aware of the potential to turn his fame into cold cash. For a libretto for Puccini (which in the end was never written), he signed a contract with Ricordi in 1906 under which he would receive 20,000 lire in cash (5000 lire in advance and the balance payable in installments on delivery of each act), and 15 percent royalties on the sales of copies of the libretto.[13]

This was an astronomical fee for a libretto. Puccini, eager to have a libretto from D'Annunzio's pen, agreed to reduce his own fee, writing Tito Ricordi: "I understand very well . . . the firm finds my 30 percent for the new opera too high — and this is because of the sacrifices that it must make to the demands of the Poet. I propose then that you make me a contract similar to the one for *Tosca*; that is, for 28 percent [of rentals] and 40,000 lire."[14]

The typical librettist's fees, as described in the previous chapter, were not overgenerous for an effort that could take months and in some cases years of a writer's time. For most, writing libretti was not their principal source of income, but a way to supplement their modest earnings from writing plays or newspaper essays. Indeed, during the entire period from 1890 to the outbreak of the First World War, Luigi Illica was the only writer in Italy to make a comfortable living from the writing of libretti — and with the possible exception of Golisciani, toiling in obscurity in Naples, the only one to even try to do so. His good fortune was made possible by his share, however small, in the royalties from a long series of successful operas, most notably *Bohème, Tosca, Butterfly*, and *Andrea Chénier*, all of which were repeatedly performed around the world, commanding high rental fees. An educated guess would suggest that by the latter years of the first decade of the twentieth century, Illica was earning between 30,000 and 50,000 lire annually from his libretti, an income beyond the dreams of most Italians, although far less than that of Puccini or Mascagni.

Luigi Illica: Librettist to a Generation

Luigi Illica was *the* librettist of the generation, a central figure in Italy's operatic life for more than twenty-five years, the writer who helped mold the most important works not only of Puccini, but of Mascagni, Giordano, and Franchetti, as well as a host of lesser-known composers. He cut a vivid, distinctive figure in the Italian opera world, described by one friend, as "half Bohemian and half scatterbrain, with his goat-like beard, his clear and sanguine eyes peering out from under shaggy eyebrows"; and by another, "the look, half joyous and half fierce, the beard, the half of his left ear that remained after a duel; a man of powerful impulses, restless, intemperate."[15]

Son of a prosperous and straitlaced notary and government official, Illica was born in Castell'Arquato, one of Italy's most beautiful hill towns, overlooking the Emilian plain from the pre-Appenine hills southeast of Piacenza. He was a restless, unruly youth; after his mother's early death he was sent by his father to a strict boarding school in Piacenza, from which he escaped, running off to sea as a deckhand at the age of sixteen. After a few years of adventure, during which he fought with the Bulgarian irregu-

Luigi Illica, in a portrait by Pietro Guberti. *(Mascagni.org)*

lars against the Turks in the battle of Plevna in 1878, he returned to Italy. Arriving in Milan in 1881, he soon became part of the Scapigliati, the city's politically radical and socially bohemian circle. Within a few years he had earned a reputation as a fearless polemicist and a talented dramatist, whose play *I Narbonnerie La Tour* was a notable succès de scandale.

Opera was the cardinal point around which his Milanese milieu, which included such prominent musical figures as Catalani, Boito, and Smareglia, revolved, and his drift into its world during the late 1880s appears almost foreordained. A swift worker, whose mind overflowed with ideas, he was enlisted in 1887 by Catalani to tinker with Zanardini's work on *Loreley*, while at the same time writing the first of three libretti he would produce for Smareglia.[16] Those activities led to two more challenging projects in the following year, which in combination demonstrated the breadth of his talents as a librettist. During 1888 and 1889 he prepared the libretto for Catalani's next opera, *La Wally*, while simultaneously winning the commission from the city of Genoa for the libretto that would be used for Franchetti's *Cristoforo Colombo*. Before either opera had actually appeared onstage, Ricordi had already become aware of Illica's abilities, and in 1891 was already contemplating a role for him as a future librettist for his star composer, Giacomo Puccini. While building his reputation as a librettist, Illica was also becoming widely recognized as a hothead, a spendthrift, and a ladies' man, whose affairs with sopranos and other young women who frequented the Milanese theatrical world were well known.

By the end of the 1890s, when he finally married and settled down, Illica was thoroughly established as the librettist of choice for the composers of the *giovane scuola*. His success reflects not only fortuitous timing, but the exquisite juxtaposition of his talents with the needs of the composers that emerged after 1890. Illica was part of their generation, and shared their interests and preoccupations. In passages like the embarkation scene in *Manon Lescaut*, the second act of *Bohème*, and the greater part of *Andrea Chénier*, he showed a remarkable ability to create powerful and fast-moving dramatic situations, in which the public and private spheres of action were superimposed on one another, and the most intimate emotions expressed without halting, or even measurably slowing down, the often breakneck dramatic pace. As I have suggested earlier, Illica was the most cinematic of Italian librettists, his skills perfectly adapted for the dramatic exigencies of the new bourgeois opera.

In an environment where most librettists' abilities went no further than the more or less competent adaptation of existing works for the operatic stage, Illica's ability to create original stories and settings was a boon to the composers of the time in their constant search for theatrical novelty. He moved comfortably from the discovery of America to the French Revolution, from pre-Western Japan to the rigors of Siberian prison camps, and from the High Middle Ages to Greek antiquity, investing each with superficial but effective historic, geographic, or ethnographic color. While today many of these dramas seem only to reshuffle the clichés of jealousy and fatal love into superficially new combinations — particularly in libretti such as *Germania* for Franchetti or *Siberia* for Giordano — they satisfied the needs of the time. However tired the underlying dramatic situation might be, the stories were effective, fast-moving, even compelling drama, particularly well-suited for musical settings.

Although he may have outshone his competitors, Illica had severe weaknesses as a librettist, both of talent and of temperament. Illica's poetic abilities were limited, as Baldacci, a prominent scholar of the opera libretto, has pointed out: "Although as a poet he never fell to the depths or the vulgarity of a Targioni-Tozzetti, his gifts for the vocation of wordsmith were modest ones, particularly at a point when D'Annunzio was establishing parameters for linguistic craftsmanship that could not be ignored."[17] He is not a *bad* writer, and is rarely less than competent, particularly in his action scenes, which are generally taut and effective. His ability to find the *parola scenica* — the words that capture the emotional essence of a dramatic moment — is considerable, a talent that particularly endeared him to the composers with whom he worked.[18] His attempts at greater poetic expressivity fall short of true poetry, however, much as his attempts at wordplay, most notably in his libretto for Mascagni's *Le Maschere*, fall short of true wit.

Although it is difficult to illustrate this flatness in translation, an example from his *Siberia*, set with some success by Giordano in 1903, may illustrate this point. In the second act, Vassili, the young officer beloved by the courtesan Stephana, has been sent to Siberian exile for having wounded her protector in a duel. In the misery of the Siberian steppes, he is miraculously reunited with Stephana, who has followed him there. The entire act has built up to this highly charged romantic moment; Vassili cries out, "Stephana?! . . . You? . . . Here with me?" and she responds with impassioned declamation. The words, however, fall flat:

Il nido del piacer, oro, splendore	The pleasure nest, golden, splendid
Dove me fu gridato	Where you cried out to me
Da te la prima volta il nome	For the first time the name "Love!"
"Amore!"	

Ai poveri ho donato!	I have given to the poor!
Son io! Vedi? Son Io!	It is I! Do you see? It is I!
Qui per voler di cuore,	Here by the will of my heart,
Voler di Dio!	The will of God!

In Vassili's response, Illica falls back on the clichés of *mammismo*, which were already a commonplace for the Italian audience of 1903:

È la clemenza degli angioli!	It is the mercy of the angels!
È la mia mamma là che prega! . . .	It is my mama up there praying!
Mia mamma morta, che prega in cielo! . . .	My dead mother, praying in Heaven!

And so forth, all of it cloaked in music in Giordano's most rapturous vein.

Illica's poetic limitations could often be disguised or minimized by the music, but were compounded by his personality. He was an intensely emotional, irascible individual, deeply invested in his work, and often lacking in self-control. As Mosco Carner describes him: "Illica . . . was prone to be carried away by a momentary enthusiasm for a subject or for a solution proposed by him for some dramatic problem or other, and with his prediction for picturesque details in the plot would indulge in soaring flights of fancy."[19] While the excitement that he brought to his creative efforts could be infectious, once he had come up with a dramatic stratagem, he would often dig in his heels, and resist future changes even under pressure. In short, Illica was a difficult person to share what is, above all, a collaborative process — and one who became increasingly difficult to work with as the years went on.

Except for Puccini, even the most established composers found themselves treating Illica with kid gloves. Although bound to one another by deep personal affection, Mascagni and Illica fought often during the course of composing *Iris* and *Le Maschere*. Mascagni, himself a notably combative individual, showed Illica extraordinary forbearance all his life, taking his most outrageous behavior in good grace. In 1897, in a letter to Ricordi, commenting on Illica's reaction to the composer's suggested changes to the third act of *Iris,* he wrote: "I got a response from him, making such a splendid joke of it, showing me up as an idiot in such an endearing fashion, that I cannot wait to congratulate him in person on his refined *esprit.*"[20] Mascagni backed down more often than Illica. In mid-December 1899, he suggested to Illica that the writer reconsider the device that ends the second act of *Le Maschere,* a magic powder that sets the entire cast to babbling; writing, "Oh, that damn 'powder'! Is there no way to change its effects? Just think!"[21] Illica's response no longer exists, but can be imagined, since less than a week later, Mascagni wrote again, "So be it: the second act finale stays."[22]

Giordano, whose theatrical instincts were finely honed, and who was less concerned with the wording than with the dramatic pace of his libretti, was constantly aware that he needed to tread carefully with Illica, introducing the subject of changes to *Siberia* in one letter by writing self-effacingly, "you have always permitted discussion, and always allowed me to say whatever came into my head,"[23] and a month or so later, mixing flattery and critique: "Your prologue is wonderful, and you have my compliments. It is so powerful that it seems to me perhaps too strong and out of proportion as the opening of our drama of passion. Before you set it into verses, I'd like to discuss it closely with you."[24] Indeed, many of Giordano's most determined efforts were devoted to restraining the exuberance of Illica's flow of ideas. At the end of August 1901, he wrote Illica again: "Believe me, Illica, leave the libretto the way it is. Let us keep it to three acts, because a fourth would make the opera heavy and dull. . . . After two acts in darkest Siberia and full of powerful dramatic situations, no more is needed. . . . Away with nihilism and Decembrism, away with history, away with it all. Nothing more than simple lyricism and human passions."[25] Bit by bit, Giordano got the libretto he wanted.

Puccini, however, was a special case. Impressed with Illica's work on *Manon Lescaut,* the astute Guile Ricordi decided that he would become Puccini's librettist, setting him in 1892 to find a subject for his protégé's new opera. Illica was ambivalent about the task, writing Ricordi in January 1893:

> Regarding Puccini — with the frankness that is my habit — I must confess to you that between me and him . . . something is rotten in the state of Denmark! . . . With all this, I am not refusing to prepare a libretto for Puccini, only — as I've already told you and you've agreed — that the structure of this libretto for Puccini will be firmly set in place and will stay that way. Do you want to have the pleasure again of dealing with the indecisions of *Manon?* I don't think so. And you know that this instability of Puccini's is nothing new.[26]

Ricordi needed Illica's talents. Responding, in all likelihood, to a similar, earlier screed from the librettist, he had already written him at the end of 1892, "I tell you, very frankly, that I haven't the slightest desire to turn to any other [librettist]."[27] Just the same, Ricordi decided that for both literary and psychological reasons, a collaboration between Illica and Puccini, without the involvement of a third party, was a highly problematic venture.

To serve both as a versifier and psychological buffer, Ricordi enlisted Giuseppe Giacosa (1847–1906), one of Italy's preeminent playwrights, famous for his sensitive, naturalistic plays of bourgeois life — most notably *Tristi amori* written for Eleanora Duse. Even earlier, Ricordi had attempted to recruit Giacosa to help fix *Manon Lescaut*. The playwright had demurred, but recommended the younger Illica in his place. Ricordi was more successful in convincing Giacosa to join forces with Illica on Puccini's new operatic project, an adaptation of Murger's *Scènes de la vie de bohème*. The collaboration that began in 1893 continued for eleven years, and included Puccini's *Tosca* and *Madama Butterfly* as well as *La bohème*.

Giacosa was a man of "meditative, avuncular countenance,"[28] as Carner describes him, whose heavy, well-rounded figure and long, flowing beard, coupled with his quiet, undemonstrative manner led Ricordi and Illica to call him the "Buddha." While Illica's sense of dramatic structure and effect was unparalleled, Giacosa was a far more subtle, nuanced writer. As a result, a division of responsibility quickly emerged. The principal responsibility for the adaptation and the dramatic structure of the opera was given to Illica; the principal responsibility for the versification was given to Giacosa. The ultimate product, however, was very much the result of a collaborative effort in which Puccini as well as Giulio Ricordi were intimate partners. Puccini, by the time of *Bohème*, had become thoroughly clearheaded about both the nature and the value of his talents as a composer, and was single-minded in his determination to pursue his vision at all costs without regard for his collaborators' sensitivities. Ricordi, in his turn, was the ultimate mediator, the court of appeal to whom all three collaborators ultimately turned for confirmation, encouragement, or consolation.

It was a more trying process for Giacosa, who lacked not only Illica's combative spirit, but his inexhaustible energy and his ability to bounce back the next day with the battle forgotten and a host of new ideas to put forward. Moreover, Giacosa could never rid himself entirely of the feeling that writing libretti, even for Puccini, was not his true métier, and that in some fashion he was both wasting valuable time and compromising himself in the bargain. His dissatisfaction began early in the creation of *Bohème*, where we find him writing Ricordi in July 1893: "The trouble is that the work I'm doing on this libretto is not artistic work, but minute pedantry and most wearisome. [I]t is work that does not stimulate or possess inner warmth."[29] Only two months later, he was at the end of his tether: "I'm giving up the job. I'm sending you what little of all that I've done that seems presentable to me, and I am laying down my arms, and confessing that I am powerless. This second part of the first act stands before me like a boulder I can't climb over. I don't feel it, I can't get inside it."[30]

Although Ricordi patched things up, Giacosa's frustrations continued; with the libretto near completion, he once again wrote Ricordi: "I am sick and tired of this continual reworking, retouching, adding, correcting, cutting, gluing, pushing out on the right to tuck in on the left. If it were not for our close friendship and because I like Puccini, at this point I would liberate myself [even if] it became unpleasant. . . . I swear to you that I will never get caught doing a libretto ever again."[31]

Yet within months he was back at work, by now on *Tosca*. The tone of resignation, however, as he wrote to Ricordi about Scarpia's monologue in December was palpable: "You tell me that the piece works musically, and I can't argue with you on that point. But to me, dramatically and psychologically [it] seems absurd. I will put my hand to it, but I refuse to take any responsibility for it."[32] For all his frustrations, however, Giacosa continued.[33] The collaboration was not only productive at the highest artistic levels; without any doubt it was also personally rewarding, as any sustained contact between such creative individuals is likely to be. It is more than likely that Giacosa, as well as Illica and Puccini, shared Ricordi's feelings, as he wrote Illica, shortly after the premiere of *Bohème*: "we all have clear consciences, we have worked from the heart, without preconceptions, serenely wrapped up in the pure atmosphere of art."[34]

After Giacosa's death in 1906, Illica wrote an obituary that appeared in *La Lettura*, the magazine Giacosa had edited for the last five years of his life. Remembering the "battles in which . . . entire acts were torn to pieces, scene after scene sacrificed," he concluded: "Giacosa was for us the equilibrium, in dark moments he was the sun, on stormy days the rainbow. . . . In that uproar of voices expressing different views and conceptions, Giacosa's voice was the delightful, persuasive song of the nightingale."[35]

Earlier, as Giacosa entered his final illness, Ricordi had written Illica in slightly lighter tone: "Giacosa was like a feather pillow, the true neutral zone between the volcanic Illica, the uncertainties of Puccini, and the impatience of the publisher. . . . It was a happy marriage, to such a degree that, as in a true miracle, one doesn't regret even the fights!"[36]

For four years after *Butterfly*, following Giacosa's death, Puccini and Illica continued to look for a new project on which they could collaborate, but without success. While the two explored a wide variety of ideas, ranging from Victor Hugo's *Notre-Dame de Paris* to the short stories of Maxim

Gorky, their discussions regularly returned to a project that had become almost an idée fixe with Illica, a historical drama on the life and death of Marie Antoinette. This project had first been broached in 1897, set aside for *Tosca* and again for *Butterfly*. While working on *Butterfly* for Puccini, Illica had sought to interest Mascagni in his *Maria Antonietta*, but for a variety of reasons nothing came of it.[37]

Early in 1905, after Puccini had abandoned Victor Hugo and Ricordi had vetoed Gorky, Illica convinced Puccini to look at *Maria Antonietta* once again. By December, however, Puccini was convinced that it needed to be completely rewritten, transformed from Illica's epic historical canvas that took the ill-fated queen from her youth in Vienna to the guillotine. He wrote Illica: "It is necessary to give up the idea of a 'from then to now' chronicle, and take it into the heart of the Revolution, where the misfortunes and miseries of Marie Antoinette begin, and from which point that unfortunate queen begins to be interesting."[38] He then put both Illica and *Maria Antonietta* out of his mind for the next nine months, while pursuing an ultimately unsuccessful partnership with D'Annunzio.[39] That, in turn, was followed by a brief flurry of interest in Pierre Louÿs' novel of sadomasochism and sexual obsession, *La femme et le pantin* (The woman and the puppet). Louÿs' reaction to Illica's proposed treatment was negative, and after a few months Puccini lost interest in pursuing the subject further.[40] In May 1907, Puccini once again asked Illica to take *Maria Antonietta* up again; this time, however, he wrote: "Not a beautiful long drama as you conceived it, as faithful as possible to history but which I've found impossible to set to music, but instead a harsh vision, powerful, completely without anything usual or conventional."[41]

Despite Illica's efforts over the next few months, Puccini was unsatisfied, finally writing him in September, using his most tactful tones to raise a highly sensitive issue: "The duty to rework and undo is not a pleasant one, and seeing as you yourself told me, back when you agreed to work for me the way I wanted, that you would take on a collaborator of my choice, I am now telling you that it is time for you to do so, thus dividing up the effort the way we did in those good days with dear old Giacosa."[42] Illica exploded, writing back a letter that began, "You have never spoken to me about collaborations, thus you are . . . dreaming, let's say," and concluded, "thus, if I chose to be impertinent, I could, and perhaps with greater truth and justice, respond suggesting that you find a decent musician as your collaborator."[43] A few weeks later, he wrote again at greater length, attempting to explain himself in detail: "after *Germania* Franchetti asked me to work with Fontana on *Antigone*, and I told him no. . . . [T]hen Giordano fancied himself a Puccini and suggested a collaboration with Stecchetti (a friend of mine), and I responded suggesting that he collaborate with the cook at his father-in-law's hotel, or the doorman at Casa Sonzogno."[44] This exchange of letters represented the end of the last attempt at collaboration between Puccini and Illica. They would have little contact with one another for the next few years, resuming a fitful correspondence only in 1912.

As Illica grew older, his irascibility grew greater and his tolerance for other human beings less. In 1901, he and his young wife abandoned Milan, first for Cassano D'Adda, a town fifteen miles east of Milan, and then in 1903 back to his birthplace, Castel'Arquato. He wrote little after 1910, when he completed his last substantial libretto, *Isabeau*, for Mascagni. *Isabeau*, however, had been sketched out years earlier, in 1904, and offered subsequently to Bossi,[45] Puccini, and Franchetti without success, before Mascagni accepted it in 1908. A final effort with Franchetti ended fruitlessly in 1912, while Illica broke off his relationship with Mascagni the following year, when the two found themselves on opposing sides in the family battle over Edoardo Sonzogno's publishing empire.

When the First World War broke out, Illica became a passionate interventionist with nothing but contempt for those, including Puccini and Mascagni, who were less enthusiastic about their country entering an increasingly bloody war. When Italy entered the war, Illica enlisted in the army at the age of fifty-eight, insisting on being sent to the front as a common soldier. He was discharged a year later, his health broken by a winter in the trenches. He spent the next three years as an invalid on a small farmstead he had purchased outside Castel'Arquato, where he died on December 16, 1919.

Mascagni attended the funeral, and the next day wrote his mistress Anna Lolli from Piacenza: "Of composers, *I was the only one there*. A disgrace! We all owe our good fortune to Illica. *Imagine: Puccini didn't show up!* . . . He didn't even send a wreath, just a perfunctory telegram. Franchetti did the same. Giordano at least sent a wreath. The libretto of *Chénier* deserved better. . . . I said a few words that came from my heart, in the middle I broke down and cried" (emphasis in original).[46]

The Fin de siècle Libretto

A truly successful libretto is a far more difficult achievement than it may seem. Although the librettist's work is often considered to be subordinated to the music, it is subordinated only in the sense that a foundation is subordinated to the superstructure of a building, not in the sense of it being inferior or less important. Indeed, the libretto must be crafted with particular care to serve the music in two distinct, equally important respects. First, the dramatic shape of the work must be suited to musical representation (a task more difficult than it appears). Second, the individual words must be appropriate for musical setting, while still conveying meaning in themselves.

The idea that the words sung in opera are a sort of harmless gibberish, if ever true, was certainly not true in late-nineteenth-century Italy.[47] The words were written in Italian, sung — for the most part — by native Italian-speaking singers, for an Italian audience, many of whom sat in the theater with libretto in hand. Practices that had once made understanding the words more difficult, such as extended melismas, coloratura display, or the repetition of individual words or vowels for musical effect — common in baroque opera and still present in the works of the first part of the century — had all but disappeared from the Italian operatic vocabulary.[48] In their place, use of *parlando*, a sort of "semi-speech," as well as actual spoken tones — from the cry of "Hanno ammazzato compare Turiddu" in *Cavalleria* to the musings of the eight-year-old Totò in *Zazà* — all designed to make the words stand out more clearly, had become common.

As Dahlhaus writes, "the libretto provides musical drama with the condition of possibility." The librettist needed not only to provide the composer with a subject that would both appeal to him and to the operatic audience, but had to be able to organize that subject in a way that it would work as a drama driven by the music, rather than a spoken play. As Dahlhaus points out, this demanded "presentation of the essential structure and sense of the action on stage, in the drama's present time . . . [and] attention to contemporary ideas about what can and cannot be set to music."[49] By the end of the nineteenth century, the scope of the possible was rapidly growing in terms of what could be set to music; at the same time, however, the scope of the libretto's actual subject matter was becoming increasingly impoverished.

With the collapse of the traditional moral order, the ability to create dramas based on that order, or to impose them on the contemporary audience, had disappeared. While some writers under the sway of naturalism and positivism might see that as a by-product of the triumph over obscurantism and superstition, it deprived both writers and composers of the powerful themes that had driven both spoken drama and opera for hundreds of years: the demands of honor, family, or kingdom; the conflict of love and duty; or the unfolding of the consequences of an action over time, each with their many potential variations and ramifications. While one can reasonably argue that the "political" dramas of the early-nineteenth century, such as Bellini's *I puritani* and Donizetti's Elizabethan trilogy, trivialize those subjects, they nonetheless offer a level of dramatic complexity and depth that in important respects was lost by the end of the century. Verdi's *Simon Boccanegra* was the last Italian opera, until perhaps Dallapiccola's 1949 *Il prigionero*, to take political themes seriously.

In their place, the 1890s brought forth first the grim, truculent, and often highly arbitrary, emotional triangles of the verismo operas with their invariably violent resolution. These were soon followed by the more extensively elaborated permutations of the possible outcomes of relationships between men and women in the bourgeois operas of Puccini, Giordano, and others. Stripped to their dramatic essentials, these operas are simple in the extreme, distinguished from one another largely by their setting and details. The number of potential permutations is small: a man and a woman love one another, but a malign environment condemns them, and they die (*Tosca, Andrea Chénier*); a woman loves a man, but he behaves badly, and she dies, or is miserable (*Madama Butterfly, Zazà, Héllera*[50]); a man loves a woman, things go wrong in some fashion, and she dies (*Manon Lescaut, La bohème, Fedora, Siberia*); the same, but *he* dies (*L'Arlesiana*). By the early years of the twentieth century, librettists and composers alike were coming to realize that the themes of bourgeois opera were, in their way, as much of a creative dead end as had been the fad for lower-depths opera that preceded it.

Perhaps the only prominent libretto of this period that made a serious attempt to link tangled emotional relationships with larger political conflict — and the opportunities it offered for nobility and self-sacrifice — was Illica's *Germania*, written for Franchetti. Of all the *giovane scuola*, Franchetti was the only one drawn to such themes, as reflected by *Cristoforo Colombo*, in which, for all its flaws, he created perhaps the only operatic hero of the 1890s for whom the term "noble" is not inappropriate. Franchetti's choice of adjectives to describe the *Germania* scenario after reading it for the first time, is telling; he wrote his father that "Illica has never produced anything so grand, so powerful and elevated."[51] Illica himself wrote Franchetti *père* that with *Germania* the writer would "lead [your] son back from those blind alleys of *Fior d'Alpe* and *Pourceaugnac* to the grand highway of *Asrael* and *Colombo* that his mind, his heart and his destiny had led him, upright, luminous and secure."[52]

The story that elicited this hyperbolic praise is set in Germany under the Napoleonic occupation between 1806 and 1813. The prologue takes place in a mill, where the printer Johannes Palm is being hidden from the French by a band of student revolutionaries. Carlo Worms, a leader of the students, and Ricke, whom Worms has seduced during the absence of her fiancé, Federico Loewe, await news of her brother and her fiancé. Worms convinces her not to tell Loewe, pointing out that both he and Loewe are needed for the revolution. Loewe arrives, bearing news that her brother is dead; moments later, the police raid the mill, and they flee.

In the first act, some months later, Worms is believed dead and Loewe and Ricke are hiding in a cottage in the Black Forest, where Pastor Stapps arrives and marries them. Moments later, the emaciated Worms appears, having escaped from prison, and brings Loewe word of a gathering of revolutionary leaders in Königsberg. When he learns of the marriage, he insists on leaving immediately. As Loewe walks off with Worms, Ricke writes out a confession, leaving it behind for Loewe as she flees. The second act takes place in Königsberg. Loewe denounces Worms and demands a duel. Worms admits his guilt, and vows to pay for his sins by dying on the battlefield. In an epilogue, after the battle of Leipzig, Ricke, wandering across the battlefield, finds the dying Loewe. He begs her to forgive Worms, who has died bravely by his side, and she gives the dead man her blessing. In the distance Napoleon's army is seen slowly retreating, as Loewe dies in Ricke's arms, in his eyes a vision of a liberated Germany.

Illica was a passionate patriot, and when he began work on this libretto, the disastrous battle of Adowa, which dealt a crushing blow not only to Italy's colonial aspirations, but its national pride, was still very much on people's minds. The story appears to be original with Illica, although the conflict between two comrades in arms over the same woman, and their ultimate reconciliation in death on the battlefield, are strongly suggestive of Verdi's *Il battaglia di Legnano*. The text is heavily laden with patriotic outbursts and invocations to die for the fatherland, encapsulated in Federico's aria "Studenti! — udite:"[53]

> Students, listen, friends new and old!
> Wipe away your tears! End your complaints!
> He who dies for the fatherland, does not die!

Illica clearly intends for the listener to see the patriots of the Risorgimento, particularly Mazzini and his Young Italy movement, in his young Germans:

> Germany is one! All a single land!
> One language, one soul, one homeland!

In contrast to *Tosca* and *Andrea Chénier*, where the protagonists are civilian victims of the struggle around them, Worms and Loewe are protagonists in the struggle, with no object other than to die for "holy Germany." Whatever may happen among Loewe, Worms, and Ricke is meant to be far less important than the struggle against Napoleon.

The patriotic drumbeat is so relentless, and the personal dimension of the unhappy triangle so clearly subordinated to the patriotic story, that the drama offers little conflict or development, other than the modest level of suspense provided by the question, what will happen when Loewe finds out? In contrast to *Il battaglia di Legnano*, where Lida's emotional ties to both Arrigo and Ronaldo create internal emotional conflict for her, and dramatic tension in the story as a whole, Ricke's conflict is not emotional but at most tactical; that is, where or when to reveal the truth to Loewe. To compensate for the lack of dramatic movement, Illica has surrounded his three protagonists with a level of background detail well beyond even his usual practices. Historical or quasi-historical episodes, such as the arrest of the printer Johannes Palm, are re-created, after a fashion, and historical figures, including Palm, General Lützow, and the pastor Stapps, all play significant roles.[54] Two well-known German songs, the "Gaudeamus Igitur" and Carl Maria von Weber's "Lützow's Wilde Jagd" (Lützow's wild ride) are interpolated at length at frequent intervals, and become an important part of the work's musical texture.[55] Indeed, the layering of historical detail is carried on to such an extent that one writer characterizes the opera as having an "excess of *inverisimilitude*."[56]

Although Illica's libretti may not read well on the printed page, they come powerfully to life when set to music. For all its pretensions and its abstract, death-obsessed characters, the libretto for *Germania*, has a vitality that could well have served as the basis for a successful opera. Sadly, as an opera *Germania* is largely stillborn. While the composer may have aimed, in Budden's words, "at a plain, rather symmetrical style of melody"[57] to reflect the setting and to fit with the musical interpolations, the effect is — with rare exceptions — worse than uninteresting, as melody after melody begins bravely only to fall into aimless, formulaic repetition and note-spinning. For me, the only exceptions in a long score are the aforementioned "studenti! — udite" and the opera's Big Tune, a patriotic hymn to German freedom that is as rhythmically square as the rest of the score yet has a genuinely uplifting quality. Perhaps suspecting that it will turn out to be the only memorable idea in the opera, Franchetti mines it ruthlessly. It is sung first by Worms in the first act ("Appena il suolo santo"), repeated by the chorus of revolutionaries in the second, and sung again by the dying

Closing scene of *Germania*, from a souvenir postcard. *(Author's Collection)*

Loewe in the epilogue. We hear it one last time at the very end of the opera, as the sun sets on the battlefield and Loewe dies in Ricke's arms. Although this closing scene still has the power to move an audience, it is too little, too late, and cannot redeem the opera. In the end, *Germania* reveals that, after little more than a decade on the operatic scene, Franchetti's powers of invention were largely exhausted. Although it had a brief vogue after its 1902 debut, assiduously promoted by Ricordi in the interval between Puccini operas, it soon faded from sight. It was the last of Franchetti's operas to attract public attention to even that limited extent.

Germania sparked no revival of interest in patriotic opera. While Leoncavallo's 1904 opera, *Der Roland von Berlin,* could be said to have a patriotic theme, the subject, the medieval origins of Germany's Hohenzollern dynasty and their bond with the German people, was selected by Germany's Kaiser Wilhelm, who had commissioned the opera, and had no resonance for Italian audiences.[58]

The direction toward which Italian opera turned as it sought to break out of the confines of bourgeois opera was not political, but mythic. Although Italian composers had long since assimilated Wagner's musical vocabulary into their language, the early years of the new century marked what might be called a neo-Wagnerian moment in Italian opera. Composers, deeply influenced by the writings of Gabriele D'Annunzio, turned back to the German master not for musical inspiration, but as a spiritual guide into a realm of myth and symbolism that had hitherto been absent from the Italian operatic world. Not only Mascagni, whose musical thinking during the decade before the First World War would be dominated by the specter of Wagner (and above all *Tristan und Isolde*), but many of the emerging younger generation of composers, such as Zandonai and Montemezzi, would be swept into the Wagnerian orbit. The raw material for these operas would be taken, not from the French boulevards but from Italy's own past, from D'Annunzio's feverish reimagining of medieval and Renaissance life to the Venetian comedies of Goldoni. Even Puccini, whose musical genius permitted him to extract more from the matrix of bourgeois opera than any of the others of the *giovane scuola*, would ultimately embrace the mythic realm with his last opera, *Turandot*.

Part III

After 1900

Chapter 11

The *giovane scuola* Grows Older

For most of the composers of the *giovane scuola*, the last decade of the nineteenth century represented the high-water mark of their creative careers. Although all were still young and continued to compose well into the twentieth century, after the first few years of the century few of their new works seemed either to elicit a strong response from the public, or to reflect a serious effort to grapple with the creative questions that began to arise, not only in Italy, but throughout Europe. This was not true of all of these composers: Puccini and Mascagni continued to grow as creative artists, although in radically different fashion, expanding their musical vocabularies and exploring new themes and ideas well into the third decade of the century. The other composers of the school, however, all gradually retreated from a creative engagement with the world, repeating timeworn themes and ideas, turning to less challenging genres (such as operetta), or falling entirely into a premature silence. After 1900 in Leoncavallo's case, 1902 in the case of Franchetti and Cilèa, and 1903 in Giordano's, these composers — although living and writing music for many years to come — added little of significance either to their reputations or to the musical world of which they were a part. Even with respect to Mascagni, who struggled hard to expand his musical horizons, the jury remains out on whether he was in fact able to do so, and the extent to which his later efforts — in particular the hugely ambitious *Parisina* — do indeed represent genuinely new directions in his creative trajectory.

At least part of this decline can be attributed to forces beyond the control of the individual composers. The new cultural winds of fin de siècle decadence and D'Annunzian aestheticism, blowing both from within and without Italy, were in many respects fundamentally alien to a generation of composers who had been trained in an aesthetic dominated by Verdi and early Wagner, and for whom the notes of verismo brutality and bourgeois sentimentality represented the farthest extent of their creative breakthrough from the old order. Neither the verismo of *Cavalleria* nor the sentimentality of *Bohème*, however, could serve as a true foundation for a generation of composers' creative growth; meanwhile, time's chariot was galloping on, and new dramatic models and ways of combining musical materials, from Maeterlinck's dramas to the new sounds of Strauss, Mahler, and Debussy, were appearing elsewhere and commanding attention.

Despite these winds of change, some life remained in the bourgeois model — at least in the hands of a genius, as shown by Puccini's career after the turn of the century. With his antennae exquisitely sensitive both to the public taste for the exotic and to the European musical currents around him, he was able to achieve great popular success with *Madama Butterfly* and to a lesser extent with *La fanciulla del West*, works of substantial creative power and vitality, rooted nonetheless in the conventions of bourgeois opera. To the extent that Puccini sought to break free from those conventions, that break came later, if at all, with *Turandot*.

Other composers lacked both Puccini's genius as well as his unremitting determination to select subjects that would be both most appropriate for his talents and for his audience. Other composers found themselves, in Riccardo Allorto's words, "in a state of lost grace," constantly moving "the direction of their choices, passing from the lyric sketch to the ostentatious epic, from the dazzling comedy to decadent decoration, with lapses into the violent realism of the *tranche de vie* and sidesteps into the operetta genre."[1] For Leoncavallo and Franchetti in particular, the phrase "a state of lost grace" seems particularly apt. Both spent the rest of their lives trying, in various ways but without success, to recapture their brief season of fame. Cilèa, confronted by the same difficulty, took a different path, in keeping with his reserved personality. After the failure of his 1907 *Gloria*, he simply withdrew, never writing another opera during his remaining forty-three years of life.

Leoncavallo's Moment Passes

Leoncavallo's first biographer Rubboli has written: "It is as if in 1900 a steel shutter came down on Leoncavallo's life. The day before, he knew youth's joys, a culture's adulation, international adventures, a path to success that brought him glory. Every day after found him fading, as if the light of Fortune was dying away behind him." For the next nineteen years, until

Leoncavallo and the cast of the first performance of *Zazà* in 1900; *from left*, Edoardo Garbin, Rosina Storchio, Leoncavallo, an unidentified comprimaria, and Mario Sammarco. *(Author's Collection)*

his death in 1919, his dream would be to "recapture the magic moment of *Pagliacci*."[2] The magic moment had passed, however. The quantity of music that Leoncavallo produced between 1900 and 1919, almost to the day of his death, is astonishing, including four operas, at least six (some say nine) operettas, and a plethora of salon pieces; none of it, though, except perhaps for the evergreen song "Mattinata," has withstood the test of time.

After *Zazà*, Leoncavallo finally turned to *Der Roland von Berlin* (in Italian, *Il Rolando*), the opera that had been commissioned by the kaiser in 1894, which he had set aside first for *La bohème* and then for *Zazà*. Leoncavallo was not only renowned in Germany for *Pagliacci*, but was a personal favorite of the kaiser, who admired the composer's Italian Renaissance epic *I Medici*, and considered him the "foremost of the Italian opera composers."[3] Although eager to maintain good relations with the kaiser, Leoncavallo made only fitful progress on the opera, his work regularly interrupted by the need to churn out songs and piano pieces, an abortive project to compose a one-act opera to pair with *Pagliacci*,[4] and even a libretto for a little-known Neapolitan composer, to pay off his debts and maintain his elegant Swiss villa on the shores of Lake Maggiore. For the rest of his life, the threat of bills and promissory notes coming due, and the need to raise cash to pay them, would be constant.

Der Roland, set in fifteenth-century Berlin and based on a patriotic novel in which the kaiser's distant ancestor, the Hohenzollern Elector Friedrich, takes the people's side against the arrogant nobility, made its debut in Berlin in December 1904, where it was warmly received, particularly by the kaiser, who subsequently arranged for extended selections from the score to be recorded by the original cast. The Berlin performance was followed immediately in January 1905 by the opera's Italian debut at Naples' San Carlo theater; although the work had a brief vogue in Germany, where, assiduously promoted by the imperial court, it received forty performances between 1904 and 1908, neither its subject matter nor its music appealed to Italian audiences, and it soon disappeared from the repertory.[5]

Listening to *Roland* today, it is not hard to understand why. Although certainly a competent, well-crafted work, with moments of beauty and power, it has neither the boulevard vivacity nor the sentimental charm that combine to make *Zazà*, for all its limitations, such an appealing theatrical experience when the title role is sung by a singer of vocal flair and exuberant temperament. In *Roland*, Leoncavallo tried hard to write an opera that would have a distinctly German quality without being merely another Wagnerian clone; he incorporated old German songs and dances into his score, while deliberately giving other passages a self-consciously "German" flavor, using the characteristic intervals and rhythms of German folk music. It was a futile exercise. Despite his efforts, the specter of Wagner, particularly *Meistersinger*, is often present, while in moments of high emotion, Leoncavallo reverts to the style of *Pagliacci*. Other passages seem more suited to an operetta in the vein of Johann Strauss or Lehar than to a high-minded patriotic opera.

From the twelve minutes of hollow posturing that make up the overture to the opera's end on a mingled chime two and a half hours later, a sense of strain is rarely absent from *Roland*. Leoncavallo's muse was ill-equipped for this subject, and the spectacle of the composer attempting to write self-consciously important music is unedifying. To the Italian public, moreover, it was, if not openly inappropriate, disconcerting for one of the nation's most prominent composers to devote such effort to an opera in German on a German patriotic theme. *Roland* was not only an unsuccessful opera, but an unpopular gesture that would come back to haunt the composer ten years later.

Leoncavallo never again tried anything so ambitious. His next two operas, the 1910 *Maia* and the 1912 *I Zingari* (The gypsies), were uninspired verismo efforts: the first set among the shepherds and horse-tamers of the Camargue; the second, a tale of the fatal love of a townsman for a Gypsy woman, reminiscent of *Carmen*.[6] At the same time, his never-ending search for money led him to begin writing operettas in 1908, with *Malbruk*, which made its debut in January 1910. His operettas are not memorable, but at least one, *La candidata* (The candidate), has an entertaining premise. Set in an imaginary European country in 1990, by which time women have finally won the right to vote, its heroine is the nation's first female parliamentary candidate, the glamorous Aurora Legleur. After various adventures, she and her opponent, Prince Franz, fall in love; both relinquish their political careers and go off to a life of wedded bliss.[7]

With Italy's entry into World War I, Leoncavallo returned briefly to the public eye. Somewhat surprisingly, in view of his largely apolitical, cosmopolitan, background — not to mention his expatriate life in Switzerland — he emerged as a passionate supporter of Italy's war effort, writing his friend Belvederi in June 1915, a few weeks after Italy had entered the war, that "this war will be good for everyone. After this terrible but glorious moment, a new Italy and a new France will rise up, radiant with a new light."[8] A week earlier, he had written Luigi Illica, who had volunteered for the army at fifty-eight and was on his way to the front: "All I can do is embrace you and express my jealousy that I cannot do likewise. But my only thought is to provide for the two women who need me more than ever in this terrible moment. . . . I will limit myself to serving my country by writing (as I have written the Queen Mother) a patriotic Italian opera to celebrate our victory."[9]

Although the image of the fifty-eight-year-old and by now morbidly obese composer in uniform is risible, his determination to write a patriotic opera was sincere and intense. After exploring and abandoning a number of ideas, he settled in June 1915 on the story of Goffredo Mameli, a hero of Garibaldi's ill-fated but romantic Roman republic of 1848. *Mameli*, subtitled *Alba Italica* (Italic dawn),[10] was produced in record time, aided by extensive borrowings from the composer's earlier works.[11] Beginning work on the libretto with Belvederi no earlier than June 1915, Leoncavallo completed the opera early in 1916, and conducted its first performance in Genoa in April 1916.

For all its noble intentions and the patriotic chords it struck, *Mameli* was a failure. Worse, Leoncavallo found himself under attack for having written the opera, most vehemently by Mussolini's prowar *Popolo d'Italia*, which wrote in brutal tones: "[Leoncavallo], who only a few years ago filled up Roland's paunch with notes on behalf of the German Emperor,

now pretties up that dead soldier [Mameli] for us and makes him sing a romance and a duet. We don't want it, Leoncavallo. Because you're looking
too much like a scoundrel to us. Leave our heroes alone. Just as we didn't
want your Roland, we don't even want this Mameli of yours."[12] The Socialist newspaper *Avanti* published a cartoon showing Mameli rising from the
grave to reproach the composer, who appears, significantly, dressed in the
livery of the German imperial court.

Leoncavallo could and did protest that when he had written *Roland* in
1905 Italy and Germany had been allies, but his protests were in vain. His
grand patriotic gesture had left his name and reputation only further tar-
nished. That fall he suffered a further blow when he was forced to sell his
Swiss villa to settle his debts. Moving back to Italy, he settled in the Tuscan
spa town of Montecatini, where he continued writing operas and operettas
until his death in August 1919. His last opera was *Edipo Re*, a one-act treatment of the Oedipus story written for Titta Ruffo, which the great baritone
performed in Chicago in 1920, and again in New York in 1921. While there
is little doubt that the opera made an effect with Ruffo in the demanding
title role, its music is largely pallid and lacking distinctive character. Indeed, at the opera's climactic moment, where the blind Oedipus laments
his fate and consoles his daughters before being led off to exile, the fading
composer's resources failed him entirely: the music is borrowed, almost
note for note, from Alda's lament for the dead Henning in *Roland*.

The Long Winter of Alberto Franchetti

With *Germania's* success in 1902, Franchetti appeared to have regained his
standing as a leading member of the *giovane scuola*, after the failure of two
earlier operas, *Fior d'Alpe* (1894) and a comedy based on a play by Molière,
Il signore di Pourceagnac (1898).[13] His next opera was awaited with great
public interest, particularly when it became known that the opera would
be a setting of the popular play by Gabriele D'Annunzio, *La figlia di Jorio*.
D'Annunzio, whose role in Italian culture generally and in its operatic
world in particular will be discussed in detail in the following chapter, was
Italy's most famous writer, and a central figure in the nation's cultural life.
La figlia di Jorio, a powerful tale of sexuality and violence in the primitive
region known as the Maiella (the most isolated part of Italy's remote
Abruzzi mountains), was an immediate success on its appearance in 1904,
cementing his reputation as Italy's preeminent playwright as well as poet
and novelist.[14]

Franchetti had fallen in love with the story after reading a synopsis in a periodical, but D'Annunzio's financial demands were excessive; fortunately, as Franchetti later recounted, "matters did not end there": "Shortly afterward I was in Parma to see my dear father. He asked for news of my work, and when he learned that I was setting an opera on a Greek subject, he seemed rather unhappy with my choice: 'There could be,' I said, "a magnificent libretto: *La figlia di Jorio*, but D'Annunzio is asking too much. 'I'll pay for the libretto,' my father said."[15] Franchetti, in his midforties, was still emotionally immature and financially dependent on his father. Not fully stable himself, Franchetti's marriage to an even more unstable and unhappy woman had ended not long before, after a long series of bitter separations and tearful reconciliations.[16] A profile of him, written at the time, describes him as "most careless of his personal appearance, anything but immaculate in his attire, and peculiar and absent-minded to a degree."[17]

Franchetti immediately moved into a villa in Settignano in order to supervise D'Annunzio's adaptation of his play into a libretto. *La figlia di Jorio* was the first of the poet's works to be turned into a libretto, and D'Annunzio — although glad enough for the money — was unenthusiastic about the task, writing sarcastically to his confidant Tom Antongini, "at this moment I can hear the roar of Franchetti's automobile, who has come to beg me to smash the granite of the Maiella into little pills to be taken by the hour."[18] By "accentuating the melodramatic dimension, shrinking the original text, and adjusting it to function as a fairly traditional operatic structure," as Tedeschi writes,[19] D'Annunzio significantly weakened the qualities that gave the play its distinctive power, while failing to provide anything that would bring out Franchetti's particular talents.[20]

The new opera made its highly anticipated debut at La Scala on March 29, 1906. Driven by the high expectations for the work and the intense public interest, and helped by a stellar cast that included Giovanni Zenatello and Angelica Pandolfini, *La figlia di Jorio* received twelve performances during its initial appearance. The opera failed, however, to sustain the interest of either the general public or the musical world. Even worse, it came to be seen almost as an object lesson in poor judgment, and in the effects of incompatibility between the composer and his subject. Franchetti was, as Tedeschi puts it, intimidated by D'Annunzio's poetry and reputation, "accepting, instinctively, a subordinate position."[21] Franchetti as much as admitted it himself, writing that, in contrast to his previous "Wagnerian" efforts, "this time I wanted *La figlia di Jorio* to be D'Annunzio's *La figlia di Jorio*; I wanted the words to have their own value, that the music would almost be subordinated to it."[22]

This is a dangerous credo for an operatic composer, but was only the beginning of the work's failure. To the extent that D'Annunzio's play transcended the clichés of peasant violence, it was because he was able to add an almost mythic, timeless dimension to the violence and barbarity of his characters' lives, a quality that has enabled the play to remain alive, albeit tenuously, after a hundred years. Much of this quality was lost in the translation of the play to a libretto. Of all of the composers of his generation, moreover, Franchetti was most probably the least suited to the task of turning such a story into a successful opera; his stolid muse was incapable of finding a musical counterpart to D'Annunzio's poetry, through which his Abruzzi mountain folk could either acquire individuality or transcend it. Few operas have been more harshly condemned or utterly dismissed. One later critic has written, "the unbridgeable distance of attitude and taste between poet and composer produced an absolute void."[23] Another wrote, "taken as a whole, the music of Alberto Franchetti unequivocally cheapened [D'Annunzio's] figlia di Jorio, and turned it into an utterly worthless, ugly, opera."[24]

After La figlia di Jorio, Franchetti turned once again to Illica, who had written the libretti for his two most successful works, Cristoforo Colombo and Germania. Although they worked on a subject, referred to in the composer's letters as Macboulè,[25] off and on for six years, the project never came to fruition. The relationship between Franchetti and Illica had become difficult; by this time, Illica had become even more cantankerous and disinclined to accommodate his collaborators, while Franchetti himself had grown more eccentric and unpredictable. The conflict-ridden collaboration was finally abandoned in 1912.[26] By the time Franchetti's next opera, Notte di leggenda, to a libretto by Giovacchino Forzano, appeared at La Scala in 1915, his reputation had waned. Both Colombo and Germania had disappeared from the repertory, and the younger generation thought of him, if at all, as a figure of little more than historical interest. Neither Notte di leggenda nor his next opera, Glauco, based on Greek myth, which made its debut at the San Carlo in Naples in 1922, did anything to restore his standing.[27] Although Franchetti continued to compose steadily, writing at least three more operas before his death in 1942, none of them were ever performed either at the time or since.

Franchetti's life continued on a downward trajectory. The composer's dealings with women had always been problematic. A sexual entanglement on his part during his student days in Munich had required parental intervention, along with the dispatch of a family retainer with "a suitable sum to resolve the problem."[28] Late in 1919, the nearly sixty-year-old composer befriended a girl of fifteen. At some point the friendship turned into a sexual relationship, and when they married in April 1922, she was already five months pregnant. Nine years later, she left him and their daughter for another man. With little left of his once-substantial fortune, and with little contact with friends and family, after years of wandering, he settled into a modest home in Viareggio in 1934, where he lived until his death in 1942.[29]

Franchetti's last years were to become even more bitter, after the Fascist regime enacted anti-Semitic laws in 1938, banning further performances of his works. Although Mascagni pled with Mussolini on his behalf to permit a revival of *Colombo*, it was in vain; the duce "carefully read the petition that Mascagni handed him, but then, closing the folder, wrote on it a large 'no,' followed by his 'M.'"[30] Franchetti was desperately lonely in his last years, almost pathetically grateful for the occasional letters he received, writing Mascagni late in 1941, "your letter was a great comfort for me — now I no longer feel alone, abandoned by all." He had just completed his last opera, a comic opera entitled *Don Bonaparte*, writing Mascagni in the same letter: "I have only one desire, which is to hear what I have written before I die. Even to have the opera performed under another's name, to renounce *all* [emphasis in original] of the eventual benefits of the work, that is, to remain morally and materially hidden."[31] It was not to be, and the opera has never been performed. Franchetti died alone, all but forgotten by the musical world of his day, on August 4, 1942.

Adriana Lecouvreur *and Cilèa's Silence*

Cilèa's unhappy experience with the 1898 premiere of *L'Arlesiana* and his treatment by Sonzogno had deeply unsettled the sensitive young composer. Unlike the quixotic Mascagni or self-assured Giordano, Cilèa was diffident and self-doubting, hesitant to assert himself or fight for his position in the intense world of opera with its many intrigues and conflicts. As he recalled years later, "the conflicts and disappointments of that sad period caused me such discomfort that, having won the competition for a position at the Florence conservatory, I didn't hesitate for a moment to accept the Chair in Harmony, and — turning my back on theater, publishers and the like — move to my new base and plunge head first into the quiet waters of teaching."[32] Sonzogno, however shabbily he may have treated Cilèa before, was well aware of the composer's ability. He sought Cilèa out in Florence and arranged for Arturo Colautti, the Dalmatian poet who had recently adapted *Fedora* for Giordano, to write him a libretto. Of the many ideas that Colautti suggested, Cilèa chose a play by Eugène Scribe and Ernest Legouvé on the romantic life and death of the eighteenth-century French actress Adrienne Le Couvreur, written in 1848 as a vehicle for the famous actress Rachel.

Cilèa began work on the opera, which had been baptized *Adriana Lecouvreur*, near the end of 1900, writing during the long vacations that the conservatory's schedule offered, and completing it in September 1902. *Adriana* made its debut in November 1902 at the Lirico in Milan. Renzo Sonzogno, the publisher's nephew, who was determined to ensure a first-rate production — and perhaps atone for the firm's half-hearted treatment of *L'Arlesiana*'s debut — had assembled a stellar cast, including Pandolfini as Adriana, Caruso as Maurizio, and De Luca as Michonnet under Campanini's baton. In addition to Cilèa's fellow Italian composers, the audience included Jules Massenet, who wrote the composer a warmly admiring letter, writing "your score is full of movement and seduction, and will have a great success."[33]

The opera's complex romantic intrigues revolve around Adriana's love for the adventurer Maurice of Saxony (Maurizio), and the jealousy of the Princess de Bouillon, who loves Maurizio and has lost him to Adriana. The Princess takes revenge on her rival by sending her a casket containing a bouquet of violets that she has infused with a powerful poison. When Adriana, believing them from Maurizio, presses them to her lips, she absorbs the poison, and dies.[34] It is an old-fashioned libretto, almost a throwback to an earlier era, redeemed by the rich delineation of the title role, and by the character of Michonnet, who plays the theater manager, a kindly older man who is in love with Adriana and, knowing his love will never be returned, has devoted his life selflessly to her service.

Adriana Lecouvreur is Cilèa's most successful and most unified opera, a rich blend indeed of movement and seduction, full of memorable melody, including such perennial favorites as Adriana's "Io son l'umile ancella" (I am the humble handmaiden) and Maurizio's "La dolcissima effigie" (the sweet image), both sung first in the opening act, and appearing as recurrent themes throughout the opera. At the same time, it is in some respects less original, less personal, than *L'Arlesiana*, in which Cilèa's distinctive voice is more consistently present. The influence of the first act of Giordano's *Andrea Chénier*, from which Cilèa appears to have learned how to compose music for an eighteenth-century French setting, is pervasive, from the bustling music that opens the opera to the third-act Pastorale sung by female voices. Equally pervasive, as Scherer points out, is Cilèa's use of the rhythmic and melodic patterns of operetta at times in ways that, how-

Poster for the first performance of *Adriana Lecouvreur,* 1902. *(Casa Musicale Sonzogno)*

ever charming, seem incongruous or out of place—as in the patter duet between the Prince of Bouillon and the Abbé de Chazeuil in the first act, or the actors' quartet in the fourth.[35]

Ultimately, the greatest strength of *Adriana* lies in the title role, rich both dramatically and musically, that has drawn great sopranos to the opera from Stehle, Bellincioni, and Cavalieri in its early years to Tebaldi, Olivero, and Freni in more modern times. Adriana is a histrionic actress, a tender lover, and a passionate rival, yet a simple woman beneath it all who yearns for love, marriage, and a quiet home. In this and other respects, *Adriana* bears a close resemblance to *Zazà,* which made its debut two years earlier, roughly at the same time that Cilèa began work on his opera. From the standpoint of today's audiences, *Adriana* offers a more straightforward, more distanced theatrical experience, a costume drama with neither the excess of sentimentality nor the whiff of the sordid that complicate today's reception of *Zazà.*

Adriana Lecouvreur's debut was highly successful; within the next year it had appeared in theaters not only in a host of Italian cities, but in Buenos Aires, Mexico City, Lisbon, Barcelona, Warsaw, Cairo, and Alexandria. As quickly as it spread, however, it began to disappear from the stage. Although it made its Paris debut in 1905, and appeared at the Met with Caruso, Cavalieri, and Scotti in 1907, by then it had already all but vanished from Italian theaters.[36] One explanation was put forward by Gavazzeni, who wrote many years later: "Ricordi, Sonzogno's rival, put into effect all of his tricks to block the course of *Lecouvreur*. These are historic facts, not legends. . . . If an impresario wanted to rent certain operas of Verdi or Puccini and had put *Adriana* into his season's program, then Signor Giulio would require him to pull Cilèa before renting him Ricordi's authors."[37] The effect of Ricordi's hostility may have been exacerbated by Sonzogno's continued ambivalence to his own composer; as Cilèa himself told a friend years later, not without bitterness, "my own editor's lack of interest in my operas finally wore me out."[38] *Adriana Lecouvreur* only began to return to the repertory toward the end of the 1920s, when the Ricordi-Sonzogno duopoly was a thing of the past, and Piero Ostali, the new owner of the Casa Sonzogno and a great admirer of Cilèa's music, began assiduously to promote the composer's operas.

In the meantime, however, the initial success of *Adriana* rekindled Cilèa's desire for an operatic career, and convinced Sonzogno to commission two more operas from the composer. Cilèa was eager to test himself on a subject that would be "more dramatic and on a larger scale, in which the chorus would actively enter into the mainstream of the action,"[39] while his years in Florence had stirred his interest in Renaissance Tuscany. Unable to get Sonzogno to pay D'Annunzio the sum he was seeking for *Francesca da Rimini*, and lacking Franchetti's means, the composer returned to Colautti. Weaving together themes from two different plays with a common Renaissance setting, Sardou's *La haine* (Hate) and Maeterlinck's *Mona Vanna*, Colautti constructed a melodramatic story of clan warfare, love, and revenge in fourteenth-century Siena, entitled *Gloria* after its heroine.[40] In order to devote all of his time to composing, Cilèa resigned from the Florence Conservatory, moving to Varazze, a small town on the Ligurian coast. By the end of 1906 he had completed *Gloria*, and the opera had been set for the upcoming *carnevale–quaresima* season at La Scala, to which Toscanini had returned after a four-year absence.

Despite Toscanini's conducting and an outstanding cast, which included Salomea Krusceniski as Gloria, Giovanni Zenatello as her lover Lionetto, and Pasquale Amato as her brother, the opera was not a success. While many found passages to praise, such as Pozza who wrote in the *Corriere della sera:* "it is rich in exquisite details, and some episodes have pages as dense in inspiration as [they are] in admirable workmanship," the opera as a whole failed to convince either critics or audience.[41] After a handful of productions, *Gloria* disappeared. Even Ostali's determined missionary efforts for it during the 1930s produced no sustained results.[42]

If *Gloria* can be seen as an attempt by Cilèa to test himself against a more difficult subject, working on a larger canvas, he would appear to have failed the test. His talents were for the romantic intrigues of *Adriana* or the delineation of his characters' febrile emotions in *L'Arlesiana*, not for battles, blood rivalries, and revenge. *Gloria* has long passages during which Cilèa appears to have no clear idea how to represent the drama unfolding on stage in meaningful musical terms, in which he resorts repeatedly to the melodramatic clichés of generations of Italian opera composers, brought up-to-date with slightly more adventuresome harmonies and rhythms. Even the romantic exchanges between Gloria and Lionetto, although more harmonically sophisticated and elaborately organized than in Cilèa's earlier operas, rarely catch fire, while truly distinctive melodic lines or motifs are few and far between.

The defects of the music are set into greater relief by the absence of any qualities in the libretto that might offer a springboard for a less than traditional musical treatment. Colautti's libretto, while bearing superficial similarities to D'Annunzio's medievalist works such as *Francesca da Rimini*, is actually an old-fashioned melodramatic story in the vein of *Ernani* or *Trovatore*, with neither distinctive characters nor a greater mythic or political dimension to lend it weight. Cilèa, torn between an innate conservatism and a cautious receptivity to the modern musical innovations seeping into Italy from the north, lacked the resources to turn such a libretto into a successful opera.

Indeed, it is questionable whether any composer of the time could have done so. Cilèa's failure with *Gloria* was not merely a personal one; it was a reflection of the waning of the cultural moment that had given rise to the *giovane scuola*, and the need for the Italian opera world to come to grips with that reality. It is notable that the other Italian premiere of the 1907 La Scala season, along with *Gloria*, was Richard Strauss's *Salome*. How to bridge the musical and dramatic gap between those two operas was about to become the central task for Italian composers, both the *giovane scuola* and the new generation, such as Zandonai and Montemezzi, that was beginning to emerge.

This was not a task, however, that Cilèa however, would pursue. While his contract with Sonzogno called for another opera to follow *Gloria*, neither he nor the publisher seemed to consider it a matter of great urgency. Cilèa only began working with Renato Simoni on "a sentimental fable of [Simoni's] own invention" in 1911; soon thereafter, having completed only the first act, Simoni left for an extended trip to China.[43] By the time Cilèa had completed revising his early *L'Arlesiana* for a 1912 production, the dis-

integration of the Casa Sonzogno was already well under way. With Riccardo in charge, a man Cilèa considered personally hostile, he saw no
point in pursuing matters further. In contrast to Mascagni, who threw himself into the publisher's internal battles, Cilèa, who described himself as
"no fighter," withdrew.[44] He applied for the position of director at the
Palermo Conservatory, to which he was appointed in September 1913.

Cilèa lived until 1950. He never wrote another opera, and, except for a
handful of miniatures and a new prelude to L'Arlesiana, largely written in
a modest burst of creative activity between 1930 to 1932, he wrote no music
at all. He had a distinguished career as an educator, leaving Palermo in 1916
to become director of his alma mater, the San Pietro a Maiella Conservatory
in Naples, where he remained until 1935. When asked, he would patiently
explain that his duties at the conservatory made it impossible for him to
pursue, "new, important, personal projects."[45] This is, of course, highly
doubtful; the conservatory, with its neat hierarchy and orderly structure, was
for him a far more congenial atmosphere than the highly pressured world of
opera with its intrigues and conflicts. As one biographer has written: "His
extreme shyness, his gentlemanly reserve, his horror of the hubbub of the
press, his love of quiet and his study, all made him a sort of poor cousin in
the noisy, emotional family that was the giovane scuola."[46] Moreover, as the
composer wrote, "each of my operas left some effect on my health. And in
the end, the excessive effort I made to complete Gloria by the publisher's
deadline utterly wore me out. The effect on my nervous system led to
frightening dizzy spells, where I felt as if everything in me was spinning."[47]

Cilèa may have believed that he had more operas within him, and that
external, rather than internal, circumstances had led to his long silence; he
wrote Ostali in 1923, "if you had been by my side in 1913, I would never have
given up my [operatic] career to find refuge in the conservatories."[48] This
is unlikely: Cilèa was a born teacher but a reluctant composer. Moreover,
as a composer he was a figure of the past, rooted in his late-nineteenth-
century Neapolitan milieu. Cilèa was a thoughtful man, however, and
well aware of the changing musical world in which he was living. He may
have realized, even while writing Gloria, that he had little to add to what
he had already written; one is tempted to conjecture that the mental and
physical difficulties he experienced composing that work had more to do
with his recognition of its problematic nature, and its fundamental irrele-
vance to the condition or direction of Italian opera at that moment, than
with any problems of schedule or deadlines. While his long silence may
have been a source of personal suffering for him, one doubts that it left any
void in the larger world of opera.

Puccini and the Apotheosis of Bourgeois Opera

In 1900, Puccini was firmly established on top of the Italian opera world. After a somewhat equivocal debut marred by a bomb scare, *Tosca* quickly established itself as an audience favorite equal to *Bohème*, rapidly making the rounds of the major theaters both in Italy and overseas. By midyear it had already been presented in Turin, Milan, Verona, and Genoa, and in July its composer traveled to London for its debut at Covent Garden. In London, Puccini saw David Belasco's play *Madame Butterfly*; while Belasco's account — in which Puccini came after the performance to the green room, embraced the playwright and with tears in his eyes begged Belasco to permit him to use it for an opera — was undoubtedly somewhat embroidered, it was not long before Puccini indeed decided to make *Madame Butterfly* his next opera.[49]

Butterfly, both in Belasco's play and in the subsequent treatment by Illica and Giacosa, is the quintessential blend of the exotic and the conventional (a blend not unusual among the operas of the time), designed to have the greatest possible appeal to the bourgeois audience. Mascagni had already used a Japanese setting, although a far less literal one, in *Iris*, while Giordano was working on *Siberia*, his second opera on a Russian theme.[50] For all its exotic setting, the story is conventional; indeed, in its sentimental triangle, it closely resembles two of the operas most recently seen on the Italian stage, *Zazà* and *Adriana Lecouvreur*. All three have as their central figure a strong-willed woman of character, who loves a cad of a tenor not wisely but too well, while receiving moral support from a sensible, decent baritone.

While both Puccini's orchestral palette and his harmonic vocabulary, enlivened with an increasingly sophisticated use of the whole-tone scale, had become richer and more distinctive in the few years since *Tosca*, *Madama Butterfly* still fit comfortably within the musical as well as dramatic parameters with which his bourgeois audience was familiar. Puccini's harmonic innovations, as well as his appropriation of traditional Japanese melodies, while giving the opera a distinctive *tinta*, do not challenge the ears of those who had become accustomed to the composer's earlier works. What *Butterfly* does offer, however, is Butterfly herself, "Madama F. B. Pinkerton," Puccini's greatest and most fully realized operatic character.

From the opening of the opera, when the soon-to-be married Pinkerton, in the presence of the disapproving Sharpless, drinks a toast, "to the day I'll have a real wedding, and a real American bride," her fate is sealed. It is not the inevitability of her fate, however, that raises her story from melodrama to tragedy. Her end is not a matter of chance, or sordid manipulation by an evil villain. It is a tragedy of character, as Girardi writes, "the psychological drama rests in large part on the contrast — which grows more and more distressing — between the stubborn fixity of Butterfly's convictions and the surrounding world to which she is essentially alien."[51] Butterfly's tragedy flows from her decision to make a pure, moral choice, accepting the consequences of that choice in an immoral world. The three acts of *Madama Butterfly* are the inexorable unfolding of her tragedy, as the course of events compels her to make her final decision, the only decision, given the moral clarity of her vision, that she can make.

In creating an opera that builds steadily and inexorably to its end, Puccini demonstrates a mastery of his craft going far beyond that of any of his contemporaries; using, as Girardi points out, "leitmotivic elaboration in the Wagnerian sense"[52] more than in any other of his operas, he has created a tightly woven opera in which every detail reinforces the whole, full of telling nuances and details. Craft, for Puccini, however, is a means to an end. His object is always to convey feeling and to engage his audience in the story unfolding before them, manipulating their emotional responses with a precision unmatched by any other operatic composer, before or since. As the history of *Butterfly* over more than a hundred years has shown, he was completely successful. Few people are capable of remaining unmoved by Butterfly's story as it is filtered through Puccini's music.

That *Madama Butterfly*'s La Scala debut on February 17, 1904, was a fiasco, "a black mark on the history of La Scala," in Ashbrook's words,[53] continues to intrigue opera historians. Although the opera in its initial version had its longueurs and awkward moments, that cannot begin to explain the intense, even vicious hostility that greeted it at its premiere, with vociferous catcalls, shouts, and mockery from Butterfly's entrance in the first act to the end, which, to Gatti-Cassazza, was even worse: "An absolutely glacial silence! Not one iota of applause! Not one shush- shush-shush! Not one shout! Nothing! It seemed that the opera was dead and buried."[54]

It is hard to challenge Carner's assertion that "the fiasco of the first *Madama Butterfly* was largely engineered."[55] Whether it reflected resentment over Puccini's success or was engineered by Sonzogno as a way of striking a blow against his hated rival remains a matter of speculation. It is clear, however, that Sonzogno had everything to gain by undermining the new opera.[56] By 1904, Puccini had become the mainstay of the Ricordi firm, with each new opera from his pen relied upon to provide a steady stream of rentals as well as income from ancillary products such as scores, arrangements, libretti, and miscellaneous knickknacks. Anything that would cast doubt on the viability of Puccini's new opera, and discourage other theaters from staging it, would affect Ricordi's balance sheet, not only for the moment, but for years to come.

Although Ricordi immediately withdrew *Madama Butterfly* from the La Scala stage, its setback was only temporary.[57] Extensively reworked, and with the lengthy second act divided into two separate acts, the opera was mounted with great success only three months later, with largely the same cast, in Brescia. From then onward, although Puccini continued to tinker with the opera over the next three years, its success was assured. Although Ricordi had never been so enthusiastic about *Butterfly* as he had been about its predecessors, it soon became as profitable to the firm as *Bohème* or *Tosca*.

Having completed *Butterfly*, Puccini found himself at a particularly difficult moment in his creative life. He was well aware that the sentimental genre of *Bohème* and *Butterfly* was increasingly seen as old-fashioned, even trivial, in light of the musical and dramatic trends sweeping Italy and Europe since the end of the century. Within little more than a week of *Butterfly*'s debut, he was writing Illica to suggest a new direction, perhaps thinking about D'Annunzio's *Francesca da Rimini*, which had appeared in 1902: "I too share Signor Giulio's opinion to avoid the 19th or 20th centuries and the tail coats and straw hats. A beautiful, poetic and cruel Middle Ages, avoiding the anti-poetic; that is, the purely decorative: a Middle Ages understood as it really was, and not as history has colored or exaggerated it."[58] Over the next three and a half years, Puccini would engage in a frantic effort to find a subject for a new opera that would represent a break with the conventional subjects that he had addressed up to now, while still engaging his muse to the same extent as before. The medieval theme would recur often over the next three years, not only with Illica (with whom Puccini explored a treatment of Hugo's *Notre-Dame de Paris*), but with other putative librettists. In mid-1904, he wrote the young playwright Valentino Soldani,[59] who had offered him a number of ideas: "I am thinking about something (perhaps) more modern. . . . I'm not sure. . . . We must surprise our blessed public, giving them a victim more modernly original and developed in a new fashion . . . hard to explain. . . . Have you read *Pelléas et Mélisande* by Maeterlinck? Have you read any of Maxim Gorky's stories?"[60] By September, they were working together on a project based on the life of the thirteenth-century saint, Margherita of Cortona, which would occupy at least part of Puccini's energy (although in all like-lihood never a large part) until the beginning of 1906, when he wrote Sol-dani, "Finally, my dear Soldani, it sorrows me a great deal to write this harshly: we're not there at all."[61]

In the meantime, Puccini had been bombarding Illica with both gen-eral thoughts and specific ideas, including a trilogy based on the Gorky sto-ries he had previously commended to Soldani (which may have provided the germ of the idea later to bear fruit in his *Trittico*), an opera buffa, and finally a French play, prompting Illica to write Ricordi in frustration: "The matter is close to becoming a farce. And who could have the nerve to sug-gest subjects to Puccini, not because of the delicate difficulty that it will en-counter, but — I confess to you — that our Doge's behavior is totally lack-ing in judgment and common sense! Last week was Gorky. Yesterday was much worse! He sent me Mirbeau's *Les mauvais bergers!* Imagine: *Avanti* [the Socialist newspaper] on stage!"[62] At the beginning of 1906, with Sol-dani out of the picture and with Puccini's tepid interest in Illica's *Maria Antonietta* waning further, the composer embarked on two new adven-tures in his search for a new libretto. The first was with D'Annunzio, with whom the composer had crossed paths briefly twice before.

Ironically, in 1894, it had been D'Annunzio who was reluctant to lower himself to what he perceived as the inferior medium of the libretto, not to mention the cultural level of the composers of the *giovane scuola*.[63] In 1900, efforts to bring the two together were rejected by the composer, who wrote Illica, "Oh marvel of marvels! D'Annunzio my librettist! But not for all the gold in the world. Too many drunken vapors, and I want to stay on my feet."[64] In 1906, D'Annunzio, desperately in need of money and pleased with the financial if not artistic outcome of *La figlia di Iorio*, was far more eager to write libretti than he had earlier been. While Puccini in 1900 was comfortably settled both with his writing team of Illica and Gia-cosa, as well as with the fundamentally conventional products that they provided him, neither situation prevailed by 1906.

In the end, however, neither of the subjects the poet offered him — *Parisina*, which D'Annunzio would later write for Mascagni, and *La rosa di Cipro* (The rose of Cyprus), appealed to Puccini, who wrote the poet in August, in a far more formal, literary style than his usual epistolary man-ner: "I don't want a 'realism' which you could painfully approach, but a 'quid medium' [middle ground] that takes hold of the audience through its facts of love and sorrow, which logically live and breathe in a poetic halo of life rather than in a dream."[65] Although his encounter with D'Annunzio was unfruitful, Puccini at this point believed that he would find the "poetic halo of life" he was seeking among the decadents, busying himself briefly with Wilde's *Florentine Tragedy*,[66] but at considerably greater length and seriousness of intent with Pierre Louÿs' *La femme et le pantin* (The woman and the puppet).

Both stories are grounded in sadomasochism and sexual perversity — as were, to a lesser extent, the stories proposed to Puccini by D'Annunzio. *La femme et le pantin*, which occupied the composer intensely well into 1907, set in the Seville of guitars and cigarette factories familiar from *Carmen*, is the story of the middle-aged Don Mateo's obsessive pursuit of the teenage temptress Conchita. She alternatively leads him on and rejects him until ultimately, goaded beyond endurance, he beats her, at which point she gladly submits to his sexual advances.[67] Puccini's attitude toward this work was not dissimilar to that of Conchita toward Mateo, alternating between enthusiasm and aversion. Only days after writing enthusiastically about the new work to Ricordi's associate Carlo Clausetti, he wrote Sybil Seligman, "what frightens me is *her* character and the plot of the play — and then all the characters seem to be unlovable, and that's a very bad thing on the stage."[68]

Whether Puccini was drawn to *La femme et le pantin* by Conchita's perversity of character — or more probably, by the direct, unbridled expression of sexual tension on its pages — he finally concluded that it would not make a successful opera. He wrote Ricordi, who by this point had invested a substantial amount of money in the project, at length in April 1907 to justify his decision.[69] Stressing that "it was not fear of the 'pruderies' of the Anglo-Saxon public," his reasons had far more to do with the difficulty of making Conchita's character comprehensible to the audience, the lack of a strong baritone role to offset what was in essence a two-character work, and finally, the ending: "which (not even speaking of the brutal part) I believe impossible to be performed, or rather, to be accepted on the stage unless one puts on a spectacle so crude that even Aretino would not have dared it."[70] By this point, however, Puccini was already moving closer to selecting the subject that would become his next opera, a subject far closer in plot and characters to his earlier works than any of those he had explored so assiduously during the past three years.

The subject he finally chose was David Belasco's *The Girl of the Golden West*, a popular sentimental tale of California's Gold Rush days from the same author who had provided Puccini with his source for *Madama Butterfly*. Set in a mining camp in the Sierras presided over by the virginal but tough-minded Minnie, the story is the customary triangle, in which Minnie rejects the advances of the baritone (the largely, but not entirely evil,

Act 3 of *La fanciulla del West*, from the Metropolitan Opera premiere in 1911, with Emmy Destinn, Enrico Caruso, and Pasquale Amato. *(Metropolitan Opera Archive)*

sheriff Jack Rance), while falling in love with the tenor (the largely, but not entirely good, bandit Ramerrez aka Dick Johnson). In the end, however, rather than either of the protagonists dying, Minnie rescues Ramerrez from the gallows where he is about to be hanged by Rance, and the two ride off into the brilliant sunrise to a new life together.[71]

Puccini had seen Belasco's play, along with others, in New York in February 1907 when visiting that city for the American premiere of *Madama Butterfly*, and had not been greatly impressed, writing Tito Ricordi: "I like the Western atmosphere, but in all the plays that I saw I found only a few scenes here and there [that I liked]. Never straightforward progress, always a jumble, and at times, bad taste or tired clichés."[72] Over the next few months his opinion of the play changed considerably. By summer, Ricordi had already recruited Carlo Zangarini, a Bolognese writer who had the special advantage of having an American mother and being fluent in English, in addition to solid professional qualifications, to prepare the libretto. Although it was not until the fall of that year that Puccini finally made his break with Illica (who was still pressing him to accept his *Maria Antonietta*), the drought was finally over.

That Puccini, after his extensive excursions into medievalism and fin de siècle sexual depravity, should select a conventional, sentimental Victorian melodrama for his next opera, suggests the extent to which he was still emotionally committed to the traditional dramatic themes of late-nineteenth-century opera, reflecting not only his desire to satisfy his audience, but also his personal tastes and inclinations. However adventurous Puccini might be in the development of his musical language, in other respects he was the archetypal Italian *homme moyen sensuel*, a man of conventional values, with few if any serious political or intellectual pursuits, whose nonmusical activities were largely limited to hunting wildfowl, driving fast automobiles, and pursuing beautiful women.

The Girl, nonetheless, offered certain possibilities that appealed to Puccini, who, largely unfamiliar with American culture, may not have appreciated the extent to which Belasco's work was riddled with the clichés of Victorian melodrama.[73] The California setting, particularly in Belasco's highly evocative staging, was certainly a new and fresh form of exoticism for both Puccini and his Italian audience,[74] while the character of Minnie as well as the redemptive dimension he saw in the work's ending both appealed deeply to the composer.[75]

Minnie, or the Girl, as she is called in Belasco's play, is a unique figure in Puccini's gallery of heroines. Virginal, an innocent romantic seeking true love, she is also tough and self-reliant, a combination saloonkeeper, teacher, and surrogate mother to a band of rowdy gold miners. Although she has some characteristics in common with Butterfly, she is no victim. As she tells Rance, who tells her that she needs a man behind her: "don't worry about me — I can look after myself. I carry a little weapon (*touching her pocket to show that she has a pistol*). I'm independent — I'm happy — the Polka's paying, and — ha! — it's all bully!" Unlike Butterfly and Tosca, who have at least some of Minnie's spirit, but are doomed to be destroyed by their cruel environments — or by what Carner characterizes, perhaps a bit tendentiously, as Puccini's "subtle, slow-working . . . sadism"[76] — Minnie not only survives, but triumphs.[77]

Puccini's behavior as a seemingly compulsive seducer, his long list of affairs with women, and the way in which he destroys his female characters from Manon to Liù, have always engendered considerable comment, not to mention outright disapproval. His attitude toward women, both in life and in art, however, was complex and equivocal, and far from dismissive. It seems clear, however, that he was looking for human connection and emotional support as much as sexual satisfaction in many of his relationships; in all likelihood, many of the women in his life found him a loving, attentive companion.[78] Many of the women to whom he was drawn, including Elvira, were strong, distinctive individuals, whose traits may well be reflected in many of his operatic characters.

In this light, and in light of the departure represented by *La fanciulla del West*, it is useful to consider the composer's relationship with Sybil Seligman and her influence on the opera. Seligman was the wife of a wealthy English banker, a talented singer, and in Budden's words, "a lover of all things Italian." That Puccini had an affair with Seligman in 1904, when they first met, is likely but not certain. Most writers believe that he did, although Budden, citing her son's comment "that his mother's aversion to sex was such that he himself wondered how he had been conceived," chooses to leave the matter open.[79] Whether or not their relationship began in bed, it soon became a deep, abiding and non-sexual friendship that lasted until his death. Characterizing her importance in Puccini's life as second only to that of Giulio Ricordi, Budden adds: "She . . . offered him subjects for his operas, smoothed his path with English managements, and in general provided him with a shoulder to cry on, if mostly at a distance. 'You are the person,' he wrote her, 'who has come nearest to understanding my nature.'"[80] Dieter Schickling called her Puccini's "mother-confessor."[81] Puccini wrote her nearly every week for twenty years.[82]

Seligman played a critical, perhaps even a determining, role in Puccini's decision to set Belasco's *Girl*, encouraging him to make the choice, arranging for the play to be translated into Italian, and providing him with constant moral support during his many moments of artistic uncertainty and personal crisis from 1907 through 1910, when *Fanciulla* was finally completed.[83] Although it would not do to overstate the point, there is a great deal of Seligman in Minnie.

In this light, the third act, and Minnie's deliverance of Ramerrez/Johnson, became critical — and the one act where the libretto deviates significantly from Belasco's play. In the play, the third act, which is set in the Polka Saloon, contains a good deal of nonessential talk and action, including the scene of Minnie's school, which the librettists changed and moved to the first act. It is followed by a brief fourth act, set in "the boundless prairies of the West" at dawn, in which Minnie and Ramerrez bid farewell to California. The critical point at the end of the third act, however, from the moment that Minnie realizes that "her boys" are about to hang Ramerrez to his deliverance at her hands, is brief, even perfunctory; as soon as the miners realize that Minnie loves him, they turn him free without further ado, in an exchange that lasts barely a minute.

In the opera, this casual exchange has become a massive *concertato*, containing more then two hundred bars of music, and running nearly ten minutes, segueing directly into the closing "Farewell, my California" moment, as Minnie and Ramerrez ride off into the dawn. As his letters to Zangarini and to Seligman make clear, this change was Puccini's idea.[84] Aside from its far greater dramatic efficacy and suitability for musical treatment, the revision brought into clear relief—far more explicitly than in the play—Minnie's role as guide, mentor, teacher, and "mother-confessor" to the miners, the same role that Seligman had come to play in Puccini's life, as well as the central redemptive theme of the opera.

Although *Fanciulla* may be considered dramatically old-fashioned, it represents a major musical departure for Puccini: he embraced the harmonic tenets of modernism (represented most significantly by Debussy's *Pelléas*), not as decorative elements superimposed on a more traditional substructure, but as the essence of the musical structure. From the block whole-tone chords of the prelude's opening motif, there is hardly a bar that does not reflect the most advanced harmonic sensibilities of the age. Budden writes: "In addition to the soft dissonances of piled-up thirds widely spaced, *Fanciulla* takes in sharper clashes of seconds, major and minor, a wealth of tritones, and of discords resolved late or not at all."[85] All of this harmonic experimentation is embedded in a rich, multilayered orchestral texture.

Puccini, however, reverts to more conventional tonality for the tender moments: for the music with which Minnie and Ramerrez declare their love, based in part on the naïve waltz tune in the third act; Ramerrez's solo in the last act, "Ch'ella mi creda libero" (let her believe me free); and above all, Jake Wallace's minstrel song and its glorious reprise at the opera's end, as the lovers sing "Addio, mio California," and the dejected miners bid them farewell to a blazing E Major resolution.

The minstrel song is the symbol of the central subtext of *Fanciulla*, the sense of uprootedness and loss that pervades Puccini's opera. The mining camp is no more than a temporary shelter for men who have left their loved ones behind, and who sing sadly:

> What will my old folks do?
> Will they think I'll never come back?
> What will my old folks do?
> Will they weep if I never come back?

They are in a clearing in the middle of the wilderness, a Dantean limbo on earth. Home, and happiness, are always somewhere else. Rance and

Ramerrez are both lost souls looking to Minnie for their deliverance. Rance sings:

> No one has ever loved me,
> I have never loved,
> Nothing has ever given me happiness.

Ramerrez, albeit somewhat implausibly, is a highwayman not by choice, but by the twist of a malign fate.

The one person keeping the camp from being hell is Minnie, who maintains the rudiments of civilization and decorum, which are constantly at threat of breaking down. What she offers, however, is not salvation, but a temporary truce. She is looking for her true love, and the men vie for that love; Sonora and Trin yearn for it, Rance demands it, and finally Ramerrez wins it. Yet the price of his salvation, and his redemption from the life of a highwayman, is the doom of the others. At the end, the pity overcomes the joy of Ramerrez's rescue, as the miners sing, over and over again, "Mai più ritornerai, no, mai più" (you will never return, no, never again).

For all *Fanciulla*'s power and brilliance, it raises troubling questions of means and ends, of the seeming incongruity between the rich, complex texture of the music and the lives of the simple folk being depicted in its pages. While in many respects it may have become the musicologists' favorite Puccini opera, it has never had the popular appeal of its predecessors, the famous trilogy of *Bohème, Tosca,* and *Butterfly.* Although melodically rich, it has fewer of the soaring melodies or memorable motifs that make those operas so enjoyable, while the absence of clearly recognizable harmonic resolution over extended periods can be frustrating to the listener who senses, underneath it all, that a clearer version of tonality is yearning to break free. Although *Fanciulla* will always have its admirers — certainly more in recent years than in the days when a respectable opera history could call it "almost as hopeless musically as it is theatrically"[86] — it will continue to be the one Puccini opera that, while recognizably a great work, is unlikely ever to be completely taken to the public's bosom.

Although Puccini had begun his quest for a libretto with the conviction that it was necessary for him to explore new themes and genres, he ultimately circled back to a subject of essentially conventional cut, not so much out of coherent conviction as from his exhaustion with what he had come to see as the essentially fruitless effort of reconciling his creative needs with the dramatic themes that were coming to supplant the late-nineteenth-century melodrama. While Puccini recognized the need for artistic renewal as much as any other composer of his generation, as Girardi points out, "according to Puccini, the way to renewal was not principally through the subject, but through the development of musical language."[87] While he was not entirely correct in this premise, he was arguably the only living European composer (with the possible exception of his contemporary Richard Strauss) who could still find renewal in the old forms. That ability would be demonstrated twice more, first with the remarkable *Trittico* and finally with the composer's last work, *Turandot*.

Chapter 12

Comic Opera

The Problem of Comedy

Comic opera, or opera buffa, has a long and glorious history in Italian opera, emerging in the eighteenth century, reaching its highest point with the works of Mozart, Paisiello, Cimarosa, and Rossini in the later eighteenth and early-nineteenth centuries. Its tangled roots can be traced back to such prototypes as the sixteenth-century *intermedio*, the seventeenth-century *contrascene*, and above all the commedia dell'arte. By the late-nineteenth century, however, its status had markedly deteriorated. Comic opera had come to occupy a distinctly inferior position in the opera world's hierarchy, well below the serious operas being written by Verdi and Puccini and performed at the *teatri massimi*, and only barely above operetta, a French import that by the end of the century had become a popular entertainment staple in Italy's smaller towns, and in the lesser theaters of its larger cities.

During the decade of the 1880s not a single opera buffa was performed at either La Scala or Venice's La Fenice. The pattern was similar elsewhere, except when financial pressures led to the theater's being rented out, as when Livorno's Goldoni was rented in 1886–1887 to the impressively named Compagnia italiana d'Opera Buffe, Semiserie e Balli for a season of comic opera.[1] Rome's Teatro Costanzi, which unlike the other *massimi* received little or no public subsidy, often had to resort to similar expedients; during the years prior to the end of the nineteenth century, it was rented to companies performing light opera, prose theater, and even at one point to a Spanish company performing zarzuelas. Except for these aberrations, opera buffa rarely invaded the grander precincts of Italian opera; when Toscanini in 1901 decided to revive *L'elisir d'amore* at La Scala, the *Gazzetta musicale di Milano* marveled that the conductor had "chosen an opera so far removed from the particular criteria that guide the programs at La Scala today."[2] The natural habitat of comic opera was the *politeama*, the multipurpose theater catering to the mass audience with its inexpensive seats and undemanding repertory.

Composers continued to carry on the tradition of Cimarosa and Rossini, but their ranks became thinner as the century progressed. In midcentury, the two brothers Luigi and Federico Ricci produced a series of popular comic operas; their 1850 opera *Crispino e la comare* (Crispino and the fairy godmother), whose charms are still apparent today, was nearly as popular as *Barbiere* in the late-nineteenth century. It was joined in the buffa repertoire by *Don Bucefalo* and *Papà Martin* by Antonio Cagnoni (1828–1896), and the works of two slightly younger composers, Enrico Sarria (1836–1883) and Emilio Usiglio (1841–1910), whose *L'educande di Sorrento* (The convent girls of Sorrento) rivaled those of his older contemporaries in popularity. Cagnoni's *Papà Martin*, however, written in 1871, was the last of the operas to find a substantial audience. As the century went on, composers found the writing of comic operas less and less rewarding, both financially and artistically.

By the 1880s and 1890s, *opera buffa* was no longer seen as an activity appropriate for a "serious" operatic composer, as it had been in the time of Rossini and Donizetti. More important, perhaps, the musical language of opera buffa had largely stood still, while that of serious opera, reflecting Verdi's transformation of the genre and the influence of Wagner, had changed dramatically. None of the features of the operas of the *giovane scuola* — the complex harmonic language, the continuous texture, the central role of the orchestra, and the intense, plethoric vocal style — seemed in the least adapted to comic opera.

Many observers of the Italian opera scene recognized this state of affairs as problematic. As discussed in an earlier chapter, Verdi saw *Falstaff* at least in part as a polemic, albeit a subtle one, against the decay of Italian opera. Ippolito Valetta, an important critic, wrote in 1898: "Complaints about the sad state of opera are heard almost daily, and of all the genres, the one that has faded most is operatic comedy, the honest expression of happy laughter that according to the old saying adds a strand to the texture of life."[3]

Although Valetta could write that "many feel the importance of not allowing this branch of truly Italian art to wither away completely," few composers during the 1890s took up the challenge, nor, despite the attention given its debut, did *Falstaff* significantly affect the choices being made by younger composers. Indeed, of the dozens of operas written by the composers of the *giovane scuola* during the decade, only one was a comic opera: *Il signor de Pourceagnac* by Alberto Franchetti, based on Molière's play *Le monsieur de Pourceaugnac*, as adapted by Ferdinando Fontana. Although some critics, including Valetta, greeted it warmly on its appearance in 1897, it failed to win favor with the public. Although it has its delightful moments, it is burdened with a clumsy libretto and goes on far too long; in the final analysis, the opera is more a tribute to Franchetti's intentions than his ability to carry them out. The composer's somewhat ponderous muse was not well suited to comedy.

The reawakening of interest in operatic comedy began immediately after the turn of the century. Ironically, the operatic project that contributed most to that reawakening was not a success, but one of the most clamorous fiascos of operatic history, the famous premiere of Pietro Mascagni's *Le Maschere* (The Masks).

Mascagni's Le Maschere and Its Seven Premieres

Mascagni, who was known for his verbal agility, satirical observations and witty remarks, was passionately devoted to Rossini, Pergolesi, and the opera buffa tradition. Not surprisingly, he began to show an interest in comic opera not long after his successful debut with *Cavalleria*; early in 1895, a newspaper reported that "he has a great desire to test himself in the [comic opera] field."[4] The composer had, indeed, approached the poet Lorenzo Stecchetti seeking such a libretto; Mascagni's thinking, which ultimately led to the creation of *Le Maschere*, was described some years later by his collaborator, Luigi Illica:

> [Steccheti] proposed an adaptation of Goldoni's *Baruffe chiozzotte*.[5] While that subject didn't fit the composer's ideas, who, looking for a better option along the same lines, had briefly hoped to set *Basi e bote*, the exquisite original Venetian comedy . . . written by Arrigo Boito.[6] As his plans gradually matured, he thought about choosing a folk subject [*soggetto tipico*], which would capture the spirit of our traditional musical comedy, reaching back into his roots and finding his way to that which is unmistakable and unalterable in Italian theater. From this starting point it was natural that his researches would turn to that inexhaustible treasure of the Italian comic genius, the commedia dell'arte.[7]

In August 1896, while Mascagni and Illica were in the midst of their collaboration on *Iris*, the composer proposed that the two also collaborate on a commedia dell'arte subject. Illica agreed enthusiastically, and the project, still no more than an idea, was quickly accepted by Sonzogno, to whom Mascagni still owed an opera.[8]

The commedia dell'arte, which dominated Italian theatrical life during the sixteenth and seventeenth centuries, was only a faint cultural memory to most Italians in the 1890s. An improvisational comedy based on a series of stock characters — Pantalone, the miserly father; Arlecchino or Harlequin, the clever, amoral servant; the Doctor, pompous and pretentious; the Lovers, and so forth — it represented a unique blend of verbal virtuosity, slapstick, and dance movement, into which musical numbers were regularly interpolated. While the words were improvised, the plots, often elaborate and convoluted, were concocted in advance; indeed, books of scenarios, either published or handwritten, were part of the equipment of any commedia company, as were the masks that were distinctive to particular characters, or the particular ways in which an actor was to perform what were known as "lazzi," (routines), specific to each classic character.

The intrigues of the commedia grew out of the social reality of the times. The plots, however complex or far-fetched, were always based on the difficulties of intimate relationships, between fathers and children, brothers and sisters, married couples, or illicit lovers. The characters were types recognizable in any Italian town, while their conflicts, grounded in love, jealousy, ambition, or greed, resonated with anyone who had ever shared any of those feelings. As Vernon Lee wrote, in one of the first works to reawaken the late-nineteenth century's interest in the commedia: "The Comedy of Masks was not an invention, not a revelation, it was a natural product; it did not seize hold of national taste, it sprang up and developed everywhere because its seeds had long existed in the Italian mind. . . . From the humbler quarters of the towns it spread to the nobler, until the high-born and learned Academicians . . . were interrupted by the yells of laughter of the spectators of Pantaloon and Harlequin over the way."[9]

By the eighteenth century, however, the commedia dell'arte was fading; as Lee writes, "The life of the style was fast ebbing; no new types appeared; the old became stereotyped; the jokes and gestures and acrobatic feats became traditional. . . . The day of its dethronement was fast approaching."[10]

Although echoes of the the commedia dell'arte can be heard in the opera buffa repertoire well into the nineteenth century, by the latter part of the century the genre itself was long gone. While everyone knew Harlequin and Punch, few remembered that they had once been part of a rich, intricate theatrical milieu. During the 1880s and 1890s the first historic studies of the commedia began to appear, while writers like Boito dis-

covered it as a source for their own creative energies. Even so, the commedia dell'arte in its rich variety was still little known to all but a handful of scholars. Its very remoteness made it that much more appealing to
Illica and Mascagni, still seeking out alternatives to the tired formulas of
operatic melodrama beyond even *Iris*, the radical opera on which they
were already working.

For Mascagni, as with everything, the decision to write an opera based
on the commedia dell'arte, the "symbol of the Italic spirit," as he referred
to it, was not only artistic, but a contribution to the polemic on the state of
opera. "Today, the public goes to the theater to make itself miserable, to
ruin their digestion with violent emotions," he wrote. "We, the authors, no
longer know how to laugh on stage," he added in typically Mascagnian
rhetorical vein: "To revive the commedia dell'arte seems to me an undertaking worthy of an artist of conscience. . . . Why, since [Rossini], has not
one of us dared to allow into the murky atmosphere of the contemporary
theater a glimmer of that smile, that light-hearted and serene satire, to link
our activities of today with that glorious tradition, already too far from our
times and our souls?"[11] The ambitions of Mascagni and Illica went far beyond the mere re-creation of a sixteenth-century dramatic genre; indeed,
they led to the composer and librettist coming to see their work as a self-
referential or metatheatrical commentary, both on the commedia dell'arte
as well as on the operatic world of their time. Such an approach to opera,
unprecedented at this point — and not only in Italy — would thoroughly
mystify their audience when the work finally appeared.

Mascagni and Illica sought to create a historically layered work through
their self-conscious revival of an ancient art form, juxtaposing the conventions of commedia dell'arte with those of contemporary opera, and in so
doing commenting on the theatricality of that art form, as well as their
own. For Mascagni, that objective called for a musical treatment that
would reflect the work's historicity by making the score, at least in part, "a
satirical review of the musical styles of all periods, from Mozart to today."[12]
He pursued this program by weaving affectionate parodies of the music of
composers past and present (including himself) into the texture of the work.
Illica took the idea of the work as commentary on itself even further, using
the customary practice of the commedia dell'arte, as described by a classic
1699 text, as his point of departure: "The manager . . . must lay out the subject before it is performed. [His] duty is not just to read the subject but to
explain [to the company] the characters with their special names and characteristics, the plot of the tale, the setting in which it takes place."[13]

Le Maschere opens with a Prologue, described in the libretto as "before

Souvenir postcard from the premiere of Mascagni's *Le Maschere*, 1901. *(Author's Collection)*

the performance." The stage directions for the opera call for the curtain to be up and the stage lit "as for a rehearsal," as the conductor enters and gives the downbeat for the orchestra to begin the overture. After a few bars: "Giocadio (the stage manager) . . . rushes on stage, slightly out of breath, begs the conductor to break off the performance; then, as director, calls the performers together and explains 'the idea' and 'the subject,' and then invites them to express their own impressions of their characters." Giocadio's discourse is not only spoken rather than sung, but is to be improvised by the actor playing the role.[14] The singers enter still dressed in street clothes,[15] and each one steps forward, singing a few bars about his or her character. At the end of the Prologue, as they leave for their dressing rooms, Giocadio informs the conductor that he may now begin the overture, and instructs the stagehands to lower the curtain.

While the device of the prologue that recognizes and manipulates the theatricality of the stage event was a staple of Roman comedy and probably goes back to the earliest days of theater, it had largely disappeared from both prose theater and opera by the nineteenth century. The prologue in Leoncavallo's *Pagliacci* is an isolated and limited exception, designed more to accentuate the work's verismo character than to comment on its theatricality. Mascagni and Illica go far in the opposite direction, setting their opera in a series of stylized, symbolic frames that give the work, in one writer's words, a "surreal, fabulous, antirealistic theatricality."[16] The Prologue not only makes it clear that a theatrical event is to be performed, but that the characters themselves are not to be taken seriously *as characters*, because they are masks; the actors are playing stock figures, which are in turn playing at being characters in a drama. The self-conscious play of the masks *as masks* that is initiated in the Prologue is a recurrent theme in the libretto, in which the characters repeatedly move back and forth between their fixed identities as dramatic characters and their mobile identities as masks, culminating in the second-act finale, in which the effects of a magic powder drive the entire cast — accompanied by music that is itself a parody of the similar finale in Rossini's *Barbiere* — to shout out all of the many names by which their characters are known in a kind of giddy cacophony.

For the most part the opera maintains a light touch suitable to its subject; yet periodically it gives way to a need to invest the masks with a symbolic, even patriotic weight, in the process treating their irreverence with a reverence that undermines the entire undertaking. Illica's libretto is at its weakest at the very end, when the entire cast comes forward and intones a hymn to the masks:

> O inspired Italian masks, you gave
> The entire world the inspired art, that
> As in life, alternates laughter and tears,
> Hail, O grandmother of ours, you have returned!

and

> They tried to bury you, but you, not dead,
> Went on obstinately throbbing in your tomb;
> And vainly shouted to the gravedigger of oblivion:
> "I still live!" And, indeed, you have risen again!

In modern productions, rather than end *Le Maschere* with this hymn, it has become customary to conclude the opera in less sententious and more entertaining fashion by following the hymn with a reprise of the brilliant, lively Furlana from the second-act ballroom scene.[17]

The first performance of *Le Maschere* soon became a major issue in itself, with the decision to have the opera make its debut simultaneously in seven theaters across the Italian peninsula becoming a matter of controversy and derision. The idea's origins are obscure; Mascagni's early biographer Pompei writes that it originated in a difference between the composer and his publisher: "[Mascagni] had promised the premiere to the Costanzi, and the publisher was, instead, obligated to give the work to La Scala; neither wanting, or able, to give way to the other, they had recourse to the expedient of giving the opera in both theaters on the same night."[18] While plausible enough as far as it goes, it hardly explains how two theaters would expand into seven, something that appears most likely to have sprung from Sonzogno's fertile and publicity-minded brain.[19] Arranging for an opera to be inserted simultaneously into the schedules of seven separate opera houses was a difficult matter, though not beyond the publisher's organizing capacities. Fortunately for Sonzogno, Ricordi, who was still hoping for another Mascagni opera to follow *Iris*, chose not to use his power to block the houses he controlled from mounting the new opera. Responding to an unusually deferential letter from the composer, he sent Mascagni a telegram assuring him that he would never "make impositions that could damage our excellent relationship."[20]

On January 17, 1901, after a barrage of publicity, *Le Maschere* made its debut simultaneously in six opera houses, the Naples performance having been delayed because of the illness of the tenor Anselmi. The six theaters, in addition to La Scala and the Costanzi, were La Fenice in Venice, the Regio in Turin, the Carlo Felice in Genoa, and the Filarmonico in Verona. Mascagni was on the podium in Rome, with Celestina Boninsegna, Bice Adami, and Amadeo Bassi. In Milan, Toscanini conducted a cast that included Caruso and Emma Carelli. Maria Farneti, still a student at the Liceo Rossini, sang the female lead in Venice, under the baton of Agide Jacchia, another Mascagni student.

Except in Rome, where the opera was greeted enthusiastically, the premiere of *Le Maschere* was perhaps the most unequivocal, spectacular, and ignominious fiasco in the history of Italian opera, dwarfing, if only in its sheer scale, the disaster of *Madama Butterfly* three years later. The Prologue was greeted with stunned incomprehension; as the first act unfolded, as a reviewer of the Milan performance wrote, "the public seemed truly seized by an untamable furor."[21] The occasion was the first of the composer's affectionate parodies, a parody of an aria from his own *Iris*: "A long mocking cry of amazement escaped from a thousand mouths. The public recognized the theme. . . . From that moment the theater boiled over. A relentless hunt for plagarisms, recollections, resemblances began. One voice cried '*La bohème!*' another responded 'Viva Puccini!'[22]

The shouting and whistling continued through the second act. By the third act of what was a very long opera, the public was tired, and the end came with neither applause nor condemnation. The audience filed out almost in silence. In Genoa, during the course of the last act the whistles and boos became so loud and continuous that the singers could not be heard, and the management ordered the curtain brought down even before the opera was over.[23] The outcome, although more decorous, was little better in Turin, Venice, or Verona.

Listening to *Le Maschere* today, it is hard to imagine the reasons for this intense, even viciously hostile reception. In part, it was a reaction to the excessive publicity and preposterously overblown claims made for the work, which Ashbrook aptly characterizes as "a deft comedy . . . too slender to withstand the exaggerations of its launching."[24] Valetta noted that "every paradoxical device of *réclame* was put to work to blow up the importance of the event in advance," including "a flood of more or less illustrated special editions, commemorative postcards in which the composer's head appeared crowned with a laurel wreath, and on and on with every bizarre touch of the most absurd attention-grabbing activity was put in motion."[25] Another writer commented that the "hubbub of advance, out of place, publicity was destined to create an atmosphere of utter distaste. . . . God protect me from my friends!"[26] Adding fuel to the flames, a rumor, unfounded but widely accepted as true, spread across Italy that the composer had dedicated the opera "to myself, as a token of my great esteem and unshakeable affection."[27]

While a reaction to the excessive claims made for the work played a part in its reception, so did the near-total incomprehension of its creators' intentions. While the Prologue prompted little more than stunned silence, Mascagni's affectionate parodies and associations were seen as improper or offensive by the 1901 audience. Not only did the audiences react violently; critics castigated the composer for his behavior, seen as outright plagarism or at best lèse-majesté. One critic took Mascagni severely to task for setting Columbina's sexual longings to a Bellinian cantilena reminiscent of "Casta diva," calling it "ridiculous and inappropriate."[28] To the nineteenth-century mind, with its insistence on originality in art, parody, especially self-parody, was not acceptable practice for a serious composer. *Le Maschere*, in many respects, was a work well ahead of its time, for which an audience had not yet come into being.

These circumstances might well have sunk a masterwork. Unfortunately, *Le Maschere*, while delightful, falls short of such stature. The Roman premiere, with its two intermissions, took more than four hours, ending well past one in the morning. For a comic opera with an exiguous plot, offering little opportunity for the audience to engage emotionally with its stylized characters, this was far too long to sustain their interest. While Illica had the intellectual ability to conceive of a dazzling commedia dell'arte entertainment, he lacked the creative resources to bring it into being. His intrigues, rather than being devious and complex in the true commedia tradition, are simplistic, while his language lacks the verbal dexterity the genre demands.[29]

Mascagni, however, is at his best throughout much of the opera. The opportunity to write for a small orchestra, compose set pieces in a traditional vein, adopt a largely diatonic vocabulary, manipulate the conventions of Italian opera, and indulge his taste for musical play that found no outlet in his more "serious" works brought forth some of the most melodically rich music he had ever written. The delights of the score range from the sparkling overture — a small masterwork in itself — to arias, duets, dances, ensembles, and the spectacular *concertato* that concludes the first act, a homage to Ponchielli modeled after the third-act finale of *La Gioconda*, in which the lovers' cantilena — into which a thinly veiled parody of the composer's famous aria "Apri la tua finestra" from *Iris* is embedded — soars over the orchestra and chorus. *Le Maschere*, however, tends to lose its momentum as it proceeds. The first act is the strongest, while in the third act, precisely when Illica's dramatic invention has clearly run out of steam, the composer's melodic vein — on which everything depends in this opera — begins to falter. The outcome is anticlimactic, both musically and dramatically.

Mascagni never lost faith in *Le Maschere*. He reworked it extensively, cutting it drastically, for a Roman revival in 1905, and again — restoring some of the 1905 cuts — for a 1931 revival at La Scala, after which it received a considerable number of performances in Italy up to the outbreak of the war. In recent years, it has been revived intermittently with some success, but not to the extent that it appears likely to move into the repertoire. The significance of *Le Maschere*, however, aside from its musical merits, lies in its role as precursor to a new genre of opera. In addition to the works of Ermanno Wolf-Ferrari, which I discuss below, the emergence of the modern sensibility in European music in the second and third decades of the twentieth century enabled a new generation of composers, including Malipiero and Casella in Italy, and Busoni, Strauss, and Stravinsky further afield, to discover "a kinship — real or imagined — with the commedia dell'arte and opera buffa traditions, leapfrogging backward over a century of Romantic excess." [30] Gianandrea Gavazzeni's conclusion that "Mascagni and Illica stand behind that world with [their] innovative genius" is perhaps an exaggeration, but not an outrageous one.[31]

Ermanno Wolf-Ferrari

Wolf-Ferrari and the Goldoni Operas

The one Italian composer of the generations that followed Verdi who created a substantial body of comic operas was Ermano Wolf-Ferrari. Although a contemporary of Zandonai and Montemezzi, as well as Casella and Malipiero, he inhabited a world thoroughly different in both musical language and spirit from their worlds. Wolf-Ferrari was a sensitive, emotionally delicate individual, whose cultural formation was rooted in the German classics of Bach, Handel, and Mozart. A colleague wrote of him: "[He] yearned for nature and its uncontaminated innocence. Everything that came from the humanity of today seemed to him ruined by bad counsel, by intellectual dishonesty, by lying egoism, which destroy, as he has written, the child that is alive in us from birth."[32] Timid and reclusive, he lived most of his life in isolation from his fellow human beings; to those he admitted into his friendship, however, he radiated a quiet decency of an almost spiritual quality.

Wolf-Ferrari's father was a German painter named August Wolf from the small town of Ladenburg, on the Neckar River near Heidelberg. Sent to Italy by a Bavarian nobleman to make copies of Renaissance paintings for the nobleman's collection, Wolf fell in love with a young Venetian woman named Emilia Ferrari, married her, and settled in Venice, where he remained for the rest of his life. Ermanno Wolf-Ferrari — who adopted the double-barreled name at nineteen[33] — was their first child, born in 1876. He was the product of an unusually multicultural household, speaking three languages from childhood (including the distinctive Venetian dialect) and exposed from infancy to both Italian and German music and art. Although he lived most of his adult life in Germany, and may indeed have personally felt more at home there, as a composer he thought of himself as Italian first and foremost, writing all but one of his thirteen operas to Italian texts.

In contrast to the childhoods of many of his contemporaries, his upbringing was sheltered and supportive. The Wolf household was materially comfortable and part of a cultured milieu in which evenings of Bach and long philosophical discussions on the meaning of life were commonplace, and in which artistic aspirations were to be nurtured rather than discouraged. When Wolf-Ferrari was twelve, his father took him to La Fenice to see Rossini's *Barbiere,* and a year later to Bayreuth to be introduced to Wagner's music.[34] Although the young Wolf-Ferrari showed gifts both as a painter and a musician, at the age of sixteen he decided to devote himself to music and entered the Akademie der Tonkunst in Munich, where he studied with Rheinberger and Abel.

After finishing his studies at Munich in 1895, Wolf-Ferrari returned to Italy, where over the course of the next few years he directed a German choral society in Milan, while composing a number of large-scale chamber and choral works, including two oratorios on biblical themes. By the fall of 1899 he had completed his first opera, *Cenerentola* (Cinderella). Staged at La Fenice early in 1900 in a production subsidized by the composer's family and friends, it was a disaster, with "laughter, whistling, shouts, that resumed implacably with every succeeding act."[35] The mortified and hypersensitive composer immediately withdrew the opera, soon thereafter fleeing Venice and Italy entirely for what he hoped would be a more receptive musical environment in Germany.

In retrospect, the Venetian fiasco of *Cenerentola* is more understandable than the opera's subsequent modest German success. *Cenerentola* is, of course, a retelling of the Cinderella story; in the treatment by Wolf-Ferrari and his librettist, the Venetian poetess Maria Pezzè-Pascolato, it becomes a vast Wagnerian canvas that totally overwhelms the modest fairy tale. The opera's tone is established with its opening, an intensely chromatic prelude patently derivative of its counterpart in *Tristan*. The prelude is followed by a lament sung by Cinderella running some 250 bars, which, after a long orchestral interlude, is followed by an even longer choral scene, culminating in a vision of Cinderella's mother in heaven enshrined on a golden throne among the Blessed. *Cenerentola* is scored for a massive orchestra, including bells, organ, and glockenspiel; the cast requires fourteen solo roles along with, as described in the score, "chamberlains, wise men, pages, courtiers, guests, heralds, servants, angels, sylphides, youths, common people, etc., etc." The story is inflated to such an extent, and set by the composer in such an overblown, ponderous Wagnerian manner that it is rendered all but indigestible.

Wolf-Ferrari's first opera, indeed, has far more in common with the works of contemporary German composers such as Humperdinck and Pfitzner than it does with anything being written in Italy at the time. Perhaps for that reason, after reappearing in Bremen in 1902 as *Aschenbrödel*, it had a modest although short-lived success in German opera houses. In the meantime, however, the composer's musical direction had changed dramatically. The change was prompted by his attending the January 1901 Venice premiere of Mascagni's *Le maschere*, the opera that set him on a new course, leading to the series of comic operas that would make his reputation. Mascagni's opera, however, was not a model to be followed literally. As Wolf-Ferrari later wrote: "Mascagni and Illica had called back to life the old masks of the commedia dell'arte, but had presented them as they found them in the storeroom, dusty, hard, wooden like puppets. Had the great reforms of Goldoni, who had been inspired by the masks, but presented them in a new light of extraordinary brilliance, recreating their fundamental traits through direct observation of the Venetian people, capturing their types, their characters, their aspects, and rendering them in inimitable language, been in vain?"[36]

Wolf-Ferrari concluded that the commedia dell'arte could serve as the starting point for a modern comic opera, but that "it was necessary to place them in a setting in which they were truly alive, rather than in Illica's symbolic manner."[37] The comedies of Carlo Goldoni, which were the staple of Venetian prose theater during his youth and with which he was intimately familiar, offered him a dramatic model to set alongside the musical model suggested by *Le Maschere*. By the following year he had decided to adapt Goldoni's *Le donne curiose* (The curious women) for his next opera, and found a collaborator in Count Luigi Sugana, a popular although dissolute local poet and café habitué. While preparing himself for his new project, Wolf-Ferrari, an extraordinarily fecund composer, dashed off another oratorio, a setting of Dante's *La vita nuova* for baritone, soprano, chorus, and orchestra.[38]

Carlo Goldoni (1707–1793), often dubbed "the father of Italian comedy," was the central figure in the transformation of the commedia dell'arte from the improvisational comedy of stereotypes into a written comedy of character grounded in the scenes and figures of Venetian life. In a series of plays written largely in the 1740s and 1750s he gradually deemphasized the roles of the traditional masked characters of the commedia, ultimately doing away with them completely. In their place, he created a vivid gallery of gondoliers, porters, lawyers, doctors, and merchants, all drawn from the streets and *campi* of his native Venice. Goldoni's plays vividly captured the texture of Venetian life; in Lee's description: "He enjoyed giving, as it were a vertical section of a middle-class house, showing at the same time the inhabitants of the various floors, letting us see the richer and poorer inmates at their amusements and occupations; displaying two or three households at once, with their efforts to make a fine show to each other, with their whole life not only of the parlor and the office but of the staircase and house door."[39]

In plays such as *Le donne curiose* and *I rusteghi* (The bumpkins), Goldoni created a host of distinctive characters who interact with one another in plots that, although sometimes complex in their interactions and relationships, never lose their direct connection with the social reality of the time, or with their ultimate goal: to bring about the union of young lovers and the restoration of comity among their families and friends. Goldoni had a strongly democratic spirit and, by the standards of the time, was something of a feminist; his women are usually stronger figures than his men, and generally have the better of them in the end. In *La locandiera* (The inn-keeper), one of his best works, the pretty innkeeper, an independent, successful woman, juggles the affections of a number of more or less silly noblemen, ending up marrying the man of her choice, her devoted retainer Fabrizio.

Wolf-Ferrari and Sugana set to work in the summer of 1902, retaining most of Goldoni's dialogue, while reducing his text to proportions appropriate for a libretto. Understanding that the success of the work would depend on the audience's being able to follow not only the interplay between the many characters but the individual words as well, and with the example of Mascagni's opera in his ears, Wolf-Ferrari reinvented his musical language. He abandoned the turgid chromaticism of *Cenerentola* for a light diatonic style, in which the words could be clearly understood and the action could move forward largely uninterrupted by orchestral commentary. This discovery was liberating; as de Rensis writes, most probably paraphrasing the composer's own words: "The composer's position is one of both servitude and liberty: servitude to the characters of the play, liberty, or rather liberation, from the egotistical, however proud, demands of symphonic stature."[40] In his Venetian roots, Wolf-Ferrari had found the means to exorcise Wagner's ghost and draw his inspiration from earlier composers, of whom the most important was Mozart.

Wolf-Ferrari completed *Le donne curiose* in August 1903.[41] In the meantime, he had returned to Venice, where he had been appointed head of the Liceo Benedetto Marcello, the city's conservatory. The opera, in German translation, made its debut at Munich's Residenztheater in November. It was received enthusiastically by the audience, and was soon picked up by other theaters in Germany and Austria, appearing under the batons of Pfitzner in Berlin, Mahler in Vienna, and Nikisch in Leipzig. In Italy, to the composer's bitter disappointment, there was not even an echo: "The critics didn't even show even the curiosity to inform themselves about an Italian opera acclaimed and discussed abroad, at the same time as they cared so much about operas by foreign composers. The publishers didn't even go out of their way, even for a commercial proposition."[42] Wolf-Ferrari's inability to get a hearing for his works in Italy, however popular they might be in northern Europe, was a constant source of frustration for a man who, however disinclined by temperament to fight for his music in the competitive, commercial atmosphere of the Italian opera word, was nonetheless certain of its worth.

The success, at least in Germany, of *Le donne curiose* led Sugana and Wolf-Ferrari to proceed immediately to set Goldoni's *I rusteghi*, renamed *I quattro rusteghi* (The four bumpkins) for the opera stage.[43] After Sugana's unexpected death, the libretto was taken up and completed by Giuseppe Pizzolato, a painter and poet of somewhat more reliable habits than his predecessor. *I quattro rusteghi* was finished at the beginning of 1906, and received its first performance at the Stadttheater in Munich in March, with a Berlin performance following a few days later. As with its predecessor, it soon made a successful round of German opera houses, but was ignored in Italy.

I quattro rusteghi, along with the short "comic intermezzo" *Il segreto di Susanna*, are Wolf-Ferrari's finest achievements, behind only Puccini's *Gianni Schicchi* as the finest Italian comic operas of the twentieth century. *Le donne curiose* in many respects is a work in progress; Wolf-Ferrari is trying to create a new genre, or perhaps a new subgenre of the opera buffa, but is not yet in full control of his materials. His use of the same simple figurations and rhythms becomes repetitive at times, while his melodic vein is still derivative. One hears recurrent echoes of Wagner as well as self-conscious Mozartean evocations, as in the closing duet of the two lovers. Written three years later — the product of both extensive study of eighteenth-century music in the library of the Liceo Benedetto Marcello and considerable inward reflection — *I quattro rusteghi* is a finer work, pared down to the bare essentials, in which the composer has found his own personal and distinctive melodic vein.

I quattro rusteghi is a uniquely Venetian opera; as Giorgio Vigolo writes, it is "the harmonic and melodic vibration of Venetian speech."[44] Except for the few lines of the foreigner Count Riccardo, an Italian from outside Venice, all of the dialogue in *I quattro rusteghi* is in Venetian dialect. The opera is rich in melodies that evoke the eighteenth-century spirit of Venice, while avoiding pastiche and remaining true to the composer's time. Wolf-Ferrari's melodies often begin innocently, with a series of repeated notes or a simple triad only to move with seeming inevitability in an unexpected melodic or harmonic direction, often leading, as in Filipeto's aria "Lucieta xe un bel nome" (Lucieta is a lovely name), to moments of ineffable tenderness or delight. They have strangely moving and nostalgic undercurrents, yet never fall into sentimentality. While Wolf-Ferrari is far from the equal of his two models, the Mozart of *Le nozze di Figaro* and the Verdi of *Fal-*

staff, in this opera he somehow found in himself a simplicity and purity of spirit not unlike that of those masters.

Wolf-Ferrari's decision to subordinate his music to Goldoni's text was conscious and deliberate, and therein lies the greatest weakness of *I quattro rusteghi*. For long stretches, the music, however ingeniously wrought, is no more than accompaniment to what can easily appear to be over-extended patter. For all his many delightful and evocative melodies, the composer was unable to find a way to give the opera a strong overarching musical — as distinct from dramatic — structure. Although delightful in performance, particularly for those whose grasp of Venetian dialect is adequate to follow the nuances of Goldoni's repartee, *I quattro rusteghi* leaves a far less lasting effect on the listener's mind or heart than either *Figaro* or *Falstaff*.

Wolf-Ferrari's next comic effort was *Il segreto di Susanna* (Susanna's secret), to a libretto by the veteran Neapolitan writer Enrico Golisciani, a modern version of the eighteenth-century "comic intermezzo" modeled after the genre's most famous example, Pergolesi's *La serva padrona*. The exiguous and today politically incorrect story concerns two newlyweds: the husband, smelling cigarette smoke in the home, suspects that his wife has a lover, only to discover that she has taken up smoking. In the end, they go off to bed, both smoking, arm in arm. The husband and wife are the only singing roles, accompanied by a mute servant, as in Pergolesi's work. First performed in Munich in 1909, it was staged at the Costanzi in 1911 — Wolf-Ferrari's first opera to be performed in Italy since the *Cenerentola* disaster. It was warmly received, with the critic Nicola D'Atri writing: "The archaic spirit blows gently through the work, which emerges, however, in new garb, capturing us with the charm of its harmonies and its modern instrumentation, carried out with such mastery as to render it simple, clear, and utterly delightful."[45] Both for its charm, and for its modest demands, it remains Wolf-Ferrari's most widely heard opera today.

Susanna is a musical gem. Freed from any need to defer to a revered literary source, or to allow room for complicated intrigues to unfold, Wolf-Ferrari created a work with a far more integrated and musically driven structure within its forty-five-minute compass than any of his Goldoni operas. It is a work in which words, music, and action form a single coherent whole, prompting the famous conductor Felix Mottl to comment, "strange as it may seem, this is the most Wagnerian opera I know."[46] Relieved by the work's contemporary setting of any need to re-create the atmosphere of an earlier era in his music, the composer allowed his musical imagination to become more unbuttoned, creating a charming Chopinesque melody for Susanna's piano playing, and evoking Debussy's *Prélude à l'après-midi d'un faune* to suggest the smoke rising from her cigarette. His music for the two newlyweds is romantic without being sentimental, tapping the purer qualities of the early-nineteenth-century. *Il segreto di Susanna* is, within the limits of its modest ambitions, a perfectly realized work.

The same cannot be said about Wolf-Ferrari's next opera. *I gioielli della Madonna* (The jewels of the Madonna) was something totally unexpected, a radical departure from everything that the composer had previously attempted in the world of opera. With a libretto by Golisciani and Carlo Zangarini (who was working at the same time on Puccini's *Fanciulla*), *I gioielli della Madonna* is an opera that is veristic almost to the point of parody, set in the heartland of verismo opera, the mean streets of Naples' poor quarters.[47] While beautifully crafted, as are all of Wolf-Ferrari's mature works, and not without some memorable music, the overall effect of the opera is that of a work divided in three roughly equal parts: self-conscious evocations of Neapolitan popular music, Mascagnian vocal rhetoric, and orchestral perorations in the vein of Richard Strauss's *Salome* and *Elektra*.

It is unclear whether Wolf-Ferrari was prompted by the intellectual challenge of working in a radically different genre, or whether he was seeking the popular success with Italian audiences that continued to elude him. If it was the latter, he was once again to be deeply disappointed. *I gioielli della Madonna* spread quickly after its successful Berlin debut in 1911. Performed in Chicago in the composer's presence only weeks after its Berlin debut, it soon became popular in the United States and Great Britain, as well as in German theaters, to such an extent that during the 1913–1914 season it was performed simultaneously by the French and Flemish opera houses in Antwerp.[48] Only in Italy did it fail to find an audience.

The near-total neglect of Wolf-Ferrari's operas in Italy during these years had more to do with the vicissitudes of the publishing industry then with the tastes of Italian operagoers. The rights to his operas were held by the Viennese publisher Josef Weinberger, a firm with which neither Ricordi nor Sonzogno had a relationship during the first decade of the century. Giulio Ricordi had never shown great interest in acquiring operatic rights from foreign publishers; while Edoardo Sonzogno had done so in earlier days, by the dawn of the twentieth century he had largely lost interest. It was only in 1911 that his nephew Lorenzo bought the rights to Wolf-Ferrari's operas from Weinberger, after he had broken with his uncle's firm and begun to build his own publishing house.

Il segreto di Susanna made its Roman debut in 1911, and soon began to appear elsewhere in Italy, while *Le donne curiose* appeared at La Scala in 1913, followed by productions in Brescia, Trieste, and Naples. *I quattro rusteghi* arrived at Milan's Teatro Lirico in June 1914, where it was greeted enthusiastically with "the same loud applause with which German audiences have welcomed it for many years."[49] In the 1920s, it moved into the Italian repertory, receiving at least eighteen productions during the decade. Although it failed to sustain that position, it continues to be performed intermittently in Italy.[50]

Sonzogno's similar efforts on behalf of *I gioielli della Madonna*, which he presented in 1913 at the Carlo Felice in Genoa, however, were unsuccessful. No other theater showed interest in the work, and it disappeared from the Italian stage until a 1953 Roman revival. While Italian verismo, particularly in Wolf-Ferrari's more sophisticated treatment, might find an audience overseas, and American audiences might still find a Neapolitan setting exotic, to Italian operagoers of 1913 Naples was a tired, clichéd setting, and verismo was a fad that had come and gone. A new opera in that genre had little appeal for the Italian audience.

By this point, however, Wolf-Ferrari had already made an important decision. In 1909, worn out by the conflicts at the Liceo Benedetto Marcello, and alienated from Italian musical life, he left Italy once again for Germany, retreating to the first of a series of villas near Munich. At thirty-three, he was still the sensitive, retiring figure that he had been as a small child, and his years in the public's eye had taken a toll. In Germany he found a retreat; as described by an intimate friend: "He lives a few kilometers from the village [of Planegg], on a hill, in a lovely park-like setting, half cut off from the world by woods, where he has a large, silent and withdrawn villa. In that silence he passes the entire year, alone, with his wife and his solitude. The silence is broken by the frequent cries of four immense, ferocious pure-bred dogs, that will all but assault the visitor that comes their way, not sparing him, if the maestro and his wife are not quick to call them off, a certain fleeting panic."[51]

His Bavarian hideaway was a retreat not only from a clamorous world, but from an era in which he was no longer at home. As Zanetti writes, "his clear intention was to withdraw from the evolutionary debates [of music] and to evoke thereby a golden age."[52] He continued to compose steadily, including three more operas based on Goldoni's plays, in which, however, he largely repeats himself, recycling the style he had perfected with *I quattro rusteghi*, each time becoming a little thinner and less fresh. He lifted his comic mask, however, with his second and far more deeply felt tragic opera *Sly*, first performed at La Scala in 1927; the work has been rediscovered and successfully revived in recent years. His last opera, *Gli dei a Thebes* (The gods at Thebes) was performed in 1943. He returned to Venice in 1947, where he died the following year.

Wolf-Ferrari's lifelong effort to revive Italian comic opera by finding a synthesis of new and old left two works of lasting value: *I quattro rusteghi* and *Il segreto di Susanna*. The finest Italian comic opera of the century, however, was neither of these, but Puccini's *Gianni Schicchi*, the last opera in his 1919 *Il trittico*. The story of the clever Schicchi who outwits the greedy Donati family, ensuring his own wealth and enabling his daughter to marry her beloved Rinuccio, *Gianni Schicchi* is a masterpiece of comic brio, lively and delightful from beginning to end, musically as rich as it is dramatically entertaining. Puccini's musical resources, the rich harmonic texture, and the complex motivic interplay that gives the piece an almost symphonic structure, raise *Gianni Schicchi* to a higher level than Wolf-Ferrari's works, making it the true musical descendant of Verdi's *Falstaff*.

There is a more fundamental difference, however, between Puccini's masterwork and those of Wolf-Ferrari. As Girardi writes, "Puccini's idea of comedy was wicked, often bordering on the grotesque and tinged by the macabre."[53] *Gianni Schicchi*, for all its comic brio, is a cynical, even angry work, in which most of the characters are caricatures, embodiments of greed, foils for the supposedly lovable trickster Schicchi. Yet, as the composer reminds us at the end, Schicchi was condemned to the eighth circle of hell by Dante for his trickery, where he is depicted as a goblin angrily preying on his fellow inmates for eternity.[54]

The world of Wolf-Ferrari's comedy is a sunnier, happier place. There may be misunderstandings in that world, but they are soon put to right. People may be thickheaded, pompous, or narrow-minded, but they are never evil; their conflicts are always reconciled, and the lovers always go off happily arm in arm. For Wolf-Ferrari, a man who found so much of human society so unpleasant and even unbearable, comedy was an opportunity to re-create the world, not as it was, but as it should be. His last Goldoni opera, *Il campiello*, written in the mid-1930s as dictators took power and war clouds gathered over Europe, breathes the same air and exudes the same serenity of spirit as *I quattro rusteghi*, written thirty years earlier in a different, more peaceful, era. One hundred years later, the opportunity to share Wolf-Ferrari's imaginary world still gives joy to opera audiences.

Chapter 13

Gabriele D'Annunzio and the New Generation

The Age of Giolitti

S omething important changed in Italian society and politics soon
after the dawn of the new century. Looking backward, it was almost
as if the entire nation, left and right alike, seeing itself on the brink
of collapse after the massacres of Milan in 1898 and the assassination of
King Umberto in 1900, pulled back from the brink, and entered, in the historian Martin Clark's words, into "a period of stable parliamentary government, without excitement or adventures; a period of social reforms and
economic prosperity, during which popular discontent could be 'bought
off,' and the Catholic, Radical or Socialist 'subversives' could be integrated
even further into the existing political system."[1] Under the experienced,
thoughtful, and consummately manipulative Giovanni Giolitti, who ruled
Italy from 1903 until 1913, governmental policy moved sharply toward one
of conciliation and reform. During the course of the next decade, unions
were recognized and strikes legalized, while Italy finally joined the European mainstream of social legislation, passing laws limiting child employment and working hours, establishing accident insurance, and creating a
maternity fund for employed women. In 1912, Parliament finally adopted
all but universal male suffrage, tripling the size of the electorate, and introducing Italy to the era of mass politics. Although in retrospect one can
argue that the Giolittian reforms did little more than paper over social and
economic fault lines—all of which would sooner or later reemerge with
often tragic consequences—they provided a breathing space for the nation, and a decade of social peace and economic progress.[2]

Much of this progress was made possible by what one historian has
called "an economic transformation of vast proportions."[3] Although Italy's
industrial expansion is generally considered to have begun around 1896, it
was in the first decade of the new century that Italy became an major in-

dustrial country, not only in the traditional areas of textiles and steel, but in new areas, such as shipbuilding, and above all, automobile manufacturing. Indeed, the Fabbrica Italiana Automobili Torino (FIAT), soon became one of Europe's leading firms, adopting the most advanced American manufacturing methods to make cars, trucks, buses, airplanes, and even submarine engines before 1914. Even agriculture, which remained the mainstay of the Italian economy, grew rapidly, with wheat production increasing by 30 percent from the beginning of the century to the eve of the war, and exports of fruits, olive oil, and a new product, sugar, becoming increasingly important. Despite recurrent governmental efforts to redress the imbalance, however, Italy's economic growth during these years took place almost entirely in the nation's north, in Piedmont, Liguria, and the Po Valley, exacerbating the already wide economic and social gap between north and south. While this imbalance may have been of little concern to prosperous northerners at the time, these seemingly good years hardened a divide that has persisted as perhaps the single most intractable issue in Italian society to this day.

Italian society was changing even more dramatically. Italians were living longer, marrying later, and becoming more urban. In halting, uneven fashion, the money that Italian governments had spent on education since unification had gradually borne fruit. From a largely illiterate nation, Italy was now a land of readers and writers. By 1911, nearly two-thirds of all Italian adults were literate; in the prosperous north, 80 percent could read and write. The new generations of Italians were also more Italian; increasingly, the nation's leaders, in government, politics, or culture, were men — and occasionally but rarely women — who had been born since unification, and had no memory of either the divided land, or the efforts of Garibaldi and Cavour to make it a nation. For them, Italy was more a reality than an issue that needed to be resolved.

Intellectual and cultural life were also changing, as Italy became increasingly part of the European world of ideas. Above all, as Clark notes, the dominant intellectual mode of the new century was "a revolt against positivism."[4] Positivism, with its materialist, determinist, and evolutionary view of human behavior and society, was now seen as a tired doctrine, discredited by decades of dull and corrupt government. It was no longer a cause that could motivate people; it lacked the aesthetic and spiritual values for which a younger generation of intellectuals were yearning. As Benedetto Croce, Italy's leading philosopher of the time, wrote, "nothing could arrest the inward decay of this doctrine, which, forty years earlier, had been received with so much favor and had engendered so many hopes."[5]

The revolt against positivism ushered in a brief period of intellectual ferment and variety of a sort that modern Italy had not experienced before, as a host of fresh 'isms', including idealism, aestheticism, spiritualism, nationalism and Futurism, competed for attention in the newly opened bazaar of ideas. In contrast to earlier dissidents like the Scapigliati, who withdrew from the public realm and talked only to one another, the new intellectuals aggressively promoted their ideas to a growing public eager to listen. Magazines and journals of all descriptions proliferated, as energetic young journalists and writers created vehicles through which to promote their new doctrines. Although Croce — who used his journal *La Critica* to advocate the complex principles of idealism, which sought to create a synthesis of the spiritual and the rational — was universally respected, in practice, as Clark writes, "positivism was challenged not so much by idealism as by irrational, mystical doctrines in philosophy, and by nationalism in politics."[6]

Applied to the arts, these doctrines had one thing in common. They rejected the realistic, commonplace, and mundane, and demanded a revival of the elevated discourse of earlier times. In the absence of the religious and social fabric that once provided the underpinnings for that discourse, they looked to more modern values, such as the cult of Beauty, or the idealized vision of a revived, warlike, and powerful Italy. Among the composers of the *giovane scuola*, whose vision had been formed in the very different cultural atmosphere of the 1880s and 1890s, most showed little interest in exploring the new directions for operatic subjects suggested or demanded by these new doctrines — Mascagni being the most notable exception. For the composers coming of age in the new century, however, matters were entirely different. In company with their contemporaries among the intellectuals and writers of the time, they rejected the conventions of verismo and bourgeois opera, and actively looked for a body of dramatic ideas that would serve as the musical counterparts of aestheticism and nationalism. They found them in the works of Gabriele D'Annunzio, who exerted, as I shall discuss below, a powerful, even overpowering, effect on the composers of this period.

The Rise of the New Generation

Along with the forces transforming the Italian social and cultural landscape, the musical and dramatic dimensions of Italian opera also began to shift, changes in their way as momentous as the manner in which verismo had emerged from the equivocations of late-nineteenth-century opera in 1890. The changes reflected the growing feeling that the conventions that had propelled opera during the 1890s had lost their ability to inspire musical invention; even more, they reflected the extent to which Italian music was increasingly permeated by the music of the larger world known to Italians as *oltr'alpe* (beyond the Alps).

A new, younger generation of composers, as well as older composers such as Puccini and Mascagni, were not only influenced by Wagner, whose works were now common fare in Italian opera houses, but by younger composers, particularly Debussy and Richard Strauss. *Pelléas et Mélisande* first appeared in 1902, *Salome* in 1905, and *Elektra* in 1909. Although *Pelléas* had to wait until 1908 for its Italian premiere, Strauss's two pathbreaking operas were picked up quickly in Italy, with *Salome* making its La Scala debut at the end of 1906, and *Elektra* making its appearance in April 1909, less than three months after its debut in Dresden.

While change demanded a conscious effort of the older composers, the new music was second nature to the younger generation. Indeed, for the composers born after 1875, the question was not change itself, relative to the musical and dramatic conventions of the 1890s, but the nature and magnitude of that change. During the course of the years leading up to the First World War, a sharp cleavage emerged. In one group were those who saw their relationship to nineteenth-century Italian opera as evolutionary, and who continued to work within a traditional framework, enriching that framework and raising its cultural level with new musical techniques and dramatic themes. In the other were those who felt that Italian music needed a clear break with an operatic culture that in their eyes was little more than an artistically bankrupt, commercially driven enterprise, a stale entertainment for the bourgeoisie. For those latter composers, the times demanded the invention of a new type of opera — or even the jettisoning of opera entirely as an irrelevant, outmoded art form beyond repair.

The principal exponents of the latter group, far better known today among musical scholars than among the general musical audience, were Ildebrando Pizzetti (1880–1968), Gian Francesco Malipiero (1882–1973), and Alfredo Casella (1883–1947), who came to be known as the *generazione dell'ottanta* (generation of the eighties). These composers, whose influence on the course of Italian opera, although significant, was both delayed and indirect, will be discussed in chapter 15. Their more evolutionary-minded contemporaries were far more central to the Italian opera world prior to the war. The most notable of these composers were Italo Montemezzi (1875–1952), Franco Alfano (1876–1956), and Riccardo Zandonai

(1883–1944). Ermanno Wolf-Ferrari, discussed in the previous chapter, might also be seen as part of this group.[7]

To characterize these composers as conservative, however, is misleading. While they may be perceived as such in retrospect, from a perspective in which Stravinsky and Schoenberg represent the frame of reference for musical progress, they did not see themselves as conservative, nor were they seen as conservative at the time by either the general public or the greater part of the critical world. Zandonai, for one, furiously rejected any suggestion that he was artistically indebted to his predecessors of the *giovane scuola*, while one critic wrote at the premiere of his *Francesca da Rimini*, the music "followed the most modern among musical styles. [Zandonai's] artistic creed is certainly not very dissimilar to that of Claude Debussy."[8] Although there is arguably more Strauss than Debussy in *Francesca*, its harmonic language and its orchestral color are far removed from the most popular operas of the *giovane scuola* that were the customary fare of Italian opera houses.

These composers were a sophisticated group, with a systematic preparation that often included study abroad; Alfano followed study at San Pietro a Maiella in Naples with a year with Jadassohn in Leipzig, while Wolf-Ferrari studied in Munich. Zandonai benefited from what may well have been the finest body of teachers in any Italian conservatory, assembled by Pietro Mascagni at the Liceo Rossini in Pesaro. In contrast to the composers of the *giovane scuola*, who showed little sustained interest in writing anything other than operas, the younger generation were far more eclectic. Although opera was at the heart of all four composers' work, their non-operatic works were far from occasional efforts. Alfano's two symphonies rank among the most important Italian symphonies of the first half of the twentieth century, while Zandonai left behind a substantial corpus of orchestral and chamber works. Even Montemezzi, closest to a purely operatic composer, left an early symphony that is both well crafted and musically appealing.[9]

All three composers, although to varying degrees, can be considered operatic symphonists, not only in the sense of symphonic elaboration and coloration, which were not new, but also, as Piero Santi writes, in the sense of a new attitude toward the relationship of music and drama: "no longer was the drama to be framed by the music, but the music was to be framed by the drama." This process is seen at its most intense in Zandonai's *Francesca*, where, indeed, entire acts can be seen as symphonic poems.[10]

Operas that followed the traditional conventions, whether sentimental or verismo, were still being written. Alfano's first major opera, *Risurrezione*

(Resurrection), which appeared in 1904, is, under a sophisticated orchestral veneer, a classic bourgeois opera. Based loosely on a novel by Tolstoy, the librettists jettisoned the author's concentration on his hero's spiritual redemption, refashioning the tale into a sentimental story of a woman wronged who finds salvation in the arms of the saintly Simonson, ministering to the needs of the Siberian exiles. Despite Alfano's German training, and his years in Paris (writing, among other things, ballet scores for the Folies Bergère), the flavor of the opera is thoroughly in the Italian mainstream, with the influence of Puccini, Mascagni, and above all, Giordano apparent on nearly every page.[11] It is, nonetheless, an impressive work. It has dramatic momentum and power; while its melodies are rarely memorable, they are often effective. Although it never won a secure place in the repertoire, it was performed often through the 1920s.

Alfano's 1914 *L'ombra di Don Giovanni* (Don Giovanni's shade) — about which Waterhouse comments, "Alfano's musical language has been transformed and modernized in a manner almost impossible to believe during the ten years that separated the composition of *L'ombra* from that of *Risurrezione*" — was radically different.[12] Alfano himself wrote that "it has a physiognomy that is special, unusual, that doesn't belong to any contemporary Italian genre."[13] Although *L'ombra* was unsuccessful, his next opera, *La leggenda di Sakùntala*, which appeared in 1921, was an equally daring and far more successful work. In light of his later career it is hard to escape the conclusion that the conventional, crowd-pleasing character of *Risurrezione* was prompted less by artistic conviction and more by Alfano's powerful desire to gain enough of a name in his native land to be able to give up his life of hack work in Paris and return home.

Works such as *Risurrezione* or Montemezzi's first opera, *Giovanni Gallurese*, a 1905 verismo exercise set in eighteenth-century Sardinia, were the last manifestations of the nineteenth-century tradition. The trend during the first decade of the twentieth century was toward a strong shift in the choice of operatic subject matter, as composers began to move away from the quotidian realities of bourgeois opera and toward a heightened, aestheticized operatic discourse. While Wolf-Ferrari would find a different direction for his creative impulses, this trend was reflected not only in the works of younger composers, such as Zandonai and Montemezzi, but also in those of Mascagni, who drew upon it to feed his never-ending quest for self-renewal.

Underlying this trend one can see the effects of the new cultural politics of an idealized Italian nationalism that began to emerge in the early years of the new century. Now, when these composers viewed Wagner — above all, *Tristan und Isolde* — they did so through a D'Annunzian prism.

Gabriele D'Annunzio in a typical pose, photographed by Nunes Vais, 1906.
(*Fondazione Vittoriale*)

While the composers had listened to Wagner's music since their youth,
and drawn their own conclusions about his music, the *meaning* of Wagner
for their own creative course came to them mediated through the sensibility of a second figure: Gabriele D'Annunzio and his eclectic vision, characterized as one "made of nationalism and borrowings of European decadence, rhetorical effusion and the cult of ancient glory."[14]

In many respects, D'Annunzio can arguably be seen as the single most influential figure in Italian music during the decade preceding the First World War.[15] This was a remarkable achievement for someone who was not only neither a composer nor a performer. For all his passionate love and deep instinctive feeling for music, his actual knowledge of music in the technical sense was clearly limited, and his writings on musical subjects largely superficial and often secondhand, borrowed from other thinkers like Nietzsche or Romain Rolland.[16] For a fuller understanding of the operas written during the years leading up to the war (discussed in the following chapter), we must explore the nature of D'Annunzio's thinking and its influence on the composers of the time.

Gabriele D'Annunzio, Wagner, and Italian Opera

The oldest son of a spendthrift, sexually predatory father, Gabriele D'Annunzio was born in 1863, to a wealthy Pescara family in the Abruzzi, one of Italy's poorest and most backward regions — a combination of circumstances that may well have contributed to the overwhelming sense of entitlement and egomania that characterized his entire life. Publishing his first volume of poetry at sixteen, by the 1880s he had established himself as a major literary and social figure in Rome, a city in the throes of rapid transformation from a sleepy city of churches and villas into Italy's national capital. He was possessed by a remarkable *furor scribendi*, combined with an unerring gift for self-promotion. While continuing to publish poetry, essays for the Roman newspaper *La Tribuna,* and lurid tales of peasant life in his native Abruzzi, he published his first novel, *Il piacere* (Pleasure) in 1889, followed by *Il trionfo della morte* (The triumph of death) in 1894, *Le vergine delle rocce* (The virgins of the rocks) in 1895, and *Il fuoco* (The flame) in 1900. In 1897 he began to write plays, many written for his then-lover Eleonora Duse, beginning with *Sogno d'un mattino di primavera* (Dream of a spring morning). It was followed by *La città morta* (The dead city) in 1898, *Francesca da Rimini* in 1901, *La figlia di Jorio* (Jorio's daughter) in 1904, and *La nave* (The ship) in 1908, among many others. His collected works, published between 1927 and 1936, fill forty-eight volumes.

His importance as a writer in early-twentieth-century Italy was nearly matched by his prominence as a personality, long before his wartime exploits would make him a national hero. His blatant self-promotion, his extravagances and his debts, and above all, his scandalous lifestyle, which left a trail of abandoned mistresses and deceived husbands across Italy, were feasted

Eleonora Duse in a scene from D'Annunzio's *La città morta*. *(Fondazione Vittoriale)*

upon by the Italian public, some of whom shook their heads in disapproval, while others lived their fantasies vicariously through him. When he was elected to Italy's Parliament in 1897, that body debated for nine months whether to seat him, or deny him his seat on grounds of immorality.[17]

His discovery of Nietzsche was to do more than simply fuel his already excessive egomania. While his principal English-language biographer has written that, "the German thinker's ideas simply gave an impersonal, abstract, or theoretical justification to the self-centered behavior patterns and attitudes which D'Annunzio had adopted spontaneously since the age of 15,"[18] their significance was far greater. They provided D'Annunzio with the framework to inflate personal predilection into a program of cultural politics, in which music, as the archetypal art form of the Italian people, would play a central role.

The evolution of his self-proclaimed persona as Nietzschean *Übermensch* from the personal to the artistic sphere is traced by his novels from *Il piacere* to *Il fuoco* — all of which are organized around a central quasi-autobiographical figure. What begins as little more than a puerile hedonism, contempt for the masses, and an often tasteless desire to shock in *Il piacere* takes on a political coloration in *Le vergine delle rocce* and becomes a distinct cultural program in *Il fuoco*. As his hero and identity character, the *Übermensch* Stelio Effrena, asks himself: "Should not a new [Italian] art robust in both roots and branches, rise from ruins steeped in so much heroic blood, and should not this art sum up within itself all the forces latent in the hereditary substance of the nation?"[19] If the philosophical (if one can use that term) framework for this new art comes from Nietzsche, the artistic point of reference is unequivocally Richard Wagner.

From his youth, music was a powerful force in D'Annunzio's life. In his teens, languishing in a Prato boarding school, he could describe himself to a childhood friend as "[one] who relentlessly frequents all the Roman concerts . . . , totally impassioned by the purest and highest emanations of musical art; spending hours of oblivion listening to Chopin or Beethoven or Schumann."[20] He was a composer manqué, and music is always close to the heart of his works, either as the subject or as an organizing principle, particularly in his novels. Music references, and scenes in which the characters listen to music, or talk about music, are legion; references to musical compositions are linked to the characters' emotional states. In *Il trionfo d'amore*, for example, the hero tells his lover: "I remember, one day, at a concert, while listening to a Beethoven sonata, in which a frequent and periodic return of a sublime and passionate phase recurred, I exalted myself almost to a state of madness by the interior repetition of a poetic phrase in which your name occurred."[21] D'Annunzio uses references to musical compositions, such as a Rameau gavotte and a Bach Prelude in *Il piacere*, as quasi-Wagnerian leitmotifs within the novelistic texture.[22] While his choice of music is eclectic, it does not extend to the works of his contemporaries; nowhere in his works is a character ever sent into an emotional transport, or prompted to evoke a tender memory, by the notes of an opera by one of the *giovane scuola*.

D'Annunzio was not a Wagnerian born. His conversion to Wagner took place in 1892, by means of *Tristan*. As a friend describes the experience: "Over less than a year, I think we must have read through *Tristan und Isolde* at least ten times. This was the point that Gabriele was writing *Il trionfo della morte*. *Tristan* filled his spirit with a morbid obsession. He wanted to listen to the Prelude over and over, it nagged at him, he took notes, and his eyes almost stuck to the page where the torture of the philtre begins."[23] That it was a conversion, religious in all but external form, is left in little doubt by that novel.

Il trionfo della morte is the story of Giorgio Aurispa, a young nobleman who is sexually obsessed with Ippolita Sanzio. When Aurispa ultimately realizes that he is unable to break free of his obsession in order to become the Nietzschean *Übermensch* of which he dreams, he plunges from a cliff to his death, dragging the unwilling Ippolita with him. D'Annunzio's *Tristan* mania was transmuted into *Il trionfo*, where the music of that opera becomes the catalyst for the work's grisly denouement. Giorgio and Ippolita have taken refuge in a country cottage by the sea, where they live an isolated life of sensual preoccupation with one another. Delivery of a piano and a box of music changes their lives. As they begin listening to *Tristan*, an "immense wave of harmony irresistibly enveloped them both, closed in on them, carried them away, transported them to 'the marvelous empire.'"[24] Listening to *Tristan*, or in Giorgio's case, reliving his experience of seeing *Tristan* on his "religious pilgrimage" to Bayreuth, becomes a spiritual rite for Giorgio and Ippolita: "They believed they had transfigured themselves, that they had attained superior heights of existence. . . . Were not they also tormented by a limitless desire? Were they not also linked together by an indissoluble bond, and did they not often feel in voluptuousness the horrors of the death agony; did they not hear the rumbling of death?"[25] It is at that point that Giorgio believes that he understands the meaning of Tristan's lines, "the terrible philtre which has brought this torture upon me, I myself have brewed it." He realizes that he must kill himself, and he must persuade Ippolita to die with him, carrying out their own *Liebestod* in emulation of Tristan and Isolde.

Ultimately, D'Annunzio's only god was himself, and by 1897 he could confide to Romain Rolland that he was already sick of Wagner's music.[26] His growing political and cultural nationalism, and his glorification of the "Mediterranean" cultures over those of the "Aryan" or "Barbarian" north (ironically, influenced by the "Aryan" Nietzsche), had led him to the rediscovery of the works of earlier generations of Italian composers such as Palestrina, Monteverdi, or Marcello. Wagner had become, rather than a deity, a specter that D'Annunzio had to exorcise. That task was the mission of his 1900 novel *Il fuoco*.

In *Il fuoco* D'Annunzio has created his Italian counterpart to Wagner, Stelio Effrena, in whom — in contrast to poor Giorgio — transcendent genius, adamantine will, and sensuality are fused into an integrated, harmonious whole. The greatest poet *and* composer of his time, he has been sarcastically dubbed "il futuro kunstgesamtwerkista italico" by one writer.[27] Effrena is the vehicle by which the Italian race will demonstrate its creative superiority over the barbarians to the north, building on the achievements of Wagner to create something even greater. As Effrena tells his faithful disciple Daniele Glauro, "I shall not revive an antique form; I shall invent a new form, obeying my instinct and the genius of my race only, as the Greeks did. . . . For a long time the three arts of music, poetry and dancing have separated from each other."[28] For this new art form, Effrena is having the Theater of Apollo, the Italian Bayreuth, built on the slopes of Rome's Gianicolo hill: "In laying the foundation stone of his theater, the poet of *Siegfried* consecrated it to the hopes and the victories of his German people. The theater of Apollo which is rapidly rising on the Janiculum . . . must be no other than the monumental revelation of the idea toward which our race is led by its genius."[29] Wagner is the model, and, indeed, the ultimate touchstone of greatness; Italy, it is clear, can only create its own great art by outdoing the Master on his own terms.

Il fuoco is set in Venice in 1883, and the presence of the aging Wagner, who has returned to Venice to die, pervades the novel. It is juxtaposed against Effrena's youthful strength and vigor, a contrast made explicit in the scene in which Effrena and Glauro help Cosima Wagner carry the frail, ailing composer from the boat to his hotel. Minutes after having held Wagner's nearly lifeless body in his arms, Effrena, standing in the midst of the rising storm, has his revelation; first, the vision of a new art, and then, the music through which he will realize it:

> The entire line of the melody had been revealed to him, was henceforth his, was immortal in his spirit and in the world. . . . He imagined it as steeped in

the symphonic sea and unfolding itself through a thousand aspects until it reached its perfection.

"Daniele, Daniele, I have found it."[30]

The novel ends with a scene laden with portentous symbolism, as Stelio, Daniele, and their friends, accompanied by two workmen from the Theater of Apollo, carry the bier of the dead Richard Wagner from his chamber to the funeral gondola, and from the boat to the train that will carry the composer's body back to his native Germany. At the end, Stelio and his companions spread branches of laurel, gathered the day before on the Gianicolo, on the coffin; the last sentence of *Il fuoco* reads, "And the laurels traveled toward the Bavarian hill still slumbering under its frost, while their noble trunks were already budding in the light of Rome to the murmur of hidden springs."[31] Italian art has triumphed.

By the time of *Il fuoco*, D'Annunzio had already begun to turn his attention toward the theater. From 1900 on, he would no longer write novels, channeling his creative energy instead into a series of plays through which he tried to realize his vision of Italian art.[32] Plays such as *Francesca da Rimini, La figlia di Jorio, La nave, Fedra*, and *Parisina*[33] all represent a systematic attempt, however unsuccessful it may appear in retrospect, to create an Italian *mythos* in the manner of Wagner. Unlike Wagner, D'Annunzio would need to find composers to complete his task.

Since 1890, Wagner's music had become widely diffused in Italy and productions of his operas common. The scale and magnificence of the composer's major works had led to their widespread use to open the *carnevale–quaresima* season, particularly at La Scala, where roughly every other season between 1890 and 1915 was initiated with a Wagner work. In contrast to earlier years, during which the Italian audience rarely heard Wagner operas other than *Lohengrin* and *Tannhäuser*, others, including the *Ring* cycle and *Tristan und Isolde*, were now heard across the Italian peninsula.

Of all of Wagner's operas, *Tristan* struck the most responsive chord in the Italian audience. All but unknown except through piano readings or pilgrimages to Bayreuth before the turn of the century, it began to move rapidly into the Italian repertory during the following decade, as shown in table 2. Verdi singled it out as the Wagner work he most admired,[34] and when Pietro Mascagni, newly appointed director of Rome's Teatro Costanzi, assembled his program for the 1909–1910 *carnevale–quaresima* season, he chose *Tristan* for the gala season-opening performance.

By this time, Italian composers' relationship to Wagner was very different from that in the late 1880s and early 1890s, when the German composer was

Table 2

Performances of Tristan in Italy 1888–1914*

Year	Place	Year	Place
1888	Bologna	1907	Bologna, Naples
1897	Turin	1908	Parma, Genoa
1899	Trieste**	1909	Venice, Palermo, Cesena, Rome Turin
1900	Milan	1911	Turin, Verona, Milan, Naples
1902	Ravenna	1912	Bologna, Padua
1903	Rome	1913	Fiume,** Ancona, Treviso, Modena, Trieste
1906	Brescia, Trieste	1914	Mantua, Milan, Genoa

*The information here is from Giorgio Gualerzi's *Wagner in Italia* (Venice: Ente Autonomo Teatro la Fenice, 1972).
**Prior to World War One, Trieste and Fiume (modern Rijeka), although ethnically and culturally Italian, were still politically part of the Austro-Hungarian Empire.

still a subject of contention and attitudes tended to be limited either to a naïve Wagnerism, reflected in works such as Franchetti's *Asrael*, or to an equally naïve anti-Wagnerism, reflected in many of the critical reactions to Mascagni's *Cavalleria rusticana*. For a younger composer like Zandonai, Wagner was part of the musical landscape; as he commented in a 1908 interview, "who doesn't admire Wagner today?"[35] By 1905, Mascagni saw Wagner's works as forming a powerful defining reality with which any serious composer had to deal, not slavishly but seriously. Long before his direct contact with D'Annunzio, he shared the poet's idea of creating a body of Italian art to set explicitly against the Master's Teutonic works. On the eve of the premiere of his new opera *Amica*, he discussed this question with Pompei: "Wagner is the first and the greatest of the modern musicians who has been able to put his music at the service of the most daring poetic ideas, and by means of music drama, has been able to bring completely new persons and characters into the poetic domain. In this sense alone I feel myself profoundly Wagnerian, while in spirit and form I remain more than ever Italian."

Mascagni suggested that an Italian counterpart could be found to the Nordic *mythos* that served as inspiration to Wagner: "The warmer, more dramatic and more passionate Italian musical temperament permits us to move away from myths and legends and to create and give life to human personages that also represent, however, symbol and significance. Human figures, therefore, real personages, but the expression of ideals, aspirations, sentiments, passions and sorrows, not individual, but of all of our people, must live and shine in the modern opera."[36] *Amica*, a drama of elemental passions set in the mountains of the Haute-Savoie, strives to achieve this goal. In the end, however, its efforts to invest its simple peasant folk with mythic significance are largely unsuccessful. Despite many powerful passages — including the highly Wagnerian intermezzo — the opera suffers from a serious imbalance, in which the characters, rather than becoming archetypes or symbols, tend to be swallowed up by the over-insistent music.[37]

The Wagnerian frame of reference led Italian composers to want to compose operas that would deal with greater themes than those customary in bourgeois opera, treating them in a manner that was elevated, rather than quotidian. The musicologist Guido Gatti put it somewhat sardonically: "Everywhere one hears a phrase that might be called the slogan of the new era: *Let us elevate ourselves.* Let us elevate Art to a level of ideality that verismo has seemingly banished; let us abandon chronicled facts and subjects of crude realism to expand in an atmosphere more pure and spiritual. We must infuse an element of poetry into the librettos; we must poetize our subjects."[38] The traditional means by which art was elevated from the mundane, by giving it a strong religious or moral dimension, was no more available to this generation than to their immediate predecessors. A society united by a common body of religious and moral values was a long-forgotten artifact of Italy's distant past. The available alternative, which was seized upon eagerly by the writers and musicians of the time, was aestheticism, the doctrine of art for art's sake, the cult of Beauty, or its corollary, the elevation of ordinary experience by treating it as an aesthetic object.

The aestheticization of opera was also seen, in an age when nationalism was emerging as an important political and cultural force, as a means toward its becoming a more intrinsically national art. Ironically, for all its popular success and deep roots in Italian mass society, verismo and bourgeois opera were considered by the ideologues of the new nationalism as almost the antithesis of true national opera. In the writings of such key critical figures of the period as Giannotto Bastianelli and Fausto Torrefranca, one finds an almost total rejection of the efforts of the *giovane scuola* — Mascagni, for Bastianelli, being a solitary exception. Indeed, Torrefranca contemptuously dismisses Puccini's music as embodying "all the decadence of today's Italian music, all its cynical commercialism, all its miserable impotence and the triumphal vogue of internationalism."[39]

It is precisely at this point, early in the new century, that D'Annunzio began to occupy center stage in Italian operatic life. He had already made his contribution to the climate in which Italy's composers would find it necessary to test themselves against Wagner in his writings. He had already come to embody as well, both in his writings and his life, the values of the now au courant aestheticism. By 1902, with *Francesca da Rimini*, he also began to create a body of dramatic works that were to become the starting point for the new Italian opera, both as operatic libretti in themselves, as well as models for other playwrights and librettists such as Sem Benelli.

D'Annunzio may not have seen his plays at first as potential operatic libretti. However much he may have fantasized himself as midwife to a new Italian musical art, the idea that his words might be subordinated to the music of another artist was repugnant to the egomaniac D'Annunzio. His plays, however, as with all his works, reflect the pervasive place of music in his creative life. It is not difficult to imagine D'Annunzio thinking of many of these works, particularly *Francesca da Rimini,* as operas; his lines have a musical quality that is unique among the writers of his time, while the plays themselves are designed to accommodate numerous musical moments. D'Annunzio certainly conceived of *Francesca* in *Gesamtkunstwerk* terms, even if it was necessary for him to commission musical interludes and songs for the play from someone else, rather than being able to write them himself.[40] As one commentator describes D'Annunzio's staging of his own play: "In contrast to the traditionally central position of the actor, or rather the protagonist . . . D'Annunzio brought a polycentric and dynamic idea of a scenic interplay, toward which he sought to utilize all possible elements to build the spectacle, including the introduction of music, song, and dance."[41]

Ultimately, however, the opportunities presented by operatic treatment, as with those that soon emerged in the growing Italian cinema industry, were too great to resist. Not only was the adaptation of his plays a particularly lucrative source of money for the spendthrift and continually financially needy D'Annunzio, but as an artist he came to see the translation of his works into films or operas not as an artistic compromise but as a re-creation of his work on a larger, more grandiose scale. Over the course of slightly more than a decade — beginning with Franchetti's setting of *La figlia di Jorio* in 1906 — a total of seven D'Annunzio plays were turned into operas, and two more into what might be called "mixed theater pieces," blends of music, dance, and recitation.[42] A list of these works is given in table 3. Meanwhile, Turin's Ambrosio Studios produced films of no fewer than six D'Annunzio works in a single year, 1911–1912.[43]

The outcomes of these operas, and the extent to which they could be considered exponents of a new Italian musical drama, varied widely. The fiasco of Franchetti's opera has already been described, while Boulanger and Pugno's *La ville morte,* a setting of a French-language version by D'Annunzio of his play *La città morta,* was never finished during its composers' lifetimes.[44] The most significant of these works are Zandonai's *Francesca da Ri-*

Table 3

Operas from D'Annunzio's Plays

Opera	Composer	Date
La figlia di Jorio	Alberto Franchetti	1906
	Ildebrando Pizzetti	1954
La ville morte (La città morta)	Nadia Boulanger and Raoul Pugno	1912
Sogno d'un tramonto d'autunno	Gian Francesco Malipiero	1913
Parisina	Pietro Mascagni	1913
Francesca da Rimini	Riccardo Zandonai	1914
Fedra	Ildebrando Pizzetti	1915
La nave	Italo Montemezzi	1918

mini and Mascagni's *Parisina* — although a case can be made for Pizzetti's *Fedra*, which Gatti referred to as "the most 'anti-D'Annunzian' opera that I know."[45] Of all of these operas, the only one that could be considered even moderately successful in terms of finding a place in the Italian repertory is Zandonai's work. Another opera, however, set to a libretto by Sem Benelli that is luridly D'Annunzian almost to the point of parody,[46] was arguably the most successful of the operas of this period or genre: Italo Montemezzi's *L'amore dei tre re* (The love of three kings), which appeared in 1911.

Tristan is a constant presence in these works, always hovering behind the scenes. In *Parisina*, the song of the nightingale reminds Parisina of the story of Tristan and Isolde; later she tells her lover Ugo,

> Carry me to the forest,
> Take me far away,
> Like Isolde the Blond-Haired,
> You with your bow and sword,
> I with only my love.

Francesca da Rimini was modeled even more directly on *Tristan*, and Isolde's presence pervades that play.

Both *Parisina* and *Francesca*, indeed, were nothing less than efforts by their composers, under D'Annunzio's influence, to craft the Italian *Tristan und Isolde*. Along with their perhaps less ambitious but no less important counterpart *L'amore dei tre re*, they will be the subject of the next chapter. While they did not succeed, their attempt led to the last upsurge of operatic creativity before the First World War brought down the curtain on Italy's last great operatic age.

Chapter 14

Tristan's Children

Pietro Mascagni, Isabeau, *and* Parisina

Tristan's most important Italian progeny were Zandonai's *Francesca da Rimini* and Mascagni's *Parisina,* which were both written to D'Annunzio libretti, along with Montemezzi's *L'amore dei tre re,* which appeared in 1911. Although *Parisina* would be the most ambitious effort to craft an Italian *Tristan,* Mascagni would prepare the ground for that work by an earlier Tristanesque opera, the less important but more approachable *Isabeau.*

Mascagni and Sonzogno ended their five-year estrangement in 1906, and the composer began a search for a new libretto. He had never completely broken with Illica, despite their harsh words over the ill-fated *Maria Antonietta.* In the meantime (most probably in 1903 or 1904), after putting that effort aside, Illica had written a libretto on a medieval theme entitled *Isabeau* without any particular composer in mind; over the next few years, he offered it to Bossi, Puccini, and Franchetti without attracting more than passing interest. In 1908, he presented it to Mascagni, who accepted it immediately, seeing in it the ideal vehicle for his creative self-renewal, a revival in modern musical garb of "the romanticism that inspired so much of Italian opera." As he told Pompei: "It seems to me that verismo in opera, of which I was once a passionate follower, has had its day; I don't feel the classicism of Greek or Roman tragedy, and even less the symbolism of philosophical concepts; thus I have turned to Romanticism, in the sense that that term had fifty years ago: that Romanticism that manifested itself with the imaginary and sentimental re-evocation of a Middle Ages proud and gentle, bitter and chivalrous, passionate and cruel."[1] In Illica's medieval evocation, Mascagni saw characters and settings to which he could give not only reality, but symbolism and a significance that transcended their individual identities.

Although a medieval setting was not in itself unusual for Illica,[2] the fusion of a highly symbolic, metaphoric tale with a highly aesthetized Pre-Raphaelite Middle Ages was a new departure. While Illica's interest in such a theme may have been prompted to some extent by the appearance of D'Annunzio's *Francesca da Rimini* in 1902, his direct influences are to be found elsewhere, in the poetry of the French symbolists, and above all, in the plays of Maeterlinck, in which many of the themes pursued in *Isabeau* can be found.[3] While the plot of *Isabeau* is built around a nude cavalcade suggested by Tennyson's *Lady Godiva*, it otherwise has nothing to do with that poem; it deals with the spiritual transformation of Princess Isabeau under the influence of the mystical woodsman Folco, who has discovered that true reality is found in dreams, and her surrender to his world of pure love and inner perception. Although they reach a sort of spiritual fusion, they are destroyed by the world of outer reality, lynched by a mob stirred up by the evil counselor Cornelius.[4]

Although Mascagni was enthusiastic about the subject, he made slow progress at first, working on it fitfully and completing only a few scattered passages, and then setting it entirely aside in the fall of 1909 when his new duties as director of the Teatro Costanzi came to occupy all his time. By the summer of 1910, however, not only was he no longer occupied with the Costanzi, but a dramatic change in his life provided the impetus for a sudden revival of his creative juices.

In April 1910, Pietro Mascagni, forty-six years old, dutifully married, and the father of three children, met the twenty-one-year-old Anna Lolli and fell passionately in love, beginning an intense relationship that would last until his death thirty-five years later.[5] In June, the composer, overwhelmed by his emotional turmoil, fled Rome to seek refuge in Illica's home in Castell'Arquato. Three weeks later, after resolving her own feelings, Lolli joined him there. From that point on, he worked at a feverish pace; on September 10, Lolli's twenty-second birthday, he presented her with the draft of the Intermezzo, the last part of the short score to be completed, inscribed to "Annuccia, divine inspiration of my music." All but a few passages of the most ambitious and complex opera Mascagni had ever composed were written in barely three months.

Isabeau is a powerful but uneven opera. While Illica crafted a dramatically effective story, he lacked the virtuoso linguistic skills of D'Annunzio. His verbal talents were ill-suited to the symbolic poetic drama *Isabeau* aspires to be, and his use of archaic words and phrases (such as "reginotta" for "principessa") is precious rather than convincing. Neither Isabeau nor Folco are plausible characters. The contemporary critic Barini was harsh, but not unreasonable when he described them as "puppets of straw and cardboard, whose mental imbalance is reflected throughout the work."[6] Mascagni's music at its best brings the work's characters to vivid life; at its weakest, it tries valiantly but without success to capture the mystical, symbolic dimension of the work.

Mascagni was determined to create something fundamentally new with *Isabeau*; as he grandiosely wrote Illica at the end of 1908: "[I must] create a work that will signify a new era in opera: I intend that *Isabeau* will be something completely new and that it will represent the precise and complete expression of my concept of modern opera."[7] His effort to "modernize" his musical language is apparent throughout the opera, yet the overall effect is uneven. The shadows of Wagner and of the Strauss of *Salome* and *Elektra* hover over the work. Sharp, acrid dissonances — coloristic rather than structural — are common, while rich chromatic and whole-tone sequences, including Wagner's famous "*Tristan* chord," dominate the harmonic texture. They coexist, often uneasily, with more diatonic passages, as well as with Mascagni's penchant for resolving even some of his most complex and recherché harmonic sequences with bald V–I cadences. It is a chameleonlike score. While some critics could stress the work's modernity, others saw it as a repetition of Mascagni's earlier works. One critic even found it a relief from modernism, writing: "In a period like ours of musical 'byzantinism,' while opera, even here, is becoming more French and German, beautiful, pure and sweet Italian melody . . . was greeted with joy."[8] *Isabeau*, whatever its limitations, is powerful musical theater, arguably one of those operas that is far more effective onstage than in recorded form. Despite the critics' ambivalence, it was popular with Italian audiences, and was performed regularly in Italian opera houses until the Second World War. Its public reception was far more successful than that of Mascagni's second and more ambitious effort to confront the same themes, this time in partnership with D'Annunzio himself.

Parisina began as a commercial speculation. In 1911, Lorenzo Sonzogno was aggressively hunting for material for his new firm. A close follower of the Parisian musical scene, he was much taken with *Le martyre de St. Sébastien*, a collaborative "choreographic poem" by Gabriele D'Annunzio and Claude Debussy. The work, which has been described as "a synthesis of orchestral and vocal music, speech, mime and dancing."[9] made its debut on May 22, 1911, at the Théâtre du Châtelet. Although the five-hour work, which featured D'Annunzio's latest conquest, the American dancer Ida Rubenstein, was not successful, it convinced Sonzogno that an operatic collaboration between D'Annunzio and Debussy would be a spectacular commercial coup for his fledgling firm.

Sonzogno approached D'Annunzio at the beginning of 1912, and found the author agreeable. D'Annunzio was, as always, in need of money, and had a subject in mind that he had previously suggested, without success, to Puccini in 1906.[10] The subject, taken from Italian Renaissance history, was the tragic love affair of Ugo, son of Niccolò, duke of Ferrara, and his father's young bride, Parisina. Discovered in flagrante by the duke, they were executed, perhaps as D'Annunzio imagined it, on

> . . . the same block,
> under the same ax;
> Two heads, and two bloods,
> making a single pool.

As early as 1902, D'Annunzio contemplated writing *Parisina* to follow *Francesca da Rimini* as the second part of a Malatesta trilogy, a project that was never completed.[11]

Debussy was not interested, however, and Sonzogno returned to Italy, writing D'Annunzio in April: "I am working on the composer, who must be at the same level as [your] grand artistic concept. . . . The subject of the tragedy is exactly right for the temperament of Maestro Mascagni, who is the one truly Italian composer left, and who has the creative strength not to turn back in the face of difficulties."[12] D'Annunzio was agreeable, and on April 20, to the fury of Lorenzo's cousin Riccardo, Mascagni signed a contract with Lorenzo Sonzogno to compose *Parisina* to the poet's libretto.

News of the collaboration between Mascagni and D'Annunzio was greeted with incredulity by the Italian media. Many remembered "Il capobanda" (The bandmaster), the vituperative attack launched by the young aesthete D'Annunzio in the pages of *Il Mattino* against the composer in 1892, not long after *Cavalleria rusticana* had made him famous. As Guido Treves wrote in *l'illustrazione italiana*: "Who would have dared predict twenty years ago, at the time of the success of *Cavalleria* that triggered such indignation on the part of the combative poet, that the names of Mascagni and D'Annunzio would be united in the same work of art?"[13] Others, still thinking of Mascagni as the composer of *Cavalleria*, did not appreciate how long an artistic journey the composer had traveled over the twenty years after his initial success. Over those years, first with *Iris* and then with *Isabeau*, Mascagni had reached a point where he felt himself ready to confront the highest challenges that the Italian opera world presented. As I have written elsewhere, "*Isabeau* had been a watershed for the composer. After nearly a decade of frustration, he had written his most am-

D'Annunzio, Mascagni, and Lorenzo Sonzogno in Paris, 1912. *(Museo Mascagnano, Bagnara di Romagna)*

bitious work and had been rewarded by public and critical acclaim. He had dared greatly and had prevailed. . . . [H]e felt himself ready to create the work in which he would fuse words and music into a transcendent whole, even—although he would never be so presumptuous to say so in public—create an Italian *Tristan*."[14]

As Mascagni had matured, he had turned away from the representation of action to a vision of a music focusing on internal psychological states. He wanted, as he told an interviewer, "not to comment on [the words], but to create a fusion of words and music,"[15] a conception of the *parola scenica* as a vehicle for illuminating the essence of his characters' psychology. For Mascagni, the quality of D'Annunzio's poetry in *Parisina*, and the musical opportunities it gave him, transcended the dramatic weaknesses of the libretto. He was well aware of those weaknesses, writing Illica days after signing the contract for the opera, "in substance, it contains only a single situation and . . . it's not in the final act."[16] Despite his qualms, the attractions of D'Annunzio's libretto, at least at first, far outweighed its risks.

Mascagni began work on *Parisina* in July 1912, renting a villa in a suburb of Paris, both to be close to D'Annunzio in his French exile and to share a few idyllic months with Anna Lolli away from the composer's increasingly difficult domestic situation.[17] By the end of the year, however, with most of the opera written, the composer was assailed by increasingly insistent doubts, writing D'Annunzio early in November: "I am very distressed when I calculate that *Parisina* will contain more than four hours of music: it will be an unperformable opera, or at a minimum, will lack that practicality [of execution] that is essential if an opera is to succeed."[18] And later that month, "You understand that an opera must be written for the theater; a performance cannot go beyond the limits of theatrical custom and human endurance."[19] There was no turning back, however; the composer persevered, finishing the opera in short score at the end of March 1913, and the orchestration by November.

Parisina made its much-heralded debut at La Scala on December 15, 1913, under the composer's baton. Ugo and Parisina were sung by two of Italy's most talented young singers, Hipòlito Làzaro and Tina Poli-Randaccio, while the role of Niccolò was sung by the famous baritone Carlo Galeffi. As the composer feared, it was a long opera. Although Mascagni gave the downbeat at 8:30 P.M., it was 1:35 A.M. when Ugo and Parisina finally walked forward to the execution block, and the curtain fell on the opera's last notes. Although the audience reaction at the end of the first act was enthusiastic, it became cooler as the night went on. One writer described the intermission chatter: "Some said that when music goes on so long, it becomes ugly. Others observed instead that it is so beautiful that it manages to save itself despite its length. 'Beautiful but long,' say the admirers, 'long, but not so beautiful' say others."[20] At the end of the opera, there was a rush for the doors. The next day, Giovanni Pozza, the authoritative critic for the *Corriere della sera*, concluded a thoughtful and appreciative discussion of the opera and its virtues by writing, "even the most passionate admirer of the Maestro must hope that the surest and simplest remedy will be adopted: cut, cut, cut."[21]

Mascagni responded swiftly and arbitrarily. For the second performance, the second-act postlude, the third-act prelude, and the entire fourth act were removed, shortening the opera by nearly an hour, but removing some of its finest music. Thus curtailed, the opera had a successful run of twelve performances to considerable public acclaim. Despite that apparent success, albeit in truncated form, few theaters took up *Parisina*. After a handful of productions in the course of the following year, it fell into near-oblivion, and has been only seen twice in modern times, in a Rome production of 1979 and more recently, drastically cut, in a 1999 performance in Montpellier.[22]

Parisina is a drama of psychology and emotion, with little dramatic action in the conventional sense. The first act presents the four principal characters — Ugo, his father, the Duke, his mother, Stella dell'Assassino the Duke's spurned mistress, and Parisina, the Duke's new bride, and their conflicts. The second act, set at the Shrine of Loreto on Italy's Adriatic coast, is an extended duet, occasionally broken by choral passages, in which Ugo and Parisina discover and then consummate their love at the foot of the statute of the Virgin. In the third act, Niccolò interrupts a tryst between Ugo and Parisina and sentences them to death, while in the fourth act, in the dungeons of the ducal castle in Ferrara, the lovers are alone, awaiting the dawn. As Ugo's mother, who has come for one last visit to her son, looks on in agony, the couple go calmly forward to their death.

This story, with its implicit and explicit echoes of *Tristan*, corresponded precisely to Mascagni's creative needs. Not only was D'Annunzio's poetry a powerful stimulus to his creative impulse, but the libretto, while offering little action, offered a gallery of rich characters thrown into intensely emotional conflicts — such as the first-act scene in which Ugo's mother tries to inflame him with her hatred of Parisina, or the mingled anger and suffering of Niccolò in the third act as he confronts the lovers. Above all, Parisina herself, who grows during the course of the opera from a childish, guilt-ridden woman to a transcendent spirit who can peacefully contemplate death, inspired Mascagni to compose some of the most powerful and beautiful music that ever came from his pen.

In *Parisina*, Mascagni blends declamation and arioso to create a rhythmically free, continuous, and intensely melodic line, buttressed by a rich orchestral texture, constantly commenting upon and reinforcing — but never supplanting — the voices. The often awkward harmonic eccentricities of *Isabeau* have been refined; the composer has assimilated a sophisticated chromatic harmonic palette, and his music flows freely from clearly defined tonality to passages in which key relations are fleeting, or barely present. As Bernardoni has written, "Mascagni interpreted the drama of *Parisina* with an incomparable modernist tension that has scarcely an equal in the Italian works of its time."[23]

No other Mascagni opera contains the musical riches of *Parisina*, and yet the composer's misgivings, which he expressed to D'Annunzio as he wrote the opera, were sadly justified. *Parisina* is all but unperformable. The combination of the opera's inordinate length with its near-total lack of overt dramatic events ultimately cannot be overcome. Even *Tristan*, hardly a fast-paced melodrama, offers far more overt dramatic action than does *Parisina*. It is questionable whether any other composer could have made D'Annunzio's libretto into a viable theatrical work, but it is clear that Mascagni did not have the creative resources to achieve such a goal.

Mascagni tries to compensate for the lack of action with what Bernar-doni characterizes, not unfairly, as "a spider's web of pastiche *strambotti* and mediaeval litanies," but, again, while often beautiful, the music does not solve the central problem: that of sustaining this often exquisite, but dramatically exiguous, work. In his attempt to compose the Italian *Tristan*, Mascagni rose to creative heights that he had never achieved before nor would ever reach again. Although he did not succeed, he nonetheless cre-ated a remarkable work that has yet to receive the recognition it deserves.

Italo Montemezzi and L'Amore dei Tre Re

Of all the Italian children of *Tristan*, the one that came closest to becom-ing a true repertory opera is the work of a composer who is more thor-oughly unknown beyond his one success than any other figure of the time. While even moderately serious opera buffs know of Mascagni's *L'amico Fritz* and *Iris* or Leoncavallo's *Zazà*, it is hard to imagine anyone but a true specialist who can name another Montemezzi opera, or proffer even the most minimal information that might illuminate who he was, and how this shadowy figure came to write this one notable opera.

Italo Montemezzi was born in 1875 in the village of Vigasio, in the pros-perous farming country south of the ancient city of Verona. His father's work fabricating and restoring clocks in the many clock towers of the Veneto had made it possible for him to build a large house with a vineyard and a garden in his native village. Although highly successful in his de-manding trade, he sought a higher social status for his son Italo, who had been born only nine years after the Veneto had become part of the Italian nation and named in the new nation's honor. He wanted his son to be-come an engineer. The young Montemezzi was not interested, however; an indifferent student, he had little aptitude for science or mathematics, a modest but not passionate interest in music, and a true passion only for "playing billiards and going hunting."[24]

At nineteen, instead of enrolling in the Polytechnic in Milan as ex-pected, he defied his father and took the entrance examination for the Milan Conservatory, which, given his scattered and unsystematic studies up to that point, he failed miserably, as he did again the following year. After the second failure, however, a momentous change appears to have come over him. Overnight, he became a serious student. After a year spent in a determined effort to overcome years of casual self-study, he was admit-ted to the conservatory on his third attempt. From that point on, he was utterly dedicated to his studies. Determined to make up for the time he had lost, he completed the remaining six years of the obligatory program in four years, receiving his diploma in 1900, a few months short of his twenty-fifth birthday.[25] His graduation exercise was a setting of the Song of Songs for soprano, mezzo-soprano, chorus, and orchestra.

By graduation, Montemezzi had already decided that his future lay in the world of opera, and he set to work immediately on his first effort, a one-act opera set in Sardinia and entitled *Giovanni Gallurese*. He submitted the work to the 1902 Sonzogno Competition, but without success. After that initial failure, and most probably with the help of some of his father's money, his librettist, the otherwise unknown Francesco D'Angelantonio, agreed to revise the libretto into a full-length three-act opera.[26]

The manner in which *Giovanni Gallurese* reached the stage, and Montemezzi began his career, reflects the burdens as well as opportunities facing a young, ambitious opera composer. Montemezzi sent the score to his friend Tullio Serafin, who was at the time beginning his conducting career at the Teatro Vittorio Emanuele, a secondary house in Turin. Serafin thought highly of the work, and recommended it to the impresario, Luigi Piontelli, Verdi's bête noire and Ricordi's faithful ally. In keeping with custom, Piontelli agreed to stage the young composer's opera in return for a subsidy to cover the costs of the production, an amount he set at 7000 lire. Such a sum, needless to say, was well beyond the means of either the composer or his father.

The determined Montemezzi, however, was able to capitalize on the intersection between the social value placed on opera in Italy and the intense local patriotism that is characteristic, even today, of Italian life. Returning to Verona, he convinced the city's two newspapers to mount a joint campaign to raise the funds needed to have his opera produced. Within a short period the necessary amount had been collected. With the funds raised from Montemezzi's fellow citizens, *Giovanni Gallurese* made its debut in Turin in January 1905.[27] While breaking no new operatic ground, *Giovanni Gallurese* was the work of a fresh new voice in Italian opera, and was well received for its lyrical qualities and its bright, distinctive orchestral color.

The timing of the new work was propitious: Tito Ricordi, who was taking over the reins at the Casa Ricordi from his father, was actively seeking out new talent for the firm. Ricordi bought the rights to *Giovanni Gallurese*, and commissioned a second opera from Montemezzi, providing the composer with a libretto by Luigi Ilica.[28] The second opera, entitled *Héllera* and based on *Adolphe*, a popular early-nineteenth-century sentimental

novel by the French writer Benjamin Constant, was less successful. Its failure, in view of the considerable beauties of its score, may have been in part
a matter of timing: by 1909, the Italian audience was losing interest in sentimental dramas of bourgeois life, however well wrought.[29] Ricordi was
willing to allow his emerging composers an occasional failure, however,
and agreed to commission a second opera from the composer, now well
into his thirties.

Soon after *Héllera*'s debut, Montemezzi's eyes fell on a new play by the
Tuscan playwright Sem Benelli. The play, which was Benelli's first and, as
it turned out, only substantial popular success, was *La cena delle beffe*, which
became, many years later, an opera by Giordano. Much to Montemezzi's
dismay, however, by the time he approached Benelli, the playwright had
already sold the operatic rights, all but giving them away to another musician, Tommaso Montefiore.[30] Although, with Ricordi offering to pay for
the rights, Benelli attempted to buy them back for substantially more than
Montefiore had paid for them, he was unwilling to sell, and *La cena delle
beffe* remained unavailable.[31]

Eager to assuage the composer's frustration, Benelli offered him the
rights to make an opera out of his next play. A contract was soon executed
with Ricordi for the rights to a play, as yet unwritten, entitled *L'amore dei
tre re* (The love of three kings). Although the play itself, when performed
in 1910, failed, Montemezzi had faith in its viability as an opera and convinced Tito Ricordi to allow him to go forward with the project. After two
years of steady work in the paternal home in Vigasio, his lifelong retreat
and haven, the opera was completed, making its debut under Serafin's
baton at La Scala on April 10, 1913. The cast contained the distinguished
singers Nazzareno De Angelis as Archibaldo and Carlo Galeffi as Manfredo, along with lesser known singers as the tenor and soprano leads. It
was an immediate success, and within months *L'amore dei tre re* began
making its way into opera houses in Italy and around the world. It made its
debut under Toscanini in January 1914 at the Metropolitan Opera, where
it was performed frequently until 1949.[32]

Sem Benelli (1877–1949), if not literally a disciple of D'Annunzio, was
his imitator, both in his extravagant, flowery language and in his penchant
for a Grand Guignol theater of extravagant sensuality and violence. Predictably, he was thoroughly detested by D'Annunzio.[33] In *L'amore dei tre
re*, although his poetry is crude and unimaginative compared to that of his
model, he was successful in blending a highly aestheticized nationalism,
almost fetishistic sensuality, and taste for recherché cruelty into a compelling narrative stew worthy of the master. The play is set in northern Italy

in the Dark Ages. The German invader Archibaldo has conquered the Italian kingdom of Altura. Eager to make peace with the natives, he has married his son Manfredo to the Italian princess Fiora. Although Manfredo, a gentle soul, loves her passionately and desperately wants her to love him, Fiora loves only Avito, the erstwhile heir to the Alturan throne to whom she was once betrothed. Now old and blind, Archibaldo paces the castle halls at night, suspecting that Fiora is seeing a lover while her husband is off in battle.

In the second act, Archibaldo surprises Fiora and Avito together. Although Avito escapes, Archibaldo strangles Fiora. Determined to learn who her lover is, the old king has her lips coated with poison as she is laid in the crypt, so that her lover — who will be unable to resist one last kiss — will die in turn. Avito enters the crypt, kisses Fiora, and falls dying to the floor. A moment later, Manfredo enters, finding his rival at his feet. Jealous of the love that Avito and Fiora shared and unable to imagine himself living without her, he too kisses her lips. As he lies dying, Archibaldo enters, gloating over his triumph; as he recognizes his son, he cries out in agony.

Beneath the gruesome melodrama lies a powerfully nationalistic subtext, of a sort not unusual in Italy in the second decade of the twentieth century, and particularly congenial to the patriotic Montemezzi, whose next opera would be a setting of D'Annunzio's hypernationalistic *La nave* (The ship). Although Italy was nominally allied to Germany and Austria-Hungary at the time through the Triple Alliance, patriotic Italians were well aware that the Italian provinces of Trent and Trieste were under Austrian rule, still awaiting liberation. In *L'amore dei tre re*, Italy may be conquered, but is neither dominated nor truly ruled by her conqueror. Fiora, who symbolizes Italy, has already drawn Manfredo away from his violent barbarian roots; she defies and, in the end, ultimately destroys her conqueror. In its way, the play reflects the state of mind, hardly universal but nonetheless widespread, that led Italy two years later to renounce the Triple Alliance and go to war against Germany and Austria-Hungary.

With a strong cast, and particularly with a strong orchestra led by a energetic figure on the podium, the opera has a dramatic impetus that sustains it from its opening notes to its grim conclusion. It is the orchestra that drives the drama, more than in any previous Italian opera. From mature Verdi on, the role of the orchestra in Italian opera had extended far beyond the traditional one of supporting the voices, by creating atmosphere and commenting on or adding emphasis to the vocal line. In Montemezzi's work, the role of the orchestra goes well beyond that, to the point where not only the rhythmic, but the melodic impetus of the music is derived from the orchestra; the vocal line, often uninteresting in itself, becomes little more than another instrument in the rich orchestral texture.

Montemezzi is brilliant at the distinctive orchestral effect that can be achieved from unusual juxtapositions of timbre, from crescendi, and from sudden sforzandi. As he told an interviewer early in his career, he "had not learned [orchestration] at the Conservatory, but from the gallery of La Scala, listening attentively . . . to the play of instruments during the performance of the most important operas."[34] During his Milan years as a student and as a struggling composer, he would have heard many Wagner operas, performed under Toscanini's baton.

Two major set pieces in the first act, Archibaldo's account of his conquest of Italy, "Italia! Italia . . . è tutto il mio ricordo," and Manfredo's passionate avowal of his love, "Fiora! Fiora!" are far more orchestral than vocal. In the first, a constantly shifting texture, with sudden outbursts from brass and timpani, combined with the appearance of a restless "galloping" motif, convey the excitement of conquest. The strings gradually come to dominate, steadily rising in intensity as Archibaldo's memories of his first encounter with Italy become more sensual and sexually charged:

> And this goddess, swimming between two seas,
> Seemed alone to us. . .
>   . . . And here we sat with her
> and here we lay and here we loved her, and
> never will any of us abandon her, our new lover . . .

If Archibaldo's narrative is a play of orchestral contrasts, Manfredo's paean to his beloved is a web of thick chromatic harmonies and pulsating string melody, culminating in an eruption of sound, as horns intone a repeated short motif against fortissimo strings — reminiscent of nothing so much as the climax of Siegfried's and Brünnhilde's love scene in *Siegfried*.

The comparison is appropriate: *L'amore dei tre re* is the most Wagnerian of Italian operas. Montemezzi's Wagner is not the composer of *Lohengrin* and *Tannhäuser*, as he was for the earlier generation, but the composer of the *Ring* and *Tristan*. As Manfredo is reminiscent of Siegfried, the second-act love scene between Avito and Fiora is intensely Tristanesque. Wagner is present in the orchestral interludes, and in the composer's use of leitmotifs, of which the most distinctive are the halting, irregular rhythmic pattern associated with Archibaldo, a noble two-bar motif for Manfredo; and the scurrying, galloping motif associated not only with the arrival and departure of Manfredo and his army, but with the idea of conquest and the underlying nationalist theme of the opera.

Montemezzi's loyalty to his Wagnerian influences extends to what is, by the standards of that decade, an unusually conservative harmonic vocabulary. However chromatic it may occasionally become, it never departs much from the roots of late-nineteenth-century tonality, and is decidedly old-fashioned in comparison to that of the contemporary works of composers as diverse as Puccini, Mascagni, and Zandonai. Despite what some commentators have written, there is little of Debussy's influence in *L'amore dei tre re*, while the influence of Strauss is found largely in the cut of some of the melodic lines or in particular orchestral effects rather than any deeper connection. Montemezzi's harmonic language is echt Wagner, the language of *Der Ring des Nibelungen*.

Montemezzi makes it his own, however, giving his opera a distinctive and unusual musical quality. In contrast to his contemporaries Zandonai and Alfano, who at this point in their careers were still unable to free themselves from the direct influence of their predecessors, Montemezzi is already his own man. His musical ideas in *L'amore dei tre re* seem to have come from a unique source, suspended in midtrajectory between Italian and German origins and influences, and sounding unlike the work of any other composer. At the same time, while many of his musical ideas are effective, particularly on first hearing, they are less compelling than those of greater masters. A New York reviewer, who had clearly heard the work often over the years, wrote in 1941: "this music drama has not survived the passage of time entirely unscathed. . . . [W]ith some memorable exceptions, its basic musical ideas seemed less individual, less readily grasped and recalled than they had been; the romanticism seemed at times to be of a kind that may not necessarily survive."

The reviewer concluded, however, that "prophecy here would be rash."[35] The prophecy, unfortunately, was apt; within a few years, *L'amore dei tre re* would begin to lose its position in the operatic repertory.

The success of *L'Amore dei Tre Re* however, had fired Montemezzi's ambition. Believing himself capable of even greater things, his attention turned during 1914 to a daunting work by D'Annunzio, the poet's 1908 play *La Nave*. In a memoir, the composer confessed his ambivalence about the project: "I felt that, to confront it and translate it into music, one would need enormous courage. . . . But so beautiful! I spent week after week studying its proportions, digging deeply into its characters. Impossible! I felt that I would be drawn into a labyrinth and I dropped the idea. I turned to reading other things, simpler, more instrumental; but those epic figures that occupied that gigantic frame, they pounded on me, and gave me no peace. . . . Months passed that way, between renunciation and definite plans, without a positive result."[36]

La nave is indeed an overwhelming work, a play of such extravagant proportions and megalomaniacal ambition that it renders the writer's earlier plays modest by comparison, a work characterized by one modern writer as an "extraordinary (and now ridiculous) blend of patriotic rhetoric, phony mysticism and sado-masochistic sex."[37] In *La nave*, D'Annunzio has left *Tristan* far behind, superimposing an ardent nationalism on an even bloodier than usual strain of his customary conflation of sexuality and violence. The play depicts the horrible revenge of the beautiful but deadly Basiliola (characterized by one writer as "an *Übermensch* in skirts"[38] against the Gràtico brothers, who have brutally tortured her father and brothers, and her ultimate self-immolation, set against a lavishly re-created background of a half-barbaric, half-Christian Venice of the sixth century. The dominant message of the play, however, is nationalist, a call for Italy to fulfill her manifest destiny, reflected in Marco Gràtico's cry, a cry that once resounded throughout Italy:

> Arm the prow and sail out against the world,
> Make of all the oceans our sea!

Gràtico's cry was read, as D'Annunzio intended, as a call to the Italian people to redeem, by force of arms if necessary, the 'unredeemed' provinces of Trent and Trieste, and make the Adriatic the Italian lake that the nationalists of the early-twentieth century considered their nation's due, the so-called Adriatic Idea.

Montemezzi might have remained suspended indefinitely in his ambivalent state had it not been for the outbreak of war: "The Adriatic Idea took on vast proportions, as did my desire to create an opera that would be a work of propaganda. My courage knew no more obstacles, and I set about achieving my dream."[39] For all his sophisticated veneer, Montemezzi was and would remain an unreflective, passionate Italian patriot, with a strong religious, even superstitious, streak. With Leoncavallo, he was an uncritical supporter of Italy's intervention in the First World War, more than susceptible to the nationalistic fervor of *La nave*. His works are permeated with nationalism. Both *Giovanni Gallurese* and *L'amore dei tre re* had nationalistic subtexts, and his last work was an orchestral "rhapsody," entitled *Italia mia! Nulla fermerà il tuo canto!* (My Italy! Nothing will hold back your song!). Written in 1946, after more than a decade of musical silence, the work's character can be elicited from one writer's description: "trumpet calls, galloping strings, deft woodwind flourishes, pounding battle cries, hymns of victory. Apotheoses, with massed peals of bells."[40]

Tito Ricordi, who was enthusiastic about *La nave*, performed the necessary cuts to render the play more or less suitable for operatic treatment, and Montemezzi began work on April 25, 1915, deliberately choosing to begin an act he saw as one of quasi-religious, quasi-patriotic devotion on the feast day of Saint Mark, patron saint of Venice. With the help of D'Annunzio, who arranged to have the composer's military service obligation waived, the work was completed by mid-1918, and made its debut at La Scala on November 3, 1918. The event was as much a patriotic rite as an operatic debut. The performance was preceded by forty-five minutes of national hymns and, as Serafin was preparing to give the downbeat to open the second act, Ricordi rushed onstage holding a telegram, informing the audience that that morning Italian troops had entered Trieste, and Trent that afternoon. The news sent the audience into a patriotic frenzy that lasted some time before the performance could resume.[41] Years later, Montemezzi would refer to this moment as "sent by God."[42]

Although its patriotic associations prompted a warm reception for *La nave* at its debut, Montemezzi's intended magnum opus failed to generate the enthusiasm that alone would have led to further productions. The casting and scenic demands of the opera were exorbitant, including, for the final act, "the great ship 'Totus Mundus,' still in shadow against the rising sun against the wharf, solidly built, with a quarterdeck on the poop and a turret on the prow, with Latin rigging and armaments, and thirty covered rowers' banks, already ready to descend into the Adriatic"[43] Even at the premiere, the warmly positive review in Milan's *Corriere della sera* noted that although its outcome "had all the grandeur of a sincere success, [it] was rarely truly enthusiastic."[44] Although performed in 1919 in Chicago and once again in 1923 in the composer's native Verona, *La nave* subsequently disappeared from the repertory.

Despite its failure to attract an audience, Montemezzi was convinced that *La nave*, rather than the far more successful *L'amore dei tre re*, was his masterpiece. Beginning in 1930, the composer bombarded Mussolini with letters pleading for a Roman revival of the opera. Failing in his effort to have the work mounted in commemoration of the tenth anniversary of the March on Rome, he wrote again to Mussolini, as war clouds grew in the spring of 1935, reminding him of the opera's patriotic origins: "What opera could be more suitable for a major Italian theater at this particular moment than *La nave*? . . . The people of *La nave* resound as one with the

Italian people. The opera written in a moment of passion, at the great moment of war, as Adriatic propaganda, finds its true moment today as propaganda for *italianità*."[45] Although the governor of Rome wrote Mussolini's secretary, at the behest of the management of the Rome Opera — now government-owned and known as the Teatro Reale — that "it does not seem to me a good idea for the Teatro Reale to put on an opera that represents a certain and unjustifiable financial loss,"[46] *La nave* finally reached the Roman stage in 1938 under Serafin's baton, with Gina Cigna as Basiliola. Greeted respectfully, but without enthusiasm, it was withdrawn after three performances. It has never been performed since.

Montemezzi's creative drive seems to have been largely exhausted with the composition of *La nave*, and he wrote little music during his remaining more than three decades of life.[47] Marrying an American heiress named Katherine Leith in 1921, he spent long periods in the United States, where he could bask in his American fame as the composer of *L'amore dei tre re*. Indeed, the work was assiduously promoted by the *New York Times*'s critic Olin Downes, who described it as "the most sincere and idealistic score which has come from Italy in the modern period — in fact, since the period of Wagner and Verdi," and "a work without which the modern repertory would be incomplete."[48] Traveling in the United States as war broke out in Europe in 1939, Montemezzi decided to remain, buying a Beverly Hills mansion and resigning himself to the life of a celebrity. In 1949, he returned to Italy, returning to the house in Vigasio in which he had been born, where he died in 1952.

Riccardo Zandonai and Francesca da Rimini

Riccardo Zandonai was the last of Italy's operatic master craftsmen, musicians in a long line beginning with Monteverdi and his contemporaries, for whom opera was as much a craft as an art, and who made the writing of operas their lifelong calling. After Zandonai, although many Italian composers continued to write operas, none would show the same consistent dedication to that pursuit, or would produce such a substantial, even impressive, body of work. Over a career of some forty years starting in the early years of the twentieth century, Zandonai composed a total of thirteen operas, the last of which, *Il bacio*, was left unfinished and not performed until after his death. Of all of his works, however, while many are still of interest, only one holds even a modest position in the contemporary operatic repertory, the Tristanesque *Francesca da Rimini*.

Riccardo Zandonai *(Konrad Claude Dryden)*

Zandonai was born in 1883 in Sacco, a small village along the Adige River in the shadow of the much larger town of Rovereto, into which it has long since been absorbed. Lying in a narrow mountain valley at the southern edge of the Tyrol, until 1919 Sacco and Rovereto were in the Austro-Hungarian Empire, forming part of the "unredeemed" Italy that was the obsession of Italian nationalists during the years that preceded the First World War. Along with his teacher Mascagni, he was one of the few composers of the time to have sprung from a working-class background. His father was a poor cobbler, while his mother worked in the tobacco factory that provided the livelihood for most of Sacco's citizens. An only child, he became accustomed to strict discipline and hard work from an early age, foreshadowing the driven, work-obsessed adult he would become. His passion for music was also apparent from early childhood; at the age of four, he was taken in hand by an uncle who was impressed by the child's response to the sound of his guitar, and by age six he had mastered the instrument.[49]

Despite the straitened circumstances of his childhood, his path into the musical world was a smooth one. Zandonai's father, a proud member of the Sacco municipal band, encouraged his musical aspirations, and the young composer-to-be was fortunate, as his talent became known, to find not only a supportive musical mentor in Vincenzo Gianferrari, director of the local music school, but encouragement and financial support from members of Rovereto's prosperous middle class as well. In 1898, at fifteen, he was admitted to the Liceo Musicale Rossini in Pesaro, in order to continue his musical studies under the guidance of Pietro Mascagni.

Since taking charge of the Liceo Rossini in 1895, Mascagni had transformed what had been a modest provincial conservatory into one of the nation's premier centers for musical education, reorganizing the curriculum and recruiting an outstanding faculty from across Italy. The enrollment had quickly doubled, and the demand for places in the student body had grown even greater, with young men and women coming to study there from across Italy, Europe, and the United States. Although within a few years, Mascagni's conflicts with the liceo's governing board and the city's politicians, and his abrupt departure, would become a national cause célèbre, in 1898 that was still in the future, and the school was at the height of its brief season of fame.

Zandonai was quickly recognized by Mascagni and his other teachers as an outstanding student, not only for his considerable talent, but for his extraordinary energy and determination. Studying constantly and pushing himself to the limits of his physical ability, he completed the conservatory program in three years, graduating with all but perfect grades in 1901 at the early age of eighteen. Years later, he described himself as a student: "I always studied seriously with great intensity, and I never cared for lack of discipline or excessive liveliness, with the excuse that at that age everything is permitted outside class."[50] His powerful ego, and his unshakable belief in the value of his talent and the soundness of his opinions, made a strong impression. As his classmate Francesco Balilla Pratella, who achieved considerable fame some years later as leader of the musical wing of the Futurist movement recalled: "Zandonai was younger than I, but graduated two years ahead of me. He was, well before then, the most promising talent at the Liceo Rossini. He always came out first, in composing, in conducting, in arguing. With an iron will and a persistent nature, he even got into arguments with maestro Mascagni."[51] His graduation work, which received favorable attention well beyond the walls of the Liceo Rossini, was a cantata for orchestra, chorus, and soprano and baritone soloists on the poem "Il ritorno di Odisseo" by the poet Giovanni Pascoli.

After graduation, Zandonai's path to recognition as a composer continued to be smooth, with few of the vicissitudes and hardships experienced by such composers as Leoncavallo or Mascagni. After a few uncertain years, he arrived in Milan early in 1905, still only twenty-two, where he was taken in hand by Arrigo Boito, and introduced by the elderly literary lion to Tito Ricordi, who had already taken over much of the responsibility for managing the family firm from his father.

Zandonai's arrival was fortuitous. Ricordi saw the young man as a potentially important future composer, and immediately offered him a libretto, an adaptation by the journalist Cesare Hanau of the Dickens tale *The Cricket on the Hearth* (*Il grillo al focolare*). The opera, which Zandonai completed in 1907, was modestly successful in its Turin debut the following fall; it was recognized as a work, if not of a mature composer, yet one of great promise. As one newspaper wrote, it was the work "of a youth, an authentic youth, who really has something to say and who knows how to say it."[52] Zandonai was still only twenty-five, and his next work was anticipated with considerable interest.

To Ricordi's dismay, even before *Il grillo* had appeared, Zandonai had already begun a new opera entitled *Melenis*, based on what the publisher considered a tedious, old-fashioned libretto set in ancient Rome. Hoping to dissuade the composer from pursuing that project, Ricordi offered him *Conchita*, the libretto that had initially been prepared for Puccini from Pierre Louÿs' *La femme et le pantin*, which Puccini had finally rejected, after considerable reflection, the year before. Zandonai abandoned

Melenis — although only temporarily — and took up the composition of *Conchita*, which he completed by the middle of 1910. While waiting for Ricordi to set a time and place for the premiere of *Conchita*, the composer resumed work on *Melenis*.[53]

Conchita made its debut at Milan's Dal Verme theater in October 1911, with the soprano Tarquinia Tarquini — who would soon become the composer's lover and later his wife — in the title role. It was a great success, running for fourteen performances to packed houses. While some listeners were revolted by the story's sadomasochistic overtones and others found it exciting for the same reason, critics and audience were all left in awe of Zandonai's brilliant orchestral palette and the powerfully atmospheric quality of his music, characteristics that overwhelm and all but submerge the claustrophic sexual dance of Mateo and Conchita. As one reviewer wrote: "He is a powerful orchestrator, a wonderfully effective creator of color, full of resources, a technique not cold, but alive. . . . Zandonai has the temperament of a symphonist."[54]

Another, accurate only in part, wrote: "Zandonai has distanced himself completely from the paths beaten by Mascagni and Puccini. The orchestral texture is totally different from that of any other contemporary Italian opera."[55] On initial hearing, *Conchita* makes a far more radical impression, even today, than is sustained by closer listening. Underneath the dazzling orchestral and atmospheric color, however, the contours of Zandonai's melodic line, as it emerges in the sequence of duets between Mateo and Conchita that make up the heart of the opera, are still firmly rooted in the conventions of the *giovane scuola*, above all in the language of Mascagni, especially *Iris*, the sole Mascagni opera whose virtues Zandonai was willing to acknowledge. This characteristic of Zandonai's style remained intact well beyond *Conchita*; fourteen years later, in 1925, reviewing the composer's latest work, *I cavalieri di Ekebù*, Adriano Lualdi wrote, "last night Riccardo Zandonai, after a number of years of incomplete confessions and hesitancies, openly declared his faith: Mascagni."[56]

Zandonai, who missed few opportunities to denigrate his immediate predecessors, took pains to deny his stylistic indebtedness to his teacher, and nurtured a lifelong bitterness over his being characterized as "Mascagni's student." He never acknowledged the extent to which doors had opened for him through his connection to Mascagni; instead, Mascagni's worldwide fame, as well as his powerful physical presence and personal magnetism, were a source of jealousy and resentment. If asked about his studies, Zandonai would defensively respond that his Rovereto mentor Gianferrari, and not Mascagni, had been his teacher.[57]

Zandonai, indeed, was a difficult, contradictory individual. Possessed of an almost overweening ego, certain of his worth, even greatness, as a composer, he combined that with a deeply rooted insecurity, perhaps associated with his short stature — he was only 5′3″ or 5′4″ — his coarse, unprepossessing features, his working-class origins, or his lack of social graces. Hard-working and driven to the point of obsession, he would regularly suffer from psychosomatic ailments that would send him to his bed for long periods, finding respite only in his beloved mountains, where he would hunt for days, alone with his dogs. Although there was a side to his personality that would win him devoted friends, there was a harsher side that was often in evidence: his treatment of his wife, as described by his biographer Dryden, often verged on the abusive, while his routine denigration of Mascagni and Puccini, whom he dubbed "a third-class craftsman,"[58] suggests an almost Oedipal need to destroy his artistic parents in order to buttress his sense of his own worth.[59]

The success of *Conchita* confirmed Tito Ricordi's conviction that in Zandonai he had found his heir to Puccini, much as his father had found Verdi's heir in Puccini. Convinced that Zandonai was growing into a mature artist capable of producing his best work, Ricordi was eager to give his protégé the opportunity to demonstrate his abilities on a larger, more ambitious scale. In the cultural context of the time, it was all but inevitable that for an opera to be seen as important it would have to be Tristanesque, with a libretto written, if not by D'Annunzio himself, then by someone else in the same vein. Fortunately, if only because no composer or publisher had previously seen fit to meet D'Annunzio's financial demands, the poet's *Francesca da Rimini* was still available. *Francesca*, first performed by Eleonora Duse in December 1901, a "poem of blood and lust," in the author's words, was, along with *La figlia di Jorio*, the most successful of his many works for the theater, in terms both of its dramatic vitality and its public reception.

Ricordi's negotiations with D'Annunzio on Zandonai's behalf for *Francesca* took place simultaneously with Sonzogno's negotiations with the poet for *Parisina*; it can not unreasonably be seen as a matter of pure chance that Zandonai set *Francesca* and Mascagni *Parisina* rather than the other way around. While Ricordi was able to reduce D'Annunzio's demands modestly, he was more successful with Zandonai, who, by this point all but desperate to obtain the rights to *Francesca*, agreed to relinquish the lion's share of his customary advance in order to accommodate the poet.[60] On May 14, 1912, the delighted composer sent a telegram to his friend and confidant Nicola D'Atri: "*Francesca* è assicurata!" (*Francesca* is in the bag!).[61]

Francesca da Rimini recounts the story of the tragic lovers Paolo and Francesca immortalized by Dante, who encountered the two in his descent into hell, describing them in canto 5 of his *Inferno*. Francesca, with the silent Paolo by her side, describes how the two "one day, for pleasure, read of Lancelot," and then:

> But one particular moment alone it was
> Defeated us: *the longed-for smile*, it said,
> *Was kissed by that most noble lover:* at this,
> This one, who will now never leave my side,
> Kissed my mouth, trembling . . .
>   . . . that day we read
> No further.[62]

Francesca, daughter of Guido da Polenta, lord of Ravenna, was married to Giovanni (Gianciotto) Malatesta, lord of Rimini.[63] She fell in love with Gianciotto's brother Paolo, and when Gianciotto discovered their affair, he killed them both. That much is history; although the exact dates are uncertain, it is generally believed that the murder took place in 1285, when Dante himself was a young man.

Nearly a hundred years later, when Boccaccio retold the story in his commentary on Dante's *Divine Comedy*, he added a telling detail, which may or may not have had any historic basis. In his account, Guido felt it necessary to marry his daughter to Gianciotto Malatesta in order to end the feud between the two families, but was concerned that she would reject the deformed bridegroom. As a result, according to Boccaccio, Gianciotto's handsome brother Paolo was enlisted to perform a proxy marriage on his brother's behalf with Francesca, a deception that the young woman only discovered on her subsequent arrival in Rimini.

D'Annunzio elaborated on Boccaccio's tale, inventing a third brother, the monster Malatestino, whose warped lust for Francesca ultimately leads him to betray her secret to her husband, and extending the story into four extended acts rich with decorative detail. The first act describes the arrival of Paolo in Ravenna, and the lovers' first meeting, while the second, on the battlements of the Malatesta castle, depicts their first reluctant acknowledgment of their love for one another. In the third act, in Francesca's chambers, D'Annunzio has re-created the scene from Dante, in which Paolo and Francesca read the story of Lancelot and fall into one another's arms, while the fourth act depicts their betrayal by Malatestino and subsequent murder by Gianciotto, Francesca's husband.

D'Annunzio's play, written in the wake of his Wagner-obsessed novel *Il fuoco*, is rich in carefully wrought parallels with *Tristan*, in the dramatic events themselves, and in his invention of the third brother Malatestino as a counterpart to Melot, although the character owes as much to Tonio in *Pagliacci* as to the Wagnerian figure. D'Annunzio weaves a web of cross-references to the story of Tristan and Isolde itself, beginning with the minstrel's account of Isolde's story in the first act, drawing close parallels between the episode in the second act of *Francesca* in which Paolo and Francesca drink from a wine goblet served by Francesca's maid Smaragdi, and the scene in which Tristan and Isolde drink from the chalice proffered by Brangäne in Wagner's opera.

By mid-June of 1912 Tito Ricordi had turned D'Annunzio's prolix text into a workable libretto, reducing the number of verses by more than a quarter, eliminating many decorative episodes as well as more substantive episodes less directly germane to the central love story. The cuts were approved by the poet at the end of June, and Zandonai began work immediately. His exalted state of mind, as well as his expectations for the new work, were reflected in a letter to a childhood friend written in October: "These days, I've written the first scene, which to my eyes has come out a little jewel of color, freshness and clarity. . . . Let us hope that the remaining acts are equal in merit to the first. Who knows, perhaps an Italian *Tristan und Isolde* is being born?"[64] Working at a pace that reflected both his intense excitement and his disciplined work habits, he completed the opera *Francesca da Rimini* in short score a year later, and orchestrated it during the fall of 1913.

Francesca made its debut at Turin's Teatro Regio on February 19, 1914. While the first two acts were greeted warmly but with some reserve, the third act moved the audience to true enthusiasm, as reflected in a subsequent review: "He who has written this third act is not only a learned musician, but a man who feels and knows how to express the palpitations and the ardor of a human and profound passion."[65]

From that point, *Francesca* moved steadily into theaters in Italy and elsewhere, reaching Rome in 1915 and La Scala in 1916, where it appeared with Rosa Raisa as Francesca, and the young tenor Aureliano Pertile as Paolo, becoming something of a repertory work in Italy during the years preceding the Second World War. Although it is no longer part of the standard repertory, it is revived periodically, including a memorable 1984 production at New York's Metropolitan Opera with Renata Scotto and Placido Domingo.

Francesca da Rimini is the richest of Zandonai's scores, a work of beauty and passion. In addition to its musical riches, it is a work of compelling dramatic power. Through Ricordi's extensive but judicious cuts, D'Annunzio's play was turned into one of the finest libretti of the period, a drama in which each act not only moves inexorably to its own dramatic climax, but contributes to the cumulative effect of the work as a whole. The opera that Zandonai crafted from that libretto is a work of dazzling, shimmering orchestral color. Through his use of the orchestra, the composer captures the magic of the moment when Paolo and Francesca first set eyes on one another, the grim bloodiness of the Malatesta battlements, or Francesca's conflicted feelings as she awaits Paolo in her perfumed chambers. In contrast to Montemezzi's orchestra, which drives the drama in *L'amore dei tre re*, Zandonai's orchestra never usurps the central dramatic role of the voices; while the role of the orchestra is atmospheric, it carries out that role with an intensity and richness never heard before in Italian opera. As one commentator wrote: "The most immediate impression of [Zandonai's] music is that of color; that his powers of evocation enable him to express in sound not only the most tenuous nuances of feeling, but the soul of things."[66] Through their orchestral garb, resonance and significance are often added to even the most commonplace vocal lines.

Zandonai's harmonic palette is equally rich, that of a composer who has not only fully assimilated Wagner, but is thoroughly au courant with the most recent works of Debussy and Richard Strauss, including the latter's operas through *Der Rosenkavalier*.[67] His vocabulary is intensely chromatic and freely modulatory, making extensive use of whole tone chords, to such a degree that he largely dispenses with key signatures for all but the most heightened romantic moments — such as the meeting of Francesca and Paolo at the end of the first act, at which point the chromatic clouds part and the music takes on a radiant diatonic D Major tonality.

A brilliant modulation creates the most magical moment in the entire score, the opening of the third-act scene between Paolo and Francesca. Her handmaidens have left, and the two look at each other silently for a moment, as a combination of muted trumpets, oboe, and the lowest notes of the harp establish a D-flat Major tonality. Finally, after we can almost wait no longer for something to happen between them, Francesca sings "Benvenuto, signore mio cognato" (Welcome, my lord brother-in-law), a simple, almost formal, limpid melody to the accompaniment of quiet string chords. The phrase begins in D-flat Major, rising slowly and seemingly predictably in a D-flat Major scale, but on the second syllable of "cognato" the vocal line moves from D-flat to E-natural, and the underlying harmony from D-flat Major to an A Major seventh chord, which resolves into D Major, the totemic key of the lover's first meeting.

Zandonai's ability to create distinctive melodic lines is not adequate to maintain a two-character love scene lasting nearly twenty minutes at a consistently high level, and he is unable to sustain the magic of the scene's opening for long. While there is much beauty in this music, there is also empty vocality, including Paolo's famous *scena* "Nemica ebbi la luce, amica ebbi la notte" (Daylight was my enemy, the night my friend), which rather than the revelatory moment that was intended, is largely stale Mascagnian rhetoric.[68] Zandonai was not without a melodic gift; it can be heard not only in Francesca's "Benvenuto, signore mio cognato," but also in the haunting viola theme that heralds Paolo's entrance in the first act, and returns to frame the fatal kiss at the end of the third. What Zandonai lacked was the gift that both Puccini and Mascagni had: the ability to give even less important moments their own hallmark, so that even minor vocal passages take on an individuality and resonance of their own. It is that quality, indeed, that redeems *Parisina*, and makes it, despite its longeurs, a rewarding listening experience. In *Francesca*, by contrast, one finds oneself often listening more for the piquant details of orchestration than following the singers' vocal lines.

If part of the explanation for why *Francesca da Rimini* falls short of greatness can be found in the limitations of Zandonai's creative gift, other reasons may be more deeply rooted in the nature of operatic composition in Italy in the new century. It is noteworthy how often Zandonai's music is characterized as Wagnerian, or alternatively Debussyan or Straussian. Leaving aside the extent to which one should credit, or blame, any of these composers for the merits or weaknesses of Zandonai's music, the characterization reflects a painful underlying reality: Italian opera after Verdi — after a brief interlude during which the members of the *giovane scuola*, in particular Puccini and to a lesser extent Mascagni, appeared to be creating new ways by which distinctively Italian operas could be written — had reverted to the status of a derivative culture. Whatever the distinctively Italian characteristics of the operas of the *giovane scuola* might have been — a subject still in dispute — it is clear that they were not substantial enough or deeply enough rooted to provide a foundation on which a new generation of composers could build a language that would be both distinctively Italian and uniquely their own. Instead, with the tropes of verismo opera already turning into clichés by the early years of the twentieth century, the younger generation of composers sought inspiration by assimilating the most advanced tendencies of French and German music, absorbing those tendencies as best they could into their music, where they coexisted uneasily with the composers' musical inheritance from the *giovane scuola*.

Francesca da Rimini, completed not long after the composer's thirtieth birthday, was the high point of Zandonai's operatic career. His next project, selected within a few months after *Francesca's* debut, was a light comedy based on a Eugène Scribe farce, turned into a libretto by Giuseppe Adami, librettist of Puccini's *La rondine* and *Il tabarro.* Entitled *La via della finestra* (The way through the window), the new work made its debut in Zandonai's adopted home of Pesaro in 1919, but with only modest success. Despite its charms, most critics agreed that "Zandonai was not born for comedy."[69] The work has not survived.

Although the choice of subject reflected Zandonai's desire to treat a lighter subject as a change from the intensity of *Francesca,* not only *La via della finestra* but the composer's subsequent works suggest that for all his preoccupation with his musical craft, Zandonai's choice of operatic subjects seems to have been based less on careful consideration than on whim or chance. Once the subject had been determined, and the overall structure of the opera established, he seems to have paid little attention to his libretti. Adami's experience, as he described it many years later, was a very different one from that of librettists who worked for Puccini or Mascagni: "The theme was well considered and established, the length of the acts and scenes were well discussed and approved. When the verses were composed [Zandonai] quietly put the libretto in his pocket, left for Pesaro or for Sacco . . . and for months and months I did not hear from him. . . . Zandonai did not ask for verses to be adapted to his music, but composed music to verses already written."[70] The laborious and painful iterative process through which Puccini, Illica, and Giacosa created *Tosca* and *Bohème,* or by which Illica and Mascagni created *Iris* and *Isabeau,* was foreign to Zandonai. His last six operas were written to libretti by Arturo Rossato, a mediocre writer at best, whose products the composer accepted largely uncritically. These works are largely forgotten: although his 1925 *I cavalieri de Ekebù,* based on the Swedish writer Selma Lagerlöf's *Gösta Berling,* is a work of considerable power, in the final analysis, it lacks the individuality or melodic distinction that would enable it to survive. Mascagni's comment on the opera, in a letter to his daughter, is harsh but not entirely unreasonable: "Zandonai is a first-rate musician," he wrote, "but his imagination is limited, and his temperament can never capture the feeling of passion."[71]

Chapter 15

The End of the Era

The Crisis of the Tradition

D uring their brief heyday, the composers of the *giovane scuola* fashioned an operatic synthesis that grafted new ideas coming from sources as different as Wagner and Massenet onto a Verdian trunk, imbuing the traditional Italian vernacular in which they had been raised with a new energy and dynamism. This new synthesis, while far from unsophisticated musically, was emotionally direct and easily approachable; it was also particularly well suited to the subjects, from the violent quarrels of Sicilian peasants and Neapolitan slum-dwellers to the exotic miseries of Puccini's Butterfly or Mascagni's Iris, that fit the tastes of the fin de siècle bourgeoisie that had come to dominate the Italian audience during the late-nineteenth century. During barely more than a decade following the premiere of *Cavalleria rusticana*, not only Puccini, but Mascagni, Cilèa, Giordano, and Leoncavallo all presented that audience with a series of operas that not only engendered passionate interest at the time, but to an extraordinary degree have remained integral to the worldwide operatic repertory more than a hundred years later.[1] No other period of such short duration, in any country, has contributed so much to the modern operatic repertory.

After 1902, however, none of these composers except for Puccini produced a work that has lasted to the present, and few works indeed that even attracted much attention at the time. Although Mascagni's *Isabeau* and two later operas, the 1917 *Lodoletta*, and his 1921 *Il piccolo Marat*, all experienced short-lived popularity — as did Giordano's 1915 *Madame Sans-Gêne* — they have not survived, while not one of the many works written after 1902 by Leoncavallo, Cilèa, or Franchetti attracted more than momentary attention. The moment of the *giovane scuola* was over almost before it began. Their achievement, however notable in itself, was incapable of serving as a basis for a more extended revival of Italy's operatic fortunes.

The ground under the Italian musical world had shifted, and these composers were unable to move with it. As the twentieth century began, Italy had finally become firmly joined to the larger European musical environment. While Franchetti's German training had been a curiosity twenty years earlier, aspiring Italian composers now studied in France and, above all, in Germany, where they were exposed to a far more sophisticated musical culture than that which existed at home. Italian audiences now regularly heard not only *Tristan* and the *Ring*, but also the latest works by Strauss, Debussy, and their contemporaries, often only months after their first performances in their homelands. The provincial culture of nineteenth-century Italy, a comfortable cocoon for all but a handful of intellectuals, had been opened to the world; the younger generation, exposed to German musical culture and to German and French operas performed in Turin or Milan, had discovered their native musical culture to be shamefully backward. If there was one matter on which every thoughtful young Italian composer or critic — and not a few members of the older generation as well — agreed, it was that change was desperately needed.

The importance of modernizing one's musical garb was not lost on Puccini and Mascagni, the two members of the *giovane scuola* who were most open to the changing winds blowing from across the Alps. Their efforts, however, reflected most dramatically in *Fanciulla* and *Parisina*, must be seen as a willed effort to graft a new vocabulary onto the language in which they had been raised. For the younger Zandonai and his contemporaries the new ideas of Strauss and Debussy were part of their cultural formation. For Zandonai, assimilating those ideas into a personal style, albeit one rooted in the Italian tradition of Puccini and Mascagni, was second nature. Zandonai and Montemezzi, in their musical language and in their exploration of Tristanesque themes reflected through the D'Annunzian prism, saw themselves in a very different light from their predecessors, and believed that they were introducing something significantly new and different to Italian opera.

Yet both composers are not unreasonably seen today as little more than epigones of verismo, composers who, if they demonstrated anything at all, established the outer limits of the musical culture of the *giovane scuola*. As Zanetti writes: "with *Francesca*, Zandonai brought to its end — along with the Puccini of *Turandot*, albeit in different fashion — the course of traditional Italian opera, carried to the ultimate degree of exhaustion and corruption."[2] The achievement of the generation that followed the *giovane scuola* was, in the final analysis, hollow. Their synthesis represented little more than an effort to graft a modernist surface derived from foreign models onto the nineteenth-century Italian model of operatic activity on which they had been raised — an effort that prompted Bastianelli to dub Zandonai a "Debusstrausian and Mascagnian" composer.[3] Zandonai and his peers failed to realize that the problem was not one of harmonic vocabulary or orchestral technique, but one of the fundamental premises of the model: its wider economic and cultural role as well its musical and dramatic content. Unknowingly perhaps, their efforts reinforced the sense of Italian musical culture as a subaltern culture, subordinate to and dependent on the creative energies of the dominant cultures to the north. As a result, as an adversarial intellectual culture emerged in Italy early in the century, opera came to be seen as part of the cultural problem to be overcome, rather than a vehicle through which Italy could build a new, stronger, and more independent cultural life.

During the decade from 1905 to 1915, all of the premises of Italian operatic life would come under sustained attack, while the beleaguered tradition would find few active defenders. Although to a casual observer Italian operatic culture might seem still to be intact, by the end of the First World War, it had already been fatally undermined. It was more attenuated, and more detached from its historic roots in a distinctive national cultural matrix, and had already become less central to the tastes and interests of the larger Italian audience. Although operas continued to be composed and performed, the process by which a body of cultural practices that had maintained their vitality for hundreds of years would be transformed from a living organism into a museum artifact had begun.

The Challenge of the Intellectuals

The adversarial intellectual culture that set itself up in opposition to bourgeois society and positivistic doctrine in the early years of the twentieth century found a highly visible target in Italian operatic culture, economically rooted as it was in its appeal to the bourgeois audience and musically retrograde by comparison to the works being written elsewhere in Europe. A precursor of the more systematic attack that would later emerge had begun as early as the mid-1890s in the pages of the *Rivista musicale italiana,* Italy's first systematic journal of music criticism and scholarship, which began publication in 1894. Under the direction of Luigi Torchi, a pioneering musicologist and passionate Wagnerian whose seven-volume anthology of early Italian music is still to be found in libraries,[4] the *Rivista* saw its mission, at least in part, as one of deflating the pretensions of the *giovane scuola* and calling attention to the inferior, even primitive, character of their efforts. Between 1895 and 1902, Torchi devoted hundreds of pages of the *Rivista* to a series of almost interminably extended and ponderously scornful reviews of the new operas of Mascagni, Puccini, and others, dissecting them in minute detail and making their inferiority to the iconic works of Wagner painfully clear.[5]

Torchi's diatribes, however much they may have impressed his likeminded colleagues, had little effect on the wider musical world. It was not until the operatic critique became part of a larger cultural critique of bourgeois society that it began to have a significant effect. By the early years of the twentieth century that larger critique had become pervasive, as a generation of public intellectuals had begun to take aim at the sterility and philistinism of the dominant strain of Italian society and culture. Applied to music by a number of writers, most notably Giannotto Bastianelli (1883–1927) and Fausto Torrefranca (1883–1955), the critique of opera went far beyond the assessment of the musical language of individual composers to encompass the operatic industry with its distinctive social and economic arrangements, proposing a fundamental reinterpretation of the role of opera in Italian music and society. To both Bastianelli and Torrefranca, the operatic world into which they were born was hopelessly corrupt, compromised by its commercialism and its conformity to the tastes of the bourgeois audience on which it was economically dependent.

Both writers were part of the circle that grew around Giuseppe Prezzolini and Giovanni Papini and the Florentine journal *La Voce*. *La Voce*, which exerted a strong influence over Italian cultural thinking during its short life from 1908 to 1914, was committed, in the words of its manifesto, "to the renewal of Italy . . . to the creation of a new environment of truth, of sincerity, and of realism."[6] Prezzolini had, indeed, during the years leading up to the first publication of *La Voce*, passed through a period where he was in thrall to D'Annunzio and his concept of the superman, only to abandon that under the influence of Benedetto Croce's philosophy of idealism in search of a more elevated mission more deeply grounded in Italian reality. For Prezzolini, that ambitious mission — which has been characterized as nothing less than an "intellectual crusade"[7] designed to renew Italian culture — could not be achieved through D'Annunzio's decadent aestheticism.

From his first days as editor of *La Voce*, Prezzolini recognized the important role that the purification of Italian music would play in this revival, reflected in the invitation he extended to the famous French writer Romain Rolland to write for his journal: "A violent attack against our horrible and effeminate Puccini, Leoncavallo, etc. would be most welcome. Your name and your authority could not be better used than to assist us in the battle we are fighting against the cowardice of our contemporaries."[8] Prezzolini made room in his journal not only for Bastianelli and Torrefranca, but also for the rising young composer Ildebrando Pizzetti.

Bastianelli was a remarkable and tragic figure, a talented composer and gifted pianist, the most brilliant and incisive musical critic of his time, yet so psychologically unstable that he spent much of his life living from hand to mouth, dying at forty-four, almost certainly by his own hand, in a shabby hotel room in Tunis. While recognizing the importance of opera as a reflection of the Italian spirit and tradition, Bastianelli was dismissive of the works of the *giovane scuola*, which he characterized as the "obscene coupling of Massenet and Wagner, mellifluous singing sentimentality, and bombastic orchestral transcendentalism."[9] Although he had initially seen some hope for a revival of Italian opera in the decadent aesthetic of D'Annunzio's musical followers, he ultimately saw the position of composers in a world he characterized as "saturated" as a largely hopeless one: "They try to invent some crude trick to surprise the public; or — at worst — enslave themselves to the publishers, fabricating falsifications of the public's preferred genre, or — at best — lean on some big name of a librettist, like D'Annunzio." In the latter case, however, Bastianelli concludes that they condemn themselves to "a distance from the public, which is fatal, since in no form of art is communication between public and composer as critical as in the theater," and that the composers "have satiated the public and created a rigid publishing monopoly."[10]

To Bastianelli, Italian opera had reached a dead end. It could not go back to the pernicious clichés of the *giovane scuola*, yet to go forward into D'Annunzian rhetoric and a specious modernism was no more productive. Ultimately, Bastianelli reluctantly concluded that while one could dream of a rebirth of opera, Italy's musical future might well lie in the sphere of pure, instrumental, music. In his last work, *Il nuovo dio della musica* [The new god of music], left unfinished at his death, Bastianelli put forward a vision of the future of twentieth-century music dominated by a cerebral, Apollonian mentality, contrasting with the Dionysian character of the nineteenth century.

Although Bastianelli could be harshly critical, his polemics reflected his often tortured effort to arrive at the essence of the matter in all its complexity. Torrefranca's style was far more overtly polemical, and his critique far less carefully nuanced than that of Bastianelli. In his 1912 diatribe *Giacomo Puccini e l'arte internazionale*, Torrefranca tears Puccini's music apart, denouncing it with an almost pathological intensity. Torrefranca's purpose, however, is less to denounce Puccini's music as such than to use it as an exemplar of the decadence and corruption of the operatic enterprise, and to set the stage for his platform of cultural renewal. He writes:

> [This moment] is a decisive point for Italian culture in general and music in particular. It signifies the battle between the young generation, which aspires to the most intense spiritual life, and the generation — already grown old — represented by those whose spiritual mediocrity has formed the basis for their guaranteed successes and lavish earnings. Today's opera defames our culture in the world because those who package it for export and send it off — composers, librettists, publishers and musical journalists — all display an intellectual squalidness that contact with foreign audiences and critics cannot but bring to light.[11]

For Torrefranca, this state of affairs was not the product of a few years or decades, but the ultimate grotesque outcome of more than a hundred years of cumulative misdirection in Italian music. To him, the history of Italian music is not the history of opera, and, as he stresses throughout, an opera composer (*operista*) is not a musician (*musicista*), or a true artist (*artista*), but someone "incapable of producing music that can stand on its own, without the help of words and staging."[12] As a result of its having lost its true roots in instrumental music, contemporary Italian music — that is to say, opera — has been "de-nationalized"; as a result, opera has "not a word to say to the world that is truly hers, truly characteristic, or deeply expressive of her historic moment."[13]

Although it is easy enough at this late date to dismiss Torrefranca's humorless dogmatism, he was seen by his contemporaries as an important critical figure, and his contemptuous rejection of the operatic milieu of the time, if not necessarily his rejection of opera itself as a genre, was widely shared. Pizzetti was one of those with similar feelings; as he wrote in 1911: "With the operas of Mascagni, Leoncavallo, and Puccini no art truly expressive of the rich spiritual life of the Italian people was created; rather, [they created] a petty bourgeois art, which was just what the Italian theatrical public, who inspired it, wanted."[14] Pizzetti believed that a new form of opera was needed that would reflect a rich spiritual, or moral, sense, rather than pandering to the tastes of the tired bourgeoisie, a conviction reflected in the many operas he wrote in a career lasting nearly five decades. Also in 1911, he joined Bastianelli and three other young musicians to form *I cinque italiani* (The Italian Five), for the purpose of advocating "the *risorgimento* of Italian music . . . depressed and circumscribed by commercialism and philistinism."[15]

The commercialism of opera, and the domination of the industry by the two giant publishers, was the focus of a similarly vehement attack by the musical wing of the Futurist movement: "The great publisher-merchants rule: they assign commercial limits to operatic forms, proclaiming as the models that may not be exceeded the base, stunted, and vulgar works of Puccini and Giordano. The publishers pay poets to waste their time and intelligence fabricating and preparing—following the recipes of that grotesque pastry chef called Luigi Illica—that fetid cake which people call a libretto."[16] The philistinism of the bourgeois audience and the commercial interests of the publishers who fed that audience were part and parcel of the same phenomenon.

Alfredo Casella, who later became Italy's most passionate promoter of new music, and who would undoubtedly have been part of the Five had he not still been studying in Paris, later wrote: "To understand the severity of the most fundamental problem that our generation had to confront: that, at all costs, we had to get out of the atmosphere in which we had been born and raised, which was that of the opera (which means, in the final analysis, the modest Italy of those times of the petty bourgeoisie and the petty politics of the status quo)."[17] One of Casella's further comments on opera is particularly dismissive, and for that reason worth noting: "the fact that the nineteenth-century opera, which by its very nature was based essentially on immediate and spontaneous impulses and was fundamentally 'small-town' (*paesano*) (in the sense that it hardly participated in the great evolution of European music during the nineteenth century) made it a convenient excuse for all those who wanted to see art brought down to their modest abilities as provincial, inadequate artists."[18]

The idea that popular opera could also be great art, which was part of the credo of Italian composers of the late-nineteenth century, was no longer intellectually respectable. All of these writers share a fundamental conviction: art can either be great or appeal to a popular audience, but not both. The popularity of Italian opera to the mass audience was seen by the younger intellectuals as a defect *d'origine*. Because the taste of the bourgeois audience was ipso facto philistine, by definition no opera written for that audience could hope to rise above that level.

To this critique tradition had no response. While Mascagni or Zandonai would grumble in letters to their friends or newspaper interviews, and individual critics continued to write appreciative reviews of new operas from their pens, not one figure emerged to mount a coherent, systematic defense of either the music of the popular opera composers of the time, or the popular nature of the operatic enterprise. This too reflected the climate of the times: although the Italian establishment under Giolitti was building a nation that was not only more prosperous, but in many respects more just, than ever before, few if any intellectuals found anything good to say or write about it. Never had the chasm between the established order and the nation's intellectuals been greater.

The Modernist Challenge and the Generazione dell'Ottanta

The rise of the critique of Italian operatic culture to prominence coincided with an explosion of new ways of writing music. Throughout Europe, change was in the air. Modernism, as it was to be known, had not yet hardened into dogma; instead, it was an open, fluid state, a condition in which composers of all persuasions consciously distanced themselves from the formal practices in which they had been trained and sought to find new creative paths for themselves. Younger composers explored a dazzling array of new ways in which music could be written, from Bartók's explorations of Hungarian folk music to Schoenberg's dismemberment of tonality in his 1908 Second String Quartet and the *Book of the Hanging Gardens*, which appeared the following year.

Modernism reflected more than the personal predilections of artists; as Conrad has written, "innovations in art are attuned to changes in the way people behave, the way society works, the way the universe is constructed: that is what modernity was all about."[19] Society and behavior had been changing, albeit gradually, for decades. With the acceleration of technology, the advent of the automobile, the telephone and the cinema, people had come to believe by the beginning of the twentieth century, rightly or wrongly, that they were living in a world that was radically different from that their fathers occupied.

The most vivid expression of this consciousness appears in the "Manifesto del futurismo" (Futurist manifesto), written by F. T. Marinetti, founder of the Futurist movement, and first published in the Paris newspaper *Le Figaro* in 1909. The manifesto contains the famous line that "a roaring motor car, which seems to run on machine-gun fire, is more beautiful than the Victory of Samothrace." Marinetti wrote, excited by his own vivid imagery: "We will sing of the great crowds agitated by work, pleasure and rebellion; the multi-colored and polyphonic signs of revolutions in modern capitals; the vibrant nocturnal excitement of the arsenals and the workshops, set on fire by their violent electric moons . . . factories suspended from the clouds by the winding threads of their smoke . . . and the gliding flight of aeroplanes."[20] Marinetti and his followers had a taste for publicity and a readiness to take their ideas to the public, not only through manifestos, but through newspapers, posters, speaking tours, and demonstrations, to the point that "in the Italy of that time there was no one who had not heard of Futurism."[21]

In retrospect, Futurism was more engaged in further undermining tradition than in offering useful directions — except in the plastic arts, where the works of Futurists like Boccioni, Carrà, and others represented a major contribution to European art of the time. Futurism had a musical side. Luigi Russolo, a Futurist painter turned musician, developed a theory of the Art of Noises, and realized it through the construction of machines he called *Intonarumori*, or Noise Tuners, which came in various types, including Exploders, Cracklers, Buzzers, and Scrapers.[22] His works written for this medium, with titles such as "Awakening of the City" or "Meeting of Automobiles and Aeroplanes," predictably promoted controversy, and the demonstrations that accompanied public performances were highly gratifying to the Futurist love of publicity. Just the same, despite its brief notoriety, Futurist music was little more than a curiosity, with little lasting effect on the course of Italian music.

The direction that Italian music would follow over the coming decades was set most strongly by the three composers who came to be known as the *generazione dell'ottanta*, Ildebrando Pizzetti, Gian Francesco Malipiero, and Alfredo Casella. Of these three, Pizzetti and Malipiero devoted a large part of their creative energy to the opera, redefining — albeit in radically different fashion — the musical and dramatic content of opera in Italy, as well as its relationship to the Italian audience. As Massimo Mila has written, comparing their efforts to the great tradition of "Bellini to Mascagni, Verdi to Puccini": "The musicians of the 'ottanta' could not but take account of the changed conditions of culture, taste and habits, as a result of which it was no longer possible, even had they wanted, to write successfully operas of that sort."[23] In the polemical environment of which they were a part and to which they contributed, they did not see their works as a continuation of the tradition represented by the operas of their predecessors; instead, they both perceived their efforts and presented them to the public as a repudiation, painful perhaps but necessary, of the exhausted tradition of Verdi and Puccini — exhausted not only musically, but also in the societal role they once played.

Of the *generazione dell'ottanta*, the only one who made a significant mark on the operatic scene prior to the outbreak of the First World War was Pizzetti, who emerged in 1901 from his studies at the Parma Conservatory firmly set on a personal mission of reviving Italian operatic culture. Although his first operatic effort — a one-act opera entitled *Il Cid*, written for the 1903 Sonzogno competition — was stillborn, he came to the public's attention after winning a 1905 competition for a choral setting of a D'Annunzio poem, a passage taken from the prologue of the poet's latest play, *La nave*. Delighted with the young composer's effort, D'Annunzio commissioned him to write the incidental music for the play. After its debut in 1908, Pizzetti found himself with the beginning of a reputation, as well as a burgeoning connection to Italy's most famous writer.

D'Annunzio, who rebaptized Pizzetti as "Ildebrando da Parma" in medieval fashion, saw him not only as a promising disciple but as his musical alter ego, a gifted composer who, under the writer's Svengali-like influence, would willingly subordinate his gifts to D'Annunzio's greater genius, providing the poet with the musical frame he had always dreamed of for his words. Between 1905 and 1915, D'Annunzio and Pizzetti would exist in an almost connubial relationship. The diffident, high-minded composer admired neither the poet's ideas nor his morals, but he was spellbound by the rich poetic qualities of D'Annunzio's work; while the famous poet's attentions had an all but hypnotic effect on the younger man. In 1909, when the poet learned of Pizzetti's interest in making an opera from Euripides' *Hippolytus*, he offered to write the composer a libretto on the subject.[24] Pizzetti later wrote: "That D'Annunzio, as he told me one day . . . was ready to write a *Fedra* specifically for me, was something I could not believe . . . but his offer so utterly moved and exalted me that from that moment I felt that could neither think about any other opera until I had finished that which his poetry inspired in me."[25]

Both D'Annunzio and Pizzetti saw *Fedra* as a major departure in Italian opera. As the poet made clear in a letter to Giulio Ricordi, written soon after Pizzetti had begun work on the opera: "We want to attempt something new in Italian music drama, about which we finally have a very clear idea, without any Wagnerian predilections . . . any Straussian excesses, or any Debussyan affectations."[26] After more than two years, the work was still far from complete. Pizzetti found himself forced into protracted periods of inactivity as he waited for D'Annunzio, distracted by his new life and new projects in France, to make the cuts and other changes to the prolix text that Pizzetti needed. Finally, in January 1912, after an extended stay with the poet in his French retreat in Arcachon, the composer was satisfied, and was able to complete the opera. That fall, he returned to Arcachon, where

Ildebrando Pizzetti

he presented *Fedra* to an enraptured D'Annunzio. After still further delays,[27] *Fedra* finally made its debut at La Scala in March 1915 with Edoardo di Giovanni[28] as Ippolito and Salomé Krusceniski as Fedra.

Despite a barrage of publicity and the prominent cast, *Fedra* was at most a *succès d'estime*, and was withdrawn after a mere four performances.[29] Since then, it has been revived only at rare intervals. Despite its limited popular success, *Fedra* is not only of some musical interest, but of considerable historical importance as the first major Italian opera to be written on the basis of a explicit program of operatic reform, not only differentiating itself sharply from its predecessors, but offering itself as a model around which the reinvention of Italian opera could begin to take place.

Pizzetti's intellectual point of departure was his firm conviction, unusual for a composer, that in opera the words should dominate the music, rather than the music the words. In a lecture early in 1913, not long after completing *Fedra*, he argued that in opera the drama was the active, and the music the passive element. Therefore, as paraphrased by Bastianelli, "The aria, and every similar lyrical effusion . . . represent nothing less than the overwhelming of the *poetic* element by the *musical*. Good for the musician, as composer, who writes beautiful arias, duets, and orchestral interludes, but from a dramatic standpoint, he shoots himself in the foot (*dà la zappa sui piedi*)."[30] To Pizzetti, at least as Bastianelli understood him, every Italian opera written since the age of Monteverdi was little more than a glorified cantata.

While *Fedra* cannot avoid showing some influence of *Pelléas* and Dukas's *Ariane et Barbe-Bleu*, it nonetheless represents a composer adhering closely to his principles.[31] The vocal lines are entirely declamatory, resting — except for momentary bursts of emotional stress — within the central register of the voices. Rather than their rhythmic structure emerging from a musical or melodic logic, the vocal lines follow the rhythm of D'Annunzio's verses in literal fashion, moving upward and down largely in intervals of seconds and thirds, in keeping with the style of Gregorian chant, which Pizzetti considered to be similar to ancient Greek music. These lines, which only at rare intervals and for the briefest of moments give way to something more recognizable as operatic melody, are supported by a continuous orchestral flux, moving, in Tedeschi's words, "in slow spirals of contiguous sounds," often more eloquent musically than the music given to the voices.[32]

Pizzetti gives his orchestra more overtly melodic material than he gives his voices, building complex orchestral textures from his principal melodic cells, particularly the tortuous line played by unison violas that opens the opera, which the composer breaks down over the course of the first act into a series of separate, distinct, motivic cells. Many of his melodies have a distinctly modal character, a feature that was to become one of Pizzetti's compositional trademarks. While his strict moral principles might seem to demand an austere harmonic vocabulary of unisons and fifths, this does not appear to be the case. Pizzetti was never so much of a "modernist" as the others in the *generazione dell'ottanta*: the composer's harmonic language is, if not conventional, recognizably diatonic, albeit only loosely tied to recognizable tonal centers, and heavily reliant on chains of lush seventh, ninth, and eleventh chords occasionally reminiscent of the music of Scriabin. Despite its elaborate harmonic and melodic texture, however, the orchestra is always subordinated, creating a frame in which the voices stand out clearly, adding a dimension to the realization of the drama without ever distracting the listener's attention from the nearly continuous *parlando* recitation.

Fedra is not a cold, bloodless opera. From a musical standpoint, however, its moments of passion and intensity seem largely unprepared, rising suddenly out of the flux only to subside moments later. Despite the composer's careful efforts at thematic development and interconnection, the opera lacks an underlying *musical* — as distinct from dramatic — logic. Taruskin's comment on Dargomizhsky's *Stone Guest* applies equally to *Fedra*: "it might best be viewed as a gigantic through-composed art song in which the whole shaping force, save at the pettiest level, is exercised by the text."[33] For those who listen carefully, it has many pages of "severe and moving beauty," in Bastianelli's words, including beautifully wrought choral passages; ironically, however, it seems less an opera than a musical elaboration of the text, a sort of continuously flowing incidental music to D'Annunzio's tragedy.[34] That subservient quality is undoubtedly what endeared the work so thoroughly to the egomaniacal poet, who reacted to it with far more wholehearted enthusiasm than to any of the many other operatic treatments of his works.

Pizzetti's relationship with D'Annunzio was short-lived. As Bastianelli, who admired Pizzetti's music but clearly felt that his pretensions made him a slightly comic figure, wrote: "the marriage did not last long. The husband — D'Annunzio — was constantly unfaithful. Pizzetti, meanwhile — like an emancipated wife — wanted to begin to stand on his own two feet."[35] *Fedra* had not come easily to Pizzetti. Morally and psychologically, its characters and their behavior were remote from, in one critic's words, "the innate vocation of sacrifice and redemption" Pizzetti sought in his characters.[36] He worked hard to impose his values on D'Annunzio's characters, using his music to give Fedra's death a redemptive quality not only absent in, but alien to, the libretto. Pizzetti henceforth wrote the libretti for all of his major operas. Pursuing his increasingly rarified dramatic vision, over the next more than fifty years until his death in 1968, he produced a series of carefully wrought operas largely on religious or ethical themes, never departing significantly from the principles he had adopted in his youth.

Although by the 1930s he had put his youthful relationship with D'Annunzio behind him, the aging poet still remembered it with nostalgic tenderness. In the summer of 1936, D'Annunzio, conscious of his advancing age and infirmity, wrote the composer giving him the rights to his 1904 play, *La figlia di Jorio:* "Ildebrando, I give you *La figlia di Jorio*, free, fresh, ageless like a folk song. Without conditions and without obligation I give it to you. . . . Accept it as a *pignus ac monimentum amoris*.[37] Like so many of D'Annunzio's gifts over the years, it had a catch; contrary to the poet's words, Alberto Franchetti still held the rights to *La figlia di Jorio*. When Pizzetti finally turned to the work in the 1950s, however, Franchetti's estate generously relinquished its rights in his favor. Pizzetti's second opera to a text by D'Annunzio made its debut at Naples' San Carlo Theater in December 1954.

Pizzetti's vision was to return Italian opera to what he saw as its roots. As Barigazzi writes: "setting aside the modest homes and daily life brought onto the stage by the *veristi*, in order to return to a timeless theater: to myth, and, regarding musical material, to the roots of Italian opera, the theater of Monteverdi, Cavalli, Legrenzi and the seventeenth century in general."[38] In pursuing that vision, his attitude to the Italian opera audience was ambivalent. In contrast to many of his successors, for whom a mass audience was irrelevant, or even undesirable, Pizzetti wanted (or believed he wanted) to reach a wide audience — but only on his uncompromising terms. He sought to redirect their attention to a higher artistic plane, awakening them to the error of their ways and opening their ears to works that would restore not only dramatic and musical integrity, but moral integrity as well to Italian opera. He sought to lead, but the audience, unresponsive as always to coerced moral uplift, failed to follow.

Pizzetti was an intermediate figure, looking backward as much as forward. His dramaturgical model was not fundamentally different from that of the Italian operatic tradition, stripped of its cruder elements and with a higher moral tone not markedly out of keeping with the Metastasian origins of that tradition. The composer who would break completely with the tradition and bring Italian opera fully into the modernist mainstream — and, in the process, out of the public eye — was his younger colleague, Gian Francesco Malipiero.

If Pizzetti was a moralist, guided "by his philosophical and dramaturgical ideals," in Waterhouse's words, Malipiero's "extraordinary output can appear the simple result of an irresistible urge to compose, compared to which external and environmental factors appear secondary."[39] During his long life from 1882 to 1973, Malipiero composed eleven symphonies, six piano concertos, eight string quartets, innumerable miscellaneous vocal, orchestral, and chamber, works, and some thirty to forty operas, the number varying widely based on whether unpublished works should be included and on the compiler's definition of what constitutes an opera. A prolific writer of prose as well, he wrote or adapted nearly all of his libretti, while publishing seventeen books of criticism or music history, as well as more than one hundred articles and essays.

An elusive figure, described by Nicolodi as "disillusioned and sharply ironic, in constant conflict with himself and the world,"[40] Malipiero was yet another one of the psychologically traumatized souls that his generation appeared to produce in large numbers, who wrote that "there is not a single human being, friend or enemy, to whom I have ever taken into my confidence."[41] Except for those occasions when he reluctantly took teaching positions in order to make enough money to survive, he lived apart from humanity for most of his life, in an isolated house in the hill town of Asolo, northwest of his native Venice, surrounded by the canine and feline companions he found more congenial than human company.[42]

A descendant of ancient Venetian nobility, raised in a household with a strong family musical tradition, Malipiero received his diploma from the conservatory in Bologna and continued his studies with Max Bruch in Berlin.[43] His first known operatic effort, entitled *Elen e Fuldano*, from the time of his German studies, remains unpublished and unperformed, while a second opera, *Canossa*, written in 1911–1912, won a competition sponsored by the city of Rome, leading to a January 1914 production at the city's Costanzi opera house. It was an abject failure, harshly dealt with by the critic for *Il Messaggero*: "This is not an 'opera' but a 'symphonic digression' made up of a succession of brief episodes whose dramatic action is clear in the libretto, but not on stage. . . . The significance of the scenes performed and their connection eluded us last night, as did that which is more important in opera, the connection between the words declaimed and the orchestral symphony that overwhelmed them."[44] Malipiero, feeling that the production had not done his work justice, withdrew it from the stage, passionately but vainly protesting his mistreatment to a variety of municipal officials.[45]

Canossa was soon little more than an annoying memory. On a visit to

Paris, on May 29, 1913, Malipiero's eyes were opened at the first performance of Stravinsky's *Rite of Spring*. By his own account, he had been largely
unaware of the more advanced currents of European music, and the experience was transformative.[46] Later, he would write that "on the evening of
May 28 [*sic*], 1913, I woke up from a long and dangerous lethargy."[47] On his
return to Italy, his music began to take on a dramatically different coloring.
Over the next few years, his contact with Casella and others of similar
mind, his studies of early Italian music and literature, and the traumatic effect of the war all combined to precipitate a dramatic change in his ideas
about opera, and theatrical music in general.

His *Sette canzoni* (Seven songs), which became the first and central part
of his epochal work *L'Orfeide* (The Orpheid; or, the epic of Orpheus),
which was written largely in 1918, is the product of that change. Some years
later, he put forward the rationale for the work: "Nauseated by recitative,
by false 'verismo,' and by everything that serves to flavor that overly sweet
mixture called opera, I had abandoned musical theater, only to fall back
too soon into its tentacles. If verismo seemed to me to be a caricature in
bad taste of life, historic and mythological subjects seemed to me to be far
more dangerous than satisfying. The *Sette canzoni* were thus seven episodes from my experience, which I felt I could translate into music while
remaining true to myself."[48] The "seven songs" are seven fragments, linked
by orchestral interludes. In each a brief dramatic episode is enacted. As
one character sings a song, the others mime their parts, with occasional interjections by an offstage chorus. The songs themselves have been adapted
by Malipiero from early Italian poetry by Poliziano, Jacopone da Todi, and
others. In one, a young lover sings a serenade to his love; wondering why
she does not respond, he enters the house to find her crying over a dead
body. In another, a bell-ringer rings a bell in a tower, singing a ditty about
an old woman who yearns for him but whom he despises, as a fire rages in
the town below. When he finishes singing, he looks down and sees that the
fire has been put out. While the *Sette canzoni* was first performed separately, and was most probably initially conceived by Malipiero as a self-
contained work, he soon added two further sections to form *L'Orfeide*.
The work opens with *La morte delle maschere* (The death of the masks),
written last, in 1921–1922, followed by the *Sette canzoni*, and concludes
with *Orfeo, ovvero l'ottava canzone* (Orpheus; or, the eighth song), written
in 1919–1920.

In *La morte delle maschere*, an impresario calls seven masked commedia dell'arte characters forward. As each explains his distinctive qualities,
they begin to dance. A masked man appears, chases the impresario away, and

forces the masks into a closet. He reveals himself as Orpheus, announces that the masks must die to make way for reality, and introduces the characters of the *Sette canzoni*. The *Sette canzoni* then follow. After the curtain falls on the last of the seven songs, it rises again to reveal a stage in a baroque court. The emperor Nero, made up like a marionette, takes the stage, watched by the king, the queen, and an audience of old fogies and young blades. While he sings, a pantomime of murder and destruction is enacted around him. Orpheus appears, dressed as a clown in white. He sings the eighth song, accompanying himself on the lute, as all but the queen gradually fall asleep. When he finishes, he kisses the queen, and the two leave together as the curtain falls.

L'Orfeide is, in the context of the times, an anti-opera. No work calling itself an opera had been presented before in Italy — and arguably in Europe — that not only so thoroughly dispensed with the conventions, both musical and dramatic, of opera as they had evolved over the previous three hundred years, but held them up to ungentle mockery in the bargain. At one level, indeed, *L'Orfeide* is "about" the exhaustion of the operatic genres of those three hundred years. The first part proclaims the death of the masks, and the commedia dell'arte — with perhaps a swipe at Mascagni's *Le Maschere*[49] — while the last part does the same for the kings, queens, and mythological heroes of baroque opera. *Sette canzoni*, in its turn, deconstructs the conventions of *ottocento* opera, reconfiguring its beloved themes of love and death into fragmentary images devoid of character or dramatic interaction. In another work written at much the same time, *Tre commedie goldoniane* (Three Goldoni comedies), Malipiero similarly deconstructs three of Goldoni's plays, boiling each down to a concentrated broth of disembodied Goldonian essence, connected only tangentially to the characterizations or dramatic action of Goldoni's originals.

L'Orfeide dispenses with the idea, essential to the *ottocento* tradition, of opera as a distinct musical theater form, containing unique and exclusive features that distinguish it from all other forms of musical theater. For Malipiero there were no more barriers between opera and other forms of musical theater. In *L'Orfeide*, song, mime, and marionettes are combined in a dramatically static environment. Its immediate predecessor in Malipiero's work was *Pantea*, a powerful monodrama for a single female dancer, who experiences a series of hallucinations depicted by an offstage chorus and an orchestra that juxtaposes "hectically piled-up dissonances in the fiercer passages with the luminous yet searingly poignant *cantabilità* of the more lyrical sections."[50]

Orpheus, although he appears only at the end of the first and third parts, is the central defining figure of Malipiero's opera, reflecting how the work is also "about" song and the nature of operatic music. Orpheus, a figure largely ignored by nineteenth-century Italian composers, took on an iconic power in European music in the 1920s that he had not had since the early days of Peri, Rossi, and Monteverdi.[51] To Malipiero and his colleagues, Orpheus was a figure uncontaminated by nineteenth-century romanticism or by the excesses of the recent Italian opera tradition; he could embody their collective desire to leap backward over that tradition in order to return to a purer era when the integrity of Italian song still remained intact. That this was Malipiero's intention is little in doubt: deeply immersed in the music of sixteenth and seventeenth-century Italy, his choice of early Italian poetry was prompted, as he wrote, by the fact that "in it one rediscovers the rhythm of our music, that is to say, that truly Italian rhythm which, little by little during three centuries, was becoming corrupted in operatic melodrama."[52]

The presence of Orpheus signifies that in the final analysis *L'Orfeide*, is about music, not in the service of drama, but as an independent force in its own right. For Malipiero at this point in his artistic evolution, opera was song, purified of its romantic and veristic accretions, and returned to its essence, not in literal imitation of seventeenth-century models, but as a re-creation of their elemental character using the vocabulary of the twentieth century. While Pizzetti's goal may have been a moral cleansing of Italian opera, in which music was subordinated to drama, Malipiero's was a *musical* purification of opera, in which the musical element was its own justification for existence, and the dramatic element, if present at all, was not to be found in conventional characters and dramatic interactions, but through the clash of musical ideas and intellectual constructs.

For all its self-conscious archaism, and the somewhat incongruous juxtaposition of its three parts, *L'Orfeide* is an important work, not only for its historic and cultural significance, but for its beauty and — in some not entirely fathomable manner — its dramatic effect. The songs and orchestral interludes of *Sette canzoni* have an unusual but often deeply moving lyrical quality. While one can find echoes of Debussy, Stravinsky, and, in a sort of affectionate parody, even Puccini, they are nonetheless the work of a composer with a distinctive individual voice. The later parts of the opera are more astringent, particularly in their orchestral garb, where unusual timbres and inventive motifs, superimposed on a largely diatonic texture of unisons, fourths, and fifths, give the work a delightful, piquant quality. More than eighty years after its first performance — during which time Malipiero's heresies have become the common currency of modern music — it is possible to appreciate *L'Orfeide* for what it is, a delightful, highly individ-ualistic work of musical theater.

First with *Fedra*, and most significantly with *L'Orfeide*, the younger gen-eration's critique of the conventions of *ottocento* opera and the *giovane scuola* took concrete form, making complete their split with those, such as Alfano or Zandonai, whom they saw as perpetuating the conventions. The division was not about harmonic structure or other questions of musical technique; it was about fundamental questions of what opera was to be, and for whom it was to be written. From *Conchita* on, Zandonai employed a musical vocabulary as "advanced" as that of the *generazione dell'ottanta*, yet was treated by them with derision. Pizzetti characterized him to Malip-iero as a "crafty speculator" (*affarista furbo*),[53] while Bastianelli, borrow-ing Torrefranca's distinction between "musician" and "opera-maker," wrote about Zandonai: "[he has] technical perfection of orchestration, is a mod-ern and often powerful harmonist, . . . but these are, of course, qualities held in common by the musician and the opera-maker."[54] Zandonai's crime was that he continued to write operas for the commercial opera in-dustry and for its traditional bourgeois audience. As he told a reporter: "The assertion [by younger composers] that 'we don't write for the public' is a fundamentally wrong idea, because the theater exists basically for the public, and cannot be a proving ground for doctrinaire exhibitions, espe-cially those too far removed from the musical instincts of the people."[55]

Yet that industry was gradually disintegrating, and its audience was gradually dissipating, gradually being lost to other pursuits. Before the end of the 1920s, even Mascagni, a passionate defender of the operatic tradi-tion, realized that his was at best a rearguard action. In 1929, he spoke to a throng assembled in Rome for the National Congress on Popular Arts: "Yes, the twentieth-centuryists (*novecentisti*) have won. But their victory is nothing but the imposition of the ugly, the grotesque, the absurd, and the immoral."[56]

The Rise of the Cinema and the Capture of the Opera Audience

As Italian society changed over the century that stretched from the begin-nings of the Golden Age of Rossini, Bellini, and Donizetti to the outbreak of the First World War, the manner in which that society entertained itself changed in equal measure. For the largely agrarian and illiterate society that preceded the *Risorgimento*, opera was the unique exception in a world where recreations were few and, other than the occasional traveling theater troupe, largely homegrown: saints' days, fairs, and local festivals like Siena's Palio or Pisa's *Giuoco del ponte* (Battle of the bridge).With unification and the growth of literacy and the middle class, a national market in entertainment began to emerge, transforming the nation's leisure habits. Theater gained in respectability, while operetta and the *café chantant*, both French imports, appeared, sharing much of the same audience that attended the opera. Italians began to develop a taste for vacations in the late-nineteenth century, as bourgeois families began to travel to the shore and the mountains; at the same time, spectator sports, including bicycle racing and "English football" or soccer, emerged. An increasingly literate population read newspapers and popular novels, aided in those pursuits by the gradual diffusion of electricity from the 1880s onward.

Through the end of the nineteenth century, none of these options seriously threatened Italy's opera industry and its hold on the heart of the bourgeois audience. The aristocratic customs of pre-unification days, when noble families would spend nearly every evening at the opera during the season, were a thing of the past, carried on by no one but a handful of old-fashioned box-holders and a coterie of fanatics. Most operagoers, particularly at the smaller theaters, would go regularly but not constantly, alternating their opera visits with visits to a *café chantant*, a prose theater performance, or even the circus. When not presenting opera, the *politeamas*, many smaller houses, and even a few of the *massimi* would house a dramatic or operetta troupe, performing in the summer or fall for many of the same people who would go to the opera during the *carnevale–quaresima* season. While large numbers of people enjoyed operetta or theater, they were clearly seen as secondary recreations, and were no threat to opera's hegemony. Within less than a decade, this state of affairs would be dramatically transformed by the emergence of a new medium, the cinema.

The cinematic era in Italy began in March 1896, when a traveling representative of the Lumière brothers set up his projection equipment in a Roman photography store, entrancing a delighted audience with his flickering moving pictures of street scenes. Italians quickly took to moving pictures, and movie theaters began to open immediately. While the first were little more than large rooms with a white sheet hung from one wall, substantial theaters began to open as early as 1897; many of them, however, combined short movies with variety and *café chantant*.[57] Rome's Moderno, which was opened by Filoteo Alberini in 1904, seated four hundred in a large, high-ceilinged, and ornately decorated hall.[58]

Like so many Italian cultural movements, Italian cinema originated in France. Nearly all the early films came from France, interspersed with rudimentary, locally made newsreels rarely running more than two or three minutes. What is generally considered the first indigenous Italian film was the 1905 *La presa di Roma* (The capture of Rome), a ten-minute-long re-enactment in seven tableaux of the 1870 rout of the papal forces by the Italian army. Its debut was a major event, with thousands in attendance. Blending patriotism and pretensions to historical accuracy with spectacle, and using well-known stage actors, it was a work of considerable ambition.[59]

From that point on, the film industry grew exponentially, as dozens of studios opened, flooding the market with hundreds of new films. As a 1907 journalist wrote: "Movies . . . movies! Where do you not see that magic word printed these days? One can't walk a step, cross a busy downtown artery or a dark suburban alley without seeing it. . . . And where has a movie theater not been set up? In the grand theaters, in the cafés, in the beer gardens . . . from the slums of the working class to the salons of the nobility! From the bottom to the top of the social scale, everywhere."[60] In 1907, the city of Livorno contained fifteen movie theaters. Eight of them decorated the city's principal commercial street, the Via Vittorio Emanuele, often within a few doors of one another, while four more theaters were operating in the city's outlying suburban districts.[61] A year later, the magazine *Cine-Fono* reported that Milan contained seventy movie theaters, adding, "Where will it end? Milan is in danger of becoming one big movie theater."[62]

Although individual theaters and studios came and went, by the end of the decade, substantial movie theaters, often seating well over a thousand people, were part of the landscape of every Italian city. Major studios such as Alberini's Cines Studios in Rome and the Ambrosio and Itala studios in Turin had become solid, well-capitalized operations, turning out films with industrial efficiency and, from 1907 on, exporting hundreds of films to the rest of Europe, the United States, and Latin America.

The next milestone was in 1911, when the first full-length feature film, *L'Inferno*, came from an Italian studio. This remarkable work attempted nothing less than to re-create the atmosphere of Dante's *Inferno* by "giving life and movement not so much to Dante's text as to its most noted and widely distributed visual interpretation, the form and iconography of Doré's famous woodcuts."[63] From then on, the Italian studios began to produce a steady stream of feature films, often two hours or more long. The most famous, and the ones that attracted the greatest attention outside Italy, were the epic historical films set in ancient Rome: *Marcantonio e Cleopatra*, *Spartaco*, *Quo Vadis?* and most notably *Cabiria*. The studios produced movies in every genre, however, including slapstick comedies, sentimental tales of petty bourgeois couples, and what came to be known as the *cinema in frac* ("top hat and tails" movies), escapist films of life and love in the upper crust.[64] *Cabiria*, which became the single most famous cinematic achievement of the period, combined a number of genres, weaving together the epic tale of the Punic Wars with the rescue of the Roman waif Cabiria, kidnapped by Carthaginian pirates and destined to be sacrificed to the god Moloch, and the doomed love of the Carthaginian princess Sofonisba for her Numidian prince.

The arrival of the feature film was the decisive point that secured the position of cinema as Italy's dominant art form during the early part of the second decade of the twentieth century. While cinema had already begun to exert a strong influence on the tastes and spending habits of Italy's working class and petty bourgeoisie, with the arrival of the feature film it was embraced by the nation's intellectual and financial elite. The premiere of *L'Inferno* took place not at a movie theater, but at Naples' Teatro Mercadante, a historic operatic venue. Highly publicized, and covered by the national press, the premiere was attended by such notable literary figures as Roberto Bracco and Matilde Serao, and by Benedetto Croce, perhaps Italy's leading public intellectual. The evening was transformative for Serao, as she wrote later, completely changing her perception of the artistic value of the cinema.[65]

While maintaining his ties to the world of opera, Gabriele D'Annunzio, ever the taste-setter, embraced the cinema, an engagement that began with his approving the cinematic adaptation of his works, and culminated in his taking part in the making of *Cabiria* in 1914.[66] Although motivated to a large extent by both the money and publicity that association with the cinema would provide, he was also enthralled by the medium. In a 1914 essay entitled "On the Cinema as an Instrument of Liberation and an Art of Transfiguration," he hailed its new "aesthetic of movement," seeing something not only new, but also distinctively "Mediterranean" in the juxtaposition of the white screen — which he found reminiscent of the white marble walls of Ancient Greece — with the dynamism of the modern.[67]

As cinema established its artistic bona fides with Italy's literary and intellectual elites, it became an almost universal art form, reaching an audience broader than even that of opera at its most popular. Early in the second decade of the twentieth century, aided by the ease of transporting films and projection equipment, an elaborate hierarchy of filmgoing venues had come into being, from grand first-run motion picture palaces frequented by the prosperous bourgeoisie in prominent locations in the major cities, to second-run theaters in urban neighborhoods and smaller towns, down to the ambulatory projectionists who would set up equipment in tents and village piazzas. Second-run theaters charged as little as ten centesimi for a ticket, well within the reach of Italy's working class, while comfortable seats in first-run theaters could cost as much as 1.50 lire. By 1917, movie theaters in Milan sold nine million movie tickets. The average Milanese adult went to the cinema twenty times in the course of the year.[68]

Cinema became a popular entertainment for the wealthy and well connected; the Palace, situated on Milan's stylish Corso Vittorio Emanuele, was characterized as the "preferred gathering-place of the Milanese aristocracy."[69] Giving the royal stamp of approval in 1913, Italy's king and queen attended the premiere of *Quo vadis?* — notably held not in a movie theater, but in Rome's Teatro Quirinale, also used as an operatic venue.[70] In keeping with this trend, during this decade, Italian cinema became not only grander and more artistic, but also in some respects more politically conventional, more "establishment." Unique among Italian cultural or artistic media, however, the cinema bridged the gap not only between social classes, but between the political and economic establishment and the adversarial intellectual culture.

Italian cinema after 1911 provided its audiences with an intense dramatic and aesthetic experience, exceeding the operatic experience in its visual qualities and the immediacy of the relationship between the audience and the screen actors, particularly the *dive*, or screen goddesses. The cinematography of the Italian silent film paralleled the epic scale of its dramatic imagination; after more than ninety years, scenes from *Cabiria*, including the flight from the eruption of Mount Etna, the burning of the Roman fleet at Syracuse, and above all, the sacrificial scene in the temple of Moloch (accompanied by Pizzetti's Symphony of Fire), have lost none of their visceral impact.

Italians began to feel an intense connection with the principal actors, whom they saw up close on the screen, beyond that they had felt for even the greatest opera stars, whom only a handful were fortunate enough actually to see and hear in the *teatri massimi*. While the *dive* were the heirs of the *prime donne* of the opera stage, *divismo* in the cinema was in many respects a new phenomenon. The intensely expressive facial gestures of Francesca Bertini and the sinuous, subliminally erotic, body language of Lyda Borelli — seen in the close-ups that became more common as the technology improved and the film language became more sophisticated — exerted a unique fascination, prompting an emotional response that outdid any previous collective expression by the Italian audience. Millions of young Italian women modeled themselves after Borelli, whom Brunetta describes as "the priestess of a new religiosity."[71] The word *borelleggiare* (to act like Borelli) entered Italian dictionaries.

The *dive* were, with one exception, female. There were no Carusos or De Lucias in the Italian cinema. In contrast to Bertini or Borelli, whose personality and allure transcended any of the many characters they played, the only male actor who attracted a comparable following was known far more for his single character, Maciste, than by his own name. Maciste, slave and sidekick to the Roman noble Fulvius in *Cabiria*, combined super-human strength and bravery with a gentleness of manner and an easygoing acceptance of life's vicissitudes that endeared him to the Italian public — in particular to the working-class audience, who knew that Maciste was Bartolomeo Pagano, a former longshoreman from Genoa who had never acted before. As Maciste, Pagano became a cult figure, making some twenty films between 1914 and 1926, including such titles as *Maciste alpino*, *Maciste innamorato*, *Maciste in vacanza*, and *Maciste e il nipote di America*.[72] No other form of art, or entertainment, had ever offered Italy's working-class audience a figure who was so clearly one of their own, and with whom they could so readily identify.

Ironically, Italian film, as it supplanted opera in the public imagination, was heavily dependent on opera for its imagery and style. The visual im-agery and the mise-en-scène of the epic cinema is that of grand opera writ large, while domestic dramas like the famous 1915 *Assunta Spinta* with Bertini were equally indebted to the bourgeois opera of the 1890s for their visual and gestural language. In many respects, the Italian films of this de-cade could not unreasonably be called "silent opera."

These films were not, of course, actually silent. Films were screened to the continuous accompaniment of music, which played a critical role in creating and maintaining the dramatic tension of the film. Surprisingly, in light of the serious artistic intentions of the filmmakers, few commissioned original music for their films, and those few rarely sought out composers of note. Indeed, the only important composer of the time to compose a com-plete film score was Pietro Mascagni, whose score for the 1915 expression-istic drama *Rapsodia satanica* represents a musical high point in the Italian silent film.[73] Much of the music that accompanied films came, indeed, from the operatic repertoire, which not only comprised a vast collection of music with strong dramatic qualities, but offered the added value that its familiarity could be counted on to trigger the appropriate emotional re-sponses from the audience, further heightening their identification with the characters and events on the screen.

Many modest movie halls supplemented the ubiquitous upright piano

Alba, played by Lyda Borelli, discovers the lifeless body of her spurned lover Sergio, in the film *Rapsodia satanica*, with music by Pietro Mascagni. *(Mascagni.org)*

with a phonograph and a stack of recorded arias, which would be played for particularly important or emotional scenes. Entire operatic scenes would be played in instrumental arrangement by the pianist to magnify the impact of the scene. As a 1920 writer noted, "[using] a love duet for a passionate scene, or for a death scene, the third-act prelude of *La traviata* or the finale of *La bohème*" was commonplace. The author added, however, that "the proceedings seem not very artistic, and any self-respecting musician would not deign to crank out what the French call a 'pastiche.'" [74] There were more than enough musicians, however, willing to do so. The process was facilitated by the Casa Ricordi, which began in this decade to publish the first of a series of volumes entitled *Biblioteca cinema* containing instrumental versions of operatic excerpts for film use.

The grander theaters had orchestras, often of symphonic caliber. Mascagni conducted such a professional orchestra for the film *Rapsodia satanica* twice daily for a month in Turin in 1918. Although paid the considerable sum of 1,000 lire per day, Mascagni found the experience depressing, writing Anna Lolli, "It's at a movie theater, it is a beautiful one, grand and elegant, and I know that they are organizing everything very nicely, but it's a movie theater just the same. You see how far I have sunk."[75]

By that point, however, the world had changed decisively. Although opera would continue to be an important part of the Italian experience, it had already lost a substantial part of its audience, and no longer played the hegemonic role that it had for so many years. Moreover, particularly after 1911, opera was supplanted by the cinema in what was the most important realm of all: the ability to bring forward regularly new creative works capable of attracting and exciting a broad audience, diverse both by social class and intellectual tendency. After the end of the nineteenth century, fewer and fewer new Italian operas were able to do so. By the second decade of the twentieth century, opera in Italy was already set on a path toward a repertory dominated by works of the past, in which the few new operas that were performed were as likely to be French or Russian as Italian. In contrast, Italian film studios were producing hundreds of new works every year, a dazzling variety of products that appealed to every social class or demarcation of taste represented in the Italian population.

Few opera premieres during this decade generated the excitement of the debuts of *L'Inferno, Quo vadis?* or *Cabiria.* Although the increasingly beleaguered *teatri massimi* would continue to present opera, many of the secondary houses closed, or were converted to movie theaters. Milan premieres of new films were often held in the Teatro Lirico, which had once been the venue for the latest operas from the House of Sonzogno, while Rome's Costanzi was rented for the night by the film studios for their most prestigious Roman cinema debuts. In a sign of the times, in 1913, Renzo Sonzogno began to invest his firm's resources in the cinema, beginning with a spectacular film version of the ballet *Excelsior.*[76] The excitement of the new had decisively shifted to the cinema.

Chapter 16

Epilogue

Summing up

As with any period distinguished by unusual creative energy, the flowering of operatic life during the short period that began in 1890 grew not out of any single factor, but from the juxtaposition of many different strands, coming together to foster the expression of a distinctive type of creative activity within a social and cultural milieu for which it was particularly appropriate. The coming of age of a new generation of composers molded by a body of cultural experiences and musical training fundamentally different from that of their predecessors, coupled with the demand for new and different operatic experiences from a new audience in a changing society, formed the matrix in which Puccini, Mascagni, and their contemporaries could create a body of operas that not only made a distinctive and unique contribution to their historic moment, but that would survive to become a mainstay of today's operatic repertoire.

Nearly fifty years passed between the rise of Verdi and the rise of the generation that came to be known as the *giovane scuola*. During those years, Italy went from a collection of backward, largely isolated, semifeudal states to a European nation. As Italy became a nation, its musical world also changed from a self-contained, almost hermetic environment to one increasingly permeated by the operatic innovations coming across the Alps, from Wagner in Germany, and from a generation of French composers from Gounod to Massenet and Bizet. Their operas made those being written in Italy — always excepting those of Verdi — appear tired and stale by comparison.

That staleness changed with the arrival of the *giovane scuola*, a generation of composers born around 1860 and reaching artistic maturity in the 1890s. They were the first generation of Italian composers to assimilate the new ideas and techniques from France and Germany into their music, creating a musical synthesis that brought a new dynamism and intensity of expression to Italian opera. The extent of that synthesis varied, but should not be underestimated; even Leoncavallo, far from the most thoughtful of the *giovane scuola*, engages in thematic and motivic manipulations in his operas in ways that are far from naïve or unsophisticated. The new dynamism of Italian opera was reflected only in part in the ways the new operas were organized. Even more important, perhaps, was the new sound of Italian opera: an extroverted, emphatic, harmonically adventurous style that used a variety of orchestral and vocal techniques to accentuate the emotional immediacy of the moment to an extent previously unknown in opera.

One cannot say that the composers of the *giovane scuola* were necessarily more gifted, in whatever imprecise and uncertain way such assessments are made, than their forgotten predecessors of the 1850s and 1860s.[1] The fundamental difference is that they had gained access to a body of techniques unavailable to their predecessors. It was their access to these techniques, coupled with their immersion in the popular music of their time, from the operetta and *café chantant* to the Neapolitan songs that grace Giordano's *Mala vita*, that unleashed the energy of composers like Leoncavallo, Mascagni, and Giordano, and that enabled all of them — and not only Puccini — to compose fresh, vital music that was, as Guido Pannain said of *Cavalleria*, "like a door that suddenly blew open onto a sealed room." Their music represented something genuinely new on the Italian operatic scene.

Opera, however, is more than music. It is a dramatic and a cultural experience. It was the great fortune of the composers of the time that their new, emphatic musical language perfectly suited the dramatic experience actively sought by the audience of the time. The second half of the nineteenth century saw a dramatic change in the character of the Italian operatic audience. From one dominated by an aristocracy with traditional cultural values and musical tastes, the Italian audience had shifted to a bourgeois one, made up of individuals whose values were grounded in the modern cult of positivism, and whose tastes were formed as much by the popular adventure or sentimental novels of the time as by the church, the village, or the other traditional themes of Italian culture.

The bourgeois audience were no longer interested seeing composers recycle the traditional themes of Italian opera that had been the staples of Donizetti and Verdi operas. They were looking for operas that would offer them greater emotional immediacy in their sentimentality or their sexualized brutality, reflecting the blend of sentimentality and sexuality that characterized the emerging late-nineteenth-century Italian society. They had long been awaiting the Italian composer whose musical language would satisfy their yearning for a new type of opera that would be not only new, but distinctly Italian. While quasi-Wagnerian efforts like Franchetti's *Asrael* or Catalani's *Loreley,* or a hypertrophied Verdian work like Ponchielli's *La Gioconda* were momentarily tantalizing, they were clearly not the answer to the question, posed by Primo Levi, who spoke for this audience as he plaintively asked where Italy would find "the man destined to . . . extend, or better, to begin anew, the tradition of our great ones, to open it to the future? To demonstrate if there will be an opera of tomorrow, and what it will be?"[2] The operas of the *giovane scuola* provided both the new musical language and the new dramatic themes that fit the desires of the new audience, an audience whose tastes and values were closer to the twenty-first-century operatic audience than to its precursors of only a generation or two before.

It is important to put Puccini clearly into this setting; recent criticism has tended to separate him from his environment rather than see him in context. Far from an isolated figure, Puccini was the quintessential *giovane scuola* composer, quick to assimilate the lessons of Wagner and the French masters, and even closer by taste and temperament than many of his colleagues to his bourgeois audience, the values and preoccupations of which he mirrored so brilliantly in the immortal triad of *Bohème, Tosca,* and *Butterfly.* If Puccini stands out among his generation today, particularly by comparison to Mascagni, who during their lifetimes was seen as his closest rival and competitor, the distinction does not lie in any fundamental difference in their musical or cultural premises. Rather, it lies in Puccini's extraordinary mastery of both musical and dramatic craft, his clear-sighted vision of his capabilities as a composer, and, of course, his unique compositional gifts.

Within little more than a decade after 1890, an entirely new operatic repertoire had been created for Italy's bourgeois audience and disseminated not only across the Italian peninsula but throughout Europe, the Mediterranean, and the Americas. That rapid dissemination, in turn, reflected yet another characteristic of the age: the emergence of a modern society of mass literacy, and of modern methods of marketing and diffusion of commercial products. The fin de siècle Italian opera was a commercial product par excellence.

While Italian opera has had its commercial dimension since the first opera houses were opened in early-seventeenth-century Venice, that dimension had previously been limited by opera's role as an aristocratic entertainment and source of patronage, and by its localized, preindustrial character. The late-nineteenth century saw a different operatic milieu emerge, in which power moved from the local impresario into the hands of publishers working at a national or even international scale, and in which speedy transportation by ocean liners and by rail could move entire opera companies across Europe in a few days, or between Europe and the Americas in a few weeks. Led by Sonzogno and Ricordi, with a host of agents, promoters, managers and impresarios following in their wake, operas and their music were diffused far more widely, both socially and geographically, than ever before: not only in opera houses, but in the salons of the bourgeoisie, the choral societies of the industrial working class, and the bands of the village piazzas. Opera earned plutocratic wealth for successful composers and singers like Mascagni or Caruso, and created entire industries devoted to meeting its needs in Milan and other Italian cities. By the end of the century, fostered by a burgeoning middle class, increased literacy, and the growth of the cities, the audience for opera in Italy had grown far larger than it ever had been — although, as would soon become apparent, far less steadfast in its devotion to this traditional Italian art.

The moment of the *giovane scuola* was short-lived. Their musical language, however exciting and refreshing at first, was self-limiting. It offered little opportunity for creative growth, while their themes of verismo, sentimentality and exotic violence soon came to be seen as repetitive and clichéd, particularly to a new generation driven by the poetic effusions of D'Annunzio or the idealism of Benedetto Croce. Their music came to be seen as less interesting; it appeared backward by comparison with the new sounds of Debussy and Richard Strauss coming into Italy from across the Alps, and reminded Italians that, for all their glorious history, their culture was still in many respects a subaltern culture, responding to and absorbing dominant French and German influences rather than creating genuinely new cultural structures. Within little more than a decade after they first appeared, composers such as Giordano, Cilèa, or Leoncavallo had run out of new ideas. The young composers that emerged after 1900 such as Zandonai, Alfano, and Montemezzi — who sought to remain within the tradition while reflecting both the new music and cultural values in their operas — were scorned by a rising modernist generation who condemned them as much for their continued servitude to the commercialization of opera as for their music. While Mascagni tried valiantly, only Puccini was able to incorporate the emerging music of the twentieth century into an artistically unified and coherent whole.

As the excitement that opera had provoked in the 1890s faded, a new medium that both engendered creative endeavor and provided public entertainment emerged to take its place. Early in the second decade of the twentieth century, the Italian public began to shift its attention away from opera to the cinema, which offered the same audience the same dramatic themes — and often the same music — with greater immediacy and even wider public diffusion. The emergence of the cinema as Italy's dominant form of both art and entertainment — a position it has largely retained to this day — was not only a reflection of the vitality of the new medium, but of the exhaustion of the creative energy of Italian opera, after three hundred years.

The Last Hurrah of the giovane scuola

Italy emerged from the First World War battered and diminished. Nominally among the victors, the nation had lost more than 600,000 men, and the political system that had led a divided, ill-prepared nation into war was in ruins. While the Socialist strikes and agitation in the years immediately after the war never led to the revolution that millions of Italians either yearned for or feared, the radicalism of the Left was soon overtaken by the more determined radicalism of the Right. In October 1922, the Fascists came to power under Mussolini, and Liberal Italy was no more.

In this turbulent period, a handful of operas — by the surviving lions of what was already coming to be seen through the haze of nostalgia as a golden age — caught the attention of the Italian audience. Although Cilèa, Leoncavallo, and Franchetti had been all but forgotten, Mascagni and Puccini were still very much in the public eye, both still vigorous and creative as they approached their sixties. During the years after the war both would present operas that briefly appeared to rekindle the flame of earlier years and, in the case of Puccini's *Trittico* and *Turandot*, would bring the era to a glorious end.[3]

Perhaps the most notable operatic event of the years immediately following the war, however, was the 1921 premiere of Mascagni's *Il piccolo Marat* (The little Marat). Set in Nantes during the French Revolution, it juxtaposed a sentimental love story against the violence and excesses of the Terror under a local despot known only as The Ogre.[4] With Mascagni widely considered a Socialist sympathizer,[5] the knowledge that he was writing an opera set in the French Revolution prompted unusual interest, both musical and political. The premiere, at Rome's Costanzi opera house, was packed with both Socialists and Fascists, both ready to demonstrate for or against the composer's new opera.[6] In the end, both sides came together to hail the new work. As I have written elsewhere: "Whatever qualms people may have felt about Mascagni's own politics, they were dispelled as the first notes of his new opera were heard. As the chorus rushed onstage and the opening scene unfolded, the audience was electrified; at the end of the first scene a wave of enthusiastic applause brought the opera to a halt for several minutes."[7]

The success, as reported in the *Giornale d'Italia*, "assum[ed] unbeliev-able proportions after the second act, as two thousand people jumped to their feet in the overflowing boxes . . . in the filled galleries, in a splendid, delirious, manifestation of enthusiasm."[8] At the end, Mascagni and the company were called back for fifty curtain calls, until Emma Carelli, gen-eral manager of the Costanzi, came on stage and begged the audience to go home.

Marat is the work of a composer fully conversant with the most recent musical developments, who has written an opera that juxtaposes a conven-tional diatonic vocabulary in the intimate scenes between the Prince and Mariella against a more dissonant modern language, in which striking and often unusual orchestral timbres are used to great effect to represent the Ogre's brutal rule. Although many of the lyrical passages were greeted en-thusiastically at the time (particularly the extended love duet that ends the second act), it is the harsher, more "modern" sections that seem more con-vincing today, and that might justify a revival of the work. The more con-ventional passages, including the duet, seem forced by comparison, an at-tempt to reawaken a fading melodic gift or revisit a language that had already come to seem stale.

The unbridled enthusiasm with which *Il piccolo Marat* was received was as much political as musical. Appearing to be a politically engaged work, but lacking anything resembling a clear ideological stance either on the Right or the Left, the opera served as a mirror for the entire spectrum of political attitudes represented in the audience. Its considerable dramatic power, moreover, offered a signal to devotees of the opera tradition that life still remained in that tradition. The success of its debut propelled it into the repertory for a decade, but by the 1930s its vogue had largely passed.[9] Except for a brief flurry of revivals in the 1960s — promoted by the basso Nicola Rossi-Lemeni, for whom the Ogre was a favorite role — it has largely disappeared from the opera stage.

Although its premiere was less widely publicized, and the work initially received with less frenetic enthusiasm, Puccini's *Il trittico* (The triptych) two years earlier in 1919 was to be of far more lasting significance. The idea of combining a group of short operas on contrasting themes into a single evening had long intrigued Puccini, and had occupied him off and on since he had first encountered the grim one-act play *La houppelande* (The cloak), by the French author Didier Gold some years earlier.[10] With Gold's play turned into *Il tabarro* (with a libretto by Giuseppe Adami), and two additional short operas, *Suor Angelica* and *Gianni Schicchi* (both with libretti by Giovacchino Forzano),[11] *Il trittico* was completed in 1918, and given its world premiere that December at the Metropolitan Opera in New York. It made its Italian debut at the Costanzi a month later, on January 11, 1919.

Il trittico was Puccini's crowning achievement. Rather than break new dramatic ground, it represents the composer's summing-up of the major themes of Italian opera, a nostalgic look back at (or perhaps an unconscious farewell to) three cardinal genres: verismo in *Il tabarro*, bourgeois sentimentality in *Suor Angelica*, and opera buffa in *Gianni Schicchi*. These genres were emblematic of an era that had all but run its course. In *Il trittico*, Puccini is at the height of his powers as a composer. He has fully assimilated the most sophisticated harmonic ideas of his time into a seamless personal style. His melodic flights, culminating in Lauretta's evergreen "O mio babbino caro," and his use of terse, telling motifs are all of a piece with and flow effortlessly out of the rich, complex orchestral and harmonic texture he creates throughout the work.

The great age of Italian opera did not quite end with *Il trittico*, but in more dramatic and poignant fashion seven years later with the posthumous production of Puccini's last opera, *Turandot*. As Budden writes, after the failure of *Edgar* in 1889, "Puccini had made clear his desire to escape from the incubus of 'grand opera' which had dominated the Italian stage for the last two decades. With *Turandot* he returned to it, not as a prisoner but as a conqueror."[12]

Turandot is an evocation of the older tradition of grand opera, a work in which pageantry and exoticism are intermingled with intimate sentiment, all designed to culminate in the transfiguration scene that Puccini was unable to complete.[13] In many respects, however, it represents a falling off from the seamless beauty and dramatic clarity of *Il trittico*. For all the brilliance of its scoring, its set pieces and chinoiserie make *Turandot* a far more conventional work than its predecessor. In the end, it has a chilling quality about it, dominated as it is by the brutal princess Turandot and the obsessive, callous prince Calaf. As Budden writes, "only a miracle of musical transcendence could redeem the two principals, and that is something that lay outside Puccini's range."[14]

The Opera Museum

With *Turandot*, the Italian opera tradition as a living, vital spectacle truly came to an end, although as with any such long-lived tradition, signs of life continued to appear, growing gradually fainter, for many years. Operas containing all of the external features of the tradition continued to be written, by once well-regarded and now forgotten figures such as Adriano Lu-aldi, Giuseppe Mulè, or Riccardo Pick-Mangiagalli. Their operas were given premieres at La Scala or at the Teatro Reale, but their efforts mattered less and less. It was not just that these composers were lesser talents; the operas of more substantial figures such as Riccardo Zandonai or Ottorino Respighi fared no better. Aesthetically, their works were exhumations of a vocabulary and a style that could no longer be rendered new; culturally, their works were no longer important to the society, or to the preservation of a vital living art.[15]

There was no lack of trying. During the 1930s, the Fascist government made a determined effort to promote the works of living Italian composers, particularly after 1935, when Mussolini announced the doctrine of autarchy, or self-sufficiency, in art as well as in the Italian economy. Between 1935 and 1940, the Teatro Reale, which had become the regime's operatic show-case, presented ten world premieres and eighteen Roman premieres of new Italian operas that had made their debuts elsewhere.[16] Whatever might have been the merits of individual works, the effort was in vain, and its effects ephemeral at best. The Fascist regime, largely dominated by individuals whose cultural formation predated the First World War, showed dogged determination in their attempts to maintain Italy's operatic life. Even after the outbreak of the Second World War, they continued to devote considerable resources to the effort. Their ability to do so, however, gradually dwindled, and with it their self-conscious promotion of works for which little or no audience existed.

As Italian culture regained its vitality after the war, its new creative energy found expression not in opera, but in a revival of the cinema, beginning with the neo-realists and continuing into the 1960s and 1970s with figures such as Fellini, Antonioni, and Bertolucci. The Teatro Reale, again renamed and now the Teatro dell'Opera, reverted largely to a diet of Verdi, Wagner, and Puccini, making room only intermittently for new works by venerable established figures such as Pizzetti or the latest verismo epigone, Menotti. It is impossible to tell to what extent this reflects a lack of imagination and energy, or simply the absence of appealing raw material. Certainly, the lack of successful new Italian operas cannot be ignored. No Italian opera written since *Turandot* (with the possible exception of Dallapiccola's *Il prigioniero*) has entered even the fringes of the contemporary repertory. No Italian composer born in the past hundred years has created a body of new operas that could even bear comparison with the oeuvre of composers such as Britten, Henze, or Sallinen, or an individual work that has established itself to the same extent as *Moses and Aaron*, *Dialogues of the Carmelites* or *War and Peace*.

The operatic institutions deteriorated. After the war, the entrepreneurial publishers were no more. Tito Ricordi was forced out of the house of Ricordi in 1919 and the firm was taken over by bureaucrats. While remaining a solid firm, it never regained its dominant position, and was ultimately absorbed in 1994 into the German media conglomerate Bertelsmann. The house of Sonzogno, in the hands of the Ostali family after 1923, has remained a family firm, but become largely a curatorial enterprise devoted to preserving and promoting their patrimony, the works of the *giovane scuola*. The smaller opera houses were turned into movie theaters, or closed their doors, while the *massimi* continued to struggle. La Scala, under wartime pressure and faced with the increased reluctance of the Visconti di Modrone family and their friends to support the institution, closed its doors in 1918, reopening only in 1921, reconstituted as a private, independent nonprofit corporation.

Over the succeeding decades, Italy's national government became more and more embroiled in the never-ending task of reorganizing the *teatri massimi* and keeping them afloat. Today, fourteen opera houses, under statutes enacted in 1996 and 2000, have been given the status of charitable foundations charged with the museumlike mission of "conserving their historic-cultural patrimony" by performing opera, ballet, and orchestral concerts.[17] Still living from hand to mouth, heavily dependent on corporate and government subvention, they keep alive an art form that means less and less to the Italian in the street, who goes to the movies, listens to the San Remo song festival, and above all, watches television.

Italy's opera houses today are just another stop on the international circuit. While many fine singers still come from Italy, today's international opera star is no more likely to be Italian than American, Ukrainian, or Korean. It has been a long time since opera houses around the world looked to Italy for what was best and most exciting in opera, would-be singers from across Europe and the Americas came to Milan in search of training and opportunity, or Milan agents assembled entire Italian opera companies and shipped them off to perform throughout the Mediterranean and Latin America.

The years from 1890 to 1915 in Italian opera were hardly golden in many respects. New operas were often crude and derivative, productions were often slapdash and uneven, while the industry itself was often corrupt and manipulative, rewarding a few lavishly while ruthlessly exploiting many others. It was a world, however, in which opera was a living, dynamic tradition, to which its practitioners brought new life and energy. In that world, opera was a pivotal part of the fabric of an entire society, offering the Italian people a measure of cohesion and identity as a nation otherwise largely absent in their lives. It was a world in which the latest work of Puccini or Mascagni was not merely of interest to a small body of opera fanatics, but to a great part of the nation. That world is gone, but it left us its legacy in a body of operas that still move and excite audiences to this day.

Notes

1. Prologue: The Unification of Italy and the World of Opera to 1890
(pages 3–20)

1. These are the most widely accepted time and location for the famous "incontro di Teano." Eyewitness as well as subsequent accounts differ considerably, however, placing the event at other locations and different times. See Pietro Zerella, "Garibaldi, Vittorio Emanuele II e l'incontro di Teano," *Il Sannio Quotidiano* (various dates, 2001).

2. John Dizikes, *Opera in America* (New Haven, CT: Yale University Press, 1993), 29.

3. Giandonato Crico, ed., *Lucia di Lammermoor, libretto e guida all'opera* (Rome: Gremese Editore, 1988), 19.

4. Lorenzo Bianconi, "Italy" in *The New Grove Dictionary of Opera* (London: Macmillan, 1992), 2:838.

5. Fulvio Venturi, *L'Opera lirica a Livorno, 1847–1999* (Livorno: Circolo Musicale Galliano Masini, 2000), 163–64. The total may actually have been eighteen, as a production of an obscure opera entitled *Le prigioni di Edimburgo*, by an unidentified composer, not mentioned in Venturi's comprehensive catalogue, is cited in *La fabbrica del"Goldoni": Architettura e cultura teatrale a Livorno* (Venice: Cataloghi Marsilio, 1988), 181.

6. Reliable and complete information on the number of performances of each opera only becomes consistently available from the 1880s. Figures provided by Venturi for five of the 1847 productions, as well as additional information about productions in the Teatro Leopoldo from *La fabbrica del "Goldoni,"* suggest an average of 6.2 to 8.2 performances per production, from which the above estimate has been derived.

7. Rafaella Valsecchi, "Teatri d'opera a Milano: 1861–1880" in Bianca Maria Antolini, ed., *Milano musicale, 1861–1897,* (Lucca: Libreria Musicale Italiana, 1999). Between 1861 and 1890, operas were performed at eighteen different ven-

ues in Milan; only five, however, offered operatic seasons in ten or more years during that thirty-year period, with La Scala the only theater that offered seasons every year.

8. John Roselli, *Music and Musicians in Nineteenth-Century Italy* (Portland, OR: Amadeus, 1991), 59. The manner in which the audience was distributed among the social classes of the community varied widely, of course, by city, by theater, and even by the type of opera being performed, with the audience for opera seria tending to be more aristocratic and less plebian than that for comic opera performances in the same theater. Roselli provides a more nuanced picture of these variations in his essay "Opera Production, 1780–1880," in Lorenzo Bianconi and Giorgio Pestelli, eds., *Opera Production and its Resources* (Chicago: University of Chicago Press, 1998), 81–89.

9. These were not mutually exclusive or homogenous categories. A large part of the agricultural population lived in towns, in some cases large towns, while many farmworkers supplemented the family income by working seasonally in towns and cities. More than half of Italy's population in 1871 lived in towns containing a center of more than 6,000 population: see Martin Clark, *Modern Italy, 1871–1982* (London: Longman Group, 1984), 31. A moderately successful agricultural smallholder living in a town might well be part of the operatic audience, while his counterpart living on a more isolated farmstead would almost certainly not be.

10. See generally, Robert Leydi, "The Dissemination and Popularization of Opera," in Lorenzo Bianconi and Giorgio Pestelli, eds., *Opera in Theory and Practice, Image and Myth* (Chicago: University of Chicago Press, 2003). This seminal essay is discussed further in chapter 8. Leydi's sources, however, rarely predate the late nineteenth or early twentieth century. The extent to which and the manner in which opera was diffused beyond urban areas to the dispersed peasantry during the period prior to unification is a subject for which there appears to be little solid information. It would be intriguing to explore, assuming that it would still be possible at this point, the extent to which operatic performances, musical selections, arrangements, and so forth, may have been part of the experience at the various fairs, festivals, and markets that were the principal vehicles by which rural Italians shared entertainment and engagement during this period.

11. Clark, *Modern Italy*, 31, 35–36.

12. Under the Italian constitution — which was in substance the 1848 constitution of the Kingdom of Sardinia — the king retained far more power than in modern constitutional monarchies. In addition to appointing the prime minister, the king had substantial executive powers over the Italian armed forces, as well broad power to conduct foreign relations with little responsibility to Parliament except to inform them after the fact.

13. Indro Montanelli, *L'Italia dei notabili* (Milan: Biblioteca universale Rizzoli, 1973), 95.

14. Clark, *Modern Italy*, 44.

15. Gianni Toniolo, *An Economic History of Liberal Italy, 1850–1918* (New York: Routledge, 1990), 65.

16. Giuseppe Mery, quoted in David G. LoRomer, *Merchants and Reform in Livorno, 1814–1868* (Berkeley and Los Angeles: University of California Press, 1987), 66.

17. Fulvio Cammarano "The Professions in Parliament," in Maria Malatesta, ed. *Society and the Professions in Italy, 1860–1914* (Cambridge: Cambridge University Press, 1995), 281.

18. An Italian website for high school and university students characterizes positivism as "the ideological expression of the rise of the bourgeois to power;" www .skuola.net/italiano/positivismo.asp (accessed January 6, 2005).

19. It is clear that positivism and Darwinism, or evolution, had significant points of intellectual contact, although Darwin's thought was far less value-laden than Comte's. The implicit connection was made explicit by Herbert Spencer, who built the doctrine of social Darwinism by fusing a distorted version of Darwinian evolution with Comte's positivism.

20. "Al lettore" in *Excelsior* libretto (Milan: G. Ricordi, n.d.), 5.

21. Giuseppe Barigazzi, *La Scala racconta* (Milan: RCS Rizzoli Libri, 1991), 241. Manzotti and his musical partner, Romualdo Marenco, collaborated on two more spectacle-ballets, *Amor* and *Sport*, but neither had the success of *Excelsior*, or captured the zeitgeist so effectively.

22. Letter to Alfredo Soffredini of May 25, 1882, quoted in Natale Gallini, "Mascagni a Milano," in Mario Morini, ed. *Pietro Mascagni* (Milan: Casa Musicale Sonzogno, 1964), 2:80

23. Gertrud Lenzer, introduction to *Auguste Comte and Positivism: The Essential Writings* (New York: Harper & Row, 1975), xlv.

24. Quoted in "The Zola Pages," www.sunderland.ac.uk/~osOtmc/zola/zola .htm (accessed January 9, 2005).

25. Giovanni Verga, "L'amante di Gramigna," in *Tutte le novelle* (Milan: Arnaldo Mondadori Editore, 1942), 192.

26. Giovanni Verga, preface to *I Malavoglia* (Milan: Biblioteca Moderna Mondadori, 1939), 11. Verga only finished the first two of the projected five novels, both dealing with modest fishermen and workers. The other three, in which he planned to focus on the aristocracy, the new political class, and the emerging world of the industrial entrepreneur, remained unwritten.

27. Specifically, *La battaglia di Legnano, Stiffelio*, the first version of *Simon Boccanegra*, and *Aroldo*, a reworking of the score of *Stiffelio*.

28. The number of operas produced in Livorno dropped from seventeen in 1847 to six in 1848; while the city's opera houses recovered in the late 1850s, the number of productions never again returned to the level of 1847, and dropped off to an average of fewer than ten per year after unification. Venturi, *L'Opera lirica a Livorno*, 164–75.

29. Budden, *The Operas of Verdi*, 3 vols. (Oxford University Press, 1981), 3:271. The chapter "A Problem of Identity" in Budden's book from which this quotation is taken provides an outstanding assessment of the musical world of Italian opera between 1860 and 1890, to which this author is thoroughly indebted. I have covered some of the same ground in my *Pietro Mascagni and his Operas* (Boston: Northeastern University Press, 2002), 61–65.

30. Although Nicolai was German by birth and upbringing, he lived in Italy, and wrote *Il Templario* for Turin's Teatro Regio.

31. Thirteen of twenty-eight productions were Meyerbeer operas, including *Robert le diable* (4 productions), *L'africaine* (3), *Dinorah* (3), *Les huguenots* (2) and *Le prophète* (1). Meyerbeer's only close competitor was Gounod, with seven productions of *Faust* during these years. Venturi, *L'Opera lirica a Livorno*.

32. See Marion S. Miller, "Wagnerism, Wagnerians and Italian Identity," in David C. Large and William Weber, eds., *Wagnerism in European Culture and Politics* (Ithaca, NY: Cornell University Press, 1984), 172.

33. Barigazzi, *La Scala racconta*, 269.

34. Miller, "Wagnerism," 178.

35. Julian Budden, *Puccini: His Life and Works* (Oxford: Oxford University Press, 2002), 22.

36. The *Ring* appeared in a number of Italian cities in 1883, presented by a German touring company organized by the Austrian impresario Angelo Neumann. Giovannina Lucca, perhaps still resentful of the Milanese treatment of *Lohengrin*, blocked Neumann's scheduled Milan performances. Bangazzi, *La Scala racconta*, 269–70.

37. Budden, *Puccini*, 22.

38. Letter to Alfredo Soffredini of February 18, 1883, quoted in Gallini, "Mascagni a Milano," 86.

39. Daniele Pistone, *Nineteenth-Century Italian Opera from Rossini to Puccini* (Portland, OR: Amadeus, 1995), 92–93.

40. Boito was most famous or notorious for his *Ode all'arte italiana* [Ode to Italian art], written to celebrate the premiere of his friend Franco Faccio's opera *I profughi fiamminghi* in 1863, in which he wrote "May [Italian art] soon escape from the prison of the old and the stupid . . . perhaps the one has already been born who will raise up that art, modest and pure, on the altar that has been fouled like the wall of a brothel." Verdi was not amused by what he — and the rest of the Italian musical world — not unreasonably saw as an attack on himself, and did not forgive Boito for many years.

41. Quoted in Rubens Tedesci, *Addio, fiorito asil: il melodramma italiano da Boito al verismo* (Milan: Feltrinelli Editore, 1978), 19.

42. Mallach, *Pietro Mascagni*, 63.

43. Primo Levi [L'italico], "La *Cavalleria rusticana* e il maestro del giorno," in *Paesaggi e figure musicali* (Milan: Treves, 1913), 266.

2. *"Abbiamo un maestro"*: Cavalleria Rusticana *and Its Progeny (pages 21–46)*

1. Eugenio Checchi ("Tom") writing in *Fanfulla* after the premiere, quoted in Edoardo Pompei, *Pietro Mascagni nella vita e nell'arte* (Rome: Tipografia Editrice Nazionale, 1912), 83.

2. *Capitan Fracassa*, May 19, 1890, quoted in Vittorio Frajese, *Dal Costanzi all'Opera*, (Rome: Edizioni Capitolium, 1977), 1:108.

3. Bellincioni interview with Alberto Gasco, quoted in Mario Rinaldi, "Mascagni a Roma," in Mario Morini, ed., *Pietro Mascagni*, (Milan: Casa Musicale Sonzogno, 1964), 2:97.

4. Although difficult if not impossible to convert meaningfully to modern dollars, 2,000 lire was adequate to provide a young composer with a small family with a modest but middle-class standard of living for six to nine months.

5. At its premiere, *Cavalleria rusticana* was followed by a ballet, presumably on a classical theme, entitled *Antiope*. It appears that few of the audience stayed for the ballet.

6. Eugenio Gara, "Cantanti mascagnani tra pregiudizio e verità" in Morini, ed., *Pietro Mascagni*, 1:206.

7. Salvatore DeCarlo, *Mascagni parla*, (Milan: DeCarlo, 1945), 27–28. This book, the product of extensive oral interviews conducted by a young journalist with the elderly composer in 1942, contains a great deal of useful detail about Mascagni's life (in which, however, it is often difficult to separate fact from fiction).

8. Rafaella Valsecchi and Bianca Maria Antolini, "Cronologia sintetica delle rappresentazioni d'opera nei teatri milanesi, 1861–1897," in Antolini, ed., *Milano musicale*, 54.

9. Francesca Bascialli, "L'attività concertistica: la programmazione," in Antolini, ed., *Milano musicale*, 105–46.

10. Letter of April 8, 1887, quoted in Morini, ed., *Pietro Mascagni*, 1:273.

11. Quoted in Tedeschi, *Addio, fiorito asil*, 9 (my translation).

12. Pietro Mascagni, "Prima di *Cavalleria*," in *Fanfulla della Domenica* (December 4, 1892); quoted in Morini, ed., *Pietro Mascagni*, 2:133.

13. Quoted in Alfredo Jeri, *Mascagni* (Milan: Garzanti Editore, 1940), 26. Although Jeri does not specify either the date or the recipient of the letter, it rings true.

14. William Weaver, *Duse* (New York: Harcourt Brace Jovanovich, 1984), 15. Weaver is referring to traveling prose theater companies, but there was little difference between the two.

15. DeCarlo, *Mascagni parla*, 53.

16. Much of the material in the following section is similar to the discussion in my *Pietro Mascagni and His Operas*, 45–48. The first version of the story was originally part of Verga's novel *I Malavoglia*, but the author eliminated it and converted it into a self-contained story, which was published in a Sunday supplement in 1880, and included in the collection of stories *Vita dei campi* (Country life), published

later that year. The episode on which it is based is described in Alfred Alexander, *Giovanni Verga* (London: Grant & Cutler, 1972), 97–98.

17. Verga may have received some assistance in the process from his friend Giuseppe Giacosa, an experienced Milanese playwright, and later co-librettist with Luigi Illica for Puccini's best-known works.

18. Marco Vallora, "Per un'analisi delle tre Cavallerie," in G. Aulenti and M. Vallora, eds., *Quartetto della maledizione* (Milan: Ubulibri, 1985), 62.

19. Most notably by Tedeschi, who devotes three long paragraphs in *Addio, fiorito asil* to denouncing Mascagni's "inability to express the people in their reality" (75), an assessment that seems driven more by the author's fervent left-wing convictions than by thoughtful analysis of the music.

20. Both the play and the story are written in standard Italian, not, as some believe, in Sicilian dialect. The use of imagery and phraseology characteristic of Sicilian speech is far more extensive, however, in the story than in the play.

21. Mallach, *Pietro Mascagni and His Operas*, 65–70.

22. E. Checchi, "*Cavalleria rusticana*," in *Pietro Mascagni, 1890–1920: Dalla Cavalleria al piccolo Marat* (Milan: Casa Musicale Sonzogno, 1920), unpaginated.

23. Guido Pannain "*Cavalleria rusticana*," in *Rassegna musicale Curci* 17, no. 4 (December 1963): 2. This article was originally written in 1940.

24. The words Mascagni used for Turiddu's serenade at the beginning of the opera, which are the only use of dialect in the opera, were taken from a volume of Sicilian dialect poems collected or written by Beniamino De Zerbi, a friend of the composer in Cerignola.

25. This important subject has been addressed, to my knowledge, by only one previous writer on *Cavalleria*, the prominent Italian musicologist Roman Vlad, "Modernità di *Cavalleria rusticana*," in Ostali and Ostali, eds. *Cavalleria rusticana, 1890–1990: Cento anni di un capolavoro* (Milan: Casa Musicale Sonzogno, 1990), 15–40.

26. Matteo Sansone, "Verismo From Literature to Opera" (Ph.D. diss., University of Edinburgh, 1987), generally 156–72. Sansone consistently compares both the libretto and music of *Cavalleria* unfavorably to those of *Mala vita*, although grudgingly recognizing that the former has better tunes.

27. Roberto Bracco in the *Corriere di Napoli*, quoted in Sansone, "Verismo," 170. Five years later, Giordano reworked the opera, toning it down so drastically as to remove not only its realism, but its dramatic coherence, and presented it as *Il voto*. It was, if anything, even less successful than the earlier version.

28. Marcello Conati, "Un indicatore stradale: Mascagni, Leoncavallo & C. nei teatri tedeschi: 1890–1900," *Musica/Realtà* (1999), 60, p. 155.

29. Ibid., 156.

30. Stefano Scardovi, *L'opera dei bassifondi* (Lucca: Libreria Musicale Italiana, 1994). The verismo tendency was not limited to Italy, but spread throughout Europe. Two of the better known of the many operas written under the direct influence of *Cavalleria rusticana* are Massenet's *La Navarraise* (1894) and Rach-

maninoff's *Aleko*, a one-act opera written as his graduation piece from the Saint Petersburg Conservatory.

31. Ibid., 80–81. Ugo Dallanoce, who wrote the libretto as well as the music to this opera, was a Bolognese composer born in 1869.

32. With the appearance of Konrad Dryden's *Leoncavallo: Life and Works* (Lanham, MD: Scarecrow Press, 2007), a serious biography of the composer is now available. By contrast, Daniele Rubboli's earlier *Ridi Pagliaccio* (Lucca: Maria Pacini Fazzi Editore, 1985), which tells his life story in a breezy, informal fashion, is riddled with errors and completely lacking in documentation. Virtually the only source available for the composer's early years in an undated typewritten document entitled *Appunti vari delle autobiografici di R. Leoncavallo* ("Miscellanous autobiographical notes regarding R. Leoncavallo") preserved in the Sonzogno archives, and written by the composer, most probably in 1895. The admirable Leoncavallo Archive (Fondo Leoncavallo) at the Ticino Cantonal Library in Locarno has virtually no materials on the composer's life prior to the 1892 premiere of *Pagliacci* other than a photocopy of this document. Despite Dryden's efforts, he is unable to add a great deal to the story of those years in the composer's life.

33. Both in interviews and in "Appunti" (1), Leoncavallo consistently gave his birthday as March 8, 1858, a date that appears in many reference works, although his actual birth date of April 25, 1857, has been well documented.

34. Carducci won the Nobel Prize for Literature in 1906. Despite that, his reputation has largely failed to stand the test of time, and he is generally regarded today more as a significant historical figure than poet.

35. Letter to Francesco Carlo Tonolla, quoted in Luca Zopelli, "*I Medici* e Wagner," in Jürgen Maehder and Lorenza Guiot, eds., *Ruggero Leoncavallo nel suo tempo: Atti del I° convegno internazionale di studi su Ruggero Leoncavallo* (Milan: Casa Musicale Sonzogno, 1993), 152.

36. Leoncavallo describes an encounter with Wagner in Bologna in 1876 in which he described his trilogy project to Wagner, receiving his strong encouragement ("Appunti," 24). It is highly unlikely that this encounter ever took place, particularly as it is uncertain that Leoncavallo had even arrived in Bologna by the time of Wagner's visit; see Julian Budden, "Primi rapporti fra Leoncavallo e la casa Ricordi: dieci missive finora sconosciute," in Maehder and Guiot, eds. *Ruggero Leoncavallo nel suo tempo*, 49.

37. Leoncavallo, "Appunti," 24.

38. Leoncavallo later wrote that he had put up 3,000 lire for the production, and that the impresario had stolen the money and abruptly left Bologna. Budden, in "Primi rapporti" casts doubt on that story as well (54–56).

39. According to Leoncavallo's account, he married Berthe Rambaud in Paris in 1888. Although that was the name by which she was known as the composer's wife, her actual name was Marie Rose Jean, and the two were not actually married until 1895; Dryden, *Leoncavallo*, 25 and Teresa Lerario, in "Ruggero Leoncavallo e il soggetto di *Pagliacci*" in *Chigiana: Rossegna annuale di studi musicologi*, XXVI–

XXVII: 115–22 (1971). Leoncavallo would not have been the only composer of his generation who lived for some time with a woman to whom he was not married.

40. Leoncavallo, "Appunti," 64.

41. The word *commedia* in Italian does not mean "comedy" in the English sense, but applies to plays in general.

42. Leoncavallo's position is detailed in a letter he wrote to Edoardo Sonzogno dated September 3, 1894. The letter (in English translation) appears in H. E. Krehbiel, *A Second Book of Operas* (Garden City, NY: Garden City Publishing, 1917) 110–11.

43. Cited in Matteo Sansone, "The 'Verismo' of Ruggero Leoncavallo: A Source Study of *Pagliacci*," *Music & Letters* 70, no. 3 (August 1989): 347.

44. Lerario, "Ruggero Leoncavallo," 117–19. Lerario reproduces the actual summaries of the trial proceedings.

45. Leoncavallo is likely to have seen Tamayo's play as well, as it had been a popular offering of Italian theater companies since the late 1860s.

46. Both Pessard and Ferrier's opera and Mendès' play, and their relationship to the libretto of *Pagliacci*, are discussed in detail in Sansone, "The 'Verismo' of Ruggero Leoncavallo."

47. In Tamayo's play, the situation revolves around Yorick, an older man, who is married to the much younger Alicia, who loves the handsome, young Edmundo. Walton, who hates Yorick, slips him the evidence of the affair; during the play, in which the events and characters parallel real life, Yorick is blinded with jealous rage, and stabs Edmundo to death. The most significant difference between this and *Pagliacci* is Tamayo's added twist that Edmundo is Yorick's son, and Alicia's stepson.

48. Leoncavallo was not above borrowing from himself; the "vesti la giubba" theme appears prominently in *I Medici* (page 12 of the vocal score) and the "love" motif from *Pagliacci* reappears in *Zazà*.

49. This connection (at pages 79–80 and again at 300, 323–324, of the vocal score) is noted in Abele Engelfred, "*I Medici* di R. Leoncavallo: La musica," *Rivista musicale italiana* 1 (1894): 101–2 and 107.

50. Pages 118–19 of the vocal score. The parallels are described in Budden, "Primi rapporti," 51–52.

51. The borrowing, which has not been previously noted, appears near the end of the opera, just after rehearsal mark 130 and again at 133. The source is bars 14–15 of the *adagio ma non troppo* of the sonata.

52. One of Leoncavallo's most effective strokes in this passage is to bring back the love motive, which has been heard steadily throughout the opera, transformed into a clarion call, but still clearly recognizable, for Nedda's line "My love is stronger than your contempt for me" (page 214 of the vocal score).

53. Quoted in Sansone, "Verismo" 10.

54. Adriana Guarnieri Corazzol, "Opera and Verismo: Regressive Points of View and the Artifice of Alientation," *Cambridge Opera Journal* 5, no. 1 (1993): 42.

55. Rovetta (1851–1910), author of *Mater Dolorosa* and *Il baraonda* [The hulla-

baloo], is all but forgotten today, but was one of Italy's most popular writers and playwrights between 1890 to 1910.

56. See Arthur Groos, "From 'Addio, del passato' to 'le patate son fredde': Representations of Consumption in Leoncavallo's *I Medici* and *La bohème*," in Lorenza Guiot and Jürgen Maehder, eds., *Letteratura, musica e teatro all tempo di Ruggero Leoncavallo: Atti del 2° convegno internazionale di studi su Ruggero Leoncavallo* (Milan: Casa Musicale Sonzogno, 1995).

57. Michele Girardi, *Puccini: His International Art* (Chicago: University of Chicago Press, 2000), 141.

58. Girardi, ibid., rather gratuitously tries to argue that this is not a verismo gesture (143). Throughout his important work, he seems determined to defend Puccini from any possible charge that he was a "verismo" composer, which he clearly seems as a term of opprobrium; see also page 149, regarding *Tosca*.

3. *Catalani, Franchetti, and the Rise of Puccini (pages 47–78)*

1. The first onset of Catalani's tuberculosis is generally dated to his Paris year, when he was eighteen; see Maria Menichini, *Alfredo Catalani alla luce di documenti inediti* (Lucca: Maria Pacini Fazzi Editore, 1993), 20. It is hard to overstate the effect of tuberculosis on life in nineteenth-century Italy. Catalani's parents and both of his siblings died of TB, while Mascagni's mother and two of his siblings also died of the same disease.

2. Ibid., 14.

3. Pacini was a prominent mid-nineteenth-century opera composer, who was Sicilian by birth but Lucchese by adoption. The conservatory was subsequently renamed for Boccherini, the name it continues to bear today.

4. The orchestra for which Catalani scored his symphony — which is actually a single allegro movement preceded by a slow introduction — is large only by the small-town standards of the time; the work, however, is a skillfully constructed and appealing piece, although marred by the excessive repetition of a perky, but ultimately seriously annoying, short motive throughout the work.

5. The Italian musical historian Carlo Gatti devoted considerable time and effort during the 1950s to an attempt to trace Catalani's Parisian activities, discovering virtually no documentary record of his presence in the French capital; see Michelangelo Zurletti, *Catalani* (Torino, EDT/Musica, 1982), 15–16.

6. Ibid.,16.

7. In *La Perseveranza*, July 21, 1875; quoted in Menichini, *Alfredo Catalani*, 22.

8. Although the woman in the painting is sometimes believed to be Teresa Junck, it is actually Lisetta Cagnoli, Catalani's sister-in-law, although it is more than likely that she was intended to be a stand-in for Catalani's mistress. The painting was, however, purchased from Cremona by Benedetto Junck, Teresa's husband.

9. Zanardini also prepared the first version of the libretto for Mascagni's *L'amico Fritz*.

10. Dejanice, a courtesan, loves Admeto, a pirate, who loves Argelia, grand-daughter of Dardano, ruler of Syracuse, who has forbidden her to marry Admeto. In the end, after various adventures, Dejanice kills Dardano and then herself, in order to render Admeto and Argelia free to live and marry.

11. It was widely known in Milan musical circles that the same subject was already being adapted by another writer for the composer Carlos Gomes. Catalani sought and received assurances from Ghislanzoni that the differences between the two treatments were substantial; see Zurletti, *Catalani*, 133. Gomes's opera on the same theme, *Lo schiavo*, did not appear until 1890, four years after *Edmea*.

12. Edmea, an orphan raised in the castle of the Count of Leitmeritz, loves the Count's son Oberto, who loves her. She is also loved by the Count's steward, Ulmo. Oberto leaves, and the Count forces Edmea to marry Ulmo. She throws herself into the Elbe, followed by Ulmo. She survives, but goes insane, and wanders the countryside protected by Ulmo, whom she believes to be her brother. They arrive at the castle, where she and Oberto recognize each other, and she regains her sanity. When Oberto learns she is married to Ulmo, he threatens to kill him, but is forestalled by the devoted Ulmo, who has taken poison in order to relieve Edmea of her vows and allow her and Oberto to marry.

13. Giuseppe Depanis, *Alfredo Catalani, Appunti-Ricordi* (Turin: Tip. L.Roux, 1893), 14.

14. I have written about *Edmea* at greater length in a review of a recording of the opera; *Opera Quarterly* 9, no. 3 (Spring 1993): 190–92.

15. Walter is betrothed to Anna but secretly loves Loreley, an orphan. Pressed by his friend Hermann, Walter tells Loreley that he is marrying Anna. Hermann, who secretly loves Anna, calls upon the Rhine gods to avenge her honor, while Loreley, in despair, plunges into the Rhine and is transformed into the golden-haired seductress of the river. At the wedding, Anna and Walter are confronted by Loreley. Walter pursues her, but she eludes him and slips into the Rhine, as Anna collapses and dies. Accursed, Walter implores Loreley to come back to him, but she spurns him and returns to her rock, as Walter drowns trying to reach her.

16. Quoted in Menichini, *Alfredo Catalani*, 33–34.

17. Quoted in Mosco Carner, *Puccini* (New York: Holmes & Meier, 1958), 30.

18. This connection was noted in the 1890s by Franchetti; see Menichini, *Alfredo Catalani*, 42. While *Loreley* appeared after *Edgar*, the funeral march was largely unchanged from the earlier *Elda*.

19. Instead of having the harp play the customary arpeggios against the violin tremolo, Catalani has the harp play scales, an unusual and effective touch.

20. Zurletti, *Catalani*, 179–80. The title literally means "Wally the vulture." The reader should bear in mind that the vultures of the Tyrol, where the story is set, are magnificent wild creatures, far grander than the image that modern Americans have of vultures. The meaning may perhaps better be captured by translating the title as "Wally the wild woman," or "the untamed Wally."

21. In a letter to Depanis on January 8, 1889, Catalani vented his fury at Verdi

for recommending to the city of Genoa that Franchetti, rather than himself, be given the commission to write an opera on Christopher Columbus to commemorate the 400th anniversary of the discovery of America; Zurletti, *Catalani*, 175. The thought of Catalani even trying to write a grand opera pageant on the discovery of America is ludicrous.

22. These letters, which make fascinating although depressing reading, were edited by Carlo Gatti and published in Italy in 1946, and have since been published in English translation. As the originals have apparently disappeared, it is not clear whether the published versions are complete. Richard M. Berrong, ed., *The Politics of Opera in Turn-of-the-century Italy: As Seen Through the Letters of Alfredo Catalani* (Lewiston, NY: Edwin Mellen Press, 1992).

23. Julian Budden, *The Operas of Verdi* (New York: Oxford University Press, 1981), 3:290.

24. Zurletti, *Catalani*, 191.

25. A detailed comparison between the original Chanson Groënlandaise and "Ebben? . . . N'andrò lontana" can be found in Menichini, *Alfredo Catalani*. Catalani also used his piano nocturne *A sera* (Toward evening) as the prelude to act 3 of *La Wally*.

26. Menichini, *Alfredo Catalani*, 39. This was unusually Scrooge-like behavior, even for the financially cautious Ricordi. In view of Catalani's health, and the fact that he did not live long enough to collect the final installment, it appears particularly grasping.

27. Although not too much of one. A cursory web search suggests that in addition to a 12 square mile landholding (roughly the size of many small American industrial cities) at Cavazzone in the Appenines south of Reggio Emilia, and a tract of comparable size along the northeast coast at Càorle, Baron Franchetti had substantial villas or palaces near Turin and Treviso, and in Venice.

28. www.blackmarketgold.com/news.html, citing www.wmagazine.com, (accessed August 3, 2005). As the Italian proverb goes, "se non è vero, è ben trovato."

29. Family information from www.sardimpex.com/files/FRANCHETTI.htm (accessed March 17, 2005). The Palazzo Franchetti, which Baron Raimondo bought in 1876 for his family, is now part of the headquarters of the Venice Institute of Science, Letters, and Art. The Franchetti family is a fascinating story in its own right. Alberto's brother Giorgio was a famous collector of medieval and Renaissance art, who restored the famous Ca' d'Oro in Venice, donating it along with his collection to the Italian nation. His first cousin Leopoldo was a prominent politician and philanthropist, who coauthored the first serious investigation of social and economic conditions in Italy's deep south and, together with his American wife Alice Hallgarten, founded a network of Montessori schools in Umbria early in the twentieth century. The composer's oldest son Raimondo was a famous aviator and explorer, who died in a mysterious airplane crash in East Africa in 1935, while *his* son, named Nanuk, in memory of his father's North Pole explorations, was a boon companion of Ernest Hemingway. Nanuk's sister Afdera (named after

an Ethiopian volcano) was Henry Fonda's fourth wife, and reputedly had a brief affair with John F. Kennedy not long after his inauguration. Baron Alberto Franchetti, Nanuk's son and the composer's great-grandson, lives in a Venetian palazzo today; his personality and lifestyle are described affectionately by former Python Michael Palin at www.palinstravels.co.uk.

30. Some of the material in this section is adapted from my earlier essay on Franchetti, "Alberto Franchetti e il suo *Cristoforo Colombo*," *Nuova rivista musicale italiana* 36 (April–June 1992): 193–211, which appeared in English in *Opera Quarterly* 9, no. 2 (Winter 1992): 12–30. One of Franchetti's early teachers in Venice was Puccini's uncle Fortunato Magi, who also taught both Puccini and Catalani.

31. According to family tradition, Franchetti's mother studied with Chopin. Alessia Ferraresi, "Alberto Franchetti: una biografia dalle lettere" *Fonti musicale italiane* 3 (1998): 215. Given that Luisa Sarah Rothschild was born in 1834, it is possible, but as the family lived in Vienna, it is unlikely that the lessons were more than occasional.

32. Particularly Strauss's symphony, op. 12, written at the same time.

33. See Ferraresi, "Alberto Franchetti," 218–19. A complete chronology of the composition of *Asrael* is not available, but a letter of Fontana to Puccini indicates that Franchetti had completed the first act early in 1886; quoted in ibid., 219.

34. Alfredo Colombani, *L'opera italiana nel secolo XIX* (Milan: Edizione del "Corriere della sera," 1900), 296.

35. Ferraresi, "Alberto Franchetti," refers to a character in the Moore poem named Nefta, but this is an error, as no such character appears in the poem.

36. The challenge is a staring contest. Apparently Lidoria's training in the magic arts has given her the ability to outstare any mere mortal.

37. Giannino Degani and Maria Grotti, eds. *Teatro Municipale Reggio Emilia: Opere in musica, 1857–1976* (Reggio Emilia: Teatro Municipale, 1976), 2:152. A chorus of one hundred is actually not a large number by the standards of the time. In a review of the Rome premiere of *Asrael*, Gino Monaldi comments that the chorus, with eighty members, was clearly too small, and notes that in an earlier Florence production, directed by Franchetti himself, the chorus had numbered at least 150; "Per l'*Asrael*," *Nuova Antologia* (January 1, 1897): 157. Ferraresi, *Alberto Franchetti*, quoting Spaggiari, *I baroni Franchetti a Reggio* (6–7), suggests that the Reggio chorus may have been larger than one hundred.

38. One can only speculate whether any of these productions were subsidized from the more than ample resources of Franchetti *père*. That is most likely in the case of the production in Treviso, a theater with modest resources in an area where the Franchetti family was particularly prominent.

39. Letter to Depanis of January 8, 1889, quoted in Zurletti, *Catalani*, 175.

40. Monaldi, Per l'*Asrael*," 150ff., singled out the heaven scene of the first act, and the entire fourth act, along with the love scene, as the outstanding sections of the score.

41. It is tempting, but wildly speculative, to suggest that his tendencies stemmed, at least in part, from his aristocratic upbringing.

42. Gino Roncaglia, "Dimenticato," *La Scala*, no. 13 (November 1950): 59. According to Roncaglia, Franchetti had made Verdi's acquaintance as early as 1881, and visited the older composer often in Genoa.

43. Ferraresi, *Alberto Franchetti*, 221

44. Illica's libretto for these two acts bears more than a passing resemblance to the libretto of an earlier *Colombo*, written by Felice Romani for Francesco Morlacchi, and first performed in Genoa in 1828. While it is unlikely that Illica ever saw Morlacchi's opera, he might well have found a copy of the published libretto.

45. *Colombo* had five productions in 1894, and six in 1895, and then averaged fewer than one per year from 1896 through 1916. Of these subsequent productions, three were in Milan, and four were in Buenos Aires. Since then productions have been rare; although it was given concert performances in Frankfurt in 1991 and Montpellier in 1992, and staged in Miami in 1992, it has not appeared in Italy since World War II. See Mario Morini, "Appunti per una cronologia: *Cristoforo Colombo* di Franchetti," *Discoteca alta fedeltà* 15 no. 143 (September 1974): 25–28.

46. In 1922, with a text provided by the writer Arturo Rossato, Franchetti composed a new third act set in the Spanish port of Palos, on the explorer's return to Spain. It was performed once, in Rome in 1923, without success, and was never published.

47. See Luca Zoppelli, "The Twilight of the True Gods: *Cristoforo Colombo, I Medici* and the Construction of Italian History," *Cambridge Opera Journal* 8, no.3 (November 1996): 251–70, for an interesting exegesis of the political subtext of *Colombo* in the Italian political climate of the 1890s.

48. See e.g., Alfredo Colombani, *L'opera italiana*, 253–54.

49. See www.teamdan.com/archive/gen/upto1903/1900.html (accessed August 7, 2005).

50. In contrast to Catalani or Franchetti, Puccini is exceptionally well served by biographical and critical works in English, including four substantial surveys (three of which have appeared since 2000) currently in print. The first, Mosco Carner's *Puccini*, first appeared in 1958, and has since been extensively revised by the author (3rd ed.; New York: Holmes & Meier, 1992). It is notable not only for its wealth of information, but for its idiosyncratic, psychoanalytically influenced analysis of the composer. The more recent books are Michele Girardi, *Puccini: His International Art* (Chicago: University of Chicago Press, 2000); Mary Jane Phillips-Matz, *Puccini: A Biography* (Lebanon, NH: University Press of New England, 2002); and Julian Budden, *Puccini: His Life and Works* (Oxford: Oxford University Press, 2002). A valuable earlier work, now out of print, is William Ashbrook's *The Operas of Puccini* (Ithaca, NY: Cornell University Press, 1968). Of these, Budden's work in many respects offers the best combination of a biography and a critical study of the composer's works, as well as being enlivened by the author's dry wit. There is also a substantial shelf of studies of individual operas as well as col-

lections of essays in English, as well as, needless to say, a vast Puccini bibliography in Italian.

51. Quoted in Carner, *Puccini*, 17.

52. Bazzini (1818–1897) was a distinguished violinist as well as composer, and most of his better-known works are violin solos and chamber works, including five string quartets. He joined the faculty of the Milan Conservatory in 1873, and became its director in 1882. His only operatic attempt was the unsuccessful *Turanda*, based on the same Carlo Gozzi play that Puccini used for *Turandot*.

53. Ibid., 28.

54. Quoted in Budden, *Puccini*, 34.

55. Karr (1808–1890) was a French journalist and writer best known during his lifetime for his sketches of Parisian life known as *Les guêpes* (The wasps); *Les guêpes* are best remembered for introducing the famous sentence "Plus ça change, plus c'est la même chose" (The more things change, the more they stay the same). Interestingly, his role as the source of Puccini's *Le Villi* was not generally recognized until Julian Budden's "The Genesis and Literary Sources of Giacomo Puccini's First Opera," *Cambridge Opera Journal* 1, no.1 (1989) appeared, although the phrase "Le Willis Alphonse Karr" is written on one page of Puccini's manuscript score; Girardi, *Puccini*, 25. A synopsis of Karr's story appears in Budden, *Puccini*, 41–42. Another story by Karr was later intended to be an opera by Mascagni, but the composer was unable to obtain the literary rights; Mallach, Pietro *Mascagni*, 93.

56. Eugenio Gara, ed., *Carteggi pucciniani* (Milan: Ricordi, 1958), 6.

57. The two winners were Luigi Mapelli's *Anna e Gualberto* and Guglielmo Zuelli's *La fata del nord*, the latter presumably another northern, romantic tale by a fellow student of Puccini's at the conservatory. Both operas sank without a trace, and neither composer even made it into the *New Grove Dictionary of Opera*.

58. E.g., Carner, *Puccini*, 41 and Budden, *Puccini*, 43.

59. Girardi, *Puccini*, 22–23.

60. Although hardly proving anything, this fact would tend to support Girardi's "Ricordi hypothesis" with respect to the outcome of the Sonzogno competition.

61. Quoted in Gara, *Carteggi pucciniani*, 11.

62. Girardi points out that, in addition to the dances, a great deal of the rest of the opera is in waltz meter; *Puccini*, 28.

63. Ibid., 31.

64. A reference to *Parsifal* is not unexpected; as was noted earlier, Puccini and his then roommate Mascagni had pooled their funds early in 1883 to buy a score of that opera. The prelude to *Parsifal* was performed in Milan in April 1883.

65. The chord, which reads C, F, B-flat, D, G in *Le Villi* and C, G, B-flat, D, F in the opening of *Cavalleria*, can best be characterized as a G Minor seventh chord on a C pedal. It could also be considered a C^{11} chord missing a third.

66. Although there is no reason to believe that Mascagni owned a copy of the score of *Le Villi* in Cerignola, he traveled to Naples to visit Puccini and attend the local premiere of the opera in the spring of 1888, less than a year before beginning

work on *Cavalleria*. Mascagni had a photographic musical memory, and could easily have remembered much of the score, either from the Naples performance or the Milan production four years earlier.

67. Letter to Carlo Clausetti (Ricordi's Naples representative) dated August 9, 1895, in Gara, *Carteggi puccinani*, 117. This sort of outburst was atypical of Puccini; later in the letter he adds "I am in a bitter mood at the moment!"

68. The extent to which Puccini's relationship with Elvira is related to his clearly distressed state after his mother's death is a matter of some dispute, with Carner considering it a central factor, and Girardi tending to dismiss it. I would suggest that in all likelihood, given Puccini's lifelong tendency to embark casually on sexual relationships with women, the relationship itself may not bear so much connection to his emotional state, but the fact that, unlike others, this relationship became a sustained — and in the end permanent — one suggests a level of atypical emotional dependency at this point that may be related to his mother's death.

69. Budden, *Puccini*, 63.

70. A synopsis can be found in Budden, *Puccini*, 58–59.

71. Ibid., 87.

72. This point should be qualified by the fact that a substantial amount of the music originally written for Tigrana was deleted when Puccini revised *Edgar* and turned it from a four-act to a three-act opera. It is possible, but not likely, that she was a more vital, independent, figure in the earlier version.

73. Carner, *Puccini*, 57.

74. Girardi, *Puccini*, 45.

75. Ibid., 61.

76. Quoted in ibid., 89. Budden notes that this quotation may be apocryphal.

77. Oliva (1860–1917) was a man of considerable accomplishment and versatility: lawyer, politician, political journalist, editor, literary critic, and poet. His libretto for *Manon Lescaut* was apparently his only effort in that genre.

78. Leoncavallo takes credit for having more or less completely rewritten the original libretto by Praga and Oliva, a claim that, given his fabulist tendencies, cannot be given great weight; see Leoncavallo, "Appunti," 62–63.

79. The libretto uses the term *landa*, which is an obscure Italian word for a heath, moor, or barren land.

80. Des Grieux does not die, but in the novel lives to recount the tale to the Abbé Prevost. The novel supplies the key connective tissue, describing how Des Grieux fights a duel over Manon with the nephew of the all-powerful Governor of New Orleans. Believing that he has killed the man, he and Manon flee into the wastelands, where she dies. The nephew, however, recovers and in his remorse sends a search party into the wastelands to look for the couple. They find Des Grieux, who has recovered enough to bury his lover, still sobbing over her grave.

81. Budden, *Puccini*, 105.

82. Quoted in ibid., 105. Colombani, Budden points out, was also the author of a book on Beethoven's symphonies, ibid., 105.

83. Quoted in ibid., 107.

84. Quoted in Arnaldo Fraccaroli, *La vita di Giacomo Puccini* (Milan: G. Ricordi & C. Editori, 1925), 68.

85. For an insightful analysis of how Puccini uses this and other motifs in *Manon Lescaut,* see Girardi, *Puccini,* 67–81.

86. Budden, 88–89; Girardi, *Puccini,* 57. Puccini also saw *Parsifal,* and may have seen *Tristan* during his visit to Bayreuth.

87. Budden, 130. In the 1984 Sinopoli version with Domingo and Freni as the lovers, act 4 takes slightly more than twenty-two minutes.

88. Carner, *Puccini,* 75.

4. *The* giovane scuola *Comes of Age: Giordana, Cilèa, and the House of Sonzogno (pages 79–103)*

1. Nandi Ostali, "Storia della Casa Editrice Sonzogno e della Casa Musicale Sonzogno," in *Casa Sonzogno: testimonianze e saggi* (Milan: Casa Musicale Sonzogno, 1995), 1:10.

2. Galli also served as editor of Sonzogno's *Il Teatro illustrato* and as a judge in the publisher's opera competitions. In 1878 he became professor of the history and aesthetics of music at the Milan Conservatory, a position he held until 1903. Although his musical compositions attracted little interest, his theoretical and didactic books, including *Estetica della musica* and a treatise on counterpoint, were widely read and studied by the Italian musicians of his time.

3. In *Il Teatro illustrato* (May 1892), quoted in Mario Morini, ed., *Umberto Giordano* (Milan: Casa Musicale Sonzogno, 1968), 230. This massive volume of essays and documents, published on the 100th anniversary of Giordano's birth, represents the most substantial biographical and critical collection on this composer.

4. Letter of October 14, 1890, in Gaetano Pittaresi, *Lettere a Francesco Cilèa, 1878–1910* (Reggio Calabria: Laruffa Editore, 2001), 41.

5. Francesco Cilèa, *Ricordi,* in Domenico Ferraro et al. eds., *Francesco Cilèa* (Milan: Casa Musicale Sonzogno, 2000), 137.

6. It is not clear when the term was first used, or by whom. The *New Grove Dictionary of Opera,* in the entry on "giovane scuola" refers to it first being used "about 1890" (2:428) which appears slightly premature; the entry on "Italy" refers to it first being used "around 1892") (2:854), which appears more likely.

7. While both Puccini and Franchetti were generally considered to be part of the *giovane scuola,* neither was available to Sonzogno because they were under contract to Ricordi. In addition to the five operas already mentioned, the program included a short work, *Il biricchino* (The rascal) by Leopoldo Mugnone. Mugnone, more talented as a conductor than as a composer, was Sonzogno's house conductor, and the work was probably included in the program as a favor to him. It was the only work presented in the Vienna season that was wholly unsuccessful: ac-

cording to Mascagni's later recollections, a Viennese critic wrote "the title was in error: it should have been in the plural. There were two rascals, the other being the composer"; Salvatore De Carlo, ed., *Mascagni parla* (Milan: De Carlo, 1945), 107.

8. Marcello Conati, "Un indicatore stradale: Mascagni, Leoncavallo & C. nei teatri tedeschi," *Musica/Realtà* p. 158.

9. De Carlo, *Mascagni parla*, 108.

10. Michael Henstock, *Fernando De Lucia* (Portland, OR: Amadeus, 1990), 140. More than thirty years later, in 1923, Mascagni was still greeted as a conquering hero on his arrival in Vienna; see Mallach, *Pietro Mascagni*, 254.

11. Letter of September 28, 1892: quoted in Daniele Cellamare, *Umberto Giordano* (Rome: Fratelli Palombi Editore, 1967), 47.

12. Eduard Hanslick, *Funf Jahre Musik (1891–1895)*; quoted in Morini, *Umberto Giordano*, 124.

13. Although of medieval origins, Foggia was largely destroyed by an earthquake in the late eighteenth century, so that little remains other than the much-restored cathedral. It was also extensively bombed during World War II and has more than doubled in size since then, so that today it presents a largely postwar appearance.

14. Cellamare, *Umberto Giordano*, 24. His father was a passionate amateur fencer, and there is no question that he studied fencing, as there is a charming photograph of him, aged perhaps eight or nine, in fencing costume and pose, reproduced in Amintore Galli, *Umberto Giordano nell'arte e nella vita* (Milan: Edizioni. Sonzogno, 1915), 5. Nonetheless, the idea that a solid bourgeois of the time would see fencing as more than an avocation seems far-fetched. Giordano himself, in a 1923 interview, stated that his father wanted him to become a doctor; Morini, *Umberto Giordano*, 225.

15. Morini, *Umberto Giordano*, 226.

16. In 1881, the population of Naples was 494,300, while that of Italy's second-largest city, Milan, was a modest 321,800, and Rome's population was 300,500. By the 1920s both Milan and Rome would overtake Naples, but it has remained Italy's third city, with a current population slightly under one million.

17. Among other works, Martucci conducted the Italian premieres of Wagner's *Tristan und Isolde* and Debussy's *Prelude to the Afternoon of a Faun*.

18. Guido Confalonieri, "Umanità di Giordano" in Morini, *Umberto Giordano*, 261.

19. Although Giordano's womanizing has not been subjected to the almost obsessive attention given to Puccini's, recurrent references make it clear that he was highly active in that department.

20. Golisciani (1848–1919) composed some eighty libretti during his long career, including in later years, two of Wolf-Ferrari's most successful operas, the comedy *Il segreto di Susannah* and the hyperveristic *I gioelli della Madonna*.

21. A detailed description of the story, play, and libretto, and the similarities and differences between each, will be found in the essay by Matteo Sansone, "Gior-

dano's *Mala vita*: A 'Verismo' opera too true to be good," *Music & Letters* 75 (1994), 381–400.

22. Ibid., 385. Sansone is describing the play rather than the libretto, but the substance is the same.

23. Writing as "T. O. Cesardi" in *Don Marzio*; quoted in Morini, *Umberto Giordano*, 232. Sacerdoti was the founder and director of *Don Marzio*, and a widely respected Neapolitan man of letters.

24. Letter dated April 30, 1892, in Concetta Pennella, *Lettere inedite di Umberto Giordano* (Naples: Società Editrice Napoletana, 1977), 44.

25. Arturo Luzzatto in *La Tribuna*, February 23, 1892; quoted in Morini, *Umberto Giordano*, 120.

26. Saint-Saëns's opera, although written in 1877, had not yet been performed in Italy at the time Giordano was writing *Mala vita*, which may explain why, although the reference is unmistakable, none of the initial reviewers or commentators noted the resemblance. Given the opera's reputation as an important French contemporary work, however, it can reasonably be assumed that the score was available at the San Pietro a Maiella Conservatory, and that the assiduous Giordano would have had some familiarity with it. References to Saint-Saëns's score in Cilèa's *Gina* are noted by Cesare Orselli in "Fonti francesi per il debutto operistico di Cilèa: *Gina*," in Johannes Streicher, ed. *Ultimi Splendori: Cilèa, Giordano, Alfano* (Rome: Ismez Editore, 2000), 145. These references, written in 1889, confirm that the score was available at San Pietro a Maiella.

27. The only commercially available recording of *Mala vita*, a 2002 production from Foggia, has a total duration of 74 min., 9 sec. The famous 1940 recording of Cavalleria conducted by Mascagni lasts 83 min., 9 sec.

28. "Europe ends at Naples, and ends there quite badly." Augustin François Creuzé de Lesser, *Voyage en Italie et en Sicilie* (Paris: Didôt l'Aîné, 1806), 86.

29. Quoted in Ugo Bernardini Marzolla, "Da un carteggio perduto," in *Pietro Mascagni: Contributi alla conoscenza della sua opera nel 1° centenario della nascita* (Livorno: Comitato onoranze nel 1° centenario della nascita, 1963), 104.

30. Writing in *Il Mattino*, March 6, 1894; quoted in Morini, *Umberto Giordano*, 127.

31. Florimo (1800–1888) was born in S. Giorgio Morgeto, a small town in the Aspromonte mountains barely twelve miles (as the crow flies) from Palmi. His devotion to the music and memory of Bellini became legendary in his later years, something Cilèa conceivably may have known and capitalized on. Intensely devoted to preserving and recording the rich Neapolitan musical tradition, he was a towering figure in the city's musical culture.

32. Tomasino d'Amico, *Francesco Cilèa* (Milan: Edizioni Curci, 1960), 28–29. This book is an uneven but valuable mixture of adulation and insight.

33. The term *maestro* not only means "teacher" but was used as a term of honor to refer to musicians, particularly those who had graduated from a conservatory.

34. D'Amico, *Francesco Cilèa*, 34.

35. The play was the subject of an earlier opera by the obscure Neapolitan composer Fortunato Rajentroph, *L'astuccio d'oro*, performed in Naples in 1838. In the opera, Gina's brother Uberto is about to be drafted into the imperial army. Seeing how distressed Gina and Uberto's fiancée Lilla are over Uberto's departure, an unknown admirer of Gina secretly substitutes himself for Uberto in the ranks, while Gina promises to marry her admirer on his return. Subsequently, Uberto joins the army just the same, and in the last act, he returns with Giulio, a fellow soldier who has saved his life at the battle of Austerlitz. After some minor complications, Giulio is revealed as the secret admirer, and all ends happily.

36. Francesco Cilèa, *Ricordi*, in Ferraro, *Francesco Cilèa*, 136.

37. Ibid., 135.

38. Ibid., 137.

39. Quoted in Morini, *Umberto Giordano*, 123.

40. D'Amico, *Francesco Cilèa*, 38. The discussion of *Tilda* above owes much to the detailed analysis by Francesco Cesari, "Aspetti del teatro musicale di Cilèa fra *Tilda e Adriana Lecouvreur*," in Streicher, ed., *Ultimi Splendori*, 160–78.

41. Pierluigi Alverà, *Giordano* (Milan: Treves, 1986), 27.

42. Samara (1861–1917), although born in Greece and a graduate of the Paris Conservatory, spent most of his adult life in Italy, where he was a member of Sonzogno's "stable" and can be considered a minor member of the *giovane scuola*. *La martire* was his most successful opera.

43. M. Incaglati, "Giordano rievoca," in *La Lettura* (1937); quoted in Morini, *Umberto Giordano*, 234.

44. Franchetti's note is reproduced in facsimile in Cellamare, *Umberto Giordano*, 61. It is hard to understand why Franchetti insisted on being reimbursed for his expenditure, bearing in mind his great wealth and Giordano's relative poverty, unless it was his way of enabling Giordano to save face by couching the transaction as a business matter, rather than an offer of charity.

45. Smareglia (1854–1929) was a composer from Trieste, which was part of the Austro-Hungarian Empire until 1918. He brought a distinctive German-Italian sensibility to his operas, most of which are in a poetic vein that shows clearly the powerful influence of both Wagner and the Scapigliatura—not surprising for a classmate of Catalani at the Milan Conservatory in the 1870s. *Nozze istriane* is his one exercise in the verismo genre, and is an effective work, although with strong Mascagnian overtones.

46. Morini, *Umberto Giordano*, 235.

47. Cellamare, *Umberto Giordano*, 64.

48. Yet another story of the composition of *Chénier*, found in different versions in different sources, depicts Giordano confronting Illica with a revolver, demanding that he resume work on the libretto, or make changes the librettist was resisting (depending on the version), and threatening either to kill himself or Illica (de-

pending on the version); in all versions, after the frightened Illica has agreed to do the composer's bidding, Giordano reveals that the revolver is made of cardboard painted black; see, e.g., Cellamare, *Umberto Giordano*, 66–67.

49. Ibid., 68. The phrase cited by Cellamare, "non vale un fico" or "not worth a fig" is a particularly dismissive phrase.

50. According to various accounts, either or both Leoncavallo and Samara were also called in, but all agree that Mascagni's intervention was the decisive point. Cellamare adds an entertaining, and most probably apocryphal, story to this episode: when Giordano finally found Mascagni, he was among a group of dignitaries who were about to get on a tram in order to dedicate a new line. Distracted by Giordano's pleas, Mascagni let the tram go without boarding, only to watch in horror as "after only a few hundred meters, the brakes failed, and [the tram] went straight into a wall, and among the passengers a number were killed or badly hurt" (*Umberto Giordano*, 68–69).

51. Among other matters, the first two tenors retained for the performance withdrew, and Borgatti was only found, again fortuitously, little more than two weeks before the opening; moreover, Illica, apparently upset at last-minute cuts in the text, withdrew to his home at Castell'Arquato, rejecting telegraphic pleas from both Giordano and Sonzogno to attend the performance.

52. Quoted in *Casa Sonzogno: testimonianze e saggi*, 2:184.

53. *Il Secolo*, from Cellamare, *Umberto Giordano*, 79; Nappi, from Morini, *Umberto Giordano*, 132.

54. The cinematic nature of *Chénier* has been noted by a number of thoughtful writers, including Rubens Tedeschi, *Addio, fiorito asil: il melodramma italiano da Boito a verismo* (Milan: Feltrinelli, 1978), 95–100; and most notably, Francesco Mastromatteo, *Umberto Giordano tra verismo e cinematografia* (Rome: Bastogi Editrice Italiana, 2003), 31–41.

55. Wagner, of course, used the change of light to powerful effect both in *Tristan* and *Die Meistersinger*.

56. This is discussed in some detail in Marcello Conati, "Il linguaggio musicale in *Andrea Chénier* di Giordano," in Streicher, ed., *Ultimi Splendori*, 339–43.

57. Although the power of the phrase is derived less in the melodic line as such than from the unexpected harmonic movement under the vocal line, I → II/9 (B flat → C9).

58. The musical line forces the singer to sing "a'mor" rather than the prosodically correct "a-mor'" Not that anyone is likely to notice.

59. Giordano's letter to Illica in January 1894, or roughly four months earlier, in Morini, *Umberto Giordano*, 273. The exact reference is to "[i] volumi di Sonzogno di cinque soldi," referring to the publisher's inexpensive editions of popular novels. A soldo was 5 centesimi, so five soldi were a quarter of a lira, or roughly equivalent to one dollar in contemporary American currency. "Cinque soldi," however, was also used as a phrase to denote a small expenditure, or an inexpensive object, regardless of the actual cost.

60. And, apparently, the spirit of our age as well, judging by the increased number of performances not only of *Chénier* but also of Giordano's next opera, *Fedora*, in recent years.

5. The Greatest Living Italian: The Last Decade of Giuseppe Verdi
(pages 104–121)

1. Denis Mack Smith, *Italy and its Monarchy* (New Haven, CT: Yale University Press, 1989), 71.

2. Roger Parker, "Verdi," in *New Grove Dictionary of Opera*, 4:944.

3. The account, although universally believed, was largely mythical; see Mary Ann Smart, "Verdi, Italian Romanticism and the Risorgimento," in Scott Balthazar, ed., *The Cambridge Companion to Verdi* (Cambridge: Cambridge University Press, 2004), 29–45.

4. Mary Jane Phillips-Matz, "Verdi's Life: A Thematic Biography," in Balthazar, *Cambridge Companion to Verdi*, 12.

5. Charles Osborne, *Verdi: A Life in the Theatre* (New York: Knopf, 1988), 319.

6. Today one out of twelve Italians is over seventy-five.

7. *Statistica della cause di morte* (Rome: Direzione generale della statistica, 1903). According to *Sommario di statistiche storiche dell'Italia, 1861–1965* (Rome: Istituto Centrale di Statistica, 1968), the principal generalized causes of death between 1887 and 1896 were infections and parasites (25%), respiratory conditions (principally tuberculosis and pneumonia) (20%), and intestinal diseases (15%).

8. Other than with respect to Mascagni's mother, the cause of death seems unclear. Biographies do not mention a cause of death for either Cilèa's or Puccini's father, while Rubboli, in his often unreliable biography of Leoncavallo, refers to his mother's death as caused by "a malady of the breast, developed as a result of breast-feeding her third son" (*Ridi, Pagliaccio*, 17). Forty was an advanced age for child-bearing in the 1870's, and it is possible that Virginia D'Auria died from some condition connected with her pregnancy or delivery. Ironically, most of the *giovane scuola* lived to a ripe old age, with Mascagni, Giordano, Cilèa, and Franchetti all surviving into their eighties.

9. Verdi's landholdings exceeded 669 hectares, or roughly 2.6 square miles of prime Po Valley farmland; see Francesco Cafasi, *Giuseppe Verdi: Fattore di Sant'Agata* (Parma: Edizioni Zara, 1994), 58.

10. Quoted in Hans Busch, ed., *Verdi's Falstaff in Letters and Contemporary Reviews* (Bloomington: Indiana University Press, 1997), xxxv.

11. Verdi served briefly in 1859 as a deputy in the Assembly of the Parma Provinces after the abolition of the duchy, and then from 1861 to 1865 as a member of Italy's first Parliament. He was later named a senator, a more honorary position, but never participated in the largely symbolic activities of that body. Piroli (1815–1890) was born in Busseto, the town in which Verdi was raised, and was a child-

hood friend of the composer. He was a prominent Risorgimento figure in the Duchy of Parma, and served along with Verdi as a deputy from Parma in the first Parliament.

12. Letter of February 5, 1888, in Alessandro Luzio, ed., *Carteggi verdiani* (Rome: Accademia Nazionale dei Lincei, 1947), 3:187.

13. Letter of February 10, 1889, in ibid., 3:190–91.

14. In smaller cities with more limited opera seasons such as Treviso, Reggio Emilia or Bologna, the need to accommodate an increasingly diverse repertory — which included not only Italian but a growing number of French operas, as well as the occasional Wagner production — meant that Verdi operas made up a smaller part of the total. This was particularly true in Bologna, where the local predilection for Wagner — including the Italian premieres of the *Ring* cycle and *Tristan und Isolde* — led to Verdi getting less attention, and only one out of ten Bologna productions. Bologna, however, was an anomaly in a largely Verdi-oriented nation.

15. More than half of all productions of Verdi's pre-*Rigoletto* operas in Genoa, Livorno, and Milan were productions of *Ernani*.

16. Harvey Sachs, *Toscanini* (New York: Harper & Row, 1978), 80.

17. H.F.G., "An Interview with Verdi," in Marcello Conati, ed. *Encounters with Verdi* (Ithaca, NY: Cornell University Press, 1984), 268.

18. Gara, *Carteggi Pucciniani*, 4:12.

19. Letter to Giuseppe Perosio, critic for the Genoa newspaper *Corriere mercantile*, in Luzio, *Carteggi Verdiani*, 4:106.

20. This phrase began to appear in the Italian press little more than a month after the first performance of *Cavalleria*; see Conati, *Encounters with Verdi*, 241–42.

21. Letter to Giovanni Tebaldini, from Gino Roncaglia, "Il tribunale di Busseto," *La Scala* 6 (April 1950). Tebaldini (1864–1952) was a prominent musicologist and educator, and can be considered a reliable witness. His visits with Verdi took place in the late 1890s, during which period he was director of the Parma Conservatory.

22. Letter of November 6, 1891; quoted in Conati, *Encounters with Verdi*, 223–24.

23. Quoted in Conati, *Encounters with Verdi*, 224. Marchese Gino Monaldi (1847–1932) was a music critic and occasional impresario, who produced a large number of books for a general audience on the musical world of his times, including biographies of Puccini and Mascagni and numerous books on Verdi. He was widely seen as an opportunistic individual who would readily trade on his connections; Ricordi comments, in a letter to Verdi, that he "[doesn't] know whether Monaldi is more a rascal or an ass — perhaps both", Busch, *Verdi's Falstaff*, 385.

24. Quoted in Luzio, *Carteggi Verdiani*, 4:94.

25. Letter to Ricordi of March 29, 1893, in Busch, *Verdi's* Falstaff, 385.

26. Pietro Mascagni, "Verdi (ricordi personali)"; quoted in Conati, *Encounters with Verdi*, 313–14.

27. Amintore Galli et al., *Umberto Giordano*, 66; quoted in Conati, *Encounters with Verdi*, 374.

28. Although Verdi's comments reflect considerable respect for Puccini's work, particularly his dramatic acumen, there is no evidence of any more than occasional or casual personal interaction between him and Puccini.

29. Alverà, *Giordano*, 42. This is not a highly reliable source, and the story may be apocryphal.

30. A detailed account of the visit in a letter from Giordano to his father is reproduced in Cellamare, *Umberto Giordano*, 91–92.

31. Marcello Conati and Mario Medici, eds., *The Verdi-Boito Correspondence* (Chicago: University of Chicago Press, 1994), 198–99.

32. A comment is often attributed to Verdi about Mascagni's *Guglielmo Ratcliff*, "A deeply felt opera, rich and vibrant in inspiration, that must succeed despite the dreariness of the subject" (Confalonieri, "Mascagni e Verdi," 56). A slightly different version appears in the composer's 1942 reminiscences, where Mascagni describes Verdi as telling him, shortly after the opera's debut at La Scala, "it is a deeply felt opera, rich and vibrant in inspiration; pity that the subject is so dreary. But the opera will succeed just the same" (De Carlo, *Mascagni parla*, 203). While the tone of the latter version appears a bit more plausible, the aging Mascagni's memory was notoriously unreliable. I am inclined to consider the comment most probably apocryphal, but the jury remains out.

33. Maffei was the husband of Clarina Maffei, the famed Milan hostess and Verdi's close friend, and a friend of Verdi in his own right. Mascagni used Maffei's translation of Heinrich Heine's *William Ratcliff* almost word for word as his libretto.

34. When Verdi was not in Milan, Mascagni would stay in Verdi's rooms.

35. Confalonieri, "Mascagni e Verdi" 66.

36. Quoted in E. Gragnani, "Prospetto cronologico della vita e delle opere di Pietro Mascagni," in *Pietro Mascagni: Contributi alla conoscenza della sua opera nel primo centenario della nascita* (Livorno: Comitato onoranze, 1963), 621. According to Mascagni's later recollections, he had previously received a letter from Verdi, who had written, "I will call my doctors and try to get permission to travel to Pesaro. I want to hear this great performance" (De Carlo, *Mascagni parla*, 205).

37. Pietro Mascagni, "Il genio di Verdi" (lecture given in 1941, on the 40th anniversary of Verdi's death), in Morini, *Mascagni*, 2:175.

38. Letters to Boito of July 6 and 10, 1889, in Conati and Medici, eds., *Verdi-Boito Correspondence*, 138–39, 143.

39. Detailed information on the composition of *Falstaff* is widely available in English. A comprehensive documentary history is provided by Busch, *Verdi's Falstaff*. James A. Hepokoski's *Falstaff (Cambridge Opera Handbook)* (Cambridge: Cambridge University Press, 1983), contains excellent chapters on the creation of the libretto and the composition of the opera.

40. Quoted in Guido Piamonte, "Prima rappresentazione della commedia *Falstaff*," in *Falstaff* (Program book from 1980–81 season; Milan: Teatro alla Scala), 92.

41. Letter of December 3, 1890, in Busch, *Verdi's Falstaff*, 97.

42. Piamonte, "Prima rappresentazione," 95. While 200 lire is technically con-

sidered to be approximately equivalent to $1000 today, which is outrageous enough, that actually understates the significance of this figure in light of the salaries and purchasing power of the time.

43. Ibid., 96–97.

44. The tour continued to Venice, Trieste, Vienna, and Berlin, but without Verdi's presence.

45. Busch, *Verdi's Falstaff*, 389. Vittorio Emanuele's "cry of pain" is a reference to a famous 1859 address by the then king of Sardinia that "we are not insensitive to the cry of pain that calls to us from so many parts of Italy."

46. It is likely that, while eager to honor Verdi, King Umberto, who was not widely popular, was also hopeful that some of the national hero's luster would rub off on him, adding to his own popular support. This episode had an uncanny echo some thirty years later, in the spring of 1924, when Mussolini attended a performance of Mascagni's *Iris* in the Sicilian city of Catania. During the interval, Mussolini invited the composer, who was conducting the opera, to his box, from which he ostentatiously presented the composer to the audience, which responded — as in Rome — with a long standing ovation. At the time, there is little doubt that Mascagni was far more popular in Sicily than Mussolini.

47. Mary Jane Phillips-Matz, *Verdi: A Biography* (Oxford: Oxford University Press, 1993), 720.

48. Piamonte, "Prima rappresentazione," 97.

49. Raffaello Barbiera, quoted in ibid., 97.

50. Quoted in Confalonieri, "Muscasni e Verdi" 61.

51. Letter of January 11, 1895; Busch, *Verdi's Falstaff*, 361.

52. The other Verdi operas performed were *Oberto, Nabucco, Un ballo in maschera, Don Carlo,* and *Aida*.

53. Roger Parker, "*Falstaff* and Verdi's Final Narratives," in Parker, *Leonora's Last Act: Essays in Verdian Discourse* (Princeton, NJ: Princeton University Press, 1997), 105–6. An extreme example is Verdi's letter to Giuseppina Negroni Prati, written October 26, 1891. Although in the middle of his most intense period of work on *Falstaff*, he could still write, "Meanwhile, to pass the time, and when I feel like it, I still scribble a few notes" (Busch, *Verdi's Falstaff*, 160).

54. Parker, "*Falstaff*," 111.

55. While his reaction to *L'amico Fritz* was similar, he did not read that opera until work on *Falstaff* was already well under way. Mascagni's opera confirmed all of his worst fears about the tendencies of the younger generation.

56. Quoted in Edoardo Pompei, *Pietro Mascagni nella vita e nell'arte* (Rome: Tipografia Editrice Nazionale, 1912), 308.

57. Interview with Jules Huret, April 1894, in Conati, *Encounters with Verdi*, 258.

58. Parker, "*Falstaff*," 113. I disagree with Parker, however, with respect to the significance of Verdi's use of chromaticism in *Falstaff*.

59. Letter to Francesco Florimo of January 5, 1871; the text of the letter is reproduced at www.organisti.it/verdi.htm (accessed July 6, 2006).

60. Quoted in Osborne, *Verdi*, 302.
61. Busch, *Verdi's Falstaff*, 469–70.

6. *The Rise of Bourgeois Opera in a Changing Nation (pages 122–150)*

1. The Socialists chose to hold their convention in Genoa in order to take advantage of the specially reduced railroad fares that were being offered in conjunction with the festivities taking place in Genoa in honor of Christopher Columbus and the 400th anniversary of the discovery of America.

2. The phrase is from Napoleone Colajanni, a prominent figure of the Left of the time; quoted in Giorgio Candeloro, *Storia dell'Italia moderna* (Milan: Feltrinelli Editore, 1974), 7:55.

3. One of those sentenced to exile was a young Socialist named Walter Mocchi, who would become during the second decade of the twentieth century perhaps Italy's most prominent opera impresario and promoter; his career is described later in these pages. Exile, generally to isolated islands off the Italian coast, but sometimes to equally isolated villages in Italy's deep south, was a common punishment during this period, as well as during the Fascist era, enabling the government to isolate the prisoner without being responsible for his support. Such a punishment was meted out during the 1930s to Carlo Levi, an anti-Fascist agitator from Turin, who wrote the classic memoir *Christ Stopped at Eboli* about his experiences in a small town in Italy's remote Basilicata region.

4. This description of the events of 1898 is generally based on Candeloro, *Storia dell'Italia moderna*, 7:51–63.

5. Quoted in ibid., 7:56.

6. Ferdinando Fontana, "I teatri di Milano," in *Milano 1881* (Milan: Giuseppe Ottino, 1881), 252–53.

7. Marenco (1831–1899), whose father was a famous playwright in pre-Unification Piedmont, was a professor of Latin literature and author of a number of verse plays, which one commentator describes as being "more notable for their lyrical qualities than for the excellence of dramatic technique"; www.Newadvent.org/cathen/09651b.htm (accessed October 3, 2005).

8. Daudet's play was based on his short story of the same name, which appeared as one of his *Lettres de mon moulin* (Letters from my windmill), published in 1869. The play, with Bizet's famous incidental music, appeared first without success in 1872. After an 1885 revival, however, it became one of the most popular plays in France through the first half of the twentieth century. In addition to Cilèa's opera, *L'Arlésienne* has spawned innumerable ballets, at least three movies, and a TV film. Marenco's libretto follows the story of the play very closely.

9. Cilèa, *Ricordi*, in Ferraro et al., ed., *Francesco Cilèa*, 140.

10. Both Federico's father and mother appear in Daudet's original short story,

but not in the play, on which the opera was based. Making Rosa a widow clearly accentuated the sentimental qualities of the story.

11. Amelia is a mother in *Un ballo in maschera*, but her being a mother is far less important than her being a wife, and an unfaithful one. The drama would lose little or nothing if she and Renato had been childless.

12. After largely fading from the repertory early in the twentieth century, it was revived in 1935, with minor modifications and a new prelude by the author, from which point it was performed frequently through the 1950s. Since then, however, it has been heard only rarely.

13. Girardi, *Puccini*, 118.

14. Dalhaus, completely misreading *Bohème* in his *Nineteenth-Century Music* by arguing that it be treated as an exotic opera, writes "nineteenth century Paris was a milieu fully as unusual, and therefore as picturesque, as China and Japan" (354). This is almost perversely off the mark; the significance of *Bohème* is that it is arguably the least exotic of all of the operas of the period, as Budden clearly understands (*Puccini*, 178–79).

15. Budden, *Puccini*, 136.

16. Fedele D'Amico "La jeunesse qui n'a qu'un temps," in William Weaver and Simonetta Puccini, eds., *The Puccini Companion* (New York: Norton, 1994), 144.

17. In addition to the major works by Girardi, Budden, and Carner previously cited, the volume edited by Arthur Groos and Roger Parker, *Giacomo Puccini: La Bohème* (Cambridge: Cambridge University Press, 1986), is invaluable.

18. Letter of March 21, 1893, in Gara, *Carteggi Pucciniani*, 81–82.

19. Rubboli, *Ridi pagliaccio*, 157.

20. Quoted in Girardi, *Puccini*, 106 (my translation). In actuality, the outcome was far from as one-sided as Puccini's characterization. Leoncavallo's opera was welcomed cordially, if not effusively, by both the critics and the public.

21. The play has also been the basis of five different movies, including two silent films, one starring Gloria Swanson, and a 1938 version with Claudette Colbert and Herbert Marshall. A 1944 Italian version had an uncredited screenplay by Alberto Moravia, and music by Nino Rota.

22. There is no Quai Mazarin in Paris. It is likely that Berton and Simon were thinking of the Quai de Conti, on the Left Bank across from the Ile de la Cité, on which stands the former Collège Mazarin, now the Institut de France. Needless to say, it is an elegant address.

23. While it is easy to understand the need for the revisions made by the composer, it is impossible to understand the motivation of the Casa Musicale Sonzogno, which commissioned Renzo Bianchi in 1947 to prepare a "performing version" of the opera, in the course of which not only were extensive cuts made, but large parts of the score were rewritten, the overall effect being one of mutilation rather than enhancement.

24. Augusto Carelli, *Emma Carelli: Trent'anni di vita lirica* (Rome: P. Maglione, 1932), 79. The Met performed *Zazà* twenty-three times between 1920 and 1922, at

which point it disappeared permanently from the theater's repertory. Geraldine Farrar sang all of the performances in the title role, while Cascart was sung by Amato and De Luca, and Dufresne by Crimi and Martinelli.

25. See Matteo Sansone, "Il verismo di *Fedora* e di *Zazà*," in Jürgen Maehder and Lorenza Guiot, eds., *Ruggero Leoncavallo nel suo tempo* (Milan: Casa Musicale Sonzogno, 1993), 170–173.

26. Art nouveau was and is known in Italy as *stile liberty*, named after the famous London department store whose fabrics played an important role in the dissemination of art nouveau imagery in Italy.

27. Tom Antongini, *D'Annunzio* (Boston: Little, Brown, 1938), 59.

28. Luigi Barzini, *Memories of Mistresses: Reflections from a Life* (New York: Macmillan, 1986), 60.

29. Ibid., 62–63.

30. This is my translation, attempting to render the meaning as closely as possible into idiomatic English, rather than to match the verse scheme or meter. This passage is often bowdlerized in English translations of the libretto; one example is the English translation (by a W. Grist and P. Pinkerton) of the libretto used at the Metropolitan Opera during the first half of the twentieth century, which rendered the first lines:

As through the streets I wander onward merrily,
    See how the folk look round,
Because they know I'm charming,
    A very charming girl.

31. Arturo Colautti (1851–1914) was a Dalmatian writer, already known for his novel *Il figlio* (The son), a blend of intimate family drama and political melodrama. He also wrote the libretti for Francesco Cilèa's *Adriana Lecouvreur* and *Gloria*.

32. The word *bigotto* (bigot) in Italian does not have the same meaning as in English, but is used exclusively in a religious context; i.e., to mean a sanctimonious, religiously intolerant person.

33. Clark, *Modern Italy*, 89. An extensive discussion of anticlericalism in the Italy of Puccini's time is John Anthony Davis's "The Political and Cultural Worlds of Puccini's *Tosca*: Anticlericalism in Italy at the Turn of the Century," in Deborah Burton et al., eds., *Tosca's Prism: Three Moments of Western Cultural History* (Boston: Northeastern University Press, 2004), 135–46. A discussion of the use of anticlericalism in *Tosca* specifically appears in Susan Vandiver Nicassio, *Tosca's Rome: The Play and the Opera in Historical Perspective* (Chicago: University of Chicago Press, 1999), 18–24. Although this latter book makes far too much of debunking the historical inaccuracies in *Tosca*, which are largely beside the point, it is consistently interesting.

34. Girardi, *Puccini*, 158.

35. As a result, *Tosca* can be relocated to modern times and other places without doing violence to its essential qualities. Girardi describes a highly successful Maggio Musicale production that set the opera in 1944 Nazi-occupied Rome, with

Scarpia as a secret police official, and Cavaradossi as a Resistance fighter; ibid., 192–93.

36. Quoted in ibid., 176.

37. Budden, *Puccini*, 222.

38. Although there is a substantial body of serious literature, both critical and descriptive, dealing with *Iris* in Italian (including at least three books devoted entirely to the opera), there is—with the sole and severely limited exception of the discussion in my biography of Mascagni—no serious treatment of this important opera available in English.

39. Quoted in Mario Morini, "*Iris* e I progetti non realizzati," *Pietro Mascagni: Contributi alla conoscenza della sua opera nel primo centenario della nascita* (Livorno: Comitato Onoranze, 1963), 193.

40. Mascagni's attitude toward *Silvano* was best reflected in an account that appeared in the *Gazzetta dei teatri*: "when asked by [a] reporter, on the eve of the first performance, what, in his opinion, was the best moment in his new opera, Mascagni replied 'the pistol shot that ends it.'"

41. Gianotto Bastianelli, *Pietro Mascagni* (Naples: Ricciardi, 1910), 80.

42. The circumstances are described later in this book in chapter 7.

43. A memorandum by Illica dated July 24, 1894, in which he agreed to prepare this libretto for Franchetti, refers to the subject as being based on the Japanese legend "L'innamorata dei fiori" (which can be translated as either "the girl who loved flowers" or "the girl beloved by flowers"); quoted in Morini, "Iris," 195. No such legend appears in any compilation or reference known to me, while the distinguished scholar of Japanese literature Donald Keene, in a communication to me, considered it highly unlikely that *Iris* had a Japanese source.

44. In his tendency to uncritically sprinkle foreign terms in the interest of creating local color, Illica occasionally slips, referring to the "djin" and "dragomanni" in the streets of Edo. Both terms, however, are Middle Eastern, or Arabic, rather than Far Eastern. Illica appears to have been a voracious, but not a careful, reader.

45. Frederick H. Martens, *A Thousand and One Nights of Opera* (New York: Appleton, 1926), 32.

46. Mallach, *Pietro Mascagni*, 125–26.

47. Cesare Orselli, *Le occasioni di Mascagni* (Siena: Edizioni di Barbablù, 1990), 62.

48. One wonders whether, in writing these lines, Illica was thinking about their parallelism—from the woman's vantage point—with Musetta's Waltz Song in *Bohème*.

49. Mallach, *Pietro Mascagni*, 126.

50. Alberto Gasco, *Da Cimarosa a Stravinsky* (Rome: De Santis, 1939), 187.

51. Letter of January 21, 1899, in Gara, *Carteggi pucciniani*, 173.

52. The Mascagni discography in Roger Flury, *Pietro Mascagni: A Bio-Bibliography* (Westport, CT: Greenwood, 2001), 306–8, lists sixty-one different versions of

"Apri la tua finestra," including renditions by Anselmi, Caruso, De Lucia, Di Stefano, Domingo, Gigli, Martinelli, Pertile, Schipa, Tucker, and many others.

53. Mallach, *Pietro Mascagni*, 128.

7. The Land of Opera (pages 153–180)

1. Fiamma Nicolodi, "Opera Production from Italian Unification to the Present," in Lorenzo Bianconi and Giorgio Pestelli, eds., *Opera Production and its Resources* (Chicago: University of Chicago Press, 1998), 168.

2. John Roselli, in *Music and Musicians in Nineteenth-Century Italy*, points out that operagoing offered "the further advantage of getting away from an immense palazzo largely unheated and unheatable. The theater . . . at least offered the warmth of other bodies" (58).

3. The manner in which the audience was distributed by social class varied widely by city, by theater, and even by the type of opera being performed, with the audience for opera seria tending to be more aristocratic and less plebian than that for comic opera performances in the same theater. Roselli provides a nuanced picture of these variations in his "Opera Production, 1780–1880," in Lorenzo Bianconi and Giorgio Pestelli, eds., *Opera Production and its Resources* (Chicago: University of Chicago Press, 1998), 81–89.

4. Nicolodi, "Opera Production," 168.

5. www.teatromassimo.it/visita_en.php (accessed October 26, 2005).

6. Subsequently, it was reconfigured to reduce capacity to 2,200. Today, after further reconfiguration to reflect both modern standards of comfort, circulation, and fire codes, its capacity has been reduced to 1,350.

7. As late as the 1870s urban Rome hardly extended more than a few short blocks east of the Corso, except for small clusters of development at the foot of the Quirinale and around the church of Santa Maria Maggiore. Nearly everything one sees in this area today, from the Quirinale to the far side of the Stazione Termini, was the product of the property boom from the 1870s through the 1890s.

8. Vittorio Frajese, *Dal Costanzi all'Opera* (Rome: Edizioni Capitolium, 1977), 1:24.

9. For financial reasons, at times one or another of the *massimi* would present a curtailed season, either *carnevale* or *quaresima*, for one or two months, rather than both. This happened on a number of occasions during this period at La Fenice.

10. Fontana, "I teatri di Milano," in *Milano 1881* (Milan: G. Ottino Editore, 1881), 244–45.

11. Nicolodi, "Opera Production," 173–74.

12. Not even the season opener was sacred. Opening night at La Scala was postponed four times between 1880 and 1899 (1880, 1883, 1889, and 1892) because of the indisposition of one or more singers. This is evidence of the thin casting and

the absence of "covers" for major roles, typical of the opera houses of the time. That, once again, reflects the financial stringencies affecting their operations.

13. Incomes from Louise A. Tilly, *Politics and Class in Milan, 1881–1901* (New York: Oxford University Press, 1992), 84; expenses from Donald Howard Bell, *Sesto San Giovanni: Workers, Culture and Politics in an Italian Town, 1880–1922* (New Brunswick, NJ: Rutgers University Press, 1986), 38. These figures illustrate the massive disparity between official conversions between lire of the period and contemporary dollars. In round numbers, a modern American family of similar socioeconomic character—a working-class family, struggling but well above the official poverty line, with two full-time wage earners—might be earning $25,000 to $30,000 per year. Ironically, while the contemporary American family would be paying far less for its food, it would most probably be spending far more for shelter.

14. Although there is a vast literature in Italian about the country's opera houses, the treatment of the secondary houses in the major cities is extremely sparse. It would make a good field of inquiry for an energetic scholar, with respect both to the houses' activities generally, and their role in the diffusion of opera in Italian society. The most extensive treatment deals with the secondary theaters of Genoa, addressed in Roberto Iovino and Ines Aliprandi. *I palcoscenici della lirica: Dall'impresariato all'ente lirico* (Genoa: Sagep Edtrice, 1992). Some information is available from other sources about secondary theaters: in Livorno, in Fulvio Venturi, *L'opera lirica a Livorno 1847–1999: dall'inaugurazione del Teatro Leopoldo al nuovo millenio* (Livorno: Circolo Musicale Galliano Masini, 1992; in Bari, in Alfredo Giovane, *Opera in musica in teatri di Bari (statistica delle rappresentazoni dal 1830 al 1969)* (Bari: Biblioteca dell'Archivio delle tradizioni popolari baresi, 1969); and in Milan, in Bianca Maria Antolini, "Teatri d'opera a Milano: 1881–1897," in *Milano musicale 1861–1897*, ed. Antolini (Lucca: Libreria Musicale Italiana, 1999).

15. Fontana, "I teatri di Milan," 249.

16. Ibid., 249. Salvatore Auteri-Manzocchi (1845–1924) was a composer who had a short burst of popularity during the 1870s and 1880s, beginning with his 1875 *Dolores*. The Dal Verme hosted the Milan premiere of that work, and later gave the premiere of his *Il Conte di Gleichen* in 1887. Manzotti, of course, went on to fame at La Scala with *Excelsior*.

17. Edwart, "La musica in Milano," in *Mediolanum* (Bologna: Casa Editrice Dott. Francesco Vallardi, 1881), 1:431. Both this publication and *Milano 1881* were meant as cultural guides to the city for visitors to the 1881 Exposition.

18. Ibid., 1:431.

19. www.Cini.it/english/foundation/07.perf/mostre/duse/crono.htm (accessed November 2, 2005).

20. Both of these composers had their first operas premiered at the Manzoni, Leoni in 1890 and Cipollini in 1891. Although Gaetano Cipollini (1855–1935) had at best a modest career, Franco Leoni (1864–1949), who emigrated to England in

1901 had a notable success with his one-act verismo effort *L'oracolo*, set in San Francisco's Chinatown.

21. GMM, May 20, 1894, quoted in Antolini, "Teatri d'opera a Milano," 35.

22. Iovino and Aliprandi, *I palcoscenici della lirica*, 49–50.

23. Iovino, I. Aliprandi, S. Licciardello, and K.Tocchi, *I palcoscenici della lirica: Cronologia dal Falcone al nuovo Carlo Felice* (Genoa: Sagep Editrice, 1993), 222–242.

24. Venturi, *L'opera lirica a Livorno*, 32.

25. This was not the Livorno debut of the Puccini opera, which had first appeared a year earlier at the city's grander Goldoni theater, where it had run for sixteen performances; Venturi, *L'opera lirica a Livorno*, 193.

26. Mauro Calvetti, *Galliano Masini* (Livorno: Belforte Editore Libraio, 1986), 25.

27. Although generally known as La Scala, the theater's official name is the Teatro alla Scala, or the "theater at La Scala," named after the medieval church of Santa Maria della Scala, known itself at the time as "La Scala," which was demolished in 1776 to create the site for the new opera house.

28. Giuseppe Barigazzi, *La Scala racconta* (Milan: RCS Rizzoli Editore, 1994), 250.

29. Nicola Tabanelli, "La 'questione della Scala' dal punto di vista storico e guiridico," *Rivista musicale italiana* 8 (1901): 189.

30. The Kingdom of Sardinia, which included Piedmont and Liguria, introduced limited suffrage in 1848. No other pre-unification Italian state followed suit.

31. Irene Piazzoni, *Spetacolo istituzioni e società nell'Italia postunitaria* (1860–1882) (Rome: Archivio Guido Izzi, 2001), 54. The other theaters that received subsidies collected substantially less, from 155,000 lire for Parma, down to the theater in the Tuscan town of Massa, which received 336 lire, or barely the cost of a second-rank singer for a single performance.

32. The generic term for municipal entities in Italy, whether a major city or a small rural township, is *comune* (pl. *comuni*).

33. Moreover, under Italian law, the franchise for local government elections was far broader than for national elections, so that the municipal electorate tended to be more representative and thus more demanding of services (and less supportive of "frills") than the national one. Roughly 40 percent of the adult male population of Milan was eligible to vote in local elections.

34. Fiamma Nicolodi, "Opera Production," 166. This point is also made by Julian Budden in *The Operas of Verdi* (Oxford: Oxford University Press, 1981), 3:267.

35. A hilarious account of such an event at Milan's Santa Radegonda theater in 1879 appears in Fontana, "I teatri di Milano," 261–64.

36. See R. Iovino, I. Mattio, and G. Tanasini, *I palcoscenici della lirica: dal Falcone al Carlo Felice* (Genoa: Sagep Editore, 1990), 117–18. The litigation was initiated in 1854 and not resolved with finality until 1885.

37. Nicolodi, "Opera Production," 166.

38. Quoted in ibid., 175.

39. While the Italian word *questione* can mean "question" in the modern Eng-

lish sense, it is often — as in this case — used to reflect a problematic condition rather than an inquiry; a reasonable translation of the phrase would be "the La Scala problem."

40. Tabanelli, "La 'questione della Scala,'" 181–82.

41. Irene Piazzoni, *Dal "Teatro dei palchettisti" all'Ente autonomo: la Scala, 1897–1920* (Florence: La Nuova Italia Editrice, 1995), 6.

42. The sole significant exception to this pattern between 1878 and 1900 was the 1881 season, when spring and fall seasons were added to complement the international exposition taking place in Milan that year. During the early 1860s, the fall season alone typically included fifty to sixty performances of five or more operas.

43. Fillipo Fillipi, "La musica a Milano," in *Milano 1881*, 281–82.

44. Bianca Maria Antolini, "Teatri d'opera a Milano: 1881–1897," in her *Milano Musicale, 1861–1897*, 26.

45. Verdi to Ricordi, June 2, 1891, in Busch, *Verdi's Falstaff*, 139. Ricordi went to great lengths to try to convince Verdi that Piontelli was a capable impresario; failing that, that he (Ricordi) would make sure that matters went smoothly; see Ricordi to Verdi of June 5, 1892, in ibid., 200–201.

46. Enrico Corti was the proprietor of the café-ristorante Cova, around the corner from La Scala. At the turn of the century, the corner table at Cova was famous as the regular lunchtime gathering place for Milan's most prominent industrialists and business leaders.

47. Quoted in Piazzoni, *Dal "Teatro deo palchettisti*, 9.

48. Quoted in ibid., 28–29.

49. Ibid., 40–41.

50. Visconti di Modrone's lineage, which went back unbroken to the Middle Ages, was probably the most distinguished of any of the numerous branches of the Visconti clan. His full title was fourth duke of Visconti di Modrone, sixth marquis of Vimodrone, tenth count of Lonate Pozzato, lord of Corgero, co-lord (*cosignore*) of Somma, Crenna, and Agnadello, and patrician of Milan. Far from being an aristocratic *rentier*, he was a major textile manufacturer and president of the Banca Lombarda. The famous director Luchino Visconti was his grandson.

51. Fontana, "I teatri di Milano," 243.

52. Piazzoni, *Dal "Teatro dei palchettisti,"* 52–53.

53. Ibid., 49.

54. Ibid., 53.

55. Ibid., 62.

56. Giulio Gatti-Casazza, *Memories of the Opera* (London: John Calder, 1977), 64.

57. An advisory referendum on the question "Should the municipality participate in the cost of operating La Scala?" was held by the municipality in 1901. Although only 19,000 out of 57,000 eligible voters participated, the outcome was strongly negative, with 11,500 (61 percent) voting no. A detailed discussion of the

referendum campaign and its outcome appears in Piazzoni, *Dal "Teatro dei palchettisti,"* 96–112.

58. See Barigazzi, *La Scala racconta*, 463–64, for an entertaining discussion of Duke Uberto's extramusical interests.

59. A fascinating subject well beyond the scope of this book is the extent to which the dissemination of operatic music tended, particularly in those parts of Italy closest to the operatic mainstream such as the Po Valley or Naples, to supersede the patterns of traditional folk music, and to lead to the creation of new "folk" genres that were strongly influenced by operatic melody and rhythm. This subject is touched upon, albeit briefly, in the magisterial essay by the late ethnomusicologist Roberto Leydi, "The Dissemination and Popularization of Opera," in Bianconi and Pestelli, *Opera in Theory and Practice, Image and Myth*, 301–6. A number of the folk melodies collected by Leydi and published in his *I canti popolari italiani* (Milan: Arnaldo Mondadori Editore, 1973), have clear affinities with the opera house.

60. Antonio Carlini, "Le bande musicale nell'Italia dell'ottocento: il modello militare, I rapporti con il teatro e la cultura dell'orchestra negli organici strumentali," *Rivista italiana di musicologia* 30 (1995): 85. In Italian, the word *banda* generally refers to a band with a combination of wind and brass instruments, while a brass band is called a *fanfara*.

61. Antonio Carlini, "La banda, strumento primario di divulgazione delle opere verdiane nell'Italia rurale dell'Ottocento," in Fabrizio Della Seta et al., eds., *Verdi 2001: Atti del convegno internazionale Parma–New York–New Haven* (Florence: Leo S. Olschki Editore, 2003), 137.

62. Licia Sirch and Henry Howey, "The Doctrine of a Critical Edition of the Band Music of Amilcare Ponchielli," *Philomusica On-line* 4 (2004–2005).

63. www.cassarmonica.it/originibanda.htm (accessed July 14, 2006).

64. Carlo Pigli, *Risposta di Carlo Pigli all'apologia di F-D Guerrazzi* (Arezzo: Filippo Borghini Editore, 1852), 89. Pigli was a member of the revolutionary junta that took control from the dukes of Tuscany during the abortive 1849 uprising.

65. Carlini, "La banda," 138.

66. Dryden, *Riccardo Zandonai*, 31.

67. Carlini, "La banda," 139.

68. Carlini, "Le bande," 91.

69. Carlini, "La banda," 137–38.

70. Mario Rinaldi, "Mascagni a Roma," in Morini, ed., *Pietro Mascagni*, 2:98.

71. "Tom" (Eugenio Checchi) quoted in ibid.

72. Ibid., 99.

73. The Casa Musicale Sonzogno currently offers band transcriptions for *Adriana Lecouvreur*, *Andrea Chénier*, *Fedora*, *Pagliacci*, and *L'amico Fritz*, as well as *Cavalleria*.

74. Carlini, "La banda," 140.

75. Antonio Carlini, "Le bande a Milano nella seconda metà dell'Ottocento,"

in Antolini, ed., *Milano musicale, 1861–1897*, 296–97. The author's opinion is that Carlini overstates this point; sometimes, after all, a band is just a band.

76. Leydi, "Dissemination and Popularization of Opera," 324.

77. The role of choral societies in Italy has been stressed by the sociologist Robert Putnam in recent years, who has cited them as the archetypal organizations of civil society: "If we draw a map of Italy in 1993 according to wealth, we will find that communities with many choral societies are also more advanced economically. I originally thought that these fortunate communities had more choral societies because they were wealthy. . . . But if we look closely at the historical record it becomes clear that I had it exactly backward. Communities don't have choral societies because they are wealthy; they are wealthy because they have choral societies — or more precisely, the traditions of engagement, trust and reciprocity that choral societies symbolize"; "What Makes Democracy Work," *National Civic Review* 82 (Spring 1993): 105–6.

78. www.comune.bagno-a-ripoli.firenze.it/I/3A699F57.htm (accessed July 15, 2006).

79. Percy M. Young, "Chorus," in *New Grove Dictionary of Music and Musicians*, 4:356.

80. Francesco Del Puglia, "Il tesoro della memoria" at www.associazioni.prato .it/guidomonaco/storia/htm/fatti.htm (accessed July 13, 2006).

81. www.coritoscana.it/ita/cori/prato/cori_verdi.html (accessed July 15, 2006).

82. One of Italy's most venerable and respected choral societies, the "Euridice" society of Bologna, was founded in 1880 to perform operatic music, but from the 1920s on shifted its repetory, becoming a polyphonic choir by midcentury.

83. Leydi, "Dissemination and Popularization of Opera," 341–44, cites a number of examples of these adaptations, including versions of *Aida* and *Lohengrin*.

84. Rinaldi, "Mascagni a Roma," 2:99.

85. Leydi, "Dissemination and Popularization of Opera," generally, but especially 315–20 and 333–37.

8. Performing Opera (pages 181–207)

1. While France, Germany, and Austria had strong homegrown operatic industries that were far from dependent on Italian talent, the rest of the world where opera was produced was largely oriented to Italy.

2. "Cenni statistichi sulla Scala," in *La Perseveranza* (December 13, 1901); cited in Irene Piazzoni, *Dal "Teatro dei palchettisti" all'Ente autonomo: la Scala, 1897–1920* (Florence: La Nuova Italia Editrice, 1995), 14.

3. *Gazzetta dei Teatri* (Feburary 18, 1897); cited in Piazzoni, *Dal "Teatro dei palchettisti,"* 15.

4. Gerolamo Sala; quoted in Piazzoni, *Dal "Teatro dei palchettisti,"* 15.

5. There is a vast literature on opera singers and singing; the entry "Singing: A

Bibliography," *New Grove Dictionary of Opera*, 4:386–401, includes well over a thousand entries on fifteen pages. Perhaps the best general work on the subject is John Rosselli, *Singers of Italian Opera* (Cambridge: Cambridge University Press, 1992), which also contains a valuable appendix on further reading. Sergio Durante's essay, "The Opera Singer," in *Opera Production and its Resources*, 345–417, is also valuable, although it tends to touch on the period of this book lightly, if at all. It also contains a useful bibliography. Most of the material for the period from 1890 through 1915 is found in individual singers' biographies and autobiographies. While the literature on Caruso dwarfs that of other singers of the period, there is a great deal of material on other singers, including autobiographies by Titta Ruffo, Beniamino Gigli, and Gemma Bellincioni. Two of the best biographies are Michael Henstock's *Fernando di Lucia* (Portland, OR: Amadeus, 1990) and Augusto Carelli's biography of his sister, *Emma Carelli: Trent'anni di vita lirica* (Rome: P. Maglione, 1932). Detailed studies of the singing styles and vocal characteristics of these singers can be found in J. B. Steane, *The Grand Tradition* (Portland, OR: Amadeus, 1993); and Michael Scott, *The Record of Singing*, 2 vols. (London: Duckworth, 1977). In addition to published works, there is an increasing amount of information about singers on the Web, in particular at sites such as www.granditenori.com, www.marstonrecords.com, and www.mrichter.com/opera/bobolink.

6. Scott, *Record of Singing*, 1:133.

7. It is not certain that he ever did learn.

8. Mauro Calvetti, *Galliano Masini* (Livorno: Belforte Editore, 1986), 23–49. The quotation is at 31.

9. Henstock, *Fernando di Lucia*, 4, 6.

10. Bianca Stagno Bellincioni, *Roberto Stagno e Gemma Bellincioni intimi* (Florence: Casa Editrice Monsalvato, 1943), 1–3.

11. When Storchio was growing up, her father was a *maresciallo*, a rank roughly equivalent to sergeant.

12. Howard Greenfeld, *Caruso* (New York: Da Capo, 1983), 19–20. Some years later, Caruso brought suit to invalidate this contract. Ultimately, an agreement was reached under which Vergine relinquished his claims to Caruso's earnings for a lump sum payment of 20,000 lire.

13. Calvetti, *Galliano Masini*, 33. If Laura demanded of Masini an agreement similar to the one Vergine required of Caruso, Calvetti does not acknowledge it.

14. Carelli, *Emma Carelli*, 28.

15. Roselli, *Singers*, 112.

16. According to the late Mario Morini, dean of Mascagni scholars, there was a recurrent rumor that Farneti was, either then or later, Mascagni's mistress. While it is certainly possible, I have never found anything to substantiate the rumor.

17. Fernando Battaglia, *L'arte del canto in Romagna* (Bologna: Edizioni Bongiovanni, 1979), 59.

18. Robert Rideout, "Celestina Boninsegna," at www.mrichter.com/opera/bobolink.bonin.htm (accessed January 2, 2006).

19. Carelli, *Emma Carelli*, 51.

20. Ibid., 52.

21. Ibid., 55. Sachs, *Toscanini*, 84, puts Carelli's fees at 12,000 and 36,000 lire respectively. This particular increase grated on Toscanini, confirming his conviction that he was being underpaid and exploited.

22. Greenfeld, *Caruso*, 182.

23. Pacini was actually born in Portugal, the child of an émigré Italian musical family.

24. Mallach, *Pietro Mascagni*, 194–95.

25. Henstock, *Fernando di Lucia*, 74, 87.

26. Titta Ruffo, *My Parabola* (Dallas: Baskerville, 1995 [English translation of a work that first appeared in Italian in 1937], 212, 264–65.

27. Ibid., 110.

28. Ibid., 159, 240.

29. John Mesereau, Jr., and Dadiv Lapeza, "Russian Romanticism," in Roy Porter and Mikulas Teich, eds., *Romanticism in National Context* (Cambridge: Cambridge University Press, 1988), 308.

30. Gatti-Cassaza, *Memories*, 303. Caruso routinely earned $6000 to $9000 (30,000–45,000 lire) per performance on tour in Latin America.

31. Roselli, *Singers*, 138.

32. Greenfeld, *Caruso*, 105–6.

33. Répetiteur is the closest available translation, in that it suggests greater status and responsibility than "coach" or "accompanist." The scope of the *concertatore's* duties, however, often went well beyond those associated with a répetiteur.

34. Michelangelo Zurletti, *La direzione d'orchestra* (Milan: Ricordi/Giunti Martello, 1985), 131.

35. "Angelo Mariani" in *New Grove Dictionary of Music and Musicians*, 11:679.

36. The description of Mancinelli's early career is largely based on Antonio Mariani, *Luigi Mancinelli: La Vita* (Lucca: Akademos, 1998). Mancinelli's older brother Marino also became a conductor and had a solid although less distinguished career.

37. Ibid., 6.

38. Emilio Usiglio (1841–1910), while a respected conductor, was better known as the composer of comic operas, among which *L'educande di Sorrento* and *Le donne curiose* were popular in the smaller theaters of Italian cities during the 1870s and 1880s.

39. Ibid., 7.

40. This pattern was not unique to Italy, but applied in Germany and Austria as well. Nikisch was twenty-four when he was appointed principal conductor in Leipzig, while Weingartner took his first conducting position, in Königsberg, at the age of twenty-one, becoming Kapellmeister at the Berlin Orchestra and conductor of the royal symphony concerts at twenty-eight. Mahler was twenty-five when he was appointed principal conductor of the Prague opera, and twenty-eight when he

accepted a similar position in Budapest, the second city of the Austro-Hungarian Empire.

41. Antonio Mariani, *Luigi Mancinelli* 10–11.

42. Quoted in Sachs, *Toscanini*, 42.

43. Letter to Giulio Ricordi of June 24, 1898, in Morini et al. ed. *Pietro Mascagni: Epistolario*, 1:205.

44. Letter to Giulio Ricordi, in Morini, *"Iris,"* 222.

45. Mascagni and Mascheroni did not speak to one another again for nearly twenty-two years. Eventually, in the summer of 1920 they made their peace. After a careful exchange of written courtesies, they shared a cordial lunch in Mascagni's villa near Livorno, and parted warmly, remaining on friendly terms for the rest of their lives.

46. Letter of March 26, 1915, in Gara, *Carteggi pucciniani*, 435.

47. Letter to Gualtiero Belvederi of December 1, 1914, in Fondo Leoncavallo Locarno, Sistema Bibliotecario Ticinese.

48. The situation is reversed today, particularly in orchestras where the contract provides for full-time employment for the musicians. At the New York Philharmonic, for example, musicians receive typically between $100,000 and $200,000 per year for a 52-week year, while Lorin Maazel receives a salary of $2.28 million for fourteen weeks in residence and a tour of two to three weeks. As a result, the conductor has far more ability to multiply his earnings with other assignments — including potentially a second "full-time" position — than his musicians.

49. Specifically, Toscanini was seeking an increase to 20,000 lire, not unreasonable in light of his work up to that point, as well as the salary increases being given the company's principal singers. Uberto Visconti di Modrone, who had but recently taken over for his father as overseer of La Scala, countered pettily with 18,000 lire — a gesture that given Toscanini's temperament, could not but infuriate him. See Sachs, *Tuscanini* 84.

50. Antonio Mariani, *Luigi Mancinelli*, 156–226.

51. J. B. Steane, *The Grand Tradition* (Portland, OR: Amadeus, 1993), 42.

52. Andrea Della Corte, *Arturo Toscanini* (Turin: Edizioni Studio Tesi, 1981), 71.

53. Ruffo, *My Parabola*, 243.

54. Quoted in Harvey Sachs, *Reflections on Toscanini* (Rocklin, CA: Prima, 1993), 52.

55. From *Gazzetta musicale di Milano* (March 16, 1899); quoted in Guglielmo Barblan, *Toscanini e La Scala* (Milan: Edizioni della Scala, 1972), 47. Ricordi has been accused of bias against Toscanini, and certainly there were conflicts between them, but they did not prevent Ricordi from praising other performances by the conductor.

56. Viviani, in *Rivista Teatrale Melodrammatica* (March 18, 1900), quoted in Barblan, *Toscanini e La Scala*, 68.

57. Letter to Giulio Ricordi of July 8, 1897, in Morini, *"Iris,"* 227–28.

58. Roger Parker offers some interesting thoughts on the reasons for this neglect

in his essay "Reading the *Livrets*, or the Chimera of 'Authentic' Staging," in his *Leonora's Last Act: Essays in Verdian Discourse*, 126–48.

59. www.teatrolafenice.it/teatro/altre_sedi/index.jsp?sezione=malibran&categoria=nel_settecento (accessed December 31, 2005).

60. Quoted in Gerardo Guccini, "Directing Opera," in Lorenzo Bianconi and Giorgio Pestelli, eds., *Opera on Stage* (Chicago: University of Chicago Press, 2002), 137.

61. Quoted in Fabrizio della Seta, "The Librettist," in Lorenzo Bianconi and Giorgio Pestelli, eds., *Opera Production and its Resources* (Chicago: University of Chicago Press, 1998), 260.

62. "Lo czar del Teatro Costanzi in Roma," *Ars et Labor* 64, no. 11 (November 1909).

63. Quoted in www.andreaconti.it/toscano2.html (accessed December 31, 2005).

64. Phillips-Matz, *Verdi*, 715.

65. Hepokoski, *Falstaff*, 124.

66. Quoted in Parker, *Leonora's Last Act*, 127n.

67. Roselli, *Music and Musicians*, 147.

68. Arnold Jacobshagen, "Staging at the Opéra-Comique in Nineteenth-Century Paris: Auber's *Fra Diavolo* and the *livrets de mise-en-scène*," *Cambridge Opera Journal* 13, no. 3 (November 2001): 241–42.

69. Roger Savage, "Production," in *New Grove Dictionary of Opera*, 3:1122.

70. There is a growing literature on the *disposizioni sceniche*, while the staging books themselves are increasingly widely available. Under the rubric of *Collana degli disposizioni sceniche*, ed. Francesco Degrada and Mercedes Viale Ferrero, volumes have appeared reprinting and analyzing the staging books for *Otello*, *Simon Boccanegra*, *Mefistofele*, and *Un ballo in maschera*, while the staging book for *Aida* has been reprinted in Hans Busch, *Verdi's Aida: The History of an Opera in Letters and Documents* (Minneapolis: University of Minnesota Press, 1978). A complete listing of Ricordi's staging books was published by Michaela Peterseil, "Die '*Disposizioni sceniche*' des Verlags Ricordi: Ihre Publikation und ihr Zeitpublikum," in *Studi Verdiani* 12 (1997). Although none of the Sonzogno staging books have been published in their entirety, an extended essay by Luciano Alberti, "Le messe in iscena di Casa Sonzogno" appears in Morini et al., eds., *Casa Sonzogno*, 1:33–147, including a detailed discussion of the staging book for Mascagni's *Isabeau*. There is also an even more extensive literature on the Parisian *Livrets du mise-en-scène*.

71. Busch, *Verdi's Aida*. 583.

72. Alberti, 37–39.

73. Ibid., 42.

74. Quoted in Mercedes Viale Ferrero, "Scene (immaginate, descritte, dipinte, prescritte) per il teatro d'opera di fine ottocento," in *Ruggero Leoncavallo nel suo tempo*, 41.

75. The staging book for act 3 of *Le roi de Lahore* is reproduced in the program book for the 2004 Teatro la Fenice production, 44–45.

76. Alberti, "Le messe in iscena di Casa Sonzogno," 106–7.

77. This was the case on occasion with *Otello* as well as with Puccini's *Manon Lescaut;* see Viale Ferrero, "Scene," 42–43.

78. From an unpublished memoir, quoted in Konrad Claude Dryden, *Riccardo Zandonai: A Biography* (Frankfurt am Main: Peter Lang, 1999), 176.

79. *Boston Evening Transcript* (February 28, 1894); quoted in Henstock, *Fernando De Lucia,* 179.

80. *Il Messaggero* (November 23, 1899); quoted in Frajese, *Dal Costanzi all'Opera,* 1:167.

9. Ricordi, Sonzogno, and the Power of the Publishers (pages 208–224)

1. Ricordi's grandfather Giovanni (1785–1853) was a Milan native and a journeyman theater violinist who first opened a music-copying business as a sideline in 1804, a business that grew within a few years into a full-time publishing business. Sonzogno's grandfather Giovanni Battista (1760–1822) came to Milan from a small town near Bergamo (roughly thirty miles ENE of Milan), and opened a print shop toward the end of the 1700s, soon branching out into publishing. A violinist in a theater pit band and a printer were from the same social stratum, poised between the working class and the emerging bourgeoisie.

2. Quoted in Bianca Maria Antolini, "L'editoria musicale in Italia negli anni di Puccini," in Gabriella Biagi Ravenni and Carolyn Gianturco eds., *Giacomo Puccini: L'uomo, il musicista, il panorama europeo* (Lucca: Libreria Musicale Italiana, 1997), 329.

3. Cavallotti (1842–1898), a highly romantic figure, was the leader of what was known as the "Extreme Left" in the Italian parliament in pre-Socialist days. A member of Garibaldi's Thousand at the age of eighteen, he served in Parliament from 1873 to 1898, and was perhaps the only political figure prior to the rise of the Socialist Party to have a significant following among Italy's working-class masses. A habitual duelist, he was killed in a duel with the right-wing editor of the *Gazzetta di Venezia* in March 1898. In addition to his close relationship with Sonzogno, Cavallotti was also friendly with Mascagni.

4. Antolini, "L'editoria musicale," 330.

5. Giovannina Lucca was generally regarded as both a stronger personality and more effective businessperson than her husband. In a famous quip, Richard Wagner said of her that "nature originally intended to make a man, until it realized that in Italy the men were not much use, and quickly corrected itself."

6. This included the physical plant, the engraving plates, the rights to hundreds of operas (including those of Wagner), and a catalogue containing some 48,000 items. In addition, Lucca's nephew Gustavo Strazza was given a seat on the board of the Casa Ricordi; "Ricordi," in Bianca Maria Antolini, ed., *Dizionario degli editori musicali italiani* (Pisa: Edizioni ETS, 2000), 293.

7. Nicola Tabanelli, "La ditta Ricordi contro il tenore Bonci," *Rivista musicale italiana* 8 (1901): 703–14.

8. Antolini, "L'editoria musicale," 332.

9. Ibid., 354–55.

10. Equally important commercially, although perhaps not artistically, was Sonzogno's acquisition of the rights to the body of French operettas by composers such as Offenbach, Lecocq, and Audran, which — in the absence of a body of home-grown operettas — was virtually the entire repertory of the traveling operetta companies operating across Italy, and which quietly provided the firm with a steady stream of royalties.

11. John Roselli, "Opera Production, 1780–1880," in Bianconi and Pestelli, eds., *Opera Production and Its Resources*, 158.

12. Antolini, "L'editoria musicale," 350.

13. *Musica* (December 15, 1907).

14. Eugène D'Harcourt, *La musique actuelle en Italie* (Paris: F. Durdilly, 1904), 41. Eugène D'Harcourt (1859–1918) was a well-respected French composer, who was particularly active in promoting German music in France, including Wagner's operas. He wrote extensively about the musical life of other European countries.

15. Antolini, "L'editoria musicale," 352.

16. During the 1880s nearly all of Sonzogno's operas were French operas, for which he had bought the Italian rights from their publishers, and to whom he owned payments whether or not the operas were performed. That gave him an added incentive to pursue an aggressive strategy of operatic production.

17. Mario Morini and Piero Ostali, Jr., "Cronologia della Casa Musicale Sonzogno," in Morini et al., eds., *Casa Sonzogno*, 1:297–335.

18. Barigazzi, *La Scala Racconta*, 381–82.

19. He presented nine operas in 1895 and ten in 1896. The total number of performances, however, did not change from previous years, as he presented fewer performances of each opera.

20. There seems some inconsistency between various sources with respect to whether he renounced the entire subsidy, or only agreed to operate with a substantially smaller subsidy than that previously required (the latter appears more likely). In addition, he demanded and received the right to use the La Scala chorus and corps de ballet at his Teatro Lirico, which scheduled its performances for the spring and fall, in order not to conflict with the season at La Scala. See Piazzoni, *Dal "Teatro dei palchettisti,"* 7; Antolini, "Teatri d'opera a Milano" 25.

21. In a letter to Boito of December 21, 1895, Verdi criticized Ricordi for refusing to permit Sonzogno to present *Lohengrin* and *Les Huguenots*; see Conati and Medici, eds., *Verdi-Boito Correspondence*, 235.

22. Marco Capra, "La Casa Editrice Sonzogno tra giornalismo e impresariato," in Morini et al., eds., *Casa Sonzogno*, 1:271.

23. A. Giovanetti, writing in *Gazzetta teatrale italiana* (March 25, 1890); quoted

in Marco Capra, "La Casa Editrice Sonzogno tra giornalismo e impresariato," in Morini et al., eds., *Casa Sonzogno,* 1:269.

24. Claudio Sartori, *Casa Ricordi, 1808–1958* (Milan: Casa Ricordi, 1958), 49–50, 68.

25. Bonaventura Caloro, "Sonzogno," *Milan* 10, no. 4, (January 24, 1954): 23.

26. Cilèa, *Ricordi,* in Ferraro et al., eds., *Francesco Cilèa,* 141. The singer's name was actually Mary Tracey.

27. Ibid., 142. It is not clear whether this letter was actually sent.

28. D'Harcourt, *La musique actuelle en Italie,* 46.

29. Cited in Pietro Mascagni, *Per le opere dell'ingegno* (On behalf of the products of creativity), (Rome: Officina Poligrafica Italiana, 1905), 7. The contents of this pamphlet were first published as a series of articles in the Roman magazine *Alba* during 1904.

30. "Ricordi," in Antolini, ed. *Dizionario,* 298.

31. See generally, *Mascagni contro Sonzogno: comparsa conclusionale del maestro Pietro Mascagni* (Livorno: Arti Grafiche S. Belforte, 1915). This document, the 236-page closing brief submitted by Mascagni's attorneys in his litigation with the Casa Sonzogno, contains a wealth of information about publishers' practices of the time.

32. Ibid., 37.

33. Letter to Tito Ricordi, March 26, 1906, in Gara, *Carteggi pucciniani,* 320.

34. Puccini to Alfredo Vandini, October 2, 1899, in ibid., 176.

35. This assumes 30 percent of the rental income on an opera rented for 6000 lire, or 1800 lire per rental, plus the cash payment prorated over five years; thus $(1800 \times 10) + 6000 = 24{,}000$.

36. *Mascagni contro Sonzogno,* 40–41.

37. Mascagni, *Per le opere dell'ingegno,* 8.

38. Sadly, the opera was a fiasco, and the humiliated young composer withdrew the work after the initial performance.

39. Quoted in Mascagni, *Per le opere dell'ingegno,* 11. Mascagni stresses that he has Wolf-Ferrari's permission to cite his letter.

40. In between, Mascagni, in desperation, looked abroad, and signed a contract with the French publisher Choudens. His next opera, *Amica,* was written in French, and made its debut at the Opéra de Monte Carlo with a star-studded cast that included Geraldine Farrar and Maurice Renard. Although flawed, it is a powerful work that deserves better than the near-total neglect it has suffered. After Mascagni's rapprochement with the Casa Sonzogno, Sonzogno bought the Italian rights to the opera from Choudens.

41. *Mascagni contro Sonzogno,* 48.

42. Sartori, *Casa Ricordi,* 75.

43. Carner, *Puccini,* 122.

44. Sartori, *Casa Ricordi,* 76.

45. Carner, *Puccini,* 122

46. Sartori, *Casa Ricordi,* 77.

47. At least one Ricordi remained with the firm. Tito's younger brother Manolo, whom Tito had placed in charge of the factory in 1912, remained at that position under the new management until his death in 1940.

48. The Casa Ricordi remained an independent firm until 1994, when it was acquired and absorbed into the German media conglomerate Bertelsmann.

49. Letter of July 5, 1910, in Morini, ed., *Pietro Mascagni,* 1:360.

50. Undated letter, summer 1910, in ibid.

51. Letter of June 1912, in ibid.

52. Lorenzo also obtained the soon-forgotten *Notte di legenda* from Franchetti. Giordano, although apparently not interested in joining Lorenzo, did have serious discussions with the Casa Ricordi at this point, but in the end gave his new opera, *Madame Sans-Gêne,* to Riccardo. See Morini, ed., *Umberto Giordano,* 246.

53. The general publishing arm still nominally exists, as a separate imprint within the Italian conglomerate RCS Media Group.

54. In death, Sonzogno took a sort of belated revenge on Lorenzo, leaving his entire estate to the son of his cousin Riccardo; letter of Mascagni to Anna Lolli, March 17, 1920.

55. Mascagni, who was fond of Lorenzo despite their intermittent fights, wrote bitterly of his mistress that "that American woman completely ruined Renzo, and then she killed him"; letter to Anna Lolli, April 7, 1920.

56. It continues to be, however, that admirable rarity in modern times, a family-owned and controlled firm. As of this writing, the third generation of the Ostali family, Piero, Jr., directs the Casa Musicale Sonzogno.

10. *Librettists and Libretti (pages 225–246)*

1. With rare and isolated exceptions over the centuries, operatic librettists until well into the twentieth century were male. The most notable exceptions, in late-eighteenth- and early-nineteenth-century France, are discussed in Jacqueline Letzer and Robert Adelson, *Women Writing Opera: Creativity and Controversy in the Age of the French Revolution* (Berkeley and Los Angeles: University of California Press, 2001).

2. Vernon Lee (pseud. of Violet Paget), *Studies of the Eighteenth Century in Italy* (Chicago: McClurg, 1908), 220. This precocious, brilliant book was first published in 1880, when the author was twenty-four, based on research that the author began not long after her fourteenth birthday.

3. Ibid.

4. Don Neville, "Pietro Metastasio," in *New Grove Dictionary of Opera,* 3:352.

5. Arthur Elson, *The Book of Musical Knowledge* (New York: Houghton Mifflin, 1915), 166.

6. Letter to Targioni-Tozzetti and Menasci, April 21, 1891; cited in Morini, "Nascita dell'amico Fritz," in Piero Ostali and Nandi Ostali, eds., *L'amico Fritz nel centenario della prima rappresentazione* (Milan: Casa Musicale Sonzogno, 1994), 11.

7. Targioni-Tozzetti and Menasci collaborated on *I Rantzau* (1892) and *Zanetto* (1896), while the two collaborated on extensive revisions to Daspuro's initial version of *L'amico Fritz* (1891). Targioni-Tozzetti individually prepared the libretti for *Silvano* (1895) and *Pinotta* (1932), rewrote and supplemented the original libretto for *Nerone* (1935), and made more modest additions to Forzano's libretti for *Lodoletta* (1917) and *Il piccolo Marat* (1921). Menasci made extensive revisions to Choudens's French-language libretto for *Amica* (1905), as well as preparing the Italian performing version. The only libretti that Mascagni set that neither Targioni-Tozzetti nor Menasci had a hand in were those by Illica or D'Annunzio.

8. He served both as an elected mayor prior to World War I, and as an appointed mayor — after local elections for mayor were abolished in the 1920s — under Fascism.

9. Adolfo Taddei, "Pietro Mascagni," *Liburni Civitas* 13 (1940): 26.

10. Letter to Mario Mascagni, June 8, 1933; cited in Morini, ed. *Pietro Mascagni*, 1:420.

11. Maria Chiara Mazzi, "Un'opera atipica: *Chopin* di Giacomo Orefice," http://www.fortepiano.it/Archivi/002NS/fpmat005.htm accessed (November 26, 2005).

12. Letter, August 13, 1884; cited in Jone Gaillard Corsi, *Il libretto d'autore, 1860–1930* (West Lafayette, IN: Bordighera, 1997), 56.

13. Rubens Tedeschi, *D'Annunzio e la musica* (Scandicci: La Nuova Italia Editrice, 1988), 46.

14. Letter, March 26, 1906, in Gara, ed., *Carteggi pucciniani*, 320.

15. Mario Morini, "Profilo di Illica," *La Scala* (October 1956): 43.

16. Illica's first libretto appears to have been written a year or two earlier, a "Fantasia Araba," written as a favor, and probably at no charge, for his friend Giovanni Tebaldini, a twenty-two-year-old Milan Conservatory student. Tebaldini, who would ultimately abandon composing and go on to a distinguished career as a music educator and musicologist, never completed setting the libretto. Illica subsequently recycled it for Franco Alfano as *La fonte de Enschir*; see www.tebaldini.it/illica.htm.

17. Luigi Baldacci, *La musica in italiano: libretti d'opera dell'ottocento* (Milan: Rizzoli, 1997), 166–67.

18. The concept of the *parola scenica* (scenic [or dramatic] word) was a favorite theme of Verdi, who characterized it as "those [words] that carve out a situation or a character, words that have a powerful impact on the audience." Letter to Ricordi, July 10, 1870; quoted in Busch, *Verdi's Aida*, 31.

19. Carner, *Puccini*, 86.

20. Letter, December 18, 1897, in Morini, ed., *Pietro Mascagni*, 1:318.

21. Letter to Illica, December 17, 1899, in Morini et al., eds., *Pietro Mascagni: Epistolario*, 1:223.

22. Letter, December 22, 1899, ibid., 1:224. Mail, in 1890s Italy, was invariably delivered the next day to all but the most isolated corners of the country.

23. Letter to Illica, July 1901, in Morini, ed., *Umberto Giordano*, 297.

24. Letter to Illica, August 23, 1901, in ibid., 300.

25. Letter to Illica, late August, in ibid.

26. Illica to Ricordi, January 1893, in Gara, *Carteggi pucciniani*, 78.

27. Ricordi to Illica, December 23, 1892, ibid., 79.

28. Carner, *Puccini*, 82.

29. Quoted in ibid., 89.

30. Giacosa to Ricordi, October 6, 1893, in Gara, *Carteggi pucciniani*, 89.

31. Giacosa to Ricordi, June 28, 1895, in ibid., 115.

32. Giacosa to Ricordi, December 14, 1895, in ibid., 136.

33. Although there is no doubt that Giacosa found creative and psychological satisfaction in his work with Illica and Puccini, one can also speculate that financial considerations played some part. The 3 percent share of royalties that he received for his work on Puccini's libretti most probably earned him substantially more than his income either from his plays or as editor of *La Lettura*.

34. Ricordi to Illica, February 15, 1896, in ibid., 143.

35. Quoted in Carner, *Puccini*, 84.

36. Ricordi to Illica, November 9, 1905; quoted in Morini, "Profilo di Illica," 46.

37. Mascagni and Illica explored this project from the beginning of 1902 to the beginning of 1904, but Mascagni was never completely convinced that Marie Antoinette would make a strong operatic heroine, or that Illica's epic treatment of the story was suitable for his talents. Just the same, in the absence of any other options, he pursued the project, but found Illica's slow pace — arising from his work for Puccini and others — intensely frustrating; moreover, Mascagni realized that Giacosa's involvement, which he actively sought, would delay the project even further. Finally, in March or April 1904, Mascagni signed a contract with the French publisher Choudens for an opera, at which point both Illica and Ricordi broke off further discussions with the composer. Even before Mascagni had signed with Choudens, Ricordi was suggesting to Illica that he sound out Puccini again about Marie Antoinette; see Ricordi to Illica of March 4, 1904 in Gara, *Carteggi pucciniani*, 266. The detailed story of Illica, Mascagni, and Marie Antoinette is recounted by Mario Morini in "*Iris* e I progetti non realizzatti," in *Pietro Mascagni: Contributi alla conoscenza della sua opera nel 1° centenario della nascita* (Livorno: Comitato onoranze, 1963), esp. 259–315.

38. Puccini to Illica, December 9, 1905, in Gara, *Carteggi pucciniani*, 307.

39. One of the subjects D'Annunzio unsuccessfully proposed to Puccini ultimately became Mascagni's *Parisina*.

40. Illica was charged with adapting a French libretto prepared under Louÿs' supervision by Maurice Vaucaire. Vaucaire's libretto, translated into Italian by Carlo Zangarini, was set by Riccardo Zandonai; baptized *Conchita*, it appeared in Milan in 1911, that composer's first important success. More recently, Louÿs' novel was the basis for Buñuel's famous movie, *That Obscure Object of Desire*.

41. Puccini to Illica, May 2, 1907, in Gara, *Carteggi pucciniani*, 344.

42. Puccini to Illica, September 17, 1907, in ibid., 354.

43. Illica to Puccini, September 1907 (undated), in ibid., 354–55.

44. Illica to Ricordi (quoting his response to Puccini), October 1907, in ibid., 357.

45. Marco Enrico Bossi (1861–1925) was a prominent composer and organist, and at the time, director of the Bologna Conservatory. He was principally a composer of choral, organ, and chamber music, who only rarely dabbled in opera.

46. Letter to Anna Lolli, December 20, 1919, in Morini et al., eds., *Pietro Mascagni: Epistolario*, 2:70.

47. One might argue that this is a distinctively American attitude, attributable at least in part to the long-standing practice in the United States — unusual elsewhere until recently — of singing opera in the original language, rather than in English translation.

48. These practices, in any event, were limited to arias, which traditionally were designed not to further dramatic action, but to depict a state of mind or two contrasting emotions. The words of the recitatives were certainly meant to be clearly understood by the audience.

49. Carl Dahlhaus, "The Dramaturgy of Italian Opera," in Lorenzo Bianconi and Giorgio Pestelli, eds., *Opera in Theory and Practice, Image and Myth* (Chicago: University of Chicago Press, 2003), 86.

50. A 1909 opera by Montemezzi, to a libretto by Illica based loosely on Benjamin Constant's novel *Adolphe*.

51. Letter, July 16, 1897, in Ferraresi, "Alberto Franchetti," 225.

52. Undated letter, in Ibid. *Fior d'Alpe* and *Il signor de Pourceaugnac* were the two operas written by Franchetti after *Colombo*, appearing in 1894 and 1897 respectively. Both were unsuccessful.

53. "Studenti! — Udite" was one of the first arias that Caruso recorded, on April 11, 1902.

54. Stapps, historically, was the father of Friedrich Stapps, a young German who was executed by the French after a failed attempt to assassinate Napoleon. The second act includes an extended scene, including an aria followed by a *concertato*, in which Stapps presents the company with a handkerchief dipped in his (martyred) son's blood.

55. The use of *Lützow's Wilde Jagd* by Illica's characters as a patriotic hymn seems somewhat inappropriate, inasmuch as it was not written until a year after the Battle of Leipzig, which ends the opera. Although most writers have assumed, logically enough, that Franchetti was responsible for the interpolation of these musical passages, the descriptions in the libretto strongly suggest that they were Illica's idea.

56. Entry for *Germania* by r.ma. in *Dizionario dell'Opera*; www.delteatro.it/hdoc/diz2home.asp (accessed December 5, 2005).

57. Julian Budden, "Wagnerian Tendencies in Italian Opera," in Nigel Fortune, ed., *Music and Theatre: Essays in Honor of Winton Dean* (Cambridge: Cambridge University Press, 1987), 316.

58. *Roland* is further discussed in chapter 11.

11. *The* giovane scuola *Grows Older (pages 247–273)*

1. Quoted in Danilo Prefumo, liner notes to Umberto Giordano, *Mese Mariano* and *Il re*, Dynamic CDS 231/1.

2. Rubboli, *Ridi Pagliaccio*, 101.

3. Quoted in Josef-Horst Lederer, "'Er Scheiterte an einem Beginnen, das sein Ehrgeiz ihn nicht hatte ausschlagen lassen'—Zur Zeitkritik an R. Leoncavallos historischem Drama *Der Roland von Berlin*," in Lorenza Guiot and Jürgen Maehder, eds., *Nazionalismo e cosmopolitismo nell'opera fra '800 e '900: Atti del 3° convegno internazionale "Ruggero Leoncavallo nel suo tempo"* (Milan: Casa Musical Sonzogno di Piero Ostali, 1998), 181.

4. The opera, tentatively entitled *Pazzariello* and set in Naples, was both an attempt to recapture the glory of his earlier days as well as an attempt to elicit 50,000 lire from an American impresario. See Remo Giazotto, "Uno sconosciuto progretto teatrale di Ruggero Leoncavallo," *Nuova Rivista Musicale Italiana* 2 (1968): 1162–1169.

5. In 1442 Berlin, the weaver Henning defends the interests of the people against the depredations of the wicked Grand Council. In the end, matters are set to rights by the Elector, who takes the part of the people against the arrogant nobility, but Henning is killed by mistake at the moment of his victory. The title draws a somewhat ironic parallel between the story of Henning and that of the hero of the *Chanson de Roland*. The opera is an adaptation of a "patriotic novel" (*vaterländische Roman*) by Willibad Alexis, pen name of Wilhelm Häring, a popular mid-nineteenth-century Prussian writer. The kaiser commissioned an Italian translation of the work, from which Leoncavallo created an Italian-language libretto, which was then translated into German by Georg Dröscher. See Jean-Jacques Velly, "Quelques aspects du traitement orchestral dans *Le Roland de Berlin*," in Lorenza Guiot and Jürgen Maehder, eds., *Letteratura, musica e teatro al tempo di Ruggero Leoncavallo: Atti del 2° convegno internazionale di studi su Ruggero Leoncavallo* (Milan: Casa Musicale Sonzogno, 1995), 167–74.

6. The libretto, by Enrico Cavacchioli and Guglielmo Emanuel, is based on a poem by Pushkin, which was translated by Prosper Merimée into French and was an important influence on Merimée's *Carmen*, the source for Bizet's opera. Radu, a young nobleman, is in love with the Gypsy girl Fleana. He abandons his old life to join the Gypsy band, angering Tamar, a Gypsy who also loves Fleana. A year later, Fleana's love for Radu has cooled, and she has left him for Tamar, who has become the leader of the band. When the maddened Radu sees Tamar and Fleana go into Tamar's cabin, he bars the door and sets fire to the cabin. As the other Gypsies pursue him, he runs off, laughing hysterically, as the fire rages.

7. Described in Rubboli, *Ridi Pagliaccio*, 175–76.

8. Quoted in Matteo Sansone, "Patriottismo in musica: il *Mameli* di Leoncavallo," in Guiot and Maehder, eds., *Nazionalismo e cosmopolitismo*, 101.

9. In ibid., 102. The two women were his wife and his adopted daughter.

10. The term "Italic" was widely used in nationalistic and patriotic contexts at

the time to suggest a sort of primordial or tribal "Italianity," as distinguished from the more prosaic, and perhaps compromised term "Italian."

11. Notably *Chatterton* and *Roland*; see Sansone, "Patriottismo in musica," 110–11. The first act of the opera depicts Mameli's decision to go to Rome and join Garibaldi to defend the republic, while the second depicts his heroic death in defense of the republic against the French army.

12. In ibid., 105.

13. Both of these operas have some merit, judging from a reading of the vocal scores. *Fior d'Alpe*, in particular, although hampered by a libretto that offers an unconvincing blend of adventure and sentimentality, has a melodic freshness and vitality that, in my opinion, is far superior to that of the better-known *Germania*.

14. *La figlia di Jorio* is set among shepherds and peasants in the Abruzzi mountains. Aligi, son of Lazaro di Rolo, abandons his fiancée and his family to live with Mila di Codro, a temptress believed to be a witch. When his father attempts to rape Mila, Aligi kills him. Condemned to death, he is saved when Mila testifies that she bewitched him and forced him to commit the crime. Mila is condemned, and is burned at the stake.

15. S. Cellucci Marcone, *D'Annunzio e la musica* (L'Aquila: Japadre, 1972), 40. According to Franchetti's account, the Greek opera was to be a treatment of *Antigone* being prepared for him by Fontana. It is not clear whether his father's reaction was to the Greek subject itself, or to the idea of his son setting yet another Fontana libretto.

16. This and other descriptions of Franchetti's personal vicissitudes are based, except where otherwise noted, on Ferraresi, "Alberto Franchetti."

17. Elise Lathrop "Alberto Franchetti," *The Musician* 10 (January 1905).

18. Tom Antongini, *Vita segreta di Gabriele D'Annunzio* (Milan: Mondadori, 1958), 481.

19. Rubens Tedeschi, *D'Annunzio e la musica* (Scandicci: La Nuova Italia Editrice, 1988), 42.

20. See Jürgen Maehder, "The Origins of Italian *Literaturoper*," in Arthur Groos and Roger Parker, eds., *Reading Opera* (Princeton, NJ: Princeton University Press, 1988), 110–11.

21. Ibid., 43.

22. Cellucci Marcone, *D'Annunzio e la musica*, 54.

23. Giorgio Graziosi, "Alberto Franchetti," *Enciclopedia dello spettacolo* (Rome: Casa Editrice Le Maschere, 1958), 5:593.

24. Luciano Tomelleri, "Gabriele D'Annunzio e i musicisti," *Rivista Musicale Italiana* 43: 2 (1939): 198.

25. According to his letters (quoted in Ferraresi, "Alberto Franchetti"), it was based on a novel by a French woman author, otherwise not identified. I have been unable to identify it further.

26. See Ferraresi, "Alberto Franchetti," 227–29.

27. Both *Notte di leggenda* and *Glauco* contain much beautiful music. *Notte di*

leggenda, in particular, a taut one-act opera of sexual jealousy and murder set in a Tuscan castle early in the seventeenth century on a winter night, might well be worthy of revival.

28. Ferraresi, "Alberto Franchetti," 216. Ferraresi also quotes Franchetti's daughter Elena, who described how her father had been well known years earlier in Florence for his habit of "spending entire afternoons in a bordello taking pictures, something known throughout the city by his automobile (one of the few at the time) parked in front of the building."

29. Ibid., 231.

30. Ardengo Soffici, "Fogli di diario," *Corriere della sera* (August 3, 1955). Soffici was a prominent painter who acted at times as a cultural adviser to Mussolini.

31. Letter of November 10, 1941.

32. Cilèa, *Ricordi*, in Ferraro et al., eds., *Francesco Cilèa*, 143.

33. Quoted in Ferraro, et al., eds., *Francesco Cilèa*, 44.

34. The vicissitudes of the violets are an example of the complexity of the play's intrigues. In the first act, Adriana gives them to Maurice; in the second act, he gives them to the Princess, in order to deflect her questions. When Adriana receives them — already withered — in the fourth act, she believes that Maurice has sent them as a symbol that he no longer loves her. He returns, however, and pledges his love to her, as she dies in his arms.

35. Barrymore Laurence Scherer, "The Case for *Adriana*," *Opera News* (March 19, 1994) 11.

36. The rapid fashion in which *Adriana* disappeared from the stage during the decade after its debut is quite remarkable, as shown by the following year-by-year tally of productions, as reported in "Cronologie delle opere" in Ferraro et al., eds., *Francesco Cilèa*, 558–62:

1903	25	1907	5	1911	1
1904	10	1908	0	1912	0
1905	8	1909	2	1913	0
1906	5	1910	3	1914	0

37. Gianandrea Gavazzeni, *Scena e retroscena*; quoted in Ferraro et al., eds., *Francesco Cilèa*, 80.

38. Quoted in ibid., 80.

39. Cilèa, *Ricordi*, in ibid., 153.

40. Lionetto, who has been banished from Siena, returns during a truce to see his beloved Gloria, daughter of his enemy Aquilante. When her father refuses to allow him to marry her, he and his followers abduct her and take her to his camp. Gloria's brother Bardo infiltrates the camp, tells Gloria that Lionetto's men have killed their father, and convinces her to avenge his death by killing Lionetto with a vial of poison he gives her. When Lionetto tells Gloria that he has made peace with the Sienese, she agrees to marry him. At the wedding, Bardo stabs Lionetto. Alone and locked in the chapel, he dies in Gloria's arms. She takes the poison, and dies on Lionetto's body.

41. Quoted in Morini et al., eds., *Casa Musicale Sonzogno*, 2:110.

42. At Ostali's request, Cilèa made extensive changes to *Gloria* in 1932, including substantial cuts, in the hope of improving the opera's chances.

43. Cilèa, *Ricordi,* in Ferraro et al., eds., *Francesco Cilèa*, 159. Simoni (1875–1952) was a distinguished critic and playwright, who was for many years drama critic of the *Corriere della sera,* and replaced Giacosa as editor of the Milan literary magazine *La Lettura.* He subsequently wrote the libretto for Giordano's *Madame Sans-Gêne* (1915), and collaborated on the libretto for Puccini's *Turandot.*

44. Quoted in Ferraro et al., eds., Francesco Cilèa, 80.

45. Quoted in ibid., 76.

46. Leonida Rèpaci, *Francesco Cilèa;* quoted in ibid., 77.

47. This description appears in a note appended to his reminiscences dated 1947; in ibid., 193.

48. Quoted in ibid., 75.

49. Belasco account quoted in Carner, *Puccini,* 135.

50. Exotic settings were even more common among French operas, ever since operas such as David's *Lalla Roukh* and Meyerbeer's *L'Africaine* appeared in the 1860s. In addition to Mascagni's opera, Japanese settings were not unusual, including Saint-Saëns' *La Princesse jaune* and André Messager's *Madame Chrysanthème,* based on the Pierre Loti novel that was the ultimate starting point for Belasco's play. See Girardi, *Puccini,* 207–9.

51. Ibid., 225.

52. Ibid.

53. Ashbrook, *Operas of Puccini,* 108.

54. Gatti-Casazza, *Memories of the Opera,* 134.

55. Carner, Puccini, 149.

56. In 1904 Sonzogno had little in the way of potentially profitable new operas in the pipeline. He was estranged from Mascagni, while Leoncavallo was occupied with *Rolando,* which the astute Sonzogno undoubtedly realized had little commercial potential. While Giordano's 1903 *Siberia* was a success, his next opera, the 1907 *Marcella* was a commercial failure, as was Cilèa's 1907 *Gloria.*

57. *Butterfly* never appeared again at La Scala during the composer's lifetime.

58. Letter of February 29, 1904, in Gara, *Carteggi pucciniani,* 265.

59. Soldani (1873–1935), from the island of Elba, was a novelist and playwright, who by 1904 had developed a solid although unspectacular reputation as an author of substantial historic tragedies, most notably *I Ciompi* and *Calendimaggio* (May Day).

60. Letter of June 28, 1904, in Gara, *Carteggi pucciniani,* 277.

61. Letter of January 9, 1906, in ibid., 313. The priest-composer Licinio Refice (1883–1954) composed a *Margherita da Cortona,* which made a successful debut in 1938, and was performed intermittently into the 1960s. The libretto, however, is not by Soldani.

62. Letter of May (date uncertain) 1905, in ibid., 294.

63. See Tedeschi, *D'Annunzio*, 38–39.

64. Letter of May 15, 1900, in Gara, *Carteggi pucciniani*, 196.

65. Letter of August 16, 1906, in ibid., 328.

66. Later to become a 1917 opera by Alexander von Zemlinsky.

67. Louÿs' novel, although never becoming a Puccini opera, has been the basis for at least four movies, including a silent version, Von Sternberg's 1935 *The Devil is a Woman* with Marlene Dietrich, a 1958 version with Brigitte Bardot, and Buñuel's 1977 *That Obscure Object of Desire*.

68. Quoted in Budden, *Puccini*, 286.

69. The libretto that Ricordi had commissioned was ultimately used by the younger composer Riccardo Zandonai for his 1911 opera *Conchita*.

70. Letter of April 11, 1907, in Gara, *Carteggi pucciniani*, 343. Piero Aretino (1492–1556) was a Renaissance writer and satirist, whose coarseness and porno-graphic writings were known, if not widely, at the time.

71. The circumstances of the composition of *La fanciulla del West*, as well as an extensive discussion of the opera's themes and reception, will be found in Annie J. Randall and Rosalind Gray Davis, *Puccini and The Girl* (Chicago: University of Chicago Press, 2005).

72. Letter of February 18, 1907, in Gara, *Carteggi pucciniani*, 340.

73. Belasco's play, moreover, was very much part of a genre of Western melo-drama that had existed since the mid-nineteenth century, and been popularized by the works of Bret Harte in the 1870s; see James H. McGuire, "Western American Drama to 1960," in Thomas J. Lyon, ed. *A Literary History of the American West* (Fort Worth: Texas Christian University Press, 1998).

74. The Italian audience was not completely ignorant of the American West, as a result of the travels of Buffalo Bill's Wild West show and Italian translations of the Wild West novels of the German author Karl May. Puccini attended the Wild West show in Milan in 1890, of which he wrote his brother, "[they] reproduce re-alistically scenes that happen on the frontier," adding "in eleven days, they've taken in 120 thousand lire!" (Gara, *Carteggi pucciniani*, 38).

75. The extent to which the important theme of redemption through love in *Fanciulla* reflects a Wagnerian perspective, or is largely an echo of the Victorian cliché of the redemption of a bad man through a good woman's love, is a matter of disagreement. Clearly, Puccini saw redemption as the central theme of the work, a perspective that led to the most significant change between the original play and the libretto, the climactic scene in which Minnie saves Ramerrez' life at the end of the third act. This question is discussed in Randall and Davis, *Puccini and The Girl*, 148–56.

76. Carner, *Puccini*, 305.

77. While this might be seen as a relatively uncommon outcome for a late-nineteenth-century opera, it actually reflects a far older—and in its time equally hackneyed—dramatic motif, that of the rescue opera so popular at the beginning of the nineteenth century, immortalized by Beethoven's *Fidelio*.

78. See, for example, the letters of Josephine von Stangl cited in Giorgio Magri, *L'uomo Puccini* (Milan: Mursia, 1992), 200–201.

79. Budden, *Puccini*, 275–76.

80. Ibid.

81. Quoted in Ibid., 276.

82. Puccini wrote her more than seven hundred letters between 1904 and 1924. Their friendship is described in detail in her son, Vincent Seligman, in *Puccini Among Friends* (New York: Macmillan, 1938), based largely on their correspondence.

83. The most intense crisis of this period was what is known as the Doria Manfredi affair. Manfredi, a domestic servant in the Puccini household, was accused by Elvira of having an affair with her husband and reviled by Elvira in front of her family and in public. With his home in turmoil, Puccini fled to Rome, while in his absence, Manfredi committed suicide. After an autopsy had established that Manfredi died a virgin, her family filed suit against Elvira early in 1909 for defamation of character. The resulting scandal, in Carner's words, "caused an unprecedented sensation in Italy" (*Puccini*, 199).

84. See Randall and Davis, *Puccini and The Girl*, 55–56.

85. Budden, *Puccini*, 330.

86. Wallace Brockway and Herbert Weinstock, *The World of Opera* (New York: Random House, 1966), 329.

87. Girardi, *Puccini*, 327.

12. *Comic Opera (pages 274–293)*

1. Venturi, *L'opera lirica a Livorno*, 187.

2. "Rivista Milanese," *Gazzetta musicale di Milano* (February 21, 1901): 117.

3. "Rassegna musicale," *Nuova antologia* 160 (1898): 349.

4. *L'illustrazione italiana* (March 31, 1895): 203.

5. A 1762 comedy, roughly translated as *The Brawls at Chioggia*, Chioggia being a small fishing village just south of Venice, known in the eighteenth century as Chiozza. It was later adapted by Gian Francesco Malipiero into one act of his opera *Tre commedie goldoniane* (1924).

6. *Basi e bote* was written in Venetian dialect in 1881 by Boito, using the stock characters of the commedia dell'arte. The work appears to have been written more as a libretto for musical setting than as a play for theatrical performance, but it is unclear whether he wrote the work for himself or for another composer. It was not used as a libretto until 1927, when it was set by Riccardo Pick-Mangiagalli and successfully performed at Rome's Teatro Argentina. It is not known whether Mascagni chose not to pursue this libretto of his own accord, for whatever reason, or whether Boito refused to make it available.

7. Luigi Illica in *L'Alba* (January 17, 1901); cited in Mario Morini, "*Le Maschere*: una nuova dimensione dell'arte mascagnana," program notes for 1988 Bologna production, 24–26.

8. While Mascagni's preexisting 1894 contract with Sonzogno contained an exception for *Iris*, which the composer was writing for Ricordi, Mascagni was committed by that contract to write two more operas for Sonzogno, the first of which was to be delivered by the end of 1897, after the completion of *Iris*. The comic opera that Mascagni was to write with Illica was to be the first of the two; needless to say, with no more than a germ of the idea at hand by the fall of 1896, no one could have been under any illusion that the opera would be completed by the end of 1897. The fact, however, that Mascagni was simultaneously writing an opera for Ricordi was a source of considerable resentment for Sonzogno, who worked hard to make the composer's project for his rival as difficult as possible.

9. Vernon Lee, *Studies of the Eighteenth Century in Italy*, 363.

10. Ibid., 371.

11. Quoted in Pompei, *Mascagni*, 308–9.

12. Ibid., 308.

13. A. Perrucci, *Dell'arte rappresentativa, premeditata ed all'improvviso*; reproduced in E. Petraccone, ed. *La commedia dell'arte* (Naples: Riccardo Ricciardi Editore, 1927), 193.

14. The scene also permits byplay between Giocadio and the conductor, as was the case in the 1988 Bologna production.

15. In a letter to Illica shortly before the first performance, Mascagni wrote, "Don't even talk to me about having the Prologue in costume. It is necessary that the artists be in street clothes in the Prologue. God help them if they are already dressed as masks — goodbye, the effect of the overture" letter of December 17, 1900, in Morini et al., eds., *Pietro Mascagni: Epistolario*, 1:234.

16. Alberto Paloscia, notes to Kicco recording of *Le Maschere*, at www.kiccomusic.com/dischi/0082-maschere.html (accessed April 11, 2006).

17. A furlana (or forlana) is a fast-moving Venetian dance in 6/8 meter, not unlike a tarantella.

18. Pompei, *Mascagni*, 312.

19. In the course of my work on *Pietro Mascagni and His Operas*, I made considerable efforts to find documentation of this episode. I was unsuccessful, largely as a result of the destruction of the Sonzogno archives during World War II. While many contemporary newspaper accounts tended to attribute it to Mascagni's purported megalomaniac streak, this is unlikely. At the time, Sonzogno was intensely resentful of Ricordi's success with Mascagni's *Iris*, and could easily have wanted to outdo his rival by orchestrating a publicity coup around the composer's new opera.

20. Morini et al., eds., *Pietro Mascagni, Epistolario*, 1:229. Ricordi, of course, at that time was hoping to wrest Mascagni from Sonzogno, and have another opera from the composer to follow *Iris*.

21. Giovanni Pozza, in *Corriere della sera* (January 18–19, 1901).

22. Ibid.

23. *Il Trovatore* (January 19, 1901), 2.

24. "Mascagni, Pietro" in *New Grove Dictionary of Music and Musicians*, 11:743.

25. "Rassegna musicale," *Nuova antologia* (February 1, 1901): 552.

26. Carlo Nasi, in *Gazzetta musicale di Milano* (January 24, 1901): 63.

27. See Alfredo Jeri, *Mascagni* (Milan: Garzanti, 1940), 120. This story appears as fact in the issue of Il Trovatore cited above, in which it is featured prominently.

28. *Il Trovatore* (January 19, 1901): 2.

29. Rosaura, daughter of Pantalone, is in love with Florindo, but her miserly father plans to marry her to Captain Spavento. Trying to prevent the wedding, Brighella obtains a magic powder that, mixed with the wine at the ceremony, makes the entire company babble incomprehensibly, so that it is impossible to sign the contract. In the last act, after the powder's effects have worn off, and the lovers are at their wits' end, Doctor Graziano appears with papers proving that the Captain is a swindler and bigamist. Pantalone reluctantly allows his daughter to marry Florindo, and all ends happily.

30. Mallach, *Pietro Mascagni and His Operas*, 142.

31. Gianandrea Gavazzeni, "La musica di Mascagni oggi," in Morini, ed., *Pietro Mascagni*, 1:29.

32. Giulio Cogni, "Ermanno Wolf-Ferrari uomo," biographical introduction to E. Wolf-Ferrari, *Considerazioni attuali sulla musica* (Siena: Ticci Editore libraio, 1935); accessed April 13, 2006, from www.rodoni.ch/busoni/wolfbusoni/cogni.html.

33. The composer adopted the name Wolf-Ferrari at nineteen, when his first composition, a Serenade for strings, was accepted for publication, and he was eager to distinguish himself from the many Wolfs already present in the musical world and, perhaps, as well, to acknowledge his multicultural roots. Raffaello de Rensis, *Ermanno Wolf-Ferrari: La sua vita d'artista* (Milan: Fratelli Treves Editore, 1937), 18–19. This book, cited frequently in this section, is based on a long series of interviews that its author held with Wolf-Ferrari in the fall of 1935, and much of it reads like a paraphrase of the composer's own words; at a minimum, it accurately reflects the older composer's recollection of his earlier life and artistic thought.

34. Ibid., 3–5.

35. Ibid., 49.

36. Guido Piamonte, "Ermanno Wolf-Ferrari e *I quattro rusteghi*" (notes to Fonit-Cetra recording of the opera). The origin of this citation is not entirely clear. Piamonte refers to a conversation between the composer and a friend. The same point, although in a much shorter version, appears in de Rensis, *Ermanno Wolf-Ferrari*, 63. I have been unable to find an earlier direct citation for this important episode.

37. de Rensis, *Ermanno Wolf-Ferrari*, 63.

38. Wolf-Ferrari was a prolific composer throughout his life, but never more so than during the decade following the completion of his studies at Munich, during which period he wrote, in addition to the two major operas described here, at least

426   *Notes*

six major chamber works including the Sinfonia da Camera, three oratorios, and dozens of short piano pieces, songs, and choral settings.

39. Lee, *Studies of the Eighteenth Century in Italy*, 398.

40. de Rensis, *Ermanno Wolf-Ferrari*, 65–66.

41. *Le donne curiose* is based on an early Goldoni work, in which masked commedia dell'arte characters such as Pantalone and Arlecchino interact with more realistic, unmasked figures. A group of Venetian burghers have established a club where they gather, and from which women are excluded. Their wives and fiancées are convinced that they are up to no good, and through various schemes manage to gain entrance to the club. At the end, the women realize that the men's activities were harmless, the men reconcile themselves to their wives' desire to know what they are up to, and all ends happily.

42. de Rensis, *Ermano Wolf-Ferrari*, 67.

43. The plot is a complex one, set during Carnival, and focusing on the stratagems adopted by Filberto to meet his intended Lucieta, and her efforts to convince her father to allow her to participate in the Carnival. Needless to say, it all ends happily. When performed in the United States and Great Britain, it has appeared under the title *The School for Fathers*.

44. Giorgio Vigolo, "Gusto e grazia di Wolf-Ferrari nei *quattro rusteghi*" (1958); accessed from www.rodoni.ch/busoni/wolfbusoni/vigolo2.html, April 9, 2006.

45. Quoted in Frajese, *Dal Costanzi all'Opera*, 2:58.

46. Quoted in the *Simon & Schuster Book of the Opera* (New York: Simon & Schuster, 1985), 350.

47. The opera takes place on the night of the festival of the Madonna. Gennaro, a poor blacksmith, yearns for the love of Maliella, a wild young woman who has been brought up in his household and thinks of him as her brother. Maliella is courted by Rafaele, leader of the local Camorra band, and declares her love for him. The jealous Gennaro confesses his love, and she taunts him, daring him to steal the Madonna's jewels for her. Desperate, he does so; on his return, entranced by the jewels, she yields to his passionate embraces. In the third act, she arrives at the lair of the Camorra, but when Rafaele learns she has given herself to Gennaro, he rejects her. When she displays the jewels, he curses her, and she runs off to drown herself in the sea. Gennaro arrives, and the Camorristas flee in horror. As a vengeful crowd gathers outside, Gennaro lays the jewels at the foot of the statute of the Madonna and stabs himself.

48. See www.dutchdivas.net/tenors/morrisson.html (accessed April 9, 2006).

49. *Corriere della sera* (June 3, 1914).

50. Morini et al., eds., *Casa Musicale Sonzogno*, 2:848–55.

51. Cogni, "Ermanno Wolf-Ferrari" (see note 32, this chapter).

52. Roberto Zanetti, *La Musica italiana nel novecento* (Busto Arsizio: Bramante Editore, 1985), 1:76.

53. Girardi, *Puccini*, 415.

54. *Inferno*, canto 30, lines 31–33.

13. *Gabriele D'Annunzio and the New Generation (pages 294–310)*

1. Martin Clark, *Modern Italy, 1871–1982*, 136.
2. Giolitti has generally received a bad press from historians. This treatment is arguably unfair, and appears to be largely colored by the fact that his years were followed first, by the debacle of the First World War, and second, by the even greater debacle of Fascism, both of which he seems at times to be blamed for having failed to prevent.
3. Giorgio Candeloro, *Storia dell'Italia moderna* (Milan: Feltrinelli, 1974), 7:94.
4. Clark, *Modern Italy, 1871–1982*, 173.
5. Benedetto Croce, *A History of Italy, 1871–1915* (New York: Russell & Russell, 1963), 237–38.
6. Clark, *Modern Italy, 1871–1982*, 173.
7. Ottorino Respighi (1879–1936) could also reasonably be considered part of this group of composers, although his name is occasionally added to the roster of the *generazione dell'ottanta*. Although an important composer, he did not play a significant role in Italy's operatic world until the 1920s. Even then, his operas, although not insubstantial, were generally considered to be a secondary part of his musical activity, in contrast to the other composers mentioned, for whom opera was the central theme of their musical life.
8. *Gazzetta del Popolo* (February 20, 1914); quoted in Konrad Claude Dryden, *Riccardo Zandonai: A Biography* (Frankfurt am Main: Peter Lang, 1999), 153.
9. Montmezzi's Symphony in E Minor was rediscovered in 2001 and subsequently recorded under the auspices of the town of Vigasio, the composer's birthplace south of Verona. It can be downloaded from www.comune.vigasio.vr.it/conoscere/montemezzi.asp.
10. Piero Santi, "La generazione di Zandonai," in Renato Chiesa, ed., *Atti del convegno di studi sulla figura e l'opera di Riccardo Zandonai* (Milan: Edizioni UNICOPLI, 1984), 106.
11. Giordano's opera *Siberia*, which bears many similarities to *Risurrezione*, made its debut at La Scala eleven months earlier, in December 1903. It is hard to imagine, however, that Alfano had heard any of it before he composed his opera.
12. John C. G. Waterhouse, "Da *Risurrezione* a *La leggenda di Sakùntala*" in Johannes Streicher, ed., *Ultimi Splendori: Cilèa, Giordano, Alfano* (Rome: ISMEZ Editore, 1999), 534.
13. Alfredo Della Corte, *Ritratto di Franco Alfano* (Turin: Paravia, 1935), 50.
14. Santi, "La generazione di Zandonai," 114.
15. Considering how obscure this topic may appear to the Anglophone reader, there is an extraordinarily extensive Italian literature specifically on D'Annunzio and his relationship to music and to the musical life of his time, including S. Cellucci Marcone, *D'Annunzio e la musica* (L'Aquila: Japadre, 1972); Rubens Tedeschi, *D'Annunzio e la musica* (Scandicci: La Nuova Italia, 1988); Adriana Guarnieri Corazzol, *Sensualità senza carne: La musica nella vita e nell'opera di D'Annunzio,*

(Bologna: Il mulino, 1990); Giovanni Gelati, *Il vate e il capobanda* (Livorno,: Belforte, 1992) (dealing entirely with D'Annunzio's relationship with Mascagni); Carlo Santoli, *Gabriele D'Annunzio: la musica e i musicisti* (Roma: Bulzoni Editore, 1997); Giovanni Cancan, *Impressioni musicali in Gabriele D'Annunzio* (Perugia: Guerra, 1997); and Adriano Bassi, *Caro Maestro (D'Annunzi e i musicisti)* (Genova: De Ferrari Editore, 1997). In addition, in 1939, Italy's principal scholarly journal in music, *Rivista Musicale Italiana*, devoted a special issue to D'Annunzio and Italian music (43, no. 2), as did in large part the *Quaderni del Vittoriale*, nos. 34–35 (1982). An international conference on D'Annunzio and music took place in 1988, the proceedings of which were edited by Bassi and Elena Ledda and published under the title *D'Annunzio e la musica* (Salo: Centro Cultural Rosetum, 1989). An article on the subject in English, "Gabriele D'Annunzio and the Italian Opera Composers," by Guido M. Gatti appeared in *Musical Quarterly* (April 1924): 263–88.

16. See Tedeschi, *D'Annunzio e la musica*, 7–23, including a letter suggesting that D'Annunzio's score-reading skills were at best rudimentary.

17. He was seated, but had a short and equivocal parliamentary career. Elected as a delegate of the Right, in a famous gesture he dramatically changed allegiances in mid-1900, crossing the hall to join the Socialists with the statement "as a man of intellect, I go from death to life." In the ensuing general election, however, he was defeated.

18. John Woodhouse, *Gabriele D'Annunzio: Defiant Archangel* (Oxford: Clarendon Press, 1998), 29.

19. *The Flame of Life* (English translation of *Il fuoco*) (New York: Modern Library, 1900), 126.

20. Quoted in Tedeschi, *D'Annunzio e la musica*, 9.

21. *The Triumph of Death* (English translation by Arthur Hornblow) (New York: Modern Library, n.d.), 36.

22. See Adriana Guarnieri Corazzol, *Tristano, mio Tristano: Gli scrittori italiani e il caso Wagner* (Bologna: Il Mulino, 1988), 11–12.

23. Quoted in ibid., 18. The author of these lines is Arturo Colautti, who was part of D'Annunzio's circle in Naples during those years, and who in the following years would develop a name as a librettist for Cilèa and Giordano. The phrase "the torture of the philtre" is a reference to Tristan's monologue in act 3, scene 1, which is described in *The Triumph of Death*, 375.

24. *The Triumph of Death*, 363.

25. Ibid., 379. D'Annunzio devotes fifteen pages to a detailed retelling of the story of Wagner's *Tristan und Isolde*, much of it apparently paraphrased from a French essay on the opera by Nerthal; see Tedeschi, *D'Annunzio e la musica*, 18.

26. Guarnieri Corazzol, *Sensualità senza carne*, 23.

27. Gioacchino Laza Tommasi, "Il gusto musicale di D'Annunzio e il dannunzianesimo musicale," in Fiamma Nicolodi, ed., *Musica italiana del primo novecento: la generazione dell'80* (Florence: Leo S. Olschki Editore, 1981), 397.

28. *The Flame of Life*, 201.

29. Ibid., 121.

30. Ibid., 203.

31. Ibid., 403.

32. During the decade following 1900 he would also write the greater part of his *Laudi*, a series of large-scale poetic cycles that many critics consider to be his only works of lasting literary merit.

33. Although *Parisina* was written as an operatic libretto rather than as a play to be staged on its own, it is not significantly different in style or manner from D'Annunzio's other plays; indeed, it was staged on a number of occasions in the 1920s without Mascagni's music, much to the composer's dismay.

34. Interview from 1899; quoted in Marion S. Miller, "Wagnerism, Wagnerians and Italian Identity," in David C. Large and William Weber, eds., *Wagnerism in European Culture and Politics* (Ithaca NY: Cornell University Press, 1984), 181.

35. Dryden, *Riccardo Zandonai*, 64.

36. Quoted in Edoardo Pompei, *Pietro Mascagni*, 350.

37. The story of *Amica* focuses on the rivalry of two brothers for Amica, who is promised to one but who loves the other. In the end, the brother she loves rejects her out of solidarity with his brother; rushing after him, Amica falls to her death from a mountain pass. The basic situation is strong but not unfamiliar, from the classic Schiller play *The Bride of Messina* to the twentieth-century story "The Intruder" by Borges. Echoes of Wagner appear elsewhere in the opera, including an important motif standing for the mountains and the freedom they represent that is clearly derived from the theme of the Valkyries in *Die Walküre*.

38. Guido M. Gatti, "Gabriele D'Annunzio and the Italian Opera Composers," 267. Gatti (1892–1973), who was a prominent advocate of new music in Italy for well more than half a century, also suggests that this change reflects a change in public tastes, reflecting in turn the higher level of education of the public by the early years of the twentieth century.

39. Fausto Torrefranca, *Giacomo Puccini e l'opera internazionale* (Turin: Fratelli Bocca, 1912), vii.

40. He commissioned the music from Antonio Scontrino (1850–1922), a Sicilian-born composer who taught at the Florence Conservatory, and had a modest reputation at the time, including a favorable mention by Bastianelli; see Santoli, *Gabriele D'Annunzio*, 69.

41. Giovanni Isgrò, *D'Annunzio e la "mise en scène"* (Palermo: Palumbo, 1993), 90; quoted in Santoli, *Gabriele D'Annunzio*, 68.

42. These two works, both products of D'Annunzio's Parisian "exile" beginning in 1910, were *Le martyre de Saint Sébastien*, with music by Claude Debussy (1911), and *La Pisanelle*, with music by Pizzetti (1913). The last was an adaptation by D'Annunzio of *La rosa di Cipro*, in which he had tried to interest Puccini a few years earlier.

43. Antonio Costa, "Dante, D'Annunzio, Pirandello," in Renzo Renzi, ed., *Sper-*

duto nel buio: il cinema muto italiano e il suo tempo (1905–1930) (Bologna: Cappelli Editore, 1991), 62.

44. Neither the play nor this opera have any relationship to Korngold's *Die Tote Stadt*, which is an operatic treatment of the novel *Bruges la mort* by the Belgian writer Rodenbach. The opera survived in a piano-vocal score, and was orchestrated and given its first performance in 2005.

45. Gatti, "Gabriele D'Annunzio," 287.

46. This characterization may be unfair; it can be argued that the element of self-parody in D'Annunzio, particularly in his later works, is so pervasive that it is impossible for his work to be parodied by others.

14. Tristan's *Children (pages 311–336)*

1. Pompei, *Mascagni*, 371.

2. Among other works, he wrote *Medioevo latino*, a tryptich of three one-act operas, for the Argentine conductor and composer Ettore Panizza (1875–1967), which made its debut in 1900.

3. Many of Maeterlinck's plays pursue the nexus of sensuality and spirituality that lies at the heart of *Isabeau*, including *Monna Vanna, Soeur Béatrice*, and *La princesse Maleine*. Although Illica may not have been familiar with the last, which was an early and relatively seldom performed work, there is little doubt that he would have known the first two plays mentioned above.

4. Desperate for an heir to the kingdom, King Raimondo presses his beautiful and devout daughter Isabeau to marry, mounting a "tournament of love" in which various nobles complete for her hand, watched by the falconer Folco, whom she has taken into her service. After she rejects all the suitors, the king, urged on by his evil counselor Cornelius, orders her to ride nude through the city at noon as punishment. Despite the people's edict that no one may watch her, Folco does so, strewing flowers on her as she rides by. He is arrested and cast into a dungeon. In the last act, Isabeau goes to see Folco in the dungeon, and realizes that she loves him. As she leaves to tell her father that she has chosen a husband, Cornelius incites the mob to seize and kill Folco. She returns and throws herself into the melee, dying with him.

5. The circumstances are described in Mallach, *Peitro Mascagni*, 178–82. The history of their relationship, including the more than 4,200 letters that Mascagni wrote her during those years, has been assembled in the Mascagni Museum in Bagnara di Romagna, the small village near Imola where Lolli was born.

6. Giorgio Barini, "*Isabeau* di Pietro Mascagni," *Nuova antologia* 157, no. 5 (February 1, 1912): 551.

7. Letter of December 31, 1908, in Morini, *Pietro Mascagni*, 1:344.

8. "Guido" in *L'illustrazione italiana* (January 28, 1912), 86.

9. Roger Nichols, "Debussy" in *New Grove Dictionary of Music and Musicians*, 5:297.

10. Letter to Tito Ricordi of August 1906, in Gara, *Carteggi pucciniani*, 324.

11. Morini, *Pietro Mascagni*, 1:362.

12. Letter to D'Annunzio of April 9, 1912, in Santoli, *Gabriele D'Annunzio*, 249.

13. Quoted in Morini, *Pietro Mascagni*, 1:364.

14. Mallach, *Pietro Mascagni*, 207.

15. Quoted in Armando Fraccaroli, *Celebrità e quasi* (Milan: Casa Editrice Sonzogno, 1923), 180.

16. Letter of April 25, 1912; quoted in Morini, *Pietro Mascagni*, 1:363.

17. The story of Mascagni's idyll in Bellevue from July to December 1912 is a fascinating one, treated briefly in Mallach, *Pietro Mascagni*, 201–203, and in greater length in Giovanni Gelati, *Il vate e il capobanda* (Livorno: Belforte Editore Libraio, 1992), 43–81. Mascagni's daughter Emy published a highly entertaining but wildly misleading memoir of this episode — which she shared with her father and his mistress — some years later; *S'inginocchi la più piccina* (Milan: Treves, 1936).

18. Letter of November 2, 1912, in Adrian Lualdi, "Mascagni, D'Annunzio e *Parisina*," *Quaderni Dannunziani* 30–31 (1965): 83.

19. Ibid., 85.

20. Giovanni Pozza, in *Corriere della sera* (December 16, 1913), 3.

21. Ibid.

22. The late Italian conductor Gianandrea Gavazzeni, a lifelong admirer of the opera, was responsible for bringing about the Rome performance, which included all four acts, although making discreet cuts elsewhere. His widow, the soprano Denia Mazzola Gavazzeni, sings Parisina in the Montpellier performance (which is available in recorded form), enhancing what is otherwise an undistinguished production.

23. Virgilio Bernardoni, "Puccini and the Dissolution of the Italian Tradition," in Mervyn Cooke, ed., *The Cambridge Companion to Twentieth-Century Opera* (Cambridge: Cambridge University Press, 2005), 34.

24. Giuseppe Silvestri, "La vita e le opere — Vocazione e volontà," in Luigi Tretti and Lionello Fiumi, ed., *Omaggio a Italo Montemezzi* (Verona: Comitato onoranze a Italo Montemezzi, 1952), 14.

25. The degree program at the conservatory was structured as a nine-year program, in three three-year units. Based on one's performance in the examinations, the entering student was placed at the beginning of one of the units. Montemezzi's performance on the exam placed him at the beginning of the second unit. By dint of extraordinary effort, he completed the second three-year unit by the end of his first year at the conservatory.

26. *Giovanni Gallurese* is a melodrama about the Sardinian bandit Giovanni Gallurese, who is treacherously killed by his evil Spanish rival, who lusts after the pure Maria, who loves Giovanni (although not realizing, until the end, that the man she loves is one and the same as the feared bandit Giovanni Gallurese). Despite the melodramatic plot, the character of the work is more lyrical than dra-

matic, with extended duets for Giovanni and Maria in each of the opera's three acts, as well as a number of static lyric apostrophes for Giovanni.

27. Silvestri, "La vita e le opere," 17.

28. Illica apparently tried to interest Montemezzi in his *Maria Antonietta* treatment, but had no more success with him than with Mascagni before or Puccini afterward; see Gara, *Carteggi pucciniani*, 287.

29. As far as can be determined, the subsequent performance history of *Héllera* is limited to a broadcast performance by Italian radio in 1938. A reading of the score, however, suggests that it is a beautiful work that would be well worth reviving.

30. The title is hard to translate; literally, it means "The Dinner of the Jokes," but the word "beffa" in Italian has harsh, even cruel, overtones not shared by the word "joke" in English, and is sometimes translated "mockery" or "practical joke." When Benelli's work was performed on Broadway in the 1920s, the title was rendered as *The Jest*.

31. Tommaso Montefiore (1855–1933) was better known as a writer and music critic, and left little mark as a composer. He never composed an opera based on Benelli's play, although once Giordano became interested in the subject in 1919, several years of acrimonious negotiation took place before Giordano was able to obtain the rights, by which time he had already composed the greater part of the work. Giordano's opera was first performed in 1924, with considerable success. See Morini, ed., *Umberto Giordano*, 250–52.

32. *L'amore dei tre re* was in the Met repertory almost every season through 1929, and was subsequently revived regularly, although at less frequent intervals, until the 1948–1949 season. It has not appeared at the Met since then, although it has appeared in New York, most recently in concert performances by the Teatro Grattacielo in 1997 and the Opera Orchestra of New York in 2006.

33. Santoli, *Gabriele D'Annunzio*, 162.

34. Silvestri, "La vita e le opere," 18.

35. Francis Perkins, reviewing the performance of January 7, 1941, in the *New York Herald Tribune*; from Metropolitan Opera Archives, http://66.187.153.86/archives/scripts/cgiip.exe/WService=BibSpeed/fullcit.w?xCID=1308 (accessed March 11, 2006).

36. Italo Montemezzi, "Come scrissi la musica per *La nave*," in *Scenario* (April 1938); reprinted in Santoli, *Gabriele D'Annunzio*, 159.

37. Adrian Lyttelton, *The Seizure of Power: Fascism in Italy, 1919–1929* (Princeton: Princeton University Press, 1987), 17.

38. Guido M. Gatti, "Gabriele D'Annunzio and the Italian Opera Composers," 275.

39. Santoli, *Gabriele D'Annunzio*, 159.

40. Umberto Cattini, "I poemi sinfonici di Montemezzi," in Tretti and Fiumi, eds., *Omaggio a Italo Montemezzi*, 54–55.

41. Santoli, *Gabriele D'Annunzio*, 160–161.

42. Letter to Mussolini, July 18, 1930, in Fiamma Nicolodi, *Musica e musicisti nel ventennio fascista* (Fiesole: Discanto Edizioni, 1984), 416.

43. *La nave*, piano-vocal score (Milan: Ricordi, 1919), 335.

44. Unsigned review, *Corriere della sera* (November 4, 1918). A perhaps more accurate indication of the audience's response, as noted in the review, was that there were four curtain calls after the prologue, three each after the first and second acts, but only two at the end of the opera, a lukewarm response at best.

45. Letter to Mussolini, May 7, 1935, in Nicolodi, *Musica e musicisti*, 425.

46. Letter of F. Boncompagni-Ludovisi to A. Chiavolini, June 16, 1930, in ibid., 415.

47. His entire musical production from 1918 until his death in 1952, as far as is known, consists of two short one-act operas, an extended symphonic poem entitled *Paolo e Virginia*, based on the novel by Berardin de Saint-Pierre, and the patriotic rhapsody *Italia mia* (mentioned in the text).

48. *New York Times* (February 18, 1933).

49. Vittoria Bonajuti Tarquini, *Riccardo Zandonai nel ricordo dei suoi intimi* (Milan: Ricordi, 1952), 24. Bonajuti Tarquini was Zandonai's sister-in-law.

50. Quoted in Adriano Bassi, *Riccardo Zandonai: tracce di vita* (Poggibonsi: Antonio Lalli Editore, 1982), 101.

51. Pratella, *Autobiografia*; quoted in Bruno Cagnoli, "Zandonai a Pesaro," in Renato Chiesa, ed., *Riccardo Zandonai: Atti dell convegno di studi sulla figura e l'opera di Ricardo Zandonai* (Milan: Edizioni UNICOPLI, 1984), 39.

52. *Gazzetta di Torino*; quoted in Dryden, *Riccardo Zandonai*, 67.

53. As a result of the success of *Conchita*, Ricordi agreed to take *Melenis*, which was subsequently premiered in November 1912 at the Dal Verme, with Claudia Muzio and Giovanni Martinelli. Although greeted respectfully, it was not successful, and was quietly forgotten after the success of the composer's next opera, *Francesca da Rimini*.

54. Quoted in Bonajuti Tarquini, *Riccardo Zandonai*, 66.

55. *Daily News and Leader* (London); quoted in Bassi, *Riccardo Zondonai: tracce di vita*, 32.

56. Adriano Lualdi, "*I cavalieri de Ekebù* di R. Zandonai alla scala," in *Serate musicali* (Milan: Fratelli Treves, 1928), 172.

57. See Dryden, *Riccardo Zandonai*, 46.

58. Letter to Gianferrari, May 9, 1910, in ibid., 81.

59. Zandonai's last jab at Mascagni, in the fall of 1943, was particularly vicious; after Mussolini's fall, during the brief moment between Fascist rule and German occupation in 1943, the ailing Mascagni had come out of retirement to conduct Beethoven's *Eroica* at Rome's Adriano theater, a gesture that was greeted enthusiastically by the Roman people. As paraphrased by Dryden, *Riccardo Zandonai*, 449, in a letter to an unspecified correspondent, Zandonai denounced Mascagni for having accepted the engagement, characterizing the older composer as "running to be blessed between the SS and the Pope."

60. See Dryden, *Riccardo Zandonai*, 111. Dryden somewhat misunderstands the situation, writing that "D'Annunzio's demand would be honored . . . leaving only 3000 lire to be paid the composer!" Clearly, it did not *leave* only 3,000 lire, as the Casa Ricordi could easily have come up with the 20,000 D'Annunzio demanded while still providing Zandonai with the customary 20,000 advance. Ricordi, however, seeing an opportunity in Zandonai's eagerness to set *Francesca*, saw an opportunity to save money, and insisted that Zandonai relinquish his advance in favor of the poet.

61. Quoted in Santoli, *Gabriele D'Annunzio*, 77.

62. Canto 5, lines 118–124, trans. Robert Pinsky, *The Inferno of Dante: A New Verse Translation* (New York: Farrar, Strauss & Giroux, 1994).

63. Gianciotto is a contraction of "Giovanni lo sciancato," or "Giovanni the cripple."

64. Letter to Lino Leonardi of October 14, 1912, quoted in Bassi, *Riccardo Zandonai*, 34–35.

65. *La gazzeta del popolo*, February 20, 1914, quoted in Dryden, *Riccardo Zandonai*, 152.

66. Baccio Ziliotto, *Francesca da Rimini* (Milan: Bottega di poesia, 1923), 9.

67. *Der Rosenkavalier* made its Milan debut at La Scala in March 1911. Zandonai attended at least one, and perhaps more, of the six performances of the opera; Dryden, *Riccardo Zandonai*, 86.

68. This passage, representing sixteen lines in the libretto, was specifically written for the libretto by D'Annunzio at the request of the composer, who felt — not unreasonably — that this critical dramatic moment called for an extended, more lyrical, outburst from Paolo; see Santoli, *Gabriele D'Annunzio*, 79–80.

69. Quoted in Dryden, *Riccardo Zandonai*, 204. The composer returned to comedy in 1933 with *Una farsa amorosa* (A romantic farce) based on a play by the Spanish writer Pedro de Alarcón, which also served as the basis for the better-known ballet by De Falla, *El sombrero de tres picos* (The three-cornered hat). A recent New York revival confirmed that, although reflecting Zandonai's unquestionable compositional craft, musical intelligence, and ingenuity, the composer's gift was not for comedy.

70. Quoted in Dryden, *Riccardo Zandonai*, 164–65.

71. Letter to Emy Mascagni of April 8, 1925, in Morini et al., eds., *Pietro Mascagni, Epistolario*, 2:125.

15. *The End of the Era (pages 337–362)*

1. I would characterize the following operas written by those composers to be to some degree alive as of the beginning of the twenty-first century. I list the titles within each group in chronological order. Those of the standard repertory are *Cavalleria rusticana*, *Pagliacci*, *La bohème*, *Andrea Chénier*, *Tosca*, and *Madama*

Butterfly. The regularly performed are *L'amico Fritz, Manon Lescaut, Fedora,* and *Adriana Lecouvreur.* The periodically revived are *La bohème* (Leoncavallo), *Iris, Zazà,* and *Le Maschere.*

2. Roberto Zanetti, *La musica italiana nel novecento* (Busto Arsizio: Bramante Editore, 1985), 1:84.

3. Giannotto Bastianelli, *Il nuovo dio della musica.* (Turin: Einaudi, 1978), 35.

4. In addition to his pioneering researches into Italian music, Luigi Torchi (1858–1920) also translated many of Wagner's works, including *Oper und Drama,* into Italian. A professor at the Bologna Conservatory for many years, his influence can be seen in the antiquarian interests of his student Ottorino Respighi.

5. Torchi's most extensive efforts included reviews of *Guglielmo Ratcliff,* RMI 2, no. 287 (1895); *Tosca,* RMI 7, no. 78 (1900); *Le Maschere,* RMI 7, no. 178 (1901); and Franchetti's *Germania,* RMI 9, no. 377 (1902).

6. Quoted in A. James Gregor, *Mussolini's Intellectuals* (Princeton: Princeton University Press, 2005), 26.

7. Horatio Smith, gen. ed., *Columbia Dictionary of Modern European Literature* (New York: Columbia University Press, 1947), 647. See also Beppe Benvenuto, *Giuseppe Prezzolini* (Palermo: Sollerio, 2003).

8. Fiamma Nicolodi, *Gusti e tendeze del novecento musicale in Italia* (Florence: Sansoni Editore, 1982), 16.

9. Gianotto Bastianelli, "Le nuove tedenze dell'opera italiana," in *Musicisti d'oggi e di ieri* (Milan: Studio Editoriale Lombardo, 1914), 48. He made something of an exception for Mascagni, whom he considered a "pure representative of [Italy's] old popular operatic tradition"; Bastianelli, *Pietro Mascagni* (Naples: Riccardo Ricciardi Editore, 1910), 24.

10. Giannotto Bastianelli, "La situazione della musica italiana modernissima dopo la grande guerra," in *La musica pura: commentari musicali e altri scritti* (Florence: Leo S. Olschki Editore, 1974), 82–83.

11. Fausto Torrefranca, *Giacomo Puccini e l'arte internazionale* (Turin: Fratelli Bocca, 1912), viii.

12. Ibid., 6.

13. Ibid., 24.

14. Ildebrando Pizzetti, "Giacomo Puccini," *La Voce* (1911): 499.

15. Quoted in John C. G. Waterhouse, "Giannotto Bastianelli," *New Grove Dictionary of Music and Musicians,* 2:281. The other three musicians making up the Five were Gian Francesco Malipiero, Ottorino Respighi, and Renzo Bossi.

16. Francesco Balilla Pratella, *Manifesto dei musicisti futuristi,* in Guido Salvetti, *Storia della musica IX: Il novecento I* (Turin: EDT, 1983), 206.

17. Alfredo Casella, *I segreti della giara* (Florence: Sansoni Editore, 1941), 298–99.

18. Ibid., 307.

19. Peter Conrad, *Modern Times, Modern Places* (New York: Knopf, 1999), 195.

20. Text accessed at http://it.wikipedia.org/wiki/futurismo, May 29, 2006.

21. Caroline Tisdall and Angelo Bozzolla, *Futurism* (London: Thames & Hudson, 1977), 9.

22. Ibid., 114–18.

23. Massimo Mila, *Breve storia della musica* (Milan: Bianchi-Giovini, 1946), 419; www.rodoni.ch/malipiero/milagenerazione80.html (accessed April 18, 2006).

24. The goddess Aphrodite decides to punish the chaste Hippolytus, Theseus's son, by making Theseus's young wife Phaedra fall in love with her stepson. Hippolytus is outraged when he learns about his stepmother's feelings, and she kills herself in despair. Theseus, believing that Hippolytus has killed Phaedra, sends him to exile. Hippolytus dies when the ship on which he is sailing is attacked by a sea monster. *Hippolytus* is generally considered one of Euripides' greatest plays.

25. Quoted in Vincenzo Borghetti and Riccardo Pecci, *Il bacio della Sfinge: D'Annunzio, Pizzetti e Fedra* (Turin: EDT, 1998), 42.

26. Ibid., 43. D'Annunzio was hoping that Ricordi would not only agree to publish the opera, but provide a modest stipend for the composer. He was disappointed on both counts, as the publisher saw little commercial potential in the work.

27. The delay in producing *Fedra*, which by this point was widely anticipated, at least by the more advanced members of the operatic audience, formed something of a controversy in itself: it was widely believed that Sonzogno had decided to shelve *Fedra* until after Mascagni's *Parisina*, also to a D'Annunzio libretto, could be produced and begin its round of the Italian theaters. After being threatened with a lawsuit by the composer, Sonzogno agreed to pay a substantial penalty if he failed to present the opera by April 1915, a deadline he met by little more than a week; see Borghetti and Pecci, *Il bacio della Sfinge*, 47–50.

28. Born Edward Johnson, he later served as general manager of the Metropolitan Opera for many years.

29. Sources differ on the reception of *Fedra*, and whether its curtailed run had to do with its failure, or with the growing war fever that was engulfing Milan; see Barigazzi, *La Scala Racconta*, 472–73.

30. Bastianelli, *Musicisti d'oggi e di ieri*, 87.

31. Pizzetti saw *Pelléas* and *Ariane* at La Scala during 1908, the year that preceded his beginning work on *Fedra*, and wrote extended reviews of both operas for the *Rivista musicale italiana*.

32. Tedeschi, *D'Annunzio*, 84.

33. Richard Taruskin, "Dargomizhsky," in *New Grove Dictionary of Opera*, 1:1082. Pizzetti's opera, however, is more than twice as long as *The Stone Guest*.

34. Gianotto Bastianelli, *Il nuovo dio della musica* (Turin: Einaudi, 1978), 156.

35. Ibid., 157. During the period between the completion of *Fedra* and its first performance, Pizzetti wrote incidental music for another D'Annunzio play, *La Pisanelle, ou la mort parfumée*, and began work on an operatic setting of yet another, *La fiaccola sotto il moggio*. The latter was set aside, however, after a short while, and never pursued further.

36. Vincenzo Borghetti, "Ildebrando Pizzetti — Gabrielle D'Annunzio: incon-

tro e scontro di dramma e musica," in Lorenza Guiot and Jürgen Maehder, eds., *Tendenze della musica teatrale italiana all'inizio del novecento: Atti del 4° convegno internazionale "Ruggero Leoncavallo nel suo tempo"* (Milan: Casa Musicale Sonzogno di Piero Ostali, 2005), 221.

37. Tedeschi, *D'Annunzio*, 89. Translation: "Pledge and monument of love."

38. Barigazzi, *La Scala Racconta*, 472

39. John C. G. Waterhouse, *Malipiero* (Turin: Nuova Eri, 1990), 13.

40. Nicolodi, *Musica e musicisti*, 200.

41. Quoted in Laureano Rodoni, notes to recording of Malipiero's Sonatina for Cello and Piano, at www.rodoni.ch/busoni/cdducale/bookletmalipiero.html (accessed April 23, 2006).

42. Malipiero published an essay on his dogs with the title "Cave canem? Cave hominem!" (Beware of the dog? Beware of people!).

43. The Malipiero family was prominent in Venice at least since the fifteenth century, producing doges, admirals, and other dignitaries. The composer's grandfather, Francesco Malipiero (1824–1887) was a well-respected operatic composer. He had a notable success with his *Giovanna di Napoli*, written when he was only eighteen, which was widely performed, and highly praised by Rossini.

44. Quoted in Frajese, *Dal Costanzi all'Opera*, 3:80.

45. Although the composer wrote that he had burned it, the score was discovered after Malipiero's death by the English musicologist John C. G. Waterhouse, in a trunk in the composer's Asolo home. The opera was based on a libretto by Silvio Benco, the Trieste poet who wrote many of Smareglia's libretti, and dealt in some fashion with the famous medieval confrontation between King Henry IV and Pope Gregory; Waterhouse, *Malipiero*, 36–37.

46. Ibid., 21.

47. Nicolodi, *Musica e musicisti*, 205. Remarkably, Malipiero, Casella, and Pizzetti all attended the premiere of *Sacre*. Pizzetti, however, was unimpressed. See Thomas F. Kelly, *First Nights: Five Musical Premieres* (New Haven: Yale University Press, 2000), 328.

48. G. F. Malipiero, "Voci dal mondo di là," in Franco Ciarlantini, ed., *Malipiero e le sue "Sette canzoni"* (Rome: Augustea, 1929); www.rodoni.ch/malipiero/sette canzoni/7C1.html (accessed June 10, 2006).

49. The parallelism, and the seeming direct contrast, between the prologue of *Le Maschere*, in which the impresario also calls the masks forward and invites them to describe their features, and Malipiero's work, up to Orpheus's arrival on the scene, is very close. Any suggestion that Malipiero deliberately made a connection between the two, however, is pure conjecture.

50. Waterhouse, "G.F. Malipiero's Crisis Years (1913–1919)," *Journal of the Royal Musical Association* 108 (1981): 136.

51. Guido Heldt, "Austria and Germany, 1918–1960," in *The Cambridge Companion to Twentieth-Century Opera*, 155. He identifies, in addition to Malipiero's work, major works on the Orpheus theme by Milhaud, Krenek, Weill, and Casella

between 1922 and 1932, and suggests that they may reflect insecurity about what it meant to be an artist in this period.

52. Quoted in Waterhouse, "G.F. Malipiero's Crisis Years (1913–1919)," 140.

53. Quoted in Nicolodi, "Zandonai e I suoi contemporanei," 114.

54. Bastianelli, *Musica pura*, 139.

55. Quoted in Nicolodi "Zandonai e I suoi contemporanei," 126.

56. Quoted in Alfredo Casella, *21+26* (Florence: Leo S. Olshki, 2001), 122–23.

57. Gian Piero Brunetta, *Storia del cinema italiano: Il cinema muto, 1895–1929* (Rome: Editori Riuniti, 1993), 21.

58. Pierre Sorlin, *Italian National Cinema, 1896–1996* (London: Routledge, 1996), 20.

59. Gian Piero Brunetta, "Filogenesi artistica e letteraria del primo cinema italiano," in Renzo Renzi, ed., *Sperduto nel buio: il cinema muto italiano e il suo tempo (1905–1930)* (Bologna: Cappelli Editore, 1991), 12.

60. Quoted in ibid., 14.

61. Marco Sisi, "Primi passi del cinema nella Livorno del 1900," *Livorno Non Stop* (June 13, 1998).

62. Quoted in Elena Mosconi, "'Venghino signori, si va ad incominciare!' Nascita ed evoluzione dell'esercizio ciematografico," in Raffaele De Berti, ed., *Un secolo di cinema a Milano* (Milan: Editrice Il Castoro, 1996), 108.

63. Brunetta, "Filogenesi artistica e letteraria del primo cinema italiano," 15.

64. Aldo Bernardini, "Industrializzazione e classi sociali," in Renzi, ed., *Sperduto nel buio*, 30.

65. Antonio Costa, "Dante, D'Annunzio, Pirandello," in Renzi, ed., *Sperduto nel buio*, 59–60.

66. His role was actually modest, being largely limited to elaborating the titles in his unique prose. It was generally believed, however, that he had played a significant role in directing the film, a misconception both he and the studio encouraged for its publicity value.

67. Costa, "Dante, D'Annunzio, Pirandello," 63–64.

68. Mosconi, "Venghino signori," 112. In 1911, the most recent census, the population of Milan over the age of fifteen was approximately 450,000. It is likely that the number of opera tickets sold in Milan in any one year at the peak of the industry was not more than 500,000.

69. Ibid., 111.

70. Riccardo Redi, *Cinema muto italiano (1896–1930)* (Venice: Marsilio: Biblioteca di bianco & nero, 1999), 68.

71. Brunetta, *Storia*, 81.

72. *Maciste in the Alpine Regiment, Maciste in Love, Maciste on Vacation*, and *Maciste and the Cousin from America*. The Maciste phenomenon survived its founder; the series of Hercules films produced by Italian studios in the 1950s are its direct descendent.

73. Pizzetti did not compose a score for *Cabiria*, as some references suggest, but

only a roughly ten-minute-long piece to accompany the sacrificial scene. The rest of the music for the film was cobbled together by a studio hack, using a variety of sources — including a number of recognizable Verdi tunes.

74. S. A. Luciani; quoted in Ennio Simeon, "L'ambiente musicale ufficiale e il cinema muto," in Renzi, ed., *Sperduto nel buio*, 111.

75. Letter to Anna Lolli, January 8, 1918.

76. Morini et al., *Casa Sonzogno*, 1:365.

16. Epilogue (pages 363–372)

1. One can only speculate on the extent to which a particular historical moment, with its creative opportunities and constraints, can make a composer great or at least greater, and whether a composer of great gifts would shine equally brilliantly at any point in history. This sort of speculation is particularly intriguing in the case of Puccini, whose tastes echo so closely those of the bourgeois audience for which he was writing. It is hard to imagine a Puccini of 1820 composing operas about the classic conflicts of love, family, and honor that occupied the composers of the time, or if he had done so, that they would stand out against the works of Bellini and Donizetti.

2. See chapter 1, note 43.

3. Umberto Giordano was also still actively composing, and in 1924 presented *La cena delle beffe*, an effective opera based on a quasi-D'Annunzian libretto by Sem Benelli set in Renaissance Florence. Occasional revivals have demonstrated that it remains a viable work.

4. Prince Charles de Fleury feigns Revolutionary sympathies in order to become a member of the Ogre's guard, known as the Marats, in order to rescue his mother, who is being held prisoner by the Ogre. He meets and falls in love with the Ogre's niece Mariella. In the end, after many difficulties, the Prince, his mother, and Mariella escape by boat to freedom.

5. Mascagni's visit to the Orlando shipyards in Livorno in September 1920, at a time when it along with most of Italy's major industrial establishments had been occupied by the Socialist workers, received national attention, and led most Italians to believe that he was sympathetic to the cause of Socialist — or as it was becoming known, Bolshevik — revolution; see Mallach, *Pietro Mascagni*, 239–40.

6. Morini, ed., *Pietro Mascagni*, 1:409.

7. Mallach, *Pietro Mascagni*, 241.

8. Quoted in Morini, *Pietro Mascagni*, 1:409.

9. During the 1920s *Marat* received an average of seven productions each year in Italy, as well as a substantial number of foreign productions. That diminished to three per year during the 1930s; Fulvio Venturi, *Pietro Mascagni: Biografia e cronologia artistica* (Livorno: Circolo musicale amici d'opera Galliano Masini, 2005), 312–26.

10. Budden tentatively dates Puccini's first contact with Gold's play in 1912; Budden, *Puccini*, 338.

11. Giovacchino Forzano (1884–1970) was a prominent playwright and director as well as librettist during the 1920s and 1930s. He prepared the libretti for Mascagni's *Lodoletta* and *Il piccolo Marat*, as well as that for Wolf-Ferrari's *Sly*.

12. Budden, *Puccini*, 446.

13. The extent to which Puccini completed the last act of *Turandot*, and the extent to which his inability to complete the work was not only a product of his final illness but arose from other, psychological, factors has been a bone of contention ever since Carner's suggestion that it was "a sign of the inner difficulty he experienced in identifying himself with the spiritual kernel of this scene" Carner, *Puccini*, 541. While later research has thrown doubt on this proposition, especially Janet Maguire's "Puccini's Version of the Duet and Final Scene of *Turandot*," *Musical Quarterly* 74, no. 3 (1990): 319–59, the jury is still out; see in particular William Ashbrook and Harold Powers, *Puccini's Turandot: The End of The Great Tradition* (Princeton: Princeton University Press, 1991), 88.

14. Budden, *Puccini*, 472.

15. On this theme, see also Ashbrook and Powers, *Puccini's Turandot*.

16. Frajese, *Dal Costanzi all'Opera*, 4:170–85.

17. Web site of the Ministero per I beni e le attività culturali (Ministry of Cultural Assets and Activities), http://194.242.241.200/spettacolo/lirica/fondazioni.htm (accessed June 18, 2006).

Bibliography

Books

Alexander, Alfred. *Giovanni Verga*. London: Grant & Cutler, 1972.

Alverà, Pierluigi. *Giordano*. New York: Treves, 1986.

Ambìveri, Corrado. *Operisti minori dell'ottocento italiano*. Rome: Gremese Editore, 1998.

Amici, Giovanni, et al. *Mascagni contro Sonzogno: comparsa conclusionale del maestro Pietro Mascagni*. Livorno: Arti Grafiche S. Belforte, 1915.

Antolini, Bianca Maria, ed. *Dizionario degli editori musicali italiani*. Pisa: Editzioni ETS, 2000.

———. ed. *Milano Musicale, 1861–1897*. Lucca: Libreria Musicale Italiana, 1999.

Antongini, Tom. *D'Annunzio*. Boston: Little, Brown, 1938.

———. *Vita segreta di Gabriele D'Annunzio*. Milan: Mondadori, 1958.

Arblaster, Anthony. *Viva la Libertà: Politics in Opera*. London: Verso, 1992.

Ashbrook, William. *The Operas of Puccini*. Ithaca, NY: Cornell University Press, 1968.

———, and Harold Powers. *Puccini's* Turandot: *The End of the Great Tradition*. Princeton, NJ: Princeton University Press, 1991.

Aulenti, Gae, and Marco Vallora, eds. *Quartetto della maledizione: Materiali per* Rigoletto, Cavalleria e Pagliacci, Fanciulla. Milan: Ubulibri, 1985.

Baldacci, Luigi. *La musica in italiano: libretti d'opera dell'ottocento*. Milan: Rizzoli, 1997.

Balthazar, Scott, ed. *The Cambridge Companion to Verdi*. Cambridge: Cambridge University Press, 2004.

Banti, Alberto M. *Storia della borghesia italiana*. Rome: Donzelli Editore, 1996.

Barański, Zygmunt G., and Rebecca J. West, eds. *The Cambridge Companion to Modern Italian Culture*. New York: Cambridge University Press, 2001.

Barblan, Guglielmo. *Toscanini e La Scala*. Milan: Edizioni della Scala, 1972.

Barigazzi, Giuseppe. *La Scala racconta*. Milan: RCS Rizzoli Libri, 1991.

Barile, Laura. *Le parole illustrate: Edoardo Sonzogno editore del popolo.* Modena: Mucchi Editore, 1994.

Barzini, Luigi. *Memories of Mistresses: Reflections from a Life.* New York: Macmillan, 1986.

Bassi, Adriano. *Caro Maestro (D'Annunzio e I musicisti).* Genoa: De Ferrari Editore, 1997.

———. *Riccardo Zandonai: tracce di vita.* Poggibonsi: Antonio Lalli Editore, 1982.

———. *Riccardo Zandonai.* Milan: Targa Italiana Editore, 1989.

Bastianelli, Gianotto. *La musica pura: commentari musicali e altri scritti.* Florence: Leo S. Olschki Editore, 1974.

———. *Musicisti d'oggi e di ieri.* Milan: Studio Editoriale Lombardo, 1914.

———. *Il nuovo dio della musica.* Turin: Einaudi, 1978.

———. *Pietro Mascagni.* Naples: Riccardo Ricciardi Editore, 1910.

Battaglia, Fernando. *L'arte del canto in Romagna.* Bologna: Edizioni Bongiovanni, 1979.

Bell, Donald Howard. *Sesto San Giovanni: Workers, Culture, and Politics in an Italian Town, 1880–1922.* New Brunswick, NJ: Rutgers University Press, 1986.

Bellina, Ana Laura, and Giovanni Morelli, eds. *L'Europa musicale.* Florence: Vallecchi Editore, 1988.

Bellincioni, Bianca Stagno. *Roberto Stagno e Gemma Bellincioni intimi.* Florence: Casa Editrice Monsalvato, 1943.

Bergin, Thomas Goddard. *Giovanni Verga.* New Haven, CT: Yale University Press, 1931.

Bernardoni, Virgilio. *La maschera e la favola nell'opera italiana del primo novecento.* Venice: Edizioni Fondazione Levi, 1986.

Berrong, Richard M., ed. and trans. *The Politics of Opera in Turn-of-the-century Italy: As Seen Through the Letters of Alfredo Catalani.* Lewiston, NY: Edwin Mellen Press, 1992.

Bianconi, Lorenzo, and Giorgio Pestelli, eds. *Opera in Theory and Practice, Image and Myth.* Chicago: University of Chicago Press, 2003.

———. *Opera on Stage.* Chicago: University of Chicago Press, 2002.

———. *Opera Production and its Resources.* Chicago: University of Chicago Press, 1998.

Bonajuti Tarquini, Vittoria. *Riccardo Zandonai nel ricordo dei suoi intimi.* Milan: G. Ricordi, 1952.

Borghetti, Vincenzo, and Riccardo Pecci, *Il bacio della Sfinge: D'Annunzio, Pizzetti e Fedra.* Turin: EDT, 1998.

Botteghi, Carlo. *Parisina.* Livorno: Casa Editrice Il Gabbiano, 1997.

Bowen, José Antonio, ed. *The Cambridge Companion to Conducting.* Cambridge: Cambridge University Press, 2003.

Brand, Peter, and Lino Pertile, eds. *The Cambridge History of Italian Literature.* New York: Cambridge University Press, 1996.

Brunetta, Gian Piero. *Storia del cinema italiano: Il cinema muto, 1895–1929.* Rome: Editori Riuniti, 1993.

Bryant, David, ed. *Il novecento musicale italiano tra neoclassicism e neogoticismo.* Florence: Leo S. Olschki Editore, 1988.

Budden, Julian. *The Operas of Verdi.* 3 vols. Oxford: Oxford University Press, 1981.

———. *Puccini: His Life and Works.* Oxford: Oxford University Press, 2002.

Burton, Deborah, Susan Vandiver Nicassio, and Agostino Ziino. *Tosca's Prism: Three Moments of Western Cultural History.* Boston: Northeastern University Press, 2004.

Busch, Hans. *Verdi's* Aida: *The History of an Opera in Letters and Documents.* Minneapolis: University of Minnesota Press, 1978.

———. *Verdi's* Falstaff *in Letters and Contemporary Reviews.* Bloomington, IN: Indiana University Press, 1997.

Cafasi, Francesco. *Giuseppe Verdi: Fattore di Sant'Agata.* Parma: Edizioni Zara, 1994.

Calvetti, Mauro. *Galliano Masini.* Livorno: Belforte Editore, 1986.

Cambiasi, Pompeo. *La Scala, 1778–1906: note storiche e statistiche.* Milan: G. Ricordi, 1906.

Cancan, Giovanni. *Impressioni musicali in Gabriele D'Annunzio.* Perugia: Guerra, 1997.

Candeloro, Giorgio. *Storia dell'Italia moderna.* Milan: Feltrinelli Editore, 1974.

Capra, Marco, ed., *Un piacente estate di San Martino: Saggi in onore di Marcello Conati.* Lucca: Libreria Musicale Italiana, 2000.

Carner, Mosco. *Puccini.* New York: Holmes & Meier, 1958.

———. *Tosca.* Cambridge: Cambridge University Press, 1985.

Carelli, Augusto. *Emma Carelli: Trent'anni di vita lirica.* Rome: P. Maglione, 1932.

Casella, Alfredo. *Music in My Time* [English translation of *I segreti della giara*]. Norman: University of Oklahoma Press, 1955.

———. *21+26.* Florence: Leo S. Olshki Editore, 2001.

Casini, Claudio, et al., eds., *Mascagni.* Milan: Electa Editrice, 1984.

Cellamare, Daniele. *Mascagni e la* Cavalleria *visti da Cerignola.* Rome: Fratelli Palombi Editore, 1941.

———. *Umberto Giordano.* Rome: Fratelli Palombi Editore, 1967.

Celletti, Rodolfo, ed. *Le grandi voci: dizionario critico-biografico dei cantanti.* Rome: Istituto per la collaborazione culturale, 1964.

Cellucci Marcone, Silvia. *D'Annunzio e la musica.* L'Aquila: Japadre, 1972.

Checci, Eugenio. *Pietro Mascagni, 1890–1920: Dalla* Cavalleria *al* Piccolo Marat. Milan: Casa Musicale Sonzogno, 1920.

Chiesa, Renato, ed. *Atti del convegno di studi sulla figura e l'opera di Riccardo Zandonai.* Milan: Edizioni UNICOPLI, 1984.

Ciarlantini, Franco. *Malipiero e le sue Sette canzoni.* Rome: Augustea, 1929.

Clark, Martin. *Modern Italy, 1871–1982.* London: Longman Group, 1984.

Colombani, Alfredo. *L'opera italiana nel secolo XIX.* Milan: Edizione del "Corriere della sera" 1900.

Conati, Marcello ed. *Encounters with Verdi*. Ithaca, NY: Cornell University Press, 1984.

———, and Mario Medici, eds. *The Verdi-Boito Correspondence*. Chicago: University of Chicago Press, 1994.

Conrad, Peter. *Modern Times, Modern Places*. New York: Knopf, 1999.

Cooke, Mervyn ed. *The Cambridge Companion to Twentieth-Century Opera*. Cambridge: Cambridge University Press, 2005.

Cooper, Martin, ed. *New Oxford History of Music*. Vol. 10, *The Modern Age, 1890–1960*. London: Oxford University Press, 1974.

Corazzol, Adriana Guarnieri. *Musica e letteratura in Italia tra ottocento e novecento*. Milan: Sansoni, 2000.

———. *Sensualità senza carne: La musica nella vita e nell'opera di D'Annunzio*. Bologna: Il Mulino, 1990.

———. *Tristano, mio Tristano: Gli scrittori italiani e il caso Wagner*. Bologna: Il Mulino, 1988.

Corsi, Jone Gaillard. *Il libretto d'autore, 1860–1930*. West Lafayette, IN: Bordighera, 1997.

Crico, Giandonato, ed. *Lucia di Lammermoor. Libretto e guida all'opera*. Rome: Gremese Editore, 1988.

Croce, Benedetto. *A History of Italy, 1871–1915*. New York: Russell & Russell, 1963.

Dahlhaus, Carl. *Nineteenth-Century Music*. Berkeley and Los Angeles: University of California Press, 1989.

———. *Realism in Nineteenth-Century Music*. Cambridge: Cambridge University Press, 1985.

Dalle Vacche, Angela. *The Body in the Mirror: Shapes of History in Italian Cinema*. Princeton, NJ: Princeton University Press, 1992.

D'Amico, Tomasino. *Francesco Cilèa*. Milan: Edizioni Curci, 1960.

Davis, John A., ed. *Italy in the Nineteenth Century, 1796–1900*. Oxford: Oxford University Press, 2000.

De Angelis, Alberto. *L'Italia musicale di oggi*. Rome: Ausonia, 1928.

De Berti, Raffaele, ed. *Un secolo di cinema a Milano*. Milan: Editrice Il Castora, 1996.

DeCarlo, Salvatore. *Mascagni parla*. Milan: DeCarlo, 1945.

Degani, Giannino, and Maria Grotti, eds. *Teatro Municipale Reggio Emilia: Opere in musica, 1857–1976*. Reggio Emilia: Teatro Municipale, 1976.

D'Harcourt, Eugène. *La musique actuelle en Italie*. Paris: F. Durdilly, 1904.

Della Corte, Alfredo. *Ritratto di Franco Alfano*. Turin: Paravia, 1935.

Della Corte, Andrea. *Arturo Toscanini*. Turin: Edizioni Studio Tesi, 1981.

Della Seta, Fabrizio, et al., eds. *Verdi 2001: Atti del convegno internazionale Parma–New York–New Haven*. Florence: Leo S. Olschki Editore, 2003.

Depanis, Giuseppe. *Alfredo Catalani, Appunti-Ricordi*. Turin: L. Roux, 1893.

De Rensis, Raffaello. *Ermanno Wolf-Ferrari: La sua vita d'artista*. Milan: Fratelli Treves Editore, 1937.

Dizikes, John. *Opera in America.* New Haven, CT: Yale University Press, 1993.

Dorsi, Fabrizio, and Giuseppe Rausa. *Storia dell'opera italiana.* Milan: Bruno Mondadori, 2000.

Drake, Richard. *Byzantium for Rome: The Politics of Nostalgia in Umbertian Italy, 1878–1900.* Chapel Hill: University of North Carolina Press, 1980.

Dryden, Konrad. *Leoncavallo: Life and Works.* Lanham, MD: Scarecrow Press, 2007.

——. *Riccardo Zandonai: A Biography.* Frankfurt am Main: Peter Lang, 1999.

Elson, Arthur. *The Book of Musical Knowledge.* New York: Houghton Mifflin, 1915.

Ferraro, Domenico, et al., eds., *Francesco Cilèa.* Milan: Casa Musicale Sonzogno, 2000.

Ferrone, Siro, ed. *Teatro dell Italia unita.* Milan: Il saggiatore, 1980.

Flury, Roger. *Pietro Mascagni: A Bio-Bibliography.* Westport, CT: Greenwood, 2001.

Forgacs, David. *Italian Culture in the Industrial Era, 1880–1980.* Manchester, Eng.: Manchester University Press, 1990.

Fortune, Nigel, ed. *Music and Theatre: Essays in Honor of Winton Dean.* Cambridge: Cambridge University Press, 1987.

Forzano, Giovacchino. *Come li ho conosciuti.* Turin: Edizioni Radio Italiana, 1957.

Fraccaroli, Armando. *Celebrità e quasi.* Milan: Casa Editrice Sonzogno, 1923.

——. *La vita di Giacomo Puccini.* Milan: G. Ricordi, 1925.

Frajese, Vittorio. *Dal Costanzi all'Opera.* 4 vols. Rome: Edizioni Capitolium, 1977.

Galli, Amintore. *Umberto Giordano nell'arte e nella vita.* Milan: Ed. Sonzogno, 1915.

Gara, Eugenio, ed. *Carteggi pucciniani.* Milan: Ricordi, 1958.

Gasco, Alberto. *Da Cimarosa a Stravinsky.* Rome: De Santis, 1939.

Gatti, Guglielmo. *Vita di Gabriele D'Annunzio.* Florence: Sansoni Editore, 1988.

Gatti, Guido M. *Ildebrando Pizzetti.* Milan: Ricordi, 1954.

Gatti-Cassaza, Giulio. *Memories of the Opera.* London: John Calder, 1977.

Gelati, Giovanni. *Il vate e il capobanda.* Livorno: Belforte, 1992.

Gentry, Theodore L. "Emblems of Love and Death in Italian Realist Opera." Ph.D diss., University of Kentucky, 1992.

Gervasio, Roberto, ed. *Come una coppa di champagne: Storia, vita e costume dell'Italia del nuovo secolo.* Milan: Rizzoli, 1985.

Girardi, Michele. *Puccini: His International Art.* Chicago: University of Chicago Press, 2000.

Greenfeld, Howard. *Caruso.* New York: Da Capo, 1983.

Gregor, A. James. *Mussolini's Intellectuals.* Princeton, NJ: Princeton University Press, 2005.

Groos, Arthur, and Roger Parker. *Giacomo Puccini: La Bohème.* Cambridge: Cambridge University Press, 1986.

——. *Reading Opera.* Princeton, NJ: Princeton University Press, 1988.

Gualerzi, Giorgio. *Wagner in Italia.* Venice: Ente Autonomo Teatro la Fenice, 1972.

446   *Bibliography*

Guiot, Lorenza, and Jürgen Maehder, eds. *Letteratura, musica e teatro al tempo di Ruggero Leoncavallo (Atti del 2° convegno internazionale di studi su Ruggero Leoncavallo)*. Milan: Casa Musicale Sonzogno di Piero Ostali, 1995.

———, eds. *Nazionalismo e cosmopolitismo nell'opera fra '800 e '900: Atti del 3° convegno internazionale "Ruggero Leoncavallo nel suo tempo."* Milan: Casa Musical Sonzogno di Piero Ostali, 1998.

———, eds. *Tendenze della musica teatrale italiana all'inizio del novecento: Atti del 4° convegno internazionale "Ruggero Leoncavallo nel suo tempo."* Milan: Casa Musicale Sonzogno di Piero Ostali, 2005.

Henstock, Michael. *Fernando De Lucia*. Portland, OR: Amadeus, 1990.

Hepokoski, James A. *Falstaff (Cambridge Opera Handbook)*. Cambridge: Cambridge University Press, 1983.

Hulten, Pontus, and Germano Celant. *Italian Art, 1900–1945*. New York: Rizzoli, 1989.

Iovino, Roberto. *Mascagni: l'avventuroso dell'opera*. Milan: Camunia, 1987.

———, and Ines Aliprandi. *I palcoscenici della lirica: Dall'impresariato all'ente lirico*. Genoa: Sagep Edtrice, 1992.

———, Ines Aliprandi, S. Licciardello, and K. Tocchi. *I palcoscenici della lirica: Cronologia dal Falcone al nuovo Carlo Felice*. Genoa: Sagep Editrice, 1993.

———, I. Mattio, and G. Tanasini. *I palcoscenici della lirica: Dal Falcone al Carlo Felice*. Genoa: Sagep Editrice, 1990.

Isnenghi, Mario, ed. *I luoghi della memoria: simboli e miti dell'Italia unita*. Rome: Editori Laterza, 1996.

Jeri, Alfredo. *Mascagni*. Milan: Garzanti Editore, 1940.

Kimbell, David. *Italian Opera*. Cambridge: Cambridge University Press, 1991.

Krehbiel, H. E. *A Second Book of Operas*. Garden City, NY: Garden City Publishing, 1917.

Large, David C., and William Weber, eds. *Wagnerism in European Culture and Politics*. Ithaca, NH: Cornell University Press, 1984.

Lee, Vernon [pseud. of Violet Paget]. *Studies of the Eighteenth Century in Italy*. Chicago: A. C. McClurg, 1908.

Lenzer, Gertrud, ed. *Auguste Comte and Positivism: The Essential Writings*. New York: Harper & Row, 1975.

Leoncavallo, Ruggero. "Appunti vari delle autobiografici di R. Leoncavallo." Unpublished manuscript.

Letzer, Jacqueline, and Robert Adelson. *Women Writing Opera: Creativity and Controversy in the Age of the French Revolution*. Berkeley and Los Angeles: University of California Press, 2001.

Levi, Primo. *Paesaggi e figure musicali*. Milan: Treves, 1913.

LoRomer, David G. *Merchants and Reform in Livorno, 1814–1868*. Berkeley and Los Angeles: University of California Press, 1987.

Lualdi, Adriano. *Serate musicali*. Milan: Fratelli Treves, 1928.

———. *Tutti vivi*. Milan: Dall'Oglio, 1955.

Luzio, Alessandro, ed. *Carteggi verdiani*. 4 vols. Rome: Accademia Nazionale dei Lincei, 1947.

Lyon, Thomas J., ed. *A Literary History of the American West*. Fort Worth, TX: Texas Christian University Press, 1998.

Lyttelton, Adrian. *The Seizure of Power: Fascism in Italy, 1919–1929*. Princeton, NJ: Princeton University Press, 1987.

Maehder, Jürgen, ed. *Esotismo e colore locale nell'opera di Puccini. Atti del I convegno internazionale sull'opera di Giacomo Puccini*. Pisa: Giardini Editori, 1983.

——, and Lorenza Guiot, eds. *Ruggero Leoncavallo nel suo tempo: atti del 1° convegno di studi su Ruggero Leoncavallo*. Milan: Casa Musicale Sonzogno, 1993.

Magri, Giorgio. *L'uomo Puccini*. Milan: Mursia, 1992.

Malatesta, Maria, ed. *Society and the Professions in Italy, 1860–1914*. Translated by Adrian Belton. Cambridge: Cambridge University Press, 1995.

Malipiero, Gian Francesco. *La pietra del bando*. Montebelluno: Edizioni Amadeus, 1990.

Mallach, Alan. *Pietro Mascagni and His Operas*. Boston: Northeastern University Press, 2002.

Mariani, Antonio. *Luigi Mancinelli: La vita*. Lucca: Akademos, 1998.

Mariani, Gaetano. *Ottocento romantico e verista*. Naples: Giannini Editore, 1972.

Mariani, Renato. *Verismo in musica e altri studi*. Florence: Leo S. Olschki Editore, 1977.

Marotti, Guido, and Ferruccio Pagni. *Giacomo Puccini intimo (nei ricordi di due amici)*. Florence: Vallecchi Editore, 1926.

Martens, Frederick H. *A Thousand and One Nights of Opera*. New York: D. Appleton, 1926.

Martin, George. *Verdi, His Music, Life and Times*. New York: Limelight Editions, 1992.

Martino, Daniele. *Catastrofi sentimentali: Puccini e la sindrome pucciniana*. Turin: EDT, 1993.

Mascagni contro Sonzogno; comparsa conclusionale del maestro Pietro Mascagno. Livorno: Arti Grafische S. Belforte, 1915.

Mascagni, Emy. *S'inginocchi la più piccina*. Milan: Treves, 1936.

Mascagni, Pietro. *Per le opere dell'ingegno*. Rome: Officina Poligrafica Italiana, 1905.

Mastromatteo, Francesco. *Umberto Giordano tra verismo e cinematografia*. Rome: Bastogi Editrice Italiana, 2003.

Mediolanum. Bologna: Casa Editrice Dott. Francesco Vallardi, 1881.

Menichini, Maria. *Alfredo Catalani alla luce di documenti inediti*. Lucca: Maria Pacini Fazzi Editore, 1993.

Mila, Massimo. *Breve storia della musica*. Milan: Bianchi-Giovini, 1946.

Milano, 1881. Milan: Giuseppe Ottino, 1881.

Milano e i suoi dintorni. Milan: G. Civelli, 1881.

Montanelli, Indro. *L'Italia dei notabili*. Milan: Biblioteca universale Rizzoli, 1973.

Morini, Mario, ed. *Pietro Mascagni.* 2 vols. Milan: Casa Musicale Sonzogno, 1964.

———, ed. *Umberto Giordano.* Milan: Casa Musicale Sonzogno, 1968.

———, Roberto Iovino, and Alberto Paloscia. *Pietro Mascagni: Epistolario.* 2 vols. Lucca: Libreria Musicale Italiana, 1996.

———, Nandi Ostali, and Piero Ostali, Jr., eds. *Casa Sonzogno: Cronologie, saggi, testimonianze.* 2 vols. Milan: Casa Musicale Sonzogno, 1995.

———, and Piero Ostali, ed. *Mascagni e l'Iris fra simbolism e floreale: atti del 2° convegno di studi su Pietro Mascagni.* Milan: Casa Musicale Sonzogno, 1989.

Musco, Gianfranco. *Musica e teatro in Giacomo Puccini.* Cortona: Calosci Editore, 1989.

Nicassio, Susan Vandiver. *Tosca's Rome: The Play and the Opera in Historical Perspective.* Chicago: University of Chicago Press, 1999.

Nicastro, Aldo. *Il melodramma e gli italiani.* Milan: Rusconi, 1982.

Nicolaisen, Jay. *Italian Opera in Transition, 1871–1893.* Ann Arbor: UMI Research Press, 1980.

Nicolodi, Fiamma. *Gusti e tendeze del novecento musicale in Italia.* Florence: Sansoni Editore, 1982.

———. *Musica e musicisti nel ventennio fascista.* Fiesole: Discanto Editore, 1984.

———. *Musica italiana del primo novecento: la generazione dell'80.* Florence: Leo S. Olschki Editore, 1981.

———. *Orizzonti musicali italo-europei, 1860–1980.* Rome: Bulzoni Editore, 1990.

Orselli, Cesare. *Le occasioni di Mascagni.* Siena: Edizioni di Barbablù, 1990.

Osborne, Charles. *Verdi: A Life in the Theatre.* New York: Knopf, 1988.

Ostali, Piero, and Nandi Ostali, eds. *L'amico Fritz nel centenario della prima rappresentazione.* Milan: Casa Musicale Sonzogno, 1994.

———, eds. *Cavalleria rusticana, 1890–1990: Cento anni di un capolavoro.* Milan: Casa Musicale Sonzogno, 1990.

———. *Il piccolo Marat: Storia e revoluzione nel melodrama verista.* Milan: Casa Musicale Sonzogno, 1990.

Paladini, Carlo. *Puccini, con l'epistolario inedito.* Florence: Vallecchi Editore, 1961.

Parker, Roger. *Leonora's Last Act: Essays in Verdian Discourse.* Princeton, NJ: Princeton University Press, 1997.

Pennella, Concetta. *Lettere inedite di Umberto Giordano.* Naples: Società Editrice Napoletana, 1977.

Petraccone, E. ed. *La commedia dell'arte.* Naples: Riccardo Ricciardi Editore, 1927.

Petrolli, Alberto. *Zandonai musicista.* Rovereto: A. Petrolli, 1998.

Phillips-Matz, Mary Jane. *Puccini: A Biography.* Lebanon, NH: University Press of New England, 2002.

———. *Verdi: A Biography.* Oxford: Oxford University Press, 1993.

Piazzoni, Irene. *Dal "Teatro dei palchettisti" all'Ente autonomo: La Scala, 1897–1920.* Florence: La Nuova Italia Editrice, 1995.

———. *Spetacolo istituzioni e società nell'Italia postunitaria (1860–1882).* Rome: Archivio Guido Izzi, 2001.

Pietro Mascagni: Contributi alla conoscenza della sua opera nel primo centenario della nascita. Livorno: Comitato onoranze nel primo centenario della nascita, 1963.

Pietro Mascagni, 1890–1920: Dalla Cavalleria al piccolo Marat. Milan: Casa Musicale Sonzogno, 1920.

Pistone, Daniele. *Nineteenth-Century Italian Opera from Rossini to Puccini*. Portland, OR: Amadeus, 1995.

Pittaresi, Gaetano, ed. *La docissima effigie: studi su Francesco Cilèa*. Reggio Calabria: Laruffa Editore, 1999.

———. *Lettere a Francesco Cilèa, 1878–1910*. Reggio Calabria: Laruffa Editore, 2001.

Pizzetti, Bruno, ed. *Ildebrando Pizzetti: Cronologia e bibliografia*. Parma: La Pilotta Editore, 1980.

Polo, Claudia. *Immaginari verdiani: Opera, media e industria culturale nell'Italia dell XX secolo*. Milan: Ricordi, 2004.

Pompei, Edoardo. *Pietro Mascagni nella vita e nell'arte*. Rome: Editrice Nazionale, 1912.

Porter, Roy, and M. Teich, eds. *Romanticism in National Context*. Cambridge: Cambridge University Press, 1988.

Randall, Annie J., and Rosalind Gray Davis. *Puccini and The Girl*. Chicago: University of Chicago Press, 2005.

Ravenni, Gabriella Biagi, and Carolyn Gianturco, eds. *Giacomo Puccini: L'uomo, il musicista, il panorama europeo*. Lucca: Libreria Musicale Italiana, 1997.

Redi, Riccardo. *Cinema muto italiano (1896–1930)*. Venice: Biblioteca di bianco & nero, 1999.

Renzi, Renzo, ed. *Sperduto nel buio: il cinema muto italiano e il suo tempo (1905–1930)*. Bologna: Cappelli Editore, 1991.

Rinaldi, Mario. *Musica e verismo*. Rome: Fratelli De Santis, 1932.

Roselli, John. *Music and Musicians in Nineteenth-Century Italy*. Portland, OR: Amadeus, 1991.

———. *Singers of Italian Opera*. Cambridge: Cambridge University Press, 1992.

Rossi, Salvatore. *L'età del verismo*. Palermo: Palumbo Editore, 1978.

Rubboli, Daniele. *Ridi pagliaccio*. Lucca: Maria Pacini Fazzi Editore, 1985.

———, and Walter Rubboli. *Rosina Storchio*. Dello: Museo R. Storchio, 1994.

Ruffo, Titta. *My Parabola*. Dallas: Baskerville Publishers, 1995 [English translation of *La mia parabola*, 1937].

Sabbatucci, Giovanni, and Vittorio Vidotto, eds. *Storia d'Italia*. Vol. 3, *Liberalismo e democrazia, 1887–1914*. Rome: Laterza, 1995.

Sachs, Harvey. *Opera in Fascist Italy*. London: Weidenfeld & Nicholson, 1987.

———. *Reflections on Toscanini*. Rocklin, CA: Prima, 1993.

———. *Toscanini*. New York: Harper & Row, 1978.

Salvetti, Guido. *Il melodrama italiana dell'ottocento: studie in onore di Massimo Mila*. Torino: Einaudi, 1977.

――. *Storia della musica IX: Il novecento I.* Turin: EDT, 1983.

Sansone, Matteo. "Verismo From Literature to Opera." Ph.D. diss., University of Edinburgh, 1987.

Santoli, Carlo. *Gabriele D'Annunzio: la musica e i musicisti.* Rome: Bulzoni Editore, 1997.

Sartori, Claudio. *Casa Ricordi, 1808–1958.* Milan: Casa Ricordi, 1958.

Scardovi, Stefano. *L'opera dei bassifondi.* Lucca: Libreria Musicale Italiana, 1994.

Scott, Michael. *The Record of Singing.* 2 vols. London: Duckworth, 1977.

Seligman, Vincent. *Puccini Among Friends.* New York: Macmillan, 1938.

Smith, Denis Mack. *Italy and its Monarchy.* New Haven, CT: Yale University Press, 1989.

Sorlin, Pierre. *Italian National Cinema, 1896–1996.* London: Routledge, 1996.

Southwell-Sander, Peter. *Puccini.* London: Omnibus, 1996.

Squarotti, Giorgio Barberi. *Invito alla lettura di Gabriele D'Annunzio.* Milan: Mursia, 1982.

Steane, J. B. *The Grand Tradition: Seventy Years of Singing on Record.* 2nd ed. Portland, OR: Amadeus, 1993.

Streicher, Johannes, ed. *Ultimi Splendori: Cilèa, Giordano, Alfano.* Rome: Ismez Editore, 2000.

Tedesci, Rubens. *Addio, fiorito asil: il melodramma italiano da Boito al verismo.* Milan: Feltrinelli Editore, 1978.

――. *D'Annunzio e la musica.* Scandicci: La Nuova Italia Editrice, 1988.

Terenzio, Vincenzo. *La musica italiana nell'ottocento.* Busto Arsizio: Bramante Editrice, 1976.

Tilly, Louise A. *Politics and Class in Milan, 1881–1901.* New York: Oxford University Press, 1992.

Tintori, Giampiero, ed. *Amilcare Ponchielli.* Milan: Nuove Edizioni, 1985.

――. *La Scala: cronologia opere-balletti-concerti, 1778–1977.* Bergamo: Grafica Gutenberg, 1979.

Tisdall, Caroline, and Angelo Bozzolla. *Futurism.* London: Thames & Hudson, 1977.

Toniolo, Gianni. *An Economic History of Liberal Italy, 1850–1918.* New York: Routledge, 1990.

Torrefranca, Fausto. *Giacomo Puccini e l'arte internazionale.* Turin: Fratelli Bocca, 1912.

Tretti, Luigi, and Lionello Fiumi, eds. *Omaggio a Italo Montemezzi.* Verona: Comitato onoranze a Italo Montemezzi, 1952.

Trezzini, Lamberto, and Angelo Curtolo. *Oltre le quinte: idee, cultura e organizzazione del teatro musicale in Italia.* Venice: Marsilio Editori, 1983.

Vanbianchi, Carlo. *La Scala: note storiche e statistiche (1906–1920).* Bergamo: Istituto italiano d'art grafiche, 1922.

Venturi, Fulvio, ed. *Iris, 1898–1998: Il centenario.* Livorno: Circolo musicale amici d'opera Galliano Masini, 1998.

———. *L'opera lirica a Livorno, 1847–1999.* Livorno: Circolo musicale amici d'-opera Galliano Masini, 2000.

———. *Pietro Mascagni: Biografia e cronologia artistica.* Livorno: Circolo musicale amici d'opera Galliano Masini, 2005.

Waterhouse, John C. G. *Malipiero.* Turin: Nuova ERI, 1990.

Weaver, William. *Duse.* New York: Harcourt Brace Jovanovich, 1984.

———. *The Golden Century of Italian Opera.* New York: Thames & Hudson, 1980.

———, and Simonetta Puccini, eds. *The Puccini Companion.* New York: Norton, 1994.

Wolf-Ferrari, Ermano. *Considerazioni attuali sulla musica.* Siena: Ticci Editore libraio, 1935.

Woodhouse, John. *Gabriele D'Annunzio: Defiant Archangel.* Oxford: Clarendon Press, 1998.

Zanetti, Roberto. *La musica italiana nel novecento.* Busto Arsizio: Bramante Editore, 1985.

Ziino, Agostino. *Antologia della critica wagneriana in Italia.* Messina: Pelontana, 1970.

Ziliotto, Baccio. *Francesca da Rimini.* Milan: Bottega di poesia, 1923.

Zoppelli, Luca. *L'opera come racconto.* Venice: Marsilio, 1994.

Zurletti, Michelangelo. *Catalani.* Turin: EDT/Musica, 1982.

———. *La direzione d'orchestra.* Milan: Ricordi/Giunti Martello, 1985.

Essays

Alberti, Luciano. "Le messe in iscena di Casa Sonzogno." In Morini et al., eds., *Casa Sonzogno.*

Antolini, Bianca Maria. "L'editoria musicale in Italia negli anni di Puccini." In Gabriella Biagi Ravenni and Carolyn Gianturco, eds., *Giacomo Puccini.*

Baldacci, Luigi. "I libretti di Mascagni." *Nuova rivista musicale italiana* (1985).

Barini, Giorgio. "*Isabeau* di Pietro Mascagni." *Nuova antologia,* 157, no. 5 (February 1912).

Bascialli, Francesca. "L'attività concertistica: la programmazione." In Antolini, ed., *Milano musicale, 1861–1897.*

Bastianelli, Giannotto. "Riccardo Zandonai." *Nuova rivista musicale italiana* 6 (1972).

Berardoni, Virgilio. "Puccini and the Dissolution of the Italian Tradition." in Cooke, ed., *The Cambridge Companion to Twentieth-Century Opera.*

Bernardini, Aldo. "Industrializzazione e classi sociali." In Renzi, ed., *Sperduto nel buio.*

———. "Le 'tinte' della *Fanciulla.*" *Centro Studi Giacomo Puccini,* www.puccini.it/Saggi/saggio%20fanc1.htm.

Borghetti, Vincenzo. "Ildebrando Pizzetti–Gabrielle D'Annunzio: incontro e scontro di dramma e musica." In Guiot and Maehder, eds., *Tendenze della musica teatrale italiana all'inizio del novecento.*

Brunetta, Gian Piero. "Comets and Fireflies: The Shining Dreams Great and Small of Forty Years of Italian Cinema." In Hulten and Celant, eds., *Italian Art, 1900–1945.*

———. "Filogenesi artistica e letteraria del primo cinema italiano." In Renzi, ed., *Sperduto nel buio.*

Budden, Julian. "The Genesis and Literary Sources of Giacomo Puccini's First Opera." *Cambridge Opera Journal* 1, no. 1 (1989).

———. "Primi rapporti fra Leoncavallo e la casa Ricordi: dieci missive finora sconosciute." In Maehder and Guiot, eds., *Ruggero Leoncavallo nel suo tempo.*

———. "Wagnerian Tendencies in Italian Opera." In Fortune, ed., *Music and Theatre.*

Burton, Deborah. "Home, Home on the 'Catena.'" *Playbill* (April 1, 2005).

Cagnoli, Bruno. "Zandonai a Pesaro." In Chiesa, ed., *Atti dell convegno di studi sulla figura e l'opera di Ricardo Zandonai.*

Caloro, Bonaventura. "Sonzogno." In *Milan* 10, 4, (January 24, 1954).

Cammarano, Fulvio. "The Professions in Parliament." in Malatesta, ed., *Society and the Professions in Italy, 1860–1914.*

Candida, Federico. "Ottocentista all'indice." *La Scala* 136 (1961).

Capra, Marco. "La Casa Editrice Sonzogno tra giornalismo e impresariato." In Morini et al., eds., *Casa Sonzogno.*

———. "Tra wagnerismo, sinfonismo e Giovane Scuola: gli inizi della carriera di Puccini nel racconto della stampa periodica." In Ravenni and Gianturco, eds., *Giacomo Puccini.*

Carlini, Antonio. "Le bande a Milano nella seconda metà dell'Ottocento." In Antolini, ed., *Milano musicale, 1861–1897.*

———. "Le bande musicale nell'Italia dell'ottocento: il modello militare, I rapporti con il teatro e la cultura dell'orchestra negli organici strumentali." *Rivista italiana di musicologia* 30 (1995).

———. "La banda, strumento primario di divulgazione delle opere verdiane nell' Italia rurale dell'Ottocento." In Della Seta et al., eds., *Verdi 2001.*

Carpitella, Diego. "Populismo, nazionalismo e italianità nelle avanguardie musicali italiane." *Chigiana,* 35, n.s. 15 (1978).

Casini, Claudio. "Il verismo musicale italiano." In Casini et al., eds., *Mascagni.*

Cesari, Francesco. "Aspetti del teatro musicale di Cilèa fra *Tilda* e *Adriana Lecouvreur.*" In Streicher, ed., *Ultimi Splendori.*

Checchi, Eugenio. "*Cavalleria Rusticana.*" In *Pietro Mascagni, 1890–1920.*

Cherry, James M. "Rituals of Nostalgia: Old-Fashioned Melodrama at the Millenium." *Americana: The Journal of American Popular Culture, 1900 to Present* 4 (Fall 2005).

Chiesa, Renato. "Componenti veriste della teatralità di Riccardo Zandonai." *Quaderni Zandonaiani* 2 (1989).

Conati, Marcello. "Un indicatore stradale: Mascagni, Leoncavallo & C. nei teatri tedeschi: 1890–1900." *Musica/Realtà* 60 (1999).

———. "Il linguaggio musicale in *Andrea Chénier* di Giordano." In Streicher, ed., *Ultimi Splendori*.

Confalonieri, Guido. "Umanità di Giordano." In Morini, ed., *Umberto Giordano.*

Corrazzol, Adriana Guaranieri. "Opera and Verismo: Regressive Points of View and the Artifice of Alienation." *Cambridge Opera Journal* 5 (1993).

Costa, Antonio. "Dante, D'Annunzio, Pirandello." In Renzi, ed., *Sperduto nel buio.*

Dahlhaus, Carl. "The Dramaturgy of Italian Opera." In Bianconi and Pestelli, eds., *Opera in Theory and Practice, Image and Myth.*

D'Amico, Fedele. "La jeunesse qui n'a qu'un temps." In Weaver and Puccini, eds., *The Puccini Companion.*

Davis, John Anthony. "The Political and Cultural Worlds of Puccini's *Tosca*: Anticlericalism in Italy at the Turn of the Century." In Burton et al., eds., *Tosca's Prism.*

Della Seta, Fabrizio. "The Librettist." In Bianconi and Pestelli, eds., *Opera Production and Its Resources.*

Dryden, Konrad Claude. "'Uno squarcio di vita' Vocal Aspects of Italian Verismo." www.grattacielo.or/tg_squarcio.html.

Durante, Sergio. "The Opera Singer." In Bianconi and Pestelli, eds., *Opera Production and Its Resources.*

Elgueta, Juan Dzazópulos. "Amadeo Bassi: The Tenor of Opera Premieres." www.grand-tenori.com.

Engelfred, Abele. "*I Medici* di R. Leoncavallo: La musica." *Rivista musicale italiana* 1 (1894).

Ferraresi, Alessia. "Alberto Franchetti: una biografia dalle lettere." *Fonti musicale italiane* 3 (1998).

Ferrero, Giovanni. "Crisi teatrale: appunti sul Teatro Regio di Torino." *Rivista musicale italiana* 6 (1899).

Fillipi, Fillipo. "La musica a Milano." In *Milano, 1881.*

Fontana, Ferdinando. "I teatri di Milano." In *Milano, 1881.*

Gallini, Natale. "Mascagni a Milano." In Morini, ed., *Pietro Mascagni.*

Gara, Eugenio. "Cantanti mascagnani tra pregiudizio e verità." In Morini, ed., *Pietro Mascagni.*

Gatti, Guido M. "Gabriele D'Annunzio and the Italian Opera Composers." *Musical Quarterly* (April 1924).

Gavazzeni, Gianandrea. "La musica di Mascagni oggi," In Morini, ed., *Pietro Mascagni.*

Giazotto, Remo. "Un sconosciuto progretto teatrale di Ruggero Leoncavallo." *Nuova rivista musicale italiana* 2 (1968).

Gossett, Philip. "The Case for Puccini." *New York Review of Books* (March 27, 2003).

Gragnani, Emilio. "Prospetto cronologico della vita e delle opere di Pietro Mascagni." In *Pietro Mascagni: Contributi alla conoscenza della sua opera.*

Grew, Raymond. "Culture and Society, 1796–1896." In Davis, ed., *Italy in the Nineteenth Century.*

Groos, Arthur. "From 'Addio, del passato' to 'le patate son fredde': Representations of Consumption in Leoncavallo's *I Medici* and *La bohème.*" In Guiot and Maehder, eds., *Letteratura, musica e teatro all tempo di Ruggero Leoncavallo.*

Guccini, Gerardo. "Directing Opera." In Bianconi and Pestelli, eds., *Opera on Stage.*

Heldt, Guido. "Austria and Germany, 1918–1960." In Cooke, ed., *The Cambridge Companion to Twentieth-Century Opera.*

Jacobshagen, Arnold. "Staging at the Opéra-Comique in Nineteenth-Century Paris: Auber's *Fra Diavolo* and the *livrets de mise-en-scène.*" *Cambridge Opera Journal* 13, no. 3, (November 2001).

Keller, Marcello Sorce. "A 'Bent for Aphorisms': Some Remarks About Music and About His Own Music by Gian Francesco Malipiero." *Music Review* 39 (1978).

Kimbell, David. "Opera since 1800." In Brand and Pertile, eds., *The Cambridge History of Italian Literature.*

Lathrop, Elise. "Alberto Franchetti." *The Musician*, 10, no. 1 (January 1905).

Lederer, Josef-Horst. "'Er Scheiterte an einem Beginnen, das sein Ehrgeiz ihn nicht hatte ausschlagen lassen'—Zur Zeitkritik an R. Leoncavallos historischem Drama *Der Roland von Berlin.*" In Guiot and Maehder, eds., *Nazionalismo e cosmopolitismo nell'opera fra '800 e '900.*

Leoncavallo, Ruggero. "Come nacquero i *Pagliacci.*" *L'Opera* 1–3 (1966).

Lerario, Teresa. "Ruggero Leoncavallo e il soggetto di *Pagliacci.*" In *Chigiana: Rassegna annuale di studi musicologi* 26–27, nos. 115–122 (1971).

Levi, Primo. [L'italico]. "La *Cavalleria rusticana* e il maestro del giorno." In Levi, *Paesaggi e figure musicali.*

Leydi, Roberto. "The Dissemination and Popularization of Opera." In Bianconi and Pestelli, eds., *Opera in Theory and Practice, Image and Myth.*

Longoni, Biancamaria. "Vita e opere di Ferdinando Fontana." *Quaderni Pucciniani* 4 (1992).

Lualdi, Adriano. "Mascagni, D'Annunzio e *Parisina.*" *Quaderni Dannunziani*, 30–31 (1965).

Maehder, Jürgen. "The Origins of Italian *Literaturoper.*" In Groos and Parker, ed., *Reading Opera.*

Maguire, Janet. "Puccini's Version of the Duet and Final Scene of *Turandot.*" *Musical Quarterly*, 74, no. 3 (1990).

Mallach, Alan. "Alberto Franchetti e il suo *Cristoforo Colombo.*" *Nuova rivista musicale italiana* 36 (April–June 1992).

Mancini, Roland. "Le vérisme, existe-t-il?" *L'avant-scène opéra* 50 (1983).

Martinotti, Sergio. "'Torna ai felici di . . . ': il librettista Fontana." *Quaderni Pucciniani* 3 (1992).

Marzolla, Ugo Bernardini. "Da un carteggio perduto." In *Pietro Mascagni: Contributi alla conoscenza della sua opera.*

Mascagni, Pietro. "Prima di *Cavalleria.*" *Fanfulla della Domenica* (December 4, 1892).

Mazzi, Maria Chiara."Un'opera atipica: *Chopin* di Giacomo Orefice." http://www .fortepiano.it/Archivi/oo2NS/fpmatoo5.htm.

Mesereau, John, Jr., and Dadiv Lapeza. "Russian Romanticism." In Porter and Teich, eds., *Romanticism in National Context.*

Miller, Marion S. "Wagnerism, Wagnerians and Italian Identity." In Large and Weber, eds., *Wagnerism in European Culture and Politics.*

Minardi, Gian Paolo. "Il *Cristoforo Colombo* di Alberto Franchetti." In Capra, ed., *Un piacente estate di San Martino.*

Monaldi, Gino. "Per l'*Asrael.*" *Nuova antologia* 67 (January 1, 1897).

Morelli, Giovanni. "Quelle lor belle incognite borghesi." In Bellina and Morelli, eds., *L'Europa musicale.*

Morini, Mario. "Appunti per una cronologia: *Cristoforo Colombo* di Franchetti." *Discoteca alta fedeltà* 15 no. 143 (September 1974).

———. "*Iris* e I progetti non realizzati." In *Pietro Mascagni: Contributi alla conoscenza della sua opera.*

———. "Leoncavallo in prospettiva." *L'Opera* 1–3 (1966).

———. "Lettere inedite a Luigi Illica." *La Scala*, (April 1955).

———. "*Le Maschere:* una nuova dimensione dell'arte mascagnana." Program notes for 1988 Bologna production.

———. "Nascita dell'*amico Fritz.*" In Ostali and Ostali, eds., *L'amico Fritz nel centenario della prima rappresentazione.*

———. "Nascita e vicenda di *Parisina.*" *Rassegna musicale Curci* (January 1979).

———. "Profilo di Illica." *La Scala* (October 1956).

———. "Simoni e Illica associati per un libretto." *La Scala* (December 1960).

———, and Piero Ostali, Jr. "Cronologia della Casa Musicale Sonzogno." In Morini et al., eds., *Casa Sonzogno.*

Mosconi, Elena. "'Venghino signori, si va ad incominciare!' Nascita ed evoluzione dell'esercizio cinematografico." In De Berti, ed., *Un secolo di cinema a Milano.*

Nicastro, Aldo. "Melodramma e scommessa (appunti su *Parisina*)." *Chigiana* 37, n.s. 17 (1980).

Nicolodi, Fiamma. "Opera Production from Italian Unification to the Present." In Bianconi and Pestelli, eds., *Opera Production and Its Resources.*

———. "Riccardo Zandonai e la musica italiana del primo novecento." *Quaderni Zandonaiani* 1 (1987).

———. "Riflessi neogotici nel teatro musicale del novecento." in Bryant, ed., *Il novecento musicale italiano tra neoclassicism e neogoticismo.*

Orlandi, F. "Baron Franchetti: Composer of the Opera *Germania.*" *Musical Courier* (November 6, 1901).

Orselli, Cesare. "Fonti francesi per il debutto operistico di Cilèa: *Gina.*" In Streicher, ed., *Ultimi Splendori.*

———. "Panneggi medievali per la donna decadente: Parisina e Francesca." *Chigiana* 37, n.s. 17, (1980).

Ostali, Nandi. "Storia della Casa Editrice Sonzogno e della Casa Musicale Sonzogno." in Morini et al., eds., *Casa Sonzogno.*

Pannain, Guido. "*Cavalleria rusticana.*" In *Rassegna musicale Curci* 17, no. 4 (December 1963).

Parker, Roger. "*Falstaff* and Verdi's Final Narratives," in Parker, *Leonora's Last Act.*

———. "The Sea and the Stars and the Wastes of the Desert." *University of Toronto Quarterly* 67 (1998).

Phillips-Matz, Mary Jane. "Verdi's life: A Thematic Biography." In Balthazar, ed., *The Cambridge Companion to Verdi.*

Piamonte, Guido. "Prima rappresentazione della commedia *Falstaff.*" In *Falstaff* (program book from 1980–81 season). Milan: Teatro alla Scala (1980).

Piazzoni, Irene. "La politica per il teatro tra promozione e censura (1882–1900)." Paper presented at Società italiana per lo studio della storia contemporanea, September 27, 2003.

Pinzauti, Leonardo. "Le ragioni di *Andrea Chénier.*" *Nuova rivista musicale italiana* 15 (1981).

Rinaldi, Mario. "Mascagni a Roma." in Morini, ed., *Pietro Mascagni.*

Roncaglia, Gino. "Catalani e la *Edmea.*" *La Scala* 110 (1959).

———. "Dimenticato." *La Scala* 33 (November 1950).

———. "Il tribunale di Busseto." *La Scala* 6 (April 1950).

Rose, Michael. "The Italian Tradition" in Bowen, ed., *The Cambridge Companion to Conducting.*

Roselli, John. "Opera Production, 1780–1880." in Bianconi and Pestelli, eds., *Opera Production and Its Resources.*

Salvetti, Guido. "Mascagni: la creazione musicale." In Casini et al., eds., *Mascagni.*

———. "Political Ideologies and Musical Poetics in 20th-Century Italy" *Rivista italiana di musicologia* 35 (2000).

———. "La Scapigliatura milanese e il teatro d'opera." In *Il melodramma italiana dell'ottocento.*

Sansone, Matteo. "Giordano's *Mala vita:* A 'Verismo' opera too true to be good." *Music & Letters* 75 (1994).

———. "Patriottismo in musica: il *Mameli* di Leoncavallo." In Guiot and Maehder, eds., *Nazionalismo e cosmopolitismo nell'opera fra '800 e '900.*

———. "Il verismo di *Fedora* e di *Zazà.*" in Maehder and Guiot, eds., *Ruggero Leoncavallo nel suo tempo.*

———. "The 'Verismo' of Ruggero Leoncavallo: A Source Study of *Pagliacci.*" *Music & Letters* 70, no. 3 (August 1989).

Santi, Piero. "Copyright e tempo della morte nell'opera pucciniana." In Ravenni and Gianturco, eds., *Giacomo Puccini.*

———. "D'Annunzio e il dannunzianesimo nella cultura musicale italiana." In *Studi su D'Annunzio.*

———. "La generazione di Zandonai." In Chiesa, ed., *Atti del convegno di studi sulla figura e l'opera di Riccardo Zandonai.*

———. "Nei cieli bigi . . ." *Nuova rivista musicale italiana* 1 (1967).

———. "Il rapporto col libretto all tempo dell'*Edgar.*" *Quaderni pucciniani* 3 (1992).

Satrangi, Giangiorgio. "Parola cantata e parola declamata ne *La bohème* di Puccini." *Nuova rivista musicale italiana* 1 (2000).

Scherer, Barrymore Laurence."The Case for *Adriana.*" *Opera News* (March 19, 1994).

Silvestri, Giuseppe. "La vita e le opere: Vocazione e volontà." In Tretti and Fiumi, eds., *Omaggio a Italo Montemezzi.*

Simeon, Ennio. "L'ambiente musicale ufficiale e il cinema muto." In Renzi, ed., *Sperduto nel buio.*

Smart, Mary Ann. "Verdi, Italian Romanticism and the Risorgimento." In Balthazar, ed., *The Cambridge Companion to Verdi.*

Socrate, Francesca. "Borghesie e stili di vita." In Sabbatucci and Vidotto, eds., *Storia d'Italia.*

Soffici, Ardengo. "Fogli di diario." *Corriere della sera* (August 3, 1955).

Strasser-Vill, Susanne. "Exoticism in Stage Art at the Beginning of the 20th Century." In Maehder, ed., *Esotismo e colore locale nell'opera di Puccini.*

Streicher, Johannes. "Appunti sull'opera buffa tra *Falstaff* (1893) e *Gianni Schicchi* (1918)." In Guiot and Maehder, eds., *Tendenze della musica teatrale italiana all'inizio del novecento.*

Tabanelli, Nicola. "La ditta Ricordi contro il tenore Bonci." *Rivista musicale italiana* 8 (1901).

———. "La 'questione della Scala' dal punto di vista storico e guiridico." *Rivista musicale italiana* 8 (1901).

Taddei, Adolfo. "Pietro Mascagni." *Liburni Civitas* 13 (1940).

Tommasi, Gioacchino Laza. "Il gusto musicale di D'Annunzio e il dannunzianesimo musicale." In Nicolodi, ed., *Musica italiana del primo novecento.*

Tomelleri, Luciano. "Gabriele D'Annunzio e i musicisti." *Rivista musicale italiana* 43, no. 2 (1939).

Torchi, Luigi. "*Germania* di Alberto Franchetti." *RMI* 9, no. 377 (1902).

———. "*Guglielmo Ratcliff* di Pietro Mascagni." *RMI* 2, no. 287 (1895).

———. "*Le Maschere* di Pietro Mascagni." *RMI* 8, no. 178 (1901).

———. "*Tosca* di Giacomo Puccini." *RMI* 7, no. 78 (1900).

Vallora, Marco. "Per un'analisi delle tre *Cavallerie.*" In Aulenti and Vallora, eds., *Quartetto della maledizione.*

Valsecchi, Rafaella, and Bianca Maria Antolini. "Cronologia sintetica delle rappresentazioni d'opera nei teatri milanesi, 1861–1897." In Antolini, ed., *Milano musicale 1861–1897.*

Velly, Jean-Jacques. "Quelques aspects du traitement orchestral dans *Le Roland de Berlin*" In Guiot and Maehder, eds., *Letteratura, musica e teatro al tempo di Ruggero Leoncavallo.*

Viale Ferrero, Mercedes. "Scene (immaginate, descritte, dipinte, prescritte) per il teatro d'opera di fine ottocento." In Maehder and Guiot, eds., *Ruggero Leon-cavallo nel suo tempo.*

Vigolo, Giorgio. "Gusto e grazia di Wolf-Ferrari nei *quattro rusteghi*" (1958). Posted on www.rodoni.ch/busoni/wolfbusoni/vigolo2.html.

Vlad, Roman. "Modernità di *Cavalleria rusticana.*" In Ostali and Ostali, eds., *Cavalleria rusticana, 1890–1990.*

Waterhouse, John C. G. "Da *Risurrezione* a *La leggenda di Sakùntala.*" In Streicher, ed., *Ultimi Splendori.*

——. "G. F. Malipiero's Crisis Years (1913–1919)." *Journal of the Royal Musical Association* 108 (1981).

——. "Since Verdi: Italian Serious Music, 1860–1995." In Barański and West, eds., *The Cambridge Companion to Modern Italian Culture.*

Zoppelli, Luca. "Modi narrativi scapigliati nella drammaturgia della *Bohème.*" *Nuova rivista musicale italiana* 35:2 (2001).

——. "The Twilight of the True Gods: *Cristoforo Colombo, I Medici* and the Construction of Italian History." *Cambridge Opera Journal* 8 (1996).

Index

Date Due

FEB 2 8 2008		
APR 0 9 200		